MEDITERRANEAN DIET COOKBOOK FOR BEGINNERS

A Complete Collection of 1100+ Quick, Delicious and Budget-Friendly Mediterranean Recipes | 6-Weeks Meal Plan to Kickstart Your New Healthy Lifestyle

AMY JAMESON

TABLE OF CONTENTS

INTRODUCTION

A Mediterranean diet is a diet that patterns the style of eating of the Mediterranean communities. You might like me to tell you that there are about twenty countries around the Mediterranean Sea. Many of these countries contribute in one way or another to the eating pattern now known as the Mediterranean diet. You could use the Moroccan recipe when making a Mediterranean diet. You could try Italian, Greek, Turkish, and so on. So, it is not exactly surprising that the Mediterranean diet may have the largest collection of recipes all over the world.

Just as the Keto, paleo, and other diets, the Mediterranean diet is not a single diet. It is a cluster of foods that is popular because of its uncountable health benefits. It is a style of diet that can be used to correct and encourage several health conditions in your body system.

There is no mistaking that the Mediterranean diet is completely different from any other diet that you can bring to the table. As you are beginning to realize, it is not just any diet that you would consume to fill your groaning tummy. It is a diet that has efficient and direct impacts on your health. It is used for medicinal and corrective features, which promotes it to the likes of the low-carb and keto diets. But it goes over and above the likes of the Keto diet for several reasons.

Foremost, there are no dietary limitations. There are no stringent rules about what you should and should never eat. You are allowed to eat practically everything else that you used to, except junk. You only had to make preferences. The Mediterranean diet is not only broader and sustainable, but it is also a normal style of eating that can be maintained forever. By now, you have to be wondering what kind of diet the Mediterranean diet is. It appears like an uncommon diet. It goes beyond all other classes of diet, and you are still unsure what exactly it contains or how it is eaten. We will get into that right away.

In essence, this diet requires an enormous amount of fruits, vegs, legumes, herbs and every form of plant. It is a style of diet that emphasizes eating plants than anything else.

What draws the line between the Mediterranean diet and the vegetarian diet is that a Mediterranean diet permits the consumption of meats. It is plant-based, but it does allow for the consumption of other diets, particularly animal proteins. It has a preference for fishes and seafood, and it demands that other diets that are not plants based should be consumed in far lesser quantities. Diaries are acceptable too.

Here are distinguishing features of the Mediterranean as detailed by the Harvard School of Public Health:

1. It emphasized healthy fats

The Mediterranean recommends a high intake of fats. It is a style of diet that includes diverse sources of fats, particularly avocado, walnuts, fish, omega -3 fatty acid and olive oil. This does not pose a problem to the body, however. These sources are considered healthy for the body. They supply that both are safe for the heart and healthy from the body. That is against what you would get from excess oil and butter.

2. Water is the primary beverage.

The Mediterranean strongly recommends that you go natural. Water is considered the primary beverage and wine are moderately permitted. That sounds out of this world, considering that it is the authentic beverage that our body needs. So, the priority is on needs.

3. Fish is the preferred source of protein.

Fish is considered the primary source of protein in the Mediterranean diet. It is strongly recommended that you eat fishes no less than twice a week. Next to that, you can also opt for several other sea animals, then poultry, eggs, and dairy in a smaller portion. The significant advantage that this brings to your table is that fishes are way safer, more nutritious and healthier than other sources of protein. If you have to scoff down red meats once in a while, you are not banned. You are just not encouraged to.

4. It considers natural sources against processed foods.

Another characteristic that distinguishes the Mediterranean diet is its heavy reliance on natural ingredients. From diet to drinks, this style of eating emphasizes natural ingredients as much as possible. This will not come as a surprise if you recall that the diet originated from ancient communities. Subsequent generations only maintain it.

Unlike every other diet, the Mediterranean diet does not rule out any food or ingredient. It also gives no rules about the rate of nutrients you should or should not consume. It only makes it clear that the most critical items on your plate are plants, and you should eat a surplus of them. This implies that you may never have to quit your favorite ingredient or dish. Neither do you have to skip your meals to achieve an improved quality of life. All you have to do is abide by the guidelines of the Mediterranean diet, and as the University of Sydney maintains, "you will become protected against metabolic syndrome, prevent and control diabetes, reverse fatty liver diseases, and probably slash the risk of Alzheimer's diseases." That's a lot, and only a magical food can get such stats.

6 Weeks Meal Plan

Week 1

	Breakfast	Lunch	Dinner	Dessert
Monday	Sardinian Flatbread	Turkey Sausage, Fresh Herbs & Feta	Lime Chicken with Black Beans	Lemon Cream
Tuesday	Asian Scrambled Egg	Chicken with Spanish Rice	Kale Chicken Soup	Blueberries Stew
Wednesday	Artichoke Frittatas	Italian Chicken	Honey Almond Chicken Tenders	Mandarin Cream
Thursday	Chocolate Sweet Potato Pudding	Turkey Meatloaf	Special Chops	Creamy Mint Strawberry Mix
Friday	Peanut Butter and Protein Pancake	Chicken and Tzaziki Pitas	Rib Roast	Vanilla Cake
Saturday	Tex-Mex Tofu Breakfast Tacos	Eggplant Pizza	Spicy Lamb Rounds	Pumpkin Cream
Sunday	Rosemary-Walnut Loaf Bread	Lemon Chicken Mix	Prime BBQ	Vanilla Apple Compote

Week 2

	Breakfast	Lunch	Dinner	Dessert
Monday	Prosciutto Breakfast Bruschetta	Tuna Pasta	Excellent Beef Meal	Chocolate Rice
Tuesday	Prosciutto, Avocado, and Veggie Sandwiches	Chicken and Pastina Soup	Lebanese Beef and Green Beans	Raisins Cinnamon Peaches
Wednesday	Chickpea and Hummus Patties in Pitas	Melt-in-Mouth Lamb Shoulder	Grandma Style Meatballs	Lemon Pear Compote
Thursday	Morning Creamy Iced Coffee	Tangy Lamb Loin	World's Best Lasagna	Cold Lemon Squares
Friday	Versatile Sandwich Round	Spiced Moroccan Lamb Chops	Turmeric Baked Chicken Breast	Blackberry and Apples Cobbler
Saturday	Tuna and Avocado Salad Sandwich	Rosemary Pork Chops	Chicken Tacos	Black Tea Cake
Sunday	Hearty Honey-Apricot Granola	Tender Lamb	Chicken and Butter Sauce	Green Tea and Vanilla Cream

Week 3

	Breakfast	Lunch	Dinner	Dessert
Monday	Charred Sirloin with Creamy Horseradish Sauce	Quinoa Chicken Fingers	Warm Lentil Salad	Chocolate Peanut Butter Cups
Tuesday	Low Carb Taco Bowls	Grilled Lamb Gyro Burger	Moroccan Lentil Soup	Banana Ice Cream with Chocolate Sauce
Wednesday	Surf and Turk Burgers	Pork Loin & Orzo	Quinoa Flour Pizza	Raspberry Lime Sorbet
Thursday	Greek Stuffed Mushrooms with Feta	Ground Meat Pizza	Dijon & Herb Pork Tenderloin	Baked Apples with Dried Fruit
Friday	Grilled Shrimp Scampi	Buttery Garlic Chicken	Greek Meatballs (Keftedes)	Hemp Seed Brittle

Saturday	Protein Oatcakes	Garlic and Parsley Chickpeas	Lamb with String Beans	Cardamom Date Bites
Sunday	Orange Ricotta Pancakes	Black-Eyed Peas Salad with Walnuts	Pork Tenderloin with Mediterranean Quinoa Salad	Blueberry Frozen Yogurt

Week 4

	Breakfast	Lunch	Dinner	Dessert
Monday	Mocha Oatmeal	Chilly Spring Night Chops	Escarole and Cannellini Beans on Pasta	Delectable Strawberry Popsicle
Tuesday	Black and Blueberry Protein Smoothie	Favorite Lamb Pitas	Moroccan Pumpkin Soup	Deliciously Cold Lychee Sorbet
Wednesday	Chapter Breakfast Recipes Part	Greek Spiced Pork Souvlaki	Pork with Couscous	Easy Fruit Compote
Thursday	Mango-Pear Smoothie	Sesame Shrimp Mix		Five Berry Mint Orange Infusion
Friday	Strawberry-Rhubarb Smoothie	Dijon Fish Fillets	Rustic Lamb Shanks	Strawberry Pie
Saturday	Pumpkin-Gingerbread Smoothie	Vegetarian Lasagna	Holiday Feast Lamb Shanks	Lemon Mousse
Sunday	Barley Porridge	Chickpea Pasta Salad	Succulent Leg of Lamb	Grapes Stew

Week 5

	Breakfast	Lunch	Dinner	Dessert
Monday	Smoked Salmon and Poached Eggs on Toast	Sunday Dinner Brisket	Minty Olives and Tomatoes Salad	Peach Sorbet
Tuesday	Mediterranean Eggs White Breakfast Sandwich with	Fall-Apart Tender Beef	Steak with Olives and Mushrooms	Mango Bowls

	Roasted Tomatoes			
Wednesday	Mediterranean Feta and Quinoa Egg Muffins	Deliciously Simple Beef	Spicy Mustard Chicken	Fruit Crepes
Thursday	Mediterranean Eggs	Baked Lemon-Butter Fish	Walnut and Oregano Crusted Chicken	Pumpkin Cream
Friday	Pastry-Less Spanakopita	Fish Taco Bowl	Bean Beef Chili	Phyllo Cups
Saturday	Greek Yogurt Pancakes	Scallops with Creamy Bacon Sauce	Garlic Caper Beef Roast	Vanilla Cake
Sunday	Spinach and egg scramble with raspberries	Beans and Cucumber Salad	Cauliflower Tomato Beef	Honey Stewed Apples

Week 6

	Breakfast	Lunch	Dinner	Dessert
Monday	Egg Cauliflower Salad	Artichoke and Arugula Salad	Catfish Fillets and Rice	Chocolate Almond Custard
Tuesday	Egg Salad	Baby Potato and Olive Salad	Halibut Pan	Cherry Cream
Wednesday	Eggs in Zucchini Nests	Barley, Parsley, and Pea Salad	Baked Shrimp Mix	Cocoa Brownies
Thursday	Herbed Breakfast Eggs	Turkey and Salsa Verde	Cheesy Peach and Walnut Salad	Pistachio Balls
Friday	Spinach Quiche	Chicken with Peas	Greek Chicken, Tomato, and Olive Salad	Easy Fruit Compote
Saturday	Seed Porridge	Chicken Wrap	Ritzy Summer Fruit Salad	Ruby Pears
Sunday	Avocado Baked Eggs	Almond Chicken Bites	Roasted Broccoli and Tomato Panzanella	Chocolate Mousse

CHAPTER 1: BREAKFAST RECIPES

1. Veggie Stuffed Hash Browns

Preparation Time: 10 minutes
Cooking Time: 20 minutes
Servings: 4

Ingredients:

Olive oil cooking spray
1 tablespoon plus 2 teaspoons olive oil, divided
4 ounces (113 g) baby bella mushrooms, diced
1 scallion, white parts and green parts, diced
1 garlic clove, minced
2 cups shredded potatoes
1/2 teaspoon salt
1/4 teaspoon black pepper
1 Roma tomato, diced
1/2 cup shredded Mozzarella

Directions:

Preheat the air fryer to 380°F (193°C). Lightly coat the inside of a 6-inch cake pan with olive oil cooking spray.
In a small skillet, heat 2 teaspoons olive oil over medium heat. Add the mushrooms, scallion, and garlic, and cook for 4 to 5 minutes, or until they have softened and are beginning to show some color. Remove from heat.
Meanwhile, in a large bowl, combine the potatoes, salt, pepper, and the remaining tablespoon olive oil. Toss until all potatoes are well coated.
Pour half of the potatoes into the bottom of the cake pan. Top with the mushroom mixture, tomato, and Mozzarella. Spread the remaining potatoes over the top.
Bake in the air fryer for 12 to 15 minutes, or until the top is golden brown.
Remove from the air fryer and allow to cool for 5 minutes before slicing and serving.

2. Feta and Pepper Frittata

Preparation Time: 10 minutes
Cooking Time: 20 minutes
Servings: 4

Ingredients:

Olive oil cooking spray
8 large eggs
1 medium red bell pepper, diced
1/2 teaspoon salt
1/2 teaspoon black pepper
1 garlic clove, minced
1/2 cup feta, divided

Directions:

Preheat the air fryer to 360°F (182°C). Lightly coat the inside of a 6-inch round cake pan with olive oil cooking spray.
In a large bowl, beat the eggs for 1 to 2 minutes, or until well combined.
Add the bell pepper, salt, black pepper, and garlic to the eggs, and mix together until the bell pepper is distributed throughout.
Fold in ¼ cup of the feta cheese.
Pour the egg mixture into the prepared cake pan, and sprinkle the remaining ¼ cup of feta over the top.
Place into the air fryer and bake for 18 to 20 minutes, or until the eggs are set in the center.
Remove from the air fryer and allow to cool for 5 minutes before serving.

3. Tomato, Herb, and Goat Cheese Frittata

Preparation Time: 15 minutes
Cooking Time: 25 minutes
Servings: 2

Ingredients:

1 tablespoon olive oil
1/2-pint cherry or grape tomatoes
2 garlic cloves, minced
5 large eggs, beaten
3 tablespoons unsweetened almond milk
1/2 teaspoon salt
Pinch freshly ground black pepper
2 tablespoons minced fresh oregano
2 tablespoons minced fresh basil
2 ounces (57 g) crumbled goat cheese (about ½ cup)

Directions:

Heat the oil in a nonstick skillet over medium heat. Add the tomatoes. As they start to cook, pierce some of them so they give off some of their juice. Reduce the heat to medium-low, cover the pan, and let the tomatoes soften.
When the tomatoes are mostly softened and broken down, remove the lid, add the garlic and continue to sauté.
In a medium bowl, combine the eggs, milk, salt, pepper, and herbs and whisk well to combine.
Turn the heat up to medium-high. Add the egg mixture to the tomatoes and garlic, then sprinkle the goat cheese over the eggs.
Cover the pan and let cook for about 7 minutes.
Uncover the pan and continue cooking for another 7 to 10 minutes, or until the eggs are set. Run a spatula around the edge of the pan to make sure they won't stick.
Let the frittata cool for about 5 minutes before serving. Cut it into wedges and serve.

4. Prosciutto Breakfast Bruschetta

Preparation Time: 10 minutes
Cooking Time: 20 minutes
Servings: 4

Ingredients:

1/4 teaspoon kosher or sea salt
6 cups broccoli rabe, stemmed and chopped (about 1 bunch)
1 tablespoon extra-virgin olive oil
2 garlic cloves, minced (about 1 teaspoon)
1-ounce (28 g) prosciutto, cut or torn into ½-inch pieces
1/4 teaspoon crushed red pepper
Nonstick cooking spray
3 large eggs
1 tablespoon unsweetened almond milk
1/4 teaspoon freshly ground black pepper
4 teaspoons grated Parmesan or Pecorino Romano cheese
1 garlic clove, halved
8 slices baguette-style whole-grain bread or 4 slices larger Italian-style whole-grain bread

Directions:

Bring a large stockpot of water to a boil. Add the salt and broccoli rabe, and boil for 2 minutes. Drain in a colander.
In a large skillet over medium heat, heat the oil. Add the garlic, prosciutto, and crushed red pepper, and cook for 2 minutes, stirring often. Add the broccoli rabe and cook for an additional 3

minutes, stirring a few times. Transfer to a bowl and set aside.

Place the skillet back on the stove over low heat and coat with nonstick cooking spray.

In a small bowl, whisk together the eggs, milk, and pepper. Pour into the skillet. Stir and cook until the eggs are soft scrambled, 3 to 5 minutes. Add the broccoli rabe mixture back to the skillet along with the cheese. Stir and cook for about 1 minute, until heated through. Remove from the heat.

Toast the bread, then rub the cut sides of the garlic clove halves onto one side of each slice of the toast. (Save the garlic for another recipe.) Spoon the egg mixture onto each piece of toast and serve.

5. Prosciutto, Avocado, and Veggie Sandwiches

Preparation Time: 10 minutes
Cooking Time: 0 minutes
Servings: 4

Ingredients:

8 slices whole-grain or whole-wheat bread
1 ripe avocado, halved and pitted
1/4 teaspoon freshly ground black pepper
1/4 teaspoon kosher or sea salt
4 romaine lettuce leaves, torn into 8 pieces total
1 large, ripe tomato, sliced into 8 rounds
2 ounces (57 g) prosciutto, cut into 8 thin slices

Directions:

Toast the bread and place on a large platter.

Scoop the avocado flesh out of the skin into a small bowl. Add the pepper and salt. Using a fork or a whisk, gently mash the avocado until it resembles a creamy spread. Spread the avocado mash over all 8 pieces of toast.

To make one sandwich, take one slice of avocado toast, and top it with a lettuce leaf, tomato slice, and prosciutto slice. Top with another slice each of lettuce, tomato, and prosciutto, then cover with a second piece of avocado toast (avocado-side down on the prosciutto). Repeat with the remaining ingredients to make three more sandwiches and serve.

6. Chickpea and Hummus Patties in Pitas

Preparation Time: 15 minutes
Cooking Time: 13 minutes
Servings: 4

Ingredients:

1 can chickpeas, drained and rinsed
1/2 cup lemony garlic hummus or ½ cup prepared hummus
1/2 cup whole-wheat panko bread crumbs
1 large egg
2 teaspoons dried oregano
1/4 teaspoon freshly ground black pepper
1 tablespoon extra-virgin olive oil
1 cucumber, unpeeled (or peeled if desired), cut in half lengthwise
1 (6-ounce / 170-g) container 2% plain Greek yogurt
1 garlic clove, minced
2 whole-wheat pita breads, cut in half
1 medium tomato, cut into 4 thick slices

Directions:

In a large bowl, mash the chickpeas with a potato masher or fork until coarsely smashed (they should still be somewhat chunky). Add the hummus, bread crumbs, egg, oregano, and pepper. Stir well to combine. With your hands, form the mixture into 4 (½-cup-size) patties. Press each patty flat to about ¾ inch thick and put on a plate.

In a large skillet over medium-high heat, heat the oil until very hot, about 3 minutes. Cook the patties for 5 minutes, then flip with a spatula. Cook for an additional 5 minutes.

While the patties are cooking, shred half of the cucumber with a box grater or finely chop with a knife. In a small bowl, stir together the shredded cucumber, yogurt, and garlic to make the tzatziki sauce. Slice the remaining half of the cucumber into ¼-inch-thick slices and set aside.

Toast the pita breads. To assemble the sandwiches, lay the pita halves on a work surface. Into each pita, place a few slices of cucumber, a chickpea patty, and a tomato slice, then drizzle the sandwich with the tzatziki sauce and serve.

7. Morning Creamy Iced Coffee

Preparation Time: 5 minutes
Cooking Time: 0 minutes
Servings: 1

Ingredients:

1 cup freshly brewed strong black coffee, cooled slightly
1 tablespoon extra-virgin olive oil
1 tablespoon half-and-half or heavy cream (optional)
1 teaspoon MCT oil (optional)
1/8 teaspoon almond extract
1/8teaspoon ground cinnamon

Directions:

Pour the slightly cooled coffee into a blender or large glass (if using an immersion blender).

Add the olive oil, half-and-half (if using), MCT oil (if using), almond extract, and cinnamon.

Blend well until smooth and creamy. Drink warm and enjoy.

8. Versatile Sandwich Round

Preparation Time: 5 minutes
Cook time: 2 minutes
Servings: 1

Ingredients:

3 tablespoons almond flour
1 tablespoon extra-virgin olive oil
1 large egg
1/2 teaspoon dried rosemary, oregano, basil, thyme, or garlic powder (optional)
1/4 teaspoon baking powder
1/8 teaspoon salt

Directions:

In a microwave-safe ramekin, combine the almond flour, olive oil, egg, rosemary (if using), baking powder, and salt. Mix well with a fork.

Microwave for 90 seconds on high.

Slide a knife around the edges of ramekin and flip to remove the bread.

Slice in half with a serrated knife if you want to use it to make a sandwich.

9. Tuna and Avocado Salad Sandwich

Preparation Time: 10 minutes
Cooking Time: 2 minutes
Servings: 4

Ingredients:

4 versatile sandwich rounds

2 (4-ounce/ 113-g) cans tuna, packed in olive oil
2 tablespoons roasted garlic aioli, or avocado oil mayonnaise with 1 to 2 teaspoons freshly squeezed lemon juice and/or zest
1 very ripe avocado, peeled, pitted, and mashed
1 tablespoon chopped fresh capers (optional)
1 teaspoon chopped fresh dill or ½ teaspoon dried dill

Directions:

Make sandwich rounds according to recipe. Cut each round in half and set aside.
In a medium bowl, place the tuna and the oil from cans. Add the aioli, avocado, capers (if using), and dill and blend well with a fork.
Toast sandwich rounds and fill each with one-quarter of the tuna salad, about 1/3 cup.

10. Hearty Honey-Apricot Granola

Preparation Time: 15 minutes
Cooking Time: 30 minutes
Servings: 6

Ingredients:

1 cup rolled oats
1/4 cup dried apricots, diced
1/4 cup almond slivers
1/4 cup walnuts, chopped
1/4 cup pumpkin seeds
1/4 cup hemp hearts
1/4 to 1/3 cup raw honey, plus more for drizzling
1 tablespoon olive oil
1 teaspoon ground cinnamon
1/4 teaspoon ground nutmeg
1/4 teaspoon salt
2 tablespoons sugar-free dark chocolate chips (optional)
3 cups nonfat plain Greek yogurt

Directions:

Preheat the air fryer to 260ºF (127ºC). Line the air fryer basket with parchment paper.
In a large bowl, combine the oats, apricots, almonds, walnuts, pumpkin seeds, hemp hearts, honey, olive oil, cinnamon, nutmeg, and salt, mixing so that the honey, oil, and spices are well distributed.
Pour the mixture onto the parchment paper and spread it into an even layer.
Bake for 10 minutes, then shake or stir and spread back out into an even layer. Continue baking for 10 minutes more, then repeat the process of shaking or stirring the mixture. Bake for an additional 10 minutes before removing from the air fryer.
Allow the granola to cool completely before stirring in the chocolate chips (if using) and pouring into an airtight container for storage.
For each serving, top 1/2 cup Greek yogurt with 1/3 cup granola and a drizzle of honey, if needed.

11. Polenta with Arugula, Figs, and Blue Cheese

Preparation Time: 10 minutes
Cooking Time: 40 minutes
Servings: 4

Ingredients:

1 cup coarse-ground cornmeal
1/2 cup oil-packed sun-dried tomatoes, chopped
1 teaspoon minced fresh thyme or ¼ teaspoon dried
1/2 teaspoon table salt
1/4 teaspoon pepper
3 tablespoons extra-virgin olive oil, divided
2 ounces (57 g) baby arugula
4 figs, cut into ½-inch-thick wedges
1 tablespoon balsamic vinegar
2 ounces (57 g) blue cheese, crumbled
2 tablespoons pine nuts, toasted

Directions:

Arrange trivet included with Instant Pot in base of insert and add 1 cup water. Fold sheet of aluminum foil into 16 by 6-inch sling, then rest 1½-quart round soufflé dish in center of sling. Whisk 4 cups water, cornmeal, tomatoes, thyme, salt, and pepper together in bowl, then transfer mixture to soufflé dish. Using sling, lower soufflé dish into pot and onto trivet; allow narrow edges of sling to rest along sides of insert.
Lock lid in place and close pressure release valve. Select high pressure cook function and cook for 40 minutes. Turn off Instant Pot and quick-release pressure. Carefully remove lid, allowing steam to escape away from you.
Using sling, transfer soufflé dish to wire rack. Whisk 1 tablespoon oil into polenta, smoothing out any lumps. Let sit until thickened slightly, about 10 minutes. Season with salt and pepper to taste.
Toss arugula and figs with vinegar and remaining 2 tablespoons oil in bowl, and season with salt and pepper to taste. Divide polenta among individual serving plates and top with arugula mixture, blue cheese, and pine nuts. Serve.

12. Pumpkin Layers with Honey Granola

Preparation Time: 5 minutes
Cooking Time: 0 minutes
Servings: 4

Ingredients:

1 (15-ounce / 425-g) can pure pumpkin purée
4 teaspoons honey, additional to taste
1 teaspoon pumpkin pie spice
1/4 teaspoon ground cinnamon
2 cups plain, unsweetened, full-fat Greek yogurt
1 cup honey granola

Directions:

In a large bowl, mix the pumpkin purée, honey, pumpkin pie spice, and cinnamon. Cover and refrigerate for at least 2 hours.
To make the parfaits, in each cup, pour ¼ cup pumpkin mix, ¼ cup yogurt and ¼ cup granola. Repeat Greek yogurt and pumpkin layers and top with honey granola.

13. Shakshuka with Cilantro

Preparation Time: 15 minutes
Cooking Time: 18 minutes
Servings: 4

Ingredients:

2 tablespoons extra-virgin olive oil
1 cup chopped shallots
1 cup chopped red bell peppers
1 cup finely diced potato
1 teaspoon garlic powder
1 can diced tomatoes, drained
1/4 teaspoon turmeric
1/4 teaspoon paprika
1/4 teaspoon ground cardamom
4 large eggs
1/4cup chopped fresh cilantro

Directions:

Preheat the oven to 350ºF (180ºC).
In an oven-safe sauté pan or skillet, heat the olive oil over medium-high heat and sauté the shallots, stirring occasionally, for about 3 minutes, until fragrant. Add the bell peppers, potato, and garlic

powder. Cook, uncovered, for 10 minutes, stirring every 2 minutes.
Add the tomatoes, turmeric, paprika, and cardamom to the skillet and mix well. Once bubbly, remove from heat and crack the eggs into the skillet so the yolks are facing up.
Put the skillet in the oven and cook for an additional 5 to 10 minutes, until eggs are cooked to your preference. Garnish with the cilantro and serve.

14. Pumpkin Muffins

Preparation Time: 15 minutes
Cooking Time: 15 minutes
Servings: 12 muffins

Ingredients:

Nonstick cooking spray
1½ cups granulated sugar
1/2 cup sugar
3/4 cup all-purpose flour
2 teaspoons pumpkin pie spice
1 teaspoon baking soda
1/4 teaspoon salt
Pinch nutmeg
3 mashed bananas
1 (15-ounce / 425-g) can pure pumpkin purée
1/2 cup plain, unsweetened, full-fat yogurt
1/2 cup butter, melted (optional)
2 large egg whites

Directions:

Preheat the oven to 350ºF (180ºC). Spray a muffin tin with cooking spray.
In a large bowl, mix the sugars, flour, pumpkin pie spice, baking soda, salt, and nutmeg. In a separate bowl, mix the bananas, pumpkin purée, yogurt, and butter (if desired). Slowly mix the wet ingredients into the dry ingredients.
In a large glass bowl, using a mixer on high, whip the egg whites until stiff and fold them into the batter.
Pour the batter into a muffin tin, filling each cup halfway. Bake for 15 minutes, or until a fork inserted in the center comes out clean.

15. Cardamom-Cinnamon Overnight Oats

Preparation Time: 10 minutes
Cooking Time: 0 minutes
Servings: 2

Ingredients:

1/2 cup vanilla, unsweetened almond milk (not Silk brand)
1/2 cup rolled oats
2 tablespoons sliced almonds
2 tablespoons simple sugar liquid sweetener
1 teaspoon chia seeds
1/4 teaspoon ground cardamom
1/4 teaspoon ground cinnamon

Directions:

In a mason jar, combine the almond milk, oats, almonds, liquid sweetener, chia seeds, cardamom, and cinnamon and shake well. Store in the refrigerator for 8 to 24 hours, then serve cold or heated.

16. Vanilla Raspberry Overnight Oats

Preparation Time: 10 minutes
Cooking Time: 0 minutes
Servings: 2

Ingredients:

2/3 cup vanilla, unsweetened almond milk
1/3 cup rolled oats
1/4 cup raspberries
1 teaspoon honey
1/4 teaspoon turmeric
1/8 teaspoon ground cinnamon
Pinch ground cloves

Directions:

In a mason jar, combine the almond milk, oats, raspberries, honey, turmeric, cinnamon, and cloves and shake well. Store in the refrigerator for 8 to 24 hours, then serve cold or heated.

17. Toasted Sesame Ginger Chicken

Preparation Time: 10 minutes
Cooking Time: 15 minutes
Servings: 4

Ingredients:

1 Tablespoon Toasted Sesame Ginger Seasoning (or toasted sesame seeds, garlic, onion powder, red pepper, ground ginger, salt, pepper, and lemon)
1 1/2 lbs. boneless, skinless chicken breast
4 teaspoons Olive Oil

Directions:

On a clean, dry cutting board put the chicken breasts.
Softly flatten the chicken breasts to the approx. thickness of 3/8 using a beef hammer or a frying pans backside.
Dust with some seasoning.
Heat the Olive Oil over medium-high flame in a big, nonstick frying pan.
Add the chicken and cook on one side for about 7-8 minutes, until a beautiful crust has created — it will be mildly orange.
Turn the chicken softly and cook on the other side for a further 5-6 minutes before the chicken is thoroughly cooked.
Serve hot or cooled over salad with your favorite side dish. Makes about 4 servings.

18. Tender and Tasty Fish Tacos

Preparation Time: 15 minutes
Cooking Time: 15 minutes
Servings: 4

Ingredients:

2 teaspoons Olive Oil or oil and fresh garlic your favorite taco condiments
1 capful (1 Tablespoon) Southwestern Seasoning or Phoenix Sunrise Seasoning or cumin, garlic, cilantro, red pepper, onion, parsley, paprika, salt & pepper (or low sodium taco seasoning)
1 3/4 lbs. cod or haddock (wild-caught)

Directions:

Clean your fish and slice into 1" pieces.
Sprinkle with the seasoning and toss over to coat the fish thoroughly.
Heat the Olive Oil over medium-high flame in a big, nonstick frying pan.
Add the fish and cook for about 10 to 12 minutes until the fish is transparent and splits into pieces. Be cautious not to overcook; otherwise, the fish may be dry and chewy.
With your favorite condiments, serve warm.
Makes about 4 servings.

19. Sausage Stuffed Mushrooms - an LB. D LG Recipe

Preparation Time: 5 minutes
Cooking Time: 25 minutes
Servings: 4

Ingredients:

4 large Portobello mushrooms (caps and stems)

1 capful (1 Tablespoon) Garlic & Spring Onion Seasoning or Garlic Gusto Seasoning or chopped garlic, chopped chives, garlic powder, onion powder, salt, and pepper to taste
1 1/2 pounds lean Italian sausage (85-94% lean)

Directions:

Preheat the oven to 350 ° C. Cut the mushroom stems carefully and clean both the tops and stems,
The stems are chopped into tiny pieces and placed in a bowl. Put the meat and spices to the bowl and mix all the spices well, using your fingertips. Set the smooth side of the mushroom caps on a wide cookie sheet or baking tray.
Divide 4 equal sections of the meat mixture and lightly press one section into each mushroom head.
Bake with your favorite side dishes for about 25 minutes & serve crispy. Make 4 servings or so.

20. Smoky Shrimp Chipotle

Preparation Time: 5 minutes
Cooking Time: 15 minutes
Servings: 4

Ingredients:

1 capful (1 Tablespoon) Cinnamon Chipotle or a small amount of chipotle pepper, cinnamon, salt, and pepper to taste
4 teaspoons Olive Oil or oil of your choice and fresh garlic
4 T fresh cilantro (optional)
2 lbs. wild-caught, raw shrimp shelled; deveined & tails removed
1 can (16 oz.) diced tomatoes (unflavored, no sugar added)
1 C chopped chives or scallions (greens only)
4 lime wedges (optional)

Directions:

Heat oil over medium-high heat in a medium-sized frying pan.
Put the scallions and roast, until mildly wilted and glistening, for one minute.
Include the shrimp and cook on each side for 1 minute.
Add the sauce with the tomatoes and Cinnamon Chipotle. Cook an extra 3-5 minutes, stirring regularly, until the tomatoes are hot and the shrimp is thoroughly cooked and opaque. As it can make the shrimp tough and dry, be careful not to overcook it.
If needed, sprinkle with cilantro and spritz with a wedge of lime (or for a beautiful and practical garnish, serve the lime wedge on the plate.
Serve it warm.

21. Low Carb Sloppy Joes

Preparation Time: 5 minutes
Cooking Time: 25 minutes
Servings: 4

Ingredients:

Dash of Desperation or Salt and Pepper to taste
1 C low sodium beef broth
1 Tablespoon of wine vinegar
1/2 Tablespoon Cinnamon Chipotle Seasoning or ground cinnamon, chipotle paste and garlic
1 Tablespoon (one Capful) Garlic & Spring Onion Seasoning or salt, pepper, crushed garlic, garlic powder and onion to taste
1 Tablespoon yellow mustard
1 teaspoon (one packet) powdered stevia
2 Tablespoons tomato paste
1/2 C diced green bell pepper
1 1/2 pounds lean ground beef

Directions:

In a frying pan, place the ground beef and place it over medium heat on the burner. When it is frying, split up the larger pieces of beef.
Cook the meat for about 7 minutes, then add the rest of the ingredients (EXCEPT the broth) and whisk to mix. Add the water and transform the
Heat up to medium high until combined.
When the liquid is boiling, reduce the heat to low and let it steam until the liquid is somewhat reduced and you have a lovely sauce, uncovered for around 10-15 minutes.
Serve warm & have fun!

22. Tex-Mex Seared Salmon

Preparation Time: 5 minutes
Cooking Time: 15 minutes
Servings: 4

Ingredients:

1 Tablespoon (one Capful) Phoenix Sunrise Seasoning or salt, pepper, garlic, cumin, paprika, cayenne, and onion to taste
1 1/2 pounds wild-caught salmon filet (will cook best if you have it at room temp)

Directions:

Preheat a nonstick pan for 1 min over high heat.
Swirl seasoning over the salmon during the heating process (NOT on the skin side)
Decrease the heat to medium height.
Put the fish in the pan and let it cook for about 4-6 minutes depending on the size, seasoned side down. When a "crust" has been created from the seasoning, and the fish is quickly released from the pan, you will know it's ready to flip.
Lower the heat to medium-low. Turn the fish down to the side of the skin and cook for about 4-6 more minutes. (Less for medium / rare and more for well done.) Using a meat thermometer is the safest way to search for crispiness.
We cook to 130 degrees and then let it rest for 5 minutes, not overcooked and softly yellow.
Withdraw from the flame and serve. Fish can slip on to the plate right off the skin.

23. Charred Sirloin with Creamy Horseradish Sauce

Preparation Time: 5 minutes
Cooking Time: 15 minutes
Servings: 4

Ingredients:

1-3 T horseradish (from the jar)
6 Tablespoons low-fat sour cream
1/2 capful (1/2 Tablespoon) Dash of Desperation Seasoning or salt, pepper, garlic, and onion to taste
1 1/2 pounds sirloin steaks, trimmed & visible fat removed

Directions:

Preheat the grill to a medium-high temperature.
On all sides, season the steak with Splash of Despair Seasoning.
Put on the grill and cook on either side for about 5-7 minutes, based on how thin the steak is and how fried you like your beef. For rare, you'll leave it on less and for medium-well on more. Using a meat thermometer is the perfect way to prepare your steak.
When the meat is cooked, mix the sour cream and horseradish to make the sauce. To thin the mixture to produce a sauce, add water, one teaspoon at a time. Put aside until done.
Let it sit for five min on a cutting board when the meat is done frying, then slice thinly.

24. Orange French Toast

Preparation Time: 5 minutes
Cooking Time: 15 minutes
Servings: 6

Ingredients:

1 cup unsweetened almond milk
3 large eggs
2 teaspoons grated orange zest
1 teaspoon vanilla extract
1/4 teaspoon ground cardamom
1/4 teaspoon ground cinnamon
1 loaf of boule bread, sliced 1 inch thick (gluten-free preferred)
1 banana, sliced
¼ cup Berry and Honey Compote

Directions:

Heat a large nonstick sauté pan or skillet over medium-high heat.
In a large, shallow dish, mix the milk, eggs, orange zest, vanilla, cardamom, and cinnamon. Working in batches, dredge the bread slices in the egg mixture and put in the hot pan.
Cook for 5 minutes on each side, until golden brown. Serve, topped with banana and drizzled with honey compote.

25. Sweet Potato Toast

Preparation Time: 5 minutes
Cooking Time: 15 minutes
Servings: 4

Ingredients:

2 plum tomatoes, halved
6 tablespoons extra-virgin olive oil, divided
Salt and freshly ground black pepper, to taste
2 large sweet potatoes, sliced lengthwise
1 cup fresh spinach
8 medium asparagus, trimmed
4 large cooked eggs or egg substitute (poached, scrambled, or fried)
1 cup arugula
4 tablespoons pesto
4 tablespoons shredded Asiago cheese

Directions:

Preheat the oven to 450ºF (235ºC).
On a baking sheet, brush the plum tomato halves with 2 tablespoons of olive oil and season with salt and pepper. Roast the tomatoes in the oven for approximately 15 minutes, then remove from the oven and allow to rest.
Put the sweet potato slices on a separate baking sheet and brush about 2 tablespoons of oil on each side and season with salt and pepper. Bake the sweet potato slices for about 15 minutes, flipping once after 5 to 7 minutes, until just tender. Remove from the oven and set aside.
In a sauté pan or skillet, heat the remaining 2 tablespoons of olive oil over medium heat and sauté the fresh spinach until just wilted. Remove from the pan and rest on a paper towel-lined dish. In the same pan, add the asparagus and sauté, turning throughout. Transfer to a paper towel-lined dish.
Place the slices of grilled sweet potato on serving plates and divide the spinach and asparagus evenly among the slices. Place a prepared egg on top of the spinach and asparagus. Top this with ¼ cup of arugula.
Finish by drizzling with 1 tablespoon of pesto and sprinkle with 1 tablespoon of cheese. Serve with 1 roasted plum tomato.

26. Cheesy Mini Frittatas

Preparation Time: 10 minutes
Cooking Time: 25 minutes
Servings: 6

Ingredients:

Nonstick cooking spray
1 1/2 tablespoons extra-virgin olive oil
1/4 cup chopped red potatoes (about 3 small)
1/4 cup minced onions
1/4 cup chopped red bell pepper
1/4 cup asparagus, sliced lengthwise in half and chopped
4 large eggs
4 large egg whites
1/2 cup unsweetened almond milk
Salt and freshly ground black pepper, to taste
1/2 cup shredded low-moisture, part-skim Mozzarella cheese, divided

Directions:

Preheat the oven to 350ºF (180ºC). Using nonstick cooking spray, prepare a 12-count muffin pan.
In a medium sauté pan or skillet, heat the oil over medium heat and sauté the potatoes and onions for about 4 minutes, until the potatoes are fork-tender.
Add the bell pepper and asparagus and sauté for about 4 minutes, until just tender. Transfer the contents of a pan onto a paper-towel-lined plate to cool.
In a bowl, whisk together the eggs, egg whites, and milk. Season with salt and pepper.
Once the vegetables are cooled to room temperature, add the vegetables and ¼ cup of Mozzarella cheese.
Using a spoon or ladle, evenly distribute the contents of the bowl into the prepared muffin pan, filling the cups about halfway.
Sprinkle the remaining ¼ cup of cheese over the top of the cups.
Bake for 20 to 25 minutes, or until eggs reach an internal temperature of 145ºF (63ºC) or the center is solid.
Allow the mini frittatas to rest for 5 to 10 minutes before removing from muffin pan and serving.

27. Avocado Toast with Poached Eggs

Preparation Time: 5 minutes
Cooking Time: 7 minutes
Servings: 4

Ingredients:

Olive oil cooking spray
4 large eggs
Salt and black pepper, to taste
4 pieces whole grain bread
1 avocado
Red pepper flakes (optional)

Directions:

Preheat the air fryer to 320ºF (160ºC). Lightly coat the inside of four small oven-safe ramekins with olive oil cooking spray.
Crack one egg into each ramekin, and season with salt and black pepper.
Place the ramekins into the air fryer basket. Close and set the timer to 7 minutes.
While the eggs are cooking, toast the bread in a toaster.
Slice the avocado in half lengthwise, remove the pit, and scoop the flesh into a small bowl. Season with salt, black pepper, and red pepper flakes, if desired. Using a fork, smash the avocado lightly.
Spread a quarter of the smashed avocado evenly over each slice of toast.
Remove the eggs from the air fryer, and gently spoon one onto each slice of avocado toast before serving.
Nutrition: calories: 232 fat: 14g protein: 11g carbs: 18g fiber: 6g sodium: 175mg

28. Low Carb Taco Bowls

Preparation Time: 5 minutes
Cooking Time: 15-20 minutes
Servings: 4

Ingredients:

cauliflower rice
1 large head cauliflower, steamed until soft or frozen ready-to-cook
1 1/2 pounds lean ground beef
2 C canned, diced tomatoes (no sugar added; no flavor added)
1-2 capfuls Sunrise or Southwestern Seasoning or low salt taco seasoning
Your favorite approved condiments.

Directions:

Over medium-high heat, position a large frying pan. In a wide (preferably Nonstick) skillet, add ground beef and sauté for 8-12 minutes until lightly browned. Using a spatula or a cutting implement, cut the bigger bits into smaller parts.
Add the tomatoes, then season. Stir to blend.
Reduce the heat to low and allow the mixture to simmer until the liquid is reduced by 1/2 and pleasant & solid for 5 minutes.
Use a food processor or chopping instrument to chop steamed cauliflower into rice-sized bits while cooking. Prepare it according to box Directions for using ready-to-cook cauli rice.
In a cup, add 1/2 C of cauliflower rice and finish with 1/4 of the meat mixture. Top with your favorite condiments and serve sweet.

29. Surf and Turk Burgers

Preparation Time: 5 minutes
Cooking Time: 20 minutes
Servings: 4

Ingredients:

1 Tablespoon Skinny Scampi Seasoning or garlic, lemon, parsley, onion, salt, pepper, and celery
8 medium raw shrimp, peeled, deveined, and tails removed (each shrimp should be about 1 oz. each)
1 1/4 pounds (20 oz.) ground turkey

Directions:

Preheat the 350-degree outdoor BBQ.
Place the turkey in a large bowl, sprinkle with seasoning and blend well with your hands.
Shape the turkey mixture into four different patties.
Push two raw shrimps in a heart shape softly into the top of the burger.
Place on the grill and cook on both sides for 5-7 minutes until finished. An internal temperature of 165 degrees F is required for Turkey.
Remove and enjoy with a fantastic side dish from the barbecue!

30. Greek Stuffed Mushrooms with Feta

Preparation Time:10 minutes
Cooking Time: 25-30 minutes
Servings: 4

Ingredients:

Four Portobello mushroom caps (about 4" diameter each)
1/2 C crumbled feta cheese
1/4 teaspoon Dash of Desperation Seasoning (or sea salt and fresh cracked pepper)
1 Tablespoon Mediterranean Seasoning (or basil, oregano, onion, black pepper, rosemary, sage, and parsley)
1 1/2 pounds lean ground beef (or chicken, turkey, or lamb)

Directions:

In a large dish, combine the meat, seasonings, and feta together. Gently blend the mixture with both fingertips.
Split it into four balls of the same size and leave them in the bowl.
In a baking dish, put the mushroom caps—season with a pinch of Desperation's Dash.
In a mushroom cap, put a part of the meat mixture and press softly, using your fingertips, so that the mixture fills the cap. Repeat the mechanism.
Place the baking dish in the oven and cook for 25-30 minutes or until the meat's ideal temperature is achieved.
With your favorite sides, serve warm.

31. Grilled Shrimp Scampi

Preparation Time: 15 minutes
Cooking Time: 20 minutes
Servings: 4

Ingredients:

4 teaspoons Olive Oil
1 3/4 lbs. wild-caught large shrimp, shells removed
1/2 Tablespoons Simply Brilliant Seasoning

Directions:

In a large pot, add all the ingredients and toss to cover. Let the grill sit until it heats up.
Preheat grill to medium-high (about 350 degrees). In a barbecue basket, add the shrimp and put on the barbecue.
Cook for 15-20 minutes, tossing it with tongs sometimes. When they are dark pink and opaque, you'll know they're thoroughly cooked.
Serve chilled or hot.

32. Protein Oatcakes

Preparation Time: 10 minutes
Cooking Time: 5 minutes
Servings: 1

Ingredients:

70g oatmeal
15g protein
1 egg white
1/2 cup water
1/2 teaspoon cinnamon
60g curd
1 teaspoon cacao powder
15g sugar

Directions:

Mix the oatmeal, protein, egg white, and water in a bowl.
Preheat a saucepan to medium heat.
Place the mixture into the saucepan.
While waiting, prepare the topping by mixing the curd, cinnamon, and sugar in a second bowl.
Remove the oatcake from the saucepan when it becomes golden-brown.
Serve on a plate.
Add the topping and cocoa powder.

33. Orange Ricotta Pancakes

Preparation Time: 10 minutes
Cooking Time: 5 minutes
Servings: 1

Ingredients:

3/4 cup all-purpose flour
1/2 tablespoon baking powder
2 teaspoons sugar
1/2 teaspoon salt
3 separated eggs
1 cup fresh ricotta
3/4 cup whole milk
1/2 teaspoon pure vanilla extract
1 large ripe orange

Directions:

Mix the flour, baking powder, sugar in a

large bowl.
Add a pinch of salt.
In a separate bowl, whisk egg yolk, ricotta, milk, orange zest, and orange juice.
Add some vanilla extract for additional flavor.
Followed by the dry ingredients to the ricotta mixture and mix adequately.
Stir the egg white in a different bowl, and then gently fold it in the ricotta mixture.
Preheat saucepan to medium heat and brush with some butter until evenly spread.
Use a measuring cup to drop the batter onto the saucepan, ensure the pan is not crowded.
Allow cooking for 2 minutes.
Flip the food when you notice the edges begin to set, and bubbles form in the center.
Cook the meat for another 1 to 2 minutes.
Serve with any toppings of your choice.

34. Asian Scrambled Egg

Preparation Time: 10 minutes
Cooking Time: 10 minutes
Servings: 1

Ingredients:

1 large egg
1/2 teaspoons light soy sauce
1/8 teaspoon white pepper
1 tablespoon Olive oil

Directions:

Beat the eggs in a bowl.
To the beaten egg, add soy sauce, one-teaspoon Olive oil, and pepper.
Preheat a saucepan on high heat.
Add the two tablespoons oil to the saucepan.
Then add the mixture of the beaten egg.
The edges will begin to cook.
Lessen the heat to medium and carefully scramble the eggs.
Turn off heat and transfer into a bowl.
Serve hot and enjoy

35. Artichoke Frittatas

Preparation Time: 10 minutes
Cooking Time: 30 minutes
Servings: 1

Ingredients:

2.5 oz. dry spinach
1/4 red bell pepper
Artichoke (drain the liquid)
Green onions
Dried tomatoes
Two eggs
Italian seasoning
Salt - Pepper

Directions:

Preheat oven to medium heat.
Brush a bit of oil on the cast-iron skillet.
Mix all the vegetables.
Add some seasoning.
Spread the vegetables evenly in the pan.
Whisk the eggs and add some milk.
Add some salt and pepper.
Mix in some cheese (helps to make it fluffier).
Pour the egg mixture in the saucepan.
Place the pan inside the oven for about 30 minutes.
Enjoy!

36. Chocolate Sweet Potato Pudding

Preparation Time: 5 minutes
Cooking Time: 2 minutes
Servings: 1

Ingredients:

2 well-cooked sweet potatoes
2 tablespoons cocoa powder
2 tablespoons maple syrup
1/4 cups plant-based milk (for example, almond milk)
1/4 tablespoons salt
1/4 tablespoons vanilla extract

Directions:

Inside the food processor, put all the ingredients.
Blend thoroughly for about 30 seconds to 1 minute.
Voilà!

37. Peanut Butter and Protein Pancake

Preparation Time: 10 minutes
Cooking Time: 15 minutes
Servings: 1

Ingredients:

1/2 cup oat flour
1/2 cup gluten-free chocolate pancake mix
1/2 cup almond milk
1 egg
1 tablespoon coconut water
1 tablespoon peanut butter
Fresh fruits slices

Directions:

Preheat a saucepan to medium heat.
Mix the flour and the pancake mix in a mixing bowl.
Mix the almond milk and eggs with coconut water in another bowl.
Mix the dry and wet ingredients thoroughly to form a delicate batter.
Spray the preheated saucepan with some coconut oil.
Put the batter into the saucepan with a measuring cup and allow it to cook for a few minutes.
Allow to cool and top with peanut butter and fresh fruit slices.

38. Tex-Mex Tofu Breakfast Tacos

Preparation Time: 10 minutes
Cooking Time: 15 minutes
Servings: 1

Ingredients:

8 oz. firm tofu
1 cup well-cooked black bean
1/4 red onion
1 cup fresh coriander
1 ripe avocado
1/2 cup salsa
1 medium-sized lime
5 whole corn tortillas
1/2 teaspoon garlic powder
1/2 teaspoon chili powder
1/8 teaspoon of sea salt
1 tablespoon salsa
1 tablespoon water

Directions:

Dice the red onions, avocados, coriander, and keep in separate bowls.
Also, slice the limes and keep in individual bowls.
In a clean towel. Wrap the tofu and place under a cast-iron skillet.
In the meantime, heat a saucepan to medium heat.
Cook the black beans in the saucepan, add a little amount of salt, cumin, and chili powder.
Then decrease the heat to a low simmer and set aside.
Add the tofu spices and salsa into a bowl, then add some water and set aside.
Heat another skillet to medium heat.
Pour some oil into the skillet, and then crumble the tofu into it.
Stir-fry for about 5 minutes until the tofu begins to brown.
Add some seasoning and continue to cook for about 5 to 10 minutes, and then set aside.
Heat the tortillas in oven to 250°F.

Top the tortillas with tofu scramble, avocado, salsa, coriander, black beans, and lime juice.
Serve immediately.

39. Mocha Oatmeal

Preparation Time: 5 minutes
Cooking Time: 10 minutes
Servings: 1

Ingredients:

1 banana
1/2 cup oats
1 cup coffee
1/4 teaspoon salt
1 teaspoon walnut
1/2 teaspoon cacao powder
1 cup milk
Honey

Directions:

Preheat a saucepan to medium heat.
Put the oats in a saucepan.
Slice the banana, mash them, and add them to the oats.
Add coffee, walnuts, cacao powder, and salt.
Stir and you may want to wait for it to simmer, practically until the mixture becomes sticky inconsistency.
Serve in a bowl and add milk and honey as desired.
Enjoy!

40. Black and Blueberry Protein Smoothie

Preparation Time: 5 minutes
Cooking Time: 0 minutes
Servings: 1

Ingredients:

1 cup sugar-free coconut milk (or any other plant-based milk of your choice)
1 scoop vanilla or natural protein powder
6 oz. fat-free vanilla Greek yogurt
2 tablespoons of milled flaxseed
1 cup berries (black or blue)
1 cup ice

Directions:

In the food processor, place all the ingredients.
Blend until smooth.
Pour into a cup and enjoy.

41. Mango-Pear Smoothie

Preparation Time: 10 minutes
Cooking Time: 3 minutes
Servings: 1

Ingredients:

1 ripe pear, cored and chopped
1/2 mango, peeled, pitted, and chopped
1 cup chopped kale
1/2 cup plain Greek yogurt
2 ice cubes

Directions:

1.In a blender, purée the pear, mango, kale, and yogurt.
2.Add the ice and blend until thick and smooth. Pour the smoothie into a glass and serve cold.
Substitution tip: Apples can be used instead of pear. For some extra fiber, leave the skin on the fruit. Wash the skin thoroughly, though, to remove any pesticide residue if your apples are not organic.

42. Strawberry-Rhubarb Smoothie

Preparation Time: 5 minutes
Cook Time: 3 minutes
Servings: 1

Ingredients:

1 rhubarb stalk, chopped
1 cup sliced fresh strawberries
1/2 cup plain Greek yogurt
2 tablespoons honey
Pinch ground cinnamon
3 ice cubes

Directions:

Place a small saucepan filled with water over high heat and bring to a boil. Add the rhubarb and boil for 3 minutes. Drain and transfer the rhubarb to a blender.
Add the strawberries, yogurt, honey, and cinnamon and pulse the mixture until it is smooth.
Add the ice and blend until thick, with no ice lumps remaining. Pour the smoothie into a glass and enjoy cold.
Ingredient tip: Rhubarb leaves contain a compound called oxalic acid, which is toxic—use only the stems of the plant in your recipes.

43. Pumpkin-Gingerbread Smoothie

Preparation Time: 5 minutes, Plus 1 Hour Or Overnight Soaking
Cooking Time: 10 minutes
Servings: 1

Ingredients:

1 cup unsweetened almond milk
2 teaspoons chia seeds
1 banana
1/2 cup canned pure pumpkin
1/4 teaspoon ground cinnamon
1/4 teaspoon ground ginger
Pinch ground nutmeg

Directions:

In a small bowl, mix the almond milk and chia seeds. Soak the seeds for at least 1 hour. Transfer the seeds to a blender.
Add the banana, pumpkin, cinnamon, ginger, and nutmeg.
Blend until smooth. Pour the smoothie into a glass and serve.
Substitution tip: Cooked sweet potato or butternut squash works as an alternative if you do not have pumpkin handy.

44. Barley Porridge

Preparation Time: 5 minutes
Cooking Time: 25 minutes
Servings: 4

Ingredients:

1 cup barley
1 cup wheat berries
2 cups unsweetened almond milk, plus more for serving
2 cups water
1/2 cup blueberries
1/2 cup pomegranate seeds
1/2 cup hazelnuts, toasted and chopped
1/4 cup honey

Directions:

In a medium saucepan over medium-high heat, place the barley, wheat berries, almond milk, and water. Bring to a boil, reduce the heat to low, and simmer for about 25 minutes, stirring frequently until the grains are very tender.
Top each serving with almond milk, 2 tablespoons of blueberries, 2 tablespoons of pomegranate seeds, 2 tablespoons of hazelnuts, and 1 tablespoon of honey.
Substitution tip: Bulgur is a healthy protein and fiber-packed substitution for

the barley in this hot breakfast. Bulgur is a cracked, partially cooked wheat kernel.

45. Ricotta Breakfast Casserole

Preparation Time: 15 minutes
Cooking Time: 25 minutes
Servings: 4

Ingredients:

1 teaspoon extra-virgin olive oil
1 zucchini, chopped
1 cup broccoli florets, blanched or steamed
½ cup diced cooked carrots
½ red bell pepper, seeded and diced
8 large eggs
½ cup low-fat ricotta cheese
1 teaspoon chopped fresh basil
1 teaspoon chopped fresh oregano
1 teaspoon chopped fresh chives
Pinch sea salt
Pinch freshly ground black pepper

Directions:

Preheat the oven to 350°F.
Lightly grease an 8-by-8-inch baking dish with olive oil. Evenly distribute the zucchini, broccoli, carrots, and red bell pepper over the bottom of the dish.
In a large bowl, whisk together the eggs, ricotta, basil, oregano, chives, sea salt, and pepper. Pour the eggs into the prepared dish over the vegetables.
Bake the casserole for about 25 minutes, or until a knife inserted near the center comes out clean.
Substitution tip: Ricotta adds an interesting texture, but you can easily substitute goat cheese, feta cheese, or even plain cottage cheese with equally superb results.

46. Savory Lentil Waffles

Preparation Time: 10 minutes
Cooking Time: 20 minutes
Servings: 4

Ingredients

1 14.5-oz. can lentils, rinsed
1/4 small red onion, thinly sliced
1/4 c. golden raisins, chopped
3 tbsp. olive oil
3 tbsp. sherry vinegar
1 c. store-bought waffle mix
1/8 tsp. salt
1/8 tsp. pepper
4 c. baby arugula
1/4 c. roasted almonds, chopped
plain Greek yogurt, for serving

Directions

In a medium bowl, red onion, combine lentils, raisins, olive oil, and sherry vinegar.
In a large bowl, beat waffle mix, curry powder, ground coriander, salt, and pepper. Prepare and cook 2-waffles in the waffle iron according to the manufacturer's directions.
Cut the waffles into pieces and divide them with Greek yogurt if desired. Top with lentil salad.

47. Baked Dandelion Toast

Preparation Time: 10 minutes
Cooking Time: 15 minutes
Servings: 4

Ingredients

2 tbsp. olive oil
1 small red onion, thinly sliced
1/8 tsp. red pepper flakes
2 tbsp. lemon juice
1 bunch dandelion greens
1/4 tsp. salt
1/4 tsp. pepper
4 oz. feta cheese
1/4 c. plain yogurt (not Greek)
1 tsp. grated lemon zest
1 loaf ciabatta, split and toasted
2 tbsp. small mint leaves

Directions

You need to heat olive oil in a large skillet over medium heat. Add red onion and red pepper flakes and cook, occasionally stirring, until softened, 4 to 5 minutes.
Add lemon juice and cook until evaporated, about 30 seconds. Remove from heat, add dandelion greens (about 8 oz, with 5 inches of stem discarded), season with salt and pepper, and toss until it starts to wilt.
Meanwhile, crumble feta cheese in a mini food processor and pulse four times. While the food processor is running, add yogurt and then the lemon zest; puree until smooth and creamy. (You can also crumble feta very finely in a bowl and beat with yogurt and lemon zest.)
Spread over ciabatta, cover with green, and sprinkle with mint.

48. Bircher Muesli

Preparation Time: 10 minutes, Plus 6 Hours Or Overnight Soaking
Cooking Time: 5 minutes
Servings: 4

Ingredients:

1½ cups rolled oats
½ cup unsweetened shredded coconut
2 cups unsweetened almond milk
2 bananas, mashed
½ cup chopped almonds
½ cup raisins
½ teaspoon ground cinnamon

Directions:

In a large sealable container, stir together the oats, coconut, and almond milk until well combined. Refrigerate the mixture to soak overnight.
In the morning, stir in the banana, almonds, raisins, and cinnamon to serve.
Substitution tip: If you do not want a vegetarian breakfast, use 2 percent milk instead of nut milk.

49. Zucchini Fritters (Ejjeh)

Preparation Time: 10 minutes
Cooking Time: 20 minutes
Servings: 6

Ingredients:

2 zucchini, peeled and grated
1 sweet onion, finely diced
1 cup chopped fresh parsley
2 garlic cloves, minced
½ teaspoon sea salt
½ teaspoon freshly ground black pepper
½ teaspoon ground allspice
4 large eggs
2 tablespoons extra-virgin olive oil

Directions:

Line a plate with paper towels and set aside.
In a large bowl, mix the zucchini, onion, parsley, garlic, sea salt, pepper, and allspice.
In a medium bowl, beat the eggs and then pour them over the zucchini mixture. Stir to mix.
In a large skillet over medium heat, heat the olive oil. Scoop ¼-cup portions of the egg-zucchini mixture into the skillet. Cook until the bottom is set, for about 3 minutes. Flip and cook for 3 minutes more. Transfer the cooked fritters to the paper towel–lined plate. Repeat with the remaining egg zucchini mixture.
Served with pita bread, if desired.

Substitution tip: Don't like zucchini? No problem—use eggplant instead. You can also enjoy these fritters with a side of plain Greek yogurt. They make a delicious combination.

50. Spiced Almond Pancakes

Preparation Time: 10 minutes
Cooking Time: 20 minutes
Servings: 6

Ingredients:

2 cups unsweetened almond milk, at room temperature
½ cup melted coconut oil, plus more for greasing the skillet
2 large eggs, at room temperature
2 teaspoons honey
1½ cups whole-wheat flour
½ cup almond flour
1½ teaspoons baking powder
½ teaspoon baking soda
¼ teaspoon sea salt
¼ teaspoon ground cinnamon

Directions:

1.In a large bowl, whisk the almond milk, coconut oil, eggs, and honey until blended.
2.In a medium bowl, sift together the whole-wheat flour, almond flour, baking powder, baking soda, sea salt, and cinnamon until well mixed.
Add the flour mixture to the milk mixture and whisk until just combined.
Grease a large skillet with coconut oil and place it over medium-high heat.
5.Add the pancake batter in ½-cup measures, about 3 for a large skillet. Cook for about 3 minutes until the edges are firm, the bottom is golden, and the bubbles on the surface break. Flip and cook for about 2 minutes more until the other side is golden brown and the pancakes are cooked through. Transfer to a plate and wipe the skillet with a clean paper towel.
Regrease the skillet and repeat until the remaining batter is used.
Serve the pancakes warm with fresh fruit, if desired.
Cooking tip: The pancakes can be made ahead. After they cool, keep refrigerated for a cold treat topped with a spoonful of honey. You can also quickly reheat the cooked pancakes in a toaster if you prefer them warm.

51. Crustless Sun-Dried Tomato Quiche

Preparation Time: 15 minutes
Cooking Time: 25 minutes
Servings: 4

Ingredients:

6 large eggs
¼ cup goat cheese
2 tablespoons milk
Pinch cayenne pepper
1 teaspoon extra-virgin olive oil
2 shallots, finely chopped
½ teaspoon minced garlic
10 sun-dried tomatoes, quartered
1 teaspoon chopped fresh parsley
Pinch sea salt
Pinch freshly ground black pepper

Directions:

Preheat the oven to 375°F.
In a medium bowl, whisk the eggs, goat cheese, milk, and cayenne pepper to blend.
Place a 9-inch ovenproof skillet over medium-high heat and add the olive oil.
Add the shallots and garlic to the skillet, and sauté for about 2 minutes until tender.
Pour in the egg mixture. Scatter the sun-dried tomatoes and parsley evenly over the top.
Season the quiche with sea salt and pepper.
Cook the quiche, lifting the edges to allow the uncooked egg to flow underneath, for about 3 minutes until the bottom is firm.
Place the skillet in the oven and bake for about 20 minutes until the egg is cooked through, golden, and puffy.
Cooking tip: If you have leftover quiche, wrap it in a tortilla the next day for an easy, hearty lunch or breakfast.

52. Artichoke Frittata

Preparation Time: 5 minutes
Cooking Time: 10 minutes
Servings: 4

Ingredients:

8 large eggs
¼ cup grated Asiago cheese
1 tablespoon chopped fresh basil
1 teaspoon chopped fresh oregano
Pinch sea salt
Pinch freshly ground black pepper
1 teaspoon extra-virgin olive oil
1 teaspoon minced garlic
1 cup canned, water-packed, quartered artichoke hearts, drained
1 tomato, chopped

Directions:

Preheat the oven to broil.
In a medium bowl, whisk the eggs, Asiago cheese, basil, oregano, sea salt, and pepper to blend.
Place a large ovenproof skillet over medium-high heat and add the olive oil.
Add the garlic and sauté for 1 minute.
Remove the skillet from the heat and pour in the egg mixture.
Return the skillet to the heat and evenly sprinkle the artichoke hearts and tomato over the eggs.
Cook the frittata without stirring for about 8 minutes, or until the center is set.
Place the skillet under the broiler for about 1 minute, or until the top is lightly browned and puffed.
Cut the frittata into 4 pieces and serve.
Substitution tip: If you don't need a vegetarian dish, add chopped cooked chicken, cooked shrimp, or smoked salmon to this frittata for extra protein.

53. Spinach Curry Pancakes with Apple, Raisins, And Chickpeas

Preparation Time: 20 minutes
Cooking Time: 40 minutes
Servings: 6

Ingredients

2 lg eggs
1/3 C finely chopped fresh cilantro
1/4 tsp. black pepper
2 1/2 C 1% milk
1 C plus 2 tbsp all-purpose flour
1 yellow onion, chopped
1 can (15.5 oz) chickpeas, rinsed and drained
1 granny smith apple, diced
1/4 C golden raisins
2 tbsp. madras curry powder
10 oz. fresh spinach
lemon wedges, for serving

Directions

In a blender, puree eggs, cilantro, pepper, 1 cup of milk and flour, 2- tablespoons of oil, and 1/4 teaspoon of salt. Lightly brush the 10 "non-stick skillet with cooking spray and heat over medium heat. Pour 1/3 cup of batter evenly into pan and cook until edges set, 1 minute. Flip and cook for 30 seconds. Repeat for remaining pancakes. Cover to keep warm.

Heat the remaining 1- tablespoon of oil in a skillet over medium heat. Add onion and keep cooking until soften, 5-minutes. Add chickpeas, apple, raisins, and curry powder—Cook for 3 minutes. Stir in the remaining 2- tablespoons of flour through and cook for 30 seconds. Stir in the remaining 1-1/2 cup milk. Cook until thick, 2 minutes. Add spinach and the remaining 1/2 teaspoon of salt.

54. Swiss Chard Gingerbread Pan with Egg, Onion, And Tomato

Preparation Time: 0 minutes
Cooking Time: 28 minutes
Servings: 4

Ingredients

1 1/4 c. quartered cherry tomatoes
1 tbsp. red wine vinegar
2 bunches Swiss chard or rainbow chard
2 c. large chopped yellow onion
3 tbsp. extra-virgin olive oil
4 cloves garlic, minced
1/2 tsp. sea salt
1/2 tsp. freshly ground black pepper
4 large eggs

Directions

Toss cherry tomatoes with vinegar in a small bowl. Put aside.
Remove chard leaves from stems. Chop the leaves, put them in a large bowl of cold water, and flip to rinse. Transfer to a colander and leave a little water on the leaves. Rinse, dry, and thinly slice the stems.
Take a large cast-iron pan over medium heat, sauté chard stalks, and olive oil onion until soft, about 10 minutes. Lower the heat. Add garlic and cook for 1 minute. Add chard leaves, salt, and pepper. Turn up the heat and toss with tongs until the leaves wilt.
Make four notches or "nests" in Swiss chard with the back of a spoon. Break one egg in each nest. Cover pan, reduce heat slightly, and cook until yolks are medium-hard, about 4 minutes.
Add cherry tomatoes and vinegar to the pan and serve.

55. Cheesy Avocado Omelet

Preparation Time: 5 minutes
Cooking Time: 15 minutes
Servings: 2

Ingredients

1 tsp. olive oil
1 small red onion, finely chopped
Kosher salt and pepper
6 cremini mushrooms, sliced
1 c. baby spinach
4 large eggs plus 2 egg whites
2 oz. sharp Cheddar, coarsely grated
1 c. grape tomatoes halved
1/4 c. fresh flat-leaf parsley, chopped
1/2 small avocado

Directions

You need to heat oil in a large non-stick frying pan over medium heat. Add the onion, season with 1/4 teaspoon salt and pepper, and cook, occasionally stirring for 4 minutes. Add the mushrooms and cook, occasionally stirring, until soft, 4 minutes. Stir in the spinach and cook until it starts to wilt.
Add eggs & start cooking; keep stirring for 1-minute, then cook without stirring until edges are browned, 2-3 minutes. Sprinkle with cheese and fold half over the other to make a semicircle.
Toss tomatoes with parsley and avocado and serve with a spoon over the omelet.

CHAPTER 2: SNACKS AND APPETIZERS

56. Burrata Caprese Stack

Preparation Time: 5 minutes
Cooking Time: 0 minutes
Servings: 4

Ingredients:

1 large organic tomato
½ teaspoon salt
¼ teaspoon black pepper
1 (4-ounce) ball burrata cheese
8 fresh basil leaves
2 tablespoons extra-virgin olive oil
1 tablespoon red wine

Directions

Slice the tomato into 4 thick slices, removing any tough center core and sprinkle with salt and pepper. Place the tomatoes, seasoned-side up, on a plate.
On a separate rimmed plate, slice the burrata into 4 thick slices and place one slice on top of each tomato slice. Top each with one-quarter of the basil and pour any reserved burrata cream from the rimmed plate over top.
Drizzle with olive oil and vinegar and serve with a fork and knife.

57. Zucchini-Ricotta Fritters with Lemon-Garlic Aioli

Preparation Time: 30 minutes
Cooking Time: 25 minutes
Servings: 4

Ingredient:

1 large zucchini
1 teaspoon salt, divided
½ cup whole-milk ricotta cheese
2 scallions
1 large egg
2 garlic cloves
2 tablespoons fresh mint (optional)
2 teaspoons grated lemon zest
¼ teaspoon freshly ground black pepper
½ cup almond flour
1 teaspoon baking powder
8 tablespoons extra-virgin olive oil
8 tablespoons Roasted Garlic Aioli

Directions

Place the shredded zucchini in a colander or on several layers of paper towels. Sprinkle with ½ teaspoon salt and let sit for 10 minutes. Using another layer of paper towel, press down on the zucchini to release any excess moisture and pat dry.
In a large bowl, combine the drained zucchini, ricotta, scallions, egg, garlic, mint (if using), lemon zest, remaining ½ teaspoon salt, and pepper and stir well.
Blend almond flour and baking powder. Mix in flour mixture into the zucchini mixture and let rest for 10 minutes.
In a large skillet, working in four batches, fry the fritters. For each batch of four, heat 2 tablespoons olive oil over medium-high heat. Add 1 heaping tablespoon of zucchini batter per fritter, pressing down with the back of a spoon to form 2- to 3-inch fritters. Cover and let fry 2 minutes before flipping. Fry another 2 to 3 minutes, covered.
Repeat for the remaining three batches, using 2 tablespoons of the olive oil for each batch.
Serve with aioli.

58. Salmon-Stuffed Cucumbers

Preparation Time: 10 minutes
Cooking Time: 0 minute
Servings: 4

Ingredients:

2 large cucumbers, peeled
1 (4-ounce) can red salmon
1 medium very ripe avocado
1 tablespoon extra-virgin olive oil
Zest and juice of 1 lime
3 tablespoons chopped fresh cilantro
½ teaspoon salt
¼ teaspoon black pepper

Directions:

Slice the cucumber into 1-inch-thick segments and using a spoon, scrape seeds out of center of each segment and stand up on a plate.
In a medium bowl, mix salmon, avocado, olive oil, lime zest and juice, cilantro, salt, and pepper.
Spoon the salmon mixture into the center of each cucumber segment and serve chilled.

59. Sfougato

Preparation Time: 9 minutes
Cooking Time: 13 minutes
Servings: 4

Ingredients:

½ cup crumbled feta cheese
¼ cup bread crumbs
1 medium onion
4 tablespoons all-purpose flour
2 tablespoons fresh mint
½ teaspoon salt
½ teaspoon ground black pepper
1 tablespoon dried thyme
6 large eggs, beaten
1 cup water

Directions:

In a medium bowl, mix cheese, bread crumbs, onion, flour, mint, salt, pepper, and thyme. Stir in eggs.
Spray an 8" round baking dish with nonstick cooking spray. Pour egg mixture into dish.
Place rack in the Instant Pot® and add water. Fold a long piece of foil in half lengthwise. Lay foil over rack to form a sling and top with dish. Cover loosely with foil. Seal lid, put steam release in Sealing, select Manual, and time to 8 minutes.
When the timer alarms, release the pressure. Uncover. Let stand 5 minutes, then remove dish from pot.

60. Goat Cheese–Mackerel Pâté

Preparation Time: 10 minutes
Cooking Time: 0 minute
Servings: 4

Ingredients:

4 ounces olive oil-packed wild-caught mackerel
2 ounces goat cheese
Zest and juice of 1 lemon
2 tablespoons chopped fresh parsley
2 tablespoons chopped fresh arugula
1 tablespoon extra-virgin olive oil
2 teaspoons chopped capers
2 teaspoons fresh horseradish (optional)

Directions:

In a food processor, blender, or large bowl with immersion blender, combine

the mackerel, goat cheese, lemon zest and juice, parsley, arugula, olive oil, capers, and horseradish (if using). Process or blend until smooth and creamy.
Serve with crackers, cucumber rounds, endive spears, or celery.

61. Baba Ghanoush

Preparation Time: 9 minutes
Cooking Time: 11 minutes
Servings: 8

Ingredients:

2 tablespoons extra-virgin olive oil
1 large eggplant
3 cloves garlic
½ cup water
3 tablespoons fresh flat-leaf parsley
½ teaspoon salt
¼ teaspoon smoked paprika
2 tablespoons lemon juice
2 tablespoons tahini

Directions:

Press the Sauté button on the Instant Pot® and add 1 tablespoon oil. Add eggplant and cook until it begins to soften, about 5 minutes. Add garlic and cook 30 seconds.
Add water and close lid, click steam release to Sealing, select Manual, and time to 6 minutes. Once the timer rings, quick-release the pressure. Select Cancel and open lid.
Strain cooked eggplant and garlic and add to a food processor or blender along with parsley, salt, smoked paprika, lemon juice, and tahini. Add remaining 1 tablespoon oil and process. Serve warm or at room temperature.

62. Instant Pot® Salsa

Preparation Time: 9 minutes
Cooking Time: 22 minutes
Servings: 12
Size/ Portion: 2 tablespoons

Ingredients:

12 cups seeded diced tomatoes
6 ounces tomato paste
2 medium yellow onions
6 small jalapeño peppers
4 cloves garlic
¼ cup white vinegar
¼ cup lime juice
2 tablespoons granulated sugar
2 teaspoons salt
¼ cup chopped fresh cilantro

Directions:

Place tomatoes, tomato paste, onions, jalapeños, garlic, vinegar, lime juice, sugar, and salt in the Instant Pot® and stir well. Close it, situate steam release to Sealing. Click Manual button, and time to 20 minutes.
Once timer beeps, quick-release the pressure. Open, stir in cilantro, and press the Cancel button.
Let salsa cool to room temperature, about 40 minutes, then transfer to a storage container and refrigerate overnight.

63. Taste of the Mediterranean Fat Bombs

Preparation Time: 15 minutes + 4 hours
Cooking Time: 0 minute
Servings: 6

Ingredients:

1 cup crumbled goat cheese
4 tablespoons jarred pesto
12 pitted Kalamata olives
½ cup finely chopped walnuts
1 tablespoon chopped fresh rosemary

Directions:

Mix goat cheese, pesto, and olives. Cool for 4 hours to harden.
Create the mixture into 6 balls, about ¾-inch diameter. The mixture will be sticky.
In a small bowl, place the walnuts and rosemary and roll the goat cheese balls in the nut mixture to coat.

64. Cream of Cauliflower Gazpacho

Preparation Time: 15 minutes
Cooking Time: 25 minutes
Servings: 6

Ingredients:

1 cup raw almonds
½ teaspoon salt
½ cup extra-virgin olive oil
1 small white onion
1 small head cauliflower
2 garlic cloves
2 cups chicken stock
1 tablespoon red wine vinegar
¼ teaspoon freshly ground black pepper

Directions:

Boil almonds to the water for 1 minute. Drain in a colander and run under cold water. Pat dry. Discard the skins.
In a food processor or blender, blend together the almonds and salt. With the processor running, drizzle in ½ cup extra-virgin olive oil, scraping down the sides as needed. Set the almond paste aside.
In a stockpot, cook remaining 1 tablespoon olive oil over medium-high heat. Sauté onion for 4 minutes. Add the cauliflower florets and sauté for another 3 to 4 minutes. Cook garlic for 1 minute more.
Add 2 cups stock and bring to a boil. Cover, reduce the heat to medium-low, and simmer the vegetables until tender, 8 to 10 minutes. Pull out from the heat and allow to cool slightly.
Blend vinegar and pepper with an immersion blender. With the blender running, add the almond paste and blend until smooth, adding extra stock if the soup is too thick.
Serve warm, or chill in refrigerator at least 4 to 6 hours to serve a cold gazpacho.

65. Passion Fruit and Spicy Couscous

Preparation Time: 15 minutes
Cooking Time: 15 minutes
Servings: 4

Ingredients:

1 pinch of salt
1 pinch of allspice
1 teaspoon of mixed spice
1 cup of boiling water
2 teaspoons of extra-virgin olive oil
½ cup of full-fat Greek yogurt
½ cup of honey
1 cup of couscous
1 teaspoon of orange zest
2 oranges, peeled and sliced
2 tablespoons of passion fruit pulp
½ cup of blueberries
½ cup of walnuts, roasted and unsalted
2 tablespoons of fresh mint

Directions:

In a mixing bowl, combine the salt, allspice, mixed spice, honey, couscous, and boiling water. Cover the bowl and allow to rest for five to ten minutes, or until the water has been absorbed. Using a fork, give the mixture a good stir, then add the diced walnuts.
In a separate bowl, combine the passion fruit, yogurt, and orange zest.
To serve, dish the couscous up into four bowls, add the yogurt mixture, and top

with the sliced orange, blueberries, and mint leaves.

66. Honey and Vanilla Custard Cups with Crunchy Filo Pastry

Preparation Time: 25 minutes
Cooking Time: 2 hours
Servings: 4

Ingredients:

1 vanilla bean, cut lengthways
2 cups of full-fat milk
1/3 cup of honey
1 tablespoon of brown sugar
2 tablespoons of custard powder
4 to 6 ripe figs, quartered
1 sheet of filo pastry
2 tablespoons of raw pistachios

Directions:

Situate saucepan over medium heat, simmer vanilla bean, milk, and honey
In a heatproof dish, combine the sugar and custard powder. Transfer the milk mixture into the bowl containing the custard powder. Using a whisk, combine well and then transfer back into the saucepan.
Bring to a boil, constantly whisking until the custard thickens. Remove the vanilla bean.
Pour the custard into cups and allow to chill in the refrigerator for 2 hours.
Heat your oven to 350 F and line a baking tray with parchment.
Put the pastry sheet onto an even surface and spray lightly with olive oil cooking spray.
Sprinkle half the pistachios over the pastry and then fold the pastry in half. Heat up 2 tablespoons of honey in the microwave, then coat the pastry.
Place the pastry into the oven and allow to bake for 10 minutes. Remove from heat and allow it to cool.
Gently break the filo pastry into pieces, then top the custard with the shards and fresh-cut figs.

67. Citrus Cups

Preparation Time: 15 minutes
Cooking Time: 15 minutes
Servings: 4

Ingredients:

½ cup of water
1 tablespoon of orange juice
3 cups of full-fat Greek yogurt
1 vanilla bean
1 ruby grapefruit
2 mandarins
1 orange
6 strips of mandarin rind
1/3 cup of powdered sugar
1 small handful of fresh mint leaves

Directions:

Slice open the vanilla bean lengthways and transfer the seeds into a medium saucepan. Add the pod to the saucepan as well, followed by the water, sugar, and mandarin rind.
Bring the mixture to a boil, then turn down to a simmer and cook for five minutes or until the syrup has thickened. Allow to cool, remove the pod, and stir in the orange juice.
Pour the syrup over the sliced citrus fruits and allow to rest.
Dish the yogurt up into four bowls, top with the citrus and syrup, sprinkle with a bit of mint, then serve.

68. Bananas Foster

Preparation Time: 5 minutes
Cooking Time: 6 minutes
Servings: 4

Ingredients

2/3 cup dark brown sugar
1/4 cup butter
3 1/2 tablespoons rum
1 1/2 teaspoons vanilla extract
1/2 teaspoon of ground cinnamon
3 bananas, peeled and cut lengthwise and broad
1/4 cup coarsely chopped nuts
vanilla ice cream

Direction

Melt the butter in a deep-frying pan over medium heat. Stir in sugar, rum, vanilla, and cinnamon.
When the mixture starts to bubble, place the bananas and nuts in the pan. Bake until the bananas are hot, 1 to 2 minutes. Serve immediately with vanilla ice cream.

69. Cranberry Orange Cookies

Preparation Time: 20 minutes
Cooking Time: 16 minutes
Servings: 24

Ingredients:

1 cup of soft butter
1 cup of white sugar
1/2 cup brown sugar
1 egg
1 teaspoon grated orange peel
2 tablespoons orange juice
2 1/2 cups flour
1/2 teaspoon baking powder
1/2 teaspoon salt
2 cups chopped cranberries
1/2 cup chopped walnuts (optional)
Icing:
1/2 teaspoon grated orange peel
3 tablespoons orange juice
1 ½ cup confectioner's sugar

Directions:

Preheat the oven to 190 ° C.
Blend butter, white sugar, and brown sugar. Beat the egg until everything is well mixed. Mix 1 teaspoon of orange zest and 2 tablespoons of orange juice. Mix the flour, baking powder, and salt; stir in the orange mixture.
Mix the cranberries and, if used, the nuts until well distributed. Place the dough with a spoon on ungreased baking trays.
Bake in the preheated oven for 12 to 14 minutes. Cool on racks.
In a small bowl, mix icing ingredients. Spread over cooled cookies.

70. Vinegar Beet Bites

Preparation Time: 10 minutes
Cooking Time: 30 minutes
Servings: 4

Ingredients:

2 beets, sliced
Pinch of sea salt and black pepper
•1/3 cup balsamic vinegar
•1 cup olive oil

Directions:

Spread the beet slices on a baking sheet lined with parchment paper, add the rest of the ingredients, toss and bake at 350 degrees F for 30 minutes.
Serve the beet bites cold as a snack.

71. Mediterranean White Bean Harissa Dip

Preparation Time: 5 minutes
Cooking Time: 1 hour
Servings: 1½ cups

Ingredients:

1 whole head of garlic
½ cup olive oil, divided
1 (15-ounce / 425-g) can cannellini beans, drained and rinsed

1 teaspoon salt
1 teaspoon harissa paste (or more to taste)

Directions:

Preheat the oven to 350ºF (180ºC).
Cut about ½ inch off the top of a whole head of garlic and lightly wrap it in foil. Drizzle 1 to 2 teaspoons of olive oil over the top of the cut side. Place it in an oven-safe dish and roast it in the oven for about 1 hour or until the cloves are soft and tender.
Remove the garlic from the oven and let it cool. The garlic can be roasted up to 2 days ahead of time.
Remove the garlic cloves from their skin and place them in the bowl of a food processor along with the beans, salt, and harissa. Purée, drizzling in as much olive oil as needed until the beans are smooth. If the dip seems too stiff, add additional olive oil to loosen the dip.
Taste the dip and add additional salt, harissa, or oil as needed.
Store in the refrigerator for up to a week.
Portion out ¼ cup of dip and serve with a mixture of raw vegetables and mini pita breads.

72. Healthy Trail Mix

Preparation Time: 10 minutes
Cooking Time: 10 minutes
Servings: 4 cups

Ingredients:

1 tablespoon olive oil
1 tablespoon maple syrup
1 teaspoon vanilla
½ teaspoon cardamom
½ teaspoon allspice
2 cups mixed, unsalted nuts
¼ cup unsalted pumpkin or sunflower seeds
½ cup dried apricots, diced or thin sliced
½ cup dried figs, diced or thinly sliced
Pinch salt

Directions:

Combine the olive oil, maple syrup, vanilla, cardamom, and allspice in a large sauté pan over medium heat. Stir to combine.
Add the nuts and seeds and stir well to coat. Let the nuts and seeds toast for about 10 minutes, stirring frequently.
Remove from the heat, and add the dried apricots and figs. Stir everything well and season with salt.
Store in an airtight container.

73. Seared Halloumi Cheese with Tomato

Preparation Time: 5 minutes
Cooking Time: 4 minutes
Servings: 2

Ingredients:

3 ounces (85 g) Halloumi cheese, cut crosswise into 2 thinner, rectangular pieces
2 teaspoons prepared pesto sauce, plus additional for drizzling if desired
1 medium tomato, sliced

Directions:

Heat a nonstick skillet over medium-high heat and place the slices of Halloumi in the hot pan. After about 2 minutes, check to see if the cheese is golden on the bottom. If it is, flip the slices, top each with 1 teaspoon of pesto, and cook for another 2 minutes, or until the second side is golden.
Serve with slices of tomato and a drizzle of pesto, if desired, on the side.

74. Cucumber Cups with Bean Dip and Tomato

Preparation Time: 5 minutes
Cooking Time: 0 minutes
Servings: 2

Ingredients:

1 (8-ounce / 227-g) medium cucumber (8 to 9 inches long)
½ cup hummus (any flavor) or white bean dip
4 or 5 cherry tomatoes, sliced in half
2 tablespoons fresh basil, minced

Directions:

Slice the ends off the cucumber (about ½ inch from each side) and slice the cucumber into 1-inch pieces.
With a paring knife or a spoon, scoop most of the seeds from the inside of each cucumber piece to make a cup, being careful to not cut all the way through.
Fill each cucumber cup with about 1 tablespoon of hummus or bean dip.
Top each with a cherry tomato half and a sprinkle of fresh minced basil.

75. Arabic Mixed-Spiced Roasted Chickpeas

Prep time: 15 minutes
Cook time: 25 minutes
Servings: 2

Ingredients:

For the Seasoning Mix:
¾ teaspoon cumin
½ teaspoon coriander
½ teaspoon salt
¼ teaspoon freshly ground black pepper
¼ teaspoon paprika
¼ teaspoon cardamom
¼ teaspoon cinnamon
¼ teaspoon allspice

For the Chickpeas:

1 (15-ounce / 425-g) can chickpeas, drained and rinsed
1 tablespoon olive oil
¼ teaspoon salt

Directions:

Make the Seasoning Mix
In a small bowl, combine the cumin, coriander, salt, freshly ground black pepper, paprika, cardamom, cinnamon, and allspice. Stir well to combine
Make the Chickpeas
Preheat the oven to 400ºF (205ºC) and set the rack to the middle position. Line a baking sheet with parchment paper.
Pat the rinsed chickpeas with paper towels or roll them in a clean kitchen towel to dry off any water.
Place the chickpeas in a bowl and season them with the olive oil and salt.
Add the chickpeas to the lined baking sheet (reserve the bowl) and roast them for about 25 to 35 minutes, turning them over once or twice while cooking. Most should be light brown. Taste one or two to make sure they are slightly crisp.
Place the roasted chickpeas back into the bowl and sprinkle them with the seasoning mix. Toss lightly to combine. Taste, and add additional salt if needed. Serve warm.

76. Apple Chips with Maple Chocolate Tahini

Preparation Time: 10 minutes
Cooking Time: 0 minutes
Servings: 2

Ingredients:

2 tablespoons tahini
1 tablespoon maple syrup

1 tablespoon unsweetened cocoa powder
1 to 2 tablespoons warm water (or more if needed)
2 medium apples
1 tablespoon roasted, salted sunflower seeds

Directions:

In a small bowl, mix together the tahini, maple syrup, and cocoa powder. Add warm water, a little at a time, until thin enough to drizzle. Do not microwave it to thin it, it won't work.
Slice the apples crosswise into round slices, and then cut each piece in half to make a chip.
Lay the apple chips out on a plate and drizzle them with the chocolate tahini sauce.
Sprinkle sunflower seeds over the apple chips.

77. Strawberry Caprese Skewers with Balsamic Glaze

Preparation Time: 5 minutes
Cooking Time: 10 minutes
Servings: 2

Ingredients:

½ cup balsamic vinegar
16 whole, hulled strawberries
12 small basil leaves or 6 large leaves, halved
12 pieces of small Mozzarella balls (ciliegine)

Directions:

To make the balsamic glaze, pour the balsamic vinegar into a small saucepan and bring it to a boil. Reduce the heat to medium-low and simmer for 10 minutes, or until it's reduced by half and is thick enough to coat the back of a spoon.
On each of 4 wooden skewers, place a strawberry, a folded basil leaf, and a Mozzarella ball, repeating twice and adding a strawberry on the end. (Each skewer should have 4 strawberries, 3 basil leaves, and 3 Mozzarella balls.)
Drizzle 1 to 2 teaspoons of balsamic glaze over the skewers.

78. Eggplant Dip

Preparation Time: 10 minutes
Cooking Time: 40 minutes
Servings: 4

Ingredients:

1 eggplant, poked with a fork
2 tablespoons tahini paste
2 tablespoons lemon juice
2 garlic cloves, minced
1 tablespoon olive oil
Salt and black pepper to the taste
1 tablespoon parsley, chopped

Directions:

Put the eggplant in a roasting pan, bake at 400 degrees F for 40 minutes, cool down, peel and transfer to your food processor. Blend the rest of the ingredients except the parsley, pulse well, divide into small bowls and serve as an appetizer with the parsley sprinkled on top.

79. Veggie Fritters

Preparation Time: 10 minutes
Cooking Time: 10 minutes
Servings: 8

Ingredients:

2 garlic cloves, minced
2 yellow onions, chopped
4 scallions, chopped
2 carrots, grated
2 teaspoons cumin, ground
½ teaspoon turmeric powder
Salt and black pepper to the taste
¼ teaspoon coriander, ground
2 tablespoons parsley, chopped
¼ teaspoon lemon juice
½ cup almond flour
2 beets, peeled and grated
2 eggs, whisked
¼ cup tapioca flour
3 tablespoons olive oil

Directions:

In a bowl, combine the garlic with the onions, scallions and the rest of the ingredients except the oil, stir well and shape medium fritters out of this mix.
Preheat pan over medium-high heat, place the fritters, cook for 5 minutes on each side, arrange on a platter and serve.

80. Mediterranean Mezze Dish

Preparation Time: 20 minutes
Cooking Time: 30 minutes
Servings: 4

Ingredients

1/2 cup of kalamata or other flavorful olives
½-cup plain Greek yogurt stirred with a pinch of salt and a drizzle of olive oil
1 cup of hummus (homemade or store-bought)
1 cup of Easy Muhammara
2/3 of an English cucumber, sliced
1 cup of cherry tomatoes
1-large carrot, sliced diagonally
A small bunch of grapes
4 ounces of feta cheese, broken into pieces, lightly drizzled with olive oil and a pinch of herbs
3-pita bread, quartered, lightly brushed with olive oil, and heated in the oven

Directions:

Set out a large bowl or a generous cutting board. Place the olives, yogurt, hummus, and muhammara in small bowls and add to the bowl. Arrange the cucumber, tomatoes, carrots, grapes, and feta on the dish. Fill in the warm pita bread just before serving.

81. Marinated Feta and Artichokes

Preparation Time: 10 minutes + 4 hours
Cooking Time: 0 minute
Servings: 3

Ingredients:

4 ounces traditional Greek feta, cut into ½-inch cubes
4 ounces drained artichoke hearts, quartered lengthwise
1/3 cup extra-virgin olive oil
Zest and juice of 1 lemon
2 tablespoons roughly chopped fresh rosemary
2 tablespoons roughly chopped fresh parsley
½ teaspoon black peppercorns

Directions:

In a glass bowl, combine the feta and artichoke hearts. Add the olive oil, lemon zest and juice, rosemary, parsley, and peppercorns and toss gently to coat, being sure not to crumble the feta.
Cover and chill for 4 hours before serving.

82. Citrus-Marinated Olives

Preparation Time: 10 minutes + 4 hours
Cooking Time: 0 minute
Servings: 4

Ingredients:

2 cups mixed green olives with pits
¼ cup red wine vinegar
¼ cup extra-virgin olive oil

4 garlic cloves, finely minced
Zest and juice orange
1 teaspoon red pepper flakes
2 bay leaves
½ teaspoon ground cumin
½ teaspoon ground allspice

Directions:

In a jar, mix olives, vinegar, oil, garlic, orange zest and juice, red pepper flakes, bay leaves, cumin, and allspice. Cover and chill for 4 hours, tossing again before serving.

83. Olive Tapenade with Anchovies

Preparation Time: 70 minutes
Cooking Time: 0 minute
Servings: 4

Ingredient:

2 cups pitted Kalamata olives
2 anchovy fillets
2 teaspoons capers
1 garlic clove
1 cooked egg yolk
1 teaspoon Dijon mustard
¼ cup extra-virgin olive oil

Directions:

Wash olives in cold water and drain well.
In a food processor, mix drained olives, anchovies, capers, garlic, egg yolk, and Dijon.
With the food processor running, slowly stream in the olive oil.
Wrap and refrigerate at least 1 hour. Serve with Seedy Crackers.

84. Greek Deviled Eggs

Preparation Time: 45 minutes
Cooking Time: 15 minutes
Servings: 4

Ingredients:

4 large hardboiled eggs
2 tablespoons Roasted Garlic Aioli
½ cup feta cheese
8 pitted Kalamata olives
2 tablespoons chopped sun-dried tomatoes
1 tablespoon minced red onion
½ teaspoon dried dill
¼ teaspoon black pepper

Directions:

Slice the hardboiled eggs in half lengthwise, remove the yolks, and place the yolks in a medium bowl. Reserve the egg white halves and set aside.
Smash the yolks well with a fork. Add the aioli, feta, olives, sun-dried tomatoes, onion, dill, and pepper and stir to combine until smooth and creamy.
Spoon the filling into each egg white half and chill for 30 minutes, or up to 24 hours, covered.

85. Manchego Crackers

Preparation Time: 55 minutes
Cooking Time: 15 minutes
Servings: 4
Size/ Portion: 10 pieces

Ingredients:

4 tablespoons butter, at room temperature
1 cup Manchego cheese
1 cup almond flour
1 teaspoon salt, divided
¼ teaspoon black pepper
1 large egg

Directions:

Using an electric mixer, scourge butter and shredded cheese.
Mix almond flour with ½ teaspoon salt and pepper. Mix almond flour mixture to the cheese, mixing constantly to form a ball.
Situate onto plastic wrap and roll into a cylinder log about 1½ inches thick. Wrap tightly and refrigerate for at least 1 hour.
Preheat the oven to 350°F. Prep two baking sheets with parchment papers.
For egg wash, blend egg and remaining ½ teaspoon salt.
Slice the refrigerated dough into small rounds, about ¼ inch thick, and place on the lined baking sheets.
Egg wash the tops of the crackers and bake for 15 minutes. Pull out from the oven and situate in wire rack.
Serve.

86. Labneh and Veggie Parfaits

Preparation Time: 10 minutes
Cooking Time: 0 minutes
Servings: 2

Ingredients:

For the Labneh:
8 ounces (227 g) plain Greek yogurt (full-fat works best)
Generous pinch salt
1 teaspoon za'atar seasoning
1 teaspoon freshly squeezed lemon juice
Pinch lemon zest
For the Parfaits:
½ cup peeled, chopped cucumber
½ cup grated carrots
½ cup cherry tomatoes, halved

Directions:

Make the Labneh
Line a strainer with cheesecloth and place it over a bowl.
Stir together the Greek yogurt and salt and place in the cheesecloth. Wrap it up and let it sit for 24 hours in the refrigerator.
When ready, unwrap the labneh and place it into a clean bowl. Stir in the za'atar, lemon juice, and lemon zest.
Make the Parfaits
Divide the cucumber between two clear glasses.
Top each portion of cucumber with about 3 tablespoons of labneh.
Divide the carrots between the glasses.
Top with another 3 tablespoons of the labneh.
Top parfaits with the cherry tomatoes.
Nutrition:

87. Balsamic Artichoke Antipasto

Preparation Time: 5 minutes
Cooking Time: 0 minutes
Servings: 4

Ingredients:

1 (12-ounce / 340-g) jar roasted red peppers, drained, stemmed, and seeded
8 artichoke hearts, either frozen (thawed), or jarred (drained)
1 (16-ounce / 454-g) can garbanzo beans, drained
1 cup whole Kalamata olives, drained
¼ cup balsamic vinegar
½ teaspoon salt

Directions:

Cut the peppers into ½-inch slices and put them into a large bowl.
Cut the artichoke hearts into quarters, and add them to the bowl.
Add the garbanzo beans, olives, balsamic vinegar, and salt.
Toss all the ingredients together. Serve chilled.

88. Mascarpone Pecans Stuffed Dates

Preparation Time: 5 minutes
Cooking Time: 5 minutes
Servings: 12 to 15

Ingredients:

1 cup pecans, shells removed
1 (8-ounce) container Mascarpone cheese
20 medjool dates

Directions:

Preheat the oven to 350°F (180°C). Put the pecans on a baking sheet and bake for 5 to 6 minutes, until lightly toasted and aromatic. Take the pecans out of the oven and let cool for 5 minutes.
Once cooled, put the pecans in a food processor fitted with a chopping blade and chop until they resemble the texture of bulgur wheat or coarse sugar.
Reserve ¼ cup of ground pecans in a small bowl. Pour the remaining chopped pecans into a larger bowl and add the Mascarpone cheese.
Using a spatula, mix the cheese with the pecans until evenly combined.
Spoon the cheese mixture into a piping bag.
Using a knife, cut one side of the date lengthwise, from the stem to the bottom. Gently open and remove the pit.
Using the piping bag, squeeze a generous amount of the cheese mixture into the date where the pit used to be. Close up the date and repeat with the remaining dates.
Dip any exposed cheese from the stuffed dates into the reserved chopped pecans to cover it up.
Set the dates on a serving plate; serve immediately or chill in the fridge until you are ready to serve.

89. Peppery Potatoes

Preparation Time: 10 minutes
Cooking Time: 18 minutes
Servings: 4

Ingredients:

4-pcs large potatoes, cubed
4-tbsp extra-virgin olive oil (divided)
3-tbsp garlic, minced
½-cup coriander or cilantro, finely chopped
2-tbsp fresh lemon juice
1¾-tbsp paprika
2-tbsp parsley, minced

Directions:

Place the potatoes in a microwave-safe dish. Pour over a tablespoon of olive oil. Cover the dish tightly with plastic wrap. Heat the potatoes for seven minutes in your microwave to par-cook them.
Cook 2 tablespoons of olive oil in a pan placed over medium-low heat. Add the garlic and cover. Cook for 3 minutes. Add the coriander, and cook 2 minutes. Transfer the garlic-coriander sauce in a bowl, and set aside.
In the same pan placed over medium heat, heat 1 tablespoon of olive oil. Add the par-cooked potatoes. Do not stir! Cook for 3 minutes until browned, flipping once with a spatula. Continue cooking until browning all the sides.
Take out the potatoes and place them on a dish. Pour over the garlic-coriander sauce and lemon juice. Add the paprika, parsley, and salt. Toss gently to coat evenly.

90. Turkey Spheroids with Tzatziki Sauce

Preparation Time: 10 minutes
Cooking Time: 20 minutes
Servings: 8

Ingredients:

For Meatballs:
2-lbs ground turkey
2-tsp salt
2-cups zucchini, grated
1-tbsp lemon juice
1-cup crumbled feta cheese
1½-tsp pepper
1½-tsp garlic powder
1½-tbsp oregano
¼-cup red onion, finely minced
For Tzatziki Sauce:
1-tsp garlic powder
1-tsp dill
1-tbsp white vinegar
1-tbsp lemon juice
1-cup sour cream
½-cup grated cucumber
Salt and pepper

Directions:

Preheat your oven to 350 °F.
For the Meatballs:
Incorporate all the meatball ingredients in a large mixing bowl. Mix well until fully combined. Form the turkey mixture into spheroids, using ¼-cup of the mixture per spheroid.
Heat a non-stick skillet placed over high heat. Add the meatballs, and sear for 2 minutes.
Transfer the meatballs in a baking sheet. Situate the sheet in the oven, and bake for 15 minutes.
For the Tzatziki Sauce:
Combine and whisk together all the sauce ingredients in a medium-sized mixing bowl. Mix well until fully combined. Refrigerate the sauce until ready to serve and eat.

91. Cheesy Caprese Salad Skewers

Preparation Time: 15 minutes
Cooking Time: 0 minute
Servings: 10

Ingredients:

8-oz cherry tomatoes, sliced in half
A handful of fresh basil leaves, rinsed and drained
1-lb fresh mozzarella, cut into bite-sized slices
Balsamic vinegar
Extra virgin olive oil
Freshly ground black pepper

Directions:

Sandwich a folded basil leaf and mozzarella cheese between the halves of tomato onto a toothpick.
Drizzle with olive oil and balsamic vinegar each skewer. To serve, sprinkle with freshly ground black pepper.

92. Leafy Lacinato Tuscan Treat

Preparation Time: 10 minutes
Cooking Time: 0 minute
Servings: 1

Ingredients:

1-tsp Dijon mustard
1-tbsp light mayonnaise
3-pcs medium-sized Lacinato kale leaves
3-oz. cooked chicken breast, thinly sliced
6-bulbs red onion, thinly sliced
1-pc apple, cut into 9-slices

Directions:

Mix the mustard and mayonnaise until fully combined.
Spread the mixture generously on each of the kale leaves. Top each leaf with 1-oz. chicken slices, 3-apple slices, and 2-red onion slices. Roll each kale leaf into a wrap.

93. Greek Guacamole Hybrid Hummus

Preparation Time: 10 minutes
Cooking Time: 0 minute
Servings: 1

Ingredients:

1-15 oz. canned chickpeas
1-pc ripe avocado
¼-cup tahini paste
1-cup fresh cilantro leaves
¼-cup lemon juice
1-tsp ground cumin
¼-cup extra-virgin olive oil
1-clove garlic
½ tsp salt

Directions:

Drain the chickpeas and reserve 2-tablespoons of the liquid. Pour the reserved liquid in your food processor and add in the drained chickpeas.
Add the avocado, tahini, cilantro, lemon juice, cumin, oil, garlic, and salt. Puree the mixture into a smooth consistency.
Serve with pita chips, veggie chips, or crudités.

94. Oven-Roasted Fresh Balsamic Beets

Preparation Time: 10 minutes
Cooking Time: 35 minutes
Servings: 8 to 10

Ingredients:

10 medium fresh beets
4 tablespoons extra-virgin olive oil, divided
1 teaspoon salt
3 teaspoons fresh thyme leaves, stems removed
1/3 cup balsamic vinegar
1/2 teaspoon freshly ground black pepper

Directions:

Preheat the oven to 400°F (205°C).
Cut off the stems and roots of the beets. Wash the beets thoroughly and dry them with a paper towel.
Peel the beets using a vegetable peeler. Cut the beets into ½-inch pieces and put them into a large bowl.
Add 2 tablespoons of olive oil, the salt, and thyme to the bowl. Toss together and pour out onto a baking sheet. Spread the beets so that they are evenly distributed.
Bake for 35 to 40 minutes, turning once or twice with a spatula, until the beets are tender.
When the beets are done cooking, set them aside and let cool for 10 minutes.
In a small bowl, whisk together the remaining olive oil, vinegar, and black pepper.
Transfer the beets into a serving bowl, spoon the vinegar mixture over the beets, and serve.

95. Ultimate Mediterranean Spicy Roasted Potatoes

Preparation Time: 10 minutes
Cooking Time: 25 minutes
Servings: 5

Ingredients:

1½ pounds (680 g) red potatoes or gold potatoes
3 tablespoons garlic, minced
1½ teaspoons salt
¼ cup extra-virgin olive oil
½ cup fresh cilantro, chopped
½ teaspoon freshly ground black pepper
¼ teaspoon cayenne pepper
3 tablespoons lemon juice

Directions:

Preheat the oven to 450°F (235°C).
Scrub the potatoes and pat dry.
Cut the potatoes into ½-inch pieces and put them into a bowl.
Add the garlic, salt, and olive oil and toss everything together to evenly coat.
Pour the potato mixture onto a baking sheet, spread the potatoes out evenly, and put them into the oven, roasting for 25 minutes. Halfway through roasting, turn the potatoes with a spatula; continue roasting for the remainder of time until the potato edges start to brown.
Remove the potatoes from the oven and let them cool on the baking sheet for 5 minutes.
Using a spatula, remove the potatoes from the pan and put them into a bowl.
Add the cilantro, black pepper, cayenne, and lemon juice to the potatoes and toss until well mixed.
Serve warm.

96. Goat-Mascarpone Cheese Stuffed Bell Peppers

Preparation Time: 10 minutes
Cooking Time: 8 minutes
Servings: 8 to 10

Ingredients:

20 to 25 mini sweet bell peppers, assortment of colors
1 tablespoon extra-virgin olive oil
4 ounces (113 g) Goat cheese, at room temperature
4 ounces (113 g) Mascarpone cheese, at room temperature
1 tablespoon fresh chives, chopped
1 tablespoon lemon zest

Directions:

Preheat the oven to 400°F (205°C).
Remove the stem, cap, and any seeds from the peppers. Put them into a bowl and toss to coat with the olive oil.
Put the peppers onto a baking sheet; bake for 8 minutes.
Remove the peppers from the oven and let cool completely.
In a medium bowl, add the Goat cheese, Mascarpone cheese, chives, and lemon zest. Stir to combine, then spoon mixture into a piping bag.
Fill each pepper to the top with the cheese mixture, using the piping bag.
Chill the peppers in the fridge for at least 30 minutes before serving.

97. Mediterranean-Style Trail Mix

Preparation Time: 10 minutes
Cooking Time: 0 minutes
Servings: 6

Ingredients:

1 cup roughly chopped unsalted walnuts
½ cup roughly chopped salted almonds
½ cup shelled salted pistachios
½ cup roughly chopped apricots
1/2 cup roughly chopped dates
1/3 cup dried figs, sliced in half

Directions:

In a large zip-top bag, combine the walnuts, almonds, pistachios, apricots, dates, and figs and mix well.

98. Savory Mediterranean Spiced Popcorn

Preparation Time: 10 minutes
Cooking Time: 2 minutes
Servings: 4 to 6

Ingredients:

3 tablespoons extra-virgin olive oil
1/4 teaspoon garlic powder
1/4 teaspoon freshly ground black pepper
1/4 teaspoon sea salt
1/8 teaspoon dried thyme
1/8 teaspoon dried oregano
12 cups plain popped popcorn

Directions:

In a large sauté pan or skillet, heat the oil over medium heat, until shimmering, and then add the garlic powder, pepper, salt, thyme, and oregano until fragrant.
In a large bowl, drizzle the oil over the popcorn, toss, and serve.

99. Turkish Spiced Mixed-Nuts

Preparation Time: 10 minutes
Cooking Time: 5 minutes
Servings: 4 to 6

Ingredients:

1 tablespoon extra-virgin olive oil
1 cup mixed nuts (walnuts, almonds, cashews, peanuts)
2 tablespoons paprika
1 tablespoon dried mint
1/2 tablespoon ground cinnamon
1/2 tablespoon kosher salt
1/4 tablespoon garlic powder
1/4 teaspoon freshly ground black pepper
1/8 tablespoon ground cumin

Directions:

In a small to medium saucepan, heat the oil on low heat.
Once the oil is warm, add the nuts, paprika, mint, cinnamon, salt, garlic powder, pepper, and cumin and stir continually until the spices are well incorporated with the nuts.

100. Honey Fig-Pecan Energy Bites

Preparation Time: 10 minutes
Cooking Time: 0 minutes
Servings: 6

Ingredients:

¾ cup diced dried figs
½ cup chopped pecans
¼ cup rolled oats (old-fashioned or quick oats)
2 tablespoons ground flaxseed or wheat germ (flaxseed for gluten-free)
2 tablespoons powdered or regular peanut butter
2 tablespoons honey

Directions:

In a medium bowl, mix together the figs, pecans, oats, flaxseed, and peanut butter. Drizzle with the honey, and mix everything together. A wooden spoon works well to press the figs and nuts into the honey and powdery ingredients. (If you're using regular peanut butter instead of powdered, the dough will be stickier to handle, so freeze the dough for 5 minutes before making the bites.)
Divide the dough evenly into four sections in the bowl. Dampen your hands with water—but don't get them too wet or the dough will stick to them. Using your hands, roll three bites out of each of the four sections of dough, making 12 total energy bites.
Enjoy immediately or chill in the freezer for 5 minutes to firm up the bites before serving. The bites can be stored in a sealed container in the refrigerator for up to 1 week.

101. Citrus-Thyme Chickpeas

Preparation Time: 5 minutes
Cooking Time: 23 minutes
Servings: 4

Ingredients:

1 (15-ounce / 425-g) can chickpeas, drained and rinsed
2 teaspoons extra-virgin olive oil
1/4 teaspoon dried thyme or ½ teaspoon chopped fresh thyme leaves
1/8 teaspoon kosher or sea salt
1/2 teaspoon zest of ½ orange

Directions:

Preheat the oven to 450ºF (235ºC).
Spread the chickpeas on a clean kitchen towel, and rub gently until dry.
Spread the chickpeas on a large, rimmed baking sheet. Drizzle with the oil, and sprinkle with the thyme and salt. Using a Microplane or citrus zester, zest about half of the orange over the chickpeas. Mix well using your hands.
Bake for 10 minutes, then open the oven door and, using an oven mitt, give the baking sheet a quick shake. (Do not remove the sheet from the oven.) Bake for 10 minutes more. Taste the chickpeas (carefully!). If they are golden but you think they could be a bit crunchier, bake for 3 minutes more before serving.

102. Crispy Seedy Crackers

Preparation Time: 10 minutes
Cooking Time: 10 minutes
Servings: 24 crackers

Ingredients:

1 cup almond flour
1 tablespoon sesame seeds
1 tablespoon flaxseed
1 tablespoon chia seeds
¼ teaspoon baking soda
¼ teaspoon salt
Freshly ground black pepper, to taste
1 large egg, at room temperature

Directions:

Preheat the oven to 350ºF (180ºC).
In a large bowl, combine the almond flour, sesame seeds, flaxseed, chia seeds, baking soda, salt, and pepper and stir well.
In a small bowl, whisk the egg until well beaten. Add to the dry ingredients and stir well to combine and form the dough into a ball.
Place one layer of parchment paper on your counter-top and place the dough on top. Cover with a second layer of parchment and, using a rolling pin, roll the dough to 1/8-inch thickness, aiming for a rectangular shape.
Cut the dough into 1- to 2-inch crackers and bake on parchment until crispy and slightly golden, 10 to 15 minutes, depending on thickness. Alternatively, you can bake the large rolled dough prior to cutting and break into free-form crackers once baked and crispy.
Store in an airtight container in the fridge for up to 1 week.

103. Feta Zucchini Roulades

Preparation Time: 10 minutes
Cooking Time: 10 minutes
Servings: 6

Ingredients:

1/2 cup Feta
1 garlic clove, minced
2 tablespoons fresh basil, minced
1 tablespoon capers, minced
1/8 teaspoon salt
1/8 teaspoon red pepper flakes
1 tablespoon lemon juice
2 medium zucchini
12 toothpicks

Directions:

Preheat the air fryer to 360ºF (182ºC). (If using a grill attachment, make sure it is inside the air fryer during preheating.)
In a small bowl, combine the Feta, garlic, basil, capers, salt, red pepper flakes, and lemon juice.
Slice the zucchini into 1/8-inch strips lengthwise. (Each zucchini should yield around 6 strips.)
Spread 1 tablespoon of the cheese filling onto each slice of zucchini, then roll it up and secure it with a toothpick through the middle.
Place the zucchini roulades into the air fryer basket in a single layer, making sure that they don't touch each other.
Bake or grill in the air fryer for 10 minutes.
Remove the zucchini roulades from the air fryer and gently remove the toothpicks before serving.

104. Cucumber Sandwich Bites

Preparation Time: 5 minutes
Cooking Time: 0 minute
Servings: 12

Ingredients:

1 cucumber, sliced
8 slices whole wheat bread
2 tablespoons cream cheese, soft
1 tablespoon chives, chopped
¼ cup avocado, peeled, pitted and mashed
1 teaspoon mustard
Salt and black pepper to the taste

Directions:

Spread the mashed avocado on each bread slice, also spread the rest of the ingredients except the cucumber slices. Divide the cucumber slices on the bread slices, cut each slice in thirds, arrange on a platter and serve as an appetizer.

105. Yogurt Dip

Preparation Time: 10 minutes
Cooking Time: 0 minute
Servings: 6

Ingredients:

2 cups Greek yogurt
2 tablespoons pistachios, toasted and chopped
A pinch of salt and white pepper
2 tablespoons mint, chopped
1 tablespoon kalamata olives, pitted and chopped
¼ cup zaatar spice
¼ cup pomegranate seeds
1/3 cup olive oil

Directions:

Mix the yogurt with the pistachios and the rest of the ingredients, whisk well, divide into small cups and serve with pita chips on the side.

106. Olives and Cheese Stuffed Tomatoes

Preparation Time: 10 minutes
Cooking Time: 0 minute
Servings: 24

Ingredients:

24 cherry tomatoes, top cut off and insides scooped out
2 tablespoons olive oil
¼ teaspoon red pepper flakes
½ cup feta cheese, crumbled
2 tablespoons black olive paste
¼ cup mint, torn

Directions:

In a bowl, mix the olives paste with the rest of the ingredients except the cherry tomatoes and whisk well. Stuff the cherry tomatoes with this mix, arrange them all on a platter and serve as an appetizer.

107. Pepper Tapenade

Preparation Time: 10 minutes
Cooking Time: 0 minute
Servings: 4

Ingredients:

7 ounces roasted red peppers, chopped
½ cup parmesan, grated
1/3 cup parsley, chopped
14 ounces canned artichokes, drained and chopped
3 tablespoons olive oil
¼ cup capers, drained
1 and ½ tablespoons lemon juice
2 garlic cloves, minced

Directions:

In your blender, combine the red peppers with the parmesan and the rest of the ingredients and pulse well. Divide into cups and serve as a snack.

108. Coriander Falafel

Preparation Time: 10 minutes
Cooking Time: 10 minutes
Servings: 8

Ingredients:

1 cup canned garbanzo beans
1 bunch parsley leaves
1 yellow onion, chopped
5 garlic cloves, minced
1 teaspoon coriander, ground
A pinch of salt and black pepper
¼ teaspoon cayenne pepper
¼ teaspoon baking soda
¼ teaspoon cumin powder
1 teaspoon lemon juice
3 tablespoons tapioca flour
Olive oil for frying

Directions:

In your food processor, combine the beans with the parsley, onion and the rest the ingredients except the oil and the flour and pulse well. Transfer the mix to a bowl, add the flour, stir well, shape 16 balls out of this mix and flatten them a bit.
Preheat pan over medium-high heat, add the falafels, cook them for 5 minutes on both sides, put in paper towels, drain excess grease, arrange them on a platter and serve as an appetizer.

109. Chickpeas and Red Pepper Hummus

Preparation Time: 10 minutes
Cooking Time: 0 minute
Servings: 6

Ingredients:

6 ounces roasted red peppers, peeled and chopped
16 ounces canned chickpeas, drained and rinsed
¼ cup Greek yogurt

3 tablespoons tahini paste
Juice of 1 lemon
3 garlic cloves, minced
1 tablespoon olive oil
A pinch of salt and black pepper
1 tablespoon parsley, chopped

Directions:

In your food processor, combine the red peppers with the rest of the ingredients except the oil and the parsley and pulse well. Add the oil, pulse again, divide into cups, sprinkle the parsley on top and serve as a party spread.

110. Hummus with Ground Lamb

Preparation Time: 10 minutes
Cooking Time: 15 minutes
Servings: 8

Ingredients:

10 ounces hummus
12 ounces lamb meat, ground
½ cup pomegranate seeds
¼ cup parsley, chopped
1 tablespoon olive oil
Pita chips for serving

Directions:

Preheat pan over medium-high heat, cook the meat, and brown for 15 minutes stirring often. Spread the hummus on a platter, spread the ground lamb all over, also spread the pomegranate seeds and the parsley and serve with pita chips as a snack.

111. The Ultimate Mediterranean Appetizer Dish

Preparation Time: 5 minutes
Cooking Time: 10 minutes
Servings: 17

Ingredients:

Fruit and vegetables:
Diced melon and slices wrapped in prosciutto
green and purple grapes, fresh pears, sliced and an assortment of kalamata olives
sliced carrots, cucumbers, celery, and cherry tomatoes
Bread and crackers:
Cheeses:
Old gouda and raw gouda cut into cubes
Greek feta drizzled with Mediterranean oregano
Soft goat cheese topped with fig paste above link I Deli always about 120 grams of a piece of fresh soft goat cheese sliced

Directions:

Freshly crumbled feta with jalapeno (preferably sheep's milk)
8 oz feta, mix with chopped jalapeno (start with a teaspoon and add more to taste) or mix with chopped sun-dried tomatoes to taste. I also like to combine the two! Tomatoes and jalapeno together. Drizzle the cheese mixture with extra virgin olive oil and spread it on crackers or as a dip for chips or pita bread.

112. Mediterranean Nachos

Preparation Time: 20 minutes
Cooking Time: 30 minutes
Servings: 4

Ingredient

4-5 pita bread, each cut into 8-triangles
1/2 cup chickpeas, drained and rinsed
1-teaspoon of olive oil + more for drizzle
Salt and pepper to taste
1-teaspoon of onion powder
1-teaspoon of garlic powder
1-teaspoon paprika
1/2 medium cucumber, cut into small cubes
1/4 cup kalamata olives, pitted and sliced
¼ cup of green olives
1-large tomato, finely chopped
1/2 cup banana peppers, sliced
¼ red onion, thinly sliced
1/2 cup of feta crumbles
2-green onions, sliced for garnish
Paperchains for garnish
2–3 TBSP fresh parsley, chopped for garnish
Pinch of Za'atar spice for garnish
Hummus, Tzatziki for serving

Directions:

Start with preheating the oven to 375° F. Then line 2-baking trays with parchment paper and divide pita triangles over them; Lightly drizzle olive oil along with salt and pepper and toss evenly. Place the chickpeas on a second baking tray and mix with 1-teaspoon olive oil, salt, pepper, garlic powder, paprika, and onion powder. Now place both sheets in the oven & bake. Bake pita bread for 10 minutes and chickpeas for 15-20 minutes, stirring in between. Check for desired crunchiness and remove from the oven.
When the pita bread comes out of the oven, place them on a tray/plate.
Top pita nachos with all toppings (optional: you can return the nachos to the oven for 4 minutes if you want the toppings to be warm too!). Garnish with a pinch of za'atar evenly spread over French fries, freshly ground pepper, green onion, and chopped parsley. Serve immediately with hummus and tzatziki sauce. See images for plating inspiration

113. Smoked Salmon and Avocado Summer Rolls

Preparation Time: 15 minutes
Cooking Time: 30 minutes
Servings: 4

Ingredients:

12 round rice paper wrappers
6-slices of smoked salmon
1-avocado, thinly sliced
2-3 cups of raw sprouts or cooked vermicelli
1-cucumber, seeded, and cut into strips
miso sesame dressing or vissaus vinaigrette, dipping into

Directions:

Take a rice paper wrapper and immerse it completely in a bowl of hot tap water for 10-15 seconds. Place the wrapper on a plate or cutting board - it will get softer as you assemble your roll. Add fillings as desired: avocado smoked salmon, cucumbers, Brussels sprouts, or noodles. Start folding the bottom half of the wrap over the filling, holding the fold in place, fold in the sides, and roll. Repeat if necessary. Dip in the miso sesame dressing or fish sauce vinaigrette and enjoy!
Roll the mixture into small balls, about 1-2 tablespoons per ball. Place in an airtight container and store in the refrigerator for up to 2 weeks. You can also store the balls in the freezer for up to 1 month.

114. Healthy Lemon Bars

Preparation Time: 15 minutes
Cooking Time: 40 minutes
Servings: 12

Ingredients:

For the crust:
¼ cup coconut sugar (or 2-3 tablespoons honey or maple syrup)

¼-cup melted and cooled coconut oil
1-egg, at room temperature
¼ teaspoon of almond extract
1-cup packed fine almond flour
3-tablespoons of coconut flour
1/4 teaspoon of salt
For the filling:
Peel of 1 lemon
½-cup freshly squeezed lemon juice
½ cup of honey
4-large eggs
1-egg yolk
1-tablespoon coconut flour, sifted (or sub tapioca flour or arrowroot flour)
To garnish:
Icing sugar (sifted)
Lemon peel

Directions:

Start with preheating the oven to 325 degrees F. Line an 8x8 inch pan with parchment paper. (Do not use a glass pan as this will likely burn the bottom of the crust.)
You need to make the crust: In a medium bowl, add the coconut oil, coconut sugar, egg, and almond extract. Mix until smooth. Add almond flour, coconut flour, and salt. Mix again until a dough form. Then start pressing the dough evenly into the prepared pan with your hands. Bake for 10 minutes, remove from oven and let cool for two minutes before adding your filling.
While your crust is baking, you can make the filling: In a medium bowl, whisk the lemon zest, lemon juice, honey, eggs, egg yolks, and coconut flour. Pour over the crust. Bake for 18-25 minutes or until filling is set and no longer shaking. Allow to cool completely on a wire rack, then refrigerate for at least 4 hours to set the bars. Once ready to serve, use a sharp knife to cut into 12 bars. I recommend garnishing them with icing sugar and a little lemon zest before serving. To enjoy!

115. Mediterranean Baking Tray With Halloumi Pieces

Preparation Time: 0 minutes
Cooking Time: 45 minutes
Servings: 2

Ingredients

400 g (14 oz) baby potatoes, waxed
4-carrots tops removed and scrubbed
2-red (paprika) peppers (paprika), core and seeds removed
1-zucchini (zucchini), garnished with a tail
1-garlic bulb
1-lemon washed
2-sprigs of fresh rosemary
60 ml extra virgin olive oil
sea salt and freshly ground black pepper
250 g (8¾ oz) Haloumi
12 black Kalamata olives, drained and pitted
To serve
rocket (arugula) or mesclun
roasted pine nuts
sea salt and freshly ground black pepper
balsamic vinegar from extra virgin olive oil

Directions

Start heating the oven to 200° C (400° F / Gas mark 6) & line a baking tray with parchment paper.
Cut the potatoes, carrots, bell pepper (bell pepper), & zucchini into bite-sized pieces, cut the garlic crosswise in half, and cut the lemon into thin wedges. Place on the baking tray and add the rosemary. Drizzle over the oil, season with salt and pepper, and mix until well coated. Bake for 25-30 minutes or until vegetables is almost cooked.
Divide the halloumi into bite-sized pieces and divide it over the vegetables along with the olives. Change the oven setting to grill, increase the temperature and grill the halloumi, olives, and vegetables for 5–10 minutes or until the halloumi is soft and golden and the vegetables are soft and golden brown.
Serve with a handful of arugulas, a drizzle of pine nuts and herbs, and a drizzle of oil and vinegar.

CHAPTER 3: PASTA AND COUSCOUS

116. Simple Pesto Pasta

Preparation Time: 10 minutes
Cooking Time: 10 minutes
Servings: 4

Ingredients:

1 lb. spaghetti
4 cups fresh basil leaves, stems removed
3 cloves garlic
1 tsp. salt
1/2 tsp. freshly ground black pepper
1/4 cup lemon juice
1/2 cup pine nuts, toasted
1/2 cup grated Parmesan cheese
1 cup extra-virgin olive oil

Directions:

Bring a large pot of salted water to a boil. Add the spaghetti to the pot and cook for 8 minutes.
Put basil, garlic, salt, pepper, lemon juice, pine nuts, and Parmesan cheese in a food processor bowl with chopping blade and purée.
While the processor is running, slowly drizzle the olive oil through the top opening. Process until all the olive oil has been added.
Reserve ½ cup of the pasta water. Drain the pasta and put it into a bowl. Immediately add the pesto and pasta water to the pasta and toss everything together. Serve warm.

117. Flat Meat Pies

Preparation Time: 20 minutes
Cooking Time: 15 minutes
Servings: 4

Ingredients:

½ lb. ground beef
1 small onion, finely chopped
1 medium tomato, finely diced and strained
½ tsp. salt
½ tsp. freshly ground black pepper
2 sheets puff pastry

Directions:

Preheat the oven to 400°F.
In a medium bowl, combine the beef, onion, tomato, salt, and pepper. Set aside.
Line 2 baking sheets with parchment paper. Cut the puff pastry dough into 4-inch squares and lay them flat on the baking sheets.
Scoop about 2 tbsp. of beef mixture onto each piece of dough. Spread the meat on the dough, leaving a ½-inch edge on each side.
Put the meat pies in the oven and bake for 12 to 15 minutes until edges are golden brown.

118. Meaty Baked Penne

Preparation Time: 10 minutes
Cooking Time: 40 minutes
Servings: 6

Ingredients:

1 lb. penne pasta
1 lb. ground beef
1 tsp. salt
1 (25-oz.) jar marinara sauce
1 (1-lb.) bag baby spinach, washed
3 cups shredded mozzarella cheese, divided

Directions:

Bring a large pot of salted water to a boil, add the penne, and cook for 7 minutes. Reserve 2 cups of e pasta water and drain the pasta.
Preheat the oven to 350°F.
In a large saucepan over medium heat, cook the ground beef and salt. Brown the ground beef for about 5 minutes.
Stir in marinara sauce, and 2 cups of pasta water. Let simmer for 5 minutes.
Add a handful of spinach at a time into the sauce, and cook for another 3 minutes.
To assemble, in a 9-by-13-inch baking dish, add the pasta and pour the pasta sauce over it. Stir in 1½ cups of the mozzarella cheese. Cover the dish with foil and bake for 20 minutes.
After 20 minutes, remove the foil, top with the rest of the mozzarella, and bake for another 10 minutes. Serve warm.

119. Mediterranean Pasta with Tomato Sauce and Vegetables

Preparation Time: 15 minutes
Cooking Time: 25 minutes
Servings: 8

Ingredients:

8 oz. linguine or spaghetti, cooked
1 tsp. garlic powder
1 (28 oz.) can whole peeled tomatoes, drained and sliced
1 tbsp. olive oil
1 (8 oz.) can tomato sauce
½ tsp. Italian seasoning
8 oz. mushrooms, sliced
8 oz. yellow squash, sliced
8 oz. zucchini, sliced
½ tsp. sugar
½ cup grated Parmesan cheese

Directions:

In a medium saucepan, mix tomato sauce, tomatoes, sugar, Italian seasoning, and garlic powder. Bring to boil on medium heat. Reduce heat to low. Cover and simmer for 20 minutes.
In a large skillet, heat olive oil on medium-high heat.
Add squash, mushrooms, and zucchini. Cook, stirring, for 4 minutes or until tender-crisp.
Stir vegetables into the tomato sauce.
Place pasta in a serving bowl.
Spoon vegetable mixture over pasta and toss to coat.
Top with grated Parmesan cheese.

120. Very Vegan Patras Pasta

Preparation Time: 5 minutes
Cooking Time: 10 minutes
Servings: 6

Ingredients:

4-quarts salted water
10-oz. gluten-free and whole-grain pasta
5-cloves garlic, minced
1-cup hummus
Salt and pepper
1/3-cup water
½-cup walnuts

½-cup olives
2-tbsp dried cranberries (optional)

Directions:

Bring the salted water to a boil for cooking the pasta.
In the meantime, prepare for the hummus sauce. Combine the garlic, hummus, salt, and pepper with water in a mixing bowl. Add the walnuts, olive, and dried cranberries, if desired. Set aside.
Add the pasta in the boiling water. Cook the pasta following the manufacturer's specifications until attaining an al dente texture. Drain the pasta.
Transfer the pasta to a large serving bowl and combine with the sauce.

121. Cheesy Spaghetti with Pine Nuts

Preparation Time: 10 minutes
Cooking Time: 10 minutes
Servings: 4

Ingredients:

8 oz. spaghetti
4 tbsp. (½ stick) unsalted butter
1 tsp. freshly ground black pepper
½ cup pine nuts
1 cup fresh grated Parmesan cheese, divided

Directions:

Bring a large pot of salted water to a boil. Add the pasta and cook for 8 minutes.
In a large saucepan over medium heat, combine the butter, black pepper, and pine nuts. Cook for 2 to 3 minutes or until the pine nuts are lightly toasted.
Reserve ½ cup of the pasta water. Drain the pasta and put it into the pan with the pine nuts.
Add ¾ cup of Parmesan cheese and the reserved pasta water to the pasta and toss everything together to evenly coat the pasta.
To serve, put the pasta in a serving dish and top with the remaining ¼ cup of Parmesan cheese.

122. Creamy Garlic-Parmesan Chicken Pasta

Preparation Time: 5 minutes
Cooking Time: 25 minutes
Servings: 6

Ingredients:

2 boneless, skinless chicken breasts
3 tbsp. extra-virgin olive oil
1½ tsp. salt
1 large onion, thinly sliced
3 tbsp. garlic, minced
1 lb. fettuccine pasta
1 cup heavy (whipping) cream
¾ cup freshly grated Parmesan cheese, divided
½ tsp. freshly ground black pepper

Directions:

Bring a large pot of salted water to a simmer.
Cut the chicken into thin strips.
In a large skillet over medium heat, cook the olive oil and chicken for 3 minutes.
Next add the salt, onion, and garlic to the pan with the chicken. Cook for 7 minutes.
Bring the pot of salted water to a boil and add the pasta, then let it cook for 7 minutes.
While the pasta is cooking, add the cream, ½ cup of Parmesan cheese, and black pepper to the chicken; simmer for 3 minutes.
Reserve ½ cup of the pasta water. Drain the pasta and add it to the chicken cream sauce.
Add the reserved pasta water to the pasta and toss together. Let simmer for 2 minutes. Top with the remaining ¼ cup Parmesan cheese and serve warm.

123. Chicken Spinach and Artichoke Stuffed Spaghetti Squash

Preparation Time: 10 minutes
Cook Time: 23 minutes
Servings: 4

Ingredients:

4 oz reduced-fat cream cheese, cubed and softened
1/4 tsp ground pepper
3 tbsp water
1/4 tsp salt
Crushed red peppers
3 lb spaghetti squash, halved lengthwise and seeded
1/2 cup shredded parmesan cheese
5 oz pack baby spinach
10 oz pack artichoke hearts, chopped
Diced fresh basil

Directions:

On a microwaveable dish, place your squash halves with the cut side facing up. Add 2 tbsp of water to the squash. Set the microwave to high and cook without covering the dish for about 15 minutes. You can also place the squash on a prepared baking sheet (rimmed) and bake at 400 degrees F for 40 minutes.
Set your stove to medium heat and place a large skillet containing 1 tbsp of water on it. Add spinach into the pan and stir while it cooks for about 5 minutes, or until the vegetable wilts. Drain the spinach and place in a bowl.
Place the rack in the upper third region of your oven, then preheat your broiler.
Using a fork, scrape squash from each shell half, and place them in a bowl. Add artichoke hearts, pepper, salt, cream cheese, and ¼ cup parmesan into the bowl of squash. Mix well. Place squash shells on a baking sheet, and add the squash mixture into the shells. Add the remaining parmesan on top and broil for 3 minutes.
Garnish with red pepper and basil, and serve.

124. Angel Hair with Asparagus-Kale Pesto

Preparation Time: 10 minutes
Cooking Time: 10 minutes
Servings: 6

Ingredients:

¾ pound asparagus, woody ends removed, and coarsely chopped
¼ pound kale, thoroughly washed
½ cup grated Asiago cheese
¼ cup fresh basil
¼ cup extra-virgin olive oil
Juice of 1 lemon
Sea salt
Freshly ground black pepper
1-pound angel hair pasta
Zest of 1 lemon

Directions:

In a food processor, pulse the asparagus and kale until very finely chopped.
Add the Asiago cheese, basil, olive oil, and lemon juice and pulse to form a smooth pesto.
Season with sea salt and pepper and set aside.

Cook the pasta al dente according to the package directions. Drain and transfer to a large bowl.
Add the pesto, tossing well to coat
Sprinkle with lemon zest and serve.
Cooking tip: You can make the asparagus pesto up to 3 days ahead. Keep it refrigerated until you need it.

125. Spicy Pasta Puttanesca

Preparation Time: 10 minutes
Cooking Time: 20 minutes
Servings: 4

Ingredients:

2 teaspoons extra-virgin olive oil
½ sweet onion, finely chopped
2 teaspoons minced garlic
1 (28-ounce) can sodium-free diced tomatoes
½ cup chopped anchovies
2 teaspoons chopped fresh oregano
2 teaspoons chopped fresh basil
½ teaspoon red pepper flakes
½ cup quartered Kalamata olives
¼ cup sodium-free chicken broth
1 tablespoon capers, drained and rinsed
Juice of 1 lemon
4 cups cooked whole-grain penne

Directions:

In a large saucepan over medium heat, heat the olive oil.
Add the onion and garlic, and sauté for about 3 minutes until softened.
Stir in the tomatoes, anchovies, oregano, basil, and red pepper flakes. Bring the sauce to a boil and reduce the heat to low. Simmer for 15 minutes, stirring occasionally.
Stir in the olives, chicken broth, capers, and lemon juice.
Cook the pasta according to the package directions and serve topped with the sauce.
Ingredient tip: Do not mistake sardines for anchovies, although they are both small, silvery fish sold in cans. Anchovies are usually salted in brine and matured to create a distinctive, rich taste.

126. Roasted Vegetarian Lasagna

Preparation Time: 25 minutes
Cooking Time: 50 minutes
Servings: 6

Ingredients:

1 eggplant, thickly sliced
2 zucchini, sliced lengthwise
1 yellow squash, sliced lengthwise
1 sweet onion, thickly sliced
2 tablespoons extra-virgin olive oil
1 (28-ounce) can sodium-free diced tomatoes
1 cup quartered, canned, water-packed artichoke hearts, drained
2 teaspoons minced garlic
2 teaspoons chopped fresh basil
2 teaspoons chopped fresh oregano
Pinch red pepper flakes
12 no-boil whole-grain lasagna noodles
¾ cup grated Asiago cheese

Directions:

Preheat the oven to 400°F.
Line a baking sheet with aluminum foil and set aside.
In a large bowl, toss together the eggplant, zucchini, yellow squash, onion, and olive oil to coat.
Arrange the vegetables on the prepared sheet and roast for about 20 minutes, or until tender and lightly caramelized.
Chop the roasted vegetables well and transfer them to a large bowl.
Stir in the tomatoes, artichoke hearts, garlic, basil, oregano, and red pepper flakes
Spoon one-quarter of the vegetable mixture into the bottom of a deep 9-by-13-inch baking dish.
Arrange 4 lasagna noodles over the sauce.
Repeat, alternating sauce and noodles, ending with sauce.
Sprinkle the Asiago cheese evenly over the top. Bake for about 30 minutes until bubbly and hot.
Remove from the oven and cool for 15 minutes before serving.
Substitution tip: If having a vegetarian meal is not a requirement, lean ground beef (92%) or ground chicken can be added to the roasted vegetable sauce for a more robust meal. Brown the ground meat in a skillet and add it to the finished sauce before assembling the lasagna.

127. Artichoke Chicken Pasta

Preparation Time: 20 minutes
Cooking Time: 5 minutes
Servings: 4

Ingredients:

2 cloves garlic, crushed
2 lemons, wedged
2 tbsp. lemon juice
14 oz. artichoke hearts, chopped
1-lb. chicken breast fillet, diced
½ cup feta cheese, crumbled
1 tbsp. olive oil
16 oz. whole-wheat (gluten-free) pasta of your choice
3 tbsp. parsley, chopped
½ cup red onion, chopped
2 tsp. oregano
1 tomato, chopped
Ground black pepper and salt, to taste

Directions:

Pour the water into a deep saucepan and boil it. Add the pasta and some salt; cook it as per package directions. Drain the water and set aside the pasta.
Over medium stove flame, heat the oil in a skillet or saucepan (preferably of medium size).
Sauté the onions and garlic until softened and translucent, stir in between.
Add the chicken and cook until it is no longer pink.
Mix in the tomatoes, artichoke hearts, parsley, feta cheese, oregano, lemon juice and the cooked pasta.
Combine well and cook for 3-4 minutes, stirring frequently.
Season with black pepper and salt. Garnish with lemon wedges and serve warm.

128. Spinach Beef Pasta

Preparation Time: 30 minutes
Cooking Time: 10 minutes
Servings: 4

Ingredients:

1 ¼ cups uncooked orzo pasta
¾ cup baby spinach
2 tbsp. olive oil
1 ½ lb. beef tenderloin
¾ cup feta cheese
2 quarts water
1 cup cherry tomatoes, halved
¼ tsp. salt

Directions:

Rub the meat with pepper and cut into small cubes.
Over medium stove flame; heat the oil in a deep saucepan (preferably of medium size).
Add and stir-fry the meat until it is evenly brown.
Add the water and boil the mixture; stir in the orzo and salt.
Cook the mixture for 7-8 minutes. Add the spinach and cook until it wilts.
Add the tomatoes and cheese; combine and serve warm.

129. Asparagus Parmesan Pasta

Preparation Time: 25 minutes
Cooking Time: 4 minutes
Servings: 2

Ingredients:

1 tsp. extra-virgin olive oil
1 tsp. lemon juice
¾ cup whole milk
½ bunch asparagus, trimmed and cut into small pieces
½ cup parmesan cheese, grated
2 tbsp. garlic, minced
2 tbsp. almond flour
2 tsp. whole grain mustard
4 oz. whole-wheat penne pasta
1 tsp. tarragon, minced
Ground black pepper and salt, to taste

Directions:

Pour the water into a deep saucepan and boil it. Add the pasta and some salt; cook it as per package directions. Drain the water and set aside the pasta.
Take another pan, pour 8 cups of water and let it come to boiling. Add the asparagus and boil until it is soft. Drain and set aside.
In a mixing bowl, combine the milk, flour, mustard, black pepper and salt. Set aside.
Over medium stove flame, heat the oil in a skillet or saucepan (preferably of medium size).
Sauté the garlic until softened and fragrant, stirring in between.
Add the milk mixture and let it simmer. Add the tarragon, lemon juice and lemon zest; mix to combine.
Add the cooked pasta, asparagus, and simmer until the sauce thickens, stirring frequently.
Top with parmesan cheese and serve warm.

130. Mussels Linguine Delight

Preparation Time: 20 minutes
Cooking Time: 10 minutes
Servings: 4

Ingredients:

1 lb. mussels, cleaned and debearded
1 tbsp. olive oil
½ tsp. oregano
½ tsp. basil, chopped
1 clove garlic, minced
1 lemon, wedges
8 oz. whole-wheat linguine pasta
1 pinch pepper flakes, crushed
1 (14.5 oz.) can tomatoes, crushed
¼ cup white wine

Directions:

Pour the water into a deep saucepan and boil it. Add the pasta and some salt; cook it as per package directions. Drain the water and set aside the pasta.
Over a medium stove flame; heat the oil in a skillet or saucepan (preferably medium size).
Sauté the garlic until softened and fragrant, stir in between.
Add the tomatoes, basil, pepper flakes and oregano. Reduce the heat and simmer the mix.
Add the mussels, wine and increase the heat. Cook for 3-5 minutes.
Wait for the mussels to cook and open. Mix in the pasta.
Garnish with the parsley; serve with some lemon wedges on the side.

131. Arugula Pasta Soup

Preparation Time: 15 minutes
Cooking Time: 5 minutes
Servings: 6

Ingredients:

7 oz. chickpeas, rinsed
4 eggs, lightly beaten
2 tbsp. lemon juice
3 cups arugula, chopped
6 tbsp. parmesan cheese
6 cups chicken broth
1 pinch of nutmeg
1 bunch scallions, sliced (greens and whites sliced separately)
1 1/3 cups whole-wheat pasta shells
2 cups water
Ground black pepper, to taste

Directions:

In a cooking pot or deep saucepan, combine the pasta, scallion whites, chickpeas, water, broth and nutmeg.
Heat the mixture; cover and bring to a boil.
Take off the lid and simmer the mixture for about 4 minutes. Add the arugula and cook until it is wilted.
Mix in the eggs and season with black pepper and salt.
Mix in the lemon juice and scallion greens. Top with the parmesan cheese; serve warm.

132. Pasta With Garlic And Hot Pepper

Preparation Time: 25 minutes
Cooking Time: 4 minutes
Servings: 4

Ingredients:

400g Spaghetti
8 tbsp. Extra virgin olive oil
4 cloves garlic, chopped
1 Chili pepper
Coarse salt

Directions:

Put the water to boil, when it comes to a boil add salt and dip the spaghetti.
Meanwhile, in a saucepan heat the oil with the garlic deprived of the inner and chopped germ and the chopped peppers.
Be careful: the flame should be sweet and the garlic should not darken.
Halfway through cooking, remove the spaghetti and continue cooking in the pan with the oil and garlic, adding the cooking water as if it were a risotto.
When cooked, serve the spaghetti.

133. Stuffed Pasta Shells

Preparation Time: 15 minutes
Cooking Time: 10 minutes
Servings: 4

Ingredients:

5 Cups Marinara Sauce
15 Oz. Ricotta Cheese
1 ½ Cups Mozzarella Cheese, Grated
¾ Cup Parmesan Cheese, Grated
2 tbsp. Parsley, Fresh & Chopped
¼ Cup Basil Leaves, Fresh & Chopped
8 Oz. Spinach, Fresh & Chopped
½ tsp. Thyme
Sea Salt & Black Pepper to Taste
1 lb. Ground Beef
1 Cup Onions, Chopped
4 Cloves Garlic, Diced
2 tbsp. Olive Oil, Divided
12 Oz. Jumbo Pasta Shells

Directions:

Start by cooking your pasta shells by following your package instructions. Once they're cooked, then set them to the side.
Press sauté and then add in half of your olive oil. Cook your garlic and onions, which should take about four minutes. Your onions should be tender, and your garlic should be fragrant.

Add your ground beef in, seasoning it with thyme, salt, and pepper, cooking for another four minutes.
Add in your basil, parsley, spinach and marinara sauce.
Cover your pot, and cook for five minutes on low pressure.
Use a quick release, and top with cheeses.
Press sauté again, making sure that it stays warm until your cheese melts.
Take a tbsp. of the mixture, stuffing it into your pasta shells.
Top with your remaining sauce before serving warm.

134. Homemade Pasta Bolognese

Preparation Time: 20 minutes
Cooking Time: 10 minutes
Servings: 4

Ingredients:

Minced meat 17 oz.
Pasta 12 oz.
Sweet red onion1 piece
Garlic 2 cloves
Vegetable oil 1 tbsp.
Tomato paste 3 tbsp.
Grated Parmesan Cheese 2 oz.
Bacon3 pieces

Directions:

Fry finely chopped onions and garlic in a frying pan in vegetable oil until a characteristic smell.
Add minced meat and chopped bacon to the pan. Constantly break the lumps with a spatula and mix so that the minced meat is crumbly.
When the mince is ready, add tomato paste, grated Parmesan to the pan, mix, reduce heat and leave to simmer.
At this time, boil the pasta. I don't salt water, because for me tomato paste and sauce as a whole turn out to be quite salty.
When the pasta is ready, discard it in a colander, arrange it on plates, add meat sauce with tomato paste on top of each serving.

135. Asparagus Pasta

Preparation Time: 10 minutes
Cooking Time: 25 minutes
Servings: 6

Ingredients:

8 Oz. Farfalle Pasta, Uncooked
1 ½ Cups Asparagus, Fresh, Trimmed & Chopped into 1 Inch Pieces
1 Pint Grape Tomatoes, Halved
2 tbsp. Olive Oil
Sea Salt & Black Pepper to Taste
2 Cups Mozzarella, Fresh & Drained
1/3 Cup Basil Leaves, Fresh & Torn
2 tbsp. Balsamic Vinegar

Directions:

Start by heating the oven to 400°F, and then get out a stockpot. Cook your pasta per package instructions, and reserve ¼ cup of pasta water.
Get out a bowl and toss the tomatoes, oil, asparagus, and season with salt and pepper. Spread this mixture on a baking sheet, and bake for fifteen minutes. Stir twice in this time.
Remove your vegetables from the oven, and then add the cooked pasta to your baking sheet. Mix with a few tbsp. of pasta water so that your sauce becomes smoother.
Mix in your basil and mozzarella, drizzling with balsamic vinegar. Serve warm.

136. Penne Bolognese Pasta

Preparation Time: 15 minutes
Cooking Time: 20 minutes
Servings: 2

Ingredients:

Penne pasta 7 oz.
Beef 5 oz.
Parmesan Cheese 1 oz.
Celery Stalk 1 oz.
Shallots 26 g
Carrot 1.5 oz.
Garlic 1 clove
Thyme 1 g
Tomatoes in own juice 6 oz.
Parsley 3 g
Oregano 1 g
Butter 20 g
Dry white wine 50 ml
Olive oil 40 ml

Directions:

Pour the penne into boiling salted water and cook for 9 minutes.
Roll the beef through a meat grinder.
Dice onion, celery, carrots and garlic in a small cube.
Fry the chopped vegetables in a heated frying pan in olive oil with minced meat for 4–5 minutes, salt and pepper.
Add oregano to the fried minced meat and vegetables, pour 50 ml of wine, add the tomatoes along with the juice and simmer for 10 minutes until the tomatoes are completely softened.
Add the boiled penne and butter to the sauce and simmer for 1-2 minutes, stirring continuously.
Put in a plate, sprinkle with grated Parmesan and chopped parsley, decorate with a sprig of thyme and serve.

137. Spicy Italian Bean Balls with Marinara

Preparation Time: 20 minutes
Cooking Time: 30 minutes
Servings: 2 to 4

Ingredients:

Bean Balls:
1 tablespoon extra-virgin olive oil
½ yellow onion, minced
1 teaspoon fennel seeds
2 teaspoons dried oregano
½ teaspoon crushed red pepper flakes
1 teaspoon garlic powder
1 (15-ounce / 425-g) can white beans (cannellini or navy), drained and rinsed
½ cup whole-grain bread crumbs
Sea salt and ground black pepper, to taste
Marinara:
1 tablespoon extra-virgin olive oil
3 garlic cloves, minced
Handful basil leaves
1 (28-ounce / 794-g) can chopped tomatoes with juice reserved
Sea salt, to taste

Directions:

Make the Bean Balls
Preheat the oven to 350°F (180°C). Line a baking sheet with parchment paper.
Heat the olive oil in a nonstick skillet over medium heat until shimmering.
Add the onion and sauté for 5 minutes or until translucent.
Sprinkle with fennel seeds, oregano, red pepper flakes, and garlic powder, then cook for 1 minute or until aromatic.
Pour the sautéed mixture in a food processor and add the beans and bread crumbs. Sprinkle with salt and ground black pepper, then pulse to combine well and the mixture holds together.
Shape the mixture into balls with a 2-ounce (57-g) cookie scoop, then arrange the balls on the baking sheet.
Bake in the preheated oven for 30 minutes or until lightly browned. Flip the balls halfway through the cooking time.
Make the Marinara

While baking the bean balls, heat the olive oil in a saucepan over medium-high heat until shimmering.
Add the garlic and basil and sauté for 2 minutes or until fragrant.
Fold in the tomatoes and juice. Bring to a boil. Reduce the heat to low. Put the lid on and simmer for 15 minutes. Sprinkle with salt.
Transfer the bean balls on a large plate and baste with marinara before serving.
Tips: Wet your hands while shaping the bean balls to avoid sticking.
To make this a complete meal, you can serve the balls and the sauce with all kinds of cooked pasta, such as pappardelle pasta, corkscrew pasta, farfalle pasta, or shell pasta.

138. Easy Walnut and Ricotta Spaghetti

Preparation Time: 15 minutes
Cooking Time: 10 minutes
Servings: 6

Ingredients:

1 pound (454 g) cooked whole-wheat spaghetti
2 tablespoons extra-virgin olive oil
4 cloves garlic, minced
¾ cup walnuts, toasted and finely chopped
2 tablespoons ricotta cheese
¼ cup flat-leaf parsley, chopped
½ cup grated Parmesan cheese
Sea salt and freshly ground pepper, to taste

Directions:

Reserve a cup of spaghetti water while cooking the spaghetti.
Heat the olive oil in a nonstick skillet over medium-low heat or until shimmering.
Add the garlic and sauté for a minute or until fragrant.
Pour the spaghetti water into the skillet and cook for 8 more minutes.
Turn off the heat and mix in the walnuts and ricotta cheese.
Put the cooked spaghetti on a large serving plate, then pour the walnut sauce over. Spread with parsley and Parmesan, then sprinkle with salt and ground pepper. Toss to serve.
Tip: How to cook the spaghetti: Bring a large pot of water to a boil, then add the spaghetti and cook for 10 minutes or until al dente. Drain the spaghetti in a colander before using.

139. Herb-Topped Focaccia

Preparation Time: 20 minutes
Cooking Time: 2 hours
Servings: 10

Ingredients:

1 tbsp. dried rosemary or 3 tbsp. minced fresh rosemary
1 tbsp. dried thyme or 3 tbsp. minced fresh thyme leaves
1/2 cup extra-virgin olive oil
1 tsp. sugar
1 cup warm water
1 packet active dry yeast
2 1/2 cups flour, divided
1 tsp. salt

Directions:

In a small bowl, combine the rosemary and thyme with the olive oil.
In a large bowl, whisk together the sugar, water, and yeast. Let stand for 5 minutes.
Add 1 cup of flour, half of the olive oil mixture, and the salt to the mixture in the large bowl. Stir to combine.
Add the remaining 1½ cups flour to the large bowl. Using your hands, combine dough until it starts to pull away from the sides of the bowl.
Put the dough on a floured board or countertop and knead 10 to 12 times. Place the dough in a well-oiled bowl and cover with plastic wrap. Put it in a warm, dry space for 1 hour.
Oil a 9-by-13-inch baking pan. Turn the dough onto the baking pan, and using your hands gently push the dough out to fit the pan.
Using your fingers, make dimples into the dough. Evenly pour the remaining half of the olive oil mixture over the dough. Let the dough rise for another 30 minutes.
Preheat the oven to 450°F. Place the dough into the oven and let cook for 18 to 20 minutes, until you see it turn a golden brown.

140. Caramelized Onion Flatbread with Arugula

Preparation Time: 10 minutes
Cooking Time: 25 minutes
Servings: 4

Ingredients:

4 tbsp. extra-virgin olive oil, divided
2 large onions, sliced into ¼-inch-thick slices
1 tsp. salt, divided
1 sheet puff pastry
1 (5-oz.) package goat cheese
8 oz. arugula
½ tsp. freshly ground black pepper

Directions:

Preheat the oven to 400°F.
In a large skillet over medium heat, cook 3 tbsp. olive oil, the onions, and ½ tsp. of salt, stirring, for 10 to 12 minutes, until the onions are translucent and golden brown.
To assemble, line a baking sheet with parchment paper. Lay the puff pastry flat on the parchment paper. Prick the middle of the puff pastry all over with a fork, leaving a ½-inch border.
Evenly distribute the onions on the pastry, leaving the border.
Crumble the goat cheese over the onions.
Put the pastry in the oven to bake for 10 to 12 minutes, or until you see the border become golden brown.
Remove the pastry from the oven, set aside. In a medium bowl, add the arugula, remaining 1 tbsp. of olive oil, remaining ½ tsp. of salt, and ½ tsp. black pepper; toss to evenly dress the arugula.
Cut the pastry into even squares. Top the pastry with dressed arugula and serve.

141. Quick Shrimp Fettuccine

Preparation Time: 10 minutes
Cooking Time: 10 minutes
Servings: 4

Ingredients:

8 oz. fettuccine pasta
1/4 cup extra-virgin olive oil
3 tbsp. garlic, minced
1 lb. large shrimp (21-25), peeled and deveined
1/3 cup lemon juice
1 tbsp. lemon zest
1/2 tsp. salt
1/2 tsp. freshly ground black pepper

Directions:

Bring a large pot of salted water to a boil. Add the fettuccine and cook for 8 minutes.
In a large saucepan over medium heat, cook the olive oil and garlic for 1 minute.
Add the shrimp to the saucepan and cook for 3 minutes on each side. Remove the shrimp from the pan and set aside.
Add the lemon juice and lemon zest to the saucepan, along with the salt and pepper.

Reserve ½ cup of the pasta water and drain the pasta.
Add the pasta water to the saucepan with the lemon juice and zest and stir everything together. Add the pasta and toss together to evenly coat the pasta. Transfer the pasta to a serving dish and top with the cooked shrimp. Serve warm.

142. Hearty Butternut Spinach, and Cheeses Lasagna

Preparation Time: 30 minutes
Cooking Time: 3 hours 45 minutes
Servings: 4 to 6

Ingredients:

2 tablespoons extra-virgin olive oil, divided
1 butternut squash, halved lengthwise and deseeded
½ teaspoon sage
½ teaspoon sea salt
¼ teaspoon ground black pepper
¼ cup grated Parmesan cheese
2 cups ricotta cheese
½ cup unsweetened almond milk
5 layers whole-wheat lasagna noodles (about 12 ounces / 340 g in total)
4 ounces (113 g) fresh spinach leaves, divided
½ cup shredded part skim Mozzarella, for garnish

Directions:

Preheat the oven to 400°F (205°C). Line a baking sheet with parchment paper.
Brush 1 tablespoon of olive oil on the cut side of the butternut squash, then place the squash on the baking sheet.
Bake in the preheated oven for 45 minutes or until the squash is tender.
Allow to cool until you can handle it, then scoop the flesh out and put the flesh in a food processor to purée.
Combine the puréed butternut squash flesh with sage, salt, and ground black pepper in a large bowl. Stir to mix well.
Combine the cheeses and milk in a separate bowl, then sprinkle with salt and pepper, to taste.
Grease the slow cooker with 1 tablespoon of olive oil, then add a layer of lasagna noodles to coat the bottom of the slow cooker.
Spread half of the squash mixture on top of the noodles, then top the squash mixture with another layer of lasagna noodles.
Spread half of the spinach over the noodles, then top the spinach with half of cheese mixture. Repeat with remaining 3 layers of lasagna noodles, squash mixture, spinach, and cheese mixture.
Top the cheese mixture with Mozzarella, then put the lid on and cook on low for 3 hours or until the lasagna noodles are al dente.
Serve immediately.
Tip: To make this a complete meal, you can serve it with fresh cucumber soup and green leafy salad.

143. Minestrone Chickpeas and Macaroni Casserole

Preparation Time: 20 minutes
Cooking Time: 7 hours 20 minutes
Servings: 5

Ingredients:

1 (15-ounce / 425-g) can chickpeas, drained and rinsed
1 (28-ounce / 794-g) can diced tomatoes, with the juice
1 (6-ounce / 170-g) can no-salt-added tomato paste
3 medium carrots, sliced
3 cloves garlic, minced
1 medium yellow onion, chopped
1 cup low-sodium vegetable soup
½ teaspoon dried rosemary
1 teaspoon dried oregano
2 teaspoons maple syrup
½ teaspoon sea salt
¼ teaspoon ground black pepper
½ pound (227-g) fresh green beans, trimmed and cut into bite-size pieces
1 cup macaroni pasta
2 ounces (57 g) Parmesan cheese, grated

Directions:

Except for the green beans, pasta, and Parmesan cheese, combine all the ingredients in the slow cooker and stir to mix well.
Put the slow cooker lid on and cook on low for 7 hours.
Fold in the pasta and green beans. Put the lid on and cook on high for 20 minutes or until the vegetable are soft and the pasta is al dente.
Pour them in a large serving bowl and spread with Parmesan cheese before serving.
Tip: Instead of chickpeas, you can also use kidney beans, great northern beans, or cannellini beans.

144. Roasted Butternut Squash and Zucchini with Penne

Preparation Time: 15 minutes
Cooking Time: 30 minutes
Servings: 6

Ingredients:

1 large zucchini, diced
1 large butternut squash, peeled and diced
1 large yellow onion, chopped
2 tablespoons extra-virgin olive oil
1 teaspoon paprika
1/2 teaspoon garlic powder
1/2 teaspoon sea salt
1/2 teaspoon freshly ground black pepper
1-pound (454 g) whole-grain penne
1/2 cup dry white wine
2 tablespoons grated Parmesan cheese

Directions:

Preheat the oven to 400°F (205°C). Line a baking sheet with aluminum foil.
Combine the zucchini, butternut squash, and onion in a large bowl. Drizzle with olive oil and sprinkle with paprika, garlic powder, salt, and ground black pepper. Toss to coat well.
Spread the vegetables in the single layer on the baking sheet, then roast in the preheated oven for 25 minutes or until the vegetables are tender.
Meanwhile, bring a pot of water to a boil, then add the penne and cook for 14 minutes or until al dente. Drain the penne through a colander.
Transfer ½ cup of roasted vegetables in a food processor, then pour in the dry white wine. Pulse until smooth.
Pour the puréed vegetables in a nonstick skillet and cook with penne over medium-high heat for a few minutes to heat through.
Transfer the penne with the purée on a large serving plate, then spread the remaining roasted vegetables and Parmesan on top before serving.
Tip: Instead of dry white wine, you can use the same amount of low-sodium chicken broth to replace it.

145. Small Pasta and Beans Pot

Preparation Time: 20 minutes
Cooking Time: 15 minutes
Servings: 2 to 4

Ingredients:

1 pound (454 g) small whole wheat pasta
1 (14.5-ounce / 411-g) can diced tomatoes, juice reserved
1 (15-ounce / 425-g) can cannellini beans, drained and rinsed
2 tablespoons no-salt-added tomato paste
1 red or yellow bell pepper, chopped
1 yellow onion, chopped
1 tablespoon Italian seasoning mix
3 garlic cloves, minced
¼ teaspoon crushed red pepper flakes, optional
1 tablespoon extra-virgin olive oil
5 cups water
1 bunch kale, stemmed and chopped
½ cup pitted Kalamata olives, chopped
1 cup sliced basil

Directions:

Except for the kale, olives, and basil, combine all the ingredients in a pot. Stir to mix well. Bring to a boil over high heat. Stir constantly.
Reduce the heat to medium high and add the kale. Cook for 10 minutes or until the pasta is al dente. Stir constantly.
Transfer all of them on a large plate and serve with olives and basil on top.
Tip: You can use the small whole-wheat pasta like penne, farfalle, shell, corkscrew, macaroni, or alphabet pasta.

146. Swoodles with Almond Butter Sauce

Preparation Time: 20 minutes
Cooking Time: 20 minutes
Servings: 4

Ingredients:

Sauce:
1 garlic clove
1-inch piece fresh ginger, peeled and sliced
1/4 cup chopped yellow onion
3/4 cup almond butter
1 tablespoon tamari
1 tablespoon raw honey
1 teaspoon paprika
1 tablespoon fresh lemon juice
1/8 teaspoon ground red pepper
Sea salt and ground black pepper, to taste
1/4 cup water
Swoodles:
2 large sweet potatoes, spiralized
2 tablespoons coconut oil, melted
Sea salt and ground black pepper, to taste
For Servings:
½ cup fresh parsley, chopped
½ cup thinly sliced scallions

Directions:

Make the Sauce
Put the garlic, ginger, and onion in a food processor, then pulse to combine well.
Add the almond butter, tamari, honey, paprika, lemon juice, ground red pepper, salt, and black pepper to the food processor. Pulse to combine well. Pour in the water during the pulsing until the mixture is thick and smooth.
Make the Swoodles:
Preheat the oven to 425°F (220°C). Line a baking sheet with parchment paper.
Put the spiralized sweet potato in a bowl, then drizzle with olive oil. Toss to coat well. Transfer them on the baking sheet. Sprinkle with salt and pepper.
Bake in the preheated oven for 20 minutes or until lightly browned and al dente. Check the doneness during the baking and remove any well-cooked swoodles.
Transfer the swoodles on a large plate and spread with sauce, parsley, and scallions. Toss to serve.
Tips: To make this a complete meal, you can serve it along with cashew slaw.
You can use the store-bought swoodles or spiralize the sweet potatoes with spiralizer yourself.

147. Tomato Sauce and Basil Pesto Fettuccine

Preparation Time: 15 minutes
Cooking Time: 15 minutes
Servings: 4

Ingredients:

4 Roma tomatoes, diced
2 teaspoons no-salt-added tomato paste
1 tablespoon chopped fresh oregano
2 garlic cloves, minced
1 cup low-sodium vegetable soup
½ teaspoon sea salt
1 packed cup fresh basil leaves
¼ cup pine nuts
¼ cup grated Parmesan cheese
2 tablespoons extra-virgin olive oil
1 pound (454 g) cooked whole-grain fettuccine

Directions:

Put the tomatoes, tomato paste, oregano, garlic, vegetable soup, and salt in a skillet. Stir to mix well.
Cook over medium heat for 10 minutes or until lightly thickened.
Put the remaining ingredients, except for the fettuccine, in a food processor and pulse to combine until smooth.
Pour the puréed basil mixture into the tomato mixture, then add the fettuccine. Cook for a few minutes or until heated through and the fettuccine is well coated.
Serve immediately.
Tip: How to cook the fettuccine: Bring a large pot of water to a boil, then add the fettuccine and cook for 8 minutes or until al dente. Drain the fettuccine in a colander before using.

148. Garlic Shrimp Fettuccine

Preparation Time: 10 minutes
Cooking Time: 15 minutes
Servings: 4 to 6

Ingredients:

8 ounces (227 g) fettuccine pasta
1/4 cup extra-virgin olive oil
3 tablespoons garlic, minced
1 pound (454 g) large shrimp, peeled and deveined
1/3 cup lemon juice
1 tablespoon lemon zest
1/2 teaspoon salt
1/2 teaspoon freshly ground black pepper

Directions:

Bring a large pot of salted water to a boil. Add the fettuccine and cook for 8 minutes. Reserve ½ cup of the cooking liquid and drain the pasta.
In a large saucepan over medium heat, heat the olive oil. Add the garlic and sauté for 1 minute.
Add the shrimp to the saucepan and cook each side for 3 minutes. Remove the shrimp from the pan and set aside.
Add the remaining ingredients to the saucepan. Stir in the cooking liquid. Add the pasta and toss together to evenly coat the pasta.
Transfer the pasta to a serving dish and serve topped with the cooked shrimp.

149. Broccoli and Carrot Pasta Salad

Preparation Time: 5 minutes
Cooking Time: 10 minutes
Servings: 2

Ingredients:

8 ounces (227 g) whole-wheat pasta
2 cups broccoli florets

1 cup peeled and shredded carrots
¼ cup plain Greek yogurt
Juice of 1 lemon
1 teaspoon red pepper flakes
Sea salt and freshly ground pepper, to taste

Directions:

Bring a large pot of lightly salted water to a boil. Add the pasta to the boiling water and cook until al dente. Drain and let rest for a few minutes.
When cooled, combine the pasta with the veggies, yogurt, lemon juice, and red pepper flakes in a large bowl, and stir thoroughly to combine.
Taste and season to taste with salt and pepper. Serve immediately.

150. Bean and Veggie Pasta

Preparation Time: 10 minutes
Cooking Time: 15 minutes
Servings: 2

Ingredients:

16 ounces (454 g) small whole wheat pasta, such as penne, farfalle, or macaroni
5 cups water
1 (15-ounce / 425-g) can cannellini beans, drained and rinsed
1 (14.5-ounce / 411-g) can diced (with juice) or crushed tomatoes
1 yellow onion, chopped
1 red or yellow bell pepper, chopped
2 tablespoons tomato paste
1 tablespoon olive oil
3 garlic cloves, minced
¼ teaspoon crushed red pepper (optional)
1 bunch kale, stemmed and chopped
1 cup sliced basil
½ cup pitted Kalamata olives, chopped

Directions:

Add the pasta, water, beans, tomatoes (with juice if using diced), onion, bell pepper, tomato paste, oil, garlic, and crushed red pepper (if desired), to a large stockpot or deep skillet with a lid. Bring to a boil over high heat, stirring often.
Reduce the heat to medium-high, add the kale, and cook, continuing to stir often, until the pasta is al dente, about 10 minutes.
Remove from the heat and let sit for 5 minutes. Garnish with the basil and olives and serve.

151. Roasted Ratatouille Pasta

Preparation Time: 10 minutes
Cooking Time: 30 minutes
Servings: 2

Ingredients:

1 small eggplant (about 8 ounces / 227 g)
1 small zucchini
1 portobello mushroom
1 Roma tomato, halved
½ medium sweet red pepper, seeded
½ teaspoon salt, plus additional for the pasta water
1 teaspoon Italian herb seasoning
1 tablespoon olive oil
2 cups farfalle pasta (about 8 ounces / 227 g)
2 tablespoons minced sun-dried tomatoes in olive oil with herbs
2 tablespoons prepared pesto

Directions:

Slice the ends off the eggplant and zucchini. Cut them lengthwise into ½-inch slices.
Place the eggplant, zucchini, mushroom, tomato, and red pepper in a large bowl and sprinkle with ½ teaspoon of salt. Using your hands, toss the vegetables well so that they're covered evenly with the salt. Let them rest for about 10 minutes.
While the vegetables are resting, preheat the oven to 400°F (205°C). Line a baking sheet with parchment paper.
When the oven is hot, drain off any liquid from the vegetables and pat them dry with a paper towel. Add the Italian herb seasoning and olive oil to the vegetables and toss well to coat both sides.
Lay the vegetables out in a single layer on the baking sheet. Roast them for 15 to 20 minutes, flipping them over after about 10 minutes or once they start to brown on the underside. When the vegetables are charred in spots, remove them from the oven.
While the vegetables are roasting, fill a large saucepan with water. Add salt and cook the pasta until al dente, about 8 to 10 minutes. Drain the pasta, reserving ½ cup of the pasta water.
When cool enough to handle, cut the vegetables into large chunks (about 2 inches) and add them to the hot pasta.
Stir in the sun-dried tomatoes and pesto and toss everything well. Serve immediately.

152. Lentil and Mushroom Pasta

Preparation Time: 10 minutes
Cooking Time: 50 minutes
Servings: 2

Ingredients:

2 tablespoons olive oil
1 large yellow onion, finely diced
2 portobello mushrooms, trimmed and chopped finely
2 tablespoons tomato paste
3 garlic cloves, chopped
1 teaspoon oregano
2½ cups water
1 cup brown lentils
1 (28-ounce / 794-g) can diced tomatoes with basil (with juice if diced)
1 tablespoon balsamic vinegar
8 ounces (227 g) pasta of choice, cooked
Salt and black pepper, to taste
Chopped basil, for garnish

Directions:

Place a large stockpot over medium heat. Add the oil. Once the oil is hot, add the onion and mushrooms. Cover and cook until both are soft, about 5 minutes. Add the tomato paste, garlic, and oregano and cook 2 minutes, stirring constantly.
Stir in the water and lentils. Bring to a boil, then reduce the heat to medium-low and cook for 5 minutes, covered.
Add the tomatoes (and juice if using diced) and vinegar. Replace the lid, reduce the heat to low and cook until the lentils are tender, about 30 minutes.
Remove the sauce from the heat and season with salt and pepper to taste. Garnish with the basil and serve over the cooked pasta.

153. Spinach Pesto Pasta

Preparation Time: 10 minutes
Cooking Time: 10 minutes
Servings: 4

Ingredients:

8 oz whole-grain pasta
1/3 cup mozzarella cheese, grated
1/2 cup pesto
5 oz fresh spinach
1 3/4 cup water
8 oz mushrooms, chopped
1 tbsp olive oil
Pepper
Salt

Directions:

Add oil into the inner pot of instant pot

and set the pot on sauté mode.
Add mushrooms and sauté for 5 minutes.
Add water and pasta and stir well.
Seal pot with lid and cook on high for 5 minutes.
Once done, release pressure using quick release. Remove lid.
Stir in remaining ingredients and serve.

154. Quick & Easy Couscous

Preparation Time: 10 minutes
Cooking Time: 5 minutes
Servings: 4

Ingredients:

2 cups couscous
2 tbsp fresh parsley, chopped
2 1/2 cups vegetable stock
Pepper
Salt

Directions:

Add couscous and vegetable stock into the instant pot.
Seal pot with lid and cook on high for 5 minutes.
Once done, allow to release pressure naturally for 10 minutes then release remaining using quick release. Remove lid.
Stir in remaining ingredients and serve.

155. Couscous and Butternut Squash Bowl

Preparation Time: 8 minutes
Cooking Time: 6 minutes
Servings 4

Ingredients

1 tablespoon ghee, melted
1-pound butternut squash, peeled and sliced
1 carrot, sliced
Sea salt and white pepper, to your liking
1/2 teaspoon Spanish paprika
1 ½ cups couscous
3 cups roasted vegetable broth, preferably homemade
1/4 teaspoon ground allspice berries
1/4 teaspoon ground cumin
2 tablespoons fresh Italian parsley leaves, chopped

Directions

Press the "Sauté" button to preheat your Instant Pot; heat olive oil. Once hot, cook the butternut squash and carrot until they are tender.
Stir in the sea salt, pepper, Spanish paprika, couscous, roasted vegetable broth, allspice, and cumin.
Secure the lid. Choose the "Manual" mode and cook for 6 minutes at High pressure. Once cooking is complete, use a quick pressure release; carefully remove the lid.
Garnish with fresh Italian parsley. Bon appétit!

156. Authentic Pasta e Fagioli

Preparation Time: 6 minutes
Cooking Time: 15 minutes
Servings 4

Ingredients:

2 tablespoons olive oil
1 teaspoon garlic, pressed
4 small-sized potatoes, peeled and diced
1 parsnip, chopped
1 carrot, chopped
1 celery rib, chopped
1 leek, chopped
1 (6-ounce) can tomato paste
4 cups water
2 vegetable bouillon cubes
8 ounces cannellini beans, soaked overnight
6 ounces elbow pasta
1/2 teaspoon oregano
1/2 teaspoon basil
1/2 teaspoon fennel seeds
Sea salt, to taste
1/4 teaspoon freshly cracked black pepper
2 tablespoons Italian parsley, roughly chopped

Directions:

Press the "Sauté" button to preheat your Instant Pot. Heat the oil and sauté the garlic, potatoes, parsnip, carrot, celery, and leek until they have softened.
Now, add in the tomato paste, water, bouillon cubes, cannellini beans, elbow pasta, oregano, basil, fennel seeds, freshly cracked black pepper, and sea salt.
Secure the lid. Choose the "Manual" mode and cook for 9 minutes at High pressure. Once cooking is complete, use a quick pressure release; carefully remove the lid.
Serve with fresh Italian parsley. Bon appétit!

157. Spaghetti Squash with Sun-Dried Tomatoes

Preparation Time: 10 minutes
Cooking Time: 1 Hour & 15 minutes
Servings: 5

Ingredients:

1 Pumpkin squash
4 stalks of Oregano
2 cloves of Garlic
5 pieces of Sun-dried tomatoes
3 Green basil
25g of Parmesan cheese
80ml of Olive oil
Salt to taste
Freshly ground black pepper

Directions:

Like any vegetable, spaghetti squash can be cooked whole , and then to keep it in the oven will have twice as long. It will be faster if you cut it in half. Only need a sharp and long knife — the raw flesh of the squash is very elastic. Scrape the white pith and the seeds and put aside.
The halves of the squash should be watered and sprinkle all aromatic: it can be any set of herbs and spices like olive oil, salt and freshly ground black pepper, grated garlic and the leaves from a couple of sprigs of fresh oregano. At the end of all of this to massage into the flesh
Lay the pumpkin halves on a foil-covered cookie sheet flesh down. Put in a preheated 175-degree oven. In about an hour (more or less depending on the weight of the vegetable) it will reach the desired condition — plug should be easy to get in the flesh.
While baking the squash, scrubbing apart the core of the pumpkin and remove the seeds. Throw them in a well-heated pan, sprinkle a pinch of salt and, continually stirring, fry the seeds until Golden brown .
After an hour, remove the squash from the oven, let it cool slightly , and flip the flesh upside. Now each half is necessary to scrape with a fork — you will see how it will come out quite long noodles, the spaghetti, the origin of the vegetable.
In a large saucepan heat with a little oil, put it in the inside of the squash and add halved sun-dried tomatoes. The tomatoes have to choose softer and juicier, and it is better to do it yourself: cut in half, lay on a baking sheet flesh up, season with salt and pepper, drizzle with olive oil, and leave overnight in a preheated 80-degree oven.
When squash and tomatoes are warmed, add the fresh Basil leaves (large leaves

can tear with your hands) and a handful of grated Parmesan or Pecorino. Mix the vegetables with cheese and hold for a few seconds on the fire.
Spread the cooked vegetables on plates, pour fresh olive oil, add more cheese, salt, freshly ground black pepper, a few basil leaves, some crispy roasted sunflower seeds — all optional and in any proportions. And serve.

158. Escarole And Cannellini Beans On Pasta

Preparation Time: 20 minutes
Cooking Time: 25 minutes
Servings: 8

Ingredients:

Pepper and salt to taste
1 can 14.5-oz diced tomatoes with garlic and onion, drained
1 can 15.5-oz cannellini beans, with liquid
1 head escarole chopped
1 package 16-oz dry penne pasta

Directions:

Cook pasta according to package instructions, then drain and rinse under cold running water.
On medium high fire, place skillet and cook diced tomatoes, cannellini beans with liquid and escarole.
Season with pepper and salt and cook until boiling.
Remove from fire and mix pasta.
Serve and enjoy.

159. Pork with Couscous

Preparation Time: 10 minutes
Cooking Time: 7 hours
Servings: 6

Ingredients:

2 and ½ pounds pork loin boneless and trimmed
¾ cup chicken stock
2 tablespoons olive oil
½ tablespoon sweet paprika
2 and ¼ teaspoon sage, dried
½ tablespoon garlic powder
¼ teaspoon rosemary, dried
¼ teaspoon marjoram, dried
1 teaspoon basil, dried
1 teaspoon oregano, dried
Salt and black pepper to taste
2 cups couscous, cooked

Directions:

In a bowl, mix oil with stock, paprika, garlic powder, sage, rosemary, thyme, marjoram, oregano, salt, and pepper to taste and whisk well. Put pork loin in your crockpot.
Add stock and spice mix, stir, cover, and cook on Low for 7 hours. Slice pork return to pot and toss with cooking juices.
Divide between plates and serve with couscous on the side.

160. Beef with Tomato Spaghetti

Preparation Time: 10 minutes
Cooking Time: 20 minutes
Servings: 4

Ingredients:

12 ounces spaghetti
Zest and juice from 1 lemon
2 garlic cloves, minced
2 tablespoons olive oil
1-pound beef, ground
Salt and black pepper to taste
1-pint cherry tomatoes, chopped
1 small red onion, chopped
½ cup white wine
2 tablespoons tomato paste
Some basil leaves, chopped for serving
Some parmesan, grated for serving

Directions:

Put water in a large saucepan, add a pinch of salt, bring to a boil over medium-high heat, add spaghetti, cook according to instructions, drain and return pasta to pan.
Add lemon zest and juice and 1 tablespoon oil to pasta, toss to coat, heat up over medium heat for a couple of seconds, divide between plates and keep warm.
Meanwhile, heat a pan with remaining oil over medium heat, add garlic, stir and cook for 1 minute.
Add beef, salt, and pepper and brown it for 4 minutes.
Add tomato paste and wine, stir and cook for 3 minutes.
Divide beef on plates, add tomatoes, red onion, basil, and parmesan and serve.

161. Mushroom and Vegetable Penne Pasta

Preparation Time: 5 minutes
Cooking Time: 8 minutes
Servings: 4

Ingredients:

6 ounces penne pasta
6 ounces shitake mushrooms, chopped
1 small carrot, cut into strips
4 ounces baby spinach, finely chopped
1 teaspoon ginger, grounded
3 tablespoons oil
2 tablespoons soy sauce
6 ounces zucchini, cut into strips
6 ounces leek, finely chopped
½ teaspoon salt
2 garlic cloves, crushed
2 cups of water

Directions:

Heat the oil
Sauté and stir-fry carrot and garlic for 3-4 minutes
Add remaining ingredients and pour in 2 cups water
Cook on High pressure for 4 minutes
Quick-release the pressure
Serve and enjoy!

162. Shrimp and Leek Spaghetti

Preparation Time: 10 minutes
Cooking Time: 20 minutes
Servings: 4

Ingredients:

2 cups leek, chopped
8 oz. spaghetti, uncooked, whole-grain
1/4 cup heavy cream
1 lb. raw medium shrimp, peeled, deveined
2 teaspoons lemon zest
1 tablespoon garlic, chopped
1/2 teaspoon black pepper
2 cups baby sweet peas, frozen, thawed
1 1/2 tablespoons olive oil, divided
3/4 teaspoon kosher salt, divided
2 tablespoons fresh lemon juice
2 tablespoons fresh dill, chopped

Directions:

Cook the pasta, drain and reserve ½ cup of the cooking liquid. Cover the cooked pasta and keep warm.
In the meantime, pat dries the shrimp with the paper towels, season with pepper, and ¼ teaspoon of salt.

Heat ½ of olive oil in a nonstick skillet over high heat, then add shrimp. Cook for about 3-4 minutes as you stir often until the shrimp is cooked through. Transfer the cooked shrimp into a plate and cover it to keep warm.
Reduce the heat to medium-high and add leek to the same skillet along with garlic, remaining ½ teaspoon of salt, and the remaining oil. Cook for about 2-3 minutes as you stir often until the leek has become slightly tender.
Add the peas to the skillet along with cream, lemon juice, lemon zest and the reserved ½ cup of the cooking liquid. Reduce the heat to medium and simmer for 2-3 minutes until the sauce has slightly thickened. Add in the shrimp and toss well until coated.
When through, divide the cooked pasta among the serving bowls and top with the shrimp and sauce evenly. Sprinkle with the chopped fresh dill. Serve immediately and enjoy!

163. Pasta Salad with Tomatoes and Eggplant

Preparation Time: 10 minutes
Cooking Time: 15 minutes
Servings: 4

Ingredients:

1 tablespoon garlic, minced
8 oz. casarecce, fusilli, or penne pasta, uncooked
2 teaspoons white wine vinegar
8 oz. haricots verts (French green beans), trimmed
1/4 cup dry white wine
1 tablespoon olive oil
6 oz. burrata
2 cups Japanese eggplant, chopped
1/2 teaspoon kosher salt
2 teaspoons fresh thyme, chopped
4 cups cherry tomatoes, halved, divided
1/2 teaspoon black pepper

Directions:

Cook the pasta according to the package instructions. Next, add in the beans 3 minutes before the cooking time is over. Drain and reserve 1 cup of cooking liquid.
In the meantime, heat the oil in a skillet over medium-high heat, add in the eggplant. Cook for 4-5 minutes as you stir occasionally until the eggplant has become tender.
Add the garlic to the skillet and cook for 1 minute until fragrant, add half of tomatoes. Continue cooking for an additional 2-3 minutes.
Add the wine to the skillet as you stir often until most wine has evaporated, then add in pasta and beans. Toss well to combine. If the mixture is too dry, add in a couple of tablespoons of the reserved pasta cooking liquid at a time.
Stir the remaining tomatoes in the skillet, along with salt and vinegar. Divide the pasta mixture among the serving bowls and top with burrata, pepper, and thyme. Serve and enjoy!

164. Spaghetti Squash with Shrimp Scampi

Preparation Time: 30 minutes
Cooking Time: 30 minutes
Servings: 4

Ingredients:

2 c. chicken broth
1 small onion, chopped
2 ½ tsp. lemon-garlic seasoning
1 tbsp. butter or ghee
3 pounds spaghetti squash, cut crosswise and seeds removed
¾ pounds shrimp, shelled and deveined
Pepper and salt to taste.

Directions:

Pour broth in the Crockpot and stir in the lemon garlic seasoning, onion, and butter.
Take the spaghetti squash and cook on high for hours.
Once cooked, remove the spaghetti squash from the Crockpot and run a fork through the meat to create the strands.
Take the squash strands back to the Crockpot and add the shrimps.
Season with pepper and salt.
Continue cooking on high for 30 minutes or until the shrimps have turned pink.

165. Italian Chicken with Zucchini Noodles

Preparation Time: 1 hour and 10 minutes
Cooking Time: 6 hours
Servings: 6

Ingredients:

½ c. chicken broth
1 tsp. Italian seasoning
4 tsps. tomato paste
1-pound chicken breast
2 tomatoes, chopped
1 ½ c. asparagus
1 c. snap peas halved
Pepper and salt to taste
4 zucchini noodles, cut into noodle-like strips
1 c. commercial pesto
Parmesan cheese for garnish
Basil for garnish

Directions:

Take the chicken broth, Italian seasoning, tomato paste, chicken breasts, tomatoes, asparagus, and peas in the Crockpot. Give a swirl and season with pepper and salt to
Close the lid and then cook on low for 6 hours. Let it cool before assembling.
Assemble the noodles by placing the chicken mixture on top of the zucchini noodles. Add commercial pesto and garnish with parmesan cheese and basil leaves.

166. Alethea's Lemony Asparagus Pasta

Preparation Time: 10 minutes
Cooking Time: 20 minutes
Servings: 6

Ingredients:

1-pound spaghetti, linguini, or angel hair pasta
2 crusty bread slices
½ cup plus 1 tablespoon avocado oil, divided
3 cups chopped asparagus (1½-inch pieces)
½ cup vegan "chicken" broth or vegetable broth, divided
6 tablespoons freshly squeezed lemon juice
8 garlic cloves, minced or pressed
3 tablespoons finely chopped fresh curly parsley
1 tablespoon grated lemon zest
1½ teaspoons sea salt

Directions:

Boil a large pot of water on high heat and cook the pasta until al dente according to the instructions on the package.
Meanwhile, in a medium skillet, crumble the bread into coarse crumbs. Put 1 tablespoon of oil on the pan and then stir well to combine over medium heat. Cook for about 5 minutes while stirring it often, until the crumbs are golden brown. Remove from the skillet and set aside.
Add the chopped asparagus and ¼ cup of broth in the skillet and cook over

medium-high heat until the asparagus becomes bright green and crisp about 5 minutes. Transfer the asparagus to a very large bowl.
Add the remaining ½ cup of oil, remaining ¼ cup of broth, lemon juice, garlic, parsley, zest, and salt to the asparagus bowl and stir well.
When the noodles are cooked, drain it very well, and then add them to the bowl. Gently toss with the asparagus mixture. Before serving, stir in the toasted bread crumbs. Store leftovers in an airtight container in the refrigerator for up 2 days.

167. Pasta with Lemon and Artichokes

Preparation Time: 10 minutes
Cooking Time: 15 minutes
Servings: 4

Ingredients:

16 ounces linguine or angel hair pasta
1/4 cup extra-virgin olive oil
8 garlic cloves, finely minced or pressed
2 (15-ounce) jars water-packed artichoke hearts, drained and quartered
2 tablespoons freshly squeezed lemon juice
1/4 cup thinly sliced fresh basil
1 teaspoon of sea salt
Freshly ground black pepper

Directions:

Boil a pot of water on high heat and cook the pasta.
While the pasta is cooking, heat the oil in a skillet over medium heat and cook the garlic, stirring often, for 1 to 2 minutes until it just begins to brown. Toss the garlic with the artichokes in a large bowl.
When the pasta is cooked, drain it very carefully and add it to the artichoke mixture, then add the lemon juice, basil, salt, and pepper. Gently stir and serve.

168. Lasagna Rolls

Preparation Time: 20 minutes
Cooking Time: 30 minutes
Servings: 2

Ingredients:

2 zucchini, trimmed
1 cup Mozzarella, shredded
1 cup ground beef
½ teaspoon salt
½ teaspoon ground black pepper
½ teaspoon ground paprika
½ teaspoon dried oregano
¼ teaspoon cayenne pepper
1/3 cup tomato sauce
1teaspoon olive oil
¼ cup Cheddar cheese, shredded
1/3 cup chicken stock

Directions:

Slice the zucchini lengthwise.
In the mixing bowl, mix up together salt, ground beef, ground black pepper, ground paprika, and cayenne pepper.
Spread every zucchini slice with ground beef mixture and roll them.
Brush the casserole mold with olive oil from inside and arrange zucchini rolls.
Top every zucchini rolls with Mozzarella and Cheddar cheese.
Then mix up together tomato sauce, dried oregano, and chicken stock.
Pour the liquid over zucchini.
Cover the casserole mold with foil and secure the edges.
Bake lasagna rolls for 30 minutes at 355F.

169. Tomato Linguine

Preparation Time: 10 minutes
Cooking Time: 15 minutes
Servings: 4

Ingredients:

2 lb. Cherry Tomatoes
2 Tablespoons Balsamic Vinegar
3 Tablespoons Olive Oil
2 Teaspoons Garlic, Minced
¾ lb. Linguine Pasta, Whole Wheat
¼ Teaspoon black Pepper
¼ Cup Feta Cheese, Crumbled
1 Tablespoon Oregano, Fresh & Chopped

Directions:

Start by heating your oven to 350, and then get out a baking sheet. Line your baking sheet with parchment paper before setting it aside.
Get out a bowl and then toss two tablespoons of olive oil, garlic, balsamic vinegar, pepper, and tomatoes together until well coated. Spread your tomatoes on your baking sheet, roasting for fifteen minutes. They should soften and burst open.
Cook your pasta according to package directions, and then drain it, placing it in a bowl.
Toss your pasta with the remaining olive oil and add in your tomatoes.
Serve topped with feta and oregano.

170. Asparagus & Kale Pesto Pasta

Preparation Time: 5 minutes
Cooking Time: 10 minutes
Servings: 6

Ingredients:

¼ Cup Basil, Fresh
¾ lb. Asparagus, Trimmed & Chopped Roughly
¼ lb. Kale, Washed
½ Cup Asiago Cheese, Grated
¼ Cup Olive Oil
1 Lemon, Juiced & Zested
¼ Teaspoon Sea Salt, Fine
¼ Teaspoon Black Pepper
1 lb. Angel Hair Pasta

Directions:

Start by pulsing your kale and asparagus in a food processor until it's finely chopped. Add in your olive oil, lemon juice, basil, and asiago cheese. Continue to pulse until it forms a smooth pesto, seasoning with salt and pepper.
Cook your pasta according to package instructions before draining it and placing it in a bowl.
Add in your pesto and make sure to toss to coat. Sprinkle with lemon zest before serving.

171. Vegetarian Lasagna

Preparation Time: 15 minutes
Cooking Time: 1 hour
Servings: 6

Ingredients:

1 Sweet Onion, Sliced Thick
1 Eggplant, Sliced Thick
2 Zucchini, Sliced Lengthwise
2 Tablespoons Olive Oil
28 Ounces Canned tomatoes, Diced & Sodium Free
1 Cup Quartered, Canned & Water Packed Artichokes, Drained
2 Teaspoons Basil, Fresh & Chopped
2 Teaspoons Garlic, Minced
2 Teaspoons Oregano, Fresh & Chopped
12 Lasagna Noodles, Whole Grain & No-Boil
¼ Teaspoon Red Pepper Flakes
¾ Cup Asiago Cheese, Grated

Directions:

Start by heating your oven to 400, and then get out a baking sheet. Line it with foil before placing it to the side.
Get out a large bowl and toss your zucchini, yellow squash, eggplant, onion,

and olive oil, making sure it's coated well.
Arrange your vegetables on the baking sheet, roasting for twenty minutes. They should be lightly caramelized and tender.
Chop your roasted vegetables before placing them in a bowl.
Stir in your garlic, basil, oregano, artichoke hearts, tomatoes, and red pepper flakes, spooning a quarter of this mixture in the bottom of a nine by thirteen baking dish. Arrange four lasagna noodles over this sauce, and continue by alternating it. Sprinkle with asiago cheese on top, baking for a half hour.
Allow it to cool for fifteen minutes before slicing to serve.

172. Chickpea Pasta Salad

Preparation Time: 10 minutes
Cooking Time: 15 minutes
Servings: 6

Ingredients:

2 Tablespoons Olive Oil
16 Ounces Rotelle Pasta
½ Cup Cured Olives, Chopped
2 Tablespoons Oregano, Fresh & Minced
2 Tablespoons Parsley, Fresh & Chopped
1 Bunch Green Onions, Chopped
¼ Cup Red Wine Vinegar
15 Ounces Canned Garbanzo Beans, Drained & Rinsed
½ Cup Parmesan Cheese, Grated
Sea Salt & Black Pepper to Taste

Directions:

Bring a pot of water to a boil and cook your pasta al dente per package instructions. Drain it and rinse it using cold water.
Get out a skillet and heat up your olive oil over medium heat. Add in your scallions, chickpeas, parsley, oregano and olives. Lower the heat to low, and cook for twenty minutes more. Allow this mixture to cool.
Toss your chickpea mixture with your pasta, and then add in your grated cheese, salt, pepper and vinegar. Let it chill for four hours or overnight before serving.

173. Flavorful Mac & Cheese

Preparation Time: 10 minutes
Cooking Time: 10 minutes
Servings: 6

Ingredients

16 oz whole-grain elbow pasta
4 cups of water
1 cup can tomato, diced
1 tsp garlic, chopped
2 tbsp olive oil
1/4 cup green onions, chopped
1/2 cup parmesan cheese, grated
1/2 cup mozzarella cheese, grated
1 cup cheddar cheese, grated
1/4 cup passata
1 cup unsweetened almond milk
1 cup marinated artichoke, diced
1/2 cup sun-dried tomatoes, sliced
1/2 cup olives, sliced
1 tsp salt

Directions

Add pasta, water, tomatoes, garlic, oil, and salt into the instant pot and stir well.
Seal pot with lid and cook on high for 4 minutes.
Once done, allow to release pressure naturally for 5 minutes then release remaining using quick release. Remove lid.
Set pot on sauté mode. Add green onion, parmesan cheese, mozzarella cheese, cheddar cheese, passata, almond milk, artichoke, sun-dried tomatoes, and olive. Mix well.
Stir well and cook until cheese is melted.
Serve and enjoy.

174. Delicious Pasta Primavera

Preparation Time: 10 minutes
Cooking Time: 4 minutes
Servings: 4

Ingredients

8 oz whole wheat penne pasta
1 tbsp fresh lemon juice
2 tbsp fresh parsley, chopped
1/4 cup almonds slivered
1/4 cup parmesan cheese, grated
14 oz can tomato, diced
1/2 cup prunes
1/2 cup zucchini, chopped
1/2 cup asparagus, cut into 1-inch pieces
1/2 cup carrots, chopped
1/2 cup broccoli, chopped
1 3/4 cups vegetable stock
Pepper
Salt

Directions

Add stock, pars, tomatoes, prunes, zucchini, asparagus, carrots, and broccoli into the instant pot and stir well.
Seal pot with lid and cook on high for 4 minutes.
Once done, release pressure using quick release. Remove lid.
Add remaining ingredients and stir well and serve.

175. Tuna Pasta

Preparation Time: 10 minutes
Cooking Time: 8 minutes
Servings: 6

Ingredients

10 oz can tuna, drained
15 oz whole wheat rotini pasta
4 oz mozzarella cheese, cubed
1/2 cup parmesan cheese, grated
1 tsp dried basil
14 oz can tomato, diced
4 cups vegetable broth
1 tbsp garlic, minced
8 oz mushrooms, sliced
2 zucchini, sliced
1 onion, chopped
2 tbsp olive oil
Pepper
Salt

Directions

Add oil into the inner pot of instant pot and set the pot on sauté mode.
Add mushrooms, zucchini, and onion and sauté until onion is softened.
Add garlic and sauté for a minute.
Add pasta, basil, tuna, tomatoes, and broth and stir well.
Seal pot with lid and cook on high for 4 minutes.
Once done, allow to release pressure naturally for 5 minutes then release remaining using quick release. Remove lid.
Add remaining ingredients and stir well and serve.

176. Chicken and Pastina Soup

Preparation Time: 5 minutes
Cooking Time: 20 minutes
Servings: 6

Ingredients:

1 tablespoon extra-virgin olive oil
2 garlic cloves, minced

3 cups packed chopped kale; center ribs removed
1 cup minced carrots
8 cups no-salt-added chicken or vegetable broth
¼ teaspoon kosher or sea salt
¼ teaspoon freshly ground black pepper
¾ cup uncooked acini de pepe or pastina pasta
2 cups shredded cooked chicken (about 12 ounces / 340 g)
3 tablespoons grated Parmesan cheese

Directions:

In a large stockpot over medium heat, heat the oil. Add the garlic and cook for 30 seconds, stirring frequently. Add the kale and carrots and cook for 5 minutes, stirring occasionally.
Add the broth, salt, and pepper, and turn the heat to high. Bring the broth to a boil, and add the pasta. Reduce the heat to medium and cook for 10 minutes, or until the pasta is cooked through, stirring every few minutes so the pasta doesn't stick to the bottom. Add the chicken, and cook for another 2 minutes to warm through.
Ladle the soup into six bowls. Top each with ½ tablespoon of cheese and serve.

177. Pesto Shrimp over Zoodles

Preparation Time: 15 minutes
Cooking Time: 10 minutes
Servings: 4

Ingredients:

1 pound (454 g) fresh shrimp, peeled and deveined
Salt and freshly ground black pepper, to taste
2 tablespoons extra-virgin olive oil
½ small onion, slivered
8 ounces (227 g) store-bought jarred pesto
¾ cup crumbled goat or feta cheese, plus additional for serving
2 large zucchini, spiralized, for serving
¼ cup chopped flat-leaf Italian parsley, for garnish

Directions:

In a bowl, season the shrimp with salt and pepper. Set aside.
In a large skillet, heat the olive oil over medium-high heat. Sauté the onion until just golden, 5 to 6 minutes.
Reduce the heat to low and add the pesto and cheese, whisking to combine and melt the cheese. Bring to a low simmer and add the shrimp. Reduce the heat back to low and cover. Cook until the shrimp is cooked through and pink, about 3 to 4 minutes.
Serve the shrimp warm over zoodles, garnishing with chopped parsley and additional crumbled cheese.

178. Pasta Primavera

Preparation Time: 15 minutes
Cooking Time: 15 minutes
Servings: 4

Ingredients

1 teaspoon salt, plus more for the pasta water
1-pound rotini
1 bell pepper (any color), seeded and cut into thin strips
1/2 cup broccoli florets
1-pint cherry or grape tomatoes, halved
2 carrots, shredded
1/2 cup fresh or frozen peas
1 scallion, thinly sliced
garlic cloves, thinly sliced
1/4 cup extra-virgin olive oil
1/4 teaspoon freshly ground black pepper
1/2 cup grated Parmesan or Romano cheese
1/2 cup chopped fresh flat-leaf parsley
1/2 teaspoon red pepper flakes

Directions:

Bring a large pot of water to a boil over high heat. Once boiling, salt the water to your liking, stir, and return to a boil. Add the rotini and cook according to package directions until al dente. Drain, reserving about ½ cup of the cooking water.
Meanwhile, in a large skillet, combine the bell pepper and broccoli. Add a few tablespoons of water, cover, and cook for about 5 minutes until they start to soften. Drain any remaining water from the pan.
In a large skillet, add the tomatoes, carrots, peas, scallion, garlic, olive oil, salt, and black pepper. Stir to coat all the vegetables and cook for 3 minutes.
Put the cooked pasta, Parmesan, parsley, and red pepper flakes in a skillet. Toss to combine, adding the reserved cooking water a little at a time as needed to thin out the sauce.

179. Roasted Tomato Sauce With Pasta

Preparation Time: 5 minutes
Cooking Time: 35 minutes
Servings: 2

Ingredients:

large tomatoes, quartered
4 garlic cloves, unpeeled
3 basil sprigs, plus more for garnish
3 tablespoons extra-virgin olive oil
1 teaspoon salt, plus more for the pasta water
1/2 teaspoon freshly ground black pepper
8 ounces whole-wheat pasta
1/4 cup grated Parmesan or Romano cheese

Directions:

1.Preheat the oven to 450°F.
In a small baking dish, put the tomatoes, garlic cloves, and basil sprigs. Add the olive oil, salt, and pepper and toss to coat. Push the basil to the bottom so that it doesn't dry out.
Roast for 30 minutes.
Meanwhile, bring a large pot of water to boil over high heat. Once boiling, salt the water to your liking, stir, and return to a boil. Add the pasta and cook for 1 to 2 minutes less than the package directions for al dente, as it will continue to cook later with the sauce. Drain, reserving about ½ cup of the cooking water.
Remove the tomatoes from the oven. Discard the basil. Squeeze the roasted garlic from their skins and discard the skins.
Using a potato masher or large spoon, mash the tomato mixture. Be careful, as it will be hot, and the juices can squirt out at you. Pull out any tomato skins; they should slip right off after being roasted.
Transfer the tomato mixture to a large skillet, set over medium-low heat, and add the cooked pasta. Toss, adding the reserved cooking water as needed to achieve the desired consistency.
Add the Parmesan. Continue to cook for 2 to 3 minutes, until everything is blended.
Garnish with fresh basil.

180. Spaghetti With Garlic, Olive Oil, And Red Pepper

Preparation Time: 5 minutes
Cooking Time: 10 minutes
Servings: 2

Ingredients

Salt
8 ounces spaghetti
1/4 cup extra-virgin olive oil
garlic cloves, 3 lightly smashed, and 1 minced
1/2 teaspoon red pepper flakes
1/4 cup grated Parmesan cheese
1 tablespoon chopped fresh flat-leaf parsley

Directions

Bring a large pot of water to a boil over high heat. Once boiling, salt the water to your liking, stir, and return to a boil. Add the spaghetti and cook according to package directions until al dente. Drain, reserving about ½ cup of the cooking water.
In a large skillet, heat the olive oil over low heat. Add the smashed garlic cloves and cook until golden brown. Remove the garlic from the pan and discard.
Add the red pepper flakes to the garlic-infused oil and warm for 1 minute before turning off the heat.
Once the spaghetti is cooked, add it to the pan.
Add the minced garlic and toss the spaghetti in the oil to coat. Add the reserved pasta water, a little at a time, as needed to help everything combine.
Sprinkle with Parmesan and parsley.
COOKING TIP: When making pasta, it is important to generously salt the water for a flavorful dish. I generally use about 2 tablespoons of salt per pound of pasta. Add the salt after the water boils, stir to dissolve, and wait for the water to return to a boil, then add the pasta.

181. Spaghetti With Anchovy Sauce

Preparation Time: 5 minutes
Cooking Time: 10 minutes
Servings: 4

Ingredients:

Salt
1-pound spaghetti
1/4 cup extra-virgin olive oil
1 can oil-packed anchovy fillets, undrained
3 garlic cloves, minced
1/4 cup chopped fresh flat-leaf parsley
1 teaspoon red pepper flakes
1/4 teaspoon freshly ground black pepper
1 tablespoon bread crumbs

Directions:

Bring a large pot of water to a boil over high heat. Once boiling, salt the water to your liking, stir, and return to a boil. Add the spaghetti and cook according to package directions until al dente. Drain, reserving about ½ cup of the cooking water.
Meanwhile, in a large skillet, heat the olive oil over low heat. Add the anchovy fillets with their oil and the garlic. Cook for 7 to 10 minutes, until the pasta, is ready, stirring until the anchovies melt away and form a sauce.
Add the spaghetti, parsley, red pepper flakes, black pepper, and a little of the reserved cooking water, as needed, and toss to combine all the ingredients.
Sprinkle with the bread crumbs.

182. Lemon Linguine

Preparation Time: 5 minutes
Cooking Time: 10 minutes
Servings: 2 Preparation

Ingredients:

Salt
8 ounces linguine
1/3 cup grated Parmesan or Romano cheese
1/3 cup extra-virgin olive oil
1/4 cup freshly squeezed lemon juice
Chopped fresh basil for garnish

Directions:

Bring a large pot of water to a boil over high heat. Once boiling, salt the water to your liking, stir, and return to a boil. Add the linguine and cook according to package directions until al dente. Drain, reserving about ½ cup of the cooking water.
In a large bowl, whisk together the Parmesan, olive oil, and lemon juice.
Add the cooked pasta to the bowl and toss to combine. Add a little of the reserved cooking water as needed to help meld the flavors.
Garnish with fresh basil.

183. White Bean Alfredo Pasta

Preparation Time: 10 minutes
Cooking Time: 15 minutes
Servings: 4

Ingredients:

1 teaspoon salt, plus more for the pasta water
1-pound fettuccine
2 tablespoons extra-virgin olive oil
garlic cloves, minced
¼ teaspoon red pepper flakes
(15-ounce) cans cannellini beans, rinsed and drained
2 cups vegetable broth
½ cup almond milk
¼ cup low-fat Pecorino cheese
¼ teaspoon ground nutmeg
Chopped fresh flat-leaf parsley for garnish

Directions:

Bring a large pot of water to boil over high heat. Once boiling, salt the water to your liking, stir, and return to a boil. Add the fettuccine and cook according to package directions until al dente. Drain, reserving about ½ cup of the cooking water.
Meanwhile, in a large skillet, heat the olive oil over medium heat. Add the garlic and red pepper flakes and cook for about 1 minute, until fragrant.
Add the beans, broth, and almond milk to the pan and bring to a boil. Remove the pan from the heat.
Using a slotted spoon, transfer the beans to a food processor or blender and process until smooth.
Return the pureed beans to the skillet. Add the Romano, salt, and nutmeg and bring to a simmer.
Add the cooked pasta to the bean mixture and stir to coat, adding the reserved cooking water, a little at a time, as needed—Cook for about 2 minutes.
Garnish with parsley.

184. Fusilli Arrabbiata

Preparation Time: 5 minutes
Cooking Time: 20 minutes
Servings: 4

Ingredients

3 tablespoons extra-virgin olive oil
1 small onion, finely chopped
Splash dry red wine (optional)
½ serrano pepper, seeded and minced
2 garlic cloves, minced
1 (28-ounce) can crushed tomatoes

1 (6-ounce) can tomato paste
¾ cup water
½ to 1 teaspoon red pepper flakes
1 tablespoon dried oregano
1 teaspoon dried basil
1 teaspoon salt, plus more for the pasta water
1/2 teaspoon freshly ground black pepper
1-pound fusilli or rotini
1/4 cup grated Parmesan or Romano cheese

Directions

In a large, deep skillet, heat the olive oil over medium heat. Add the onion and cook for about 3 minutes, until just starting to soften.
Add a little red wine (if using) and cook for about 3 minutes, until the alcohol is burned off.
Add the serrano pepper and garlic and cook for about 1 minute, until fragrant.
Pour in the crushed tomatoes and stir everything together. Add the tomato paste and water and stir until the paste is blended in.
Add the red pepper flakes. You may want to do this a little at a time until you get your desired level of heat. You can always add more, but you can't take it out.
Season the recipe with oregano, basil, salt, and black pepper.
Bring the sauce to a boil, then reduce the heat to a simmer.
Bring a large pot of water to a boil over high heat. Once boiling, salt the water to your liking, stir, and return to a boil. Add the fusilli and cook according to package directions until al dente. Drain.
Ladle the sauce over the pasta and top with the Parmesan cheese.

185. Triple-Green Pasta with Cheese

Preparation Time: 5 minutes
Cooking Time: 14 to 16 minutes
Servings: 4

Ingredients:

8 ounces (227 g) uncooked penne
1 tablespoon extra-virgin olive oil
2 garlic cloves, minced
1/4 teaspoon crushed red pepper
2 cups chopped fresh flat-leaf parsley, including stems
5 cups loosely packed baby spinach
1/4 teaspoon ground nutmeg
1/4 teaspoon kosher salt
1/4 teaspoon freshly ground black pepper
1/3 cup Castelvetrano olives, pitted and sliced
1/3 cup grated Parmesan cheese

Directions:

In a large stockpot of salted water, cook the pasta for about 8 to 10 minutes. Drain the pasta and reserve ¼ cup of the cooking liquid.
Meanwhile, heat the olive oil in a large skillet over medium heat. Add the garlic and red pepper and cook for 30 seconds, stirring constantly.
Add the parsley and cook for 1 minute, stirring constantly. Add the spinach, nutmeg, salt, and pepper, and cook for 3 minutes, stirring occasionally, or until the spinach is wilted.
Add the cooked pasta and the reserved ¼ cup cooking liquid to the skillet. Stir in the olives and cook for about 2 minutes, or until most of the pasta water has been absorbed.
Remove from the heat and stir in the cheese before serving.

186. Caprese Pasta with Roasted Asparagus

Preparation Time: 5 minutes
Cooking Time: 25 minutes
Servings: 6

Ingredients:

8 ounces (227 g) uncooked small pasta, like orecchiette (little ears) or farfalle (bow ties)
1½ pounds (680 g) fresh asparagus, ends trimmed and stalks chopped into 1-inch pieces
1½ cups grape tomatoes, halved
2 tablespoons extra-virgin olive oil
1/4 teaspoon kosher salt
1/4 teaspoon freshly ground black pepper
2 cups fresh Mozzarella, drained and cut into bite-size pieces (about 8 ounces / 227 g)
1/3 cup torn fresh basil leaves
2 tablespoons balsamic vinegar

Directions:

Preheat the oven to 400ºF (205ºC).
In a large stockpot of salted water, cook the pasta for about 8 to 10 minutes. Drain and reserve about ¼ cup of the cooking liquid.
Meanwhile, in a large bowl, toss together the asparagus, tomatoes, oil, salt and pepper. Spread the mixture onto a large, rimmed baking sheet and bake in the oven for 15 minutes, stirring twice during cooking.
Remove the vegetables from the oven and add the cooked pasta to the baking sheet. Mix with a few tablespoons of cooking liquid to help the sauce become smoother and the saucy vegetables stick to the pasta.
Gently mix in the Mozzarella and basil. Drizzle with the balsamic vinegar. Serve from the baking sheet or pour the pasta into a large bowl.

187. Easy Simple Pesto Pasta

Preparation Time: 10 minutes
Cooking Time: 8 minutes
Servings: 4 to 6

Ingredients:

1-pound (454 g) spaghetti
4 cups fresh basil leaves, stems removed
3 cloves garlic
1 teaspoon salt
1/2 teaspoon freshly ground black pepper
1/2 cup toasted pine nuts
1/4 cup lemon juice
1/2 cup grated Parmesan cheese
1 cup extra-virgin olive oil

Directions:

Bring a large pot of salted water to a boil. Add the spaghetti to the pot and cook for 8 minutes.
In a food processor, place the remaining ingredients, except for the olive oil, and pulse.
While the processor is running, slowly drizzle the olive oil through the top opening. Process until all the olive oil has been added.
Reserve ½ cup of the cooking liquid. Drain the pasta and put it into a large bowl. Add the pesto and cooking liquid to the bowl of pasta and toss everything together.
Serve immediately.

188. Spaghetti with Pine Nuts and Cheese

Preparation Time: 10 minutes
Cooking Time: 11 minutes
Servings: 4 to 6

Ingredients:

8 ounces (227 g) spaghetti
4 tablespoons almond butter
1 teaspoon freshly ground black pepper

1/2 cup pine nuts
1 cup fresh grated Parmesan cheese, divided

Directions:

Bring a large pot of salted water to a boil. Add the pasta and cook for 8 minutes.
In a large saucepan over medium heat, combine the butter, black pepper, and pine nuts. Cook for 2 to 3 minutes, or until the pine nuts are lightly toasted.
Reserve ½ cup of the pasta water. Drain the pasta and place it into the pan with the pine nuts.
Add ¾ cup of the Parmesan cheese and the reserved pasta water to the pasta and toss everything together to evenly coat the pasta.
Transfer the pasta to a serving dish and top with the remaining ¼ cup of the Parmesan cheese. Serve immediately.

189. Creamy Garlic Parmesan Chicken Pasta

Preparation Time: 5 minutes
Cooking Time: 15 minutes
Servings: 4

Ingredients:

3 tablespoons extra-virgin olive oil
2 boneless, skinless chicken breasts, cut into thin strips
1 large onion, thinly sliced
3 tablespoons garlic, minced
1½ teaspoons salt
1-pound (454 g) fettuccine pasta
1 cup heavy whipping cream
3/4 cup freshly grated Parmesan cheese, divided
1/2 teaspoon freshly ground black pepper

Directions:

In a large skillet over medium heat, heat the olive oil. Add the chicken and cook for 3 minutes.
Add the onion, garlic and salt to the skillet. Cook for 7 minutes, stirring occasionally.
Meanwhile, bring a large pot of salted water to a boil and add the pasta, then cook for 7 minutes.
While the pasta is cooking, add the heavy cream, ½ cup of the Parmesan cheese and black pepper to the chicken. Simmer for 3 minutes.
Reserve ½ cup of the pasta water. Drain the pasta and add it to the chicken cream sauce.
Add the reserved pasta water to the pasta and toss together. Simmer for 2 minutes. Top with the remaining ¼ cup of the Parmesan cheese and serve warm.

190. Penne Pasta with Tomato Sauce and Mitzithra cheese

Preparation Time: 15 minutes
Cooking Time: 20 minutes
Servings: 5

Ingredients:

2 tablespoons olive oil
2 scallion stalks, chopped
2 green garlic stalks, minced
10 ounces penne
1/3 teaspoon ground black pepper, to taste
Sea salt, to taste
1/4 teaspoon cayenne pepper
1/4 teaspoon dried marjoram
1/2 teaspoon dried oregano
1/2 teaspoon dried basil
1/2 cup marinara sauce
2 cups vegetable broth
2 overripe tomatoes, pureed
1 cup Mitzithra cheese, grated

Directions:

Press the "Sauté" button to preheat your Instant Pot. Heat the oil until sizzling. Now, sauté the scallions and garlic until just tender and fragrant.
Stir in the penne pasta, spices, marinara sauce, broth, and pureed tomatoes; do not stir, but your pasta should be covered with the liquid.
Secure the lid. Choose the "Manual" mode and cook for 7 minutes at High pressure. Once cooking is complete, use a natural pressure release for 5 minutes; carefully remove the lid.
Fold in the cheese and seal the lid. Let it sit in the residual heat until the cheese melts. Bon appetite

191. All-Star Ziti Casserole

Preparation Time: 10 minutes
Cooking Time: 25 minutes
Servings: 4

Ingredients:

1 tablespoon olive oil
1 shallot, chopped
2 green garlic stalks, minced
2 bell peppers, chopped
1 teaspoon red chili pepper, minced
4 tablespoons cooking wine
2 overripe tomatoes, crushed
2 tablespoons coriander, minced
1/2 teaspoon basil
1/2 teaspoon sage
1/2 teaspoon thyme
1/2 teaspoon oregano
2 teaspoons kosher salt
Salt and red cayenne pepper, to your liking
1 cup pasta sauce
1 cup condensed cream of mushroom soup
12 ounces ziti pasta
4 ounces feta cheese, crumbled
1/4 cup Graviera cheese, grated
1/2 cup dry breadcrumbs

Directions:

Press the "Sauté" button to preheat your Instant Pot. Heat the oil until sizzling. Now, sauté the shallot, garlic, and peppers until just tender and fragrant.
Add a splash of the cooking wine to scrape up the dark spots from the bottom of the inner pot.
Add the tomatoes and bring it to a boil on "More" setting. Press the "Cancel" button. Stir in the spices, pasta sauce, condensed cream of mushroom soup, and ziti pasta.
Secure the lid. Choose the "Manual" mode and cook for 7 minutes at High pressure. Once cooking is complete, use a natural pressure release for 5 minutes; carefully remove the lid.
Transfer the mixture to an oven-safe casserole dish that is previously greased with cooking spray.
Top with the cheese and breadcrumbs. Bake in the preheated oven at 350 degrees F for 15 minutes or until it is bubbly. Let stand on a cooling rack for 10 minutes before slicing and serving. Enjoy!

192. Delicious Chicken Pasta

Preparation Time: 10 minutes
Cooking Time: 17 minutes
Servings: 4

Ingredients:

3 chicken breasts, skinless, boneless, cut into pieces
9 oz whole-grain pasta
1/2 cup olives, sliced
1/2 cup sun-dried tomatoes
1 tbsp roasted red peppers, chopped
14 oz can tomatoes, diced
2 cups marinara sauce
1 cup chicken broth
Pepper
Salt

Directions:

Add all ingredients except whole-grain pasta into the instant pot and stir well.
Seal pot with lid and cook on high for 12 minutes.
Once done, allow to release pressure naturally. Remove lid.
Add pasta and stir well. Seal pot again and select manual and set timer for 5 minutes.
Once done, allow to release pressure naturally for 5 minutes then release remaining using quick release. Remove lid.
Stir well and serve.

193. Roasted Pepper Pasta

Preparation Time: 10 minutes
Cooking Time: 13 minutes
Servings: 6

Ingredients:

1 lb. whole wheat penne pasta
1 tbsp Italian seasoning
4 cups vegetable broth
1 tbsp garlic, minced
1/2 onion, chopped
14 oz jar roasted red peppers
1 cup feta cheese, crumbled
1 tbsp olive oil
Pepper
Salt

Directions:

Add roasted pepper into the blender and blend until smooth.
Add oil into the inner pot of instant pot and set the pot on sauté mode.
Add garlic and onion and sauté for 2-3 minutes.
Add blended roasted pepper and sauté for 2 minutes.
Add remaining ingredients except feta cheese and stir well.
Seal pot with lid and cook on high for 8 minutes.
Once done, allow to release pressure naturally for 5 minutes then release remaining using quick release. Remove lid.
Top with feta cheese and serve.

194. Italian Chicken Pasta

Preparation Time: 10 minutes
Cooking Time: 9 minutes
Servings: 8

Ingredients:

1 lb chicken breast, skinless, boneless, and cut into chunks
1/2 cup cream cheese
1 cup mozzarella cheese, shredded
1 1/2 tsp Italian seasoning
1 tsp garlic, minced
1 cup mushrooms, diced
1/2 onion, diced
2 tomatoes, diced
2 cups of water
16 oz whole wheat penne pasta
Pepper
Salt

Directions:

Add all ingredients except cheeses into the inner pot of instant pot and stir well.
Seal pot with lid and cook on high for 9 minutes.
Once done, allow to release pressure naturally for 5 minutes then release remaining using quick release. Remove lid.
Add cheeses and stir well and serve.

195. Pesto Chicken Pasta

Preparation Time: 10 minutes
Cooking Time: 10 minutes
Servings: 6

Ingredients:

1 lb chicken breast, skinless, boneless, and diced
3 tbsp olive oil
1/2 cup parmesan cheese, shredded
1 tsp Italian seasoning
1/4 cup heavy cream
16 oz whole wheat pasta
6 oz basil pesto
3 1/2 cups water
Pepper
Salt

Directions:

Season chicken with Italian seasoning, pepper, and salt.
Add oil into the inner pot of instant pot and set the pot on sauté mode.
Add chicken to the pot and sauté until brown.
Add remaining ingredients except for parmesan cheese, heavy cream, and pesto and stir well.
Seal pot with lid and cook on high for 5 minutes.
Once done, release pressure using quick release. Remove lid.
Stir in parmesan cheese, heavy cream, and pesto and serve.

196. Fresh Sauce Pasta

Preparation Time: 15 minutes
Cooking Time: 15 minutes
Servings: 4

Ingredients:

1/8 teaspoon salt, plus more for cooking the pasta
1-pound penne pasta
1/4 cup olive oil
1 garlic clove, crushed
3 cups chopped scallions, white and green parts
3 tomatoes, diced
2 tablespoons chopped fresh basil
1/8 teaspoon freshly ground black pepper
Freshly grated Parmesan cheese, for serving

Directions:

Bring a large pot of salted water to a boil over high heat. Drop in the pasta, stir, and return the water to a boil. Boil the pasta for about 6 minutes or until al dente.
A couple minutes before the pasta is completely cooked, in a medium saucepan over medium heat, heat the olive oil.
Add the garlic and cook for 30 seconds.
Stir in the scallions and tomatoes. Cover the pan and cook for 2 to 3 minutes.
Drain the pasta and add it to the vegetables. Stir in the basil and season with the salt and pepper. Top with the Parmesan cheese.

197. Three Sauces Lasagna

Preparation Time: 30 minutes
Cooking Time: 45 minutes
Servings: 8

Ingredients:

1 cup ricotta
1 cup Basil Pesto, or store-bought
4 cups Basic Tomato Basil Sauce, or store-bought, divided
2 (9-ounce) packages no-boil lasagna sheets
4 cups Béchamel Sauce, divided
½ cup freshly grated Parmesan cheese

Directions:

Preheat the oven to 375°F.
In a small mixing bowl, stir together the ricotta and pesto. Set aside.
Spread 1 cup of tomato sauce on the bottom of a 9-by-13-inch baking dish.

Cover the sauce with a few lasagna sheets.
Spread 2 cups of béchamel sauce evenly on top of the lasagna sheets. Cover with a few more lasagna sheets.
Spread the ricotta and pesto mixture evenly over the lasagna sheets.
Pour 1 cup of tomato sauce over the ricotta layer and cover the sauce with a few lasagna sheets.
Spread the remaining 2 cups of béchamel sauce over the lasagna sheets. Cover with a few more lasagna sheets.
Pour the remaining 2 cups of tomato sauce over the sheets. Top with the Parmesan cheese.
Bake for 30 minutes or until the cheese on top is melted and golden brown. Let rest for 15 minutes before serving.

198. Tortellini In Mint Yogurt Sauce

Preparation Time: 15 minutes
Cooking Time: 25 minutes
Servings: 6

Ingredients:

¼ cup cornstarch
1 cup cold water
6 cups Plain Yogurt, or store-bought
¼ teaspoon ground nutmeg
½ teaspoon salt, plus more as needed
2 tablespoons Ghee, butter, or olive oil
3 garlic cloves, minced
1 tablespoon dried mint
1-pound store-bought mushroom-filled tortellini, cooked according to the package directions

Directions:

In a large bowl, whisk the cornstarch and cold water until the cornstarch dissolves. Add the yogurt and whisk well. Place a fine-mesh sieve over a medium saucepan and pour the yogurt mixture through the sieve to remove any lumps.
Stir in the nutmeg and salt. Taste and season with more salt, as needed. Place the pan over medium heat and cook, stirring continuously, for about 20 minutes or until the sauce thickens and begins to coat the back of a spoon.
In a small saucepan over medium heat, melt the ghee.
Add the garlic to the ghee and cook for 1 minute. Stir in the mint, remove from the heat, and stir the mixture into the yogurt sauce. Taste and adjust the seasoning.
Add the cooked tortellini to the yogurt sauce, stirring so they are coated. Cook over low heat for 5 minutes or until heated through.

199. Homemade Shish Barak

Preparation Time: 40 minutes
Cooking Time: 20 minutes
Servings: 40 Dumplings

Ingredients:

1/4 cup olive oil
1 onion, chopped
1-pound white mushrooms, chopped
1 garlic clove, mashed
1/2 teaspoon salt
1/2 teaspoon freshly ground black pepper
All-purpose flour, for dusting
Pita Bread dough

Directions:

In a medium sauté pan or skillet over medium heat, heat the olive oil.
Add the onion and cook for about 5 minutes until golden. Add the mushrooms and cook for about 10 minutes until their natural water evaporates, stirring often.
Stir in the garlic, salt, and pepper. Remove from the heat.
Preheat the oven to 350°F.
Dust a work surface with flour and roll out the pita dough on it to 1/8 inch thick.
Using a 2-inch round glass or cookie cutter, cut rounds from the dough.
Place ½ teaspoon of mushroom stuffing in the center of each dough circle. Fold the circle in half and pinch the edges together to form a hat-like shape. Place the tortellini on a baking sheet.
Bake for 5 minutes.
Let cool. Once cooled, use them in the Tortellini in Mint Yogurt Sauce or freeze in a freezer bag for up to 3 months.

200. Penne In Tomato And Caper Sauce

Preparation Time: 10 minutes
Cooking Time: 15 minutes
Servings: 4

Ingredients:

2 tablespoons olive oil
2 garlic cloves, minced
1 cup sliced cherry tomatoes
2 cups Basic Tomato Basil Sauce, or store-bought
1 cup capers, drained and rinsed
Salt
4 cups penne pasta

Directions:

Set a large pot of salted water over high heat to boil.
In a medium saucepan over medium heat, heat the olive oil. Add the garlic and cook for 30 seconds. Add the cherry tomatoes and cook for 2 to 3 minutes.
Pour in the tomato sauce and bring the mixture to a boil. Stir in the capers and turn off the heat.
Once boiling add the pasta to the pot of water and cook for about 7 minutes until al dente.
Drain the pasta and stir it into the sauce. Toss gently and cook over medium heat for 1 minute or until warmed through.

201. Spaghetti Pesto Cake

Preparation Time: 10 minutes
Cooking Time: 40 minutes
Servings: 6

Ingredients:

12 ounces ricotta
1 cup Basil Pesto, or store-bought
2 tablespoons olive oil
¼ cup freshly grated Parmesan cheese
Salt
1-pound spaghetti

Directions:

Preheat the oven to 400°F. Set a large pot of salted water to boil over high heat.
In a food processor, combine the ricotta and basil pesto. Purée into a smooth cream and transfer to a large bowl. Set aside.
Coat a 10-cup Bundt pan with the olive oil and sprinkle with the Parmesan cheese. Set aside.
Once the water is boiling, add the pasta to the pot and cook for about 6 minutes until al dente.
Drain the pasta well and add it to the pesto cream. Mix well until all the pasta is saturated with the sauce.
Spoon the pasta into the prepared pan, pressing to ensure it is tightly packed. Bake for 30 minutes.
Place a flat serving platter on top of the cake pan. Quickly and carefully invert the pasta cake. Gently remove the pan. Cut into slices and serve topped with your favorite sauce, if desired.

202. Artichokes, Olives & Tuna Pasta

Preparation Time: 10 minutes
Cooking Time: 15 minutes
Servings: 4

Ingredients:

¼ cup chopped fresh basil
¼ cup chopped green olives
¼ tsp freshly ground pepper
½ cup white wine
½ tsp salt, divided
1 10 oz package frozen artichoke hearts, thawed and squeezed dry
2 cups grape tomatoes, halved
2 tbsp lemon juice
2 tsp chopped fresh rosemary
2 tsp freshly grated lemon zest
3 cloves garlic, minced
4 tbsp extra virgin olive oil, divided
6 oz whole wheat penne pasta
8 oz tuna steak, cut into 3 pieces

Directions:

Cook penne pasta according to package instructions. Drain and set aside.
Preheat grill to medium high.
In bowl, toss and mix ¼ tsp pepper, ¼ tsp salt, 1 tsp rosemary, lemon zest, 1 tbsp oil and tuna pieces.
Grill tuna for 3 minutes per side. Allow to cool and flake into bite sized pieces.
On medium fire, place a large nonstick saucepan and heat 3 tbsp oil.
Sauté remaining rosemary, garlic olives, and artichoke hearts for 4 minutes Add wine and tomatoes, bring to a boil and cook for 3 minutes while stirring once in a while.
Add remaining salt, lemon juice, tuna pieces and pasta. Cook until heated through.
To serve, garnish with basil and enjoy.

203. Broccoli Pesto Spaghetti

Preparation Time:5 minutes
Cooking Time:35 minutes
Servings: 4

Ingredients:

8 oz. spaghetti
1-pound broccoli, cut into florets
2 tablespoons olive oil
4 garlic cloves, chopped
4 basil leaves
2 tablespoons blanched almonds
1 lemon, juiced
Salt and pepper to taste

Directions:

For the pesto, combine the broccoli, oil, garlic, basil, lemon juice and almonds in a blender and pulse until well mixed and smooth.
Cook the spaghetti in a large pot of salty water for 8 minutes or until al dente. Drain well.
Mix the warm spaghetti with the broccoli pesto and serve right away.

204. Spaghetti all'Olio

Preparation Time:5 minutes
Cooking Time:30 minutes
Servings: 4

Ingredients:

8 oz. spaghetti
3 tablespoons olive oil
4 garlic cloves, minced
2 red peppers, sliced
1 tablespoon lemon juice
Salt and pepper to taste
½ cup grated parmesan cheese

Directions:

Heat the oil in a skillet and add the garlic. Cook for 30 seconds then stir in the red peppers and cook for 1 more minute on low heat, making sure to only infuse them, not to burn or fry them.
Add the lemon juice and remove off heat.
Cook the spaghetti in a large pot of salty water for 8 minutes or as stated on the package, just until they become al dente.
Drain the spaghetti well and mix them with the garlic and pepper oil.
Serve right away.

205. Quick Tomato Spaghetti

Preparation Time:5 minutes
Cooking Time:15 minutes
Servings: 4

Ingredients:

8 oz. spaghetti
3 tablespoons olive oil
4 garlic cloves, sliced
1 jalapeno, sliced
2 cups cherry tomatoes
Salt and pepper to taste
1 teaspoon balsamic vinegar
½ cup grated Parmesan

Directions:

Heat a large pot of water on medium flame. Add a pinch of salt and bring to a boil then add the pasta.
Cook for 8 minutes or until al dente.
While the pasta cooks, heat the oil in a skillet and add the garlic and jalapeno. Cook for 1 minute then stir in the tomatoes, as well as salt and pepper.
Cook for 5-7 minutes until the tomatoes' skins burst.
Add the vinegar and remove off heat.
Drain the pasta well and mix it with the tomato sauce. Sprinkle with cheese and serve right away.

206. Tomato and Almond Pesto

Preparation Time: 15 minutes
Cooking Time: None
Servings: 4 cups

Ingredients:

¾ Cup slivered almonds
one 28-oz. can dice tomatoes, drained
one 14-oz. can tomato, fire-roasted, drained
¾ cup of extra-virgin olive oil
½ cup grated parmesan cheese
salt and pepper to taste
1 cup fresh basil leaves
1 tbsp red wine vinegar

Directions:

Begin by heating a frying pan over a medium to high flame. After heating the pan put the almonds into the pan and let them cook for 4 to 5 minutes.
Once the almonds have reached a golden-brown color, place it into a food processor until you reach the consistency of fine powder.
Mix into the food processor the basil, red wine vinegar, and the tomatoes. Wait until the mixture becomes smooth and add the olive oil.
Continue processing for 35 seconds before adding the salt, pepper, and Parmesan. After a few pulses, the mix is ready to serve.
You can refrigerate for a cooler mix.

207. Pasta with Pesto

Preparation Time: 10 minutes
Cooking Time: 0 minutes
Servings: 4

Ingredients:

3 tablespoons extra-virgin olive oil
3 garlic cloves, finely minced
½ cup fresh basil leaves

¼ cup (about 2 ounces) grated Parmesan cheese
¼ cup pine nuts
8 ounces whole-wheat pasta, cooked according to package instructions and drained

Directions:

In a blender or food processor, combine the olive oil, garlic, basil, cheese, and pine nuts. Pulse for 10 to 20 (1-second) pulses until everything is chopped and blended.
Toss with the hot pasta and serve.

208. Mac & Cheese

Preparation Time: 10 minutes
Cooking Time: 4 minutes
Servings: 8

Ingredients:

1 lb whole grain pasta
1/2 cup parmesan cheese, grated
4 cups cheddar cheese, shredded
1 cup milk
1/4 tsp garlic powder
1/2 tsp ground mustard
2 tbsp olive oil
4 cups of water
Pepper
Salt

Directions:

Add pasta, garlic powder, mustard, oil, water, pepper, and salt into the instant pot. Seal pot with lid and cook on high for 4 minutes. Once done, release pressure using quick release. Remove lid. Add remaining ingredients and stir well and serve.

209. Vegan Olive Pasta

Preparation Time: 10 minutes
Cooking Time: 5 minutes
Servings: 4

Ingredients:

4 cups whole grain penne pasta
1/2 cup olives, sliced
1 tbsp capers
1/4 tsp red pepper flakes
3 cups of water
4 cups pasta sauce, homemade
1 tbsp garlic, minced
Pepper
Salt

Directions:

Add all ingredients into the inner pot of instant pot and stir well.
Seal pot with lid and cook on high for 5 minutes.
Once done, release pressure using quick release. Remove lid.
Stir and serve.

210. Italian Mac & Cheese

Preparation Time: 10 minutes
Cooking Time: 6 minutes
Servings: 4

Ingredients:

1 lb whole grain pasta
2 tsp Italian seasoning
1 1/2 tsp garlic powder
1 1/2 tsp onion powder
1 cup sour cream
4 cups of water
4 oz parmesan cheese, shredded
12 oz ricotta cheese
Pepper
Salt

Directions:

Add all ingredients except ricotta cheese into the inner pot of instant pot and stir well.
Seal pot with lid and cook on high for 6 minutes.
Once done, allow to release pressure naturally for 5 minutes then release remaining using quick release. Remove lid.
Add ricotta cheese and stir well and serve.

211. Delicious Greek Chicken Pasta

Preparation Time: 10 minutes
Cooking Time: 10 minutes
Servings: 6

Ingredients:

2 chicken breasts, skinless, boneless, and cut into chunks
1/2 cup olives, sliced
2 cups vegetable stock
12 oz Greek vinaigrette dressing
1 lb whole grain pasta
Pepper
Salt

Directions:

Add all ingredients into the inner pot of instant pot and stir well.
Seal pot with lid and cook on high for 10 minutes.
Once done, release pressure using quick release. Remove lid.
Stir well and serve.

CHAPTER 4: RICE AND GRAIN

212. Garbanzo And Kidney Bean Salad

Preparation Time: 10 minutes
Cooking Time: 0 minutes
Servings: 4

Ingredients:

1 (15 ounce) can kidney beans, drained
1 (15.5 ounce) can garbanzo beans, drained
1 lemon, zested and juiced
1 medium tomato, chopped
1 teaspoon capers, rinsed and drained
1/2 cup chopped fresh parsley
1/2 teaspoon salt, or to taste
1/4 cup chopped red onion
3 tablespoons extra virgin olive oil

Directions:

In a salad bowl, whisk well lemon juice, olive oil and salt until dissolved.
Stir in garbanzo, kidney beans, tomato, red onion, parsley, and capers. Toss well to coat.
Allow flavors to mix for 30 minutes by setting in the fridge.
Mix again before serving.

213. Rice & Currant Salad Mediterranean Style

Preparation Time: 20 minutes
Cooking Time: 50 minutes
Servings: 4

Ingredients:

1 cup basmati rice
salt
2 1/2 Tablespoons lemon juice
1 teaspoon grated orange zest
2 Tablespoons fresh orange juice
1/4 cup olive oil
1/2 teaspoon cinnamon
Salt and pepper to taste
4 chopped green onions
1/2 cup dried currants
3/4 cup shelled pistachios or almonds
1/4 cup chopped fresh parsley

Directions:

Place a nonstick pot on medium high fire and add rice. Toast rice until opaque and starts to smell, around 10 minutes.
Add 4 quarts of boiling water to pot and 2 tsp salt. Boil until tender, around 8 minutes uncovered.
Drain the rice and spread out on a lined cookie sheet to cool completely.
In a large salad bowl, whisk well the oil, juices and spices. Add salt and pepper to taste.
Add half of the green onions, half of parsley, currants, and nuts.
Toss with the cooled rice and let stand for at least 20 minutes.
If needed adjust seasoning with pepper and salt.
Garnish with remaining parsley and green onions.

214. Stuffed Tomatoes With Green Chili

Preparation Time: 10 minutes
Cooking Time: 55 minutes
Servings: 6

Ingredients:

4 oz Colby-Jack shredded cheese
¼ cup water
1 cup uncooked quinoa
6 large ripe tomatoes
¼ tsp freshly ground black pepper
¾ tsp ground cumin
1 tsp salt, divided
1 tbsp fresh lime juice
1 tbsp olive oil
1 tbsp chopped fresh oregano
1 cup chopped onion
2 cups fresh corn kernels
2 poblano chilies

Directions:

Preheat broiler to high.
Slice lengthwise the chilies and press on a baking sheet lined with foil. Broil for 8 minutes. Remove from oven and let cool for 10 minutes. Peel the chilies and chop coarsely and place in medium sized bowl.
Place onion and corn in baking sheet and broil for ten minutes. Stir two times while broiling. Remove from oven and mix in with chopped chilies.
Add black pepper, cumin, ¼ tsp salt, lime juice, oil and oregano. Mix well.
Cut off the tops of tomatoes and set aside. Leave the tomato shell intact as you scoop out the tomato pulp.
Drain tomato pulp as you press down with a spoon. Reserve 1 ¼ cups of tomato pulp liquid and discard the rest. Invert the tomato shells on a wire rack for 30 mins and then wipe the insides dry with a paper towel.
Season with ½ tsp salt the tomato pulp.
On a sieve over a bowl, place quinoa. Add water until it covers quinoa. Rub quinoa grains for 30 seconds together with hands; rinse and drain. Repeat this procedure two times and drain well at the end.
In medium saucepan bring to a boil remaining salt, ¼ cup water, quinoa and tomato liquid.
Once boiling, reduce heat and simmer for 15 minutes or until liquid is fully absorbed. Remove from heat and fluff quinoa with fork. Transfer and mix well the quinoa with the corn mixture.
Spoon ¾ cup of the quinoa-corn mixture into the tomato shells, top with cheese and cover with the tomato top. Bake in a preheated 350oF oven for 15 minutes and then broil high for another 1.5 minutes.

215. Red Wine Risotto

Preparation Time: 30 minutes
Cooking Time: 25 minutes
Servings: 8

Ingredients:

Pepper to taste
1 cup finely shredded Parmigian-Reggiano cheese, divided
2 tsp tomato paste
1 ¾ cups dry red wine
¼ tsp salt
1 ½ cups Italian 'risotto' rice
2 cloves garlic, minced
1 medium onion, freshly chopped
2 tbsp extra-virgin olive oil
4 ½ cups reduced sodium beef broth

Directions:

On medium high fire, bring to a simmer broth in a medium fry pan. Lower fire so broth is steaming but not simmering.
On medium low heat, place a Dutch oven and heat oil.
Sauté onions for 5 minutes. Add garlic and cook for 2 minutes.
Add rice, mix well, and season with salt.
Into rice, add a generous splash of wine and ½ cup of broth.

Lower fire to a gentle simmer, cook until liquid is fully absorbed while stirring rice every once in a while.
Add another splash of wine and ½ cup of broth. Stirring once in a while.
Add tomato paste and stir to mix well.
Continue cooking and adding wine and broth until broth is used up.
Once done cooking, turn off fire and stir in pepper and ¾ cup cheese.
To serve, sprinkle with remaining cheese and enjoy.

216. Chicken Pasta Parmesan

Preparation Time: 10 minutes
Cooking Time: 20 minutes
Servings: 1

Ingredients:

¼ cup prepared marinara sauce
½ cup cooked whole wheat spaghetti
1 oz reduced fat mozzarella cheese, grated
1 tbsp olive oil
2 tbsp seasoned dry breadcrumbs
4 oz skinless chicken breast

Directions:

On medium high fire, place an ovenproof skillet and heat oil.
Pan fry chicken for 3 to 5 minutes per side or until cooked through.
Pour marinara sauce, stir and continue cooking for 3 minutes.
Turn off fire, add mozzarella and breadcrumbs on top.
Pop into a preheated broiler on high and broil for 10 minutes or until breadcrumbs are browned and mozzarella is melted.
Remove from broiler, serve and enjoy.

217. Orange, Dates And Asparagus On Quinoa Salad

Preparation Time: 10 minutes
Cooking Time: 25 minutes
Servings: 8

Ingredients:

¼ cup chopped pecans, toasted
½ cup white onion, finely chopped
½ jalapeno pepper, diced
½ lb. asparagus, sliced into 2-inch lengths, steamed and chilled
½ tsp salt
1 cup fresh orange sections
1 cup uncooked quinoa
1 tsp olive oil
2 cups water
2 tbsp minced red onion
5 dates, pitted and chopped
¼ tsp freshly ground black pepper
¼ tsp salt
1 garlic clove, minced
1 tbsp extra virgin olive oil
2 tbsp chopped fresh mint
2 tbsp fresh lemon juice
Mint sprigs – optional

Directions:

On medium high fire, place a large nonstick pan and heat 1 tsp oil.
Add white onion and sauté for two minutes.
Add quinoa and for 5 minutes sauté it.
Add salt and water. Bring to a boil, once boiling, slow fire to a simmer and cook for 15 minutes while covered.
Turn off fire and leave for 15 minutes, to let quinoa absorb the remaining water.
Transfer quinoa to a large salad bowl. Add jalapeno pepper, asparagus, dates, red onion, pecans and oranges. Toss to combine.
Make the dressing by mixing garlic, pepper, salt, olive oil and lemon juice in a small bowl.
Pour dressing into quinoa salad along with chopped mint, mix well.
If desired, garnish with mint sprigs before serving.

218. Tasty Lasagna Rolls

Preparation Time: 20 minutes
Cooking Time: 20 minutes
Servings: 6

Ingredients:

¼ tsp crushed red pepper
¼ tsp salt
½ cup shredded mozzarella cheese
½ cups parmesan cheese, shredded
1 14-oz package tofu, cubed
1 25-oz can of low-sodium marinara sauce
1 tbsp extra virgin olive oil
12 whole wheat lasagna noodles
2 tbsp Kalamata olives, chopped
3 cloves minced garlic
3 cups spinach, chopped

Directions:

Put enough water on a large pot and cook the lasagna noodles according to package instructions. Drain, rinse and set aside until ready to use.
In a large skillet, sauté garlic over medium heat for 20 seconds. Add the tofu and spinach and cook until the spinach wilts. Transfer this mixture in a bowl and add parmesan olives, salt, red pepper and 2/3 cup of the marinara sauce.
In a pan, spread a cup of marinara sauce on the bottom. To make the rolls, place noodle on a surface and spread ¼ cup of the tofu filling. Roll up and place it on the pan with the marinara sauce. Do this procedure until all lasagna noodles are rolled.
Place the pan over high heat and bring to a simmer. Reduce the heat to medium and let it cook for three more minutes. Sprinkle mozzarella cheese and let the cheese melt for two minutes. Serve hot.

219. Raisins, Nuts And Beef On Hashweh Rice

Preparation Time: 30 minutes
Cooking Time: 50 minutes
Servings: 8

Ingredients:

½ cup dark raisins, soaked in 2 cups water for an hour
1/3 cup slivered almonds, toasted and soaked in 2 cups water overnight
1/3 cup pine nuts, toasted and soaked in 2 cups water overnight
½ cup fresh parsley leaves, roughly chopped
Pepper and salt to taste
¾ tsp ground cinnamon, divided
¾ tsp cloves, divided
1 tsp garlic powder
1 ¾ tsp allspice, divided
1 lb. lean ground beef or lean ground lamb
1 small red onion, finely chopped
Olive oil
1 ½ cups medium grain rice

Directions:

For 15 to 20 minutes, soak rice in cold water. You will know that soaking is enough when you can snap a grain of rice easily between your thumb and index finger. Once soaking is done, drain rice well.
Meanwhile, drain pine nuts, almonds and raisins for at least a minute and transfer to one bowl. Set aside.
On a heavy cooking pot on medium high fire, heat 1 tbsp olive oil.
Once oil is hot, add red onions. Sauté for a minute before adding ground meat and sauté for another minute.
Season ground meat with pepper, salt, ½ tsp ground cinnamon, ½ tsp ground cloves, 1 tsp garlic powder, and 1 ¼ tsp allspice.

Sauté ground meat for 10 minutes or until browned and cooked fully. Drain fat.
In same pot with cooked ground meat, add rice on top of meat.
Season with a bit of pepper and salt. Add remaining cinnamon, ground cloves, and allspice. Do not mix.
Add 1 tbsp olive oil and 2 ½ cups of water. Bring to a boil and once boiling, lower fire to a simmer. Cook while covered until liquid is fully absorbed, around 20 to 25 minutes.
Turn of fire.
To serve, place a large serving platter that fully covers the mouth of the pot. Place platter upside down on mouth of pot, and invert pot. The inside of the pot should now rest on the platter with the rice on bottom of plate and ground meat on top of it.
Garnish the top of the meat with raisins, almonds, pine nuts, and parsley.
Serve and enjoy.

220. Yangchow Chinese Style Fried Rice

Preparation Time: 10 minutes
Cooking Time: 20 minutes
Servings: 4

Ingredients:

4 cups cold cooked rice
1/2 cup peas
1 medium yellow onion, diced
5 tbsp olive oil
4 oz frozen medium shrimp, thawed, shelled, deveined and chopped finely
6 oz roast pork
3 large eggs
Salt and freshly ground black pepper
1/2 tsp cornstarch

Directions:

Combine the salt and ground black pepper and 1/2 tsp cornstarch, coat the shrimp with it. Chop the roasted pork. Beat the eggs and set aside.
Stir-fry the shrimp in a wok on high fire with 1 tbsp heated oil until pink, around 3 minutes. Set the shrimp aside and stir fry the roasted pork briefly. Remove both from the pan.
In the same pan, stir-fry the onion until soft, Stir the peas and cook until bright green. Remove both from pan.
Add 2 tbsp oil in the same pan, add the cooked rice. Stir and separate the individual grains. Add the beaten eggs, toss the rice. Add the roasted pork, shrimp, vegetables and onion. Toss everything together. Season with salt and pepper to taste.

221. Cinnamon Quinoa Bars

Preparation Time: 20 minutes
Cooking Time: 30 minutes
Servings: 4

Ingredients:

2 ½ cups cooked quinoa
4 large eggs
1/3 cup unsweetened almond milk
1/3 cup pure maple syrup
Seeds from ½ whole vanilla bean pod or 1 tbsp vanilla extract
1 ½ tbsp cinnamon
1/4 tsp salt

Directions:

Preheat oven to 375oF.
Combine all ingredients into large bowl and mix well.
In an 8 x 8 Baking pan, cover with parchment paper.
Pour batter evenly into baking dish.
Bake for 25-30 minutes or until it has set. It should not wiggle when you lightly shake the pan because the eggs are fully cooked.
Remove as quickly as possible from pan and parchment paper onto cooling rack.
Cut into 4 pieces.
Enjoy on its own, with a small spread of almond or nut butter or wait until it cools to enjoy the next morning.

222. Cucumber Olive Rice

Preparation Time: 20 minutes
Cooking Time: 10 minutes
Servings: 8

Ingredients:

2 cups rice, rinsed
1/2 cup olives, pitted
1 cup cucumber, chopped
1 tbsp red wine vinegar
1 tsp lemon zest, grated
1 tbsp fresh lemon juice
2 tbsp olive oil
2 cups vegetable broth
1/2 tsp dried oregano
1 red bell pepper, chopped
1/2 cup onion, chopped
1 tbsp olive oil
Pepper
Salt

Directions:

Add oil into the inner pot of instant pot and set the pot on sauté mode.
Add onion and sauté for 3 minutes.
Add bell pepper and oregano and sauté for 1 minute.
Add rice and broth and stir well.
Seal pot with lid and cook on high for 6 minutes.
Once done, allow to release pressure naturally for 10 minutes then release remaining using quick release. Remove lid.
Add remaining ingredients and stir everything well to mix.
Serve immediately and enjoy it.

223. Chorizo-kidney Beans Quinoa Pilaf

Preparation Time: 10 minutes
Cooking Time: 35 minutes
Servings: 4

Ingredients:

¼ pound dried Spanish chorizo diced (about 2/3 cup)
¼ teaspoon red pepper flakes
¼ teaspoon smoked paprika
½ teaspoon cumin
½ teaspoon sea salt
1 3/4 cups water
1 cup quinoa
1 large clove garlic minced
1 small red bell pepper finely diced
1 small red onion finely diced
1 tablespoon tomato paste
1 15-ounce can kidney beans rinsed and drained

Directions:

Place a nonstick pot on medium high fire and heat for 2 minutes. Add chorizo and sauté for 5 minutes until lightly browned.
Stir in peppers and onion. Sauté for 5 minutes.
Add tomato paste, red pepper flakes, salt, paprika, cumin, and garlic. Sauté for 2 minutes.
Stir in quinoa and mix well. Sauté for 2 minutes.
Add water and beans. Mix well. Cover and simmer for 20 minutes or until liquid is fully absorbed.
Turn off fire and fluff quinoa. Let it sit for 5 minutes more while uncovered.
Serve and enjoy.

224. Belly-filling Cajun Rice & Chicken

Preparation Time: 45 minutes
Cooking Time: 20 minutes
Servings: 6

Ingredients:

1 tablespoon oil
1 onion, diced
3 cloves of garlic, minced
1-pound chicken breasts, sliced
1 tablespoon Cajun seasoning
1 tablespoon tomato paste
2 cups chicken broth
1 ½ cups white rice, rinsed
1 bell pepper, chopped

Directions:

Press the Sauté on the Instant Pot and pour the oil.
Sauté the onion and garlic until fragrant.
Stir in the chicken breasts and season with Cajun seasoning.
Continue cooking for 3 minutes.
Add the tomato paste and chicken broth. Dissolve the tomato paste before adding the rice and bell pepper.
Close the lid and press the rice button.
Once done cooking, do a natural release for 10 minutes.
Then, do a quick release.
Once cooled, evenly divide into serving size, keep in your preferred container, and refrigerate until ready to eat.

225. Chicken And White Bean

Preparation Time: 90 minutes
Cooking Time: 70 minutes
Servings: 8

Ingredients:

2 tbsp fresh cilantro, chopped
2 cups grated Monterey Jack cheese
3 cups water
1/8 tsp cayenne pepper
2 tsp pure chile powder
2 tsp ground cumin
1 4-oz can chop green chiles
1 cup corn kernels
2 15-oz cans shite beans, drained and rinsed
2 garlic cloves
1 medium onion, diced
2 tbsp extra virgin olive oil
1 lb. chicken breasts, boneless and skinless

Directions:

Slice chicken breasts into ½-inch cubes and with pepper and salt, season it.
On high fire, place a large nonstick fry pan and heat oil.
Sauté chicken pieces for three to four minutes or until lightly browned.
Reduce fire to medium and add garlic and onion.
Cook for 5 to 6 minutes or until onions are translucent.
Add water, spices, chilies, corn and beans. Bring to a boil.
Once boiling, slow fire to a simmer and continue simmering for an hour, uncovered.
To serve, garnish with a sprinkling of cilantro and a tablespoon of cheese.

226. Quinoa & Black Bean Stuffed Sweet Potatoes

Preparation Time: 15 minutes
Cooking Time: 60 minutes
Servings: 8

Ingredients:

4 sweet potatoes
½ onion, diced
1 garlic glove, crushed and diced
½ large bell pepper diced (about 2/3 cups)
Handful of diced cilantro
½ cup cooked quinoa
½ cup black beans
1 tbsp olive oil
1 tbsp chili powder
½ tbsp cumin
½ tbsp paprika
½ tbsp oregano
2 tbsp lime juice
2 tbsp honey
Sprinkle salt
1 cup shredded cheddar cheese
Chopped spring onions, for garnish (optional)

Directions:

Preheat oven to 400oF.
Wash and scrub outside of potatoes. Poke with fork a few times and then place on parchment paper on cookie sheet. Bake for 40-45 minutes or until it is cooked.
While potatoes are baking, sauté onions, garlic, olive oil and spices in a pan on the stove until onions are translucent and soft.
In the last 10 minutes while the potatoes are cooking, in a large bowl combine the onion mixture with the beans, quinoa, honey, lime juice, cilantro and ½ cup cheese. Mix well.
When potatoes are cooked, remove from oven and let cool slightly. When cool to touch, cut in half (hot dog style) and scoop out most of the insides. Leave a thin ring of potato so that it will hold its shape. You can save the sweet potato guts for another recipe, such as my veggie burgers (recipe posted below).
Fill with bean and quinoa mixture. Top with remaining cheddar cheese.
(If making this a freezer meal, stop here. Individually wrap potato skins in plastic wrap and place on flat surface to freeze. Once frozen, place all potatoes in large zip lock container or Tupperware.)
Return to oven for an additional 10 minutes or until cheese is melted.

227. Feta, Eggplant And Sausage Penne

Preparation Time: 20 minutes
Cooking Time: 30 minutes
Servings: 6

Ingredients:

¼ cup chopped fresh parsley
½ cup crumbled feta cheese
6 cups hot cooked penne
1 14.5oz can diced tomatoes
¼ tsp ground black pepper
1 tsp dried oregano
2 tbsp tomato paste
4 garlic cloves, minced
½ lb. bulk pork breakfast sausage
4 ½ cups cubed peeled eggplant

Directions:

On medium high fire, place a nonstick, big fry pan and cook for seven minutes garlic, sausage and eggplant or until eggplants are soft and sausage are lightly browned.
Stir in diced tomatoes, black pepper, oregano and tomato paste. Cover and simmer for five minutes while occasionally stirring.
Remove pan from fire, stir in pasta and mix well.
Transfer to a serving dish, garnish with parsley and cheese before serving.

228. Bell Peppers 'n Tomato-chickpea Rice

Preparation Time: 30 minutes
Cooking Time: 35 minutes
Servings: 4

Ingredients:

2 tablespoons olive oil
1/2 chopped red bell pepper
1/2 chopped green bell pepper

1/2 chopped yellow pepper
1/2 chopped red pepper
1 medium onion, chopped
1 clove garlic, minced
2 cups cooked jasmine rice
1 teaspoon tomato paste
1 cup chickpeas
salt to taste
1/2 teaspoon paprika
1 small tomato, chopped
Parsley for garnish

Directions:

In a large mixing bowl, whisk well olive oil, garlic, tomato paste, and paprika. Season with salt generously.
Mix in rice and toss well to coat in the dressing.
Add remaining ingredients and toss well to mix.
Let salad rest to allow flavors to mix for 15 minutes.
Toss one more time and adjust salt to taste if needed.
Garnish with parsley and serve.

229. Lipsmacking Chicken Tetrazzini

Preparation Time: 1 hour 15 minutes
Cooking Time: 3 Hours
Servings: 8

Ingredients:

Toasted French bread slices
¾ cup thinly sliced green onion
2/3 cup grated parmesan cheese
10 oz dried spaghetti or linguine, cooked and drained
¼ tsp ground nutmeg
¼ tsp ground black pepper
2 tbsp dry sherry
¼ cup chicken broth or water
1 16oz jar of Alfredo pasta sauce
2 4.5oz jars of sliced mushrooms, drained
2.5 lbs. skinless chicken breasts cut into ½ inch slices

Directions:

In a slow cooker, mix mushrooms and chicken.
In a bowl, mix well nutmeg, pepper, sherry, broth and alfredo sauce before pouring over chicken and mushrooms.
Set on high heat, cover and cook for two to three hours.
Once chicken is cooked, pour over pasta, garnish with green onion and serve with French bread on the side.

230. Seafood Risotto

Preparation Time: 15 minutes
Cooking Time: 30 minutes
Servings: 4

Ingredients:

3 cups seafood or vegetable broth
3 cups water
4 tablespoons extra-virgin olive oil, divided
1 shallot, finely chopped
1½ cups Arborio rice
1/4 cup dry white wine
1-pound mussels, scrubbed and debearded
1-pound small clams, scrubbed
1-pound large shrimp, peeled and deveined
2 garlic cloves, minced
1/2 teaspoon salt
1/2 teaspoon freshly ground black pepper
1 cup baby arugula
1/4 cup mascarpone cheese

Directions

In a small saucepan, bring the broth to a simmer. In another small saucepan, bring the water to a simmer.
In a large saucepan, heat 2 tablespoons of olive oil over medium heat. Add the shallot and cook for 3 minutes, until it starts to soften.
Add the rice and cook for 1 minute. Add the wine and cook until it evaporates, stirring constantly.
Add a ladleful of hot broth and cook until it is absorbed into the rice, continuing to stir. Then add a ladleful of hot water and cook until it is absorbed. Alternate these liquids until the rice takes on a creamy consistency, about 20 minutes total.
Meanwhile, put the mussels and clams in a large, deep skillet. Pour in ½ inch of water. Cover and cook over high heat for 3 to 5 minutes until all the clams and mussels have opened. Discard any that do not open.
In a medium skillet, heat the remaining 2 tablespoons of olive oil over low heat. Add the shrimp, garlic, salt, and pepper and cook for about 5 minutes, turning once, until the shrimp turn pink.
Once the rice is fully cooked, stir in the arugula and mascarpone cheese. Fold in the shrimp and all the pan drippings.
Divide the risotto among serving bowls. Place a few mussels and clams in each bowl, hinged-ends down.

231. Easy Rice Pilaf

Preparation Time: 5 minutes
Cooking Time: 20 minutes
Servings: 4

Ingredients:

2 tablespoons extra-virgin olive oil
1 small onion, diced
1½ cups long-grain white rice, such as jasmine
2 cups chicken broth
1 teaspoon dried oregano
1/2 teaspoon salt
1/4 teaspoon freshly ground black pepper

Directions:

In a large saucepan, heat the olive oil over medium heat. Add the onion and cook for about 3 minutes, until it starts to soften.
Add the rice and toss to coat it in the oil.
Add the chicken broth, oregano, salt, and pepper and bring to a boil. Reduce the heat to low, cover, and simmer for about 15 minutes until the liquid is fully absorbed into the rice.
Fluff with a fork before serving.

232. Baked Chicken Paella

Preparation Time: 15 minutes
Cooking Time: 1 hour 15 minutes
Servings: 4

Ingredients:

2 tablespoons extra-virgin olive oil
2 boneless, skinless chicken breasts, cut into bite-size pieces
1 teaspoon salt
1 teaspoon freshly ground black pepper
1 hot Italian pork sausage, sliced
1 medium onion, sliced
1 red or green bell pepper, seeded and sliced
3 garlic cloves, chopped
1/4 cup dry white wine
1 cup Arborio rice
3 cups chicken broth, divided
1 cup canned or cooked chickpeas
2 cup baby spinach
2 large eggs, beaten

Directions:

Preheat the oven to 350°F.
In a large ovenproof skillet or braising pan, heat the olive oil over medium heat. Add the chicken and season with salt and pepper. Brown the chicken on both sides, about 5 minutes total, then transfer to a plate.

Add the sausage, onion, bell pepper, and garlic to the skillet and cook for about 10 minutes, until the sausage is browned and the vegetables are softened. Transfer to the plate with the chicken.
Pour in the wine and deglaze the skillet, stirring to scrape up any browned bits on the bottom. Add the rice and mix with the wine until coated.
Add 1 cup of chicken broth, stir and cook for 5 minutes.
Add the chickpeas and another 1 cup of broth and stir again. Return the browned chicken to the skillet on top of the rice and chickpeas.
Add the sausage, onion, and bell pepper mixture on top of the chicken. Push the chicken, sausage, and vegetables down into the rice and chickpea mixture, but do not stir. Add the remaining 1 cup of chicken broth and bring to a boil.
Cover the skillet, transfer to the oven and bake for 40 minutes.
Uncover the skillet and take a peek at the dish. If it looks dry, add 1/3 cup water to the skillet. Add the spinach and push it down into the mixture slightly. Pour the beaten eggs on top.
Return to the oven and bake for another 10 minutes, uncovered, until the egg is completely cooked.
Let rest for 5 minutes before serving.

233. Vegetable Rice Bake

Preparation Time: 15 minutes
Cooking Time: 50 minutes
Servings: 4

Ingredients:

1½ teaspoons paprika
1½ teaspoons dried thyme
1 teaspoon Italian Herb Blend
1 teaspoon salt
2 teaspoons freshly ground black pepper
2 carrots, chopped
1 turnip, peeled and chopped
2garlic cloves, minced
1½ cups long-grain white rice
1½ cups chicken broth
1½ cups water
head broccoli, cut into florets
2 ears of corn, husks, and silks removed, cut into thirds
1 red onion, cut into large chunks
Red bell pepper, seeded and cut into chunks
1/4 cup extra-virgin olive oil

Directions

Preheat the oven to 400°F.
In a small bowl, combine the paprika, thyme, Italian herb blend, salt, and pepper.
In a 9-by-13-inch baking pan, combine the carrots, turnip, garlic, rice, broth, and water. Stir in 1 teaspoon of the spice mix. Cover with aluminum foil and bake for 20 minutes.
In a large bowl, combine the broccoli, corn pieces, red onion, and bell pepper. Add the olive oil and the remaining 5 teaspoons of spice mix and toss to coat.
Remove the baking pan from the oven and remove the foil. Increase the oven temperature to 425°F.
Scatter the broccoli and corn mixture over the surface of the rice mixture. Be sure to cover the top fully so that the rice stays hidden underneath.
Return the dish to the oven, uncovered, and bake for 30 minutes.

234. Farro With Porcini Mushrooms

Preparation Time: 15 minutes
Cooking Time: 40 minutes
Servings: 4

Ingredients:

cups vegetable broth
2 tablespoons extra-virgin olive oil
1 shallot, finely chopped
1 cup pearled farro
1/2 cup dry white wine
1/4 teaspoon red pepper flakes
1-pound porcini mushrooms, sliced
1/4 cup water
1/2 teaspoon salt
2 garlic cloves, minced
1 tablespoon cream sherry (optional)
1/4 cup grated Parmesan or Romano cheese
Chopped fresh flat-leaf parsley for garnish

Directions:

In a small saucepan, bring the vegetable broth to a gentle simmer.
In a large skillet, heat the olive oil over medium heat and cook the shallot for about 2 minutes until softened.
Add the farro and stir until coated with oil—Cook for 1 minute.
Add the wine and cook until it is absorbed, stirring constantly. Add the red pepper flakes.
Mix in the hot broth, a ladleful at a time, and cook until absorbed,
stirring frequently. Each ladleful will probably take about 5 minutes to absorb.
Meanwhile, in another skillet, combine the mushrooms, water, and salt. Cover and cook for about 5 minutes, until the mushrooms have softened. Add the garlic and sherry (if using) and continue to cook, uncovered.
When you have about 1 ladleful of broth left, add the mushroom mixture to the farro and fold it in. Add the rest of the broth and continue to cook and stir until the liquid is absorbed.
Add the Parmesan and stir to combine. Garnish with parsley.

235. Sicilian Eggplant With Israeli Couscous

Preparation Time: 10 minutes
Cooking Time: 45 minutes
Servings: 2

Ingredients

1/4 cup extra-virgin olive oil
1/4 red onion, chopped
1 small Sicilian eggplant, cut into cubes
1 garlic clove, minced
1/2 teaspoon salt
1 cup canned crushed tomatoes
1/2 teaspoon dried oregano
1½ cups water
1 cup tricolor Israeli couscous
fresh basil leaves, chopped
1/4 teaspoon smoked paprika
Pinch cayenne pepper

Directions:

In a large skillet, heat the olive oil over medium heat. Add the red onion and cook for 3 to 5 minutes, until it starts to soften.
Add the eggplant, garlic, and salt and cook for about 10 minutes until the eggplant starts to soften and break down.
Add the tomatoes and oregano. Cover and cook until fully soft, about 20 minutes.
Meanwhile, in a saucepan, bring the water to a boil over high heat. Reduce the heat to a simmer and add the couscous. Cover and simmer for 10 minutes. Fluff it up using a fork, then remove from the heat and let stand, covered, for 3 minutes.
Add the couscous to the eggplant mixture. Stir in the basil, smoked paprika, and cayenne. Stir to combine and simmer for 10 minutes to meld all the flavors.

236. Polenta With Wild Greens

Preparation Time: 10 minutes
Cooking Time: 25 minutes
Servings: 2

Ingredients:

1 pound red or Swiss green chard, trimmed
1-pound dandelion greens, trimmed
1/4 cup extra-virgin olive oil
2 celery stalks, chopped
1 small onion, finely chopped
3 garlic cloves, minced
1 teaspoon red pepper flakes
1 teaspoon Italian Herb Blend
1/2 tube firm polenta, cut into 1-inch-thick slices
Sea salt

Directions:

Bring a large pot of water to a boil over high heat. Add the chard and dandelion greens and cook for 3 to 5 minutes, until the stems are soft. Drain and set aside to cool.
In a large skillet, heat the olive oil over low heat. Add the celery, onion, garlic, red pepper flakes, and Italian herb blend. Cook for 3 minutes, stirring until the vegetables soften.
Add the polenta to the pan and stir to combine—Cook for 5 minutes. Turn the polenta over and cook for another 5 minutes.
Roughly chop the cooled greens and add them to the skillet—season with salt.
Stir everything together—some of the polenta will break up into smaller pieces at this point. Cover and cook for about 10 minutes, until the greens are tender.

237. Baked Rice With Swordfish And Mussels

Preparation Time: 10 minutes
Cooking Time: 1 hour
Servings: 4

Ingredients:

2 tablespoons extra-virgin olive oil
2 swordfish steaks, cut into bite-size pieces
1 teaspoon salt
1 teaspoon freshly ground black pepper
1 hot Italian pork sausage, sliced
1 medium onion, sliced
1 yellow or orange bell pepper, seeded and sliced
3 garlic cloves, chopped
¼ cup dry white wine
1 cup Arborio rice
3 cups seafood or vegetable broth, divided
1-pound mussels, scrubbed and debearded
2 large eggs, beaten

Directions:

Preheat the oven to 325°F.
In a large, deep ovenproof skillet, heat the olive oil over medium heat. Add the swordfish and season with salt and pepper. Brown, the fish for about 1 minute on each side, then transfer to a plate.
Add the sausage, onion, bell pepper, and garlic to the skillet and cook for about 10 minutes, until the sausage is browned and the vegetables are softened. Transfer to the plate with the swordfish.
Pour in the wine and deglaze the skillet, stirring to scrape up any browned bits on the bottom. Add the rice and mix with the wine until coated.
Add 2 cups of broth and cook for 5 minutes without stirring.
Add the swordfish, sausage, onion, and bell pepper mixture on top of the rice. Pour in the remaining 1 cup of seafood broth and bring to a boil. Do not stir.
Cover, transfer to the oven and bake for 30 minutes.
Uncover the skillet and take a peek at the dish. If it looks dry, add 1/3 cup water. Add the mussels, pushing the hinged-ends down into the rice. Pour the beaten eggs over the top of the dish.
Cook for another 10 minutes, uncovered, or until the mussels open and the egg is completely cooked. Discard any mussels that do not open.

238. Creamy Garlic and Cheese Polenta

Preparation Time: 5 minutes
Cooking Time: 30 minutes
Servings: 4

Ingredients:

4 tablespoons (½ stick) unsalted butter, divided
1 tablespoon garlic, finely chopped
4 cups water
1 teaspoon salt
1 cup polenta
¾ cup Parmesan cheese, divided

Directions:

In a large pot over medium heat, cook 3 tablespoons of butter and the garlic for 2 minutes.
Add the water and salt, and bring to a boil. Add the polenta and immediately whisk until it starts to thicken, about 3 minutes. Turn the heat to low, cover, and cook for 25 minutes, whisking every 5 minutes.
Using a wooden spoon, stir in ½ cup of the Parmesan cheese.
To serve, pour the polenta into a large serving bowl. Sprinkle the top with the remaining 1 tablespoon butter and ¼ cup of remaining Parmesan cheese. Serve warm.

239. Mushroom Risotto

Preparation Time: 10 minutes
Cooking Time: 30 minutes
Servings: 4

Ingredients:

6 cups vegetable broth
3 tablespoons extra-virgin olive oil, divided
1-pound cremini mushrooms, cleaned and sliced
1 medium onion, finely chopped
2 cloves garlic, minced
1½ cups Arborio rice 1 teaspoon salt
½ cup freshly grated Parmesan cheese
½ teaspoon freshly ground black pepper

Directions:

In a saucepan over medium heat, bring the broth to a low simmer.
In a large skillet over medium heat, cook 1 tablespoon olive oil and the sliced mushrooms for 5 to 7 minutes. Set cooked mushrooms aside.
In the same skillet over medium heat, add the 2 remaining tablespoons of olive oil, onion, and garlic. Cook for 3 minutes.
Add the rice, salt, and 1 cup of broth to the skillet. Stir the ingredients together and cook over low heat until most of the liquid is absorbed. Continue adding ½ cup of broth at a time, stirring until it is absorbed. Repeat until all of the broth is used up.
With the final addition of broth, add the cooked mushrooms, Parmesan cheese, and black pepper. Cook for 2 more minutes. Serve immediately.

240. Rice Pudding

Preparation Time: 5 minutes
Cooking Time: 15 minutes
Servings: 5

Ingredients:

1 cup brown rice
2 cups coconut milk, unsweetened
1 teaspoon cinnamon
1 teaspoon ginger
1/3 teaspoon thyme
1/3 cup almonds
2 tablespoon honey
1 teaspoon lemon zest

Directions:

Pour the coconut milk into a saucepan and heat over medium.
Add the brown rice and stir the mixture carefully.
Close the lid and cook the brown rice over medium heat for 10 minutes.
Meanwhile, crush the almonds and combine them with the lemon zest, thyme, ginger, and cinnamon.
Sprinkle the brown rice with the almond mixture and stir it carefully.
Close the lid and cook the dish for 5 minutes.
When the pudding is cooked, remove it from the saucepan and transfer to a big bowl.
Add the honey and stir the pudding.
Serve it immediately.

241. Creamy Millet

Preparation Time: 10 minutes
Cooking Time: 15 minutes
Servings: 8

Ingredients:

2 cups millet
1 cup almond milk, unsweetened
1 cup water
1 cup coconut milk, unsweetened
1 teaspoon cinnamon
½ teaspoon ground ginger
¼ teaspoon salt
1 tablespoon chia seeds
1 tablespoon cashew butter
4 oz Parmesan cheese, grated

Directions:

Combine the coconut milk, almond milk, and water together in the saucepan.
Stir the liquid gently and add millet.
Mix carefully and close the lid.
Cook the millet on the medium heat for 5 minutes.
Sprinkle the porridge with the cinnamon, ground ginger, salt, and chia seeds.
Stir the mixture carefully with a spoon and continue to cook on medium heat for 5 minutes more.
Add the cashew butter and cook the millet for 5 minutes.
Remove the millet from the heat and transfer it to serving bowls.
Sprinkle the dish with the grated cheese.
Serve it.

242. Brown Rice Salad

Preparation Time: 10 minutes
Cooking Time: 0 minutes
Servings: 4

Ingredients:

9 oz. brown rice, cooked
7 cups baby arugula
15 oz. canned garbanzo beans, drained and rinsed
4 oz. feta cheese, crumbled
¾ cup basil, chopped
A pinch of salt and black pepper
2 tbsps. lemon juice
¼ tsp lemon zest, grated
¼ cup olive oil

Directions:

In a salad bowl, combine the brown rice with the arugula, the beans, and the rest of the ingredients, toss and serve cold for breakfast.

243. Barley Risotto With Vegetables

Preparation Time: 10 minutes
Cooking Time: 30 minutes
Servings: 4

Ingredients:

1½ cups pearled barley
2 tablespoons extra-virgin olive oil
1 small onion, chopped
2 zucchinis, cut into small cubes
1 (15-ounce) can cannellini beans, rinsed and drained
3 cups vegetable broth, divided
12 cherry tomatoes, chopped
¼ cup grated Parmesan or Romano cheese
Chopped fresh basil for garnish

Directions:

In a saucepan, prepare the barley according to package directions until al dente. Drain and set aside.
In a large skillet, heat the olive oil over medium heat. Add the onion and cook for 3 to 5 minutes, until softened.
Add the zucchini, beans, and a splash of the broth and cook for 10 minutes, stirring frequently.
Add the barley and 1 cup of broth. Cook until the liquid absorbs, stirring constantly. Keep stirring in the broth, a ladleful at a time, allowing it to absorb before adding more until you use it all up.
Fold in the tomatoes and Parmesan and stir gently until combined.
Garnish with basil.

244. Curried Chicken, Chickpeas And Raita Salad

Preparation Time: 10 minutes
Cooking Time: 15 minutes
Servings: 8

Ingredients:

1 cup red grapes, halved
3-4 cups rotisserie chicken, meat coarsely shredded
2 tbsp cilantro
1 cup plain yogurt
2 medium tomatoes, chopped
1 tsp ground cumin
1 tbsp curry powder
2 tbsp olive oil
1 tbsp minced peeled ginger
1 tbsp minced garlic
1 medium onion, chopped
¼ tsp cayenne
½ tsp turmeric
1 tsp ground cumin
1 19-oz can chickpeas, rinsed, drained and patted dry
1 tbsp olive oil
½ cup sliced and toasted almonds
2 tbsp chopped mint
2 cups cucumber, peeled, cored and chopped
1 cup plain yogurt

Directions:

To make the chicken salad, on medium low fire, place a medium nonstick saucepan and heat oil.
Sauté ginger, garlic and onion for 5 minutes or until softened while stirring occasionally.
Add 1 ½ tsp salt, cumin and curry. Sauté for two minutes.
Increase fire to medium high and add tomatoes. Stirring frequently, cook for 5 minutes.
Pour sauce into a bowl, mix in chicken, cilantro and yogurt. Stir to combine and let it stand to cool to room temperature.
To make the chickpeas, on a nonstick fry pan, heat oil for 3 minutes.
Add chickpeas and cook for a minute while stirring frequently.
Add ¼ tsp salt, cayenne, turmeric and cumin. Stir to mix well and cook for two minutes or until sauce is dried.
Transfer to a bowl and let it cool to room temperature.

To make the raita, mix ½ tsp salt, mint, cucumber and yogurt. Stir thoroughly to combine and dissolve salt.
To assemble, in four 16-oz lidded jars or bowls layer the following: curried chicken, raita, chickpeas and garnish with almonds.
You can make this recipe one day ahead and refrigerate for 6 hours before serving.

245. Bulgur Tomato Pilaf

Preparation Time: 15 minutes
Cooking Time: 27 minutes
Servings: 1 Cup

Ingredients:

1 lb. ground beef
3 TB. extra-virgin olive oil
1 large yellow onion, finely chopped
2 medium tomatoes, diced
11/2 tsp. salt
1 tsp. ground black pepper
2 cups plain tomato sauce
2 cups water
2 cups bulgur wheat, grind #2

Directions:

In a large, 3-quart pot over medium heat, brown beef for 5 minutes, breaking up chunks with a wooden spoon.
Add extra-virgin olive oil and yellow onion, and cook for 5 minutes.
Stir in tomatoes, salt, and black pepper, and cook for 5 minutes.
Add tomato sauce and water, and simmer for 10 minutes.
Add bulgur wheat, and cook for 2 minutes. Remove from heat, cover, and let sit for 5 minutes. Uncover, fluff bulgur with a fork, cover, and let sit for 5 more minutes.
Serve warm.

246. Shrimp And Polenta

Preparation Time: 15 minutes
Cooking Time: 30 minutes
Servings: 4

Ingredients:

4 cups water
1 cup instant polenta
1 teaspoon salt
½ cup grated Parmesan cheese
2 tablespoons extra-virgin olive oil
4 ounces pancetta, cut into ¼-inch dice
pound large shrimp, peeled and deveined
2 cup sliced scallions
2 tablespoons chopped fresh flat-leaf parsley
1 tablespoon freshly squeezed lemon juice
garlic cloves, minced

Directions:

In a saucepan, bring the water to a boil over high heat, then reduce the heat to low. Add the polenta and salt and cook for 15 minutes, or according to package directions.
Remove the polenta from the heat and stir in the Parmesan and olive oil. Cover and set aside.
In a large skillet, fry the pancetta for about 5 minutes until it starts to brown. Add the shrimp and cook for about 3 minutes, until they turn pink. Add a little olive oil if the pan becomes too dry.
Add the scallions, parsley, lemon juice, and garlic to the pan. Cook for about 3 minutes, until fragrant.
Spoon the polenta into serving bowls and top with the shrimp mixture.

247. Algerian Vegetable Couscous

Preparation Time: 15 minutes
Cooking Time: 15 minutes
Servings: 4

Ingredients:

2 tablespoons extra-virgin olive oil
1 cup sliced cremini or white button mushrooms
1 small onion, chopped
1 carrot, grated
2 garlic cloves, minced
1¼ cups vegetable broth
1 cup couscous
¼ cup raisins
Grated zest and juice of 1 lemon
½ teaspoon ground cumin
½ teaspoon ground coriander
½ teaspoon salt

Directions:

In a large skillet, heat the olive oil over medium heat. Add the mushrooms, onion, and carrot and cook for about 5 minutes until they start to soften. Add the garlic and cook for 1 minute.
Stir in the broth, couscous, raisins, lemon zest and juice, cumin, coriander, and salt. Bring to a boil, then cover and remove the pan from heat. Let stand for 5 minutes before serving.

248. Bulgur Pilaf with Garbanzo

Preparation Time: 5 minutes
Cooking Time: 20 minutes
Servings: 4 to 6

Ingredients:

3 tablespoons extra-virgin olive oil
1 large onion, chopped
1 (1-pound / 454-g) can garbanzo beans, rinsed and drained
2 cups bulgur wheat, rinsed and drained
1½ teaspoons salt
½ teaspoon cinnamon
4 cups water

Directions:

In a large pot over medium heat, heat the olive oil. Add the onion and cook for 5 minutes.
Add the garbanzo beans and cook for an additional 5 minutes.
Stir in the remaining ingredients.
Reduce the heat to low. Cover and cook for 10 minutes.
When done, fluff the pilaf with a fork. Cover and let sit for another 5 minutes before serving.

249. Pearl Barley Risotto with Parmesan Cheese

Preparation Time: 5 minutes
Cooking Time: 20 minutes
Servings: 6

Ingredients:

4 cups low-sodium or no-salt-added vegetable broth
1 tablespoon extra-virgin olive oil
1 cup chopped yellow onion
2 cups uncooked pearl barley
1/2 cup dry white wine
1 cup freshly grated Parmesan cheese, divided
1/4 teaspoon kosher or sea salt
1/4 teaspoon freshly ground black pepper
Fresh chopped chives and lemon wedges, for serving (optional)

Directions:

Pour the broth into a medium saucepan and bring to a simmer.
Heat the olive oil in a large stockpot over medium-high heat. Add the onion and cook for about 4 minutes, stirring occasionally.
Add the barley and cook for 2 minutes, stirring, or until the barley is toasted.

Pour in the wine and cook for about 1 minute, or until most of the liquid evaporates. Add 1 cup of the warm broth into the pot and cook, stirring, for about 2 minutes, or until most of the liquid is absorbed.
Add the remaining broth, 1 cup at a time, cooking until each cup is absorbed (about 2 minutes each time) before adding the next. The last addition of broth will take a bit longer to absorb, about 4 minutes.
Remove the pot from the heat, and stir in ½ cup of the cheese, and the salt and pepper.
Serve with the remaining ½ cup of the cheese on the side, along with the chives and lemon wedges (if desired).

250. Israeli Couscous with Asparagus

Preparation Time: 5 minutes
Cooking Time: 25 minutes
Servings: 6

Ingredients:

1 1/2 pounds (680 g) asparagus spears, ends trimmed and stalks chopped into 1-inch pieces
1 garlic clove, minced
1 tablespoon extra-virgin olive oil
1/4 teaspoon freshly ground black pepper
1 3/4 cups water
1 box uncooked whole-wheat or regular Israeli couscous (about 11/3 cups)
1/4 teaspoon kosher salt
1 cup garlic-and-herb goat cheese, at room temperature

Directions:

Preheat the oven to 425°F (220°C).
In a large bowl, stir together the asparagus, garlic, oil, and pepper. Spread the asparagus on a large, rimmed baking sheet and roast for 10 minutes, stirring a few times. Remove the pan from the oven, and spoon the asparagus into a large serving bowl. Set aside.
While the asparagus is roasting, bring the water to a boil in a medium saucepan. Add the couscous and season with salt, stirring well.
Reduce the heat to medium-low. Cover and cook for 12 minutes, or until the water is absorbed.
Pour the hot couscous into the bowl with the asparagus. Add the goat cheese and mix thoroughly until completely melted.
Serve immediately.

251. Freekeh Pilaf with Dates and Pistachios

Preparation Time: 10 minutes
Cooking Time: 10 minutes
Servings: 4 to 6

Ingredients:

2 tablespoons extra-virgin olive oil, plus extra for drizzling
1 shallot, minced
1½ teaspoons grated fresh ginger
¼ teaspoon ground coriander
¼ teaspoon ground cumin
Salt and pepper, to taste
1¾ cups water
1½ cups cracked freekeh, rinsed
3 ounces (85 g) pitted dates, chopped
¼ cup shelled pistachios, toasted and coarsely chopped
1½ tablespoons lemon juice
¼ cup chopped fresh mint

Directions:

Set the Instant Pot to Sauté mode and heat the olive oil until shimmering.
Add the shallot, ginger, coriander, cumin, salt, and pepper to the pot and cook for about 2 minutes, or until the shallot is softened. Stir in the water and freekeh.
Secure the lid. Select the Manual mode and set the cooking time for 4 minutes at High Pressure. Once cooking is complete, do a quick pressure release. Carefully open the lid.
Add the dates, pistachios and lemon juice and gently fluff the freekeh with a fork to combine. Season to taste with salt and pepper.
Transfer to a serving dish and sprinkle with the mint. Serve drizzled with extra olive oil.

252. Quinoa with Baby Potatoes and Broccoli

Preparation Time: 5 minutes
Cooking Time: 10 minutes
Servings: 4

Ingredients:

2 tablespoons olive oil
1 cup baby potatoes, cut in half
1 cup broccoli florets
2 cups cooked quinoa
Zest of 1 lemon
Sea salt and freshly ground pepper, to taste

Directions:

Heat the olive oil in a large skillet over medium heat until shimmering.
Add the potatoes and cook for about 6 to 7 minutes, or until softened and golden brown. Add the broccoli and cook for about 3 minutes, or until tender.
Remove from the heat and add the quinoa and lemon zest. Season with salt and pepper to taste, then serve.

253. Italian-Style Aromatic Risotto

Preparation: 15 minutes
Cooking Time: 30 minutes
Servings: 5

Ingredients:

1 ½ cups Arborio rice
1/4 teaspoon ground bay laurel
1/4 teaspoon mustard seeds
1/2 teaspoon oregano
1/2 teaspoon basil
1/2 teaspoon thyme
2 cups roasted vegetable broth
1 cup Parmigiano-Reggiano cheese, preferably freshly grated

Directions

Place all ingredients, except for the Parmigiano-Reggiano cheese, in the inner pot of your Instant Pot.
Secure the lid. Choose the "Rice" mode and cook for 12 minutes at High pressure. Once cooking is complete, use a natural pressure release for 10 minutes; carefully remove the lid.
Ladle into serving bowls, garnish with cheese and serve immediately. Bon appétit!

254. Spanish Arroz Rojo with Beef

Preparation Time: 25 minutes
Cooking Time: 40 minutes
Servings: 4

Ingredients:

2 tablespoons olive oil
1-pound lean ground beef
1 Spanish onion, peeled and chopped
1 medium green pepper, deveined and chopped
1 Padrón pepper, deveined and minced
1/2 teaspoon fresh ginger, peeled and grated
2 garlic cloves, minced
2 tomatoes, pureed
2 tablespoons tomato paste
2 cups beef bone broth
1 teaspoon chili powder

Coarse sea salt and ground black pepper, to taste
1 cup brown rice

Directions

Press the "Sauté" button to preheat your Instant Pot and heat 1 tablespoon of olive oil. Once hot, brown the ground beef for 3 to 4 minutes or until no longer pink; make sure to crumble with a fork and set aside.
Then, heat the remaining tablespoon of olive oil and sweat the Spanish onion for 2 to 3 minutes; add the peppers, ginger, and garlic and continue cooking an additional minute or until they are fragrant.
Add in the pureed tomatoes, tomato paste, beef bone broth, chili powder, salt, black pepper, and brown rice. Add the brown beef back to the inner pot.
Secure the lid. Choose the "Manual" mode and cook for 20 minutes at High pressure. Once cooking is complete, use a quick pressure release; carefully remove the lid. Enjoy!

255. Rice with Red Sauce and Graviera Cheese

Preparation Time: 10 minutes
Cooking Time: 15 minutes
Servings: 4

Ingredients:

1 ½ cups Basmati rice
2 cups water
1 cup grape tomatoes, halved
1/2 cup ripe olives, pitted and halved
2 roasted peppers, sliced into small pieces
2 tablespoons olive oil
1/2 cup spring onions, chopped
Sea salt and red pepper flakes, to taste
1/2 teaspoon oregano
1/4 teaspoon garlic powder
4 ounces Graviera cheese
2 tablespoons fresh basil, snipped

Directions :

Place the basmati rice and water in the inner pot of your Instant Pot.
Secure the lid. Choose the "Manual" mode and cook for 4 minutes at High pressure. Once cooking is complete, use a quick pressure release; carefully remove the lid.
Transfer the cooked rice to a serving bowl. Process the tomatoes, olives, red peppers, and olive oil in your blender until creamy and smooth.
Pour the tomato/pepper sauce over cooked rice. Add the spring onions, salt, pepper, oregano, and garlic powder; stir to combine.
Top with Graviera cheese and fresh basil. Serve immediately.

256. Mediterranean Spicy Jambalaya

Preparation Time: 10 minutes
Cooking Time: 20 minutes
Servings: 4

Ingredients:

2 teaspoons olive oil
1/2-pound whole chicken, cut into bite-sized chunks
1 carrot, trimmed and chopped
1 shallot, chopped
2 sweet Italian peppers, deveined and chopped
1 red chili pepper, deveined and minced
2 cloves garlic, minced
1/2 teaspoon ground bay laurel
1 cup white rice
2 cups water
Garlic salt and ground black pepper, to taste
1 tablespoon Old Bay seasoning
1/2 teaspoon file powder
2 chicken bouillon cubes
2 Roma tomatoes, pureed
2 tablespoons tomato paste
12 ounces frozen jumbo shrimp, peeled

Directions:

Press the "Sauté" button to preheat your Instant Pot. Once hot, cook the chicken until it is no longer pink, stirring frequently; reserve.

257. Confetti Couscous

Preparation Time: 5 minutes
Cooking Time: 20 minutes
Servings: 4 To 6

Ingredients:

3 tablespoons extra-virgin olive oil
1 large onion, chopped
2 carrots, chopped
1 cup fresh peas
½ cup golden raisins
1 teaspoon salt
2 cups vegetable broth
2 cups couscous

Directions:

In a medium pot over medium heat, gently toss the olive oil, onions, carrots, peas, and raisins together and let cook for 5 minutes.
Add the salt and broth, and stir to combine. Bring to a boil, and let ingredients boil for 5 minutes.
Add the couscous. Stir, turn the heat to low, cover, and let cook for 10 minutes. Fluff with a fork and serve.
Substitution tip: You can substitute the peas or carrots for other vegetables of your choosing. Serve with fresh chopped parsley for extra flavor.

258. Lemon Orzo with Fresh Herbs

Preparation Time: 10 minutes
Cooking Time: 10 minutes
Servings: 4

Ingredients:

2 cups orzo
1/2 cup fresh parsley, finely chopped
1/2 cup fresh basil, finely chopped
2 tablespoons lemon zest
1/2 cup extra-virgin olive oil
1/3 cup lemon juice
1 teaspoon salt
1/2 teaspoon freshly ground black pepper

Directions:

Bring a large pot of water to a boil. Add the orzo and cook for 7 minutes. Drain and rinse with cold water. Let the orzo sit in a strainer to completely drain and cool.
Once the orzo has cooled, put it in a large bowl and add the parsley, basil, and lemon zest.
In a small bowl, whisk together the olive oil, lemon juice, salt, and pepper. Add the dressing to the pasta and toss everything together. Serve at room temperature or chilled.

259. Orzo-Veggie Pilaf

Preparation Time: 20 minutes
Cooking Time: 10 minutes
Servings: 6

Ingredients:

2 cups orzo
1-pint (2 cups) cherry tomatoes, cut in half
1 cup Kalamata olives
1/2 cup fresh basil, finely chopped
1/2 cup extra-virgin olive oil
1/3 cup balsamic vinegar
1 teaspoon salt

1/2 teaspoon freshly ground black pepper

Directions:

Bring a large pot of water to a boil. Add the orzo and cook for 7 minutes. Drain and rinse the orzo with cold water in a strainer.
Once the orzo has cooled, put it in a large bowl. Add the tomatoes, olives, and basil.
In a small bowl, whisk together the olive oil, vinegar, salt, and pepper. Add this dressing to the pasta and toss everything together. Serve at room temperature or chilled.

260. Earthy Lentil and Rice Pilaf

Preparation Time: 5 minutes
Cooking Time: 50 minutes
Servings: 6

Ingredients:

¼ cup extra-virgin olive oil
1 large onion, chopped
6 cups water
1 teaspoon ground cumin
1 teaspoon salt
2 cups brown lentils, picked over and rinsed
1 cup basmati rice

Directions:

In a medium pot over medium heat, cook the olive oil and onions for 7 to 10 minutes until the edges are browned.
Turn the heat to high, add the water, cumin, and salt, and bring this mixture to a boil, boiling for about 3 minutes.
Add the lentils and turn the heat to medium-low. Cover the pot and cook for 20 minutes, stirring occasionally.
Stir in the rice and cover; cook for an additional 20 minutes.
Fluff the rice with a fork and serve warm.

261. Lentils and Bulgur with Caramelized Onions

Preparation Time: 10 minutes
Cooking Time: 50 minutes
Servings: 6

Ingredients:

1/2 cup extra-virgin olive oil
4 large onions, chopped
2 teaspoons salt, divided
6 cups water
2 cups brown lentils, picked over and rinsed
1 teaspoon freshly ground black pepper
1 cup bulgur wheat #3

Directions:

In a large pot over medium heat, cook and stir the olive oil, onions, and 1 teaspoon of salt for 12 to 15 minutes, until the onions are a medium brown/golden color.
Put half of the cooked onions in a bowl.
Add the water, remaining 1 teaspoon of salt, and lentils to the remaining onions. Stir. Cover and cook for 30 minutes.
Stir in the black pepper and bulgur, cover, and cook for 5 minutes. Fluff with a fork, cover, and let stand for another 5 minutes.
Spoon the lentils and bulgur onto a serving plate and top with the reserved onions. Serve warm.

262. Bulgur and Garbanzo Pilaf

Preparation Time: 5 minutes
Cooking Time: 20 minutes
Servings: 4 To 6

Ingredients:

3 tablespoons extra-virgin olive oil
1 large onion, chopped
1 (16-ounce) can garbanzo beans, rinsed and drained
2 cups bulgur wheat #3, rinsed and drained
1½ teaspoons salt
½ teaspoon cinnamon
4 cups water

Directions:

In a large pot over medium heat, cook the olive oil and onion for 5 minutes.
Add the garbanzo beans and cook for another 5 minutes.
Add the bulgur, salt, cinnamon, and water and stir to combine. Cover the pot, turn the heat to low, and cook for 10 minutes.
When the cooking is done, fluff the pilaf with a fork. Cover and let sit for another 5 minutes.

263. Spanish Rice

Preparation Time: 10 minutes
Cooking Time: 20 minutes
Servings: 4

Ingredients:

2 tablespoons extra-virgin olive oil
1 medium onion, finely chopped
1 large tomato, finely diced
2 tablespoons tomato paste
1 teaspoon smoked paprika
1 teaspoon salt
1½ cups basmati rice
3 cups water

Directions:

In a medium pot over medium heat, cook the olive oil, onion, and tomato for 3 minutes.
Stir in the tomato paste, paprika, salt, and rice. Cook for 1 minute.
Add the water, cover the pot, and turn the heat to low. Cook for 12 minutes.
Gently toss the rice, cover, and cook for another 3 minutes.

264. Overnight Berry Chia Oats

Preparation Time: 15 minutes
Cooking Time: 5 minutes
Servings: 1

Ingredients:

1/2 cup Quaker Oats rolled oats
1/4 cup chia seeds
1 cup milk or water
pinch of salt and cinnamon
maple syrup, or a different sweetener, to taste
1 cup frozen berries of choice or smoothie leftovers
Toppings:
Yogurt
Berries

Directions:

In a jar with a lid, add the oats, seeds, milk, salt, and cinnamon, refrigerate overnight. On serving day, puree the berries in a blender.
Stir the oats, add in the berry puree and top with yogurt and more berries, nuts, honey, or garnish of your choice. Enjoy!

265. Banana Oats

Preparation Time: 10 minutes
Cooking Time: 0 minutes
Servings: 2

Ingredients:

1 banana, peeled and sliced
¾ cup almond milk
½ cup cold-brewed coffee
2 dates, pitted
2 tablespoons cocoa powder

1 cup rolled oats
1 and ½ tablespoons chia seeds

Directions:

In a blender, combine the banana with the milk and the rest of the ingredients, pulse, divide into bowls and serve for breakfast.

266. Sun-dried Tomatoes Oatmeal

Preparation Time: 10 minutes
Cooking Time: 25 minutes
Servings: 4

Ingredients:

3 cups water
1 cup almond milk
1 tablespoon olive oil
1 cup steel-cut oats
¼ cup sun-dried tomatoes, chopped
A pinch of red pepper flakes

Directions:

In a pan, mix the water with the milk, bring to a boil over medium heat.
Meanwhile, heat up a pan with the oil over medium-high heat, add the oats, cook them for about 2 minutes and transfer m to the pan with the milk.
Stir the oats, add the tomatoes and simmer over medium heat for 23 minutes.
Divide the mix into bowls, sprinkle the red pepper flakes on top and serve for breakfast.

CHAPTER 5: BREAD AND PIZZA

267. Grilled Burgers with Mushrooms

Preparation Time: 10 minutes
Cooking Time: 10 minutes
Servings: 4

Ingredients:

2 Bibb lettuce, halved
4 slices red onion
4 slices tomato
4 whole wheat buns, toasted
2 tbsp olive oil
¼ tsp cayenne pepper, optional
1 garlic clove, minced
1 tbsp sugar
½ cup water
1/3 cup balsamic vinegar
4 large Portobello mushroom caps, around 5-inches in diameter

Directions:

Remove stems from mushrooms and clean with a damp cloth. Transfer into a baking dish with gill-side up.
In a bowl, mix thoroughly olive oil, cayenne pepper, garlic, sugar, water and vinegar. Pour over mushrooms and marinate mushrooms in the ref for at least an hour.
Once the one hour is nearly up, preheat grill to medium high fire and grease grill grate.
Grill mushrooms for five minutes per side or until tender. Baste mushrooms with marinade so it doesn't dry up.
To assemble, place ½ of bread bun on a plate, top with a slice of onion, mushroom, tomato and one lettuce leaf. Cover with the other top half of the bun. Repeat process with remaining ingredients, serve and enjoy.

268. Mediterranean Baba Ghanoush

Preparation Time: 5 minutes
Cooking Time: 25 minutes
Servings: 4

Ingredients:

1 bulb garlic
1 red bell pepper, halved and seeded
1 tbsp chopped fresh basil
1 tbsp olive oil
1 tsp black pepper
2 eggplants, sliced lengthwise
2 rounds of flatbread or pita
Juice of 1 lemon

Directions:

Grease grill grate with cooking spray and preheat grill to medium high.
Slice tops of garlic bulb and wrap in foil. Place in the cooler portion of the grill and roast for at least 20 minutes.
Place bell pepper and eggplant slices on the hottest part of grill.
Grill for at least two to three minutes each side.
Once bulbs are done, peel off skins of roasted garlic and place peeled garlic into food processor.
Add olive oil, pepper, basil, lemon juice, grilled red bell pepper and grilled eggplant.
Puree until smooth and transfer into a bowl.
Grill bread at least 30 seconds per side to warm.
Serve bread with the pureed dip and enjoy.

269. Multi Grain & Gluten Free Dinner Rolls

Preparation Time: 30 minutes
Cooking Time: 20 minutes
Servings: 8

Ingredients:

½ tsp apple cider vinegar
3 tbsp olive oil
2 eggs
1 tsp baking powder
1 tsp salt
2 tsp xanthan gum
½ cup tapioca starch
¼ cup brown teff flour
¼ cup flax meal
¼ cup amaranth flour
¼ cup sorghum flour
¾ cup brown rice flour

Directions:

Mix well water and honey in a small bowl and add yeast. Leave it for exactly 10 minutes.
In a large bowl, mix the following with a paddle mixer: baking powder, salt, xanthan gum, flax meal, sorghum flour, teff flour, tapioca starch, amaranth flour, and brown rice flour.
In a medium bowl, whisk well vinegar, olive oil, and eggs.
Into bowl of dry ingredients pour in vinegar and yeast mixture and mix well.
Grease a 12-muffin tin with cooking spray. Transfer dough evenly into 12 muffin tins and leave it for an hour to rise.
Then preheat oven to 375oF and bake dinner rolls until tops are golden brown, around 20 minutes.
Remove dinner rolls from oven and muffin tins immediately and let it cool.
Best served when warm.

270. Quinoa Pizza Muffins

Preparation Time: 20 minutes
Cooking Time: 30 minutes
Servings: 4

Ingredients:

1 cup uncooked quinoa
2 large eggs
½ medium onion, diced
1 cup diced bell pepper
1 cup shredded mozzarella cheese
1 tbsp dried basil
1 tbsp dried oregano
2 tsp garlic powder
1/8 tsp salt
1 tsp crushed red peppers
½ cup roasted red pepper, chopped*
Pizza Sauce, about 1-2 cups

Directions:

Preheat oven to 350oF.
Cook quinoa according to directions.
Combine all ingredients (except sauce) into bowl. Mix all ingredients well.
Scoop quinoa pizza mixture into muffin tin evenly. Makes 12 muffins.
Bake for 30 minutes until muffins turn golden in color and the edges are getting crispy.
Top with 1 or 2 tbsp pizza sauce and enjoy!

271. Rosemary-Walnut Loaf Bread

Preparation Time: 90 minutes
Cooking Time: 45 minutes
Servings: 8

Ingredients:

½ cup chopped walnuts

4 tbsp fresh, chopped rosemary
1 1/3 cups lukewarm carbonated water
1 tbsp honey
½ cup extra virgin olive oil
1 tsp apple cider vinegar
3 eggs
5 tsp instant dry yeast granules
1 tsp salt
1 tbsp xanthan gum
¼ cup buttermilk powder
1 cup white rice flour
1 cup tapioca starch
1 cup arrowroot starch
1 ¼ cups all-purpose Bob's Red Mill gluten-free flour mix

Directions:

In a large mixing bowl, whisk well eggs. Add 1 cup warm water, honey, olive oil, and vinegar.
While beating continuously, add the rest of the ingredients except for rosemary and walnuts.
Continue beating. If dough is too stiff, add a bit of warm water. Dough should be shaggy and thick.
Then add rosemary and walnuts continue kneading until evenly distributed.
Cover bowl of dough with a clean towel, place in a warm spot, and let it rise for 30 minutes.
Fifteen minutes into rising time, preheat oven to 400oF.
Generously grease with olive oil a 2-quart Dutch oven and preheat inside oven without the lid.
Once dough is done rising, remove pot from oven, and place dough inside. With a wet spatula, spread top of dough evenly in pot.
Brush tops of bread with 2 tbsp of olive oil, cover Dutch oven and bake for 35 to 45 minutes.
Once bread is done, remove from oven. And gently remove bread from pot.
Allow bread to cool at least ten minutes before slicing.
Serve and enjoy.

272. Tasty Crabby Panini

Preparation Time: 20 minutes
Cooking Time: 10 minutes
Servings: 4

Ingredients:

1 tbsp Olive oil
French bread split and sliced diagonally
1 lb. blue crab meat or shrimp or spiny lobster or stone crab
½ cup celery
¼ cup green onion chopped
1 tsp Worcestershire sauce
1 tsp lemon juice
1 tbsp Dijon mustard
½ cup light mayonnaise

Directions:

In a medium bowl mix the following thoroughly: celery, onion, Worcestershire, lemon juice, mustard and mayonnaise. Season with pepper and salt. Then gently add in the almonds and crabs.
Spread olive oil on sliced sides of bread and smear with crab mixture before covering with another bread slice.
Grill sandwich in a Panini press until bread is crisped and ridged.

273. Sardinian Flatbread

Preparation Time: 1 hour 15 minutes
Cooking Time: 15 minutes
Servings: 6

Ingredients:

1½ cups all-purpose flour, plus more for dusting
1½ cups semolina flour
1½ cups warm water
1 (¼-ounce) packet active dry yeast
Pinch salt
Extra-virgin olive oil, for brushing

Directions:

In a large bowl, combine the flours, water, yeast, and salt and mix thoroughly to form a firm dough.
Turn out the dough onto a work surface and divide it into quarters. Set the dough pieces on a rimmed baking sheet, cover, and let rest for 1 hour.
Preheat the oven to 375°F. Lightly brush another rimmed baking sheet with olive oil.
Lightly flour a work surface and a rolling pin. Roll out one piece of dough until it is as thin as possible, then place it on the prepared baking sheet.
Bake for 2 minutes. Turn the flatbread over and bake for another 2 minutes, or until crisp.
Repeat with the remaining dough.

274. Focaccia (Italian Flatbread)

Preparation Time: 2 hours
Cooking Time: 30 minutes
Servings: 8

Ingredients:

2½ cups warm water, divided
2 teaspoons active dry yeast
Pinch sugar
6 cups all-purpose flour, divided
5 tablespoons extra-virgin olive oil, divided
2 tablespoons coarse sea salt, divided
1 tablespoon chopped fresh rosemary

Directions:

Pour ½ cup of warm water into a large bowl and sprinkle on the yeast and sugar. Stir, then let rest for 1 minute. The yeast mixture should start to look foamy.
Add the remaining 2 cups of warm water, 2 cups of flour, 2 tablespoons of olive oil, and 1 tablespoon of sea salt. Stir until smooth.
Slowly add the remaining 4 cups of flour, using your hands to combine. If the dough is too sticky, add additional flour.
Turn out the dough onto a work surface and knead until you get a smooth, springy dough.
Brush a bowl with 1 tablespoon of olive oil. Place the dough in the bowl, cover with plastic wrap, and set aside in a warm place until the dough rises to double its size, about 1½ hours.
Preheat the oven to 425°F. Brush an 11-by-17-inch baking pan with 1 tablespoon of olive oil.
Press the dough into the prepared pan in an even layer, covering the entire surface. It may take a few minutes for the dough to cooperate. Cover the dough with a damp kitchen towel and let rise until doubled in size, about 30 minutes.
Press the dough with your fingers to add dimples all over. Brush with the remaining 2 tablespoons of olive oil, allowing it to pool in the dimples. Sprinkle with the remaining 1 tablespoon of sea salt and the rosemary.
Place a baking pan filled with ice on the lowest oven shelf or on the floor of the oven to create steam. Place the baking pan on the rack above.
Bake for about 30 minutes, until golden.
Transfer the focaccia to a wire rack to cool, then cut into strips or squares.

275. Taralli (Pugliese Bread Knots)

Preparation Time: 45 minutes
Cooking Time: 25 minutes
Servings: 30 pieces

Ingredients:

2 cups all-purpose flour
1/2 teaspoon salt
1/2 cup dry white wine
1/3 cup extra-virgin olive oil
1/2 teaspoon freshly ground black pepper

Directions:

In a large bowl, combine the flour and salt. Add the wine and olive oil and mix together with a fork until the mixture starts to form a rough dough.
Turn out the dough onto a work surface and knead until smooth, sprinkling with the pepper as you work until it is all combined and the dough is smooth.
Cover the dough with a kitchen towel and let it rest for 15 minutes.
Preheat the oven to 375°F. Line a rimmed baking sheet with parchment paper. Bring a large pot of water to a boil over high heat.
For each bread knot, roll a tablespoon of the dough into a rope about 4 inches long and ½ inch thick. Form a circle with the rope, then crisscross the ends to form a knot shape and press the ends together to seal.
Drop a few knots at a time into the boiling water. When they float, after about 30 seconds, transfer them with a slotted spoon to a kitchen towel to dry.
Arrange the taralli on the prepared baking sheet in a single layer, making sure they do not touch.
Bake for 25 minutes, or until golden.
Transfer to a rack to cool a bit before serving.

276. Testaroli (Etruscan Pancakes)

Preparation Time: 5 minutes
Cooking Time: 15 minutes
Servings: 2

Ingredients:

½ cup whole wheat flour
½ cup all-purpose flour
1 cup warm water
Salt
2 tablespoons extra-virgin olive oil

Directions:

In a bowl, whisk together the flours, water, and a pinch of salt until you get a thick batter. Let the mixture rest while you heat a cast-iron skillet over high heat. At the same time, fill a large pot with warm salted water.
Brush the skillet with about 1 teaspoon of olive oil, then pour about ¼ cup of the batter into the hot pan, just enough to cover the bottom. Cook for 1 to 2 minutes, until golden brown, flip, and cook the other side until golden.
Remove the pancake from the pan and cut the testaroli like a pizza, into 6 or 8 wedges. Transfer the wedges to the pot of warm salted water and let them sit for 1 minute, then remove from the water.
Repeat with the remaining batter and oil.

277. Pesto Vegetable Bread

Preparation Time: 15 minutes
Cooking Time: 20 minutes
Servings: 4

Ingredients:

2 tablespoons extra-virgin olive oil, plus more for drizzling
½ eggplant, cut into cubes
½ fennel bulb, trimmed and sliced
1 red bell pepper, seeded and cut into strips
1 bunch broccoli rabe
1 loaf Focaccia
2 tablespoons Basil Pesto with Almond Butter or store-bought pesto
½ small onion, thinly sliced
4 radishes, sliced
1 teaspoon fresh thyme leaves
½ teaspoon salt
1 teaspoon minced garlic

Directions:

Preheat the oven to 350°F.
In a large skillet, heat the olive oil over medium heat. Add the eggplant, fennel, and bell pepper and cook for about 10 minutes, until they start to soften.
Meanwhile, bring a large pot of water to a boil over high heat. Add the broccoli rabe and cook for 3 minutes. Drain, squeeze out any excess water, and cut into bite-size pieces.
Slice the focaccia in half horizontally all the way through and brush each cut side with the pesto. Arrange the eggplant, fennel, bell pepper, and broccoli rabe on the pesto. Top with the onion and radish slices and sprinkle with the thyme and salt.
Bake for 5 to 10 minutes, until the fresh ingredients start to warm.
Turn the oven to broil and toast for 1 minute.
Remove the bread from the oven. Sprinkle with the garlic and drizzle with a bit of olive oil. Cut into slices.

278. Tomato Bruschetta

Preparation Time: 10 minutes
Cooking Time: 4 minutes
Servings: 6

Ingredients:

1 baguette, sliced
3 large tomatoes, finely chopped
1 small onion, diced
¼ cup extra-virgin olive oil
4 garlic cloves, minced
1 teaspoon dried oregano
1 teaspoon salt
¼ teaspoon freshly ground black pepper
Chopped fresh basil, for garnish

Direction;

Preheat the oven to 350°F.
Place the baguette slices on a rimmed baking sheet. Toast for 2 minutes, turn them over, and toast for another 2 minutes.
In a large bowl, combine the tomatoes, onion, olive oil, garlic, oregano, salt, and pepper and toss to mix thoroughly.
Arrange the toasted baguette slices on a serving plate and spoon the tomato mixture generously over each piece. Sprinkle with basil.

279. White Bean Crostini

Preparation Time: 5 minutes
Cooking Time: 4 minutes
Servings: 4

Ingredients:

1 baguette, sliced
1 (19-ounce) can cannellini beans, rinsed and drained
2 tablespoons extra-virgin olive oil, plus more for drizzling
1 garlic clove, peeled
1 teaspoon salt
½ teaspoon dried oregano
¼ teaspoon red pepper flakes
¼ teaspoon freshly ground black pepper

Directions:

Preheat the oven to 350°F.
Place the baguette slices on a rimmed baking sheet. Toast for 2 minutes, turn them over, and toast for another 2 minutes.
In a food processor or blender, combine the beans, olive oil, garlic, salt, oregano,

red pepper flakes, and black pepper and puree.
Spoon the bean mixture onto the toasted baguette slices and drizzle with extra-virgin olive oil.

280. Pizza Dough

Preparation Time: 15 minutes, plus 1 hour to rise
Cooking Time: 0 minutes
Servings: 4

Ingredients:

4 cups 00 flour or bread flour, plus more for dusting
½ teaspoon salt
¼ cup water
2 tablespoons extra-virgin olive oil, plus 1 teaspoon
1¼ teaspoons active dry yeast
1 teaspoon sugar

Directions:

Sift together the flour and salt onto a work surface. Make a well in the middle.
In a bowl, combine the water, 2 tablespoons of olive oil, the yeast, and sugar. Let the mixture sit for a few minutes for the yeast to activate, then pour it into the well in the flour.
Using a fork, bring the flour in gradually from the sides and swirl it into the liquid. Keep mixing, bringing in more and more flour, until it is all combined.
Knead the mixture with your hands until you get a smooth, bouncy ball of dough.
Oil a bowl with the remaining 1 teaspoon of olive oil and place the dough in it. Sprinkle the top with flour, cover the bowl with a damp kitchen towel, and set it aside in a warm place to double in size, about 1 hour.
Dust a work surface with flour and knead the dough again, releasing the air until it is back to normal size.
Divide the dough into 4 pieces and roll each piece into a round.

281. Bruschetta Pizza

Preparation Time: 10 minutes
Cooking Time: 10 minutes
Servings: 4

Ingredients:

¼ cup extra-virgin olive oil, plus 1 tablespoon
4 garlic cloves, minced, divided
1 teaspoon Italian Herb Blend
¼ teaspoon red pepper flakes
1 teaspoon salt, plus a pinch
2 rounds Pizza Dough or 12-inch store-bought pizza crusts
1 cup shredded pizza cheese (such as a mozzarella-provolone blend)
4 large tomatoes, chopped
2 tablespoons diced red onion
1 tablespoon dried oregano

Directions:

Preheat the oven to 425°F.
In a small bowl, combine ¼ cup of olive oil with half the garlic, the Italian herb blend, red pepper flakes, and a pinch of salt. Using a spoon, spread this mixture evenly over the pizza crusts.
Sprinkle the cheese on top.
Bake the pizzas for 8 to 10 minutes, until the dough is cooked through and the cheese is melted.
Meanwhile, in a bowl, toss together the tomatoes, red onion, remaining garlic, remaining 1 tablespoon of olive oil, remaining 1 teaspoon of salt, and the oregano.
Remove the pizza from the oven and turn the oven to broil.
Spoon the tomato mixture over the top of the pizzas. Broil for 1 to 2 minutes, just enough to quickly warm up the tomato mixture.
Cut into slices.

282. Pizza Bianca With Spinach

Preparation Time: 15 minutes
Cooking Time: 15 minutes
Servings: 4

Ingredients:

2 rounds Pizza Dough or 12-inch store-bought pizza crusts
2 tablespoons extra-virgin olive oil
2 garlic cloves, minced
2 cups frozen chopped spinach, thawed and drained
1 cup shredded provolone cheese
1 cup shredded mozzarella cheese
1 tablespoon dried oregano

Directions:

Preheat the oven to 450°F.
Brush the pizza crusts with the olive oil and sprinkle with the garlic and spinach.
Cover the pizzas with the cheeses and sprinkle with the oregano.
Bake for 10 to 15 minutes, until the cheese is browned and bubbling.
Let rest for 1 minute before slicing.

283. Mushroom Pesto Pita Pizza

Preparation Time: 15 minutes
Cooking Time: 10 to 15 minutes
Servings: 4

Ingredients:

1/4 cup extra-virgin olive oil
12 large mushrooms, sliced
1 teaspoon salt
1/4 teaspoon red pepper flakes (optional)
4 whole-wheat pita breads
1/2 cup Pesto (here)
1/2 cup shredded Parmesan cheese

Directions:

Preheat the oven to 375°F.
Warm a medium skillet over high heat, then add the olive oil, mushrooms, salt, and red pepper flakes (if using). Sauté until the liquid from the mushrooms has evaporated, about 5 to 7 minutes.
Place the pita breads on a baking sheet. Spread the pesto over the pitas and top with the mushrooms and Parmesan cheese.
Bake 10 to 15 minutes, or until the pizzas are lightly browned. Serve immediately.
This pizza can be made with gluten-free pita bread. To make it vegan, replace the pesto with a simple mixture of ½ cup olive oil, one garlic clove, 5 basil leaves, and ½ teaspoon salt puréed in a blender. Spread this over the pita instead of the pesto, and omit the Parmesan cheese. If you want to make your pita bread from scratch, check out the recipe for Pork Souvlaki with Tzatziki on Pita Bread here.

284. White Pizza

Preparation Time: 15 minutes
Cooking Time: 10 to 15 minutes
Servings: 4

Ingredients:

1 (14- or 16-inch) cooked pizza crust (ideally thin-crust)
1 tablespoon extra-virgin olive oil
8 ounces Fontina cheese, thinly sliced
1 leek, root and top trimmed, thinly sliced
½ fennel bulb, thinly sliced
1 teaspoon salt
1 tablespoon fresh thyme leaves

Directions:

Preheat the oven to 400°F.

Place the pizza crust on a large baking sheet. Brush with the olive oil and top with an even layer of cheese.
Arrange the sliced leek and fennel on top of the cheese.
Sprinkle salt over the toppings and bake about 10 minutes, or until the pizza is lightly browned. Top with thyme leaves.
Cooked pizza is best eaten right away. However, you can wrap leftovers in foil and refrigerate it for several days. Reheat in a hot oven or toaster oven for best results.
Fontina cheese is an Italian cow's milk cheese with a delicious buttery flavor. If you can't find Fontina, substitute Swiss or Jarlsberg cheese. The leeks and fennel can be replaced with thinly sliced onion and zucchini.

285. Chicken, Garlic, and Artichoke Pizza with Olives

Preparation Time: 15 minutes
Cooking Time: 10 to 15 minutes
Servings: 4

Ingredients:

1 (14- or 16-inch) cooked pizza crust (ideally thin crust)
1 tablespoon extra-virgin olive oil
8 ounces Yogurt Cheese (here)
2 garlic cloves, thinly sliced
3 scallions, thinly sliced
2 cups diced cooked chicken
1 (14-ounce) can artichoke hearts, drained, rinsed, cut in half
½ cup grated Parmesan cheese
½ cup pitted green olives

Directions:

Preheat the oven to 400°F.
Place the pizza crust on a large baking sheet. Brush with the olive oil.
Top with an even layer of yogurt cheese.
Arrange the garlic, scallions, chicken, artichoke hearts, Parmesan cheese, and olives over the top.
Bake about 10 minutes or until the pizza is lightly browned.
Cooked pizza is best eaten right away. However, you can wrap leftovers in foil and refrigerate it for several days. Reheat in a hot oven or toaster oven for best results.

286. Gluten-Free Zucchini and Walnut Pizza

Preparation Time: 20 minutes
Cooking Time: 20 minutes
Servings: 2

Ingredients:

FOR CRUST
¼ cup extra-virgin olive oil, plus 1 tablespoon to oil the pan
1 cup finely ground walnuts
2 cups shredded zucchini
¼ cup rice flour
1 egg
1 teaspoon salt
¼ teaspoon red pepper flakes (optional)
¼ teaspoon dried oregano
FOR THE PIZZA
½ cup sun-dried tomatoes, chopped
½ cup crumbled feta cheese
1 tablespoon chopped fresh basil
1 garlic clove, minced

Directions:

MAKE THE CRUST
Preheat the oven to 375°F.
Brush a 9-inch pie plate with olive oil and set aside.
In a medium bowl, combine the walnuts, zucchini, rice flour, egg, olive oil, salt, red pepper flakes (if using), and oregano. Mix well.
Press the crust into the prepared pan and bake about 15 to 20 minutes or until the crust is browned around the edges.
The cooked crust can be wrapped in plastic wrap and frozen for several months.
MAKE THE PIZZA
Top the baked crust with sun-dried tomatoes, feta cheese, basil, and garlic.
Return to the oven for 5 minutes to soften the feta.
Cut into wedges and serve.
Cooked pizza is best eaten right away. However, you can wrap leftovers in foil and refrigerate it for several days. Reheat in a hot oven or toaster oven for best results.
One cup of ground unsalted almonds or almond flour can be used in place of the ground walnuts. To make this pizza vegan, omit the feta and make an egg substitute by combining 1 tablespoon ground flaxseed with 3 tablespoons water and using this mixture instead of the egg.

287. Whole-Wheat Roasted Vegetable Pizza with Chèvre

Preparation Time: 15 minutes
Cooking Time: 10 minutes
Servings: 4

Ingredients:

FOR THE CRUST
1 cup warm water
1 tablespoon sugar
1 tablespoon extra-virgin olive oil
1 envelope rapid-rise yeast
1¾ cups whole-wheat flour
1 cup all-purpose flour, plus more to knead and roll the dough
1 teaspoon salt
FOR THE PIZZA
1 tablespoon extra-virgin olive oil
3 cups roasted vegetables from Couscous with Roasted Vegetables (here)
¼ teaspoon red pepper flakes (optional)
2 ounces chèvre, crumbled

Directions:

MAKE THE CRUST
Place the water, sugar, olive oil, yeast, flours, and salt in the bowl of a food processor or stand mixer and process until the mixture makes a wet dough. Or mix the dough in a large bowl using a wooden spoon. Be sure to mix well.
Scrape the dough onto a floured work surface, shape into a round, dust with flour, and let rest 10 minutes.
After 10 minutes, flatten the round and gently roll the dough into a 14-inch circle on a floured surface.
The dough can be made ahead and kept in the refrigerator overnight, or in the freezer longer. If freezing, thaw the dough overnight in the refrigerator.
MAKE THE PIZZA
Preheat the oven to 425°F.
Place the dough on a large baking sheet. Brush the top with olive oil.
Top with the roasted vegetables, red pepper flakes (if using), and chèvre.
Bake 10 to 12 minutes or until the pizza crust is golden. Serve immediately.
Cooked pizza is best eaten right away, but you can wrap leftovers in foil and refrigerate them for several days. Reheat in a hot oven or toaster oven for best results.
It's possible to make this dough with all whole-wheat flour, but it's much more difficult to handle since the gluten in white flour helps add elasticity.

288. Cumin, Lamb, and Pine Nut Pita Pizza

Preparation Time: 15 minutes
Cooking Time: 25 minutes
Servings: 4

Ingredients:

1 tablespoon extra-virgin olive oil
1 small onion, chopped
1 garlic clove, chopped
1-pound ground lamb
1 teaspoon ground cumin
½ teaspoon ground cinnamon
½ cup tomato sauce
¼ cup raisins
1 teaspoon salt
¼ teaspoon red pepper flakes (optional)
4 whole-wheat pita breads
¼ cup toasted pine nuts (pignoli)
2 ounces feta cheese, crumbled
¼ cup chopped fresh flatleaf parsley

Directions:

Preheat the oven to 375°F.
Place a large skillet over high heat. Add the olive oil, onion, and garlic, and sauté until the vegetables are soft, about 5 minutes.
Add the lamb and cook until all the pink is gone, about 5 minutes.
Add the cumin, cinnamon, tomato sauce, raisins, salt, and red pepper flakes (if using), and simmer an additional 5 minutes, or until most of the liquid in the tomato sauce has evaporated.
Place the pita breads on a large baking sheet and divide the lamb mixture among the four pita breads. Top each pita with pine nuts, feta, and parsley.
Bake about 10 minutes to heat through and toast the pita. Serve immediately.
The lamb filling can be made several days ahead. Keep in an airtight container in the refrigerator.
This topping is delicious on the whole-wheat pizza crust from Whole-Wheat Roasted Vegetable Pizza with Chèvre (here). If you want to make your pita bread from scratch, check out the recipe for Pork Souvlaki with Tzatziki on Pita Bread here.

289. Tomato Bread

Preparation Time: 30 minutes
Cooking Time: 35 minutes
Servings: 2

Ingredients:

750g flour
1 pack of dry yeast
250ml milk (lukewarm at best)
120g dried tomatoes
70g olive oil
10g sugar
10g salt
2 teaspoons thyme
½ teaspoon oregano

Directions:

First put the flour, dry yeast, sugar, salt, thyme, oregano and the dried tomatoes cut into strips in a bowl.
Then the milk and olive oil are added to the flour and kneaded into a dough. If the dough is too firm, it is advisable to add some milk. If, on the other hand, the dough is too runny, you should add a little more flour.
Now cover the dough with a warm cloth and let it rise for an hour in a warm place.
After this hour you can shape two loaves of bread out of the dough and place on a baking tray sprinkled with flour. Before baking, you should let the bread rise again for about 30 minutes at 40 ° C in the preheated oven.
The bread can then be baked in a preheated oven at 200 ° C for about 25 minutes.

290. Pork Souvlaki with Tzatziki on Pita Bread

Preparation Time: 90 minutes (less if you buy the pita)
Cooking Time: 20 minutes
Servings: 4 to 6

Ingredients:

FOR THE PITA BREAD
1 cup lukewarm water
1 package dry active yeast
½ teaspoon sugar
1 cup whole-wheat flour, divided
1¾ cups all-purpose flour, divided, plus extra for kneading and rolling
1 teaspoon salt
2 tablespoons extra-virgin olive oil
FOR THE SOUVLAKI
1½ pounds pork shoulder, cut into 1-inch pieces
¼ cup extra-virgin olive oil
2 tablespoons red wine vinegar
1 garlic clove, minced
1 teaspoon salt
1 teaspoon dried oregano
6 to 8 skewers
TO ASSEMBLE THE SANDWICHES
½ red onion, thinly sliced
1 large ripe tomato, thinly sliced
1 recipe Tzatziki (here)
1 tablespoon minced fresh oregano

Directions:

MAKE THE PITA BREAD
Place the water, yeast, and sugar in a medium bowl and stir to combine.
Add ¼ cup whole-wheat flour and ¼ cup all-purpose flour and whisk until smooth.
Place the bowl in a warm spot and let rest 15 minutes.
Add the salt, olive oil, and remaining ¾ cup whole-wheat flour and ¾ cup all-purpose flour, and mix until the mixture begins to turn into a wet sticky dough. Gradually add more all-purpose flour and knead the dough until it makes a soft, sticky dough. You may not need all the flour.
Turn the dough out onto a lightly floured work surface and knead the dough until it's smooth, elastic, and slightly sticky.
Return to the bowl, cover with plastic wrap, and leave in a warm spot to double in bulk, about 1 hour.
After the dough has risen, preheat the oven to 425°F. Punch the dough down and cut it into six equal pieces. Shape each piece into a ball, cover with plastic wrap, and let rest about 10 minutes.
Place a large heavy-duty baking sheet in the hot oven. While the baking sheet is heating, roll each piece of dough into a flat round, about 1/8 inch thick.
Remove the hot baking sheet, quickly place three of the rolled pitas on the sheet, and return it to the oven. After 2 to 3 minutes, the dough should puff up. Flip the pitas and cook the other side an additional 2 to 3 minutes. Remove the cooked pitas to a towel-lined plate to keep them warm.
Repeat the process with the remaining pita breads.
MAKE THE SOUVLAKI
Place the pork, olive oil, red wine vinegar, garlic, salt, and oregano in a medium bowl, cover, and let marinate at least 30 minutes or longer.
Preheat a grill or broiler to high.
Thread the meat on skewers. Place the meat on the grill or broiler and cook until golden brown on all sides, about 3 to 4 minutes per side.
ASSEMBLE THE SANDWICHES
Place a warm pita on a serving plate.
Remove the souvlaki from a skewer and place it on top of the pita bread.
Top with red onions, tomatoes, and tzatziki. Garnish with oregano and serve immediately.

291. Smoked Mackerel on Brown Bread with Spinach

Preparation Time: 10 minutes
Cooking Time: 5 minutes
Servings: 4

Ingredients:

4 slices dark rye bread
2 teaspoons Dijon mustard
1 cup packed baby spinach
12 thin slices cucumber
1 tablespoon chopped scallions
6 ounces smoked mackerel
¼ teaspoon salt (optional)
¼ teaspoon freshly ground black pepper (optional)

Directions:

Toast the bread.
Spread each toasted slice with the mustard.
Arrange baby spinach over the bread and top with the cucumber slices and scallions.
Divide the mackerel among the four slices of bread. Sprinkle with the salt and pepper (if using), and serve.
If you can't find smoked mackerel, you can substitute smoked salmon or trout, or use good-quality canned tuna instead.

292. Mozzarella baguette

Preparation 10 minutes:
Cooking Time: 10 minutes
Servings: 4

Ingredients:

1 stick of baguette
15 slices of mozzarella
2 tomatoes
1 clove of garlic
4 tbsp olive oil
15 slices of salami
1 pinch of salt and pepper
1 sprig of basil

Directions:

First of all, 15 even slices are cut from the baguette.
These are now briefly toasted in the oven, rubbed with a clove of garlic and drizzled with olive oil.
In the meantime, you can start washing and slicing the tomatoes.
Now tomatoes, salami and mozzarella are placed on the slices, drizzled with olive oil and refined with basil, salt and pepper.
The whole thing can now be baked for 5 minutes at 200 ° C.

293. Cheesy Fig Pizzas with Garlic Oil

Preparation Time: 1 day 40 minutes
Cooking Time: 10 minutes
Servings: 2 pizzas

Ingredients:

Dough:
1 cup almond flour
1 1/2 cups whole-wheat flour
3/4 teaspoon instant or rapid-rise yeast
2 teaspoons raw honey
1 1/4 cups ice water
2 tablespoons extra-virgin olive oil
1 3/4 teaspoons sea salt
Garlic Oil:
4 tablespoons extra-virgin olive oil, divided
1/2 teaspoon dried thyme
2 garlic cloves, minced
1/8 teaspoon sea salt
1/2 teaspoon freshly ground pepper
Topping:
1 cup fresh basil leaves
1 cup crumbled feta cheese
8 ounces (227 g) fresh figs, stemmed and quartered lengthwise
2 tablespoons raw honey

Directions:

Make the Dough:
Combine the flours, yeast, and honey in a food processor, pulse to combine well. Gently add water while pulsing. Let the dough sit for 10 minutes.
Mix the olive oil and salt in the dough and knead the dough until smooth. Wrap in plastic and refrigerate for at least 1 day.
Make the Garlic Oil:
Heat 2 tablespoons of olive oil in a nonstick skillet over medium-low heat until shimmering.
Add the thyme, garlic, salt, and pepper and sauté for 30 seconds or until fragrant. Set them aside until ready to use.
Make the pizzas:
Preheat the oven to 500ºF (260ºC). Grease two baking sheets with 2 tablespoons of olive oil.
Divide the dough in half and shape into two balls. Press the balls into 13-inch rounds. Sprinkle the rounds with a tough of flour if they are sticky.
Top the rounds with the garlic oil and basil leaves, then arrange the rounds on the baking sheets. Scatter with feta cheese and figs.
Put the sheets in the preheated oven and bake for 9 minutes or until lightly browned. Rotate the pizza halfway through.
Remove the pizzas from the oven, then discard the bay leaves. Drizzle with honey. Let sit for 5 minutes and serve immediately.
Tip: You can replace the garlic oil with homemade pesto and top the pizzas with freshly chopped tomatoes, fried potatoes, and sautéed broccoli.

294. Mashed Grape Tomato Pizzas

Preparation Time: 10 minutes
Cooking Time: 20 minutes
Servings: 6

Ingredients:

3 cups grape tomatoes, halved
1 teaspoon chopped fresh thyme leaves
2 garlic cloves, minced
1/4 teaspoon kosher salt
1/4 teaspoon freshly ground black pepper
1 tablespoon extra-virgin olive oil
3/4 cup shredded Parmesan cheese
6 whole-wheat pita breads

Directions:

Preheat the oven to 425ºF (220ºC).
Combine the tomatoes, thyme, garlic, salt, ground black pepper, and olive oil in a baking pan.
Roast in the preheated oven for 20 minutes. Remove the pan from the oven, mash the tomatoes with a spatula and stir to mix well halfway through the cooking time.
Meanwhile, divide and spread the cheese over each pita bread, then place the bread in a separate baking pan and roast in the oven for 5 minutes or until golden brown and the cheese melts.
Transfer the pita bread onto a large plate, then top with the roasted mashed tomatoes. Serve immediately.
Tip: If you want a juicier pizza, you can replace the grape tomatoes to normal large tomatoes and chopped the tomatoes into chunks to make them easier for cooking.

295. Sumptuous Vegetable and Cheese Lavash Pizza

Preparation Time: 15 minutes
Cooking Time: 11 minutes
Servings 4

Ingredients:

2 (12 by 9-inch) lavash breads
2 tablespoons extra-virgin olive oil
10 ounces (284 g) frozen spinach, thawed and squeezed dry
1 cup shredded fontina cheese
1 tomato, cored and cut into ½-inch pieces
½ cup pitted large green olives, chopped
¼ teaspoon red pepper flakes
3 garlic cloves, minced
¼ teaspoon sea salt
¼ teaspoon ground black pepper
½ cup grated Parmesan cheese

Directions:

Preheat oven to 475ºF (246ºC).
Brush the lavash breads with olive oil, then place them on two baking sheet. Heat in the preheated oven for 4 minutes or until lightly browned. Flip the breads halfway through the cooking time.
Meanwhile, combine the spinach, fontina cheese, tomato pieces, olives, red pepper flakes, garlic, salt, and black pepper in a large bowl. Stir to mix well.
Remove the lavash bread from the oven and sit them on two large plates, spread them with the spinach mixture, then scatter with the Parmesan cheese on top.
Bake in the oven for 7 minutes or until the cheese melts and well browned.
Slice and serve warm.
Tip: You can replace the tomato, spinach, and olives with broccoli, fennel and artichoke for a different lavash pizza.

296. Pineapple Pizza

Preparation Time: 10 minutes
Cooking Time: 30 minutes
Servings: 3

Ingredients:

1 large whole wheat tortilla
¼ cup tomato pizza sauce
¼ cup pineapple tidbits
¼ cup mozzarella cheese, grated
¼ cup ham slice

Directions:

Preheat your air fryer to 300° F. Place the tortilla on a baking sheet then spread pizza sauce over tortilla. Arrange ham slice, cheese, pineapple over the tortilla. Put the pizza in the air fryer basket and then cook for 10 minutes. Serve hot.

297. Air Fryer Tortilla Pizza

Preparation Time: 7 minutes
Cooking Time: 30 minutes
Servings: 6

Ingredients:

1 large whole wheat tortilla
1 tablespoon black olives
Salt and pepper to taste
4 tablespoons tomato sauce
8 pepperoni slices
3 tablespoons of sweet corn
1 medium, tomato, chopped
½ cup mozzarella cheese, grated

Directions:

Preheat your air fryer to 325° F. Spread tomato sauce over tortilla. Add pepperoni slices, olives, corn, tomato, and cheese on top of the tortilla. Season with salt and pepper. Place pizza in the air fryer basket and cook for 7 minutes. Serve and enjoy!

298. Stuffed Pita Breads

Preparation Time: 5 minutes
Cooking Time: 15 minutes
Servings: 4

Ingredients:

1 and ½ tablespoons olive oil
1 tomato, cubed
1 garlic clove, minced
1 red onion, chopped
¼ cup parsley, chopped
15 ounces canned fava beans, drained and rinsed
¼ cup lemon juice
Salt and black pepper to the taste
4 whole wheat pita bread pockets

Directions:

Heat up a pan with the oil over medium heat, add the onion, stir and sauté for 5 minutes.
Add the rest of the ingredients, stir and cook for 10 minutes more
Stuff the pita pockets with this mix and serve for breakfast.

299. Avocado Tomato Gouda Socca Pizza

Preparation Time: 20 minutes
Cooking Time: 20 minutes
Servings: 2

Ingredients:

1 and 1/4 cups of chickpea or garbanzo bean flour
1 and 1/4 cups of cold water
1/4 teaspoon of pepper and sea salt each
2 teaspoons of avocado or olive oil + 1 teaspoon extra for heating the pan
1 teaspoon of minced Garlic which will be around two cloves
1 teaspoon of Onion powder/other herb seasoning powder
10 to twelve-inch cast iron pan
1 sliced tomato
1/2 avocado
2 ounces of thinly sliced Gouda
1/4-1/3 cup of Tomato sauce
2 or 3 teaspoons of chopped green scallion/onion
Sprouted greens for green
Extra pepper/salt for sprinkling on top of the pizza
Red pepper flakes

Directions:

Mix the flour with two teaspoons of olive oil, herbs, water, and whisk it until a smooth mixture form. Keep it at room temperature for around 15-20 minutes to let the batter settle.
In the meantime, preheat the oven and place the pan inside the oven and let it get heated for around 10 minutes. When the pan gets preheated, chop up the vegetables into fine slices.
Remove the pan after ten minutes using oven mitts. Put one teaspoon of oil and swirl it all around to coat the pan.
Pour the batter into the pan and tilt the pan so that the batter spreads evenly throughout the pan. Turn down the over to 425f and place back the pan for 5-8 minutes.
Remove the pan from the oven and add the sliced avocado, tomato and on top of that, add the gouda slices and the onion slices.
Put the pizza back into the oven and wait till the cheese get melted or the sides of the bread gets crusty and brown.
Remove the pizza from the pan and add the microgreens on top, along with the toppings.

300. Thin Crust Low Carb Pizza

Preparation Time: 15 minutes
Cooking Time: 25 minutes
Servings: 6

Ingredients:

2 tablespoons tomato sauce
1/8 teaspoon black pepper
1/8 teaspoon chili flakes
1 piece low-carb pita bread
2 ounces low-moisture mozzarella cheese
1/8 teaspoon garlic powder
Toppings:
Bacon, roasted red peppers, spinach, olives, pesto, artichokes, salami, pepperoni, roast beef, prosciutto, avocado, ham, chili paste, Sriracha

Directions:

Warm the oven to 450 degrees F, then oiled a baking dish. Mix tomato sauce, black pepper, chili flakes, and garlic powder in a bowl and keep aside.
Place the low-carb pita bread in the oven and bake for about 2 minutes. Remove from the oven and spread the tomato sauce on it.
Add mozzarella cheese and top with your favorite toppings. Bake again for 3 minutes and dish out.

301. Fresh Bell Pepper Basil Pizza

Preparation Time: 15 minutes
Cooking Time: 25 minutes
Servings: 3

Ingredients:

Pizza Base:
½ cup almond flour
2 tablespoons cream cheese
1 teaspoon Italian seasoning
½ teaspoon black pepper
6 ounces mozzarella cheese
2 tablespoons psyllium husk
2 tablespoons fresh Parmesan cheese
1 large egg
½ teaspoon salt
Toppings:
4 ounces cheddar cheese, shredded
¼ cup Marinara sauce
2/3 medium bell pepper
1 medium vine tomato
3 tablespoons basil, fresh chopped

Directions:

Warm the oven to 400 degrees F and grease a baking dish. Microwave mozzarella cheese for about 30 seconds and top with the remaining pizza crust.
Add the remaining pizza ingredients to the cheese and mix. Flatten the dough and transfer to the oven.
Bake for about 10 minutes. Remove, and top the pizza with the toppings and bake for another 10 minutes. Remove pizza from the oven and allow to cool.

302. BBQ Chicken Pizza

Preparation Time: 15 minutes
Cooking Time: 30 minutes
Servings: 4

Ingredients:

Dairy-Free Pizza Crust
6 tablespoons Parmesan cheese
6 large eggs
3 tablespoons psyllium husk powder
Salt and black pepper, to taste
1½ teaspoons Italian seasoning
Toppings
6 oz. rotisserie chicken, shredded
4 oz. cheddar cheese
1 tablespoon mayonnaise
4 tablespoons tomato sauce
4 tablespoons BBQ sauce

Directions:

Warm the oven to 400 degrees F and grease a baking dish. Place all Pizza Crust ingredients in an immersion blender and blend until smooth.
Spread dough mixture onto the baking dish and transfer it to the oven. Bake for about 10 minutes and top with favorite toppings. Bake for about 3 minutes and dish out.

303. Caramelized Onion and Goat Cheese Pizza

Preparation Time: 1 hour & 15 minutes
Cooking Time: 30 minutes
Servings: 4

Ingredients:

For the crust:
2 cups flour
1 cup lukewarm water
1 pinch of sugar
1 tsp active dry yeast
¾ tsp salt
2 tbsp olive oil
For the topping:
2 tbsp butter
2 red onions, thinly sliced
Salt and black pepper to taste
1 cup crumbled goat cheese
1 tbs almond milk
1 cup fresh curly endive, chopped

Directions:

Sift the flour and salt in a bowl and stir in yeast. Mix lukewarm water, olive oil, and sugar in another bowl. Add the wet mixture to the dry mixture and whisk until you obtain a soft dough.
Place the dough on a lightly floured work surface and knead it thoroughly for 4-5 minutes until elastic. Transfer the dough to a greased bowl.
Cover with cling film and leave to rise for 50-60 minutes in a warm place until doubled in size. Roll out the dough to a thickness of around 12 inches.
Preheat the oven to 400 F. Line a pizza pan with parchment paper. Melt the butter in a large skillet and stir in the onions.
Reduce the heat to low, season the onions with salt, black pepper, and cook with frequent stirring until caramelized, 15 to 20 minutes. Turn the heat.
In a medium bowl, mix the goat cheese with the almond milk and spread on the crust. Top with the caramelized onions. Bake in the oven for 10 minutes and take out after. Top with the curly endive, slice, and serve warm.

304. Vegetarian Spinach-Olive Pizza

Preparation Time: 15 minutes
Cooking Time: 25 minutes
Servings: 4

Ingredients:

For the crust:
½ cup almond flour
¼ tsp salt
2 tbsp ground psyllium husk
1 tbsp olive oil
1 cup lukewarm water
For the topping:
½ cup tomato sauce
½ cup baby spinach
1 cup grated mozzarella cheese
1 tsp dried oregano
3 tbsp sliced black olives

Directions:

Preheat the oven to 400 F. Line a baking sheet with parchment paper. In a medium bowl, mix the almond flour, salt, psyllium powder, olive oil, and water until dough forms.
Spread the mixture on the pizza pan and bake in the oven until crusty, 10 minutes.
When ready, remove the crust and spread the tomato sauce on top.

Add the spinach, mozzarella cheese, oregano, and olives. Bake until the cheese melts, 15 minutes. Take out of the oven, slice and serve warm.

305. Chicken Bacon Ranch Pizza

Preparation Time: 1 hour & 15 minutes
Cooking Time: 20 minutes
Servings: 4

Ingredients:

For the crust:
2 cups flour
1 cup lukewarm water
1 pinch of sugar
1 tsp active dry yeast
¾ tsp salt
2 tbsp olive oil
For the ranch sauce:
1 tbsp butter
2 garlic cloves, minced
1 tbsp cream cheese
¼ cup half and half
1 tbsp dry Ranch seasoning mix
For the topping:
3 bacon slices, chopped
2 chicken breasts
Salt and black pepper to taste
1 cup grated mozzarella cheese
6 fresh basil leaves

Directions:

Sift the flour and salt in a bowl and stir in yeast. Mix lukewarm water, olive oil, and sugar in another bowl. Add the wet mixture to the dry mixture and whisk until you obtain a soft dough.
Place the dough on a lightly floured work surface and knead it thoroughly for 4-5 minutes until elastic. Transfer the dough to a greased bowl.
Cover with cling film and leave to rise for 50-60 minutes in a warm place until doubled in size. Roll out the dough to a thickness of around 12 inches.
Preheat the oven to 400 F. Line a pizza pan with parchment paper. In a bowl, mix the sauce's ingredients butter, garlic, cream cheese, half and half, and ranch mix. Set aside.
Heat a grill pan over medium heat and cook the bacon until crispy and brown, 5 minutes. Transfer to a plate and set aside.
Season the chicken with salt, pepper and grill in the pan on both sides until golden brown, 10 minutes. Remove to a plate, allow cooling and cut into thin slices.
Spread the ranch sauce on the pizza crust, followed by the chicken and bacon, and then, mozzarella cheese and basil. Bake for 5 minutes or until the cheese melts. Slice and serve warm.

306. Chicken Pizza

Preparation Time: 1 minute
Cooking Time: 10 minutes
Servings: 4

Ingredients:

2 flatbreads
1 tbsp. Greek vinaigrette
½ cup feta cheese, crumbled
¼ cup Parmesan cheese, grated
½ cup water-packed artichoke hearts, rinsed, drained and chopped
½ cup olives, pitted and sliced
½ cup cooked chicken breast strips, chopped
1/8 tsp. dried basil
1/8 tsp. dried oregano
Pinch of ground black pepper
1 cup part-skim mozzarella cheese, shredded

Directions:

Preheat the oven to 400°F. Arrange the flatbreads onto a large ungreased baking sheet and coat each with vinaigrette.
Top with feta, followed by the Parmesan, veggies and chicken. Sprinkle with dried herbs and black pepper. Top with mozzarella cheese evenly.
Bake for about 8-10 minutes or until cheese is melted. Remove from the oven and set aside for about 1-2 minutes before slicing. Cut each flat bread into 2 pieces and serve.

307. Shrimp Pizza

Preparation Time: 15 minutes
Cooking Time: 10 minutes
Servings: 1

Ingredients:

2 tbsp. spaghetti sauce
1 tbsp. pesto sauce
1 (6-inch) pita bread
2 tbsp. mozzarella cheese, shredded
5 cherry tomatoes, halved
1/8 cup bay shrimp
Pinch of garlic powder
Pinch of dried basil

Directions:

Preheat the oven to 325°F. Lightly, grease a baking sheet. In a bowl, mix together the spaghetti sauce and pesto. Spread the pesto mixture over the pita bread in a thin layer.
Top the pita bread with the cheese, followed by the tomatoes and shrimp. Sprinkle with the garlic powder and basil.
Arrange the pita bread onto the prepared baking sheet and bake for about 7-10 minutes. Remove from the oven and set aside for about 3-5 minutes before slicing. Cut into desired sized slices and serve.

308. Veggie Pizza

Preparation Time: 20 minutes
Cooking Time: 12 minutes
Servings: 6

Ingredients:

1 (12-inch) prepared pizza crust
¼ tsp. Italian seasoning
¼ tsp. red pepper flakes, crushed
1 cup goat cheese, crumbled
1 (14-oz.) can quartered artichoke hearts
3 plum tomatoes, sliced into ¼-inch thick size
6 kalamata olives, pitted and sliced
¼ cup fresh basil, chopped

Directions:

Preheat the oven to 450°F. Grease a baking sheet. Sprinkle the pizza crust with Italian seasoning and red pepper flakes evenly.
Place the goat cheese over crust evenly, leaving about ½-inch of the sides. With the back of a spoon, gently press the cheese downwards.
Place the artichoke, tomato and olives on top of the cheese. Arrange the pizza crust onto the prepared baking sheet.
Bake for about 10-12 minutes or till cheese becomes bubbly. Remove from oven and sprinkle with the basil. Cut into equal sized wedges and serve.

309. Avocado and Turkey Mix Panini

Preparation Time: 5 minutes
Cooking Time: 8 minutes
Servings: 2

Ingredients:

2 red peppers, roasted and sliced into strips
¼ lb. thinly sliced mesquite smoked turkey breast
1 cup whole fresh spinach leaves, divided
2 slices provolone cheese
1 tbsp olive oil, divided
2 ciabatta rolls

¼ cup mayonnaise
½ ripe avocado

Directions for Cooking:

In a bowl, mash thoroughly together mayonnaise and avocado. Then preheat Panini press.
Slice the bread rolls in half and spread olive oil on the insides of the bread. Then fill it with filling, layering them as you go: provolone, turkey breast, roasted red pepper, spinach leaves and spread avocado mixture and cover with the other bread slice.
3 Place sandwich in the Panini press and grill for 5 to 8 minutes until cheese has melted and bread is crisped and ridged.

310. Cucumber, Chicken and Mango Wrap

Preparation Time: 10 minutes
Cooking Time: 20 minutes
Servings: 1

Ingredients:

½ of a medium cucumber cut lengthwise
½ of ripe mango
1 tbsp salad dressing of choice
1 whole wheat tortilla wrap
1-inch thick slice of chicken breast around 6-inch in length
2 tbsp oil for frying
2 tbsp whole wheat flour
2 to 4 lettuce leaves
Salt and pepper to taste

Directions for Cooking:

Slice a chicken breast into 1-inch strips and just cook a total of 6-inch strips. That would be like two strips of chicken. Store remaining chicken for future use.
Season chicken with pepper and salt. Dredge in whole wheat flour.
On medium fire, place a small and nonstick fry pan and heat oil. Once oil is hot, add chicken strips and fry until golden brown around 5 minutes per side.
While chicken is cooking, place tortilla wraps in oven and cook for 3 to 5 minutes. Then remove from oven and place on a plate.
Slice cucumber lengthwise, use only ½ of it and store remaining cucumber. Peel cucumber cut into quarter and remove pith. Place the two slices of cucumber on the tortilla wrap, 1-inch away from the edge.
Slice mango and store the other half with seed. Peel the mango without seed, slice into strips and place on top of the cucumber on the tortilla wrap.
Once chicken is cooked, place chicken beside the cucumber in a line.
Add cucumber leaf, drizzle with salad dressing of choice.
Roll the tortilla wrap, serve and enjoy.

311. Garlic & Tomato Gluten Free Focaccia

Preparation Time: 10 minutes
Cooking Time: 20 minutes
Servings: 8

Ingredients:

1 egg
½ tsp lemon juice
1 tbsp honey
4 tbsp olive oil
A pinch of sugar
1 ¼ cup warm water
1 tbsp active dry yeast
2 tsp rosemary, chopped
2 tsp thyme, chopped
2 tsp basil, chopped
2 cloves garlic, minced
1 ¼ tsp sea salt
2 tsp xanthan gum
½ cup millet flour
1 cup potato starch, not flour
1 cup sorghum flour
Gluten free cornmeal for dusting

Directions for Cooking:

For 5 minutes, turn on the oven and then turn it off, while keeping oven door closed.
In a small bowl, mix warm water and pinch of sugar. Add yeast and swirl gently. Leave for 7 minutes.
In a large mixing bowl, whisk well herbs, garlic, salt, xanthan gum, starch, and flours.
Once yeast is done proofing, pour into bowl of flours. Whisk in egg, lemon juice, honey, and olive oil.
Mix thoroughly and place in a well-greased square pan, dusted with cornmeal.
Top with fresh garlic, more herbs, and sliced tomatoes.
Place in the warmed oven and let it rise for half an hour.
Turn on oven to 375oF and after preheating time it for 20 minutes. Focaccia is done once tops are lightly browned.
Remove from oven and pan immediately and let it cool.
Best served when warm.

312. Bread Machine Pizza Dough

Preparation Time: 15 minutes
Cooking Time: 24 minutes
Servings: 6

Ingredients:

1 cup of beer
2 tablespoons butter
2 tablespoons sugar
1 teaspoon of salt
2 1/2 cups of all-purpose flour
2 1/4 teaspoons of yeast

Directions:

Place beer, butter, sugar, salt, flour, and yeast in a bread maker in the order recommended by the manufacturer. Select the Paste setting and press Start.
Remove the dough from the bread maker once the cycle is complete. Roll or press the dough to cover a prepared pizza dish.
Brush lightly with olive oil. Cover and let stand for 15 minutes. Preheat the oven to 250 degrees (400 degrees F).
Spread the sauce and garnish on the dough. Bake until the crust is a little brown and crispy on the outside, about 24 minutes.

313. Pizza Crust

Preparation Time: 15 minutes
Cooking Time: 15-20 minutes
Servings: 15

Ingredients:

7/8 cup warm water
3/4 teaspoon salt
2 tablespoons olive oil
2 1/2 cups all-purpose flour
2 teaspoons white sugar
2 teaspoons active dry yeast

Directions:

Set the bread machine to adjust the dough and start the machine. Tap the dough into a rolling pan or a 12-inch greased round pizza pan. Let stand for 10 minutes.
Preheat the oven to 205° C (400° F).
Spread the pizza sauce on the dough.
Sprinkle the toppings over the sauce.
Bake for 15-20 minutes, or until the crust is golden brown.

314. Pizza Buns

Preparation Time: 15 minutes
Cooking Time: 41 minutes
Servings: 8

Ingredients:

8 hamburger buns, divided
1-pound ground beef
1/3 cup onion, minced
1 (15 oz) jar pizza sauce
1/3 cup grated Parmesan cheese
2 1/4 teaspoon Italian herbs
1 teaspoon garlic powder
1/4 cup Onion powder
1/8 teaspoon ground crushed red pepper flakes
1 teaspoon bell pepper
2 cups grated mozzarella cheese

Directions:

Place the oven rack about 6 centimeters from the heat source. Place the buns on a baking sheet. Grill for about 1 minute until they are toasted. Set aside.
Set the oven to 350 degrees F (175 degrees C). In a frying skillet over medium heat, cook and mix the minced beef until it is golden and crumbly, about 10 minutes. Drain the excess fat and stir in the onion.
Cook and mix the beef mixture until the onion is transparent, about 5 minutes longer, then add the pizza sauce, parmesan cheese, Italian herbs, garlic powder, onion powder, ground red pepper flakes bell pepper.
Bring the sauce to a boil and simmer for 10 to 15 minutes to mix the flavors, stirring often.
Pour the beef sauce over the baking sheet and cover each loaf with about 1/4 cup grated mozzarella cheese.
Put the rolls back in the oven and bake for about 10 minutes, until the cheese is bubbling and light brown.

315. Brick Oven Pizza (Brooklyn Style)

Preparation Time: 16 hours & 15 minutes
Cooking Time: 6 minutes
Servings: 18

Ingredients:

1 teaspoon of active dry yeast
1/4 cup of warm water
1 cup of cold water
1 teaspoon of salt
3 cups of bread flour
6 oz low-mozzarella cheese, minced
1/2 cup of crushed canned tomatoes without salt
1/4 tsp of fresh pepper
1/2 teaspoon dried oregano
3 tablespoons extra virgin olive oil
6 fresh basil leaves, torn

Directions:

Scatter the yeast over the warm water in a large bowl. Let stand for 5 minutes to check. Stir in salt and cold water, and then add about 1 cup of flour at a time.
When the dough is thick enough to be removed from the bowl, knead it on a floured surface until smooth, about 10 minutes.
Divide it in two and form a tight ball. Coat the balls with olive oil and leave them in a sealed container for at least 16 hours. Remove the dough from the fridge one hour before use.
Preheat the oven with a pizza stone on the lowest rack at 550 degrees F. Lightly dust a pizza skin with flour.
Use a dough ball at a time, sprinkle the dough lightly with flour, and gradually stretch it until it is approximately 14 inches in diameter, about the pizza stone's size. Place on the floured tin.
Place thin slices of mozzarella on the crust and then chop a generous amount of black pepper.
Sprinkle with dried oregano. Arrange the crushed tomatoes randomly and leave empty areas. Sprinkle with olive oil.
Make sure the dough comes off the skin with a quick jerk. Place the skin's tip on the back of the preheated pizza stone and remove it to leave the pizza on the stone.
Bake in the preheated oven for 4 to 6 minutes or until the crust starts to brown.
Remove from the oven by sliding the skin under the pizza.
Randomly sprinkle some basil leaves on the pizza. Cut into segments and serve.

316. Valentine Pizza

Preparation Time: 15 minutes
Cooking Time: 15-20 minutes
Servings: 12

Ingredients:

3 cups of bread flour
1 (0.25 oz) active dry yeast cover
1 1/4 cup of warm water
3 tablespoons chopped fresh rosemary
3 tablespoons extra virgin olive oil, divided
1 can of pizza sauce (14 oz)
3 cups grated mozzarella cheese
2 ripe tomatoes
15 slices of vegetarian pepperoni
1 can (2.25 oz) sliced black olives, sliced
1 zucchini, sliced

Directions:

Place the bread flour, yeast, water, and 2 tablespoons of olive oil in the bread maker in the order recommended by the manufacturer.
Select the Paste setting. Press Start. When the dough is ready, knead the rosemary into the dough.
Divide the dough into three servings. Shape each heart-shaped piece about 1/2 inch thick. Brush with remaining olive oil, then spread a thin layer of pizza sauce on each pizza.
Sprinkle cheese over pizza sauce and arrange on top with tomatoes, zucchini, pepperoni, and sliced olives. Bake for about 15 to 20 minutes.

317. Pizza Muffins

Preparation Time: 15 minutes
Cooking Time: 15-20 minutes
Servings: 12

Ingredients:

2 1/2 cups flour
1/2 teaspoon baking powder
1/2 teaspoon dried oregano
2 tablespoons white sugar
1/2 teaspoon salt
1 teaspoon dried basil leaves
3 sun-dried tomatoes
2 1/2 cups of cheddar cheese, grated, divided
4 green onions, minced
1 beaten egg
1 1/2 cup buttermilk

Directions:

Preheat the oven to 190° C. Grease the muffin cups or double them with muffin paper. Combine flour baking powder, baking powder, salt, basil, oregano, and sugar in a large bowl in a large bowl.
Stir until everything is well mixed. Mix tomatoes, 1.5 cups of cheese, and onions.
In another bowl, whisk the egg, pick up buttermilk and stir until smooth.
Place the dough halfway in the muffin pans. Sprinkle the remaining cup of cheese over the muffins.
Bake in the preheated oven for 15 to 20 minutes until a toothpick in the middle of the muffin comes out clean.

318. Pub Pizza

Preparation Time: 15 minutes
Cooking Time: 12-15 minutes
Servings: 1

Ingredients:

1 small (4 inches) pita bread
1/4 cup pizza sauce
4 slices cooked ham
1/4 cup pineapple chunks, drained
4 slices Monterey Jack cheese

Directions:

Preheat the oven to 250 degrees (400 degrees F). Place the pita bread on a small baking sheet. Cover with pizza sauce, ham, and pieces of pineapple garnish with Monterey Jack cheese.
Bake in the preheated oven for 12 to 15 minutes, until cheese is melted and light brown.

319. Alfredo Chicken Pita Pizza

Preparation Time: 15 minutes
Cooking Time: 20 minutes
Servings: 4

Ingredients:

2 tbsp olive oil, divided
6 small frozen chicken fillets, thawed and sliced
1 pinch of salt with garlic or to taste
1/4 cup of garlic hummus
4 pita bread
4 teaspoons of basil pesto
1/2 cup of prepared Alfredo sauce
1 cup of freshly chopped spinach leaves
1 jar of marinated artichoke hearts
3/4 cup mozzarella cheese
3/4 cup crumbled feta cheese
1/2 cup grated Parmesan cheese
1/2 cup sliced fresh mushrooms

Directions:

Preheat the oven to 175 degrees (350° F).
Heat 1 tablespoon of olive oil in a frying pan over medium-high heat.
Season the chicken with garlic salt; cook and stir the hot oil until it is no longer pink in the middle, in 5 minutes. Set aside to cool.
Spread 1 tablespoon of hummus on one side of each pita bread almost to the edges. Cover with layers of pesto and alfredo sauce.
Sprinkle a layer of chopped spinach on the Alfredo sauce; garnish with equal Servings of chicken, artichoke hearts, feta cheese, mozzarella, parmesan cheese, and mushrooms.
Sprinkle the pizzas with the remaining olive oil. Bake for 15 minutes.

320. Miniature Pizzas

Preparation Time: 15 minutes
Cooking Time: 12-15 minutes
Servings: 20

Ingredients:

1-pound ground beef
1 pound of fresh minced pork sausage
1 chopped onion
10 grams of processed American cheese, diced
32 grams of cocktail rye bread

Directions:

Preheat the oven to 175 degrees (350° F).
Brown ground beef and sausages.
Mix the onion in the sausage and beef mixture and cook until done. Pour the fat from the pan. Add the melted cheese to the mixture. Keep cooking until the cheese has melted.
Place spoons full of the mixture on each slice of bread. Bake 12 to 15 minutes.

321. Easy Pizza with a Pinch

Preparation Time: 15 minutes
Cooking Time: 45 minutes
Servings: 8

Ingredients:

8 hot dog buns
2 cups of tomato sauce
3 teaspoons of minced garlic
3 teaspoons dried Italian herbs
1 tbsp. Sweet pepper
1 tbsp. Kosher salt
1 teaspoon ground black pepper
1 pound of sweet Italian sausages
2 tablespoons extra virgin olive oil
1 cup of grated mozzarella cheese
1/2 cup grated Parmesan cheese
fresh oregano sprigs (optional)
Ground red pepper (optional)

Directions:

For the sauce, mix tomato sauce, garlic, pepper, salt, and pepper in a pan over medium heat.
When the sauce is bubbling, place on low heat and stir. Cover and simmer for 15 minutes on low heat.
Crumble the Italian sausages in a pan and cook them over medium heat until they are no longer pink about 15 minutes. Drain on kitchen paper. Set aside.
Preheat the oven to 400 degrees F. Combine olive oil, garlic, and 1 teaspoon in a small bowl. Put the hot dog bun on baking trays with aluminum foil.
Cover the buns with the olive oil mixture. Grill for about 5 minutes, until the edges start to brown. Remove the pan from the oven and brush each sandwich with hot tomato sauce.
Garnish with golden Italian sausages, sliced pepperoni, mozzarella, and parmesan cheese.
Put the pan in the oven and bake for 5 to 10 minutes, at 400° F, or until the cheese is bubbling. Serve garnished with fresh oregano leaves and chopped red pepper, if desired.

322. Basil & Artichoke Pizza

Preparation Time: 1 hours & 15 minutes
Cooking Time: 24 minutes
Servings: 4

Ingredients:

1 cup canned passata
2 cups flour
1 cup lukewarm water
1 pinch of sugar
1 tsp active dry yeast
¾ tsp salt
2 tbsp olive oil
1 ½ cups frozen artichoke hearts
¼ cup grated Asiago cheese
½ onion, minced
3 garlic cloves, minced
1 tbsp dried oregano
1 cup sun-dried tomatoes, chopped
½ tsp red pepper flakes
5-6 basil leaves, torn

Directions:

Sift the flour and salt in a bowl and stir in yeast. Mix lukewarm water, olive oil, and sugar in another bowl. Add the wet mixture to the dry mixture and whisk until you obtain a soft dough.
Place the dough on a lightly floured work surface and knead it thoroughly for 4-5 minutes until elastic. Transfer the dough to a greased bowl.
Cover with cling film and leave to rise for 50-60 minutes in a warm place until doubled in size. Roll out the dough to a thickness of around 12 inches.
Preheat oven to 400 F. Warm oil in a saucepan over medium heat and sauté

onion and garlic for 3-4 minutes. Mix in tomatoes and oregano and bring to a boil. Decrease the heat and simmer for another 5 minutes. Transfer the pizza crust to a baking sheet. Spread the sauce all over and top with artichoke hearts and sun-dried tomatoes.
Scatter the cheese and bake for 15 minutes until golden. Top with red pepper flakes and basil leaves and serve sliced.

323. Balsamic-Glazed Pizza with Arugula & Olives

Preparation Time: 1 hour & 20 minutes
Cooking Time: 20 minutes
Servings: 4

Ingredients:

2 cups flour
1 cup lukewarm water
1 pinch of sugar
1 tsp active dry yeast
2 tbsp olive oil
2 tbsp honey
½ cup balsamic vinegar
4 cups arugula
Salt and black pepper to taste
1 cup mozzarella cheese, grated
¾ tsp dried oregano
6 black olives, drained

Directions:

Sift the flour and ¾ tsp salt in a bowl and stir in yeast. Mix lukewarm water, olive oil, and sugar in another bowl. Add the wet mixture to the dry mixture and whisk until you obtain a soft dough.
Place the dough on a lightly floured work surface and knead it thoroughly for 4-5 minutes until elastic. Transfer the dough to a greased bowl.
Cover with cling film and leave to rise for 50-60 minutes in a warm place until doubled in size. Roll out the dough to a thickness of around 12 inches.
Place the balsamic vinegar and honey in a saucepan over medium heat and simmer for 5 minutes until syrupy. Preheat oven to 390 F.
Transfer the pizza crust to a baking sheet and sprinkle with oregano and mozzarella cheese; bake for 10-15 minutes.
Remove the pizza from the oven and top with arugula. Sprinkle with balsamic glaze and black olives and serve.

324. Pepperoni Fat Head Pizza

Preparation Time: 1 hour & 20 minutes
Cooking Time: 15 minutes
Servings: 4

Ingredients:

2 cups flour
1 cup lukewarm water
1 pinch of sugar
1 tsp active dry yeast
¾ tsp salt
2 tbsp olive oil
1 tsp dried oregano
2 cups mozzarella cheese
1 cup sliced pepperoni

Directions:

Sift the flour and salt in a bowl and stir in yeast. Mix lukewarm water, olive oil, and sugar in another bowl. Add the wet mixture to the dry mixture and whisk until you obtain a soft dough.
Place the dough on a lightly floured work surface and knead it thoroughly for 4-5 minutes until elastic. Transfer the dough to a greased bowl.
Cover with cling film and leave to rise for 50-60 minutes in a warm place until doubled in size. Roll out the dough to a thickness of around 12 inches.
Preheat oven to 400 F. Line a round pizza pan with parchment paper. Spread the dough on the pizza pan and top with the mozzarella cheese, oregano, and pepperoni slices.
Bake in the oven for 15 minutes or until the cheese melts. Remove the pizza, slice and serve.

325. Extra Cheesy Pizza

Preparation Time: 15 minutes
Cooking Time: 28 minutes
Servings: 4

Ingredients:

For the crust:
½ cup almond flour
¼ tsp salt
2 tbsp ground psyllium husk
1 tbsp olive oil
1 cup lukewarm water
For the topping
½ cup sugar-free pizza sauce
1 cup sliced mozzarella cheese
1 cup grated mozzarella cheese
3 tbsp grated Parmesan cheese
2 tsp Italian seasoning

Directions:

Preheat the oven to 400 F. Line a baking sheet with parchment paper. In a medium bowl, mix the almond flour, salt, psyllium powder, olive oil, and lukewarm water until dough forms.
Spread the mixture on the pizza pan and bake in the oven until crusty, 10 minutes. When ready, remove the crust and spread the pizza sauce on top.
Add the sliced mozzarella, grated mozzarella, Parmesan cheese, and Italian seasoning. Bake in the oven for 18 minutes or until the cheeses melt. Serve warm.

326. Za'atar Pizza

Preparation Time: 10 minutes
Cooking Time: 15 minutes
Servings: 4 To 6

Ingredients:

1 sheet puff pastry
1/4 cup extra-virgin olive oil
1/3 cup za'atar seasoning

Directions:

Preheat the oven to 350°F.
Put the puff pastry on a parchment-lined baking sheet. Cut the pastry into desired slices.
Brush the pastry with olive oil. Sprinkle with the za'atar.
Put the pastry in the oven and bake for 10 to 12 minutes or until edges are lightly browned and puffed up. Serve warm or at room temperature.
VARIATION TIP: Serve with Greek yogurt or tzatziki sauce.

327. White Pizza with Prosciutto and Arugula

Preparation Time: 10 minutes
Cooking Time: 15 minutes
Servings: 4

Ingredients:

1-pound prepared pizza dough
½ cup ricotta cheese
1 tablespoon garlic, minced
1 cup grated mozzarella cheese
3 ounces prosciutto, thinly sliced
½ cup fresh arugula
½ teaspoon freshly ground black pepper

Directions:

Preheat the oven to 450°F. Roll out the pizza dough on a floured surface.
Put the pizza dough on a parchment-lined baking sheet or pizza sheet. Put the

dough in the oven and bake for 8 minutes.
In a small bowl, mix together the ricotta, garlic, and mozzarella.
Remove the pizza dough from the oven and spread the cheese mixture over the top. Bake for another 5 to 6 minutes.
Top the pizza with prosciutto, arugula, and pepper; serve warm.
SUBSTITUTION TIP: If you don't like arugula, you can top the pizza with basil dressed with some olive oil, salt, and pepper.

328. Margherita Pizza

Preparation Time: 10 minutes
Cooking Time: 10 minutes
Servings: 4

Ingredients:

1 tablespoon olive oil
½ yield Pizza Dough, or 1 pound store-bought
8 ounces fresh mozzarella cheese, cut into 1-inch cubes
All-purpose flour, for dusting
1 teaspoon cornmeal
1 cup Basic Tomato Basil Sauce, or store-bought
½ cup chopped fresh basil, divided
1 tablespoon freshly grated Parmesan cheese

Directions:

Coat a medium bowl with the olive oil. Place the dough in the bowl, cover with a clean kitchen towel, and let rise for 1 hour or until the dough doubles in size.
Preheat the oven to 500°F.
Pat the mozzarella cheese dry with paper towels.
Dust a work surface with flour and turn the dough out on to it. Flatten the dough into a 10-inch circle. Sprinkle the cornmeal on a baking sheet. Place the dough circle on the baking sheet.
Spread the tomato sauce on the pizza, leaving a ½-inch border all around. Scatter the mozzarella and half the basil over the sauce.
Bake for about 10 minutes until the crust is golden and the cheese is bubbling.
Sprinkle with the remaining basil and the Parmesan cheese. Serve hot!

329. No-Knead Sesame Bread

Preparation Time: 20 minutes
Cooking Time: 10 minutes
Servings: 2

Ingredients:

3 tablespoons olive oil, divided
½ yield Pita Bread dough
¼ cup all-purpose flour, for dusting
1 large egg yolk
¼ cup milk
1 tablespoon white sesame seeds
1 tablespoon black sesame seeds

Directions:

Coat 2 baking sheets with 1 tablespoon of olive oil each and set aside.
Coat a large bowl with the remaining 1 tablespoon of olive oil. Place the dough in the bowl, cover with a clean kitchen towel, and let rise for 1 hour or until the dough doubles in size.
Dust a work surface with flour and turn the dough out on to it. Cut the dough into 2 balls. Keep dusting with flour to prevent sticking. Roll out the balls into ½-inch-thick flat circles. Place each dough circle on a prepared baking sheet. Cover and let rest for 30 minutes.
Preheat the oven to 450°F.5.
In a small bowl, whisk the egg yolk and milk until combined. Set aside.
Using your fingertips, dent the tops of the dough all over. Brush the dough with the egg-and-milk glaze. Sprinkle 1½ teaspoons each of white and black sesame seeds over each dough circle.
Bake for about 10 minutes or until the edges begin to brown. Serve warm.

330. Cheese And Parsley Flatbread

Preparation Time: 25 minutes
Cooking Time: 25 minutes
Servings: 4

Ingredients:

1 cup crumbled feta cheese
1 large egg
1/2 cup finely chopped fresh parsley
1/8 teaspoon freshly ground black pepper
1/2 yield Pita Bread dough
All-purpose flour, for dusting
2 tablespoons olive oil
1/2 teaspoon black sesame seeds

Directions:

In a medium bowl, stir together the feta cheese, egg, parsley, and pepper. Set aside.
Divide the pita dough into 4 balls. Dust each with flour and place each dough ball into a bowl. Cover and let rise for 10 minutes.
Dust a work surface with flour. Punch down each dough ball and roll them out into 3-by-12-inch ovals.
Preheat the oven to 400°F.
Spread a quarter of the feta filling on each piece of dough. Pinch the top and bottom of each bread, and fold the sides inward to create a boat shape. Brush the dough with olive oil and sprinkle with the sesame seeds.
Bake for 12 to 15 minutes or until golden. Let cool for 10 minutes before serving.
Variation Tip: Mix the feta cheese with 1 cup ricotta, ½ cup chopped green olives, and ½ teaspoon dried oregano for a different take.

331. Flatbread With Harissa And Sesame

Preparation Time: 25 minutes
Cooking Time: 15 minutes
Servings: 4

Ingredients:

1/2 yield Pita Bread dough
All-purpose flour, for dusting
1/4 cup olive oil
1 small onion, finely chopped
1/4 cup Harissa, or store-bought
2 tablespoons sesame seeds

Directions:

Cut the dough into 2 equal balls. Dust a work surface with flour, place the balls on the flour, cover, and let rise for 15 minutes.
In a small sauté pan or skillet over medium heat, heat the olive oil.
Add the onion and cook for about 5 minutes until transparent. Remove from the heat and stir in the harissa. Set aside.
Preheat the oven to 400°F.
Roll out each dough ball into an 8-inch circle, dusting with flour as needed to prevent sticking. Transfer the dough to a baking sheet.
Spread half the onion-harissa mixture over each dough circle and sprinkle each with 1 tablespoon of sesame seeds.
7.Bake for 10 minutes or until the edges are golden.
Variation Tip: Sprinkle with chopped cured black olives and fresh thyme before baking for a different flavor combination.

332. Rosemary Focaccia

Preparation Time: 15 minutes
Cooking Time: 20 minutes
Servings: 6

Ingredients:

1/2 cup olive oil, divided
1 yield Pizza Dough, or 2 pounds store-bought
All-purpose flour, for dusting
1/4 cup chopped fresh rosemary, plus 1 rosemary sprig
1 14 teaspoons salt, divided
1/4 cup water

Directions:

Preheat the oven to 400°F.
Coat a medium bowl with 1 tablespoon of olive oil. Place the dough in the bowl, cover with a clean kitchen towel, and let rise for 30 minutes.
Flour a work surface and turn the dough out on to it. Roll out the dough into a ½-inch-thick rectangle. Transfer the rectangle to a baking sheet.
Using your fingertips, make deep dents all over the dough. Drizzle with the remaining 7 tablespoons of olive oil and sprinkle with the chopped rosemary. Let rest for 20 minutes.
In a small bowl, stir together 1 teaspoon of salt and the water. Drizzle over the dough. Sprinkle the rosemary needles from the sprig evenly across the dough. Sprinkle on the remaining ½ teaspoon of salt.
Bake for 20 minutes or until the dough is slightly golden.

333. Sweet Anise Bread

Preparation Time: 20 minutes
Cooking Time: 1 Hour
Servings: 8

Ingredients:

2 tablespoons olive oil, plus more for preparing the pan
2 cups all-purpose flour, plus more for dusting
1 cup sugar
1½ teaspoons baking powder
1 teaspoon aniseed
½ teaspoon ground cinnamon
¼ teaspoon salt
1 large egg
½ cup milk
1 tablespoon freshly squeezed orange juice
Grated zest of 1 orange

Directions:

Preheat the oven to 375°F. Coat a 5-by-9-inch loaf pan with olive oil. Set aside.
In a medium bowl, whisk the flour, sugar, baking powder, aniseed, cinnamon, and salt. Set aside.
In a small bowl, whisk the egg, milk, olive oil, orange juice, and orange zest. Add the egg mixture to the flour mixture and mix until well combined and a smooth dough forms.
Dust a work surface with flour. Place the dough on it and flatten the dough to fit into the prepared loaf pan. Place the dough in the pan.
Bake for about 50 minutes or until golden. Let the bread rest in the pan for 10 minutes. Transfer to a wire rack to cool completely.

334. Spanish-Style Pizza de Jamon

Preparation Time: 1 hour & 15 minutes
Cooking Time: 15 minutes
Servings: 4

Ingredients:

For the crust:
2 cups flour
1 cup lukewarm water
1 pinch of sugar
1 tsp active dry yeast
¾ tsp salt
2 tbsp olive oil
For the topping:
½ cup tomato sauce
½ cup sliced mozzarella cheese
4 oz jamon serrano, sliced
7 fresh basil leaves

Directions:

Sift the flour and salt in a bowl and stir in yeast. Mix lukewarm water, olive oil, and sugar in another bowl. Add the wet mixture to the dry mixture and whisk until you obtain a soft dough.
Place the dough on a lightly floured work surface and knead it thoroughly for 4-5 minutes until elastic. Transfer the dough to a greased bowl.
Cover with cling film and leave to rise for 50-60 minutes in a warm place until doubled in size. Roll out the dough to a thickness of around 12 inches.
Preheat the oven to 400 F. Line a pizza pan with parchment paper. Spread the tomato sauce on the crust.
Arrange the mozzarella slices on the sauce and then the jamon serrano. Bake for 15 minutes or until the cheese melts.
Remove from the oven and top with the basil. Slice and serve warm.

335. Spicy & Smoky Pizza

Preparation Time: 1 hour & 15 minutes
Cooking Time: 20 minutes
Servings: 4

Ingredients:

For the crust:
2 cups flour
1 cup lukewarm water
1 pinch of sugar
1 tsp active dry yeast
¾ tsp salt
2 tbsp olive oil
For the topping:
1 tbsp olive oil
1 cup sliced chorizo
¼ cup sugar-free marinara sauce
1 cup sliced smoked mozzarella cheese
1 jalapeño pepper, deseeded and sliced
¼ red onion, thinly sliced

Directions:

Sift the flour and salt in a bowl and stir in yeast. Mix lukewarm water, olive oil, and sugar in another bowl. Add the wet mixture to the dry mixture and whisk until you obtain a soft dough.
Place the dough on a lightly floured work surface and knead it thoroughly for 4-5 minutes until elastic. Transfer the dough to a greased bowl.
Cover with cling film and leave to rise for 50-60 minutes in a warm place until doubled in size. Roll out the dough to a thickness of around 12 inches.
Preheat the oven to 400 F. Line a pizza pan with parchment paper. Heat the olive oil and cook the chorizo until brown, 5 minutes.
Spread the marinara sauce on the crust, top with the mozzarella cheese, chorizo, jalapeño pepper, and onion.
Bake in the oven until the cheese melts, 15 minutes. Remove from the oven, slice, and serve warm.

336. Turkey Pizza with Pesto Topping

Preparation Time: 15 minutes
Cooking Time: 30 minutes
Servings: 4

Ingredients:

Pizza Crust:
3 cups flour
3 tbsp olive oil
1/3 tsp salt

3 large eggs
Pesto Chicken Topping:
½ lb. turkey ham, chopped
2 tbsp cashew nuts
Salt and black pepper to taste
1 ½ tbsp olive oil
1 green bell pepper, seeded and sliced
1 ½ cups basil pesto
1 cup mozzarella cheese, grated
1 ½ tbsp Parmesan cheese, grated
1½ tbsp fresh basil leaves
A pinch of red pepper flakes

Directions:

In a bowl, mix flour, 3 tbsp of olive oil, salt, and eggs until a dough form. Mold the dough into a ball and place it in between two full parchment papers on a flat surface.
Roll it out into a circle of a ¼ -inch thickness. After, slide the pizza dough into the pizza pan and remove the parchment paper. Place the pizza pan in the oven and bake the dough for 20 minutes at 350ºF.
Once the pizza bread is ready, remove it from the oven, fold and seal the extra inch of dough at its edges to make a crust around it.
Apply 2/3 of the pesto on it and sprinkle half of the mozzarella cheese too. Toss the chopped turkey ham in the remaining pesto and spread it on top of the pizza.
Sprinkle with the remaining mozzarella, bell peppers, and cashew nuts and put the pizza back in the oven to bake for 9 minutes.
When it is ready, remove from the oven to cool slightly, garnish with the basil leaves and sprinkle with parmesan cheese and red pepper flakes. Slice and serve.

337. Baby Spinach Pizza with Sweet Onion

Preparation Time: 1 hour & 15 minutes
Cooking Time: 53 minutes
Servings: 4

Ingredients:

For the crust:
2 cups flour
1 cup lukewarm water
1 pinch of sugar
1 tsp active dry yeast
¾ tsp salt
2 tbsp olive oil
For the caramelized onion:
1 onion, sliced
1 tsp sugar
2 tbsp olive oil
½ tsp salt
For the pizza:
¼ cup shaved Pecorino Romano cheese
2 tbsp olive oil
½ cup grated mozzarella cheese
1 cup baby spinach
¼ cup chopped fresh basil leaves
½ red bell pepper, sliced

Directions:

Sift the flour and salt in a bowl and stir in yeast. Mix lukewarm water, olive oil, and sugar in another bowl. Add the wet mixture to the dry mixture and whisk until you obtain a soft dough.
Place the dough on a lightly floured work surface and knead it thoroughly for 4-5 minutes until elastic. Transfer the dough to a greased bowl.
Cover with cling film and leave to rise for 50-60 minutes in a warm place until doubled in size. Roll out the dough to a thickness of around 12 inches.
Warm olive oil in a skillet over medium heat and sauté onion with salt and sugar for 3 minutes. Lower the heat and brown for 20-35 minutes until caramelized. Preheat oven to 390 F.
Transfer the pizza crust to a baking sheet. Drizzle the crust with olive oil and top with onion. Cover with bell pepper and mozzarella. Bake for 10-15 minutes. Serve topped with baby spinach, basil, and Pecorino cheese.

338. Italian Mushroom Pizza

Preparation Time: 1 hour & 15 minutes
Cooking Time: 25 minutes
Servings: 4

Ingredients:

For the crust:
2 cups flour
1 cup lukewarm water
1 pinch of sugar
1 tsp active dry yeast
¾ tsp salt
2 tbsp olive oil
For the topping:
1 tsp olive oil
2 medium cremini mushrooms, sliced
1 garlic clove, minced
½ cup sugar-free tomato sauce
1 tsp sugar
1 bay leaf
1 tsp dried oregano
1tsp dried basil
Salt and black pepper to taste
½ cup grated mozzarella cheese
½ cup grated Parmesan cheese
6 black olives, pitted and sliced

Directions:

Sift the flour and salt in a bowl and stir in yeast. Mix lukewarm water, olive oil, and sugar in another bowl. Add the wet mixture to the dry mixture and whisk until you obtain a soft dough.
Place the dough on a lightly floured work surface and knead it thoroughly for 4-5 minutes until elastic. Transfer the dough to a greased bowl.
Cover with cling film and leave to rise for 50-60 minutes in a warm place until doubled in size. Roll out the dough to a thickness of around 12 inches.
Preheat the oven to 400 F. Line a pizza pan with parchment paper. Heat the olive oil in a medium skillet and sauté the mushrooms until softened, 5 minutes. Stir in the garlic and cook until fragrant, 30 seconds.
Mix in the tomato sauce, sugar, bay leaf, oregano, basil, salt, and black pepper. Cook for 2 minutes and turn the heat off. Spread the sauce on the crust, top with the mozzarella and Parmesan cheeses, and then, the olives. Bake in the oven until the cheese's melts, 15 minutes. Remove the pizza, slice, and serve warm.

339. Broccoli-Pepper Pizza

Preparation Time: 15 minutes
Cooking Time: 20 minutes
Servings: 4

Ingredients:

For the crust:
½ cup almond flour
¼ tsp salt
2 tbsp ground psyllium husk
1 tbsp olive oil
1 cup lukewarm water
For the topping:
1 tbsp olive oil
1 cup sliced fresh mushrooms
1 white onion, thinly sliced
3 cups broccoli florets
4 garlic cloves, minced
½ cup pizza sauce
4 tomatoes, sliced
1 ½ cup grated mozzarella cheese
½ cup grated Parmesan cheese

Directions:

Preheat the oven to 400 F. Line a baking sheet with parchment paper. In a bowl, mix the almond flour, salt, psyllium powder, olive oil, and lukewarm water until dough forms.
Spread the mixture on the pizza pan and bake in the oven until crusty, 10 minutes. When ready, remove the crust and allow cooling.

Heat olive oil in a skillet and sauté the mushrooms, onion, garlic, and broccoli until softened, 5 minutes.
Spread the pizza sauce on the crust and top with the broccoli mixture, tomato, mozzarella and Parmesan cheeses. Bake for 5 minutes.

340. Mozzarella Bean Pizza

Preparation Time: 10 minutes
Cooking Time: 15 minutes
Servings: 6

Ingredients:

2 tbsp. cornmeal
1 cup mozzarella
1/3 cup barbecue sauce
1 roma tomato, diced
1 cup black beans
1 cup corn kernels
1 medium whole-wheat pizza crust

Directions:

Preheat your oven at 400°F. Take a baking sheet, line it with parchment paper. Grease it with some avocado oil. Spread some cornmeal over the baking sheet.
In a bowl, mix together the tomatoes, corn and beans. Place the pizza crust on the baking sheet.
Spread the sauce on top; add the topping, and top with the cheese and bake until the cheese melts and the crust edges are golden-brown for 12-15 minutes. Slice and serve warm.

341. Pizza Dough Without Yeast in Milk

Preparation Time: 5 minutes
Cooking Time: 1 hour
Servings: 5

Ingredients:

Wheat flour 2 cups
Milk 125 ml
Salt 1 tsp.
Chicken egg 2 pieces
Sunflower oil 2 tbsp.

Directions:

Making pizza dough without yeast in milk is quite simple. The recipe is designed to prepare a dough, which is enough for two, but only large, baking sheets.
Combine flour and salt in one bowl. And in the second butter, milk and eggs, mix well and combine the contents of two bowls in one large container.
Wait a few minutes for the whole liquid consistency to soak in the flour, and start mixing the dough. It will take about 15 minutes. Dough, in finished form, should be elastic, soft and smooth.
Then you need to take a kitchen towel, of course clean, and soak it in water. As a result, it should be moist, but not wet. Excess fluid must be squeezed out. Wrap the dough in a towel, leave to lie down for 20 minutes.
After waiting for the set time, remove the dough and, sprinkling flour on the countertop, roll out, but only very thinly. Place it on a baking sheet and lay out the filling prepared according to your taste preferences. As a result, the finished dough will have an effect that is easy, of course, of puff pastry and has a crispy taste.

342. Ideal Pizza Dough (On A Large Baking Sheet)

Preparation Time: 10 minutes
Cooking Time: 1 hour
Servings: 5

Ingredients:

Wheat flour 13 oz.
Salt 1.5 tsp.
Dry yeast 1,799 tsp.
Sugar 1 tsp.
Water 200 ml
1 tbsp. olive oil
Dried Basil 1.5 tsp.

Directions:

We cultivate yeast in warm water. There you can add a spoonful of sugar, so the yeast will begin to work faster. Leave them for 10 minutes.
Sift the flour through a sieve (leave 2 oz. for the future) in a deep bowl. Add salt, basil, mix. Pour water with yeast into the cavity in the flour and mix thoroughly with a fork.
Somewhere in the middle of the process, when the dough becomes less than one whole, add olive oil. When the dough is ready, cover with a damp towel and put in heat for 30 minutes.
Now just lay it on a flour dusted surface and roll out the future pizza to a thickness of 2-3 mm.
The main rule of pizza is the maximum possible temperature, minimum time. Therefore, feel free to set the highest temperature that is available in your oven.

343. Vegetable Oil Pizza Dough

Preparation Time: 10 minutes
Cooking Time: 1 hour
Servings: 3

Ingredients:

Wheat flour 1 cup
Water 1 cup
Salt to taste
Vegetable oil 1 tbsp.
Dry yeast 10 g

Directions:

We mix water and yeast, leave for 40 minutes so that they disperse. You can add a tablespoon of sugar.
Then pour in the oil, add the flour; knead well and put in a warm place to increase the volume by 2 times.

344. Chicken Alfredo Pita Pizza

Preparation Time: 40 minutes
Cooking Time: 50 minutes
Servings:4

Ingredients :

Frozen chicken tenders – 6 smalls (thawed and sliced)
Garlic humus – ¼ cup
Basil pesto – 4 teaspoons
Fresh spinach leaves – 1 cup (chopped)
Olive oil (divided)
Garlic salt – 1 pinch or according to taste
Pita bread rounds – 4
Prepared Alfredo sauce – ½ cup
Marinated artichoke hearts – 1 (6.5 ounce) jar (drained and chopped)
Feta cheese – ¾ cup (crumbled)
Parmesan cheese – ½ cup (shredded)
Mozzarella cheese – ¾ cup
Fresh mushrooms – ½ cup (sliced)

Directions:

Preheat oven to 350 degrees F (175 degrees C)
In a skillet and over medium heat, heat 1 tablespoon of olive oil. Season chicken with garlic salt the cook and stir in hot oil for about five minutes or until the chicken is no longer pink in the middle. Set aside to cool.
Spread 1 tablespoon of hummus over one side of each of the pita rounds so that it is nearly touching the edges. Top with layers pesto and Alfredo sauce.

After this, top with even portions of chicken, artichoke hearts, feta cheese, mozzarella cheese, parmesan cheese and mushrooms.
Drizzle the remaining olive oil on the pizzas and bake in the preheated oven for about 15 minutes or until the cheese is melted and the crust on the pitas is slightly brown.

345. Apple and Feta Pan Fried Pizzas

Preparation Time: 35 minutes
Cooking time 40 minutes
Servings: 8

Ingredients :

Hot water – ½ cup
Feta cheese – 8 ounces (crumbled)
Fresh thyme – 1 tablespoon (chopped)
Apples – 4 (cored and chopped)
Dy pizza crust mix – 6 ½ ounces
Olive oil – 5 tablespoons
Red onion – 1 (thinly sliced)
Butter – ½ teaspoon
Ground black pepper to taste.

Directions:

Combine the contents of the pizza dough package with ½ cup of hot water in a medium-sized bowl. Stir vigorously and set the bowl in a warm place of about 85 degrees F or 35 degrees C for 5 minutes.
Turn the dough onto a floured board and divide into 8 small sections, then knead and shape into rounds.
Heat the olive oil in a large skillet, add the dough and fry until it is lightly browned on both sides.
Once this is cooked, place the circles on a cookie sheet. Sprinkle the feta, red onion and thyme on top of the circles.
Bake the pizza for about 10 to 12 minutes or until the feta begins to brown.
While the pizzas bake, heat ½ tablespoon of butter and a few sprigs of thyme in the previously used skillet.
Mix the apples into the skillet and cook until the apples are soft and golden. Put the apples on top of the pizzas, season with pepper and serve.

346. Eggplant Pizza

Preparation Time: 40 minutes
Cooking Time: 50 minutes
Servings: 4

Ingredients:

One large eggplant
1/3 Cup Olive oil
Pepper
Salt
2 cups cherry tomatoes – halved
1½ cups Shredded mozzarella cheese
1¼ cups Marinara sauce
1/2 cup Torn basil leaves

Directions:

Preheat your oven to 450°F.
Slice the eggplants into slices and arrange them on the baking sheet.
Cover each of the eggplant slices with olive oil.
Roast the eggplant slices until tender.
Spread two tbsp of the marinara sauce on each piece.
Add the cheese and arrange cherry tomato pieces on each.
Cook for about four minutes, removing when the cheese melts.

347. Avocado Tomato Pizza

Preparation Time: 42 minutes
Cooking Time: 30 minutes
Servings: 4

Ingredients:

Pizza Crust:
Two tbsp Olive oil
Two cloves of garlic minced
1 1/4 cup Chickpea flour
Sea salt and pepper
1 1/4 cup Cold water
One tsp any herbs of choice
Soccer Pizza Toppings:
Extra salt/pepper for seasoning
1 Roma tomato sliced
One half of an avocado
2 ounces of gouda (sliced thin)
1/3 cup Tomato sauce
Three tbsp Green onion (chopped)
Red pepper flakes

Directions:

Preheat your oven at 350 F.
Place pan in oven to warm.
Mix olive oil, water, flour, and herbs until smooth and let it chill for ten minutes.
Remove pan from oven after ten minutes then add a tbsp of oil to the pan, moving it around to cover the bottom of the pan then pour in your batter.
Set the oven temperature to 425F and put the pan back in the oven, until the mixture has set.
Remove pan from oven and spread the tomato sauce on top, then sliced tomato and avocado.
Put the Gouda slices on top of the tomato and avocado.
Put back in oven until the cheese melts.
Let it cool then put the fresh green onion on the top.
Drizzle a bit olive oil on top and enjoy.

348. Pizza Dough on Yogurt

Preparation Time: 10 minutes
Cooking Time: 30 minutes
Servings: 5

Ingredients:

Natural yogurt 9 oz.
Vegetable oil 5 tbsp.
½ tsp. salt
Wheat flour 2.5 cups
Baking powder 1 tsp.

Directions:

Mix flour, baking powder and salt. Add yogurt and butter, mix everything thoroughly. Preheat the oven to 190 ° C. Lubricate the pan with oil. Roll the dough very thinly and transfer to a baking sheet. Put the filling to taste. Bake for 10-15 minutes.

349. Mediterranean Whole Wheat Pizza

Preparation Time: 5 minutes
Cooking Time: 25 minutes
Servings: 4

Ingredients:

Whole-wheat pizza crust (1)
Basil pesto (4 oz. jar)
Artichoke hearts (.5 cup)
Kalamata olives (2 tbsp.)
Pepperoncini (2 tbsp. drained)
Feta cheese (.25 cup)

Directions:

Program the oven to 450°F. Drain and pull the artichokes to pieces. Slice/chop the pepperoncini and olives.
Arrange the pizza crust onto a floured work surface and cover it using pesto. Arrange the artichoke, pepperoncini slices, and olives over the pizza. Lastly, crumble and add the feta.
Bake in the hot oven until the cheese has melted, and it has a crispy crust or 10-12 minutes.

350. Fruit Pizza

Preparation Time: 15 minutes
Cooking Time: 0 minutes
Servings: 4

Ingredients:

4 watermelon slices

1 oz blueberries
2 oz goat cheese, crumbled
1 teaspoon fresh parsley, chopped

Directions:

Put the watermelon slices in the plate in one layer. Then sprinkle them with blueberries, goat cheese, and fresh parsley.

351. Sprouts Pizza

Preparation Time: 15 minutes
Cooking Time: 15 minutes
Servings: 6

Ingredients:

4 oz wheat flour, whole grain
2 tablespoons olive oil
¼ teaspoon baking powder
5 oz chicken fillet, boiled
2 oz Mozzarella cheese, shredded
1 tomato, chopped
2 oz bean sprouts

Directions:

Make the pizza crust: mix wheat flour, olive oil, baking powder, and knead the dough. Roll it up in the shape of pizza crust and transfer in the pizza mold.
Then sprinkle it with chopped tomato, shredded chicken, and Mozzarella. Bake the pizza at 365F for 15 minutes. Sprinkle the cooked pizza with bean sprouts and cut into servings.

352. Cheese Pinwheels

Preparation Time: 15 minutes
Cooking Time: 25 minutes
Servings: 6

Ingredients:

1 teaspoon chili flakes
½ teaspoon dried cilantro
1 egg, beaten
1 teaspoon cream cheese
1 oz Cheddar cheese, grated
6 oz pizza dough

Directions:

Roll up the pizza dough and cut into 6 squares. Sprinkle the dough with dried cilantro, cream cheese, and Cheddar cheese.
Roll the dough in the shape of pinwheels, brush with beaten egg and bake in the preheated to 365F oven for 25 minutes or until the pinwheels are light brown.

353. Ground Meat Pizza

Preparation Time: 15 minutes
Cooking Time: 35 minutes
Servings: 4

Ingredients:

7 oz ground beef
1 teaspoon tomato paste
½ teaspoon ground black pepper
2 egg whites, whisked
½ cup Mozzarella cheese, shredded
1 teaspoon fresh basil, chopped

Directions:

Line the baking tray with baking paper. Preheat the oven to 370F. Mix all ingredients except Mozzarella in the mixing bowl.
Then place the mixture in the tray and flatten it to get a thick layer. Top the pizza with Mozzarella cheese and bake in the oven for 35 minutes. Then cut the cooked pizza into the servings.

354. Quinoa Flour Pizza

Preparation Time: 15 minutes
Cooking Time: 15 minutes
Servings: 6

Ingredients:

1 oz pumpkin puree
3 tablespoons quinoa flour
½ teaspoon dried oregano
1 cup Mozzarella cheese, shredded
1 tomato, chopped
1 teaspoon olive oil

Directions:

Mix pumpkin puree, quinoa flour, and olive oil. Knead the dough. Roll it up in the shape of pizza crust and transfer in the lined with a baking paper baking tray.
Then top the pizza crust with tomato, oregano, and Mozzarella cheese. Bake the pizza at 365F for 15 minutes.

355. Artichoke Pizza

Preparation Time: 15 minutes
Cooking Time: 20 minutes
Servings: 4

Ingredients:

7 oz pizza crust
5 oz artichoke hearts, canned, drained, chopped
1 teaspoon fresh basil, chopped
1 tomato, sliced
1 cup Monterey Jack cheese, shredded

Directions:

Line the pizza mold with baking paper. Then put the pizza crust inside. Top it with sliced tomato, canned artichoke hearts, and basil.
Then top the pizza with Monterey Jack cheese and transfer in the preheated to 365F oven. Cook the pizza for 20 minutes.

356. 3-Cheese Pizza

Preparation Time: 15 minutes
Cooking Time: 10 minutes
Servings: 6

Ingredients:

1 pizza crust, cooked
½ cup Mozzarella, shredded
½ cup Cheddar cheese, shredded
2 oz Parmesan, grated
¼ cup tomato sauce
1 teaspoon Italian seasonings

Directions:

Put the pizza crust in the baking pan. Then brush it with tomato sauce and Italian seasonings.
After this, sprinkle the pizza with Mozzarella, Cheddar cheese, and Parmesan. Bake the pizza for 10 minutes at 375F.

357. Chickpea Pizza

Preparation Time: 15 minutes
Cooking Time: 25 minutes
Servings: 6

Ingredients:

4 tablespoons marinara sauce
7 oz pizza dough
1 tomato, sliced
1 red onion, sliced
5 oz chickpeas, canned
½ cup Mozzarella cheese, shredded

Directions:

Roll up the pizza dough in the shape of pizza crust and transfer in the pizza mold. Then brush the pizza crust with marinara sauce and sprinkle with sliced onion, tomato, and chickpeas.
Top the chickpeas with mozzarella cheese and bake the pizza for 25 minutes at 355F.

358. Hummus Pizza

Preparation Time: 15 minutes
Cooking Time: 20 minutes
Servings: 6

Ingredients:

6 oz pizza dough
5 oz hummus
3 oz Feta cheese, crumbled
1 tablespoon fresh parsley, chopped
½ cup black olives, sliced
3 sun-dried tomatoes, chopped
1 tablespoon avocado oil

Directions:

Roll up the pizza dough in the shape of the pizza crust. Then place it in pizza mold and brush with avocado oil.
Spread the pizza crust with hummus and sprinkle with parsley, black olives, and sun-dried tomatoes, and crumbled feta.
Bake the pizza at 400F for 20 minutes.

359. Pesto Pita Pizza

Preparation Time: 15 minutes
Cooking Time: 15 minutes
Servings: 4

Ingredients:

4 pita bread rounds
1/2 cup pesto
2 tomatoes, sliced
1 (4 oz) container crumbled feta cheese

Directions:

Preheat oven to 400 degrees. Arrange pita bread on a baking sheet. Bake in the preheated oven until pita is lightly toasted, about 4 minutes.
Spread pesto evenly over toasted pita bread and arrange tomato slices in a single layer. Top with feta cheese.
Continue baking until feta cheese is browned and pita bread is crisp, about 11 minutes more.

360. Veggie Pita Pizza

Preparation Time: 15 minutes
Cooking Time: 5 minutes
Servings: 1

Ingredients:

1 round pita bread
1 teaspoon of olive oil
3 tablespoons of pizza sauce
1/2 cup grated mozzarella cheese
1/4 cup sliced Cremini mushrooms
1/8 teaspoon salt with garlic

Directions:

Preheat the grill on medium heat. Spread a side of the pita with olive oil and pizza sauce. Garnish with cheese and mushrooms and season with garlic salt.
Lightly grease the grill. Place the pita pizza on the grill, cover, and cook until the cheese has completely melted about 5 minutes.

361. Mini Pizzas with Arugula & Hummus

Preparation Time: 15 minutes
Cooking Time: 0 minutes
Servings: 1

Ingredients:

2 tablespoons hummus
1 naan bread
1 cup of arugula
1 date, pitted and chopped
2 teaspoons pumpkin seeds
1 teaspoon balsamic vinegar

Directions:

Spread the hummus on naan bread; garnish with arugula, date, and pumpkin seeds. Sprinkle balsamic vinegar on pizza. Serve.

362. Grilled Buffalo Chicken Pizza

Preparation Time: 12 hours & 15 minutes
Cooking Time: 35 minutes
Servings: 2

Ingredients:

1 boneless chicken fillet
2 pinches of steak herbs
2 tablespoons hot pepper sauce
2 pieces of naan tandoori bread
1 teaspoon of olive oil
½ cup of blue cheese dressing
2 tablespoons diced red onion
8 grams of grated cheddar cheese
½ cup of grated iceberg lettuce
1 Roma tomato, seeded and minced

Directions:

Season the chicken fillet with Montreal Steak Seasoning. 1/3 cup of hot pepper sauce into the bag. Close the bag and rub the hot sauce into the chicken.
Place the bag in the refrigerator and marinate for 12 hours. Preheat an outside grill over medium heat and lightly oil the grill.
Discard the marinade. Cook the chicken on the preheated grill until it is no longer pink in the middle and the juice is clear, 5 to 7 minutes on each side.
An instant-read thermometer in the center must indicate at least 165° F (74° C). Put the chicken on a cutting board and let it sit for 5 to 10 minutes.
Cut the chilled chicken into bite-sized pieces. Mix chicken and remaining hot sauce in a bowl.
Brush every naan with olive oil; bake on the grill until golden brown and grilled on one side for 3 to 5 minutes.
Reduce the heat to low and medium and place the pieces of toasted bread on a baking sheet. Spread blue cheese vinaigrette on the grilled side of each naan.
Garnish each with diced chicken and red onion. Sprinkle with cheddar cheese.
Place the Naan on the grill and cook until the cheese has melted and the bottom is grilled and golden brown, another 5 to 10 minutes. Remove from the grill, cut into pieces and garnish with lettuce and tomato.

363. Portobello Mushroom Pizzas

Preparation Time: 15 minutes
Cooking Time: 10 minutes
Servings: 1

Ingredients:

2 2 ounces Portobello mushroom, stems removed and gills scraped out
1/4 cup Italian tomato sauce
4 ounces reduced fat shredded mozzarella cheese
2 tablespoons shredded basil

Directions:

Preheat the broiler to medium high heat.
Place the mushroom caps on a greased baking sheet lined with foil.
Broil fir 4 minutes until tender.
Spread the tomato sauce into each and top with cheese and basil.
Broil for another 3 minutes.
Nutrition:

364. Reuben Pizza

Preparation Time: 15 minutes
Cooking Time: 40 minutes
Servings: 8

Ingredients:

1 frozen whole meal bread, thawed
1/2 cup thousand island vinaigrette

2 cups of grated Swiss cheese
6 grams of salted beef, sliced
1 cup sauerkraut, rinsed and drained
1/2 teaspoon cumin seeds
1/4 cup chopped dill pickles (optional)

Directions:

Preheat the oven to 190° degrees. Oil a large pizza dish. Roll bread dough on a lightly floured surface into a large circle about 14 inches in diameter.
Transfer to the prepared pizza dish. Build the edges and pierce the center with a fork to not form a dome during cooking. Bake in the preheated oven for 30 minutes or until golden brown.
Spread half the vinaigrette over the hot crust. Sprinkle with half the Swiss cheese. Place the corned beef on the cheese and pour the rest of the vinaigrette.
Cover with sauerkraut and remaining Swiss cheese. Sprinkle with cumin seeds. Bake for another 10 min in the preheated oven until the cheese has melted and the toppings are well heated. Sprinkle with chopped pickle. Let stand for 5 minutes before cutting.

365. Grape Pizza

Preparation Time: 15 minutes
Cooking Time: 10 minutes
Servings: 4

Ingredients:

5 oz flatbread pizza crust
4 oz brie cheese, crumbled
1/3 cup red grapes, halved, seedless
¼ cup fresh arugula, chopped

Directions:

Put the flatbread pizza crust in the baking tray. Then put the halved red grapes on the pizza crust. Sprinkle the grapes with crumbled brie cheese and bake at 400F for 10 minutes.

366. Gorgonzola Pizza

Preparation Time: 15 minutes
Cooking Time: 12 minutes
Servings: 6

Ingredients:

1 pizza crust
2 pears, sliced
5 oz Gorgonzola, crumbled
2 tablespoons cream cheese
½ teaspoon Italian seasonings

Directions:

Spread the pizza crust with cream cheese. Then put the sliced peas on the pizza crust on one layer and sprinkle with gorgonzola and Italian seasonings. Bake the pizza at 400F for 12 minutes.

CHAPTER 6: MEAT RECIPES

367. Moist Shredded Beef

Preparation Time: 10 minutes
Cooking Time: 20 minutes
Servings: 8

Ingredients:

2 lbs. beef chuck roast, cut into chunks
1/2 tbsp dried red pepper
1 tbsp Italian seasoning
1 tbsp garlic, minced
2 tbsp vinegar
14 oz can fire-roasted tomatoes
1/2 cup bell pepper, chopped
1/2 cup carrots, chopped
1 cup onion, chopped
1 tsp salt

Directions:

Add all ingredients into the inner pot of instant pot and set the pot on sauté mode.
Seal pot with lid and cook on high for 20 minutes.
Once done, release pressure using quick release. Remove lid.
Shred the meat using a fork.
Stir well and serve.

368. Hearty Beef Ragu

Preparation Time: 10 minutes
Cooking Time: 50 minutes
Servings: 4

Ingredients:

1 1/2 lbs. beef steak, diced
1 1/2 cup beef stock
1 tbsp coconut amino
14 oz can tomato, chopped
1/2 tsp ground cinnamon
1 tsp dried oregano
1 tsp dried thyme
1 tsp dried basil
1 tsp paprika
1 bay leaf
1 tbsp garlic, chopped
1/2 tsp cayenne pepper
1 celery stick, diced
1 carrot, diced
1 onion, diced
2 tbsp olive oil
1/4 tsp pepper
1 1/2 tsp sea salt

Directions:

Add oil into the instant pot and set the pot on sauté mode.
Add celery, carrots, onion, and salt and sauté for 5 minutes.
Add meat and remaining ingredients and stir everything well.
Seal pot with lid and cook on high for 30 minutes.
Once done, allow to release pressure naturally for 10 minutes then release remaining using quick release. Remove lid.
Shred meat using a fork. Set pot on sauté mode and cook for 10 minutes. Stir every 2-3 minutes.
Serve and enjoy.

369. Dill Beef Brisket

Preparation Time: 10 minutes
Cooking Time: 50 minutes
Servings: 4

Ingredients:

2 1/2 lbs. beef brisket, cut into cubes
2 1/2 cups beef stock
2 tbsp dill, chopped
1 celery stalk, chopped
1 onion, sliced
1 tbsp garlic, minced
Pepper
Salt

Directions:

Add all ingredients into the inner pot of instant pot and stir well.
Seal pot with lid and cook on high for 50 minutes.
Once done, allow to release pressure naturally for 10 minutes then release remaining using quick release. Remove lid.
Serve and enjoy.

370. Tasty Beef Stew

Preparation Time: 10 minutes
Cooking Time: 30 minutes
Servings: 4

Ingredients:

2 1/2 lbs. beef roast, cut into chunks
1 cup beef broth
1/2 cup balsamic vinegar
1 tbsp honey
1/2 tsp red pepper flakes
1 tbsp garlic, minced
Pepper
Salt

Directions:

Add all ingredients into the inner pot of instant pot and stir well.
Seal pot with lid and cook on high for 30 minutes.
Once done, allow to release pressure naturally. Remove lid.
Stir well and serve.

371. Italian Style Ground Beef

Preparation Time: 10 minutes
Cooking Time: 20 minutes
Servings: 4

Ingredients:

2 lbs. ground beef
2 eggs, lightly beaten
1/4 tsp dried basil
3 tbsp olive oil
1/2 tsp dried sage
1 1/2 tsp dried parsley
1 tsp oregano
2 tsp thyme
1 tsp rosemary
Pepper
Salt

Directions:

Pour 1 1/2 cups of water into the instant pot then place the trivet in the pot.
Spray loaf pan with cooking spray.
Add all ingredients into the mixing bowl and mix until well combined.
Transfer meat mixture into the prepared loaf pan and place loaf pan on top of the trivet in the pot.
Seal pot with lid and cook on high for 35 minutes.
Once done, allow to release pressure naturally for 10 minutes then release remaining using quick release. Remove lid.
Serve and enjoy.

372. Flavorful Beef Bourguignon

Preparation Time: 10 minutes
Cooking Time: 20 minutes
Servings: 4

Ingredients:

1 1/2 lbs. beef chuck roast, cut into chunks

2/3 cup beef stock
2 tbsp fresh thyme
1 bay leaf
1 tsp garlic, minced
8 oz mushrooms, sliced
2 tbsp tomato paste
2/3 cup dry red wine
1 onion, sliced
4 carrots, cut into chunks
1 tbsp olive oil
Pepper
Salt

Directions:

Add oil into the instant pot and set the pot on sauté mode.
Add meat and sauté until brown. Add onion and sauté until softened.
Add remaining ingredient and stir well.
Seal pot with lid and cook on high for 12 minutes.
Once done, allow to release pressure naturally. Remove lid.
Stir well and serve.

373. Delicious Beef Chili

Preparation Time: 10 minutes
Cooking Time: 35 minutes
Servings: 8

Ingredients:

2 lbs. ground beef
1 tsp olive oil
1 tsp garlic, minced
1 small onion, chopped
2 tbsp chili powder
1 tsp oregano
1/2 tsp thyme
28 oz can tomato, crushed
2 cups beef stock
2 carrots, chopped
3 sweet potatoes, peeled and cubed
Pepper
Salt

Directions:

Add oil into the instant pot and set the pot on sauté mode.
Add meat and cook until brown.
Add remaining ingredients and stir well.
Seal pot with lid and cook on high for 35 minutes.
Once done, allow to release pressure naturally. Remove lid.
Stir well and serve.

374. Rosemary Creamy Beef

Preparation Time: 10 minutes
Cooking Time: 40 minutes
Servings: 4

Ingredients:

2 lbs. beef stew meat, cubed
2 tbsp fresh parsley, chopped
1 tsp garlic, minced
1/2 tsp dried rosemary
1 tsp chili powder
1 cup beef stock
1 cup heavy cream
1 onion, chopped
1 tbsp olive oil
Pepper
Salt

Directions:

Add oil into the instant pot and set the pot on sauté mode.
Add rosemary, garlic, onion, and chili powder and sauté for 5 minutes.
Add meat and cook for 5 minutes.
Add remaining ingredients and stir well.
Seal pot with lid and cook on high for 30 minutes.
Once done, allow to release pressure naturally for 10 minutes then release remaining using quick release. Remove lid.
Serve and enjoy.

375. Spicy Beef Chili Verde

Preparation Time: 10 minutes
Cooking Time: 23 minutes
Servings: 2

Ingredients:

1/2 lb beef stew meat, cut into cubes
1/4 tsp chili powder
1 tbsp olive oil
1 cup chicken broth
1 Serrano pepper, chopped
1 tsp garlic, minced
1 small onion, chopped
1/4 cup grape tomatoes, chopped
1/4 cup tomatillos, chopped
Pepper
Salt

Directions:

Add oil into the instant pot and set the pot on sauté mode.
Add garlic and onion and sauté for 3 minutes.
Add remaining ingredients and stir well.
Seal pot with lid and cook on high for 20 minutes.
Once done, allow to release pressure naturally. Remove lid.
Stir well and serve.

376. Carrot Mushroom Beef Roast

Preparation Time: 10 minutes
Cooking Time: 40 minutes
Servings: 4

Ingredients:

1 1/2 lbs. beef roast
1 tsp paprika
1/4 tsp dried rosemary
1 tsp garlic, minced
1/2 lb mushrooms, sliced
1/2 cup chicken stock
2 carrots, sliced
Pepper
Salt

Directions:

Add all ingredients into the inner pot of instant pot and stir well.
Seal pot with lid and cook on high for 40 minutes.
Once done, allow to release pressure naturally for 10 minutes then release remaining using quick release. Remove lid.
Slice and serve.

377. Italian Beef Roast

Preparation Time: 10 minutes
Cooking Time: 50 minutes
Servings: 6

Ingredients:

2 1/2 lbs. beef roast, cut into chunks
1 cup chicken broth
1 cup red wine
2 tbsp Italian seasoning
2 tbsp olive oil
1 bell pepper, chopped
2 celery stalks, chopped
1 tsp garlic, minced
1 onion, sliced
Pepper
Salt

Directions:

Add oil into the instant pot and set the pot on sauté mode.
Add the meat into the pot and sauté until brown.
Add onion, bell pepper, and celery and sauté for 5 minutes.
Add remaining ingredients and stir well.

Seal pot with lid and cook on high for 40 minutes.
Once done, allow to release pressure naturally. Remove lid.
Stir well and serve.

378. Thyme Beef Round Roast

Preparation Time: 10 minutes
Cooking Time: 55 minutes
Servings: 8

Ingredients:

4 lbs. beef bottom round roast, cut into pieces
2 tbsp honey
5 fresh thyme sprigs
2 cups red wine
1 lb carrots, cut into chunks
2 cups chicken broth
6 garlic cloves, smashed
1 onion, diced
1/4 cup olive oil
2 lbs. potatoes, peeled and cut into chunks
Pepper
Salt

Directions:

Add all ingredients except carrots and potatoes into the instant pot.
Seal pot with lid and cook on high for 45 minutes.
Once done, release pressure using quick release. Remove lid.
Add carrots and potatoes and stir well.
Seal pot again with lid and cook on high for 10 minutes.
Once done, allow to release pressure naturally. Remove lid.
Stir well and serve.

379. Jalapeno Beef Chili

Preparation Time: 10 minutes
Cooking Time: 40 minutes
Servings: 8

Ingredients:

1 lb ground beef
1 tsp garlic powder
1 jalapeno pepper, chopped
1 tbsp ground cumin
1 tbsp chili powder
1 lb ground pork
4 tomatillos, chopped
1/2 onion, chopped
5 oz tomato paste
Pepper
Salt

Directions:

Add oil into the instant pot and set the pot on sauté mode.
Add beef and pork and cook until brown.
Add remaining ingredients and stir well.
Seal pot with lid and cook on high for 35 minutes.
Once done, allow to release pressure naturally. Remove lid.
Stir well and serve.

380. Beef with Tomatoes

Preparation Time: 10 minutes
Cooking Time: 40 minutes
Servings: 4

Ingredients:

2 lb beef roast, sliced
1 tbsp chives, chopped
1 tsp garlic, minced
1/2 tsp chili powder
2 tbsp olive oil
1 onion, chopped
1 cup beef stock
1 tbsp oregano, chopped
1 cup tomatoes, chopped
Pepper
Salt

Directions:

Add oil into the instant pot and set the pot on sauté mode.
Add garlic, onion, and chili powder and sauté for 5 minutes.
Add meat and cook for 5 minutes.
Add remaining ingredients and stir well.
Seal pot with lid and cook on high for 30 minutes.
Once done, allow to release pressure naturally for 10 minutes then release remaining using quick release. Remove lid.
Stir well and serve.

381. Tasty Beef Goulash

Preparation Time: 10 minutes
Cooking Time: 30 minutes
Servings: 2

Ingredients:

1/2 lb beef stew meat, cubed
1 tbsp olive oil
1/2 onion, chopped
1/2 cup sun-dried tomatoes, chopped
1/4 zucchini, chopped
1/2 cabbage, sliced
1 1/2 tbsp olive oil
2 cups chicken broth
Pepper
Salt

Directions:

Add oil into the instant pot and set the pot on sauté mode.
Add onion and sauté for 3-5 minutes.
Add tomatoes and cook for 5 minutes.
Add remaining ingredients and stir well.
Seal pot with lid and cook on high for 20 minutes.
Once done, allow to release pressure naturally for 10 minutes then release remaining using quick release. Remove lid.
Stir well and serve.

382. Beef & Beans

Preparation Time: 10 minutes
Cooking Time: 30 minutes
Servings: 4

Ingredients:

1 1/2 lbs. beef, cubed
8 oz can tomato, chopped
8 oz red beans, soaked overnight and rinsed
1 tsp garlic, minced
1 1/2 cups beef stock
1/2 tsp chili powder
1 tbsp paprika
2 tbsp olive oil
1 onion, chopped
Pepper
Salt

Directions:

Add oil into the instant pot and set the pot on sauté mode.
Add meat and cook for 5 minutes.
Add garlic and onion and sauté for 5 minutes.
Add remaining ingredients and stir well.
Seal pot with lid and cook on high for 25 minutes.
Once done, allow to release pressure naturally. Remove lid.
Stir well and serve.

383. Delicious Ground Beef

Preparation Time: 10 minutes
Cooking Time: 10 minutes
Servings: 4

Ingredients:

1 lb ground beef
1 tbsp olive oil
1 cup chicken broth
2 tbsp tomato paste
1 tbsp Italian seasoning
12 oz cheddar cheese, shredded
Salt
Pepper

Directions:

Add oil into the instant pot and set the pot on sauté mode.
Add meat and cook until browned.
Add remaining ingredients except for cheese and stir well.
Seal pot with lid and cook on high for 7 minutes.
Once done, release pressure using quick release. Remove lid.
Add cheese and stir well and cook on sauté mode until cheese is melted.
Serve and enjoy.

384. Bean Beef Chili

Preparation Time: 10 minutes
Cooking Time: 40 minutes
Servings: 4

Ingredients:

1 lb ground beef
1/2 onion, diced
1 tsp chili powder
1 tsp garlic, chopped
14 oz can black beans, rinsed and drained
14 oz can red beans, rinsed and drained
1/2 jalapeno pepper, minced
1/2 bell pepper, chopped
1 cup chicken broth
Pepper
Salt

Directions:

Set instant pot on sauté mode.
Add meat and sauté until brown.
Add remaining ingredients and stir well.
Seal pot with lid and cook on high for 35 minutes.
Once done, release pressure using quick release. Remove lid.
Stir well and serve.

385. Garlic Caper Beef Roast

Preparation Time: 10 minutes
Cooking Time: 40 minutes
Servings: 4

Ingredients:

2 lbs. beef roast, cubed
1 tbsp fresh parsley, chopped
1 tbsp garlic, minced
1/2 tsp dried rosemary
1 onion, chopped
1 tbsp olive oil
1 tbsp capers, chopped
1 cup chicken stock
1/2 tsp ground cumin
Salt
Pepper

Directions:

Add oil into the instant pot and set the pot on sauté mode.
Add garlic and onion and sauté for 5 minutes.
Add meat and cook until brown.
Add remaining ingredients and stir well.
Seal pot with lid and cook on high for 30 minutes.
Once done, allow to release pressure naturally. Remove lid.
Stir well and serve.

386. Cauliflower Tomato Beef

Preparation Time: 10 minutes
Cooking Time: 25 minutes
Servings: 2

Ingredients:

1/2 lb beef stew meat, chopped
1 tsp paprika
1 celery stalk, chopped
1 tbsp balsamic vinegar
1/4 cup grape tomatoes, chopped
1 onion, chopped
1/4 cup cauliflower, chopped
1 tbsp olive oil
Pepper
Salt

Directions:

Add oil into the instant pot and set the pot on sauté mode.
Add meat and sauté for 5 minutes.
Add remaining ingredients and stir well.
Seal pot with lid and cook on high for 20 minutes.
Once done, allow to release pressure naturally. Remove lid.
Stir and serve.

387. Dinner Party Brisket

Preparation Time: 15 minutes
Cooking Time: 11 hours 5 minutes
Serves: 8

Ingredients:

1 fresh beef brisket, trimmed
3 tsp. dried Italian seasoning, crushed and divided
1 can diced tomatoes with basil, garlic and oregano with juice
1/2 C. olives, pitted
1 tsp. lemon peel, grated finely
Pinch salt and freshly ground black pepper, to taste
1/2 C. low-sodium beef broth
2 medium fennel bulbs, trimmed, cored and cut into wedges
2 tbsp. all-purpose flour
1/4 C. cold water

Directions:

Season the brisket with 1 tsp. of the Italian seasoning.
In a bowl, add the remaining Italian seasoning, tomatoes with juice, olives, lemon peel, salt, black pepper and broth and mix well.
In a slow cooker, place the brisket and top with fennel, followed by the tomato mixture.
Set the slow cooker on "Low" and cook, covered for about 10-11 hours.
Uncover the slow cooker and with a slotted spoon, transfer the brisket and vegetables onto a platter.
With a piece of foil, cover the meat to keep warm.
Skim off the fat from the top of cooking liquid.
In a small pan, add about 2 C. of the cooking liquid over medium heat.
In a small bowl, dissolve the flour in water.
In the pan of cooking liquid, add the flour mixture, stirring continuously.
Cook for about 2-3 minutes or until desired thickness of sauce, stirring continuously.
Cut the brisket into desired sized slices and serve with the topping of gravy.

388. Sunday Dinner Brisket

Preparation Time: 10 minutes
Cooking Time: 8 hours 10 minutes
Servings: 6

Ingredients:

2 1/2 lb. beef brisket, trimmed
Salt and freshly ground black pepper, to taste
2 tsp. olive oil
2 medium onions, chopped
2 large garlic cloves, sliced
1 tbsp. Herbs de Provence
1 (15-oz.) can diced tomatoes, drained
2 tsp. Dijon mustard
1 C. dry red wine

Directions:

Season the brisket with salt and black pepper evenly.
In a non-stick skillet, heat the oil over medium heat and cook the brisket for about 4-5 minutes per side.

Transfer the brisket into a slow cooker.
Add the remaining ingredients and stir to combine.
Set the slow cooker on "Low" and cook, covered for about 8 hours.
Uncover the slow cooker and with a slotted spoon, transfer the brisket onto a platter.
Cut the brisket into desired sized slices and serve with the topping of pan sauce.

389. Fall-Apart Tender Beef

Preparation Time: 10 minutes
Cooking Time: 11 hours
Serves: 12

Ingredients:

4 lb. boneless beef chuck roast, trimmed
2 large onions, sliced into thin strips
4 celery stalks, sliced
4 garlic cloves, minced
1 1/2 C. catsup
1 C. BBQ sauce
1/4 C. molasses
1/4 C. apple cider vinegar
2 tbsp. prepared yellow mustard
1/4 tsp. red chili powder
Fresh ground black pepper, to taste

Directions:

In a slow cooker, place all the ingredients and stir to combine.
Set the slow cooker on "Low" and cook, covered for about 8-10 hours.
Uncover the slow cooker and with 2 forks, shred the meat.
Stir the meat with pan sauce.
Set the slow cooker on "Low" and cook, covered for about 1 hour.
Serve hot.

390. Deliciously Simple Beef

Preparation Time: 10 minutes
Cooking Time: 10 hours
Servings: 4

Ingredients:

1 large onion, sliced thinly
1/4 C. extra-virgin olive oil
1 tbsp. garlic, minced
1 tsp. dried oregano
Salt and freshly ground black pepper, to taste
2 tbsp. fresh lemon juice
2 lb. beef chuck roast, cut into bite-sized pieces

Directions:

In a slow cooker, place all the ingredients except for beef cubes and stir to combine.
Add the beef cubes and stir to combine.
Set the slow cooker on "Low" and cook, covered for about 8-10 hours.
Serve hot.

391. Excellent Beef Meal

Preparation Time: 15 minutes
Cooking Time: 7 hours 4 minutes
Servings: 6

Ingredients:

1 tbsp. vegetable oil
2 lb. beef stew meat
1 can artichoke hearts
1 onion
4 garlic cloves
1 container beef broth
1 can tomato sauce
1 can diced tomatoes with juice
1/2 C. Kalamata olives, pitted
1 tsp. dried oregano
1 tsp. dried basil
1 tsp. dried parsley
1 bay leaf, crumbled
1/2 tsp. ground cumin

Directions:

In a skillet, heat the oil over medium-high heat and cook the beef for about 2 minutes per side.
Transfer the beef into a slow cooker and top with artichoke hearts, followed by the onion and garlic.
Place the remaining ingredients on top.
Set the slow cooker on "Low" and cook, covered for about 7 hours.
Serve hot.

392. Lebanese Beef and Green Beans

Preparation Time: 15 minutes
Cooking Time: 4 hours
Servings: 4

Ingredients:

1 lb. beef stew meat, cubed
1 lb. fresh green beans, trimmed and cut in 2-inch pieces
1 medium onion, chopped
1 can crushed tomatoes
1 tbsp. ground cinnamon
Salt and freshly ground black pepper, to taste
1/4 C. fresh parsley, chopped

Directions:

In a slow cooker, place all the ingredients except for parsley and stir to combine.
Set the slow cooker on "High" and cook, covered for about 4 hours.
Serve hot with the garnishing of parsley.

393. Grandma Style Meatballs

Preparation Time: 20 minutes
Cooking Time: 8 hours
Servings: 4

Ingredients:

For Meatballs:
1 lb. ground beef
1/4 C. fresh parsley, minced
1/4 C. plain breadcrumbs
1 tbsp. olive oil
1/2 tsp. ground allspice
1/2 tsp. ground cinnamon
1/2 tsp. ground cumin
1/4 tsp. cayenne pepper
Salt and freshly ground black pepper, to taste
For Veggie Sauce:
2 cans diced tomatoes
1 can tomato sauce
1 tsp. ground cumin
1 tsp. ground cinnamon
1/4 tsp. cayenne pepper
Pinch of salt and freshly ground black pepper
1 lb. frozen green beans
1/2 of sweet onion, chopped
2 garlic cloves, minced
2 tbsp. fresh parsley, chopped

Directions:

For meatballs: in a large bowl, add all the ingredients and mix until well combined.
Make 1-inch sized meatballs from the mixture.
For sauce: in a slow cooker, place the diced tomatoes, tomato sauce and spices and stir to combine.
Add the green beans, onions and garlic and stir to combine.
Place the meatballs and gently submerge into the sauce.
Set the slow cooker on "Low" and cook, covered for about 8 hours.
Serve hot with the garnishing of parsley.

394. World's Best Lasagna

Preparation Time: 15 minutes
Cooking Time: 6 hours
Servings: 4

Ingredients:

1 lb. lean ground beef

1 medium onion, chopped
1 jar pasta sauce
3-5 fresh basil leaves, chopped
Salt, to taste
2 C. mozzarella cheese, shredded and divided
1 C. Parmesan cheese, shredded
15 oz. part-skim ricotta cheese
15 uncooked lasagna noodles

Directions:

Heat a non-stick skillet over medium heat and cook the beef and onion for about 8-10 minutes.
Drain the grease from skillet.
In the skillet, add the pasta sauce, basil and salt and stir to combine.
Remove from the heat and set aside.
In a bowl, add 1 C. of the mozzarella, Parmesan and ricotta cheese and mix.
In a slow cooker, place ¼ of the beef mixture evenly and arrange 5 noodles on top, breaking them to fit in the pot.
Place half of the cheese mixture on top of the noodles.
Repeat the layer twice, ending with ¼ of the beef mixture.
Set the slow cooker on "Low" and cook, covered for about 4-6 hours.
In the last 20 minutes of cooking, sprinkle the lasagna with remaining mozzarella cheese.
Serve hot.

395. Rustic Lamb Shanks

Preparation Time: 15 minutes
Cooking Time: 4 1/4 hours
Servings: 6

Ingredients:

6 lamb shanks, frenched
1/4 C. flour
3 tbsp. olive oil, divided
2 onions, sliced
4 garlic cloves, sliced thinly
1 (14-oz.) can marinated artichoke hearts
3/4 C. Kalamata olives, pitted
2 tbsp. lemon rind, grated
1 tbsp. fresh oregano, chopped
Salt and freshly ground black pepper, to taste
1/2 C. white wine
2 1/2 C. chicken broth

Directions:

In a large plastic bag, place the lamb shanks and flour.
Seal the bag and shake to coat.
In a pan, heat 2 tbsp. of the oil and sear the lamb shanks in 2 batches for about 4-5 minutes or until browned completely.
With a slotted spoon, transfer the shanks onto a platter.
In the same pan, heat the remaining oil over medium heat and sauté the onions and garlic for about 4-5 minutes.
Remove from the heat.
In a slow cooker, place the lamb shanks and onion mixture.
Top with the remaining ingredients and stir to combine.
Set the slow cooker on "High" and cook, covered for about 4 hours.
Serve hot.

396. Holiday Feast Lamb Shanks

Preparation Time: 15 minutes
Cooking Time: 8 hours 5 minutes
Servings: 4

Ingredients:

4 lamb shanks
Salt and freshly ground black pepper, to taste
1 tbsp. olive oil
1 lb. baby potatoes, halved
1 C. Kalamata olives
1 (3-oz.) jar sun-dried tomatoes
1 C. chicken broth
3 tbsp. fresh lemon juice
2 1/2 tsp. dried oregano
1 tsp. dried rosemary
1 tsp. dried basil
1 tsp. onion powder

Directions:

Season the lamb shanks with salt and black pepper evenly.
In a large heavy-bottomed skillet, heat the olive oil over medium-high heat and sear the lamb shanks for about 4-5 minutes or until browned completely.
Remove from the heat.
In a slow cooker, place the potatoes, olives, sun-dried tomatoes, salt, black place the lamb on top and sprinkle with dried herbs and onion powder.
Set the slow cooker on "Low" and cook, covered for about 8 hours.
Serve hot.

397. Succulent Leg of Lamb

Preparation Time: 15 minutes
Cooking Time: 4 hours 8 minutes
Servings: 8

Ingredients:

1 (3-lb.) boneless leg of lamb, trimmed
Salt and freshly ground black pepper, to taste
5 tbsp. extra-virgin olive oil, divided
6 garlic cloves, sliced thinly
2 tbsp. fresh lemon juice
6 garlic cloves, minced
2 tsp. fresh thyme
2 tsp. dried rosemary
1 tsp. dried oregano
3/4 tsp. sweet paprika
1 lb. pearl onions, peeled
1 C. dry red wine
1/2 C. low-sodium beef broth

Directions:

Season the leg of lamb with salt and black pepper generously.
Set aside at room temperature for up to 1 hour.
In a large skillet, heat 2 tbsp. of the oil over medium heat and sear the lamb for about 7-8 minutes or until browned completely.
Remove from the heat and set aside to cool slightly.
With a sharp knife, cut slits into the lamb on both sides.
Insert 1 garlic slice in each slit.
In a small bowl, add the remaining oil, lemon juice, minced garlic, herbs and paprika and mix well.
Coat the leg of lamb with oil mixture evenly.
In a slow cooker, place the pearl onions, wine and broth.
Arrange the leg of lamb on top.
Set the slow cooker on "High" and cook, covered for about 3-4 hours.
Uncover the slow cooker and with 2 tongs, transfer the leg of lamb onto a serving platter.
Top with pan juices and serve.

398. Melt-in-Mouth Lamb Shoulder

Preparation Time: 10 minutes
Cooking Time: 5 hours 10 minutes
Servings: 8

Ingredients:

3 1/4 lb. bone-in lamb shoulder, trimmed
2 brown onions, sliced thinly
5-6 garlic cloves
1/4 C. beef broth
1/4 C. olive oil
1 tbsp. dried thyme
Salt and freshly ground black pepper, to taste

Directions:

Heat a large cast-iron skillet over medium-high heat and sear the lamb

shoulder for about 4-5 minutes per side.
Remove from the heat.
In a slow cooker, place the onion slices and garlic evenly and arrange the lamb shoulder on top.
Place the remaining ingredients on top.
Set the slow cooker on "High" and cook, covered for about 4-5 hours.
Uncover the slow cooker and with a slotted spoon, transfer the lamb shoulder onto a platter.
Cut the lamb shoulder into desired sized slices and serve with the topping of pan sauce.

399. Tangy Lamb Loin

Preparation Time: 15 minutes
Cooking Time: 6 hours 5 minutes
Servings: 8

Ingredients:

2 lb. lamb loin, rolled
6 garlic cloves, sliced thinly
1 bunch fresh rosemary
3 tbsp. olive oil
2 1/4 lb. potatoes, peeled and cubed
1/2 C. dry white wine
1/2 C. fresh lemon juice

Directions:

With a sharp knife, cut slits into the lamb on both sides.
Insert 1 garlic slice in each slit.
In a large skillet, heat the oil over medium-high heat and sear the lamb loin for about 4-5 minutes or until browned from all sides.
Remove from the heat and insert the rosemary into the slits with garlic.
In the bottom of a slow cooker, place the potatoes, followed by 2 rosemary stalks and lamb loin.
Place the wine and lemon juice on top.
Set the slow cooker on "Low" and cook, covered for about 6 hours.
Uncover the slow cooker and with a slotted spoon, transfer the lamb loin onto a platter.
Cut the lamb loin into desired sized slices and serve alongside the potatoes.

400. Spiced Moroccan Lamb Chops

Preparation Time: 10 minutes
Cooking Time: 4 hours
Servings: 4

Ingredients:

2 lb. lamb shoulder chops
2 tbsp. Moroccan spice rub
¼ lb. carrots, chopped
¼ C. onion, sliced
¼ C. fresh mint, chopped
¼ C. low-sodium chicken broth

Directions:

Rub the lamb chops with spice rub generously.
In a slow cooker, place all the ingredients and stir to combine.
Set the slow cooker on "High" and cook, covered for about 3-4 hours.
Serve hot.

401. Chilly Spring Night Chops

Preparation Time: 15 minutes
Cooking Time: 6 hours 5 minutes
Servings: 4

Ingredients:

1 C. dry white wine
1/4 C. butter, melted
2 tbsp. tomato paste
2 lb. lamb shoulder-blade chops
1 tbsp. fresh thyme, chopped
Salt and freshly ground black pepper, to taste
1 tbsp. extra-virgin olive oil
1 large onion, sliced thinly
2 jars marinated artichokes, drained
1/2 C. peas

Directions:

In a bowl, add the wine, butter and tomato paste and beat until well combined. Set aside.
Rub the chops with thyme, salt and black pepper evenly.
In a non-stick skillet, heat the oil over medium-high heat and sear the chops for about 4-5 minutes or until browned completely.
Remove from the heat and place the chops in a slow cooker.
Place onion slices over chops and top with wine mixture, followed by the, artichokes.
Set the slow cooker on "Low" and cook, covered for about 6 hours.
In the last 30 minutes of cooking, stir in the peas.
Serve hot.

402. Favorite Lamb Pitas

Preparation Time: 20 minutes
Cooking Time: 4 hours
Servings: 4

Ingredients:

For Meatballs:
1 lb. ground lamb
3/4 C. fresh breadcrumbs
1 large egg, beaten lightly
1/4 C. onion, chopped finely
1 tsp. dried mint leaves
1 tsp. dried oregano
Salt and freshly ground black pepper, to taste
3/4 C. chicken broth
For Yogurt Sauce:
1/4 C. plain Greek yogurt
1/4 C. cucumber, seeded and chopped finely
1 tsp. dried mint leaves
For Servings:
2 pita breads, halved
4 tbsp. feta cheese, crumbled

Directions:

For meatballs: in a large bowl, add all the ingredients except for broth and mix until well combined.
Make 16 equal-sized meatballs from the mixture.
In a slow cooker, place the meatballs and top with the broth.
Set the slow cooker on "Low" and cook, covered for about 4 hours.
Uncover the slow cooker and drain the cooked meatballs.
Meanwhile, for yogurt sauce: in a bowl, add all the ingredients and mix well.
Arrange the pita halves onto the serving plates.
Place about 4 meatballs into each pita half and top with 2 tbsp. of yogurt sauce and 1 tbsp. of the feta cheese.
Serve immediately.

403. Greek Spiced Pork Souvlaki

Preparation Time: 10 minutes
Cooking Time: 8 hours
Serves: 5

Ingredients:

1/4 C. olive oil
1/4 C. fresh lemon juice
2 tbsp. red wine vinegar
1 tbsp. dried oregano
1 tbsp. dried mint
1 tbsp. za'atar
1 tbsp. garlic powder
1 tsp. chili flakes
Salt, to taste
2 lb. boneless pork shoulder, cubed

Directions:

In a medium bowl, add all the ingredients except for pork shoulder and mix well.

In the bottom of a slow cooker, place the pork shoulder and top with oil mixture.
Set the slow cooker on "Low" and cook, covered for about 8 hours.
Uncover the slow cooker and with 2 forks, shred the meat.
With a spoon, mix the meat with pan juices and serve.

404. Lovely Smelling Pork Loin

Preparation Time: 10 minutes
Cooking Time: 8 hours
Servings: 8

Ingredients:

2 tbsp. olive oil
3/4 C. chicken broth
1/2 tbsp. paprika
1/2 tbsp. garlic powder
2¼ tsp. dried sage
1 tsp. dried basil
1 tsp. dried oregano
1/4 tsp. dried marjoram
1/4 tsp. dried rosemary
1/4 tsp. dried thyme
2½ lb. boneless pork loin, trimmed

Directions:

In a medium bowl, add all the ingredients except for pork loin and mix well.
In the bottom of a slow cooker, place the pork loin and top with oil mixture.
Set the slow cooker on "Low" and cook, covered for about 7-8 hours.
Uncover the slow cooker and with 2 forks, shred the meat.
With a spoon, mix the meat with pan juices and serve.

405. Elegant Pork Loin

Preparation Time: 15 minutes
Cooking Time: 6 hours 5 minutes
Servings: 8

Ingredients:

1 (3-lb.) boneless pork loin roast, trimmed
4 tsp. Greek seasoning
2 fennel bulbs, trimmed and sliced
4 plum tomatoes, chopped
1/3 C. plus 2 tbsp. low-sodium chicken broth, divided
Salt and freshly ground black pepper, to taste
2 tbsp. cornstarch
1½ tsp. Worcestershire sauce
¼ C. black olives, pitted and chopped

Directions:

Rub the pork loin with 1 tsp. of the Greek seasoning evenly.
In the bottom of a slow cooker, place the fennel slices and top with pork loin.
Arrange the tomatoes around the pork.
Top with 1/3 C. of the broth, followed by remaining Greek seasoning, salt and black pepper.
Set the slow cooker on "Low" and cook, covered for about 6 hours.
Meanwhile, in a small bowl, dissolve the cornstarch in remaining broth and Worcestershire sauce.
Uncover the slow cooker and with a slotted spoon, transfer the pork onto a platter.
With a piece, cover the pork to keep warm.
Through a strainer, strain the cooking liquid into a small pan.
Place the pan over medium-high heat and bring to a boil.
Add the cornstarch mixture, beating continuously until well combined.
Cook for about 1 minute, stirring continuously.
Remove from the heat and pour the sauce over pork.
Garnish with olives and serve.

406. Zero-Fussing Pork Meal

Preparation Time: 20 minutes
Cooking Time: 6 hours
Servings: 4

Ingredients:

1 lb. lean pork, cut into bite-sized cubes
2 potatoes, peeled and quartered
1 lb. fresh green beans
2 carrots, peeled and sliced thinly
2 celery stalks, sliced thinly
1 large onion, chopped
3 fresh tomatoes, grated
½ C. extra-virgin olive oil
1 tsp. dried thyme
Salt and freshly ground black pepper, to taste

Directions:

In a slow cooker, place all the ingredients and stir to combine.
Set the slow cooker on "High" and cook, covered for about 6 hours.
Serve hot.

407. Grilled Steak

Preparation Time: 10 minutes
Cooking Time: 20 minutes
Servings: 2

Ingredients

2 steaks
1 c. spinach, chopped
1 tbsp. olive oil
2 tbsps. red onions, diced
2 tbsps. feta cheese, crumbled
2 tbsps. panko breadcrumbs
1 tbsp. diced sun-dried tomato
Salt and pepper

Directions:

Preheat grill to medium-high heat.
Use a skillet to sauté the onions in the olive oil for 5 minutes.
Add the remaining ingredients, except the steaks, and stir for 2 minutes. Take off the stove and let sit.
Grill the steaks to the desired doneness.
Top each steak with the spinach mix. Cook in the broiler until the top turns brown.

408. Spicy Roasted Leg of Lamb

Preparation Time: 30 minutes
Cooking Time: 2 hours
Servings: 4

Ingredients

for the Lamb:
1 lb./450 g. leg of lamb, bone-in
Salt and pepper
3 tbsps. olive oil
5 sliced garlic cloves
2 c. water
4 cubed potatoes
1 onion, chopped
1 tsp. garlic powder
for the Lamb Spice Rub:
15 peeled garlic cloves
3 tbsps. oregano
2 tbsps. mint
1 tbsp. paprika
½ c. olive oil
¼ c. lemon juice

Directions:

Allow the lamb to rest for 1 hour at room temperature.
While you wait, put all of the spice rub ingredients in a food processor and blend. Refrigerate the rub.
Make a few cuts in the lamb using a knife. Season with salt and pepper.
Place on a roasting pan.

Heat the broiler and broil for 5 minutes on each side so the whole thing is seared. Place the lamb on the counter and set the oven temperature to 375°F/190°C.
Let the lamb cool, then fill the cuts with the garlic slices and cover with the spice rub.
To the roasting pan, set in 2 cups of water.
Sprinkle the potatoes and onions with the garlic powder, salt, and pepper. Arrange them around the leg of lamb.
Add oil to the top of lamb and vegetables.
Use aluminum foil to cover the roasting pan and place it back in the oven.
Roast the lamb for 1 hour.
Discard the foil and roast for 15 more minutes.
Let the leg of lamb sit for 20 minutes before serving.

409. Dijon & Herb Pork Tenderloin

Preparation Time: 1hr
Cooking Time: 30 minutes
Servings: 6

Ingredients

½ c. freshly chopped Italian parsley leaves,
3 tbsps. fresh rosemary leaves, chopped
3 tbsps. fresh thyme leaves, chopped
3 tbsps. Dijon mustard
1 tbsp. extra-virgin olive oil
4 garlic cloves, minced
½ tsp. sea salt
¼ tsp. freshly ground black pepper
1½ lbs./680 g. pork tenderloin

Directions:

Preheat the oven to 400°F/204°C.
In a blender or food processor, combine the parsley, rosemary, thyme, mustard, olive oil, garlic, sea salt, and pepper. Process for about 30 seconds until smooth.
Spread the mixture evenly over the pork and place it on a rimmed baking sheet.
Bake for about 20 minutes, or until the meat reaches an internal temperature of 140°F/60°C.
Allow to rest for 10 minutes before slicing and serving.
Nutritional: Calories 393 Total fat 12 g Sat. fat 4 g Carbs 5 g Fiber 3 g Sugars 1 g Protein 74 g Sodium 617 mg

410. Greek Meatballs (Keftedes)

Preparation Time: 20 minutes
Cooking Time: 25 minutes
Servings: 4

Ingredients

2 whole-wheat bread slices
1¼ lbs./560 g. ground turkey
1 egg
¼ c. whole-wheat bread crumbs, seasoned
3 minced garlic cloves
¼ red onion, grated
¼ c. chopped fresh Italian parsley leaves
2 tbsps. chopped fresh mint leaves
2 tbsps. chopped fresh oregano leaves
½ tsp. sea salt
¼ tsp. freshly ground black pepper
Water as needed

Directions:

Set your oven to preheat at 350°F/176°C.
Set a parchment paper on a baking sheet.
Run the bread under water to wet it, and squeeze out any excess. Tear the wet bread into small pieces and place it in a medium bowl.
Add the turkey and all the other ingredients to the same bowl and mix well.
Form the mixture into ¼-cup-size balls. Place the meatballs on the prepared sheet and bake for about 25 minutes, or until the internal temperature reaches 165°F/74°F.

411. Lamb with String Beans

Preparation Time: 45 minutes
Cooking Time: 1 hour
Servings: 4

Ingredients

¼ c. extra-virgin olive oil, divided
6 lamb chops, trim excess fat
1 tsp. sea salt, divided
½ tsp. freshly ground black pepper
2 tbsps. tomato paste
1½ c. hot water
1 lb./450 g. green beans, trimmed and halved crosswise
1 onion, chopped
2 tomatoes, chopped

Directions:

Over medium-high source off heat, set a large skillet in place. Heat half of olive oil until it shimmers.
Season the lamb chops with ½ teaspoon of sea salt and 1/8 teaspoon of pepper. Cook the lamb in the hot oil for about 4 minutes per side until browned on both sides. Set aside on a platter.
Return the skillet to the heat and add the remaining 2 tablespoons of olive oil. Heat until it shimmers.
Using a separate bowl, mix tomato paste and hot water. Add it to the hot skillet along with the green beans, onion, tomatoes, and the remaining sea salt and pepper. Bring to a simmer, using the side of a spoon to scrape and fold in any browned bits at the bottom.
Return the lamb chops to the pan. Bring to a boil and reduce the heat to medium-low. Simmer for 45 minutes until the beans are soft, adding additional water as needed to adjust the thickness of the sauce.

412. Pork Tenderloin with Mediterranean Quinoa Salad

Preparation Time: 30 minutes
Cooking Time: 2 hours 15 minutes
Servings: 4

Ingredients

¼ c. extra virgin olive oil
½ tsp. kosher salt
¼ tsp. freshly ground black pepper
1½ lbs./675 g. pork tenderloin
1 c. chicken broth or water
4 garlic cloves
Salt and pepper
1 c. quinoa
2 tbsps. Apple cider vinegar
½ c. minced parsley
½ c. dried cranberries
½ c. sliced almonds

Directions:

At the bottom of your cooker's pan, set in the chicken broth.
Season and pat the pork tenderloin with salt, pepper and half of the garlic then transfer into the slow cooker.
Cook about 2 hours on low or until the meat thermometer reads 160 degrees. Then pull the pork out of the slow cooker and place it on a cutting board.
Pour the liquid into a liquid measuring cup and pour back into the slow cooker 1 cup of the liquid. Add in the quinoa and cook on high for around 15 minutes or until the quinoa is cooked and fluffy.
Add the cranberries and almonds and mix.
In a bowl, mix oil, vinegar, ½ tsp. salt, and ¼ tsp. pepper, the rest of the garlic

and the parsley. Whisk until the vinaigrette is well combined.
Slice the tenderloin and serve with the quinoa.
Drizzle the vinaigrette over both.

413. Quinoa Chicken Fingers

Preparation Time: 10 minutes
Cooking Time: 10 minutes
Servings: 6

Ingredients:

2 lbs./900 g. sliced chicken breasts
2 egg whites
1½ c. quinoa, cooked
½ c. breadcrumbs
2 tbsps. olive oil
Salt, black pepper, paprika

Directions:

Season chicken with salt, pepper, and paprika.
Dip the chicken in the broken egg mix, then coat with quinoa and breadcrumbs.
Cook the chicken in oil for 5 minutes on each side.

414. Grilled Lamb Gyro Burger

Preparation Time: 15 minutes
Cooking Time: 12 minutes
Servings: 2

Ingredients:

4 oz./115 g. lean ground lamb
4 naan flatbread or pita
2 tbsps. olive oil
2 tbsps. tzatziki sauce
1 red onion, thinly sliced
1 tomato, sliced
1 bunch lettuce, separated

Directions:

Grill meat for 10 minutes.
Toast naan bread, and drizzle with olive oil.
Top two of the halves of naan bread with meat and the rest ingredients.
Cover with other halves and enjoy!

415. Pork Loin & Orzo

Preparation Time: 20 minutes
Cooking Time: 30 minutes
Servings: 4

Ingredients:

1 lb./450 g. pork tenderloin
1 tsp. coarsely ground pepper
1 tsp. kosher salt
2 tbsps. olive oil
1 c. uncooked orzo pasta
Water as needed
2 c. spinach
1 c. cherry tomatoes
¾ c. crumbled feta cheese

Directions:

Coat the pork loin with the kosher salt and black pepper and massage it into the meat. Then cut the meat into one-inch cubes.
Heat the olive oil in a cast-iron skillet over medium heat until sizzling hot. Cook the pork for about 8 minutes until there's no pink left.
Cook the orzo in water according to package directions (adding a pinch of salt to the water).
Stir in the spinach and tomatoes and add the cooked pork.
Top with feta and serve.

416. Lamb Chops

Preparation Time: 10 minutes
Cooking Time: 20 minutes
Servings: 4

Ingredients:

4 oz./115 g. trimmed lamb rib chops
4 tbsps. olive oil
1 tbsp. kosher salt
½ tsp. black pepper
3 tbsps. Balsamic vinegar
Non-stick cooking spray

Directions:

Mix one tablespoon of oil with the rind and juice into a Ziploc-type bag. Add the chops and coat well. Marinate at room temperature ten minutes.
Remove it from the bag and season with the pepper and salt.
Using the med-high heat setting; coat a pan with the spray. Add the lamb and cook two minutes per side until it's the way you like it.
Using a saucepan, pour in the vinegar (med-high) and cook until it's syrupy or about three minutes.
Drizzle the vinegar and rest of oil (1 teaspoon) over the lamb.
Serve with your favorite sides.

417. Roasted Lamb with Vegetables

Preparation Time: 20 minutes
Cooking Time: 1 hour
Servings: 4

Ingredients:

1 lb./450 g. lamb leg shanks
½ tbsp. dried Italian seasoning
¼ tsp. salt
¼ tsp. black pepper
2 tbsps. olive oil
1 cloves garlic
1 onion
2 carrots
1 potato
2 apples
2 rosemary sprigs

Directions:

Season the lamb shanks with Italian seasoning, salt, and fresh ground black pepper.
Preheat oven to 370°F/190°C.
Place lamb into the greased baking dish, cover with a foil and bake it for 40 minutes.
Meanwhile, in medium heat pan, sauté the garlic and onion in olive oil.
Add the carrots and potatoes, and sauté for another 3-5 minutes.
Transfer vegetables to the baking dish around the lamb and add the apples.
Bake the lamb with vegetables for another 20 minutes without foil until golden brown outside and tender inside.
Garnish with fresh rosemary.

418. Pan-Fried Pork Chops with Orange Sauce

Preparation Time: 10 minutes
Cooking Time: 20 minutes
Servings: 8

Ingredients:

2 lbs./900 g. lean pork chops
¾ tsp. salt
½ tsp. black pepper
2 tbsp. olive oil
1 clove garlic
½ c. orange juice
1 orange

Directions:

Apply black pepper and salt to the pork chops.

In a medium heat pan, sauté the garlic in olive oil.
Add the pork chops and sear it on both sides until tender and golden brown. Remove fried pork chops from the pan and set aside.
In the same pan, pour the orange juice. Let it simmer for 4 minutes until the sauce thickens.
In a serving plate, place the pork chops with orange sauce and orange wedges.

419. Beef Spicy Salsa Braised Ribs

Preparation Time: 30 minutes
Cooking Time: 4 hours
Servings: 12

Ingredients:

6 lbs./2.7 kg. beef ribs
4 diced tomatoes
2 chopped jalapenos
2 chopped shallots
1 c. chopped parsley
½ c. chopped cilantro
3 tbsps. Olive oil
2 tbsps. Balsamic vinegar
1 tsp. Worcestershire sauce
Salt and pepper

Directions:

Combine all the ingredients except the beef ribs.
Set in the ribs and cover with aluminum foil.
Cook in the preheated oven at 300F/150C for 3 1/3 hours.
Serve the ribs warm.

420. Chargrilled Mediterranean Beef Lasagna

Preparation Time: 25 minutes
Cooking Time: 55 minutes
Servings: 4

Ingredients

1 tbsp butter
1 tbsp sunflower oil
100 g frozen diced onion
2 cloves of garlic
500 g frozen ground beef
3 tbsp tomato paste
400 g diced tomatoes
100 ml of water hot
1 cube of beef stock
1 bay leaf
1 teaspoon of frozen basil
1 teaspoon of frozen oregano
80 g cheddar cheese
1 tbsp butter (for the sauce)
50 g cheddar cheese and Grana Padang (for the top)
Dried lasagna sheets
500 g frozen grilled Mediterranean vegetables

Directions

Preheat the oven to 180 C and lightly grease a 1.2-liter frying pan.
Heat oil and butter in a large skillet or saucepan over medium heat and gently fry the onions until they thaw and soften.
Add the ground beef and season with salt and pepper. Fry until completely brown.
Stir in the tomato paste and cook for a few more minutes. Add the canned tomatoes, herbs, stock cube, and hot water mix well, reduce the temperature and simmer over medium heat for about 10 minutes.
For the sauce, heat the butter in a medium saucepan until it starts to bubble slightly. Stir in the flour and cook, constantly stirring, for one minute. Remove from heat, whisk in milk until combined, and return to heat, occasionally stirring, while the mixture thickens. When the mixture has thickened, remove from heat and stir in 80 grams of the cheddar cheese. Put aside.
Before assembling, place a spoonful of sauce on the bottom of an oven dish. Finish with a layer of dried lasagna sheets. Spoon the remaining beef mixture over the pasta and drizzle with some Grana Padano cheese.
Add another layer of lasagna sheet and top with the frozen grilled Mediterranean vegetables. Finish with more lasagna sheets. Spoon the cheese sauce over it until the last layer of pasta is completely covered.
Sprinkle with the remaining cheddar and Grana Padang and bake in a preheated 190 C oven for 35-40 minutes, or until the top is golden and bubbly.

421. Beef Cacciatore (Italy)

Preparation Time: 20 minutes
Cooking Time: 35 minutes
Servings: 4

Ingredients

1-pound beef, thinly sliced
Buy Now 1/4 cup extra virgin olive oil
1 onion, chopped
2 red peppers, chopped
1 orange bell pepper, chopped
pepper and salt to taste
1 cup of tomato sauce
Your choice of pasta (regular or gluten-free), cooked or prepared rice

Directions

Add olive oil to a pan, heat over medium heat, and then add meat and brown well. Add onions and sauté for 1 minute. Add peppers and cook for 2 minutes. Add tomato sauce and salt and pepper to taste.
Bring to boil. Cover and cook until meat is tendered, about 40 minutes.
Remove most of the sauce with the peppers (leave the meat in the pan) and puree in a food processor. Add back to the pan and simmer for an additional 5 minutes, stirring constantly.
Serve with the pasta of your choice (you can also use gluten-free pasta or rice.

422. Green Curry Beef

Preparation Time: 10 mins
Cooking Time: 40 mins
Servings: 3

Ingredients

1 tbsp. olive oil
½ mug chopped parsley
1 mug cilantro leaves
1 white onion, chopped
1Thai green chili, chopped
2 cloves garlic, thinly sliced
¼ tsp. Turmeric
½ tsp. ground cumin
2 tbsp. Lime juice
¼ tsp. sea salt
Black pepper
16 ounces beef top round, cut into pieces
1 can light coconut milk
¼ tsp. turmeric
½ tsp. ground cumin
¼ tsp. sea salt

Directions

Green curry paste:
In a blender or blender, combine olive oil, parsley, cilantro, onion, chili pepper, garlic, turmeric, cumin, lime juice, sea salt, and pepper; process until very smooth.
Combine beef and green curry paste in a container; toss to coat.
Refrigerate for at least 30 mins.
When ready, flame a large skillet over medium to high flame and add beef along with the green curry sauce.
Lower flame and stir for about 10 mins or until the meat is browned on the outside.
Stir in coconut milk and cook for about 30 mins or until the sauce is thick.

Serve immediately.

423. Mediterranean Beef Pitas

Preparation Time: 10 mins
Cooking Time: 5 mins
Servings: 4

Ingredients

1pound ground beef
Freshly ground black pepper
Sea salt
1 ½ tsp. dried oregano
2 tbsp. olive oil, divided
¼ red onion, sliced
3/4mug store-bought hummus
2 tbsp. Flat-parsley
4 pitas
4 lemon wedges

Directions

Form beef into 16 patties; season with ¼ teaspoon ground pepper, ½ teaspoon sea salt, and oregano.
Add 1 tbsp of olive oil in a skillet set over medium heat; cook the beef patties for about 2 mins per side or until lightly browned. To serve, top pitas with the beef patties, hummus, parsley, and onion and drizzle with the remaining olive oil; garnish with lemon wedges.

424. London Broil With Bourbon-Sautéed Mushrooms

Preparation Time: 15 mins
Cooking Time: 60 mins
Servings: 3

Ingredients

½ tsp. olive oil
½ mug minced shallot
¾ lb. halved cremini mushrooms
6 tbsp. non-fat beef stock
3 tbsp. Bourbon
½ tbsp. unsalted butter
1 tbsp. pure maple syrup
Black pepper, to taste
1 lb. lean London broil
1/8 tsp. sea salt

Directions

Preflare your oven to 400°F.
Flame a nonstick skillet in the oven for about 10 mins.
Transfer and add olive oil; swirl to coat the pan.
Stir in shallots and mushrooms until well blended; return to oven and roast the mushrooms for about 15 mins, stirring once with a wooden spatula. Stir in beef stock, bourbon, butter, maple syrup, and pepper; toss and return the pan to oven; cook for 10 mins more or until liquid is reduced by half. transfer pan from oven and set aside.
Place another nonstick skillet in the oven and flame for about 10 mins.
In the meantime, sprinkle salt and ground pepper over the steak and place it in the hot pan.
Roast in the oven for about 14 mins, turning once.
Transfer the meat from the oven and warm the mushrooms.
Place steak on the cutting board & let rest for about 5 mins.
Thinly slice beef and serve top with sautéed mushrooms to serve.

425. Beef & Potatoes

Preparation Time: 1 hour
Cooking Time: 40 minutes
Servings: 6

Ingredients:

1 1/2 lb. stew beef, sliced into cubes
2 teaspoons mixed dried herbs (thyme, sage)
4 potatoes, cubed
10 oz. mushrooms
1 ½ cups red wine

Directions:

Set the Instant Pot to sauté.
Add 1 tablespoon olive oil and cook the beef until brown on all sides.
Add the rest of the ingredients.
Season with salt and pepper.
Pour in 1 ½ cups water into the pot.
Mix well.
Cover the pot.
Set it to manual.
Cook at high pressure for 20 minutes.
Release the pressure naturally.

426. Cumin Lamb Mix

Preparation Time: 10 minutes
Cooking Time: 10 minutes
Servings: 2

Ingredients:

2 lamb chops (3.5 oz each)
1 tablespoon olive oil
1 teaspoon ground cumin
½ teaspoon salt

Directions:

Rub the lamb chops with ground cumin and salt.
Then sprinkle them with olive oil.
Let the meat marinate for 10 minutes.
After this, preheat the skillet well.
Place the lamb chops in the skillet and roast them for 10 minutes. Flip the meat on another side from time to time to avoid burning.

427. Chicken and Onion Casserole

Preparation Time: 16 minutes
Cooking Time: 47 minutes
Servings: 4

Ingredients:

4 chicken breasts
4-5 large onions, sliced
2 leeks, cut
4 tbsp. extra virgin olive oil
1 tsp thyme

Directions:

Cook olive oil in a large, deep frying pan over medium-high heat. Brown chicken, turning, for 2-3 minutes each side or until golden. Set aside in a casserole dish.
Cut the onions and leeks and add them on and around the chicken, add in olives, thyme, salt and black pepper to taste. Cover it using aluminum foil and bake at 375 F for 35 minutes, or until the chicken is cooked through. Open then situate back to the oven for 6 minutes.

428. Chicken and Mushrooms

Preparation Time: 20 minutes
Cooking Time: 7 minutes
Servings: 4

Ingredients:

4 chicken breasts, diced
2 lbs. mushrooms, chopped
onion, chopped
4 tbsp. extra virgin olive oil
salt and black, pepper to taste

Directions:

Heat olive oil in a deep-frying pan over medium-high heat. Brown chicken, stirring, for 2 minutes each side, or until golden. Add the chopped onion, mushrooms, salt and black pepper, and stir to combine. Adjust heat, cover and simmer for 30 minutes. Uncover and simmer for 5 more minutes.

429. Blue Cheese and Mushroom Chicken

Preparation Time: 25 minutes
Cooking Time: 18 minutes
Servings: 4

Ingredients:

4 chicken breast halves
cup crumbled blue cheese
1 cup sour cream
salt and black pepper, to taste
1/2 cup parsley, finely cut

Directions:

Prep the oven to 350 degrees F. Grease a casserole with nonstick spray. Place all ingredients into it, turn chicken to coat. Bake for 22 minutes. Sprinkle with parsley and serve.

430. Herb-Roasted Lamb Leg

Preparation Time: 14 minutes
Cooking Time: 2 hours
Servings: 4

Ingredients:

(6-lb) boneless leg of lamb, trimmed
cups fresh spinach leaves
1/3 cup water
1 Tbsp. Italian seasoning
1 Tbsp. extra virgin olive oil

Directions:

Combine spinach, Italian seasoning and olive oil in a food processor. Process until finely chopped.
Thoroughly cover the top and sides of the lamb with this mixture.
Situate in the bottom of a big roasting pan. Pour water and cook, covered, at 300 F for approximately two hours or until cooked through.
Uncover and cook for 10 minutes more.

431. Spring Lamb Stew

Preparation Time: 34 minutes
Cooking Time: 13 minutes
Servings: 4

Ingredients:

lb. lamb, cubed
1 lb. white mushrooms, chopped
4 cups fresh spring onions, chopped
1 tbsp. extra virgin olive oil
1 tbsp. Italian seasoning

Directions:

Heat olive oil in a deep casserole. Gently brown lamb pieces for 2-3 minutes. Cook the mushrooms for 2 minutes.
Stir in Italian seasoning, cover, and cook for an hour or until tender. Add in spring onions and simmer for 10 minutes more.
Uncover and cook until almost all the liquid evaporates.

432. Pork and Mushroom Crock Pot

Preparation Time: 1 hour
Cooking Time: 8 hours
Servings: 4

Ingredients:

2 lbs. pork tenderloin, sliced
lb. chopped white button mushrooms
1 can cream of mushroom soup
1 cup sour cream
salt and black pepper, to taste

Directions:

Spray the slow cooker with nonstick spray.
Combine all ingredients into the slow cooker.
Cook on low for 8 hours, covered.

433. Slow Cooked Pot Roast

Preparation Time: 1 hour
Cooking Time: 9 hours
Servings: 4

Ingredients:

2 lb. pot roast
1-2 garlic cloves, crushed
small onion, finely cut
1/2 cup chicken broth
1 tbsp. Italian seasoning

Directions:

Spray the slow cooker with nonstick spray.
Place the roast in the slow cooker.
In a bowl, incorporate chicken broth, garlic, onions and Italian seasoning. Spread this sauce over the meat.
Cover and cook on low 9 hours.

434. Chicken Quesadilla

Preparation Time: 5 minutes
Cooking Time: 5 minutes
Servings: 2

Ingredients:

low-carbohydrate tortillas
½ cup shredded Mexican blend cheese
2 ounces shredded chicken
1 teaspoon Tajin seasoning salt
2 tablespoons sour cream

Direction

In a big skillet at medium-high heat, cook olive oil. Add a tortilla, then layer on top ¼ cup of cheese, the chicken, the Tajin seasoning, and the remaining ¼ cup of cheese. Top with the second tortilla.
Peek under the edge of the bottom tortilla to monitor how it is browning. Once the bottom tortilla gets golden and the cheese begins to melt, after about 2 minutes, flip the quesadilla over. The second side will cook faster, about 1 minute.
Once the second tortilla is crispy and golden, transfer the quesadilla to a cutting board and let sit for 2 minutes. Cut the quesadilla into 4 wedges using a pizza cutter or chef's knife.
Transfer half the quesadilla to each of two plates. Pour 1 tablespoon of sour cream to each plate, and serve hot.

435. Garlic-Parmesan Chicken Wings

Preparation Time: 10 minutes
Cooking Time: 3 hours
Servings: 2

Ingredients:

8 tablespoons (1 stick) butter
2 garlic cloves, minced
tablespoon dried Italian seasoning
¼ cup grated Parmesan cheese, plus ½ cup
1-pound chicken wings

Directions:

With the crock insert in place, preheat the slow cooker to high. Cover baking sheet with silicone baking mat.
Put the butter, garlic, Italian seasoning, and ¼ cup of Parmesan cheese in the slow cooker and season with pink Himalayan salt and pepper. Heat up the butter, and stir the ingredients until well mixed.

Add the chicken wings and stir until coated with the butter mixture.
Cover the slow cooker and cook for 2 hours and 45 minutes.
Preheat the broiler.
Transfer the wings to the prepared baking sheet, sprinkle the remaining ½ cup of Parmesan cheese over the wings, and cook under the broiler until crispy, about 5 minutes.
Serve hot.

436. Chicken Skewers with Peanut Sauce

Preparation Time: 70 minutes
Cooking Time: 15 minutes
Servings: 2

Ingredients:

1-pound boneless skinless chicken breast, cut into chunks
3 tablespoons soy sauce (or coconut amino), divided
½ teaspoon plus ¼ teaspoon Sriracha sauce
3 teaspoons toasted sesame oil, divided
2 tablespoons peanut butter

Directions:

In a large zip-top bag, mix chicken chunks with 2 tablespoons of soy sauce, ½ tsp. of Sriracha sauce and 2 tsp. of sesame oil. Cover and marinate for an hour or so in the refrigerator or up to overnight.
If you are using wood 8-inch skewers, soak them in water for 30 minutes before using.
Preheat your grill pan or grill to low. Oil the grill pan with ghee.
Shred the chicken chunks onto the skewers.
Cook the skewers at low heat for 13 minutes, flipping halfway through.
Stir the peanut dipping sauce. Stir together the remaining 1 tablespoon of soy sauce, ¼ teaspoon of Sriracha sauce, 1 teaspoon of sesame oil, and the peanut butter. Season well.
Serve with peanut sauce.

437. Braised Chicken Thighs with Kalamata Olives

Preparation Time: 10 minutes
Cooking Time: 40 minutes
Servings: 4

Ingredients:

4 chicken thighs, skin on
2 tablespoons ghee
½ cup chicken broth
lemon, ½ sliced and ½ juiced
½ cup pitted Kalamata olives

Directions:

Preheat the oven to 375 degrees F.
Dry the chicken thighs using paper towels, and season with pink Himalayan salt and pepper.
In a medium oven-safe skillet or high-sided baking dish over medium-high heat, melt the ghee. When the ghee has melted and is hot, add the chicken thighs, skin-side down, and leave them for 8 minutes.
Cook the other side for 2 minutes. Around the chicken thighs, pour in the chicken broth, and add the lemon slices, lemon juice, and olives.
Bake for 30 minutes. Add the butter to the broth mixture.
Divide the chicken and olives between two plates and serve.

438. Buttery Garlic Chicken

Preparation Time: 5 minutes
Cooking Time: 40 minutes
Servings: 2

Ingredients:

2 tablespoons ghee, melted
2 boneless skinless chicken breasts
tablespoon dried Italian seasoning
4 tablespoons butter
¼ cup grated Parmesan cheese

Directions:

Preheat the oven to 375°F. Select a baking dish that fit both chicken breasts and coat it with the ghee.
Pat-dry the chicken breasts. Season with pink Himalayan salt, pepper, and Italian seasoning. Place the chicken in the baking dish.
Using medium skillet at medium heat, melt the butter. Sauté minced garlic, for about 5 minutes.
Remove the butter-garlic mixture from the heat, and pour it over the chicken breasts.
Roast in the oven for 30 to 35 minutes. Sprinkle some of the Parmesan cheese on top of each chicken breast. Let the chicken rest in the baking dish for 5 minutes.
Divide the chicken between two plates, spoon the butter sauce over the chicken, and serve.

439. Buttery Herb Lamb Chops

Preparation Time: 10 minutes
Cooking Time: 10 minutes
Servings: .

Ingredients:

8 Lamb Chops
1 Tablespoon Olive Oil
1 Tablespoon Butter
Sea Salt & Black Pepper to Taste
4 Ounces Herb Butter.
1 Lemon, Cut into Wedges

Directions:

Season well the chops, then prep a pan.
Heat up butter in a pan at medium-high heat and then fry your chops for four minutes per side.
Arrange on a serving plate with herb butter on each one. Serve with a lemon wedge.

440. Kale Chicken Soup

Preparation Time: 12 minutes.
Cooking Time: 18 minutes.
Servings: 6.

Ingredients:

1 Tablespoon Olive Oil.
3 Cups Kale, Chopped.
1 Cup Carrot, Minced.
2 Cloves Garlic, Minced.
8 Cups Chicken Broth, Low Sodium.
Sea Salt & Black Pepper to Taste.
¾ Cup Patina Pasta, Uncooked.
2 Cups Chicken, Cooked & Shredded.
3 Tablespoons Parmesan Cheese, Grated.

Directions:

Start by getting out a stockpot over medium heat and heat your oil. Add in your garlic, cooking for half a minute. Stir frequently and add in the kale and carrots. Cook for an additional five minutes, and make sure to stir so it doesn't burn.
Add in salt, pepper, and broth, turning the heat to high. Boil before adding in your pasta.
Set the heat to medium then cook for extra ten minutes. Your pasta should be cooked all the way through, but make sure to stir occasionally so it doesn't stick to the bottom. Add in the chicken, and cook for two minutes.
Ladle the soup and serve topped with cheese.

441. Honey Almond Chicken Tenders

Preparation Time: 10 minutes.
Cooking Time: 20 minutes
Servings: 4.

Ingredients:

1 Tablespoon Honey, Raw.
1 Tablespoon Dijon Mustard.
1 Cup Almonds.
Sea Salt & Black Pepper to Taste.
1 Lb. Chicken Breast Tenders, Boneless & Skinless.

Directions:

Set oven to 425F, and then get out a baking sheet. Wrap it with parchment paper, and then put a cooking rack on it. Spray your cooling rack down with nonstick cooking spray.
Get out a bowl and combine your mustard and honey. Season with salt and pepper, and then add in your chicken. Make sure it's well coated and place it to the side.
Use a knife and chop your almonds. You can also use a food processor. You want them to be the same size as sunflower seeds roughly. Press your chicken into the almonds, and then lay it on your cooking rack.
Bake for fifteen to twenty minutes. Your chicken should be cooked all the way through.

442. Special Chops

Preparation Time: 12 minutes.
Cooking Time: 12 minutes
Servings: 2.

Ingredients:

2 Lamb Chops.
Minced Shallots 2 Tablespoons.
Balsamic Vinegar, 2 Tablespoons.
Chicken Broth, 2 Tablespoons.
Basil, ¼ Teaspoon.
Rosemary, 1 Teaspoon.
Thyme, ¼ Teaspoon.
Salt and Pepper as Needed.
Extra Virgin Olive Oil, 1 Tablespoon.
Greek Yogurt, 2 Tablespoons.

Directions:

Take a mixing bowl and mix all herbs and yogurt with seasoning.
Rub this mixture into the chops thoroughly. Leave them for a few minutes.
Heat a skillet over medium heat and cook both sides of the chops well.
When tender, brown the shallots on the skillet and add the vinegar and broth.
Top the chops with the warm sauce of broth and serve on a platter.

443. Rib Roast

Preparation Time: 10 minutes
Cooking Time: 80 minutes
Servings: 2

Ingredients:

Rib Roast, 4 Pounds.
Salt and Pepper to Taste.
Garlic, 1 Clove, Minced.
Extra Virgin Olive Oil, 1 Teaspoon.
Thyme, ¼ Teaspoon.

Directions:

Arrange the Meat in The Roasting Pan.
Take A Small Bowl, And Mix the Rest of The Ingredients.
Apply the Mixture to The Meat. Leave for One Hour.
Bake That At 500F for 25 minutes.
Then, Bake Again At 325F for 80 minutes.
Serve warm.

444. Spicy Lamb Rounds

Preparation Time: 10 minutes
Cooking Time: 12 minutes
Servings: 2

Ingredients:

Ground Lamb, 1 Pound.
Garlic, 1 Tablespoon, Chopped.
Mint Leaves, 1 Tablespoon, Chopped.
Oregano, 1 Tablespoon, Chopped.
Cilantro, 1 Tablespoon, Chopped.
Red Pepper, ½ Teaspoon.
Ground Cumin, ½ Teaspoon.
Salt and Pepper, ½ Teaspoon Each.
Feta Cheese, 4 Ounces.
Extra Virgin Olive Oil as Needed.
Greek Yogurt, 2 Tablespoons.

Directions:

Heat a grill pan over medium heat.
Meanwhile, coat the lamb with the yogurt, all the spices, seasoning, and herbs in a bowl.
Stir the rest of the ingredients, excluding the feta cheese.
Brush the grill pan with cooking oil.
Shape the lamb meat into small round cutlets or patties.
Grill them, and serve with cheese on top.

445. Prime BBQ

Preparation Time: 35 minutes
Cooking Time: 85 minutes
Servings: 2

Ingredients:

Ribs of Your Choice, 2 Pounds.
Garlic, 1 Teaspoon, Minced.
Pepper to Taste.
Salt as Needed.

Directions:

Take a large pot and apply salt, pepper, and garlic well to the ribs.
Boil the ribs in boiling water.
When tender, bake them at 325f for 15 minutes.
Cover them in aluminum foil and place a warm coal piece on the foil.
Let the ribs absorb the coal smell and taste for one hour.
Bake the ribs again.
Serve warm.

446. Pork And Chestnuts Mix

Preparation Time: 30 minutes
Cooking Time: 0 minutes
Servings: 6

Ingredients:

1 and ½ cups brown rice, already cooked
2 cups pork roast, already cooked and shredded
3 ounces water chestnuts, drained and sliced
½ cup sour cream
A pinch of salt and white pepper

Directions:

In a bowl, mix the rice with the roast and the other ingredients, toss and keep in the fridge for 2 hours before serving.

447. Steak with Olives and Mushrooms

Preparation Time: 20 minutes
Cooking Time: 9 minutes
Servings: 6

Ingredients:

lb. boneless beef sirloin steak
1 large onion, sliced
5-6 white button mushrooms
1/2 cup green olives, coarsely chopped
4 tbsp. extra virgin olive oil

Directions:

Heat olive oil in a heavy bottomed skillet over medium-high heat. Brown the steaks on both sides then put aside.
Gently sauté the onion in the same skillet, for 2-3 minutes, stirring rarely.
Sauté in the mushrooms and olives.
Return the steaks to the skillet, cover, cook for 5-6 minutes and serve.

448. Spicy Mustard Chicken

Preparation Time: 32 minutes
Cooking Time: 36 minutes
Servings: 4

Ingredients:

4 chicken breasts
2 garlic cloves, crushed
1/3 cup chicken broth
3 tbsp. Dijon mustard
tsp chili powder

Directions:

In a small bowl, mix the mustard, chicken broth, garlic and chili. Marinate the chicken for 30 minutes.
Bake in a preheated to 375 F oven for 35 minutes.

449. Walnut and Oregano Crusted Chicken

Preparation Time: 36 minutes
Cooking Time: 13 minutes
Servings: 4

Ingredients:

4 skinless, boneless chicken breasts
10-12 fresh oregano leaves
1/2 cup walnuts, chopped
2 garlic cloves, chopped
2 eggs, beaten

Directions:

Blend the garlic, oregano and walnuts in a food processor until a rough crumb is formed. Place this mixture on a plate.
Whisk eggs in a deep bowl. Soak each chicken breast in the beaten egg then roll it in the walnut mixture. Place coated chicken on a baking tray and bake at 375 F for 13 minutes each side.

450. Greek Pork

Preparation Time: 10 minutes
Cooking Time: 1 Hour And 10 minutes
Servings: 8

Ingredients:

3 lb. pork roast, sliced into cubes
1/4 cup chicken broth
1/4 cup lemon juice
2 teaspoons dried oregano
2 teaspoons garlic powder

Directions:

Put the pork in the Instant Pot.
In a bowl, mix all the remaining ingredients.
Pour the mixture over the pork.
Toss to coat evenly.
Secure the pot.
Choose manual mode.
Cook at high pressure for 50 minutes.
Release the pressure naturally.

451. Balsamic Roasted Carrots and Baby Onions

Preparation Time: 50 minutes
Cooking Time: 26 minutes
Servings: 4

Ingredients:

2 bunches baby carrots, scrubbed, ends trimmed
10 small onions, peeled, halved
4 tbsp. 100% pure maple syrup (unprocessed)
tsp thyme
tbsp. extra virgin olive oil

Directions:

Preheat oven to 350F. Line a baking tray with baking paper.
Place the carrots, onion, thyme and oil in a large bowl and toss until well coated.
Spread carrots and onion, in a single layer, on the baking tray. Roast for 25 minutes or until tender.
Sprinkle over the maple syrup and vinegar and toss to coat. Roast for 25-30 minutes more or until vegetables are tender and caramelized. Season well and serve.

452. Baked Cauliflower

Preparation Time: 13 minutes
Cooking Time: 26 minutes
Servings: 4

Ingredients:

small cauliflower, cut into florets
1 tbsp. garlic powder
1 tsp paprika
4 tbsp. extra virgin olive oil
grated Parmesan cheese, to taste

Directions:

Combine olive oil, paprika and garlic powder together. Mix in the cauliflower florets and situate in a baking dish in one layer.
Bake in a preheated to 350 F oven for 20 minutes. Take away from the oven, and drizzle with Parmesan cheese. Cook for 5 minutes more.

453. Baked Bean and Rice Casserole

Preparation Time: 8 minutes
Cooking Time: 22 minutes
Servings: 4

Ingredients:

can red beans, rinsed
1 cup water
2/3 cup rice
onions, chopped
tsp dried mint

Directions:

Cook olive oil in an ovenproof casserole dish and gently sauté the chopped onions for 1-2 minutes. Stir in the rice and cook, stirring constantly, for another minute.
Rinse the beans and add them to the casserole. Stir in a cup of water and the mint and bake in a preheated to 350 F oven for 20 minutes.

454. Okra and Tomato Casserole

Preparation Time: 25 minutes
Cooking Time: 26 minutes
Servings: 4

Ingredients:

lb. okra, trimmed
1 tomatoes, cut into wedges
1 garlic cloves, chopped
1 cup fresh parsley leaves, finely cut
1 tbsp. extra virgin olive oil

Directions:

In a deep ovenproof baking dish, combine okra, sliced tomatoes, olive oil and garlic.
Toss to combine and bake in a preheated to 350 degrees F oven for 45 minutes.
Drizzle with parsley and serve.

455. Spicy Baked Feta with Tomatoes

Preparation Time: 15 minutes
Cooking Time: 22 minutes
Servings: 4

Ingredients:

lb. feta cheese, cut in slices
ripe tomatoes, sliced
1 onion, sliced
tbsp. extra virgin olive oil
1/2 tbsp. hot paprika

Directions:

Preheat the oven to 430F
In an ovenproof baking dish, arrange the slices of onions and tomatoes overlapping slightly but not too much. Sprinkle with olive oil.
Bake for 5 minutes then place the feta slices on top of the vegetables. Sprinkle with hot paprika. Bake for 15 more minutes and serve.

456. Baked Lemon-Butter Fish

Preparation Time: 10 minutes
Cooking Time: 17 minutes
Servings: 4

Ingredients:

4 tablespoons butter, plus more for coating
2 (5-ounce) tilapia fillets
2 garlic cloves, minced
lemon, zested and juiced
tablespoons capers, rinsed and chopped

Direction

Preheat the oven to 400°F. Coat an 8-inch baking dish with butter.
Pat dry the tilapia with paper towels, and season on both sides with pink Himalayan salt and pepper. Place in the greased baking dish.
In a medium skillet at medium heat, heat up butter. Add the garlic and cook for 3 to 5 minutes, until slightly browned but not burned.
Remove the garlic butter from the heat, and mix in the lemon zest and 2 tablespoons of lemon juice.
Pour the lemon-butter sauce over the fish, and sprinkle the capers around the baking pan.
Bake for 13 minutes and serve.

457. Fish Taco Bowl

Preparation Time: 10 minutes
Cooking Time: 15 minutes
Servings: 2

Ingredients:

2 (5-ounce) tilapia fillets
4 teaspoons Tajin seasoning salt, divided
cups pre-sliced coleslaw cabbage mix
1 tablespoon Spicy Red Pepper Miso Mayo, plus more for serving
1 avocado, mashed

Direction

Preheat the oven to 425°F. Prep baking sheet with silicone baking mat.
Rub the tilapia with the olive oil, and then coat it with 2 teaspoons of Tajin seasoning salt. Place the fish in the prepared pan.
Bake for 15 minutes, or until the fish is opaque when you pierce it with a fork. Put the fish on a cooling rack and let it sit for 4 minutes.
Meanwhile, in a medium bowl, gently mix to combine the coleslaw and the mayo sauce. You don't want the cabbage super wet, just enough to dress it. Add the mashed avocado and the remaining 2 teaspoons of Tajin seasoning salt to the coleslaw, and season with pink Himalayan salt and pepper. Divide the salad between two bowls.
Shred the fish into small pieces, and add it to the bowls.
Top the fish with a drizzle of mayo sauce and serve.

458. Scallops with Creamy Bacon Sauce

Preparation Time: 5 minutes
Cooking Time: 20 minutes
Servings: 2

Ingredients:

4 bacon slices
cup heavy (whipping) cream
¼ cup grated Parmesan cheese
1 tablespoon ghee
8 large sea scallops, rinsed and patted dry

Direction

In a medium skillet at medium-high heat, fry bacon on both sides for 8 minutes.
Transfer the bacon to a paper towel–lined plate.
Lower the heat to medium. Add the cream, butter, and Parmesan cheese to the bacon grease, and season with a pinch of pink Himalayan salt and pepper. Decrease the heat to low and cook, stir constantly, for 10 minutes.
In a separate large skillet over medium-high heat, heat the ghee until sizzling.
Season the scallops with pink Himalayan salt and pepper, and add them to the skillet. Cook for just 1 minute per side. Do not crowd the scallops; if your pan isn't large enough, cook them in two batches. You want the scallops golden on each side.
Transfer the scallops to a paper towel–lined plate.
Divide the cream sauce between two plates, crumble the bacon on top of the cream sauce, and top with 4 scallops each. Serve immediately.

459. Shrimp and Avocado Lettuce Cups

Preparation Time: 10 minutes
Cooking Time: 5 minutes
Servings: 2

Ingredients:

tablespoon ghee
½ pound shrimp
½ avocado, sliced
4 butter lettuce leaves
1 tablespoon Spicy Red Pepper Miso Mayo

Direction

Preheat medium skillet over medium-high heat, cook the ghee. Add the shrimp and cook. Season with pink Himalayan salt and pepper. Shrimp are cooked when they turn pink and opaque.
Season the tomatoes and avocado with pink Himalayan salt and pepper.
Divide the lettuce cups between two plates. Fill each cup with shrimp, ½ cup grape tomatoes, and avocado. Drizzle the mayo sauce on top and serve.

460. Garlic Butter Shrimp

Preparation Time: 10 minutes
Cooking Time: 15 minutes
Servings: 2

Ingredients:

3 tablespoons butter
½ pound shrimp
lemon, halved
garlic cloves, crushed
¼ teaspoon red pepper flakes (optional)

Direction

Preheat the oven to 425°F.

Place the butter in an 8-inch baking dish, and pop it into the oven while it is preheating, just until the butter melts.
Sprinkle the shrimp with pink Himalayan salt and pepper.
Slice one half of the lemon in thin slices, and cut the other half into 2 wedges.
In the baking dish, add the shrimp and garlic to the butter. The shrimp should be in a single layer. Add the lemon slices. Sprinkle the top of the fish with the red pepper flakes (if using).
Bake the shrimp for 15 minutes, stirring halfway through.
Remove the shrimp from the oven, and squeeze juice from the 2 lemon wedges over the dish. Serve hot.

461. Seared-Salmon Shirataki Rice Bowls

Preparation Time: 40 minutes
Cooking Time: 10 minutes
Servings: 2

Ingredients:

2 (6-ounce) salmon fillets, skin on
4 tablespoons soy sauce (or coconut aminos), divided
2 small Persian cucumbers or ½ large English cucumber
1 (8-ounce) pack Miracle Shirataki Rice
1 avocado, diced

Direction

Place the salmon in an 8-inch baking dish, and add 3 tablespoons of soy sauce. Cover and marinate in the refrigerator for 30 minutes.
Meanwhile, slice the cucumbers thin, put them in a small bowl, and add the remaining 1 tablespoon of soy sauce. Set aside to marinate.
Situate skillet over medium heat, melt the ghee. Add the salmon fillets skin-side down. Pour some of the soy sauce marinade over the salmon, and sear the fish for 3 to 4 minutes on each side.
Meanwhile, in a large saucepan, cook the shirataki rice per package instructions:
Rinse the shirataki rice in cold water in a colander.
In a saucepan filled with boiling water, cook the rice for 2 minutes.
Pour the rice into the colander. Dry out the pan.
Transfer the rice to the dry pan and dry roast over medium heat until dry and opaque.
Season the avocado with pink Himalayan salt and pepper.
Place the salmon fillets on a plate, and remove the skin. Cut the salmon into bite-size pieces.
Assemble the rice bowls: In two bowls, make a layer of the cooked Miracle Rice. Top each with the cucumbers, avocado, and salmon, and serve.

462. Pork Rind Salmon Cakes

Preparation Time: 10 minutes
Cooking Time: 10 minutes
Servings: 2

Ingredients

6 ounces canned Alaska wild salmon, drained
2 tablespoons crushed pork rinds
egg, lightly beaten
1 tablespoon ghee
½ tablespoon Dijon mustard

Directions:

In a medium bowl, incorporate salmon, pork rinds, egg, and 1½ tablespoons of mayonnaise, and season with pink Himalayan salt and pepper.
With the salmon mixture, form patties the size of hockey pucks or smaller. Keep patting the patties until they keep together.
Position the medium skillet over medium-high heat, melt the ghee. When the ghee sizzles, place the salmon patties in the pan. Cook for 6 minutes both sides. Transfer the patties to a paper towel–lined plate.
In a small bowl, mix together the remaining 1½ tablespoons of mayonnaise and the mustard.
Serve the salmon cakes with the mayo-mustard dipping sauce.

463. Rosemary Pork Chops

Preparation Time: 30 minutes
Cooking Time: 35 minutes
Servings: 4

Ingredients:

4 pork loin chops, boneless
Salt and black pepper to the taste
4 garlic cloves, minced
1 tablespoon rosemary, chopped
1 tablespoon olive oil

Directions:

In a roasting pan, combine the pork chops with the rest of the ingredients, toss, and bake at 425 degrees F for 10 minutes.
Reduce the heat to 350 degrees F and cook the chops for 25 minutes more.
Divide the chops between plates and serve with a side salad.

464. Tender Lamb

Preparation Time: 2 hours
Cooking Time: 2 Hours And 5 minutes
Servings: 6

Ingredients:

3 lamb shanks
Seasoning mixture (1 tablespoon oregano, 1/4 teaspoon ground cumin and 1 tablespoon smoked paprika)
3 cloves garlic, minced
2 cups red wine
4 cups beef stock

Directions:

Coat the lamb shanks with the seasoning mixture.
Sprinkle with salt and pepper.
Cover with minced garlic.
Marinate in half of the mixture for 30 minutes.
Set the Instant Pot to sauté.
Pour in 2 tablespoons of olive oil.
Brown the lamb on all sides. Remove and set aside.
Add the rest of the ingredients.
Put the lamb back to the pot.
Cover the pot and set it to manual.
Cook at high pressure for 30 minutes.
Release the pressure naturally.
Set the Instant Pot to sauté to simmer and thicken the sauce.

465. Worcestershire Pork Chops

Preparation Time: 15 minutes
Cooking Time: 15 minutes
Servings: 3

Ingredients:

2 tablespoons Worcestershire sauce
8 oz pork loin chops
1 tablespoon lemon juice
1 teaspoon olive oil

Directions:

Mix up together Worcestershire sauce, lemon juice, and olive oil.
Brush the pork loin chops with the sauce mixture from each side.
Preheat the grill to 395F.

Place the pork chops in the grill and cook them for 5 minutes.
Then flip the pork chops on another side and brush with remaining sauce mixture.
Grill the meat for 7-8 minutes more.

466. Pork With Green Beans & Potatoes

Preparation Time: 1 hour 30 minutes
Cooking Time: 45 minutes
Servings: 6

Ingredients:

1 lb. lean pork, sliced into cubes
1 onion, chopped
2 carrots, sliced thinly
2 cups canned crushed tomatoes
2 potatoes, cubed

Directions:

Set the Instant Pot to sauté.
Add ½ cup of olive oil.
Cook the pork for 5 minutes, stirring frequently.
Add the rest of the ingredients.
Mix well.
Seal the pot.
Choose manual setting.
Cook at high pressure for 17 minutes.
Release the pressure naturally.

CHAPTER 7: POULTRY RECIPES

467. Chicken with Peas

Preparation Time: 5 minutes
Cooking Time: 30 minutes
Servings: 4

Ingredients:

Four chicken fillets
1 tsp. cayenne pepper
1 tsp. salt
1 tbsp. mayonnaise
1 cup green peas
¼ cup of water
One carrot, peeled, chopped

Directions:

Sprinkle the chicken fillet with cayenne pepper and salt.
Line the baking tray using foil and place chicken fillets in it.
Then brush the chicken with mayonnaise.
Add carrot and green peas.
Then add water and cover the ingredients with foil.
Bake the chicken for 30 minutes at 355F.

468. Chicken Wrap

Preparation Time: 10 minutes
Cooking Time: 0 minutes
Servings: 2

Ingredients:

Two whole wheat tortilla flatbreads
Six chicken breast slices, skinless, boneless, cooked, and shredded
A handful of baby spinach
Two provolone cheese slices
Four tomato slices
Ten kalamata olives, pitted and sliced
One red onion, sliced
2 tbsp. roasted peppers, chopped

Directions:

Arrange the tortillas on a working surface, and divide the chicken and the other ingredients on each.
Roll the tortillas and serve them right away.

469. Almond Chicken Bites

Preparation Time: 5 minutes
Cooking Time: 5 minutes
Servings: 8

Ingredients:

1-pound chicken fillet
1 tbsp. potato starch
½ tsp. salt
1 tsp. paprika
2 tbsp. wheat flour, whole grain
One egg, beaten
1 tbsp. almond butter

Directions:

Chop the chicken fillet on the small pieces and place it in the bowl.
Add egg, salt, and potato starch. Mix up the chicken.
Then mix up wheat flour and paprika.
Then coat every chicken piece in wheat flour mixture.
Place almond butter in the skillet and heat it.
Add chicken popcorn and roast it for 5 minutes over medium heat.
Dry the chicken popcorn with the help of a paper towel.

470. Garlic Chicken and Endives

Preparation Time: 5 minutes
Cooking Time: 15 minutes
Servings: 4

Ingredients:

1-pound chicken breasts, skinless, boneless, and cubed
Two endives, sliced
2 tbsp. olive oil
Four garlic cloves, minced
½ cup chicken stock
2 tbsp. parmesan, grated
1 tbsp. parsley, chopped
Salt and black pepper to the taste

Directions:

Heat a pan with the oil over medium-high heat, add the chicken and cook for 5 minutes.
the endives, garlic, the stock, salt, and pepper, stir, bring to a simmer and cook over medium-high heat for 10 minutes.
Add the parmesan and the parsley, toss gently, divide everything between plates and serve.

471. Butter Chicken Thighs

Preparation Time: 5 minutes
Cooking Time: 30 minutes
Servings: 4

Ingredients:

1 tsp. fennel seeds
One garlic clove, peeled
1 tbsp. butter
1 tsp. coconut oil
¼ tsp. thyme
½ tsp. salt
1 oz. fennel bulb, chopped
1 oz. shallot, chopped
Four chicken thighs, skinless, boneless
1 tsp. ground black pepper

Directions:

Rub the chicken thighs with ground black pepper.
In the skillet, mix up together butter and coconut oil.
Add fennel seeds, garlic clove, thyme, salt, and shallot.
Roast the mixture for 1 minute.
Then add fennel bulb and chicken thighs.
Roast the chicken thighs for 2 minutes from each side over high heat.
Then transfer the skillet with chicken in the oven and cook the meal for 20 minutes at 360F.

472. Chicken and Olives Salsa

Preparation Time: 10 minutes
Cooking Time: 25 minutes
Servings: 4

Ingredients:

2 tbsp. avocado oil
Four chicken breast halves, skinless and boneless
Salt and black pepper to the taste
1 tbsp. sweet paprika
One red onion, chopped
1 tbsp. balsamic vinegar
2 tbsp. parsley, chopped
One avocado, peeled, pitted, and cubed

2 tbsp. black olives, pitted and chopped

Directions:

Heat and set your grill over medium-high heat, add the chicken brushed with half of the oil and seasoned with paprika, salt, and pepper, cook for 7 minutes on each side, and divide between plates.
Meanwhile, in a bowl, mix the onion with the rest of the ingredients and the remaining oil, toss, add on top of the chicken and serve.

473. Turkey and Salsa Verde

Preparation Time: 5 minutes
Cooking Time: 50 minutes
Servings: 4

Ingredients:

One big turkey breast, skinless, boneless, and cubed
One and ½ cups Salsa Verde
Salt and black pepper to the taste
1 tbsp. olive oil
One and ½ cups feta cheese, crumbled
¼ cup cilantro, chopped

Directions:

In a roasting pan greased with the oil, combine the turkey with the salsa, salt, and pepper and bake 400 degrees F for 50 minutes.
Add the cheese and the cilantro, toss gently, divide everything between plates and serve.

474. Chili Chicken Mix

Preparation Time: 10 minutes
Cooking Time: 18 minutes
Servings: 4

Ingredients:

2 pounds chicken thighs, skinless and boneless
2 tbsp. olive oil
2 cups yellow onion, chopped
1 tsp. onion powder
1 tsp. smoked paprika
1 tsp. chili pepper
½ tsp. coriander seeds, ground
2 tsp. oregano, dried
2 tsp. parsley flakes
30 ounces canned tomatoes, chopped
½ cup black olives pitted and halved

Directions:

Set the instant pot on Sauté mode then add the oil, heat it, add the onion, onion powder, and the rest of the ingredients except the tomatoes, olives, and the chicken, stir, and sauté 10 minutes.
Add the chicken, tomatoes, and olives, put the lid on, and cook on High for 8 minutes.
Release the pressure naturally for 10 minutes, split the mix into bowls and serve.

475. Duck and Orange Warm Salad

Preparation Time: 10 minutes
Cooking Time: 25 minutes
Servings: 4

Ingredients:

2 tbsp. balsamic vinegar
Two oranges, peeled and cut into segments
1 tsp. orange zest, grated
1 tbsp. orange juice
Three shallots, minced
2 tbsp. olive oil
Salt and black pepper to the taste
Two duck breasts, boneless and skin scored
2 cups baby arugula
2 tbsp. chives, chopped

Directions:

Heat a pan with the oil over medium-high heat, add the duck breasts skin side down, and brown for 5 minutes.
Flip the duck, add the shallot and the other ingredients except for the arugula, orange, and the chives, and cook for 15 minutes more.
Transfer the duck breasts to a cutting board, cool down, cut into strips, and put in a salad bowl.
Add the remaining ingredients, toss, and serve warm.

476. Turmeric Baked Chicken Breast

Preparation Time: 5 minutes
Cooking Time: 40 minutes
Servings: 2

Ingredients:

8 oz. chicken breast, skinless, boneless
2 tbsp. capers
1 tsp. olive oil
½ tsp. paprika
½ tsp. ground turmeric
½ tsp. salt
½ tsp. minced garlic

Directions:

Make the lengthwise cut in the chicken breast.
Rub the chicken with olive oil, paprika, capers, ground turmeric, salt, and minced garlic.
Then fill the chicken cut with capers and secure it with toothpicks.
Bake the chicken breast for 40 minutes at 350F.
Remove the toothpicks from the chicken breast and slice it.

477. Chicken Tacos

Preparation Time: 10 minutes
Cooking Time: 20 minutes
Servings: 4

Ingredients:

Two bread tortillas
1 tsp. butter
2 tsp. olive oil
1 tsp. Taco seasoning
6 oz. chicken breast, skinless, boneless, sliced
1/3 cup Cheddar cheese, shredded
One bell pepper, cut on the wedges

Directions:

Pour 1 tsp. of olive oil in the skillet and add chicken.
Sprinkle the meat with Taco seasoning and mix up well.
Roast chicken for 10 minutes over medium heat. Stir it from time to time.
Then transfer the cooked chicken to the plate.
Add remaining olive oil to the skillet.
Then add bell pepper and roast it for 5 minutes. Stir it all the time.
Mix up together bell pepper with chicken.
Toss butter in the skillet and melt it.
Put one tortilla in the skillet.
Put Cheddar cheese on the tortilla and flatten it.
Then add a chicken-pepper mixture and cover it with the second tortilla.
Roast the quesadilla for 2 minutes from each side.
Cut the cooked meal on the halves and transfer it to the serving plates.

478. Chicken and Butter Sauce

Preparation Time: 5 minutes
Cooking Time: 30 minutes
Servings: 5

Ingredients:

1-pound chicken fillet
1/3 cup butter, softened
1 tbsp. rosemary
½ tsp. thyme
1 tsp. salt
½ lemon

Directions:

Churn together thyme, salt, and rosemary.
Chop the chicken fillet roughly and mix it up with churned butter mixture.
Place the prepared chicken in the baking dish.
Squeeze the lemon over the chicken.
Chop the squeezed lemon and add it to the baking dish.
Cover the chicken with foil and bake it for 20 minutes at 365F.
Then discard the foil and bake the chicken for 10 minutes more.

479. Coriander and Coconut Chicken

Preparation Time: 10 minutes
Cooking Time: 30 minutes
Servings: 4

Ingredients:

2 pounds chicken thighs, skinless, boneless, and cubed
2 tbsp. olive oil
Salt and black pepper to the taste
3 tbsp. coconut flesh, shredded
One and ½ tsp. orange extract
1 tbsp. ginger, grated
¼ cup orange juice
2 tbsp. coriander, chopped
1 cup chicken stock
¼ tsp. red pepper flakes

Directions:

Heat a pan with the oil over medium-high heat, add the chicken, and brown for 4 minutes on each side.
Add salt, pepper, and the rest of the ingredients, bring to a simmer and cook over medium heat for 20 minutes.
Divide the mix between plates and serve hot.

480. Chicken Pilaf

Preparation Time: 10 minutes
Cooking Time: 30 minutes
Servings: 4

Ingredients:

4 tbsp. avocado oil
2 pounds chicken breasts, skinless, boneless, and cubed
½ cup yellow onion, chopped
Four garlic cloves, minced
8 ounces brown rice
4 cups chicken stock
½ cup kalamata olives pitted
½ cup tomatoes, cubed
6 ounces baby spinach
½ cup feta cheese, crumbled
A pinch of salt and black pepper
1 tbsp. marjoram, chopped
1 tbsp. basil, chopped
Juice of ½ lemon
¼ cup pine nuts, toasted

Directions:

Heat a pot with 1 tbsp. avocado oil set over medium-high heat, add the chicken, salt, and pepper, brown for 5 minutes on each side, and transfer to a bowl.
Heat the pot again with the rest of the avocado oil over medium heat, add the onion and garlic and sauté for 3 minutes.
Add the rice, the rest of the ingredients except the pine nuts, return the chicken, toss, bring it to a simmer and cook over medium heat for 20 minutes.
Divide the mix between plates, top each serving with some pine nuts and serve.

481. Chicken and Black Beans

Preparation Time: 10 minutes
Cooking Time: 20 minutes
Servings: 4

Ingredients:

12 oz. chicken breast, skinless, boneless, chopped
1 tbsp. taco seasoning
1 tbsp. nut oil
½ tsp. cayenne pepper
½ tsp. salt
½ tsp. garlic, chopped
½ red onion, sliced
1/3 cup black beans, canned, rinsed
½ cup Mozzarella, shredded

Directions:

Rub the chopped chicken breast with taco seasoning, salt, and cayenne pepper.
Place the chicken in the skillet, add nut oil and roast it for 10 minutes over medium heat. Mix up the chicken pieces from time to time to avoid burning.
After this, transfer the chicken to the plate.
Add sliced onion and then garlic to the skillet. Roast the vegetables for 5 minutes. Stir them constantly. Then add black beans and stir well—Cook the ingredients for 2 minutes more.
Add the chopped chicken and mix up well. Top the meal with Mozzarella cheese.
Close the lid and cook the meal for 3 minutes.

482. Coconut Chicken

Preparation Time: 10 minutes
Cooking Time: 5 minutes
Servings: 4

Ingredients:

6 oz. chicken fillet
¼ cup of sparkling water
One egg
3 tbsp. coconut flakes
1 tbsp. coconut oil
1 tsp. Greek Seasoning

Directions:

Cut the chicken fillet into small pieces (nuggets).
Then crack the egg in the bowl and whisk it.
Mix up together egg and sparkling water.
Add Greek seasoning and stir gently.
Dip the chicken nuggets in the egg mixture and then coat in the coconut flakes.
Melt the coconut oil in the skillet and heat it until it is shimmering.
Then add prepared chicken nuggets.
Roast them for 1 minute from each or until they are light brown.
Dry the cooked chicken nuggets with the paper towels help and transfer them to the serving plates.

483. Ginger Chicken Drumsticks

Preparation Time: 10 minutes
Cooking Time: 30 minutes
Servings: 4

Ingredients:

Four chicken drumsticks
One apple, grated
1 tbsp. curry paste
4 tbsp. milk
1 tsp. coconut oil
1 tsp. chili flakes
½ tsp. minced ginger

Directions:

Mix up together grated apple, curry paste, milk, chili flakes, and minced garlic.

Put coconut oil in the skillet and melt it.
Add apple mixture and stir well.
Then add chicken drumsticks and mix up well.
Roast the chicken for 2 minutes from each side.
Then preheat the oven to 360F.
Place the skillet with chicken drumsticks in the oven and bake for 25 minutes.

484. Parmesan Chicken

Preparation Time: 10 minutes
Cooking Time: 30 minutes
Servings: 3

Ingredients:

1-pound chicken breast, skinless, boneless
2 oz. Parmesan, grated
1 tsp. dried oregano
½ tsp. dried cilantro
1 tbsp. Panko bread crumbs
One egg, beaten
1 tsp. turmeric

Directions:

Cut the chicken breast into three servings.
Then combine Parmesan, oregano, cilantro, bread crumbs, and turmeric.
Dip the chicken servings in the beaten egg carefully.
Then coat every chicken piece in the cheese-bread crumbs mixture.
Line the baking tray using the baking paper.
Arrange the chicken pieces in the tray.
Bake the chicken for 30 minutes at 365F.

485. Chicken Breasts With Stuffing

Preparation Time: 15 minutes
Cooking Time: 37 minutes
Servings: 8

Ingredients:

¼ cup crumbled feta cheese
1 large bell pepper, halved and seeded
1 tbsp minced fresh basil
2 tbsp finely chopped, pitted Kalamata olives
8 pcs of 6-oz boneless and skinless chicken breasts

Directions:

In a greased baking sheet place bell pepper with skin facing up and pop into a preheated broiler on high. Broil until blackened around 15 minutes. Remove from broiler and place right away into a re-sealable bag, seal and leave for 15 minutes.
After, peel bell pepper and mince.
Preheat grill to medium high fire.
In a medium bowl, mix well basil, olives, cheese and bell pepper.
Form a pocket on each chicken breast by creating a slit through the thickest portion; add 2 tbsp bell pepper mixture and seal with a wooden pick. (At this point, you can stop and freeze chicken and just thaw when needed for grilling already)
Season chicken breasts with pepper and salt.
Grill for six minutes per side, remove from grill and cover loosely with foil and let stand for 10 minutes before serving.

486. Turkey Sausage, Fresh Herbs & Feta

Preparation Time: 20 minutes
Cooking Time: 40 minutes
Servings: 6

Ingredients:

1 onion, sliced thinly
1 smoked turkey sausage, sliced into rounds
1 cup white rice
4 tablespoons fresh herbs, chopped (parsley, basil)
4 oz. feta cheese, crumbled

Directions:

Add 1 tablespoon olive oil in the Instant Pot.
Cook the onion and sausage for 5 minutes.
Season with a little salt and pepper.
Add the rice and stir.
Add 2 cups chicken stock.
Stir well.
Seal the pot.
Set it to manual.
Cook at high pressure for 15 minutes.
Release the pressure quickly.

487. Chicken With Spanish Rice

Preparation Time: 15 minutes
Cooking Time: 40 minutes
Servings: 12

Ingredients:

6 chicken breast fillet, sliced into cubes
4 cloves garlic, minced
1 onion, chopped
4 cups brown rice
28 oz. canned diced tomatoes with green chili

Directions:

Season the chicken with salt and pepper.
Pour 1 tablespoon into the Instant Pot.
Set it to sauté.
Brown the chicken and set aside.
Add the garlic, onion and rice.
Cook for 2 minutes.
Add the canned tomatoes with green chili and 4 ½ cups of water.
Seal the pot.
Set it to manual.
Cook at high pressure for 24 minutes.
Release the pressure naturally.
Fluff the rice and top with the chicken.

488. Italian Chicken

Preparation Time: 10 minutes
Cooking Time: 30 minutes
Servings: 6

Ingredients:

1 carrot, chopped
1/2 lb. mushrooms
8 chicken thighs
1 cup tomato sauce
3 cloves garlic, crushed

Directions:

Season the chicken with salt and pepper.
Cover and marinate for 30 minutes.
Press the sauté setting in the Instant Pot.
Add 1 tablespoon of ghee.
Cook the carrots and mushrooms until soft.
Add the tomato sauce and garlic.
Add the chicken, tomatoes and olives.
Cook and mix well.
Seal the pot.
Set it to manual.
Cook at high pressure for 10 minutes.
Release the pressure naturally.

489. Turkey Meatloaf

Preparation Time: 15 minutes
Cooking Time: 50 minutes
Servings: 6

Ingredients:

1/2 cup bread crumbs
1/4 cup onion, chopped
1 lb. lean ground turkey
1/4 cup sun dried tomatoes, diced
1/2 cup feta cheese, crumbled

Directions:

Mix all the ingredients in a bowl.
Form a loaf and cover with foil.
Pour 1 cup of water into the Instant Pot.
Add the steamer basket inside.
Place the wrapped turkey mixture on top of basket.
Cover the pot.
Set it to manual.
Cook at high pressure for 35 minutes.
Release the pressure quickly.

490. Chicken And Tzaziki Pitas

Preparation Time: 10 minutes
Cooking Time: 0 minutes
Servings: 8

Ingredients:

4 pita bread
10 oz chicken fillet, grilled
1 cup lettuce, chopped
8 teaspoons tzaziki sauce

Directions:

Cut every pita bread on the halves to get 8 pita pockets.
Then fill every pita pocket with chopped lettuce and sprinkle greens with tzatziki sauce.
Chop chicken fillet and add it in the pita pockets too.

491. Lime Chicken With Black Beans

Preparation Time: 15 minutes
Cooking Time: 30 minutes
Servings: 8

Ingredients:

8 chicken thighs (boneless and skinless)
3 tablespoons lime juice
1 cup black beans
1 cup canned tomatoes
4 teaspoons garlic powder

Directions:

Marinate the chicken in a mixture of lime juice and garlic powder.
Add the chicken to the Instant Pot.
Pour the tomatoes on top of the chicken.
Seal the pot.
Set it to manual.
Cook at high pressure for 10 minutes.
Release the pressure naturally.
Stir in the black beans.
Press sauté to simmer until black beans are cooked.

492. Lemon Chicken Mix

Preparation Time: 10 minutes
Cooking Time: 10 minutes
Servings: 2

Ingredients:

8 oz chicken breast, skinless, boneless
1 teaspoon Cajun seasoning
1 teaspoon balsamic vinegar
1 teaspoon olive oil
1 teaspoon lemon juice

Directions:

Cut the chicken breast on the halves and sprinkle with Cajun seasoning.
Then sprinkle the poultry with olive oil and lemon juice.
Then sprinkle the chicken breast with the balsamic vinegar.
Preheat the grill to 385F.
Grill the chicken breast halves for 5 minutes from each side.
Slice Cajun chicken and place in the serving plate.

493. Chicken Shawarma

Preparation Time: 15 minutes
Cooking Time: 30 minutes
Servings: 8

Ingredients:

2 lb. chicken breast, sliced into strips
1 teaspoon paprika
1 teaspoon ground cumin
1/4 teaspoon granulated garlic
1/2 teaspoon turmeric
1/4 teaspoon ground allspice

Directions:

Season the chicken with the spices, and a little salt and pepper.
Pour 1 cup chicken broth to the pot.
Seal the pot.
Choose poultry setting.
Cook for 15 minutes.
Release the pressure naturally.

494. Pomegranate Chicken

Preparation Time: 10 minutes
Cooking Time: 25 minutes
Servings: 6

Ingredients:

1-pound chicken breast, skinless, boneless
1 tablespoon za'atar
½ teaspoon salt
1 tablespoon pomegranate juice
1 tablespoon olive oil

Directions:

Rub the chicken breast with za'atar seasoning, salt, olive oil, and pomegranate juice.
Marinate the chicken or 15 minutes and transfer in the skillet.
Roast the chicken for 15 minutes over the medium heat.
Then flip the chicken on another side and cook for 10 minutes more.
Slice the chicken and place in the serving plates.

495. Chicken & Rice

Preparation Time: 25 minutes
Cooking Time: 50 minutes
Servings: 8

Ingredients:

1 whole chicken, sliced into smaller pieces.
2 tablespoons dry Greek seasoning
1 1/2 cups long grain white rice
1 cup chopped parsley

Directions:

Coat the chicken with the seasoning mix.
Add 2 cups of water to the Instant Pot.
Add the chicken inside.
Seal the pot.
Choose manual mode.
Cook at high pressure for 30 minutes.
Release the pressure naturally.
Lift the chicken and place on a baking sheet.
Bake in the oven for 5 minutes or until skin is crispy.
While waiting, strain the broth from the Instant Pot to remove the chicken residue.
Add the rice.
Seal the pot.
Set it to rice function.
Fluff the rice and serve with the chicken.

496. Chicken With Salsa & Cilantro

Preparation Time: 10 minutes
Cooking Time: 30 minutes
Servings: 6

Ingredients:

1 ½ lb. chicken breast fillets
2 cups salsa verde
1 teaspoon garlic, minced
1 teaspoon cumin

2 tablespoons fresh cilantro, chopped

Directions:

Put the chicken breast fillets inside the Instant Pot.
Pour the salsa, garlic and cumin on top.
Seal the pot.
Set it to poultry.
Release the pressure quickly.
Remove the chicken and shred.
Put it back to the pot.
Stir in the cilantro.

497. Lemon Chicken

Preparation Time: 10 minutes
Cooking Time: 20 minutes
Servings: 4

Ingredients:

1-pound chicken breast, skinless, boneless
3 tablespoons lemon juice
1 tablespoon olive oil
1 teaspoon ground black pepper

Directions:

Cut the chicken breast on 4 pieces.
Sprinkle every chicken piece with olive oil, lemon juice, and ground black pepper.
Then place them in the skillet.
Roast the chicken for 20 minutes over the medium heat.
Flip the chicken pieces every 5 minutes.

498. Greek Chicken Bites

Preparation Time: 10 minutes
Cooking Time: 20 minutes
Servings: 6

Ingredients:

1-pound chicken fillet
1 tablespoon Greek seasoning
1 teaspoon sesame oil
½ teaspoon salt
1 teaspoon balsamic vinegar

Directions:

Cut the chicken fingers on small tenders (fingers) and sprinkle them with Greek seasoning, salt, and balsamic vinegar. Mix up well with the help of the fingertips.
Then sprinkle chicken with sesame oil and shake gently.
Line the baking tray with parchment.
Place the marinated chicken fingers in the tray in one layer.
Bake the chicken fingers for 20 minutes at 355F. Flip them on another side after 10 minutes of cooking.

499. Turkey Verde With Brown Rice

Preparation Time: 15 minutes
Cooking Time: 30 minutes
Servings: 5

Ingredients:

2/3 cup chicken broth
1 1/4 cup brown rice
1 1/2 lb. turkey tenderloins
1 onion, sliced
1/2 cup salsa verde

Directions:

Add the chicken broth and rice to the Instant Pot.
Top with the turkey, onion and salsa.
Cover the pot.
Set it to manual.
Cook at high pressure for 18 minutes.
Release the pressure naturally.
Wait for 8 minutes before opening the pot.

500. Lemon Garlic Chicken

Preparation Time: 30 minutes
Cooking Time: 1 Hour And 20 minutes
Servings: 6

Ingredients:

6 chicken breast fillets
3 tablespoons olive oil
1 tablespoon lemon juice
3 cloves garlic, crushed and minced
2 teaspoon dried parsley

Directions:

Marinate the chicken breast fillets in a mixture of olive oil, lemon juice, garlic, parsley, and a pinch of salt and pepper.
Let sit for 1 hour covered in the refrigerator.
Press the sauté setting in the Instant Pot.
Pour in the vegetable oil.
Cook the chicken for 5 minutes per side or until fully cooked.

501. Turkey With Basil & Tomatoes

Preparation Time: 10 minutes
Cooking Time: 20 minutes
Servings: 4

Ingredients:

4 turkey breast fillets
1 tablespoon olive oil
1/4 cup fresh basil, chopped
1 1/2 cups cherry tomatoes, sliced in half
1/4 cup olive tapenade

Directions:

Season the turkey fillets with salt.
Add the olive oil to the Instant Pot.
Set it to sauté.
Cook the turkey until brown on both sides.
Stir in the basil, tomatoes and olive tapenade.
Cook for 3 minutes, stirring frequently.

502. Honey Balsamic Chicken

Preparation time 20 minutes
Cooking Time: 1 Hour
Servings: 10

Ingredients:

1/4 cup honey
1/2 cup balsamic vinegar
1/4 cup soy sauce
2 cloves garlic minced
10 chicken drumsticks

Directions:

Mix the honey, vinegar, soy sauce and garlic in a bowl.
Marinate the chicken in the sauce for 30 minutes.
Cover the pot.
Set it to manual.
Cook at high pressure for 10 minutes.
Release the pressure quickly.
Choose the sauté button to thicken the sauce.

503. Mediterranean Chicken

Preparation Time: 10 minutes
Cooking Time: 20 minutes
Servings: 6

Ingredients:

2 lb. chicken breast fillet, sliced into strips
Wine mixture (1/4 cup white wine mixed with 3 tablespoons red wine)
2 tablespoons light brown sugar
1 1/2 teaspoons dried oregano
6 garlic cloves, chopped

Directions:

Pour in the wine mixture to the Instant Pot.
Stir in the rest of the ingredients.
Toss the chicken to coat evenly.
Seal the pot.
Set it to high pressure.
Cook for 10 minutes.
Release the pressure naturally.

504. Turkey Lasagna

Preparation Time: 15 minutes
Cooking Time: 30 minutes
Servings: 4

Ingredients:

4 tortillas
1 1/4 cup salsa
1/2 can refried beans
1 1/2 cups cooked turkey
1 1/4 cup cheddar cheese, shredded

Directions:

Spray a small pan with oil.
Spread the refried beans on each tortilla.
Place the first tortilla inside the pan.
Add layers of the turkey, salsa and cheese.
Place another tortilla and repeat the layers.
Pour 1 cup of water inside the Instant Pot.
Place the layers on top of a steamer basket.
Place the basket inside the Instant Pot.
Choose manual setting.
Cook at high pressure for 10 minutes.

505. Mediterranean Chicken Wings

Preparation Time: 45 minutes
Cooking Time: 1 hour and 20 minutes
Servings: 4

Ingredients:

8 chicken wings
1 tablespoon garlic puree
2 tablespoons mixed dried herbs (tarragon, oregano and basil)
1 tablespoon chicken seasoning

Directions:

In a bowl, mix the garlic puree, herbs and seasoning.
Marinate the chicken in this mixture for 1 hour.
Add 1 tablespoon of coconut oil into the Instant Pot.
Set it to sauté.
Cook the chicken until brown on both sides.
Remove and set aside.
Add 1 cup of water to the pot.
Place steamer basket inside.
Put the chicken on top of the basket.
Seal the pot.
Set it to manual and cook at high pressure for 10 minutes.
Release the pressure naturally.

506. Duck and Blackberries

Preparation Time: 10 minutes
Cooking Time: 25 minutes
Servings: 4

Ingredients

4 duck breasts, boneless and skin scored
2 tablespoons balsamic vinegar
Salt and black pepper to the taste
1 cup chicken stock
4 ounces blackberries
¼ cup chicken stock
2 tablespoons avocado oil

Directions

Divide into plates and serve.

507. Ginger ducted

Preparation Time: 10 minutes
Cooking Time: 50 minutes
Servings: 4

Ingredients

2 big duck breasts, boneless and skin scored
2 tablespoons olive oil
Salt and black pepper to the taste
1 tablespoon fish sauce
1 tablespoon lime juice
1 garlic clove, minced
1 Serrano chili, chopped
1 small shallot, sliced
1 cucumber, sliced
2 mangos, peeled and sliced
¼ cup oregano, chopped

Directions

Heat up a pan with the oil over medium-high heat, add the duck breasts skin side down and cook for 5 minutes.
Add the orange zest, salt, pepper, fish sauce, and the rest of the ingredients, bring to a simmer and cook over medium-low heat for 45 minutes.
Divide everything between plates and serve.

508. Turkey and Cranberry Sauce

Preparation Time: 10 minutes
Cooking Time: 50 minutes
Servings: 4

Ingredients

1 cup chicken stock
2 tablespoons avocado oil
½ cup cranberry sauce
1 big turkey breast, skinless, boneless, and sliced
1 yellow onion, roughly chopped
Salt and black pepper to the taste

Directions

Heat up a pan with the avocado oil over medium-high heat, add the onion and sauté for 5 minutes.
Add the turkey and brown for 5 minutes more.
Add the rest of the ingredients, toss, introduce in the oven at 350 degrees F and cook for 40 minutes

509. Sage Turkey Mix

Preparation Time: 10 minutes
Cooking Time: 40 minutes
Servings: 4

Ingredients

1 big turkey breast, skinless, boneless, and roughly cubed
Juice of 1 lemon
2 tablespoons avocado oil
1 red onion, chopped
2 tablespoons sage, chopped
1 garlic clove, minced
1 cup chicken stock

Directions

Heat up a pan with the avocado oil over medium-high heat, add the turkey, and brown for 3 minutes on each side.
Add the rest of the ingredients, bring to a simmer and cook over medium heat for 35 minutes.
Divide the mix between plates and serve with a side dish.

510. Turkey and Asparagus Mix

Preparation Time: 10 minutes
Cooking Time: 30 minutes
Servings: 4

Ingredients

1 bunch asparagus, trimmed and halved

1 big turkey breast, skinless, boneless and cut into strips
1 teaspoon basil, dried
2 tablespoons olive oil
A pinch of salt and black pepper
½ cup tomato sauce
1 tablespoon chives, chopped

Directions

Heat up a pan with the oil over medium-high heat, add the turkey, and brown for 4 minutes.
Add the asparagus and the rest of the ingredients except the chives, bring to a simmer and cook over medium heat for 25 minutes.
Add the chives, divide the mix between plates, and serve.

511. Herbed Almond Turkey

Preparation Time: 10 minutes
Cooking Time: 40 minutes
Servings: 4

Ingredients

1 big turkey breast, skinless, boneless, and cubed
1 tablespoon olive oil
½ cup chicken stock
1 tablespoon basil, chopped
1 tablespoon rosemary, chopped
1 tablespoon oregano, chopped
1 tablespoon parsley, chopped
3 garlic cloves, minced
½ cup almonds, toasted and chopped
3 cups tomatoes, chopped

Directions

Heat up a pan with the oil over medium-high heat, add the turkey and the garlic, and brown for 5 minutes.
Add the stock and the rest of the ingredients, bring to a simmer over medium heat and cook for 35 minutes.
Divide the mix between plates and serve.

512. Thyme Chicken and Potatoes

Preparation Time: 10 minutes
Cooking Time: 50 minutes
Servings: 4

Ingredients

1 tablespoon olive oil
4 garlic cloves, minced
A pinch of salt and black pepper
2 teaspoons thyme, dried
12 small red potatoes, halved
2 pounds chicken breast, skinless, boneless and cubed
1 cup red onion, sliced
¾ cup chicken stock
2 tablespoons basil, chopped

Directions

In a baking dish greased with the oil, add the potatoes, chicken, and the rest of the ingredients, toss a bit, introduce in the oven and bake at 400 degrees F for 50 minutes.
Divide between plates and serve.

513. Lemony Turkey and Pine Nuts

Preparation Time: 10 minutes
Cooking Time: 30 minutes
Servings: 4

Ingredients

2 turkey breasts, boneless, skinless and halved
A pinch of salt and black pepper
2 tablespoons avocado oil
Juice of 2 lemons
1 tablespoon rosemary, chopped
3 garlic cloves, minced
¼ cup pine nuts, chopped
1 cup chicken stock

Directions

Heat up a pan with the oil over medium-high heat, add the garlic and the turkey and brown for 4 minutes on each side.
Add the rest of the ingredients, bring to a simmer and cook over medium heat for 20 minutes.
Divide the mix between plates and serve with a side salad.

514. Yogurt Chicken and Red Onion Mix

Preparation Time: 10 minutes
Cooking Time: 30 minutes
Servings: 4

Ingredients

2 pounds chicken breast, skinless, boneless and sliced
3 tablespoons olive oil
¼ cup Greek yogurt
2 garlic cloves, minced
½ teaspoon onion powder
A pinch of salt and black pepper
4 red onions, sliced

Directions

In a roasting pan, combine the chicken with the oil, the yogurt, and the other ingredients, introduce in the oven at 375 degrees F and bake for 30 minutes.
Divide the chicken mix between plates and serve hot.

515. Quick Chicken Salad Wraps

Preparation Time: 15 minutes
Cooking Time: 0 minutes
Servings: 2

Ingredients:

Tzatziki Sauce:
½ cup plain Greek yogurt
1 tablespoon freshly squeezed lemon juice
Pinch garlic powder
1 teaspoon dried dill
Salt and freshly ground black pepper, to taste
Salad Wraps:
2 (8-inch) whole-grain pita bread
1 cup shredded chicken meat
2 cups mixed greens
2 roasted red bell peppers, thinly sliced
½ English cucumber, peeled if desired and thinly sliced
¼ cup pitted black olives
1 scallion, chopped

Directions:

Make the tzatziki sauce: In a bowl, whisk together the yogurt, lemon juice, garlic powder, dill, salt, and pepper until creamy and smooth.
Make the salad wraps: Place the pita bread on a clean work surface and spoon ¼ cup of the tzatziki sauce onto each piece of pita bread, spreading it all over. Top with the shredded chicken, mixed greens, red pepper slices, cucumber slices, black olives, finished by chopped scallion.
Roll the salad wraps and enjoy.
Tips: You can cover the bottom half of each salad wrap in foil, for it's easier to eat. If you cannot find the pita bread, whole-grain naan bread will work, too.

516. Roasted Chicken Thighs With Basmati Rice

Preparation Time: 15 minutes
Cooking Time: 50 to 55 minutes
Servings: 2

Ingredients:

Chicken:

½ teaspoon cumin
½ teaspoon cinnamon
½ teaspoon paprika
¼ teaspoon ginger powder
¼ teaspoon garlic powder
¼ teaspoon coriander
¼ teaspoon salt
1/8 teaspoon cayenne pepper
10 ounces (284 g) boneless, skinless chicken thighs (about 4 pieces)
Rice:
1 tablespoon olive oil
½ small onion, minced
½ cup basmati rice
2 pinches saffron
1 cup low-sodium chicken stock
¼ teaspoon salt

Directions:

Make the Chicken
Preheat the oven to 350°F (180°C).
Combine the cumin, cinnamon, paprika, ginger powder, garlic powder, coriander, salt, and cayenne pepper in a small bowl.
Using your hands to rub the spice mixture all over the chicken thighs.
Transfer the chicken thighs to a baking dish. Roast in the preheated oven for 35 to 40 minutes, or until the internal temperature reaches 165°F (74°C) on a meat thermometer.
Make the Rice
Meanwhile, heat the olive oil in a skillet over medium-high heat.
Sauté the onion for 5 minutes until fragrant, stirring occasionally.
Stir in the basmati rice, saffron, chicken stock, and salt. Reduce the heat to low, cover, and bring to a simmer for 15 minutes, until light and fluffy.
Remove the chicken from the oven to a plate and serve with the rice.
Tip: You can substitute the boneless or bone-in chicken breasts for chicken thighs.

517. Panko Grilled Chicken Patties

Preparation Time: 10 minutes
Cooking Time: 8 to 10 minutes
Servings: 4

Ingredients:

1-pound (454 g) ground chicken
3 tablespoons crumbled feta cheese
3 tablespoons finely chopped red pepper
¼ cup finely chopped red onion
3 tablespoons panko bread crumbs
1 garlic clove, minced
1 teaspoon chopped fresh oregano
¼ teaspoon salt
1/8 teaspoon freshly ground black pepper
Cooking spray

Directions:

Mix together the ground chicken, feta cheese, red pepper, red onion, bread crumbs, garlic, oregano, salt, and black pepper in a large bowl, and stir to incorporate.
Divide the chicken mixture into 8 equal portions and form each portion into a patty with your hands.
Preheat a grill to medium-high heat and oil the grill grates with cooking spray.
Arrange the patties on the grill grates and grill each side for 4 to 5 minutes, or until the patties are cooked through.
Rest for 5 minutes before serving.
Tip: Use any leftovers to your favorite salad. You can cook the patties in a nonstick skillet over medium-high, 4 to 5 minutes per side, until cooked through.

518. Spiced Roast Chicken

Preparation Time: 10 minutes
Cooking Time: 35 minutes
Servings: 6

Ingredients:

1 teaspoon garlic powder
1 teaspoon ground paprika
½ teaspoon ground cumin
½ teaspoon ground coriander
½ teaspoon salt
¼ teaspoon ground cayenne pepper
6 chicken legs
1 teaspoon extra-virgin olive oil

Directions:

Preheat the oven to 400°F (205°C).
Combine the garlic powder, paprika, cumin, coriander, salt, and cayenne pepper in a small bowl.
On a clean work surface, rub the spices all over the chicken legs until completely coated.
Heat the olive oil in an ovenproof skillet over medium heat.
Add the chicken thighs and sear each side for 8 to 10 minutes, or until the skin is crispy and browned.
Transfer the skillet to the preheated oven and continue cooking for 10 to 15 minutes, or until the juices run clear and it registers an internal temperature of 165°F (74°C).
Remove from the heat and serve on plates.
Tip: The skin-on, bone-in chicken breasts would work just as well as chicken legs with this spice rub. The chicken breasts take longer to cook. Bake for 45 minutes until cooked through, flipping halfway through.

519. Yogurt Chicken Breasts

Preparation Time: 10 minutes
Cooking Time: 10 minutes
Servings: 4

Ingredients:

Yogurt Sauce:
½ cup plain Greek yogurt
2 tablespoons water
Pinch saffron (3 or 4 threads)
3 garlic cloves, minced
½ onion, chopped
2 tablespoons chopped fresh cilantro
Juice of ½ lemon
½ teaspoon salt
1 pound (454 g) boneless, skinless chicken breasts, cut into 2-inch strips
1 tablespoon extra-virgin olive oil

Directions:

Make the yogurt sauce: Place the yogurt, water, saffron, garlic, onion, cilantro, lemon juice, and salt in a blender, and pulse until completely mixed.
Transfer the yogurt sauce to a large bowl, along with the chicken strips. Toss to coat well.
Cover with plastic wrap and marinate in the refrigerator for at least 1 hour, or up to overnight.
When ready to cook, heat the olive oil in a large skillet over medium heat.
Add the chicken strips to the skillet, discarding any excess marinade. Cook each side for 5 minutes, or until cooked through.
Let the chicken cool for 5 minutes before serving.
Tips: If the saffron isn't available, you can use ½ teaspoon of turmeric to replace it. To make this a complete meal, serve it with your favorite salad or cooked brown rice.

520. Coconut Chicken Tenders

Preparation Time: 10 minutes
Cooking Time: 15 to 20 minutes
Servings: 6

Ingredients:

4 chicken breasts, each cut lengthwise into 3 strips
½ teaspoon salt

¼ teaspoon freshly ground black pepper
½ cup coconut flour
2 eggs
2 tablespoons unsweetened plain almond milk
1 cup unsweetened coconut flakes

Directions:

Preheat the oven to 400ºF (205ºC). Line a baking sheet with parchment paper.
On a clean work surface, season the chicken with salt and pepper.
In a small bowl, add the coconut flour. In a separate bowl, whisk the eggs with almond milk until smooth. Place the coconut flakes on a plate.
One at a time, roll the chicken strips in the coconut flour, then dredge them in the egg mixture, shaking off any excess, and finally in the coconut flakes to coat.
Arrange the coated chicken pieces on the baking sheet. Bake in the preheated oven for 15 to 20 minutes, flipping the chicken halfway through, or until the chicken is golden brown and cooked through.
Remove from the oven and serve on plates.
Tip: The chicken tenders can be served with anything you like. They taste great with a small potato with a green salad.

521. Grilled Chicken With Lemon And Fennel

Preparation Time: 25 minutes
Cooking Time: 25 minutes
Servings: 4

Ingredients:

2 cups chicken fillets
large fennel bulb
garlic cloves
1 jar green olives
1 lemon

Directions:

Pre-heat your grill to medium-high
Crush garlic cloves
Take a bowl and add olive oil and season with salt and pepper
Coat chicken skewers with the marinade
Transfer them under grill and grill for 20 minutes, making sure to turn them halfway through until golden
Zest half of the lemon and cut the other half into quarters
Cut the fennel bulb into similarly sized segments
Brush olive oil all over the garlic clove segments and cook for 3-5 minutes
Chop them and add them to the bowl with the marinade
Add lemon zest and olives
Once the meat is read, serve with the vegetable mix

CHAPTER 8: EGGS RECIPES

522. Smoked Salmon and Poached Eggs on Toast

Preparation Time: 10 minutes
Cooking Time: 4 minutes

Ingredients:

2 oz avocado smashed
2 slices of bread toasted
Pinch of kosher salt and cracked black pepper
1/4 tsp freshly squeezed lemon juice
2 eggs see notes, poached
3.5 oz smoked salmon
1 TBSP. thinly sliced scallions
Splash of Kikkoman soy sauce optional
Microgreens are optional

Directions:

Take a small bowl and then smash the avocado into it. Then, add the lemon juice and also a pinch of salt into the mixture. Then, mix it well and set aside.
After that, poach the eggs and toast the bread for some time.
Once the bread is toasted, you will have to spread the avocado on both slices and after that, add the smoked salmon to each slice.
Thereafter, carefully transfer the poached eggs to the respective toasts.
Add a splash of Kikkoman soy sauce and some cracked pepper; then, just garnish with scallions and micro greens.

523. Mediterranean Eggs White Breakfast Sandwich with Roasted Tomatoes

Preparation Time: 15 minutes
Cooking Time: 10 minutes
Servings: 2

Ingredients:

Salt and pepper to taste
¼ cup egg whites
1 teaspoon chopped fresh herbs like rosemary, basil, parsley,
1 whole grain seeded ciabatta roll
1 teaspoon butter
1-2 slices Muenster cheese
1 tablespoon pesto
About ½ cup roasted tomatoes
10 ounces grape tomatoes
1 tablespoon extra-virgin olive oil
Black pepper and salt to taste

Directions:

First, you will have to melt the butter over medium heat in the small nonstick skillet.
Then, mix the egg whites with pepper and salt.
Then, sprinkle it with the fresh herbs
After that cook it for almost 3-4 minutes or until the eggs are done, then flip it carefully
Meanwhile, toast ciabatta bread in the toaster
After that, you will have to place the egg on the bottom half of the sandwich rolls, then top with cheese
Add roasted tomatoes and the top half of roll.
To make a roasted tomato, preheat the oven to 400 degrees.
Then, slice the tomatoes in half lengthwise.
Place on the baking sheet and drizzle with the olive oil.
Season it with pepper and salt and then roast in the oven for about 20 minutes. Skins will appear wrinkled when done.

524. Mediterranean Feta and Quinoa Egg Muffins

Preparation Time: 15 minutes
Cooking Time: 15 minutes
Servings: 12

Ingredients:

2 cups baby spinach finely chopped
1 cup chopped or sliced cherry tomatoes
1/2 cup finely chopped onion
1 tablespoon chopped fresh oregano
1 cup crumbled feta cheese
1/2 cup chopped {pitted} kalamata olives
2 teaspoons high oleic sunflower oil
1 cup cooked quinoa
8 eggs
1/4 teaspoon salt

Directions:

Pre-heat oven to 350 degrees Fahrenheit, and then prepare 12 silicone muffin holders on the baking sheet, or just grease a 12-cup muffin tin with oil and set aside.
Finely chop the vegetables and then heat the skillet to medium.
After that, add the vegetable oil and onions and sauté for 2 minutes.
Then, add tomatoes and sauté for another minute, then add spinach and sauté until wilted, about 1 minute.
Place the beaten egg into a bowl and then add lots of vegetables like feta cheese, quinoa, veggie mixture as well as salt, and then stir well until everything is properly combined.
Pour the ready mixture into greased muffin tins or silicone cups, dividing the mixture equally. Then, bake it in an oven for 30 minutes or so, or until the eggs set nicely, and the muffins turn a light golden brown in color.

525. Mediterranean Eggs

Preparation Time: 15 minutes
Cooking Time: 20 minutes
Servings: 2

Ingredients:

5 tbsp. of divided olive oil
2 diced medium sized Spanish onions
2 diced red bell peppers
2 minced cloves garlic
1 teaspoon cumin seeds
4 diced large ripe tomatoes
1 tablespoon of honey
Salt
Freshly ground black pepper
1/3 cup crumbled feta
4 eggs
1 teaspoon zaatar spice
Grilled pita during serving

Directions:

To start with, you have to add 3 tablespoons of olive oil into a pan and heat it over medium heat. Along with the oil, sauté the cumin seeds, onions, garlic and red pepper for a few minutes.
After that, add the diced tomatoes and salt and pepper to taste and cook them for about 10 minutes till they come together and form a light sauce.
With that, half the preparation is already done. Now you just have to break the eggs directly into the sauce and poach them. However, you must keep in mind to cook the egg whites, but keep the

yolks still runny. This takes about 8 to 10 minutes.
While plating adds some feta and olive oil with zaatar spice to further enhance the flavors. Once done, serve with grilled pita.

526. Pastry-Less Spanakopita

Preparation Time: 5 minutes
Cooking Time: 20 minutes
Servings: 4

Ingredients:

1/8 teaspoons black pepper, add as per taste
1/3 cup of Extra virgin olive oil
4 lightly beaten eggs
7 cups of Lettuce, preferably a spring mix (mesclun)
1/2 cup of crumbled Feta cheese
1/8 teaspoon of Sea salt, add to taste
1 finely chopped medium Yellow onion

Directions:

For this delicious recipe, you need to first start by preheating the oven to 180C and grease the flan dish.
Once done, pour the extra virgin olive oil into a large saucepan and heat it over medium heat with the onions, until they are translucent. To that, add greens and keep stirring until all the ingredients are wilted.
After completing that, you should season it with salt and pepper and transfer the greens to the prepared dish and sprinkle on some feta cheese.
Pour the eggs and bake it for 20 minutes till it is cooked through and slightly brown.

527. Greek Yogurt Pancakes

Preparation Time: 10 minutes
Cooking Time: 5 minutes
Servings: 2

Ingredients:

1 cup all-purpose flour
1 cup whole-wheat flour
1/4 teaspoon salt
4 teaspoons baking powder
1 Tablespoon sugar
1 1/2 cups unsweetened almond milk
2 teaspoons vanilla extract
2 large eggs
1/2 cup plain 2% Greek yogurt
Fruit, for serving
Maple syrup, for serving

Directions:

First, you will have to pour the curds into the bowl and mix them well until creamy.
After that, you will have to add egg whites and mix them well until combined.
Then take a separate bowl, pour the wet mixture into the dry mixture. Stir to combine. The batter will be extremely thick.
Then, simply spoon the batter onto the sprayed pan heated to medium-high.
The batter must make 4 large pancakes.
Then, you will have to flip the pancakes once when they start to bubble a bit on the surface. Cook until golden brown on both sides.

528. Spinach and egg scramble with raspberries

Preparation Time: 10 minutes
Cooking Time: 10 minutes
Servings: 1

Ingredients:

One teaspoon of canola oil
One and a half cups of baby spinach (which is one and a half ounces)
Two eggs, large and lightly beaten
Kosher salt, a pinch.
Ground pepper, a pinch
One slice of whole-grain toasted bread
Half cup of fresh and fine raspberries

Directions:

Heat the oil in a non-stick and small skillet at a temperature of medium-high.
Add spinach to the plate.
Cleanly wipe the pan and add eggs into the medium heated pan.
Stir and cook twice in order to ensure even-cooking for about two minutes.
Stir the spinach in and add salt and pepper into it.
Garnish it with raspberries and toast before eating.

529. Egg Cauliflower Salad

Preparation Time: 10 minutes
Cooking Time: 14 minutes
Servings: 4

Ingredients:

4 eggs, hard-boiled, peeled and cubed
2 tbsp fresh parsley, chopped
1 tbsp vinegar
2 tbsp green onion, chopped
2 tbsp mayonnaise
1/2 cup heavy cream
1 1/2 cup vegetable stock
2 cups cauliflower florets
1/4 cup grape tomatoes, halved
Pepper
Salt

Directions:

Pour 1 1/2 cups of stock into the instant pot the place steamer basket in the pot.
Add cauliflower florets into the steamer basket.
Seal pot with lid and cook on high for 14 minutes.
Once done, allow to release pressure naturally for 10 minutes then release remaining using quick release. Remove lid.
Transfer cauliflower florets into the large mixing bowl. Add remaining ingredients into the bowl and mix well.
Serve and enjoy.

530. Egg Salad

Preparation Time: 10 minutes
Cooking Time: 8 minutes
Servings: 4

Ingredients:

4 eggs
2 tablespoon mayonnaise
¼ cup fresh dill, chopped
1 avocado, chopped
1 teaspoon lime juice
¼ teaspoon ground black pepper
1 cup water, for cooking

Directions:

Pour water in the saucepan, add eggs and close the lid.
Boil the eggs for 8 minutes.
Meanwhile, in the salad bowl combine together avocado and chopped dill.
When the eggs are cooked, chill them in the ice water and peel.
Chop the eggs and add in the salad mixture.
Sprinkle the salad with lime juice, ground black pepper, and mayonnaise.
Mix up the salad carefully.

531. Eggs In Zucchini Nests

Preparation Time: 10 minutes
Cooking Time: 7 minutes
Servings: 4

Ingredients:

4 teaspoons butter
½ teaspoon paprika
½ teaspoon black pepper
¼ teaspoon sea salt
4-ounces cheddar cheese, shredded
4 eggs
8-ounces zucchini, grated

Directions:

Grate the zucchini and place the butter in ramekins.
Add the grated zucchini in ramekins in the shape of nests. Sprinkle the zucchini nests with salt, pepper, and paprika. Beat the eggs and pour over zucchini nests.
Top egg mixture with shredded cheddar cheese. Preheat the air fryer basket and cook the dish for 7-minutes.
When the zucchini nests are cooked, chill them for 3-minutes and serve them in the ramekins.

532. Herbed Breakfast Eggs

Preparation Time: 3 minutes
Cooking Time: 17 minutes
Servings: 2

Ingredients:

4 eggs
1 teaspoon oregano
1 teaspoon parsley, dried
½ teaspoon sea salt
1 tablespoon chives, chopped
1 tablespoon cream
1 teaspoon paprika

Directions:

Place the eggs in the air fryer basket and cook them for 17-minutes at 320°Fahrenheit. Meanwhile, combine the parsley, oregano, cream, and salt in shallow bowl.
Chop the chives and add them to cream mixture. When the eggs are cooked, place them in cold water and allow them to chill. After this, peel the eggs and cut them into halves.
Remove the egg yolks and add yolks to cream mixture and mash to blend well with a fork. Then fill the egg whites with the cream-egg yolk mixture. Serve immediately.

533. Spinach Quiche

Preparation Time: 35 minutes
Cooking Time: 21 minutes
Servings: 6

Ingredients:

6-ounces cheddar cheese, shredded
1 teaspoon olive oil
3 eggs
1 teaspoon ground black pepper
½ yellow onion, diced
¼ cup cream cheese
1 cup spinach
1 teaspoon sea salt
4 tablespoons water, boiled
½ cup almond flour

Directions:

Combine the almond flour, water, and salt. Mix and knead the dough. Spray the inside of the fryer basket with olive oil. Set your air fryer to 375°Fahrenheit. Roll the dough and place it in your air fryer basket tray in the shape of the crust. Place air fryer basket tray inside of air fryer and cook for 5-minutes. Chop the spinach and combine it with the cream cheese and ground black pepper.
Dice the yellow onion and add it to the spinach mixture and stir. Whisk eggs in a bowl. When the quiche crust is cooked—transfer the spinach filling.
Sprinkle the filling top with shredded cheese and pour the whisked eggs over the top. Set the air fryer to 350°Fahrenheit. Cook the quiche for 7-minutes.
Reduce the heat to 300°Fahrenheit and cook the quiche for an additional 9-minutes.
Allow the quiche to chill thoroughly and then cut it into pieces for serving.

534. Seed Porridge

Preparation Time: 10 minutes
Cooking Time: 12 minutes
Servings: 3

Ingredients:

1 tablespoon butter
¼ teaspoon nutmeg
1/3 cup heavy cream
1 egg
¼ teaspoon salt
3 tablespoons sesame seeds
3 tablespoons chia seeds

Directions:

Place the butter in your air fryer basket tray. Add the chia seeds, sesame seeds, heavy cream, nutmeg, and salt. Stir gently.
Beat the egg in a cup and whisk it with a fork.
Add the whisked egg to air fryer basket tray.
Stir the mixture with a wooden spatula.
Preheat your air fryer to 375°F. Place the air fryer basket tray into air fryer and cook the porridge for 12-minutes.
Stir it about 3 times during the cooking process.
Remove the porridge from air fryer basket tray immediately and serve hot!

535. Avocado Baked Eggs

Preparation Time: 10 minutes
Cooking Time: 25 minutes
Servings: 2

Ingredients:

2 eggs
1 medium sized avocado, halved and pit removed
¼ cup cheddar cheese, shredded
Kosher salt and black pepper, to taste

Directions:

Preheat oven to 425 degrees and grease a muffin pan.
Crack open an egg into each half of the avocado and season with salt and black pepper.
Top with cheddar cheese and transfer the muffin pan in the oven.
Bake for about 15 minutes and dish out to serve.

536. Cottage Cheese And Berries Omelet

Preparation Time: 2-3 minutes
Cooking Time: 4 minutes
Servings: 1

Ingredients:

1 egg, whisked
1 teaspoon cinnamon powder
1 tablespoon almond milk
3 ounces cottage cheese
4 ounces blueberries

Directions:

Scourge egg with the rest of the ingredients except the oil and toss.
Preheat pan with the oil over medium heat, add the eggs mix, spread, cook for 2 minutes on each side, transfer to a plate and serve.

537. Almond Scramble

Preparation Time: 10 minutes
Cooking Time: 6 Hours
Servings: 4

Ingredients:

1 teaspoon almond butter
4 egg whites
¼ teaspoon salt
½ teaspoon paprika
2 tablespoons heavy cream

Directions:

Whisk the egg whites gently and add heavy cream.
Put the almond butter in the skillet and melt it.
Then add egg white mixture.
Sprinkle it with salt and cook for 2 minutes over the medium heat.
After this, scramble the egg whites with the help of the fork or spatula and sprinkle with paprika.
Cook the scrambled egg whites for 3 minutes more.
Transfer the meal into the serving plates.

538. Poached Egg In Bell Pepper

Preparation Time: 10 minutes
Cooking Time: 15 minutes
Servings: 2

Ingredients:

2 eggs
2 bell peppers, ends sliced off
2 slices mozzarella cheese, shredded

Directions:

Pour 1 cup water inside the Instant Pot.
Add the steamer basket.
Carefully break an egg into each bell pepper cup.
Cover with foil.
Put on top of the basket.
Seal the pot.
Cook on low for 4 minutes.
Release the pressure naturally.
Top with the cheese and wait for it to melt.

539. Eggs And Tomato Mix

Preparation Time: 5 minutes
Cooking Time: 5 minutes
Servings: 2

Ingredients:

1 tomato
2 eggs
¼ teaspoon chili flakes
¾ teaspoon salt
½ teaspoon butter

Directions:

Trim the tomato and slice it into 2 rings.
Remove the tomato flesh.
Toss butter in the skillet and melt it.
Then arrange the tomato rings.
Crack the eggs in the tomato rings. Sprinkle them with salt and chili flakes.
Cook the eggs for 4 minutes over the medium heat with the closed lid.
Transfer the cooked eggs into the serving plates with the help of the spatula.

540. Baked Eggs With Cheddar And Beef

Preparation Time: 20 minutes
Cooking Time: 20 minutes
Servings: 2

Ingredients:

3 oz ground beef, cooked
2 organic eggs
2oz shredded cheddar cheese
1 tbsp olive oil

Directions:

Switch on the oven, then set its temperature to 390°F and let it preheat.
Meanwhile, take a baking dish, grease it with oil, add spread cooked beef in the bottom, then make two holes in it and crack an organic egg into each hole.
Sprinkle cheese on top of beef and eggs and bake for 20 minutes until beef has cooked and eggs have set.
When done, let baked eggs cool for 5 minutes and then serve straight away.
For meal prepping, wrap baked eggs in foil and refrigerate for up to two days.
When ready to eat, reheat baked eggs in the microwave and then serve.

541. Eggs With Zucchini Noodles

Preparation Time: 15 minutes
Cooking Time: 11 minutes
Servings: 2

Ingredients:

2 tablespoons extra-virgin olive oil
3 zucchinis, cut with a spiralizer
4 eggs
A pinch of red pepper flakes
1 tablespoon basil, chopped

Directions:

In a bowl, combine the zucchini noodles with salt, pepper and the olive oil and toss well.
Grease a baking sheet with cooking spray and divide the zucchini noodles into 4 nests on it.
Crack an egg on top of each nest, sprinkle salt, pepper and the pepper flakes on top and bake at 350 degrees F for 11 minutes.
Divide the mix between plates, sprinkle the basil on top and serve.

542. Bread-Free Breakfast Sandwich

Preparation Time:
Cooking Time: 10 minutes
Servings: 2

Ingredients:

6-ounces ground chicken
2 slices of cheddar cheese
2 lettuce leaves
1 tablespoon dill, dried
½ teaspoon sea salt
1 egg
1 teaspoon cayenne pepper
1 teaspoon tomato puree

Directions:

Combine the ground chicken with the pepper and sea salt. Add the dried dill and stir. Beat the egg into the ground chicken mixture.
Make 2 medium-sized burgers from the ground chicken mixture. Preheat your air fryer to 380°Fahrenheit. Spray the air fryer basket tray with olive oil and place the ground chicken burgers inside of it.
Cook the chicken burgers for 10-minutes. Flip over burgers and cook for an additional 6-minutes.
When the burgers are cooked, transfer them to the lettuce leaves. Sprinkle the top of them with tomato puree and with a slice of cheddar cheese. Serve immediately!

543. Western Omelette

Preparation Time: 5 minutes
Cooking Time: 10 minutes
Servings: 4

Ingredients:

1 green pepper
5 eggs
½ yellow onion, diced
3-ounces Parmesan cheese, shredded

1 teaspoon butter
1 teaspoon oregano, dried
1 teaspoon cilantro, dried
1 teaspoon olive oil
3 tablespoons cream cheese

Directions:

In a bowl, add the eggs and whisk them. Sprinkle the cilantro, oregano, and cream cheese into the eggs.
Add the shredded parmesan and mix the egg mixture well.
Preheat your air fryer to 360°Fahrenheit. Pour the egg mixture into the air fryer basket tray and place it into the air fryer. Cook the omelet for 10-minutes. Meanwhile, chop the green pepper and dice the onion. Pour olive oil into a skillet and preheat well over medium heat.
Add the chopped green pepper and onion to skillet and roast for 8-minutes. Stir veggies often.
Remove the omelet from air fryer basket tray and place it on a serving plate. Add the roasted vegetables and serve warm.

544. Scrambled Pancake Hash

Preparation Time: 1hour 15 minutes
Cooking Time: 9 minutes
Servings: 7

Ingredients:

1 egg
¼ cup heavy cream
5 tablespoons butter
1 cup coconut flour
1 teaspoon ground ginger
1 teaspoon salt
1 tablespoon apple cider vinegar
1 teaspoon baking soda

Directions:

Combine the salt, baking soda, ground ginger and flour in a mixing bowl. In a separate bowl crack, the egg into it. Add butter and heavy cream.
Mix well using a hand mixer. Combine the liquid and dry mixtures and stir until smooth. Preheat your air fryer to 400°Fahrenheit.
Pour the pancake mixture into the air fryer basket tray. Cook the pancake hash for 4-minutes.
After this, scramble the pancake hash well and continue to cook for another 5-minutes more. When dish is cooked, transfer it to serving plates, and serve hot!

545. Morning Time Sausages

Preparation Time: 15 minutes
Cooking Time: 12 minutes
Servings: 6

Ingredients:

7-ounces ground chicken
7-ounces ground pork
1 teaspoon ground coriander
1 teaspoon basil, dried
½ teaspoon nutmeg
1 teaspoon olive oil
1 teaspoon minced garlic
1 tablespoon coconut flour
1 egg
1 teaspoon soy sauce
1 teaspoon sea salt
½ teaspoon ground black pepper

Directions:

Combine the ground pork, chicken, soy sauce, ground black pepper, garlic, basil, coriander, nutmeg, sea salt, and egg.
Add the coconut flour and mix the mixture well to combine.
Preheat your air fryer to 360°Fahrenheit. Make medium-sized sausages with the ground meat mixture.
Spray the inside of the air fryer basket tray with the olive oil.
Place prepared sausages into the air fryer basket and place inside of air fryer. Cook the sausages for 6-minutes.
Turn the sausages over and cook for 6-minutes more.
When the cook time is completed, let the sausages chill for a little bit. Serve warm.

546. Baked Bacon Egg Cups

Preparation Time: 10 minutes
Cooking Time: 12 minutes
Servings: 2

Ingredients:

2 eggs
1 tablespoon chives, fresh, chopped
½ teaspoon paprika
½ teaspoon cayenne pepper
3-ounces cheddar cheese, shredded
½ teaspoon butter
¼ teaspoon salt
4-ounces bacon, cut into tiny pieces

Directions:

Slice bacon into tiny pieces and sprinkle it with cayenne pepper, salt, and paprika. Mix the chopped bacon.
Spread butter in bottom of ramekin dishes and beat the eggs there.
Add the chives and shredded cheese. Add the chopped bacon over egg mixture in ramekin dishes. Place the ramekins in your air fryer basket.
Preheat your air fryer to 360°Fahrenheit. Place the air fryer basket in your air fryer and cook for 12-minutes.
When the cook time is completed, remove the ramekins from air fryer and serve warm.

547. Breakfast Meatloaf Slices

Preparation Time: 10 minutes
Cooking Time: 20 minutes
Servings: 6

Ingredients:

8-ounces ground pork
7-ounces ground beef
1 teaspoon olive oil
1 teaspoon butter
1 tablespoon oregano, dried
1 teaspoon cayenne pepper
1 teaspoon salt
1 tablespoon chives
1 tablespoon almond flour
1 egg
1 onion, diced

Directions:

Beat egg in a bowl. Add the ground beef and ground pork.
Add the chives, almond flour, cayenne pepper, salt, dried oregano, and butter. Add diced onion to ground beef mixture. Use hands to shape a meatloaf mixture. Preheat the air fryer to 350°Fahrenheit. Spray the inside of the air fryer basket with olive oil and place the meatloaf inside it.
Cook the meatloaf for 20-minutes. When the meatloaf has cooked, allow it to chill for a bit. Slice and serve it.

548. Baked Eggs & Sausage Muffins

Preparation Time:
Cooking Time: 20 minutes
Servings: 2

Ingredients:

3 eggs
¼ cup cream
2 sausages, boiled
Chopped fresh herbs
Sea salt to taste
4 tablespoons cheese, grated
1 piece of bread, sliced lengthwise

Directions:

Preheat your air fryer to 360°Fahrenheit. Break the eggs in a bowl, add cream, and scramble. Grease 3 muffin cups with cooking spray.

Add equal amounts of egg mixture into each. Arrange sliced sausages and bread slices into muffin cups, sinking into egg mixture.

Sprinkle the tops with cheese, and salt to taste. Cook the muffins for 20-minutes. Season with fresh herbs and serve warm.

549. Spinach & Parsley Baked Omelet

Preparation Time: 45 minutes
Cooking Time: 10 minutes
Servings: 1

Ingredients:

1 teaspoon olive oil
3 eggs
3 tablespoons ricotta cheese
1 tablespoon parsley, chopped
¼ cup spinach, chopped
Salt and pepper to taste

Directions:

Preheat your air fryer to 330°Fahrenheit. Whisk eggs adding salt and pepper as seasoning. Heat the olive oil in air fryer. Stir in the ricotta, spinach, and parsley with eggs. Pour the egg mixture into baking dish and cook in air fryer for 10-minutes. Serve warm.

550. English Breakfast

Preparation Time: 10-15 minutes
Cooking Time: 20 minutes
Servings: 4

Ingredients:

8 medium sausages
8 slices of back bacon
4 eggs
8 slices of toast
1 can baked beans
2 tomatoes, sliced, sauté
1/2 cup mushrooms, finely sliced, sauté
1 tablespoon olive oil

Directions:

Preheat your air fryer to 320°Fahrenheit. Heat olive oil in saucepan over medium-high heat. Add mushrooms to pan and sauté for a few minutes.

Remove mushrooms from pan and set aside, add tomatoes to pan and sauté for a few minutes then set aside.

Place your sausages and bacon into your air fryer and cook for 10-minutes.

Place the baked beans into a ramekin and your (cracked) eggs in another ramekin and cook for an additional 10-minutes at 390°Fahrenheit. Serve warm.

551. Italian Breakfast Frittata

Preparation Time: 30 minutes
Cooking Time: 10 minutes
Servings: 2

Ingredients:

4 cherry tomatoes, sliced into halves
½ Italian sausage, sliced
½ teaspoon Italian seasoning
3 eggs
2-ounces parmesan cheese, shredded
1 tablespoon parsley, chopped
Salt and pepper to taste

Directions:

Preheat your air fryer to 360°Fahrenheit. Put the sausage and cherry tomatoes into baking dish and cook for 5-minutes.

Crack eggs into small bowl, add parsley, Italian seasoning and mix well by whisking.

Pour egg mixture over sausage and cherry tomatoes and place back into air fryer to cook for an additional 5-minutes. Serve warm.

552. Spinach Balls

Preparation Time: 2 hours
Cooking Time: 20 minutes
Servings: 4

Ingredients:

1 carrot, peeled and grated
2 slices of bread, toasted and make into breadcrumbs
1 tablespoon corn flour
1 tablespoon nutritional yeast
½ teaspoon garlic, minced
1 egg, beaten
½ teaspoon garlic powder
½ onion, chopped
1 package fresh spinach, blanched and chopped

Directions:

Blend ingredients in a bowl, except the breadcrumbs. Make small balls with mixture and roll them over the bread crumbs.

Place the spinach balls in your air fryer at 390°Fahrenheit for a cook time of 10-minutes. Serve warm.

553. Pea Protein Breakfast

Preparation Time: 10 minutes
Cooking Time: 15 minutes
Servings: 4

Ingredients:

1 cup almond flour
1 teaspoon baking powder
3 eggs
1 cup mozzarella cheese, shredded
½ cup chicken or turkey strips
3 tablespoons pea protein
1 cup cream cheese
1 cup almond milk

Directions:

Preheat the air fryer to 390°Fahrenheit. Mix all the ingredients in mixing bowl and stir with wooden spoon. Fill muffin cups with mixture ¾ full and bake for 15-minutes and enjoy!

554. Bacon & Cheddar Scrambled Eggs

Preparation Time: 5- 10 minutes
Cooking Time: 10 minutes
Servings: 4

Ingredients:

¼ teaspoon onion powder
4 eggs, beaten
3-ounces bacon, cooked, chopped
½ cup cheddar cheese, grated
3 tablespoons Greek yogurt
¼ teaspoon garlic powder
Salt and pepper to taste

Directions:

Preheat your air fryer to 330°Fahrenheit. Whisk eggs in a bowl, add salt and pepper to taste along with yogurt, garlic powder, onion powder, cheese, and bacon, stir.

Add the egg mixture into oven-proof baking dish. Place into air fryer and cook for 10-minutes. Scramble eggs and serve warm.

555. Ham, Bacon, Eggs & Cheese

Preparation Time: 20 minutes
Cooking Time: 10 minutes
Servings: 4

Ingredients:

4 eggs
1/3 cup ham, cooked and chopped into small pieces
1/3 cup bacon, cooked, chopped into small pieces
1/3 cup cheddar cheese, shredded

Directions:

In a medium-sized mixing bowl whisk the eggs, add the ham, bacon, and cheese and stir until well combined.
Add to baking pan that is sprayed with cooking spray. Preheat the air fryer to 300°Fahrenheit and a cook time of 10-minutes.
Place pan into air fryer then remove when cooking time is completed and serve warm.

556. Asparagus Omelet

Preparation Time: 20 minutes
Cooking Time: 8 minutes
Servings: 2

Ingredients:

3 eggs
5 steamed asparagus tips
2 tablespoons of warm milk
1 tablespoon parmesan cheese, grated
Salt and pepper to taste
Non-stick cooking spray

Directions:

Mix in a large bowl, eggs, cheese, milk, salt and pepper then blend them. Spray a baking pan with non-stick cooking spray. Pour the egg mixture into pan and add the asparagus then place pan inside of baking basket. Set air fryer to 320°Fahrenheit for 8-minutes. Serve warm.

557. Air Baked Eggs

Preparation Time: 10 minutes
Cooking Time: 8 minutes
Servings: 4

Ingredients:

1 lb. of spinach, chopped
7 ounces sliced ham
4 eggs
1 tablespoon olive oil
4 tablespoons milk
Salt and pepper to taste

Directions:

Preheat your air fryer to 300°Fahrenheit for a cook time of 10-minutes.
Butter the inside of 4 ramekins. In each ramekin, place spinach on bottom, one egg, 1 tablespoon of milk, salt, and pepper. Place ramekins in air fryer basket and cook for 8-minutes.

558. Pumpkin Pie French Toast

Preparation Time: 30 minutes
Cooking Time: 20 minutes
Servings: 4

Ingredients:

2 large, beaten eggs
4 slices of cinnamon swirl bread
¼ cup milk
¼ cup pumpkin purée
¼ teaspoon pumpkin spices
¼ cup butter

Directions:

In a large mixing bowl, mix milk, eggs, pumpkin purée and pie spice. Whisk until mixture is smooth.
In the egg mixture dip the bread on both sides. Place rack inside of air fryer's cooking basket. Place 2 slices of bread onto rack.
Set the temperature to 340°Fahrenheit for 10-minutes. Serve pumpkin pie toast with butter.

559. Air Fryer Scrambled Egg

Preparation Time: 10 minutes
Cooking Time: 10 minutes
Servings: 2

Ingredients:

2 eggs
1 tomato, chopped
Dash of salt
1 teaspoon butter
¼ cup cream

Directions:

In a bowl, whisk the eggs, salt, and cream until fluffy. Preheat air fryer to 300°Fahrenheit. Add butter to baking pan and place into preheated air fryer.
Once the butter is melted, add the egg mixture to baking pan and tomato then cook for 10-minutes. Whisk the eggs until fluffy then serve warm.

560. Breakfast Cheese Bread Cups

Preparation Time: 30 minutes
Cooking Time: 15 minutes
Servings: 2

Ingredients:

2 eggs
2 tablespoons cheddar cheese, grated
Salt and pepper to taste
1 ham slice, cut into 2 pieces
4 bread slices, flatten with rolling pin

Directions:

Spray the inside of 2 ramekins with cooking spray. Place 2 flat pieces of bread into each ramekin. Add the ham slice pieces into each ramekin.
Crack an egg in each ramekin then sprinkle with cheese. Season with salt and pepper. Place the ramekins into air fryer at 300°Fahrenheit for 15-minutes. Serve warm.

561. Breakfast Cod Nuggets

Preparation Time: 15 minutes
Cooking Time: 10 minutes
Servings: 4

Ingredients:

1 lb. of cod
For breading:
2 eggs, beaten
2 tablespoons olive oil
1 cup almond flour
¾ cup breadcrumbs
1 teaspoon dried parsley
Pinch of sea salt
½ teaspoon black pepper

Directions:

Preheat the air fryer to 390°Fahrenheit. Cut the cod into strips about 1-inch by 2-inches in length.
Blend breadcrumbs, olive oil, salt, parsley and pepper in a food processor. In three separate bowls add breadcrumbs, eggs, and flour.
Place each piece of fish into flour, then the eggs and lastly the breadcrumbs. Add pieces of cod to air fryer basket and cook for 10-minutes. Serve warm.

562. Breakfast Egg on Avocado

Preparation Time: 10 minutes
Cooking Time: 15 minutes
Servings: 6

Ingredients:

1 tsp garlic powder
1/2 tsp sea salt
1/4 cup Parmesan cheese (grated or shredded)
1/4 tsp black pepper
3 medium avocados (cut in half, pitted, skin on)
6 medium eggs

Directions:

Prepare muffin tins and preheat the oven to 350°F.
To ensure that the egg would fit inside the cavity of the avocado, lightly scrape off 1/3 of the meat.
Place avocado on muffin tin to ensure that it faces with the top up.
Evenly season each avocado with pepper, salt, and garlic powder.
Add one egg on each avocado cavity and garnish tops with cheese.
Pop in the oven and bake until the egg white is set, about 15 minutes.
Serve and enjoy.

563. Breakfast Egg-artichoke Casserole

Preparation Time: 10 minutes
Cooking Time: 35 minutes
Servings: 8

Ingredients:

16 large eggs
14 ounce can artichoke hearts, drained
10-ounce box frozen chopped spinach, thawed and drained well
1 cup shredded white cheddar
1 garlic clove, minced
1 teaspoon salt
1/2 cup parmesan cheese
1/2 cup ricotta cheese
1/2 teaspoon dried thyme
1/2 teaspoon crushed red pepper
1/4 cup milk
1/4 cup shaved onion

Directions:

Lightly grease a 9x13-inch baking dish with cooking spray and preheat the oven to 350oF.
In a large mixing bowl, add eggs and milk. Mix thoroughly.
With a paper towel, squeeze out the excess moisture from the spinach leaves and add to the bowl of eggs.
Into small pieces, break the artichoke hearts and separate the leaves. Add to the bowl of eggs.
Except for the ricotta cheese, add remaining ingredients in the bowl of eggs and mix thoroughly.
Pour egg mixture into the prepared dish.
Evenly add dollops of ricotta cheese on top of the eggs and then pop in the oven.
Bake until eggs are set and doesn't jiggle when shook, about 35 minutes.
Remove from the oven and evenly divide into suggested servings. Enjoy.

564. Brekky Egg-potato Hash

Preparation Time: 10 minutes
Cooking Time: 25 minutes
Servings: 2

Ingredients:

1 zucchini, diced
1/2 cup chicken broth
½ pound cooked chicken
1 tablespoon olive oil
4 ounces shrimp
Salt and ground black pepper to taste
1 large sweet potato, diced
2 eggs
1/4 teaspoon cayenne pepper
2 teaspoons garlic powder
1 cup fresh spinach (optional)

Directions:

In a skillet, add the olive oil.
Fry the shrimp, cooked chicken and sweet potato for 2 minutes.
Add the cayenne pepper, garlic powder and salt, and toss for 4 minutes.
Add the zucchini and toss for another 3 minutes.
Whisk the eggs in a bowl and add to the skillet.
Season using salt and pepper. Cover with the lid.
Cook for 1 minute and add the chicken broth.
Cover and cook for another 8 minutes on high heat.
Add the spinach and toss for 2 more minutes.
Serve immediately.

565. Dill and Tomato Frittata

Preparation Time: 10 minutes
Cooking Time: 35 minutes
Servings: 6

Ingredients:

Pepper and salt to taste
1 tsp red pepper flakes
2 garlic cloves, minced
½ cup crumbled goat cheese – optional
2 tbsp fresh chives, chopped
2 tbsp fresh dill, chopped
4 tomatoes, diced
8 eggs, whisked
1 tsp coconut oil

Directions:

Grease a 9-inch round baking pan and preheat oven to 325oF.
In a large bowl, mix well all ingredients and pour into prepped pan.
Pop into the oven and bake until middle is cooked through around 30-35 minutes.
Remove from oven and garnish with more chives and dill.

566. Paleo Almond Banana Pancakes

Preparation Time: 10 minutes
Cooking Time: 10 minutes
Servings: 3

Ingredients:

1/4 cup almond flour
1/2 teaspoon ground cinnamon
3 eggs
1 banana, mashed
1 tablespoon almond butter
1 teaspoon vanilla extract
1 teaspoon olive oil
Sliced banana to serve

Directions:

Whisk the eggs in a mixing bowl until they become fluffy.
In another bowl, mash the banana using a fork and add to the egg mixture.
Add the vanilla, almond butter, cinnamon and almond flour.
Mix into a smooth batter.
Heat the olive oil in a skillet.
Add one spoonful of the batter and fry them on both sides.
Keep doing these steps until you are done with all the batter.
Add some sliced banana on top before serving.

567. Spinach Mushroom Omelette

Preparation Time: 5 mins
Servings: 2
Cooking Time: 5 mins

Ingredients:

2 tbsps. Olive oil
2 whole eggs
3 c. spinach, fresh
Cooking spray
10 sliced baby Bella mushrooms
8 tbsps. Sliced red onion
4 egg whites
2 oz. goat cheese

Directions:

Place a skillet over medium-high heat and add olive.
Add the sliced red onions to the pan and stir until translucent. Then, add your mushrooms to the pan and keep stirring until they are slightly brown.
Add spinach and stir until they wilted. Season with a tiny bit of pepper and salt. Remove from heat.
Spray a small pan with cooking spray and Place over medium heat.
Break 2 whole eggs in a small bowl. Add 4 egg whites and whisk to combine.
Pour the whisked eggs into the small skillet and allow the mixture to sit for a minute.
Use a spatula to gently work your way around the skillet's edges. Raise the skillet and tip it down and around in a circular style to allow the runny eggs to reach the center and cook around the edges of the skillet.
Add crumbled goat cheese to a side of the omelet top with your mushroom mixture.
Then, gently fold the other side of the omelet over the mushroom side with the spatula.
Allowing cooking for thirty seconds. Then, transfer the omelet to a plate.

568. Mushroom Spinach Omelet

Preparation Time: 3 minutes
Cook time: 15 minutes
Servings: 2

Ingredients:

1 tablespoon olive oil;
1/4 cup red onion, sliced;
green onions, diced; 1 oz. goat cheese;
cups fresh spinach;
5 baby bella mushrooms, sliced;
1 whole egg; 2 egg whites;
garlic powder, black pepper, to taste.

Directions:

Heat oil in a medium skillet on medium-high heat.
Add red onions and sauté for 2-3 minutes. Add sliced mushrooms and sauté for 4-5 minutes.
Add spinach, sauté for about 2 minutes and season with garlic powder and pepper. Then set aside.
Whisk eggs in a bowl. Pour the egg mixture into a small skillet and cook it on medium heat till eggs are no longer runny.
Put mushroom/spinach mixture on top of the omelet and sprinkle it with goat cheese.
Fold omelet in half and cook for another 30 seconds. Once cooked, put omelet onto a plate and top with green onions.

569. Green Beans and Eggs

Preparation Time: 10 minutes
Cooking Time: 15 minutes
Servings: 2

Ingredients

½ cup green beans
¼ teaspoon salt
5 eggs
1/3 cup skim milk
1 bell pepper, seeds removed
1 teaspoon olive oil

Directions:

Slice the bell pepper and combine it with the green beans.
Pour the olive oil in a skillet and transfer the vegetable mixture to the skillet.
Cook on medium heat for 3 minutes, stirring frequently.
Meanwhile, beat the eggs in a mixing bowl.
Sprinkle the egg mixture with the salt and add skim milk. Whisk well.
Pour the egg mixture over the vegetable mixture and cook for 3 minutes on medium heat.
Stir the mixture carefully so that the eggs and vegetables are well combined.
Cook for 4 minutes more.
Stir again and close the lid.
Cook the scrambled eggs for 5 minutes more.
Stir the mixture again.
Serve it.

570. Spiced Morning Omelet

Preparation Time: 10 minutes
Cooking Time: 15 minutes
Servings: 3

Ingredients:

7 eggs
1/3 cup skim milk
3 garlic cloves
¼ teaspoon nutmeg
¼ teaspoon ground ginger
1 teaspoon cilantro
1 teaspoon olive oil
1 tablespoon chives
1 teaspoon turmeric

Directions:

Beat the eggs in a mixing bowl.
Add the skim milk and whisk again.
Sprinkle the egg mixture with the nutmeg, ground ginger, cilantro, and turmeric.
Peel the garlic cloves and mince them.
Chop the chives and combine with the minced garlic.
Add the herb mixture to the eggs and stir it again.
Preheat a skillet well and pour in the olive oil.
Preheat the olive oil over medium heat and then pour the egg mixture into the pan.
Close the lid and cook the omelet for 15 minutes.
When the dish is cooked, cool slightly and cut into the serving portions.
Serve it.

571. Quinoa and Eggs Salad

Preparation Time: 5 minutes
Cooking Time: 0 minutes
Servings: 4

Ingredients:

4 eggs, soft boiled, peeled and cut into wedges
2 cups baby arugula
2 cups cherry tomatoes, halved
1 cucumber, sliced
1 cup quinoa, cooked
1 cup almonds, chopped
1 avocado, peeled, pitted and sliced
1 tablespoon olive oil
1/2 cup mixed dill and mint, chopped
A pinch of salt and black pepper
Juice of 1 lemon

Directions:

In a large salad bowl, combine the eggs

with the arugula and the rest of the ingredients, toss, divide between plates and serve for breakfast.

572. Artichokes and Cheese Omelet

Preparation Time: 10 minutes
Cooking Time: 8 minutes
Servings: 1

Ingredients:

1 teaspoon avocado oil
1 tablespoon almond milk
2 eggs, whisked
A pinch of salt and black pepper
2 tablespoons tomato, cubed
2 tablespoons kalamata olives, pitted and sliced
1 artichoke heart, chopped
1 tablespoon tomato sauce
1 tablespoon feta cheese, crumbled

Directions:

In a bowl, combine the eggs with the milk, salt, pepper and the rest of the ingredients except the avocado oil and whisk well.
Heat up a pan with the avocado oil over medium-high heat, add the omelet mix, spread into the pan, cook for 4 minutes, flip, cook for 4 minutes more, transfer to a plate and serve.

573. Cheesy Eggs Ramekins

Preparation Time: 10 minutes
Cooking Time: 10 minutes
Servings: 2

Ingredients:

1 tablespoon chives, chopped
1 tablespoon dill, chopped
A pinch of salt and black pepper
2 tablespoons cheddar cheese, grated
1 tomato, chopped
2 eggs, whisked
Cooking spray

Directions:

In a bowl, mix the eggs with the tomato and the rest of the ingredients except the cooking spray and whisk well.
Grease 2 ramekins with the cooking spray, divide the mix into each ramekin, bake at 400 degrees F for 10 minutes and serve.

574. Leeks and Eggs Muffins

Preparation Time: 10 minutes
Cooking Time: 20 minutes
Servings: 2

Ingredients:

3 eggs, whisked
¼ cup baby spinach
2 tablespoons leeks, chopped
4 tablespoons parmesan, grated
2 tablespoons almond milk
Cooking spray
1 small red bell pepper, chopped
Salt and black pepper to the taste
1 tomato, cubed
2 tablespoons cheddar cheese, grated

Directions:

In a bowl, combine the eggs with the milk, salt, pepper and the rest of the ingredients except the cooking spray and whisk well.
Grease a muffin tin with the cooking spray and divide the eggs mixture in each muffin mould.
Bake at 380 degrees F for 20 minutes and serve them for breakfast.

575. Baked Omelet Mix

Preparation Time: 10 minutes
Cooking Time: 45 minutes
Servings: 12

Ingredients:

12 eggs, whisked
8 ounces spinach, chopped
2 cups almond milk
12 ounces canned artichokes, chopped
2 garlic cloves, minced
5 ounces feta cheese, crumbled
1 tablespoon dill, chopped
1 teaspoon oregano, dried
1 teaspoon lemon pepper
A pinch of salt
4 teaspoons olive oil

Directions:

Heat up a pan with the oil over medium-high heat, add the garlic and the spinach and sauté for 3 minutes.
In a baking dish, combine the eggs with the artichokes and the rest of the ingredients.
Add the spinach mix as well, toss a bit, bake the mix at 375 degrees F for 40 minutes, divide between plates and serve for breakfast.

576. Scrambled Eggs

Preparation Time: 10 minutes
Cooking Time: 10 minutes
Servings: 2

Ingredients:

1 yellow bell pepper, chopped
8 cherry tomatoes, cubed
2 spring onions, chopped
1 tablespoon olive oil
1 tablespoon capers, drained
2 tablespoons black olives, pitted and sliced
4 eggs
A pinch of salt and black pepper
¼ teaspoon oregano, dried
1 tablespoon parsley, chopped

Directions:

Heat up a pan with the oil over medium-high heat, add the bell pepper and spring onions and sauté for 3 minutes.
Add the tomatoes, capers and the olives and sauté for 2 minutes more.
Crack the eggs into the pan, add salt, pepper and the oregano and scramble for 5 minutes more.
Divide the scramble between plates, sprinkle the parsley on top and serve.

CHAPTER 9: SEAFOOD AND FISH RECIPES

577. Fish and Orzo

Preparation Time: 10 minutes
Cooking Time: 35 minutes
Servings: 4

Ingredients:

1 teaspoon garlic, minced
1 teaspoon red pepper, crushed
2 shallots, chopped
1 tablespoon olive oil
1 teaspoon anchovy paste
1 tablespoon oregano, chopped
2 tablespoons black olives, pitted and chopped
2 tablespoons capers, drained
15 ounces canned tomatoes, crushed
A pinch of salt and black pepper
4 cod fillets, boneless
1-ounce feta cheese, crumbled
1 tablespoons parsley, chopped
3 cups chicken stock
1 cup orzo pasta
Zest of 1 lemon, grated

Directions:

Heat up a pan with the oil over medium heat, add the garlic, red pepper and the shallots and sauté for 5 minutes.
Add the anchovy paste, oregano, black olives, capers, tomatoes, salt and pepper, stir and cook for 5 minutes more.
Add the cod fillets, sprinkle the cheese and the parsley on top, introduce in the oven and bake at 375 degrees F for 15 minutes more.
Meanwhile, put the stock in a pot, bring to a boil over medium heat, add the orzo and the lemon zest, bring to a simmer, cook for 10 minutes, fluff with a fork, and divide between plates.
Top each serving with the fish mix and serve.

578. Baked Sea Bass

Preparation Time: 10 minutes
Cooking Time: 12 minutes
Servings: 4

Ingredients:

4 sea bass fillets, boneless
Sal and black pepper to the taste
2 cups potato chips, crushed
1 tablespoon mayonnaise

Directions:

Season the fish fillets with salt and pepper, brush with the mayonnaise and dredge each in the potato chips.
Arrange the fillets on a baking sheet lined with parchment paper and bake at 400 degrees F for 12 minutes.
Divide the fish between plates and serve with a side salad.

579. Fish and Tomato Sauce

Preparation Time: 10 minutes
Cooking Time: 30 minutes
Servings: 4

Ingredients:

4 cod fillets, boneless
2 garlic cloves, minced
2 cups cherry tomatoes, halved
1 cup chicken stock
A pinch of salt and black pepper
¼ cup basil, chopped

Directions:

Put the tomatoes, garlic, salt and pepper in a pan, heat up over medium heat and cook for 5 minutes.
Add the fish and the rest of the ingredients, bring to a simmer, cover the pan and cook for 25 minutes.
Divide the mix between plates and serve.

580. Halibut and Quinoa Mix

Preparation Time: 10 minutes
Cooking Time: 12 minutes
Servings: 4

Ingredients:

4 halibut fillets, boneless
2 tablespoons olive oil
1 teaspoon rosemary, dried
2 teaspoons cumin, ground
1 tablespoons coriander, ground
2 teaspoons cinnamon powder
2 teaspoons oregano, dried
A pinch of salt and black pepper
2 cups quinoa, cooked
1 cup cherry tomatoes, halved
1 avocado, peeled, pitted and sliced
1 cucumber, cubed
½ cup black olives, pitted and sliced
Juice of 1 lemon

Directions:

In a bowl, combine the fish with the rosemary, cumin, coriander, cinnamon, oregano, salt and pepper and toss.
Heat up a pan with the oil over medium heat, add the fish, and sear for 2 minutes on each side.
Introduce the pan in the oven and bake the fish at 425 degrees F for 7 minutes.
Meanwhile, in a bowl, mix the quinoa with the remaining ingredients, toss and divide between plates.
Add the fish next to the quinoa mix and serve right away.

581. Lemon and Dates Barramundi

Preparation Time: 10 minutes
Cooking Time: 12 minutes
Servings: 2

Ingredients:

2 barramundi fillets, boneless
1 shallot, sliced
4 lemon slices
Juice of ½ lemon
Zest of 1 lemon, grated
2 tablespoons olive oil
6 ounces baby spinach
¼ cup almonds, chopped
4 dates, pitted and chopped
¼ cup parsley, chopped
Salt and black pepper to the taste

Directions:

Season the fish with salt and pepper and arrange on 2 parchment paper pieces.
Top the fish with the lemon slices, drizzle the lemon juice, and then top with the other ingredients except the oil.
Drizzle 1 tablespoon oil over each fish mix, wrap the parchment paper around the fish shaping to packets and arrange them on a baking sheet.
Bake at 400 degrees F for 12 minutes, cool the mix a bit, unfold, divide everything between plates and serve.

582. Catfish Fillets and Rice

Preparation Time: 10 minutes
Cooking Time: 55 minutes
Servings: 2

Ingredients:

2 catfish fillets, boneless
2 tablespoons Italian seasoning
2 tablespoons olive oil
For the rice:
1 cup brown rice
2 tablespoons olive oil
1 and ½ cups water
½ cup green bell pepper, chopped
2 garlic cloves, minced
½ cup white onion, chopped
2 teaspoons Cajun seasoning
½ teaspoon garlic powder
Salt and black pepper to the taste

Directions:

Heat up a pot with 2 tablespoons oil over medium heat, add the onion, garlic, garlic powder, salt and pepper and sauté for 5 minutes.
Add the rice, water, bell pepper and the seasoning, bring to a simmer and cook over medium heat for 40 minutes.
Heat up a pan with 2 tablespoons oil over medium heat, add the fish and the Italian seasoning, and cook for 5 minutes on each side.
Divide the rice between plates, add the fish on top and serve.

583. Halibut Pan

Preparation Time: 10 minutes
Cooking Time: 20 minutes
Servings: 4

Ingredients:

4 halibut fillets, boneless
1 red bell pepper, chopped
2 tablespoons olive oil
1 yellow onion, chopped
4 garlic cloves, minced
½ cup chicken stock
1 teaspoon basil, dried
½ cup cherry tomatoes, halved
1/3 cup kalamata olives, pitted and halved
Salt and black pepper to the taste

Directions:

Heat up a pan with the oil over medium heat, add the fish, cook for 5 minutes on each side and divide between plates.
Add the onion, bell pepper, garlic and tomatoes to the pan, stir and sauté for 3 minutes.
Add salt, pepper and the rest of the ingredients, toss, cook for 3 minutes more, divide next to the fish and serve.

584. Baked Shrimp Mix

Preparation Time: 10 minutes
Cooking Time: 32 minutes
Servings: 4

Ingredients:

4 gold potatoes, peeled and sliced
2 fennel bulbs, trimmed and cut into wedges
2 shallots, chopped
2 garlic cloves, minced
3 tablespoons olive oil
1/2 cup kalamata olives, pitted and halved
2 pounds shrimp, peeled and deveined
1 teaspoon lemon zest, grated
2 teaspoons oregano, dried
4 ounces feta cheese, crumbled
2 tablespoons parsley, chopped

Directions:

In a roasting pan, combine the potatoes with 2 tablespoons oil, garlic and the rest of the ingredients except the shrimp, toss, introduce in the oven and bake at 450 degrees F for 25 minutes.
Add the shrimp, toss, bake for 7 minutes more, divide between plates and serve.

585. Shrimp and Lemon Sauce

Preparation Time: 10 minutes
Cooking Time: 15 minutes
Servings: 4

Ingredients:

1-pound shrimp, peeled and deveined
1/3 cup lemon juice
4 egg yolks
2 tablespoons olive oil
1 cup chicken stock
Salt and black pepper to the taste
1 cup black olives, pitted and halved
1 tablespoon thyme, chopped

Directions:

In a bowl, mix the lemon juice with the egg yolks and whisk well.
Heat up a pan with the oil over medium heat, add the shrimp and cook for 2 minutes on each side and transfer to a plate.
Heat up a pan with the stock over medium heat, add some of this over the egg yolks and lemon juice mix and whisk well.
Add this over the rest of the stock, also add salt and pepper, whisk well and simmer for 2 minutes.
Add the shrimp and the rest of the ingredients, toss and serve right away.

586. Shrimp and Beans Salad

Preparation Time: 10 minutes
Cooking Time: 4 minutes
Servings: 4

Ingredients:

1-pound shrimp, peeled and deveined
30 ounces canned cannellini beans, drained and rinsed
2 tablespoons olive oil
1 cup cherry tomatoes, halved
1 teaspoon lemon zest, grated
½ cup red onion, chopped
A pinch of salt and black pepper
For the dressing:
3 tablespoons red wine vinegar
2 garlic cloves, minced
½ cup olive oil

Directions:

Heat up a pan with 2 tablespoons oil over medium-high heat, add the shrimp and cook for 2 minutes on each side.
In a salad bowl, combine the shrimp with the beans and the rest of the ingredients except the ones for the dressing and toss.
In a separate bowl, combine the vinegar with ½ cup oil and the garlic and whisk well.
Pour over the salad, toss and serve right away.

587. Pecan Salmon Fillets

Preparation Time: 10 minutes
Cooking Time: 15 minutes
Servings: 6

Ingredients:

3 tablespoons olive oil
3 tablespoons mustard
5 teaspoons honey
1 cup pecans, chopped
6 salmon fillets, boneless
1 tablespoon lemon juice
3 teaspoons parsley, chopped
Salt and pepper to the taste

Directions:

In a bowl, mix the oil with the mustard and honey and whisk well.
Put the pecans and the parsley in another bowl.
Season the salmon fillets with salt and pepper, arrange them on a baking sheet

lined with parchment paper, brush with the honey and mustard mix and top with the pecans mix.
Introduce in the oven at 400 degrees F, bake for 15 minutes, divide between plates, drizzle the lemon juice on top and serve.

588. Salmon and Broccoli

Preparation Time: 10 minutes
Cooking Time: 20 minutes
Servings: 4

Ingredients:

2 tablespoons balsamic vinegar
1 broccoli head, florets separated
4 pieces salmon fillets, skinless
1 big red onion, roughly chopped
1 tablespoon olive oil
Sea salt and black pepper to the taste

Directions:

In a baking dish, combine the salmon with the broccoli and the rest of the ingredients, introduce in the oven and bake at 390 degrees F for 20 minutes.
Divide the mix between plates and serve.

589. Salmon and Peach Pan

Preparation Time: 10 minutes
Cooking Time: 11 minutes
Servings: 4

Ingredients:

1 tablespoon balsamic vinegar
1 teaspoon thyme, chopped
1 tablespoon ginger, grated
2 tablespoons olive oil
Sea salt and black pepper to the taste
3 peaches, cut into medium wedges
4 salmon fillets, boneless

Directions:

Heat up a pan with the oil over medium-high heat, add the salmon and cook for 3 minutes on each side.
Add the vinegar, the peaches and the rest of the ingredients, cook for 5 minutes more, divide everything between plates and serve.

590. Tarragon Cod Fillets

Preparation Time: 10 minutes
Cooking Time: 12 minutes
Servings: 4

Ingredients:

4 cod fillets, boneless
¼ cup capers, drained
1 tablespoon tarragon, chopped
Sea salt and black pepper to the taste
2 tablespoons olive oil
2 tablespoons parsley, chopped
1 tablespoon olive oil
1 tablespoon lemon juice

Directions:

Heat up a pan with the oil over medium-high heat, add the fish and cook for 3 minutes on each side.
Add the rest of the ingredients, cook everything for 7 minutes more, divide between plates and serve.

591. Salmon and Radish Mix

Preparation Time: 10 minutes
Cooking Time: 15 minutes
Servings: 4

Ingredients:

2 tablespoons olive oil
1 tablespoon balsamic vinegar
1 and ½ cup chicken stock
4 salmon fillets, boneless
2 garlic cloves, minced
1 tablespoon ginger, grated
1 cup radishes, grated
¼ cup scallions, chopped

Directions:

Heat up a pan with the oil over medium-high heat, add the salmon, cook for 4 minutes on each side and divide between plates
Add the vinegar and the rest of the ingredients to the pan, toss gently, cook for 10 minutes, add over the salmon and serve.

592. Smoked Salmon and Watercress Salad

Preparation Time: 5 minutes
Cooking Time: 0 minutes
Servings: 4

Ingredients:

2 bunches watercress
1-pound smoked salmon, skinless, boneless and flaked
2 teaspoons mustard
¼ cup lemon juice
½ cup Greek yogurt
Salt and black pepper to the taste
1 big cucumber, sliced
2 tablespoons chives, chopped

Directions:

In a salad bowl, combine the salmon with the watercress and the rest of the ingredients toss and serve right away.

593. Salmon and Corn Salad

Preparation Time: 5 minutes
Cooking Time: 0 minutes
Servings: 4

Ingredients:

½ cup pecans, chopped
2 cups baby arugula
1 cup corn
¼ pound smoked salmon, skinless, boneless and cut into small chunks
2 tablespoons olive oil
2 tablespoon lemon juice
Sea salt and black pepper to the taste

Directions:

In a salad bowl, combine the salmon with the corn and the rest of the ingredients, toss and serve right away.

594. Cod and Mushrooms Mix

Preparation Time: 10 minutes
Cooking Time: 25 minutes
Servings: 4

Ingredients:

2 cod fillets, boneless
4 tablespoons olive oil
4 ounces mushrooms, sliced
Sea salt and black pepper to the taste
12 cherry tomatoes, halved
8 ounces lettuce leaves, torn
1 avocado, pitted, peeled and cubed
1 red chili pepper, chopped
1 tablespoon cilantro, chopped
2 tablespoons balsamic vinegar
1-ounce feta cheese, crumbled

Directions:

Put the fish in a roasting pan, brush it with 2 tablespoons oil, sprinkle salt and pepper all over and broil under medium-high heat for 15 minutes. Meanwhile, heat up a pan with the rest of the oil over medium heat, add the mushrooms, stir and sauté for 5 minutes.
Add the rest of the ingredients, toss, cook for 5 minutes more and divide between plates.
Top with the fish and serve right away.

595. Sesame Shrimp Mix

Preparation Time: 10 minutes
Cooking Time: 0 minutes
Servings: 4

Ingredients:

2 tablespoon lime juice
3 tablespoons teriyaki sauce
2 tablespoons olive oil
8 cups baby spinach
14 ounces shrimp, cooked, peeled and deveined
1 cup cucumber, sliced
1 cup radish, sliced
¼ cup cilantro, chopped
2 teaspoons sesame seeds, toasted

Directions:

In a bowl, mix the shrimp with the lime juice, spinach and the rest of the ingredients, toss and serve cold.

596. Dijon Fish Fillets

Preparation Time: 15 minutes
Cooking Time: 3 minutes
Servings: 2

Ingredients:

2 white fish fillets
1 tbsp Dijon mustard
1 cup of water
Pepper
Salt

Directions:

Pour water into the instant pot and place trivet in the pot.
Brush fish fillets with mustard and season with pepper and salt and place on top of the trivet.
Seal pot with lid and cook on high for 3 minutes.
Once done, release pressure using quick release. Remove lid.
Serve and enjoy.

597. Marinated Tuna Steak

Preparation Time: 6 minutes
Cooking Time: 18 minutes
Servings: 4

Ingredients:

Olive oil (2 tbsp.)
Orange juice (.25 cup)
Soy sauce (.25 cup)
Lemon juice (1 tbsp.)
Fresh parsley (2 tbsp.)
Garlic clove (1)
Ground black pepper (.5 tsp.)
Fresh oregano (.5 tsp.)
Tuna steaks (4 - 4 oz. Steaks)

Directions:

Mince the garlic and chop the oregano and parsley.
In a glass container, mix the pepper, oregano, garlic, parsley, lemon juice, soy sauce, olive oil, and orange juice.
Warm the grill using the high heat setting. Grease the grate with oil.
Add to tuna steaks and cook for five to six minutes. Turn and baste with the marinated sauce.
Cook another five minutes or until it's the way you like it. Discard the remaining marinade.

598. Garlic and Shrimp Pasta

Preparation Time: 4 minutes
Cooking Time: 16 minutes
Servings: 4

Ingredients:

6 ounces whole wheat spaghetti
12 ounces raw shrimp, peeled and deveined, cut into 1-inch pieces
1 bunch asparagus, trimmed
1 large bell pepper, thinly sliced
1 cup fresh peas
3 garlic cloves, chopped
1 and ¼ teaspoons kosher salt
½ and ½ cups non-fat plain yogurt
3 tablespoon lemon juice
1 tablespoon extra-virgin olive oil
½ teaspoon fresh ground black pepper
¼ cup pine nuts, toasted

Directions:

Take a large sized pot and bring water to a boil
Add your spaghetti and cook them for about minutes less than the directed package instruction
Add shrimp, bell pepper, asparagus and cook for about 2- 4 minutes until the shrimp are tender
Drain the pasta and the contents well
Take a large bowl and mash garlic until a paste form
Whisk in yogurt, parsley, oil, pepper and lemon juice into the garlic paste
Add pasta mix and toss well
Serve by sprinkling some pine nuts!

599. Paprika Butter Shrimps

Preparation Time: 6 minutes
Cooking Time: 31 minutes
Servings: 2

Ingredients:

¼ tablespoon smoked paprika
1/8 cup sour cream
½ pound tiger shrimps
1/8 cup butter
Salt and black pepper, to taste

Directions:

Prep the oven to 390F and grease a baking dish.
Mix together all the ingredients in a large bowl and transfer into the baking dish.
Situate in the oven and bake for about 15 minutes.
Place paprika shrimp in a dish and set aside to cool for meal prepping. Divide it in 2 containers and cover the lid. Refrigerate for 1-2 days and reheat in microwave before serving.

600. Mediterranean Avocado Salmon Salad

Preparation Time: 6 minutes
Cooking Time: 10 minutes
Servings: 4

Ingredients:

1 lb. skinless salmon fillets
Marinade/Dressing:
3 tbsp. olive oil
2 tbsp. lemon juice fresh, squeezed
1 tbsp. red wine vinegar, optional
1 tbsp. fresh chopped parsley
2 tsp garlic minced
1 tsp dried oregano
1 tsp salt
Cracked pepper, to taste
Salad:
4 cups Romaine (or Cos) lettuce leaves
1 large cucumber
2 Roma tomatoes
1 red onion
1 avocado
1/2 cup feta cheese
1/3 cup pitted Kalamata olives

Directions:

Scourge the olive oil, lemon juice, red wine vinegar, chopped parsley, garlic minced, oregano, salt and pepper

Fill out half of the marinade into a large, shallow dish, refrigerate the remaining marinade to use as the dressing
Coat the salmon in the rest of the marinade
Place a skillet pan or grill over medium-high, add 1 tbsp oil and sear salmon on both sides until crispy and cooked through
Allow the salmon to cool
Distribute the salmon among the containers, store in the fridge for 2-3 days
To Serve: Prep the salad by putting the romaine lettuce, cucumber, roma tomatoes, red onion, avocado, feta cheese, and olives in a bowl. Reheat the salmon in the microwave for 30seconds to 1 minute or until heated through.
Slice the salmon and arrange over salad. Drizzle the salad with the remaining untouched dressing, serve with lemon wedges.

601. Moroccan Fish

Preparation Time: 9 minutes
Cooking Time: 76 minutes
Servings: 12

Ingredients:

Garbanzo beans (15 oz. Can)
Red bell peppers (2)
Large carrot (1)
Vegetable oil (1 tbsp.)
Onion (1)
Garlic (1 clove)
Tomatoes (3 chopped/14.5 oz can)
Olives (4 chopped)
Chopped fresh parsley (.25 cup)
Ground cumin (.25 cup)
Paprika (3 tbsp.)
Chicken bouillon granules (2 tbsp.)
Cayenne pepper (1 tsp.)
Salt (to your liking)
Tilapia fillets (5 lb.)

Directions:

Drain and rinse the beans. Thinly slice the carrot and onion. Mince the garlic and chop the olives. Throw away the seeds from the peppers and slice them into strips.
Warm the oil in a frying pan using the medium temperature setting. Toss in the onion and garlic. Simmer them for approximately five minutes.
Fold in the bell peppers, beans, tomatoes, carrots, and olives.
Continue sautéing them for about five additional minutes.
Sprinkle the veggies with the cumin, parsley, salt, chicken bouillon, paprika, and cayenne.
Stir thoroughly and place the fish on top of the veggies.
Pour in water to cover the veggies.
Lower the heat setting and cover the pan to slowly cook until the fish is flaky (about 40 min.

602. Nicoise-inspired Salad with Sardines

Preparation Time: 9 minutes
Cooking Time: 16 minutes
Servings: 4

Ingredients:

4 eggs
12 ounces baby red potatoes (about 12 potatoes)
6 ounces green beans, halved
4 cups baby spinach leaves or mixed greens
1 bunch radishes, quartered (about 1 1/3 cups)
1 cup cherry tomatoes
20 Kalamata or Nicoise olives (about 1/3 cup)
3 (3.75-ounce) cans skinless, boneless sardines packed in olive oil, drained
8 tablespoons Dijon Red Wine Vinaigrette

Directions:

Situate the eggs in a saucepan and cover with water. Bring the water to a boil. Once the water starts to boil, close then turn the heat off. Set a timer for minutes. Once the timer goes off, strain the hot water and run cold water over the eggs to cool. Peel the eggs when cool and cut in half.
Poke each potato a few times using fork. Place them on a microwave-safe plate and microwave on high for 4 to 5 minutes, until the potatoes are tender. Let cool and cut in half.
Place green beans on a microwave-safe plate and microwave on high for 1½ to 2 minutes, until the beans are crisp-tender. Cool.
Place 1 egg, ½ cup of green beans, 6 potato halves, 1 cup of spinach, 1/3 cup of radishes, ¼ cup of tomatoes, olives, and 3 sardines in each of 4 containers. Pour 2 tablespoons of vinaigrette into each of 4 sauce containers.

603. Broiled Chili Calamari

Preparation Time: 9 minutes
Cooking Time: 8 minutes
Servings: 4

Ingredients:

2 tablespoons extra virgin olive oil
1 teaspoon chili powder
½ teaspoon ground cumin
Zest of 1 lime
Juice of 1 lime
Dash of sea salt
1 and ½ pounds squid, cleaned and split open, with tentacles cut into ½ inch rounds
2 tablespoons cilantro, chopped
2 tablespoons red bell pepper, minced

Directions:

Take a medium bowl and stir in olive oil, chili powder, cumin, lime zest, sea salt, lime juice and pepper
Add squid and let it marinade and stir to coat, coat and let it refrigerate for 1 hour
Pre-heat your oven to broil
Arrange squid on a baking sheet, broil for 8 minutes turn once until tender
Garnish the broiled calamari with cilantro and red bell pepper
Serve and enjoy!

604. Salmon with Corn Pepper Salsa

Preparation Time: 9 minutes
Cooking Time: 12 minutes
Servings: 2

Ingredients:

1 garlic clove, grated
1/2 teaspoon mild chili powder
1/2 teaspoon ground coriander
1.4 teaspoon ground cumin
2 limes – 1, zest and juice; 1 cut into wedges
2 teaspoons rapeseed oil
2 wild salmon fillets
1 ear of corn on the cob
1 red onion, finely chopped
1 avocado, cored, peeled, and finely chopped
1 red pepper, deseeded and finely chopped
1 red chili, halved and deseeded
1/2 a pack of finely chopped coriander

Directions:

Boil the corn in water for about 6-8 minutes until tender.
Drain and cut off the kernels.

In a bowl, combine garlic, spices, 1 tablespoon of lime juice, and oil; mix well to prepare spice rub.
Coat the salmon with the rub.
Add the zest to the corn and give it a gentle stir.
Heat a frying pan over medium heat.
Cook salmon for 4 minutes on both sides.
Serve the cooked salmon with salsa and lime wedges.
Enjoy!

605. Seafood Paella

Preparation Time: 9 minutes
Cooking Time: 41 minutes
Servings: 4

Ingredients:

4 small lobster tails (6-12 oz. each)
3 tbsp. Extra Virgin Olive Oil
1 large yellow onion
2 cups Spanish rice
4 garlic cloves
2 large pinches of Spanish saffron threads
1 tsp. Sweet Spanish paprika
1 tsp. cayenne pepper
1/2 tsp. Aleppo pepper flakes
2 large Roma tomatoes
6 oz. French green beans
1 lb. prawns or large shrimp
1/4 cup chopped fresh parsley

Directions:

Using big pot, add 3 cups of water and bring it to a rolling boil
Add in the lobster tails and allow boil briefly, about 1-minutes or until pink, remove from heat
Using tongs situate the lobster tails to a plate and Do not discard the lobster cooking water
Allow the lobster is cool, then remove the shell and cut into large chunks.
Using a deep pan or skillet over medium-high heat, add 3 tbsp olive oil
Add the chopped onions, sauté the onions for 2 minutes and then add the rice, and cook for 3 more minutes, stirring regularly
Then add in the lobster cooking water and the chopped garlic and, stir in the saffron and its soaking liquid, cayenne pepper, Aleppo pepper, paprika, and salt
Gently stir in the chopped tomatoes and green beans, bring to a boil and allow it to slightly reduce, then cover and cook over low heat for 20 minutes
Once done, uncover and spread the shrimp over the rice, push it into the rice slightly, add in a little water, if needed
Close and cook for 18 minutes
Then add in the cooked lobster chunks
Once the lobster is warmed through, remove from heat allow the dish to cool completely
Distribute among the containers, store for 2 days
To Serve: Reheat in the microwave for 1-2 minutes or until heated through. Garnish with parsley and enjoy!

606. Mediterranean Pearl Couscous

Preparation Time: 4 minutes
Cooking Time: 10 minutes
Servings: 6

Ingredients:

For the Lemon Dill Vinaigrette:
1 large lemon, juice of
1/3 cup Extra virgin olive oil
1 tsp dill weed
1 tsp garlic powder
Salt and pepper
For the Israeli Couscous:
2 cups Pearl Couscous, Israeli Couscous
Extra virgin olive oil
2 cups grape tomatoes, halved
1/3 cup finely chopped red onions
1/2 English cucumber
15 oz. can chickpeas
14 oz. can good quality artichoke hearts
1/2 cup Kalamata olives
15–20 fresh basil leaves
3 oz. fresh baby mozzarella or feta cheese

Directions:

Make the lemon-dill vinaigrette, scourge lemon juice, olive oil, dill weed, garlic powder, salt and pepper then keep aside
In a medium-sized heavy pot, heat two tbsp. of olive oil
Sauté the couscous in the olive oil briefly until golden brown, then add cups of boiling water (or follow the instructed on the package), and cook according to package.
Once done, drain in a colander, set aside in a bowl and allow to cool
In a large mixing bowl, combine the extra virgin olive oil, grape tomatoes, red onions, cucumber, chickpeas, artichoke hearts, and Kalamata olives
Then add in the couscous and the basil, mix together gently
Now, give the lemon-dill vinaigrette a quick whisk and add to the couscous salad, mix to combine
Taste and adjust salt, if needed
Distribute among the containers, store for 2-3 days
To Serve: Add in the mozzarella cheese, garnish with more fresh basil and enjoy!

607. Potato and Tuna Salad

Preparation Time: 18 minutes
Cooking Time: 0 minutes
Servings: 4

Ingredients:

1-pound baby potatoes, scrubbed, boiled
1 cup tuna chunks, drained
1 cup cherry tomatoes, halved
1 cup medium onion, thinly sliced
8 pitted black olives
2 medium hard-boiled eggs, sliced
1 head Romaine lettuce
Honey lemon mustard dressing
¼ cup olive oil
2 tablespoons lemon juice
1 tablespoon Dijon mustard
1 teaspoon dill weed, chopped
Salt as needed
Pepper as needed

Directions:

Take a small glass bowl and mix in your olive oil, honey, lemon juice, Dijon mustard and dill
Season the mix with pepper and salt
Add in the tuna, baby potatoes, cherry tomatoes, red onion, green beans, black olives and toss everything nicely
Arrange your lettuce leaves on a beautiful serving dish to make the base of your salad
Top them up with your salad mixture and place the egg slices
Drizzle it with the previously prepared Salad Dressing
Serve

608. Tuna with Vegetable Mix

Preparation Time: 8 minutes
Cooking Time: 16 minutes
Servings: 4

Ingredients:

¼ cup extra-virgin olive oil, divided
1 tablespoon rice vinegar
1 teaspoon kosher salt, divided
¾ teaspoon Dijon mustard
¾ teaspoon honey
4 ounces baby gold beets, thinly sliced
4 ounces fennel bulb, trimmed and thinly sliced
4 ounces baby turnips, thinly sliced
6 ounces Granny Smith apple, very thinly sliced
2 teaspoons sesame seeds, toasted

6 ounces tuna steaks
½ teaspoon black pepper
1 tablespoon fennel fronds, torn

Directions:

Scourge 2 tablespoons of oil, ½ a teaspoon of salt, honey, vinegar, and mustard.
Give the mixture a nice mix.
Add fennel, beets, apple, and turnips; mix and toss until everything is evenly coated.
Sprinkle with sesame seeds and toss well.
Using cast-iron skillet, heat 2 tablespoons of oil over high heat.
Carefully season the tuna with ½ a teaspoon of salt and pepper
Situate the tuna in the skillet and cook for 4 minutes, giving 1½ minutes per side.
Remove the tuna and slice it up.
Place in containers with the vegetable mix.
Serve with the fennel mix, and enjoy!

609. Tuna Bowl with Kale

Preparation Time: 4 minutes
Cooking Time: 18 minutes
Servings: 6

Ingredients:

3 tablespoons extra virgin olive oil
1 ½ teaspoons minced garlic
¼ cup of capers
2 teaspoons sugar
15 ounce can have drained and rinsed great northern beans
1-pound chopped kale with the center ribs removed
½ teaspoon ground black pepper
1 cup chopped onion
2 ½ ounces of drained sliced olives
¼ teaspoon sea salt
¼ teaspoon crushed red pepper
6 ounces of tuna in olive oil, do not drain

Directions:

Place a large pot, like a stockpot, on your stove and turn the burner to high heat.
Fill the pot about 3-quarters of the way full with water and let it come to a boil.
Cook the kale for 2 minutes.
Drain the kale and set it aside.
Set the heat to medium and place the empty pot back on the burner.
Add the oil and onion. Sauté for 3 to 4 minutes.
Combine the garlic into the oil mixture and sauté for another minute.
Add the capers, olives, and red pepper.
Cook the ingredients for another minute while stirring.
Pour in the sugar and stir while you toss in the kale. Mix all the ingredients thoroughly and ensure the kale is thoroughly coated.
Cover the pot and set the timer for 8 minutes.
Put off the heat and stir in the tuna, pepper, beans, salt, and any other herbs that will make this one of the best Mediterranean dishes you've ever made.

610. Greek Baked Cod

Preparation Time: 9 minutes
Cooking Time: 13 minutes
Servings: 4

Ingredients:

1 ½ lb. Cod fillet pieces (4–6 pieces)
5 garlic cloves, peeled and minced
1/4 cup chopped fresh parsley leaves
Lemon Juice Mixture:
5 tbsp. fresh lemon juice
5 tbsp. extra virgin olive oil
2 tbsp. melted vegan butter
For Coating:
1/3 cup all-purpose flour
1 tsp ground coriander
3/4 tsp sweet Spanish paprika
3/4 tsp ground cumin
3/4 tsp salt
1/2 tsp black pepper

Directions:

Preheat oven to 400F
Scourge lemon juice, olive oil, and melted butter, set aside
In another shallow bowl, mix all-purpose flour, spices, salt and pepper, set next to the lemon bowl to create a station
Pat the fish fillet dry, then dip the fish in the lemon juice mixture then dip it in the flour mixture, brush off extra flour
In a cast iron skillet over medium-high heat, add 2 tbsp olive oil
Once heated, add in the fish and sear on each side for color, but do not thoroughly cook, remove from heat
With the remaining lemon juice mixture, add the minced garlic and mix
Drizzle all over the fish fillets
Bake for 10 minutes, for until the it begins to flake easily with a fork
Allow the dish to cool completely
Distribute among the containers, store for 2-3 days
To Serve: Reheat in the microwave for 1-2 minutes or until heated through. Sprinkle chopped parsley. Enjoy!

611. Pistachio Sole Fish

Preparation Time: 4 minutes
Cooking Time: 11 minutes
Servings: 4

Ingredients:

4 (5 ounces boneless sole fillets
Salt and pepper as needed
½ cup pistachios, finely chopped
Zest of 1 lemon
Juice of 1 lemon
1 teaspoon extra virgin olive oil

Directions:

Pre-heat your oven to 350 degrees Fahrenheit
Prep a baking sheet using parchment paper then keep side
Pat fish dry with kitchen towels and lightly season with salt and pepper
Take a small bowl and stir in pistachios and lemon zest
Place sol on the prepped sheet and press 2 tablespoons of pistachio mixture on top of each fillet
Rub fish with lemon juice and olive oil
Bake for 10 minutes until the top is golden and fish flakes with a fork
Serve and enjoy!
Meal Prep/Storage Options: Store in airtight containers in your fridge for 1-2 days.

612. Baked Tilapia

Preparation Time: 9 minutes
Cooking Time: 16 minutes
Servings: 4

Ingredients:

1 lb. tilapia fillets (about 8 fillets)
1 tsp olive oil
1 tbsp. vegan butter
2 shallots finely chopped
3 garlic cloves minced
1 1/2 tsp ground cumin
1 1/2 tsp paprika
1/4 cup capers
1/4 cup fresh dill finely chopped
Juice from 1 lemon
Salt & Pepper to taste

Directions:

Preheat oven to 375F
Prep a rimmed baking sheet using parchment paper or foil
Lightly mist with cooking spray, arrange the fish fillets evenly on baking sheet
Mix the cumin, paprika, salt and pepper
Rub the fish fillets with the spice mixture

Scourge the melted butter, lemon juice, shallots, olive oil, and garlic, and brush evenly over fish fillets
Top with the capers
Bake for 13 minutes
Pull out from oven and allow the dish to cool completely
Distribute among the containers, store for 2-3 days
To Serve: Reheat in the microwave for 1-2 minutes or until heated through. Top with fresh dill. Serve!

613. A Great Mediterranean Snapper

Preparation Time: 11 minutes
Cooking Time: 19 minutes
Servings: 2

Ingredients:

2 tablespoons extra virgin olive oil
1 medium onion, chopped
2 garlic cloves, minced
1 teaspoon oregano
1 can (14 ounces tomatoes, diced with juice
½ cup black olives, sliced
4 red snapper fillets (each 4 ounces
Salt and pepper as needed
Garnish
¼ cup feta cheese, crumbled
¼ cup parsley, minced

Directions:

Pre-heat your oven to a temperature of 425-degree Fahrenheit
Take a 13x9 inch baking dish and grease it up with non-stick cooking spray
Take a large sized skillet and place it over medium heat
Add oil and heat it up
Add onion, oregano and garlic
Sauté for 2 minutes
Add diced tomatoes with juice alongside black olives
Bring the mix to a boil
Remove the heat
Place the fish on the prepped baking dish
Season both sides with salt and pepper
Spoon the tomato mix over the fish
Bake for 10 minutes
Remove the oven and sprinkle a bit of parsley and feta
Enjoy!

614. Mediterranean Snapper

Preparation Time: 9 minutes
Cooking Time: 13 minutes
Servings: 4

Ingredients:

non-stick cooking spray
2 tablespoons extra virgin olive oil
1 medium onion, chopped
2 garlic cloves, minced
1 teaspoon oregano
1 14-ounce can dice tomatoes
½ cup black olives, sliced
4 4-ounce red snapper fillets
Salt
Pepper
¼ cup crumbled feta cheese
¼ cup fresh parsley, minced

Directions:

Preheat oven to 425 degrees Fahrenheit.
Brush a 13x9 baking dish with non-stick cooking spray.
Cook oil in a large skillet over medium heat.
Sauté onion, oregano, garlic for 2 minutes.
Add can of tomatoes and olives, and bring mixture to a boil; remove from heat.
Season both sides of fillets with salt and pepper and place in the baking dish.
Ladle the tomato mixture evenly over the fish.
Bake for 11 minutes.
Pull out from oven and sprinkle with parsley and feta.
Enjoy!

615. Mediterranean Salmon

Preparation Time: 9 minutes
Cooking Time: 16 minutes
Servings: 4

Ingredients:

½ cup of olive oil
¼ cup balsamic vinegar
4 garlic cloves, pressed
4 pieces salmon fillets
1 tablespoon fresh cilantro, chopped
1 tablespoon fresh basil, chopped
1½ teaspoons garlic salt

Directions:

Combine olive oil and balsamic vinegar.
Add salmon fillets to a shallow baking dish.
Rub the garlic onto the fillets.
Pour vinegar and oil all over, making sure to turn them once to coat them.
Season with cilantro, garlic salt, and basil.
Keep aside and marinate for 13 minutes.
Preheat the broiler to your oven.
Place the baking dish with the salmon about 6 inches from the heat source.
Broil for 15 minutes until both sides are evenly browned and can be flaked with a fork.
Make sure to keep brushing with sauce from the pan.
Enjoy!

616. Heartthrob Mediterranean Tilapia

Preparation Time: 8 minutes
Cooking Time: 16 minutes
Servings: 4

Ingredients:

3 tbsp. Sun-dried tomatoes, packed in oil
1 tbsp. capers
2 tilapia fillets
1 tbsp. oil from sun-dried tomatoes
1 tbsp. lemon juice
2 tbsp. Kalamata olives, chopped and pitted

Directions:

Pre-heat your oven to 372-degree Fahrenheit
Take a small sized bowl and add sun-dried tomatoes, olives, capers and stir well
Keep the mixture on the side
Take a baking sheet and transfer the tilapia fillets and arrange them side by side
Drizzle olive oil all over them
Drizzle lemon juice
Bake in your oven for 10-15 minutes
After 10 minutes, check the fish for a "Flaky" texture
Once appropriately cooked, top the fish with tomato mix and serve!

617. Spanish Salmon With Smoked Paprika

Preparation Time: 10 minutes
Cooking Time: 30 minutes
Servings: 4

Ingredients:

2 tablespoons extra-virgin olive oil, plus more for brushing and drizzling
4 salmon fillets (6 ounces each)
1 tablespoon smoked paprika

1 teaspoon salt, divided
½ teaspoon freshly ground black pepper
2 large tomatoes, quartered
2 yellow bell peppers, seeded and roughly chopped
1 red onion, roughly chopped
1 garlic clove, peeled
1 (1-inch) piece jalapeño, seeded
Chopped fresh flat-leaf parsley for garnish

Directions:

Preheat the oven to 400°F. Line a rimmed baking sheet with parchment paper and brush it lightly with olive oil.
Place the salmon fillets on the prepared baking sheet. Drizzle with 2 tablespoons olive oil.
In a small bowl, mix the smoked paprika, ½ teaspoon of salt, and the pepper. Rub the spice mixture into each salmon fillet.
Bake for 20 to 30 minutes, until the salmon flakes easily with a fork.
Meanwhile, in a food processor, combine the tomatoes, bell peppers, red onion, garlic, jalapeño, and remaining ½ teaspoon of salt. Pulse a few times to get a chunky salsa-like texture.
Spoon some of the tomato mixture on each serving plate and drizzle with olive oil. Lay a salmon fillet on top. Sprinkle with chopped parsley.

618. Whole Branzino With Garlic And Herbs

Preparation Time: 5 minutes
Cooking Time: 25 minutes
Servings: 2

Ingredients:

The whole branzino, scaled and gutted
thyme sprigs
marjoram sprigs
1/4 cup extra-virgin olive oil
2 garlic cloves, minced
1 teaspoon Italian Herb Blend¼ teaspoon salt

Directions:

Preheat the oven to 325°F. Line a rimmed baking sheet with parchment paper.
Place the fish on the prepared baking sheet. Place the thyme and marjoram sprigs inside each fish.
In a small bowl, stir together the olive oil, garlic, Italian herb blend, and salt. Spoon the mixture inside the fish and all around the outside as well.
Bake for 25 to 30 minutes, until the fish easily flakes with a fork.
Remove from the oven and discard the herbs. Using 2 spoons, gently remove the fish backbones.
Serve 1 fish per person, with the caution to look out for any small bones as you eat.

619. Herbed Salmon With Mashed Potatoes

Preparation Time: 15 minutes
Cooking Time: 30 minutes
Servings: 4

Ingredients:

For the salmon
2 tablespoons extra-virgin olive oil, plus more for brushing
1 salmon fillet (16 to 20 ounces)
Salt
Freshly ground black pepper
2 thyme sprigs
2 marjoram sprigs
For the potatoes
2 russet potatoes, peeled and diced
3 to 4 tablespoons whole milk
1 tablespoon unsalted butter
2 teaspoon salt
For the sauce
½ cup Dijon mustard
2 tablespoons freshly squeezed lemon juice
1 teaspoon extra-virgin olive oil
tablespoons chopped fresh dill
2 tablespoons chopped fresh basil

Directions:

Preheat the oven to 400°F. Line a rimmed baking sheet with parchment paper and brush it with olive oil.
Place the salmon, skin-side down, on the prepared baking sheet. Rub it with olive oil and season it lightly with salt and pepper. Top with the herb sprigs.
Bake for 20 to 30 minutes, until the salmon flakes easily with a fork.
Remove the herbs sprigs and discard.
To cook the potatoes
When the salmon is nearly done, bring a large pot of water to a boil over high heat. Add the potatoes and boil for 5 to 10 minutes, until soft. Drain and transfer to a bowl.
Using a hand mixer on low beat the potatoes with 2 tablespoons of milk, butter, and salt. Add the remaining 1 or 2 tablespoons of milk, a little at a time, until you reach the desired consistency.
To make the sauce
In a small bowl, whisk together the mustard, lemon juice, olive oil, dill, and basil.
Spoon the sauce over the salmon and serve with the mashed potatoes.

620. Mediterranean Snapper With Olives And Feta

Preparation Time: 10 minutes
Cooking Time: 20 minutes
Servings: 4

Ingredients:

3 tablespoons extra-virgin olive oil, divided, plus more for brushing
4 snapper fillets (4 to 5 ounces each)
½ teaspoon salt
¼ teaspoon freshly ground black pepper
1 onion, chopped
2 garlic cloves, minced
1 teaspoon dried oregano
(14.5-ounce) can diced tomatoes, undrained
½ cup chopped pitted kalamata olives
¼ cup crumbled feta cheese
2 tablespoons chopped fresh flat-leaf parsley

Directions:

Preheat the oven to 425°F. Brush a 3-quart (13 × 9 × 2 inches) baking dish lightly with olive oil.
Place the snapper in the prepared baking dish. Massage it gently with 2 tablespoons of olive oil, then sprinkle with salt and pepper.
In a large skillet, heat the remaining 1 tablespoon of olive oil over medium heat. Add the onion, garlic, and oregano and cook for about 3 minutes until the onion starts to soften.
Add the tomatoes and their juices and the olives and cook for 5 minutes to warm through and combine the flavors.
Spoon the tomato mixture over the fish.
Bake for 10 to 15 minutes, until the fish is tender and flakes easily with a fork.
Serve with a sprinkling of crumbled feta cheese and chopped parsley.

621. Moroccan Cod

Preparation Time: 10 minutes
Cooking Time: 30 minutes
Servings: 4

Ingredients:

russet potatoes, peeled and cut into large chunks
carrots, cut into large chunks
tablespoons extra-virgin olive oil, divided

1½ teaspoons salt, divided
cod fillets (6 ounces each)
½ teaspoon ground cumin
½ teaspoon paprika
¼ teaspoon ground turmeric
1 large red onion, cut into large chunks
Chopped fresh flat-leaf parsley for garnish

Directions:

Preheat the oven to 425°F. Line a rimmed baking sheet with aluminum foil.
Toss the potatoes and carrots on the prepared baking sheet with 3 tablespoons of olive oil and 1 teaspoon of salt. Spread out in a single layer and roast for 15 minutes.
Meanwhile, rub the remaining 1 tablespoon of olive oil all over the cod. In a small bowl, combine the cumin, paprika, turmeric, and remaining ½ teaspoon of salt and sprinkle the mixture over the fish.
Remove the baking sheet from the oven and move the vegetables over to clear four spots for the fish. Add the fish and red onion and roast for 15 to 20 minutes, until the fish is fully cooked and flakes easily with a fork. Garnish with parsley.

622. Tuna Puttanesca

Preparation Time: 10 minutes
Cooking Time: 30 minutes
Servings: 4

Ingredients:

1 tablespoon extra-virgin olive oil, plus more for brushing
1 (6-ounce) can tomato paste
½ cup water
3 garlic cloves, minced, divided
1 teaspoon dried oregano
½ teaspoon salt
¼ teaspoon freshly ground black pepper
2 tuna steaks (1 inch thick)
½ cup pitted kalamata olives 2 tablespoons capers
1 teaspoon red pepper flakes
8 fresh basil leaves for garnish

Directions:

Preheat the oven to 350°F. Line a rimmed baking sheet with parchment paper and lightly brush with olive oil.
In a skillet, heat the olive oil over medium heat. Add the tomato paste and water and stir to combine. Bring the mixture to a boil, then reduce the heat to a simmer.
Add 1 minced garlic clove, oregano, salt, and black pepper. Simmer for 10 minutes, then remove the pan from the heat.
Halve the tuna steaks horizontally to create four ½-inch-thick steaks. Place the tuna steaks on the prepared baking sheet.
Spoon the tomato sauce over the tuna. Cover with the olives, capers, remaining 2 minced garlic cloves, and red pepper flakes.
Bake for 20 minutes, or until the tuna steaks are cooked to your preference. Garnish with fresh basil.

623. Fish En Papillote

Preparation Time: 10 minutes
Cooking Time: 30 minutes
Servings: 4

Ingredients:

3 tablespoons extra-virgin olive oil, divided
½ green bell pepper, seeded and chopped
½ cup chopped radicchio
1 scallion, thinly sliced 2 garlic cloves, minced
1 salmon fillet (20 ounces)
½ teaspoon salt
¼ teaspoon freshly ground black pepper
3 thyme sprigs, leaves picked
3 plum tomatoes, chopped
3 cups chopped beet greens

Directions:

Preheat the oven to 400°F.
In a skillet, heat 2 tablespoons of olive oil over medium heat. Cook the bell pepper, radicchio, scallion, and garlic for about 3 minutes, until the radicchio, has just wilted. Remove from the heat.
Place the salmon on half of a large sheet of parchment paper. Brush it with the remaining 1 tablespoon of olive oil and sprinkle with salt and pepper. Top with fresh thyme leaves. Spoon the sautéed vegetables over the top of the fish. Add the tomatoes on top.
Fold the other half of the parchment paper over the fish to enclose it. To seal, start at one end and firmly fold the paper along the edges in small pleats to create a half-moon-shaped packet.
Place the packet on a rimmed baking sheet and bake for 25 minutes.
Meanwhile, in a skillet, heat ¼ inch water over medium-high heat. Add the beet greens and cook for about 10 minutes, until wilted and tender. Drain.
Remove the baking sheet from the oven. Be careful when opening the parchment packet because hot steam will be released. Serve the fish on a bed of beet greens, topped with the vegetables from the packet.

624. Baked Fish Fingers

Preparation Time: 20 minutes
Cooking Time: 10 minutes
Servings: 4

Ingredients:

For the fish fingers
Nonstick cooking spray
1-pound cod fillets
1 teaspoon salt
½ teaspoon freshly ground black pepper
1 cup all-purpose flour
1teaspoon paprika
2 large eggs
¼ cup whole milk
1 cup bread crumbs
For the dipping sauce
1 cup low-fat plain Greek yogurt
2 tablespoons extra-virgin olive oil
2 tablespoons freshly squeezed lemon juice
1 garlic clove, minced
1 teaspoon minced fresh dill
½ teaspoon salt
¼ teaspoon freshly ground black pepper

Directions:

Preheat the oven to 450°F. Line a rimmed baking sheet with parchment paper and coat with nonstick cooking spray.
Slice the cod into 1-inch-wide strips. You should get about 20 fish fingers. Season the fingers with salt and pepper.
Set up an assembly line with three shallow bowls. Mix the flour and paprika together in the first bowl, beat together the eggs and milk in the second bowl, and put the bread crumbs in the third bowl.
Dredge a fish stick in the flour, then dip it in the egg mixture, then roll it in the bread crumbs to completely coat. Place on the prepared baking sheet and repeat with the remaining fish fingers.
Bake for about 10 minutes, until the fish is cooked through.
To make the dipping sauce
In a small bowl, stir together the yogurt, olive oil, lemon juice, garlic, dill, salt, and pepper. Serve with the fish fingers.

625. Shrimp Scampi

Preparation Time: 10 minutes
Cooking Time: 10 minutes
Servings: 4

Ingredients:

3 tablespoons extra-virgin olive oil, divided
4 garlic cloves, minced, divided
1 teaspoon salt
½ teaspoon freshly ground black pepper
1-pound large shrimp, peeled and deveined
1 shallot, chopped
¼ cup dry white wine
1 tablespoon freshly squeezed lemon juice
¼ teaspoon red pepper flakes
2 tablespoons unsalted butter
¼ cup chopped arugula

Directions:

In a large bowl, whisk together 1 tablespoon of olive oil, half the garlic, the salt, and black pepper. Add the shrimp and toss to coat.
In a large skillet, heat the remaining 2 tablespoons of olive oil over medium heat. Add the shrimp and cook for 2 minutes.
Add the shallot, wine, lemon juice, remaining garlic, and red pepper flakes. Toss to coat the shrimp and cook until heated through and the liquid reduces by half.
Add the butter and arugula to the pan. Cook, stirring, until the butter melts and the arugula is wilted.

626. Shrimp Margarita

Preparation Time: 10 minutes
Cooking Time: 5 minutes
Servings: 4

Ingredients:

4 tablespoons extra-virgin olive oil, divided
2 tablespoons freshly squeezed lime juice
1 tablespoon tequila (optional)
2 garlic cloves, minced
¼ teaspoon salt
¼ teaspoon cayenne pepper
1-pound large shrimp, peeled and deveined
Easy Rice Pilaf
1 tomato, chopped
1 avocado, pitted, peeled, and sliced
2 tablespoons diced red onion
2 tablespoons chopped fresh cilantro

Directions:

In a bowl, whisk together 2 tablespoons of olive oil, lime juice, tequila (if using), garlic, salt, and cayenne. Add the shrimp and toss to coat.
In a large skillet, heat the remaining 2 tablespoons of olive oil over medium heat. Add the shrimp and cook for about 5 minutes, until the shrimp are pink and cooked through.
Divide the rice pilaf into individual serving bowls. Divide the shrimp evenly among the bowls. Scatter the tomato, avocado, and red onion on top and garnish with the cilantro.

627. Baked Flounder With Parmesan And Herbs

Preparation Time: 5 minutes
Cooking Time: 15 minutes
Servings: 4

Ingredients:

Nonstick cooking spray
flounder fillets (4 ounces each)
2 tablespoons extra-virgin olive oil
1 tablespoon dried oregano
¼ teaspoon freshly ground black pepper
¼ teaspoon salt
½ cup chopped fresh flat-leaf parsley
½ cup grated Parmesan cheese
½ cup bread crumbs

Directions:

Preheat the oven to 325°F. Line a rimmed baking sheet with parchment paper and coat with cooking spray.
Brush the flounder fillets with olive oil and sprinkle with salt, oregano, and pepper—Bake for 10 minutes.
In a small bowl, combine the parsley, Parmesan, and bread crumbs.
Sprinkle the mixture on the flounder fillets and return the baking sheet to the oven for about 5 minutes, until the topping browns and gets a bit crunchy, and the fish flakes easily with a fork.

628. Mussels And Clams In White Wine

Preparation Time: 10 minutes
Cooking Time: 10 minutes
Servings: 4

Ingredients:

2 tablespoons extra-virgin olive oil
1 shallot, minced
2 garlic cloves, minced
1 cup dry white wine
½ teaspoon red pepper flakes
1-pound clams, scrubbed
1-pound mussels, scrubbed and debearded
¼ cup chopped arugula

Directions:

In a large, deep skillet, heat the olive oil over low heat. Cook the shallot for about 5 minutes, until it starts to soften. Add the garlic and cook for 1 minute.
Stir in the white wine and red pepper flakes and cook for 1 minute to allow the alcohol to evaporate.
Increase the heat to medium and add the clams and mussels. Cover and steam for 3 to 5 minutes until the shellfish have opened. Discard any that do not open. If you need more liquid to steam them, add some water.
Remove the shellfish from the pan and top with the sauce from the pan and chopped arugula.
VARIATION TIP: You can enjoy this dish as is or serve it over linguine if you like.

629. Shrimp Fra Diavolo

Preparation Time: 15 minutes
Cooking Time: 15 minutes
Servings: 4

Ingredients:

tablespoons extra-virgin olive oil
2 cups chopped onion
2 garlic cloves, minced
(28-ounce) can whole peeled tomatoes, undrained
1/2 cup dry red wine
1 tablespoon dried oregano
1/2 teaspoon red pepper flakes
1/2 teaspoon salt, plus more for the pasta water
1/4 teaspoon freshly ground black pepper
1-pound linguine
1-pound large shrimp, peeled and deveined

Directions:

In a large skillet, heat the olive oil over medium heat. Add the onion and cook for about 3 minutes, until it starts to soften. Add the garlic and cook for another minute.
Add the tomatoes and their juices, using a potato masher or spoon to break up the tomatoes in the pan.
Add the wine, oregano, red pepper flakes, salt, and black pepper. Bring to a boil, then reduce to a simmer.

Meanwhile, bring a large pot of water to a boil over high heat. Once boiling, salt the water to your liking, stir, and return to a boil. Add the linguine and cook according to package directions until al dente.
Drain.
Add the shrimp to the simmering tomato sauce and cook for about 3 minutes, until opaque.
Serve the shrimp and sauce over the linguine.

630. Sardine Pâté

Prep time: 10 minutes
Cooking Time: 20 minutes
Servings: 4

Ingredients:

2 (7-ounce) cans oil-packed sardines, drained
2 ounces cream cheese or mascarpone
shallot, minced
scallions, thinly sliced
1 tablespoon minced fresh chives
1 tablespoon freshly squeezed lemon juice
Pinch cayenne pepper

Directions:

Put the sardines in a bowl. Remove any spines or tails. Using a fork, mash the sardines.
Add the cream cheese, shallot, scallions, chives, lemon juice, and cayenne and stir until well blended.
MAKE-AHEAD TIP: This mixture can be stored in an airtight container in the refrigerator for up to 2 days.

631. Mussels In Tomato Sauce With Pastina

Preparation Time: 10 minutes
Cooking Time: 20 minutes
Servings: 4

Ingredients:

1/4 cup extra-virgin olive oil
4 garlic cloves, sliced
1 cup dry white wine
1 (28-ounce) can whole peeled tomatoes, undrained
1 tablespoon dried oregano
1 teaspoon red pepper flakes
1 teaspoon salt
1/2 teaspoon freshly ground black pepper
2 pounds mussels, scrubbed and debearded
2 tablespoons pastina

Directions:

In a large, deep skillet, heat the olive oil over medium heat. Add the garlic and cook for 1 minute.
Add the white wine and bring to a boil.
Add the tomatoes and their juices, using a potato masher or spoon to break up the tomatoes in the pan.
Add the oregano, red pepper flakes, salt, and black pepper and stir to combine.
When the sauce starts to boil, add the mussels and cook for about 5 minutes until they all open. Discard any mussels that do not open.
Reduce the heat to low. Stir in the pastina and simmer for 7 to 8 minutes, until the pasta is cooked.
Ingredient Tip: Any small shaped pasta will work in this dish. Orzo is a good alternative if you can't find pastina.

632. Easy Fish And Papillote Recipe

Preparation Time 20 Min
Cooking Time 25 Min
Servings: 1-2

Ingredients

1 ¼ lb. cod fillet (2.5 cm thick) cut into 4 pieces
Kosher salt and black pepper
½ tomato thinly sliced into 4 rounds
½ cored green pepper, thinly sliced into 4 rounds
½ lemon cut into thin rings
A handful of pitted green olives optional
For the sauce
¼ cup of extra virgin olive oil I used Private Reserve Greek EVOO
Juice of ½ lemon
1 shallot finely chopped
2 cloves of garlic finely chopped
1 teaspoon of oregano
1 tsp paprika powder
½ teaspoon of cumin

Directions

Heat the oven to 425 degrees F.
Season the fish on both sides with kosher salt and pepper.
Prepare the sauce. Place the olive oil, lemon juice, shallots, garlic, and herbs in a small mixing bowl or measuring cup and whisk to combine.
Prepare 4 large pieces of parchment paper (about 12 inches on each side). Fold the parchment paper pieces in the middle to mark two halves.
Assemble the bags. Place each fish fillet on the bottom half of a piece of parchment paper spoon 2 tablespoons of the prepared sauce over the fish. Add 1 slice of lemon, 1 slice of tomato, and 1 slice of bell pepper.
Fold the top half of the parchment paper over the fish and vegetables and fold and secure each piece of parchment around the fish and vegetables to create a well-packed pouch.
Place the fish bags on a large baking tray. Bake on the center rack of your heated oven for 12 to 15 minutes or until the fish is cooked through and falls apart easily.
To serve, place the fish and vegetables in their closed parchment containers and place each bag on a serving platter.

633. Calamari With Tomato Sauce

Preparation Time: 20 minutes
Cooking Time: 8 minutes
Servings: 4

Ingredients:

3 lbs. calamari
1/3 cup olive oil
1 tablespoon fresh oregano
1 teaspoon lemon juice
1 tablespoon garlic, minced
¼ teaspoon chopped fresh lemon peel
¼ teaspoon crushed red pepper
¼ cup vinegar
Sauce:
1 lb. fresh whole tomatoes
3 cloves garlic, minced
1 stalk of celery, chopped
1 tablespoon olive oil
½ green bell pepper
Salt and pepper to taste
½ cup onion, chopped

Directions:

To make the sauce, mix all the sauce ingredients and add to blender.
Blend until mixture is smooth. Clean the calamari and slice it into ½-inch rings.
Season calamari with vinegar, red pepper, lemon peel, garlic, lemon juice, and oregano. Add oil to air fryer. Add calamari with its juice. Air fry for about 6-minutes.
Stir once and air fry for another 2-minutes. Serve with hot with sauce.

634. Salmon & Eggs

Preparation Time: 10 minutes
Cooking Time: 10 minutes
Servings: 2

Ingredients:

2 eggs
1 lb. salmon, seasoned and cooked

1 cup celery, chopped
1 onion, chopped
1 tablespoon olive oil
Salt and pepper to taste

Directions:

Whisk the eggs in a bowl. Add celery, onion, salt, and pepper. Add the oil to round baking tray and pour in egg mixture. Place in air fryer on 300°Fahrenheit. Let it cook for 10-minutes. When done, serve with cooked salmon.

635. Tilapia With Egg

Preparation Time: 30 minutes
Cooking Time: 15 minutes
Servings: 3

Ingredients:

2 egg yolks
4 wheat buns
1 lb. tilapia fillets, sliced
1 tablespoon nectar
1 tablespoon hot sauce
3 teaspoons of sweet pickle relish
2 tablespoons mayonnaise
1 tablespoon fish sauce

Directions:

Mix the fish sauce and egg yolks in a bowl. Add mayonnaise, sweet pickle relish, hot sauce, and nectar. Pour mixture into round baking tray.
Place tray inside air fryer with tilapia fillets inside. Cook for 15 minutes on 300°Fahrenheit.

636. Breaded Fish

Preparation Time: 5 minutes
Cooking Time: 12 minutes
Servings: 4

Ingredients:

4 fish fillets
1 egg
5-ounces breadcrumbs
4 tablespoons olive oil

Directions:

Preheat your air fryer to 350°Fahrenheit. In a bowl mix oil and breadcrumbs. Whisk egg. Gently dip the fish into egg and then into crumb mixture. Put into air fryer and cook for 12-minutes.

637. Tasty Tuna With Roast Potatoes

Preparation Time: 20 minutes
Cooking Time: 30 minutes
Servings: 2

Ingredients:

4 medium potatoes
1 teaspoon olive oil
½ tablespoon capers
Salt and pepper to taste
1 green onion, sliced
1 tablespoon Greek yogurt
½ teaspoon chili powder
½ can of tuna in oil, drained
2 boiled eggs, sliced

Directions:

Soak the potatoes in water for 30-minutes. Pat dry with kitchen towel. Brush the potatoes with olive oil. Place potatoes in air fryer and air fry for 30-minutes at 355°Fahrenheit. Put tuna in a bowl with yogurt and chili powder, mix well. Add half of the green onion plus salt and pepper. Slit potatoes length-wise. Stuff tuna mixture in middle of potatoes and place on a serving plate. Sprinkle with chili powder and remaining green onions over potatoes. Serve with capers and a salad of your choice and topped with boiled egg slices.

638. Glazed Halibut Steak

Preparation Time: 10 minutes
Cooking Time: 12 minutes
Servings: 3

Ingredients:

1 lb. halibut steak
2/3 cup soy sauce
¼ teaspoon ginger, ground
1 garlic clove, minced
¼ cup orange juice
¼ teaspoon crushed red pepper flakes
2 tablespoon lime juice
1 teaspoon liquid stevia
½ cup mirin

Directions:

Prepare teriyaki glaze by combining all ingredients except halibut steak in a saucepan. Bring mixture to a boil and then reduce heat by half.
Set aside and allow to cool.
Pour half of the glaze into re-sealable bag with halibut and place in the fridge for 30-minutes. Preheat your air fryer to 390°Fahrenheit.
Place marinated halibut in air fryer and cook for 12-minutes.
When finished, brush some of the remaining glazes over halibut steak.

639. Nacho-Crusted Shrimp

Preparation Time: 15 minutes
Cooking Time: 8 minutes
Servings: 8

Ingredients:

18 jumbo shrimps, peeled and deveined
1 egg, beaten
8-9-ounce nacho-flavored chips, crushed
Salt and pepper to taste

Directions:

Prepare two shallow dishes, one with egg and one with crushed chips. Season with a pinch of salt and pepper. Dip shrimp in the egg and then coat in nacho crumbs. Preheat your air fryer to 350°Fahrenheit. Arrange the shrimp in air fryer and cook for 8-minutes.

640. Sriracha And Honey Tossed Calamari

Preparation Time: 45 minutes
Cooking Time: 13 minutes
Servings: 2

Ingredients:

½ lb. calamari tubes, about ¼ inch wide, rinsed and patted dry
1 cup club soda
½ cup honey
Red pepper flakes to taste
1 cup almond flour
Salt and black pepper to taste
2 tablespoons sriracha

Directions:

Cover calamari rings with club soda in a bowl. Set aside for 10-minutes. In another bowl, mix flour, salt, and black pepper. In a third bowl, combine honey, sriracha, and red pepper flakes. Drain the calamari, pat dry, and cover with flour mixture. Grease your air fryer basket with cooking spray. Add calamari in one layer, leaving little space in between. Set temperature to 380°Fahrenheit and cook for 11-minutes. Shake basket a couple of times during the process. Remove the calamari from air fryer and cover with half of honey sauce and place inside air fryer again. Cook for an additional 2-minutes. When ready to serve cover with remaining sauce.

641. Kataifi-Wrapped Shrimp With Lemon Garlic Butter

Preparation Time: 30 minutes
Cooking Time: 22 minutes
Servings: 5

Ingredients:

20 large green shrimps, peeled and deveined
7 tablespoons unsalted butter
12-ounces of kataifi pastry
Wedges of lemon or lime
Salt and pepper to taste
5 cloves of garlic, crushed
2 lemons, zested and juiced

Directions:

In a pan, over low heat melt butter. Add the garlic and lemon zest, and sauté for about 2-minutes. Season with salt, pepper and lemon juice.
Cover the shrimp with half of garlic butter sauce and set aside remaining half of sauce.
Preheat your air fryer to 360°Fahrenheit and cover the tray with a sheet of foil. Remove the pastry from the bag and tease out strands.
On the countertop lay 6-inch strands. Roll shrimp and butter into pastry. Shrimp tail should be exposed.
Repeat process for all shrimp. Place the shrimp into air fryer for 10-minutes.
Flip shrimp over and place back into air fryer for another 10-minutes.
Serve with a salad and lime or lemon wedges. Dip the shrimp into remaining garlic butter sauce.

642. Fish Taco

Preparation Time: 25 minutes
Cooking Time: 8 minutes
Servings: 2

Ingredients:

1 ½ cups almond flour
1 can of beer
1 teaspoon baking powder
1 teaspoon sea salt
½ cup salsa
8-ounces fresh halibut, sliced into small strips
Corn tortillas
Cilantro, chopped
Cholula sauce to taste
2 tablespoons olive oil
2 chili peppers, sliced
Avocado Cream:
1 large avocado
¾ cup buttermilk
½ lime juiced

Directions:

Make your batter by mixing baking powder, 1 cup of flour, beer, and salt. Stir well. Cover the halibut with remaining ½ cup of flour and dip it into the batter to coat well. Preheat your air fryer to 390°Fahrenheit and grease air fry basket with olive oil. Cook the fish for 8-minutes.
Mix the avocado cream ingredients in a blender until smooth. Place the corn tortillas on a plate and cover with salsa. Set aside. Put the fish on top of tortillas and cover with avocado cream. Add Cholula sauce, sprinkle with cilantro and top with chili slices and serve.

643. Grilled Barramundi With Lemon Butter

Preparation Time: 10 minutes
Cooking Time: 40 minutes
Servings: 2

Ingredients:

1 lb. small potatoes
7-ounces barramundi fillets
1 teaspoon olive oil
¼ bunch of fresh thyme, chopped
Green beans, cooked, optional
Lemon Butter Sauce:
1 scallion, chopped
½ cup thickened cream
½ cup white wine
1 bay leaf
10 black peppercorns
1 clove garlic, chopped
8-ounces unsalted butter
1 lemon, juiced
Salt and pepper to taste

Directions:

Preheat your air fryer to 390°Fahrenheit for 5-minutes. In a bowl, add potatoes, salt, thyme and olive oil. Mix ingredients well. Put potatoes into air fryer basket and cook for 20-minutes. Layer the fish fillets in a basket on top of potatoes. Cook for another 20-minutes. Prepare the sauce on top of the stove. Heat scallion and garlic over medium-high heat and add the peppercorns and bay leaf. Pour in the wine and reduce heat to low.
Add the thickened cream and stir to blend. Add the butter and whisk over low heat. When butter has melted add salt, pepper, and lemon juice. Strain the sauce to remove peppercorns and bay leaf. Place the fish and potatoes on serving plate and add sauce and serve with green beans.

644. Cranberry Cod

Preparation Time: 5 minutes
Cooking Time: 20 minutes
Servings: 2

Ingredients:

3 filets cod
1 tablespoon olive oil
3 tablespoons cranberry jam

Directions:

Preheat your air fryer to 390°Fahrenheit. Brush the cod filets with olive oil. Spoon a tablespoon of cranberry jam on each filet. Cook for 20-minutes.

645. Cod Fish Teriyaki With Oysters, Mushrooms & Veggies

Preparation Time: 30 minutes
Cooking Time: 10 minutes
Servings: 2

Ingredients:

1 tablespoon olive oil
6 pieces mini king oyster mushrooms, thinly sliced
2 slices (1-inch) codfish
1 Napa cabbage leaf, sliced
1 clove garlic, chopped
Salt to taste
1 green onion, minced
Veggies, steamed of your choice
Teriyaki Sauce:
1 teaspoon liquid stevia
2 tablespoons mirin
2 tablespoons soy sauce

Directions:

Prepare teriyaki sauce by mixing all the ingredients in a bowl then set aside. Grease the air fryer basket with oil.
Place the mushrooms, garlic, Napa cabbage leaf, and salt inside. Layer the fish on top. Preheat your air fryer to 360°Fahrenheit for 3-minutes.
Place the basket in air fryer and cook for 5-minutes. Stir.
Pour the teriyaki sauce over ingredients in the basket. Cook for an additional 5-minutes. Serve with your choice of steamed veggies.

646. Salmon With Dill Sauce

Preparation Time: 20 minutes
Cooking Time: 23 minutes
Servings: 4

Ingredients:

1 ½ lbs. of salmon
4 teaspoons olive oil
Pinch of sea salt
Dill Sauce:
½ cup non-fat Greek yogurt
½ cup light sour cream
2 tablespoons dill, finely chopped
Pinch of sea salt

Directions:

Preheat your air fryer to 270°Fahrenheit. Cut salmon into four 6-ounce portions and drizzle 1 teaspoon of olive oil over each piece.
Season with sea salt. Place salmon into cooking basket and cook for 23-minutes.
Make dill sauce. In a mixing bowl, mix sour cream, yogurt, chopped dill and sea salt.
Top cooked salmon with sauce and garnish with additional dill and serve.

647. Grilled Salmon With Capers & Dill

Preparation Time: 30 minutes
Cooking Time: 8 minutes
Servings: 2

Ingredients:

1 teaspoon capers, chopped
2 sprigs dill, chopped
1 lemon zest
1 tablespoon olive oil
4 slices lemon (optional)
11-ounce salmon fillet
Dressing:
5 capers, chopped
1 sprig dill, chopped
2 tablespoons plain yogurt
Pinch of lemon zest
Salt and black pepper to taste

Directions:

Preheat your air fryer to 400°Fahrenheit. Mix dill, capers, lemon zest, olive oil and salt in a bowl. Cover the salmon with this mixture. Cook salmon for 8-minutes.
Combine the dressing ingredients in another bowl.
When salmon is cooked, place on serving plate and drizzle dressing over it. Place lemon slices at the side of the plate and serve.

648. Black Cod With Grapes, Pecans, Fennel & Kale

Preparation Time: 1 hour
Cooking Time: 15 minutes
Servings: 2

Ingredients:

2 fillets black cod (8-ounces)
3 cups kale, minced
2 teaspoons white balsamic vinegar
½ cup pecans
1 cup grapes, halved
1 small bulb fennel, cut into inch-thick slices
4 tablespoons extra-virgin olive oil
Salt and black pepper to taste

Directions:

Preheat your air fryer to 400°Fahrenheit. Use salt and pepper to season your fish fillets. Drizzle with 1 teaspoon of olive oil.
Place the fish inside of air fryer with the skin side down and cook for 10-minutes. Take the fish out and cover loosely with aluminum foil.
Combine fennel, pecans, and grapes. Pour 2 tablespoons of olive oil and season with salt and pepper. Add to the air fryer basket. Cook for an additional 5-minutes.
In a bowl combine minced kale and cooked grapes, fennel and pecans.
Cover ingredients with balsamic vinegar and remaining 1 tablespoon of olive oil. Toss gently. Serve fish with sauce and enjoy!

649. Air-Fried Asian Style Fish

Preparation Time: 20 minutes
Cooking Time: 20 minutes
Servings: 2

Ingredients:

1 medium sea bass
or halibut (12-ounces)
2 garlic cloves, minced
1 tablespoon olive oil
3 slices of ginger, julienned
2 tablespoons cooking wine
1 tomato, cut into quarters
1 lime, thinly cut
1 green onion, chopped
1 chili, diced

Directions:

Prepare ginger, garlic oil mixture: sauté ginger and garlic with oil until golden brown in a small saucepan over medium-heat on top of the stove.
Preheat your air fryer to 360°Fahrenheit.
Prepare fish: clean, rinse, and pat dry. Cut in half to fit into air fryer. Place the fish inside of air fryer basket then drizzle it with cooking wine.
Layer tomato and lime slices on top of fish. Cover with garlic ginger oil mixture.
Top with green onion and slices of chili. Cover with aluminum foil. Cook for 20-minutes.

650. Sweet Mustard Coconut Shrimp

Preparation Time: 30 minutes
Cooking Time: 20 minutes
Servings: 2

Ingredients:

½ cup breadcrumbs
Salt and black pepper to taste
½ cup shredded coconut, unsweetened
½ teaspoon cayenne pepper
8-ounces coconut milk
8 large shrimps
1 tablespoon sugar-free syrup
¼ teaspoon hot sauce
½ cup orange jam, sugar-free
1 teaspoon mustard

Directions:

Preheat your air fryer to 350°Fahrenheit. Place breadcrumbs, coconut, salt, pepper, and cayenne pepper in a bowl and mix.
Dip the shrimp in coconut milk first, then in breadcrumb mixture.
Line baking sheet and arrange shrimp on it.
Place in air fryer and cook for 20-minutes.
Whisk the orange jam, mustard, syrup, and hot sauce.
Add the shrimp to a serving platter and drizzle with sauce and serve.

651. Fish Sticks

Preparation Time: 10 minutes
Cooking Time: 13 minutes
Servings: 4

Ingredients:

3 eggs
2 cups breadcrumbs
1 lb. codfish

1 cup almond flour
3 tablespoons skim milk
Salt and black pepper to taste

Directions:

Whisk milk and egg together in a mixing bowl. In another bowl, add breadcrumbs, and in a third bowl combine flour.
Slice the fish into strips and season with salt and pepper.
Dip each piece into flour, then into egg mixture and then into breadcrumbs.
Preheat your air fryer to 340°Fahrenheit and cook for 13-minutes.
Turn once during cook time.

652. Fish Cakes

Preparation Time: 10 minutes
Cooking Time: 8 minutes
Servings: 4

Ingredients:

14-ounces of potatoes, boiled and mashed
10-ounces cooked salmon, flaked
1 teaspoon olive oil
¼ cup almond flour
1 handful parsley, fresh, chopped
1 handful of capers
1 teaspoon lemon zest

Directions:

Place the potatoes, flaked salmon, lemon zest, parsley, and capers in a bowl and mix well. Make 4 large cakes out of the mixture.
Dust fish cakes with flour. Place them in the fridge for an hour.
Preheat your air fryer to 350°Fahrenheit. Heat olive oil.
Add salmon cakes and cook for 8-minutes. Serve warm.

653. Parmesan-Crusted Tilapia

Preparation Time: 20 minutes
Cooking Time: 5 minutes
Servings: 4

Ingredients:

1 tablespoon olive oil
4 tilapia fillets
¾ cup grated Parmesan cheese
1 tablespoon parsley, chopped
2 teaspoons paprika
Pinch of garlic powder

Directions:

Preheat your air fryer to 350°Fahrenheit.
Brush oil over tilapia fillets. Mix the remaining ingredients in a bowl. Coat tilapia fillets with parmesan mixture. Line baking dish with parchment paper and arrange fillets. Place in air fryer and cook for 5-minutes.

654. Salmon Croquettes

Preparation Time: 45 minutes
Cooking Time: 10 minutes
Servings: 4

Ingredients:

14-ounce tin of red salmon, drained
2 free-range eggs
5 tablespoons olive oil
½ cup breadcrumbs
2 tablespoons spring onions, chopped
Salt and pepper to taste
Pinch of herbs

Directions:

Add drained salmon into a bowl and mash well. Break in the egg, add herbs, spring onions, salt, pepper and mix well.
In another bowl, combine breadcrumbs and oil and mix well.
Take a spoon of the salmon mixture and shape it into a croquette shape in your hand.
Roll it in the breadcrumbs and place inside air fryer. Set your air fryer to 390°Fahrenhiet for 10-minutes.

655. Salmon With Creamy Zucchini

Preparation Time: 15 minutes
Cooking Time: 10 minutes
Servings: 2

Ingredients:

2 (6-ounce) salmon fillets, skin on
Salt and pepper to taste
1 teaspoon olive oil
Courgette:
2 large zucchinis, trimmed and spiralized
1 avocado, peeled and chopped
Small handful of parsley, chopped
½ garlic clove, minced
Small handful cherry tomatoes, halved
Small handful of black olives, chopped
2 tablespoons pine nuts, toasted

Directions:

Preheat your air fryer to 350°Fahrenheit.
Brush salmon with olive oil and season with salt and pepper.
Place salmon in air fryer and cook for 10-minutes.
Blend the avocado, garlic, and parsley in a food processor until smooth.
Toss in a bowl with zucchini, olives, and tomatoes.
Divide vegetables between two plates, top each portion with salmon fillet, sprinkle with pine nuts, and serve.

656. Cajun-Seasoned Lemon Salmon

Preparation Time: 20 minutes
Cooking Time: 7 minutes
Servings: 1

Ingredients:

1 salmon fillet
1 teaspoon Cajun seasoning
2 lemon wedges, for serving
1 teaspoon liquid stevia
½ lemon, juiced

Directions:

Preheat your air fryer to 350°Fahrenheit.
Combine lemon juice and liquid stevia and coat salmon with this mixture.
Sprinkle Cajun seasoning all over salmon.
Place salmon on parchment paper in air fryer and cook for 7-minutes. Serve with lemon wedges.

657. The Ultimate Recipe of Tuna Salad with Olive Dressing

Preparation Time 20 Min
Cooking Time 35 Min
Servings: 4-6

Ingredients

For the salad:
3 cups of chopped kale (or mixed vegetables)
2 small apples, cored and thinly sliced
1-2 avocados, thinly sliced
A handful of halved cherry tomatoes, about 1 cup
1 small red onion, thinly sliced
1 1/4 cup cooked corn (or canned)
2/3 cup of green olives
3 hard-boiled eggs
2 tablespoons of capers
Sauce ingredients:
1/4 cup finely chopped red onions
2 spring onions, finely chopped
1/4 cup finely chopped green onions (any type, but the olives wrapped in chili are best)

3 tablespoons of granular honey mustard (or granular mustard and 1 tablespoon of honey)
1 tablespoon of chopped capers
1 jalapeno, finely chopped
1 large lemon (or 2 small)
1/4 cup finely chopped herbs (a mixture of cilantro, parsley, and usually dill)
2/3 cup extra virgin olive oil (flavored olive oil also works)
1/4 teaspoon of salt
1/4 teaspoon of pepper
2 - 3 cans of tuna, if applicable, drained and left whole

Directions

Prepare your salad ingredient and place them in a large bowl.
In another bowl, mix all the sauce ingredients until smooth. Taste and adjust the seasoning.
Take 2 tablespoons of the sauce and drizzle the tuna pieces, and set aside.
Take another 3 tablespoons of sauce (more or less to taste) and mix it with the salad ingredients.
Arrange the salad ingredients on the plate; I have clumped each ingredient separately with the vegetables in the bowl's bottom.
Then spoon the tuna over the salad and drizzle with more sauce. Serve the salad and enjoy

658. Smoked Salmon Plate

Preparation Time 14 Min
Cooking Time 45 Min
Servings: 24

Ingredients

1-pound smoked salmon
1 cucumber sliced
1 red onion sliced
1/4 cup capers, drained
1 cup of arugula
4 bagels with rye bread, toasted
Lemon slices
Avocados, radishes, tomatoes, apple slices (optional)
Garlic Lemon Herb Cream Cheese
Sweet Mustard Dill Sauce

Directions

Arrange the salmon right in the center of your serving of plater and surround the rest of the ingredients. Add more or less to your taste.
Recipe notes
Smoked salmon shell tips
Choose your favorite ingredients or whatever you have on hand.
Use different fruits for color contrast and sweetness.
Slice your ingredients so you can easily assemble the smoked salmon platter.
Use additional spices such as the sweet mustard-dill sauce.
You can use ready cream cheese or this Garlic Lemon Herb Cream Cheese.

659. Salmon Asparagus Sweet Potato Nicoise

Preparation Time 10 Min
Cooking Time 15 Min
Servings: 2

Ingredients

For the salad:
3 hard-boiled eggs
2 cups of fresh baby spinach
1 cup of seedless grapes
Cut 2 scallions into 2-inch strips
For the sweet potatoes:
1 purple sweet potato peeled and thinly sliced into 1/8-inch-thick rounds
1 orange sweet potato peeled and thinly sliced into 1/8-inch-thick rounds
1 pinch of salt
1 teaspoon of olive oil
For the salmon and asparagus:
2 large salmon fillets - about 6 ounces each cut into 1-inch-thick strips
2 bunches of asparagus tips trimmed
1/2 teaspoon of salt
1/4 teaspoon freshly cracked black pepper
1/2 teaspoon Provencal herbs (or substitute dried oregano)
1 tablespoon of olive oil
For the dressing:
Sweet Mustard Dill Sauce

Directions

Preheat the oven to 425 degrees F.
For the sweet potatoes:
Start with the sweet potatoes; mix them with a pinch of salt and olive oil and spread them in an even layer on a baking tray. When the oven is ready, roast the sweet potatoes until tender - about 15 minutes.
While the sweet potatoes are roasting, prepare the remaining salad
For the salmon and asparagus:
For the salmon and asparagus, place them in a single layer on a baking tray and sprinkle with salt, pepper, and Provencal herbs or dried oregano. Then divide the olive oil, drizzle the salmon with 1/2 tablespoon, toss the salmon pieces together, and put them back in a single layer on your baking sheet.
Drizzle the remaining 1/2 tablespoon of olive oil over the seasoned asparagus and mix well. Then divide the asparagus again in a single layer on the baking tray.
When the sweet potatoes are cooked, turn the oven to grill and grill the salmon and asparagus for 5-7 minutes (depending on the salmon's size and thickness) until the edges are golden and the salmon is cooked.

660. Mediterranean Fish Packages

Preparation Time 10 Min
Cooking Time 15 Min
Servings: 12

Ingredients

4 tilapia fillets
1/2 cup wish-bone Robust Italian dressing
1 cup plum tomatoes (sliced ripe)
4 teaspoons capers (drained (optional))
1/2 cup of kalamata olives

Directions

Preheat the oven to 350 °.
Place the fillets in the center of four 12 x 18-inch pieces of heavy aluminum foil. Divide the vegetables evenly among the fillets and sprinkle with Wish-Bone® Robust Italian Dressing. Wrap the foil loosely around the fillet and vegetables and seal the edges airtight with a double fold. Arrange the packages on the jelly roll pan. Bake for 20 minutes or until fillets flake with a fork.

661. Mediterranean Style Fish Stew

Preparation Time 25 Min
Cooking Time 55 Min
Servings: 4

Ingredients

28 grams of San Marzano whole tomatoes
3 1/2 pounds of fresh cod
1 sweet onion (large, halved, and thinly sliced, about 2 cups)
2 cloves of garlic (peeled and broken, finely chopped)
1 teaspoon of dried oregano
1 teaspoon of salt (omit if salt-sensitive)
6 tablespoons of EVOO (divided between 4 and 2)
1 dash of pepper (to taste)
1 dash of red pepper flakes (optional)
12 green olives (large, with chili, halved)

12 Greek black olives (pitted, halved, Kalamata olives)
pecorino Romano (grated as a topping, contrary to the old belief that you should not use cheese with fish it is delicious)
fresh parsley (finely chopped, for garnish, optional)

Directions

Crush the San Marzano tomatoes with your hands, reserve the liquid, and set aside.
Pat the fish dry with paper towels and cut into 4–5-inch pieces.
In a large deep skillet, heat 2 tablespoons of EVOO over medium heat. Add half of the cod and cook for 3-4 minutes on each side. Remove from pan and set aside. Repeat with the second half of the fish, remove and set aside.
In the same skillet, heat the remaining EVOO over medium heat, add onions, oregano, zucchini, garlic, salt, and pepper until tender.
Add tomatoes and liquid to the pan. Bring to the boil.
Add the cod and bring back to the boil, spoon over the sauce. Reduce heat to low and leave uncovered until fish starts to flake easily with a fork, about 5-7 minutes, no more.
Sprinkle with parsley and grated Pecorino Romano cheese.

662. Mediterranean Trout With Sautéed Vegetables

Preparation Time: 10 minutes
Cooking Time: 20 minutes
Servings: 4

Ingredients:

2 pounds (907 g) rainbow trout fillets
Salt and ground white pepper, to taste
1 tablespoon olive oil
1-pound (454 g) asparagus
4 medium golden potatoes, thinly sliced
1 garlic clove, finely minced
1 scallion, thinly sliced, green and white parts separated
2 Roma tomatoes, chopped
1 large carrot, thinly sliced
8 pitted kalamata olives, chopped
1/4 cup ground cumin
2 tablespoons paprika
2 tablespoons dried parsley
1 tablespoon vegetable bouillon seasoning
1/2 cup dry white wine

Directions:

In a bowl, rub the rainbow trout fillets with salt and white pepper. Set aside.
Heat the olive oil in a large skillet over medium heat. Sauté the asparagus, golden potatoes, garlic, and the white parts of the scallion in the oil for about 5 minutes, stirring occasionally, or until the garlic is fragrant.
Toss in the tomatoes, carrot slices and olives, then continue to cook until the vegetables are tender but still crisp, about 5 to 7 minutes.
Add the cumin, paprika, parsley, vegetable bouillon seasoning, and salt. Stir to combine well. Top with the seasoned fillets and slowly pour in the white wine.
Turn the heat down to low, cover, and bring to a simmer for about 6 minutes, or until the flesh is opaque and it flakes apart easily.
Remove from the heat and sprinkle the scallion greens on top for garnish before serving.
TIP: If you don't want to cook the whole trout fillets at a time, you can cut them into uniform pieces and cover with plastic wrap, then put in the freezer for next meal.

663. Garlicky Branzino With Fresh Herbs

Preparation Time: 10 minutes
Cooking Time: 20 minutes
Servings: 2

Ingredients:

1½ pounds (680 g) branzino, scaled and gutted
Salt and freshly ground black pepper, to taste
1 tablespoon olive oil
1 sliced lemon
3 minced garlic cloves
¼ cup chopped fresh herbs (any mixture of thyme, oregano, rosemary, and parsley)

Directions:

Preheat the oven to 425°F (220°C).
Arrange the branzino on a baking dish. Using a sharp knife, make 4 slits in the fish, about 1½ inches apart.
Generously brush the fish inside and out with salt and pepper, then drizzle with 1 tablespoon olive oil.
Place the lemon slices, garlic gloves, and fresh herbs into the cavity of the fish.
Roast the fish in the preheated oven for 15 to 20 minutes, or until the fish flakes easily with a fork and juices run clear.
Allow to cool for 5 minutes and remove the lemon slices before serving.
TIP: To make this a complete meal, serve it with sautéed mushroom and green beans as a side dish.

664. Shrimp With Black Bean Pasta

Preparation Time: 10 minutes
Cooking Time: 15 minutes
Servings: 4

Ingredients:

1 package black bean pasta
4 tablespoons olive oil
3 garlic cloves, minced
1 onion, finely chopped
1 pound (454 g) fresh shrimp, peeled and deveined
Salt and pepper, to taste
¾ cup low-sodium chicken broth
¼ cup basil, cut into strips

Directions:

Put the black bean pasta in a large pot of boiling water and cook for 6 minutes.
Remove the pasta from the heat. Drain and rinse with cold water, then set the pasta aside on a platter.
Heat the olive oil in a large skillet over medium heat. Add the garlic and onion, then cook for 3 minutes until the onion is translucent.
Add the shrimp and season with salt and pepper. Cook for 3 minutes, stirring occasionally, or until the shrimp is opaque. Pour in the chicken broth and let it simmer for 2 to 3 minutes until heated through.
Remove the shrimp from the heat to the platter of pasta. Pour the liquid over the pasta and garnish with basil, then serve.
TIP: If the black bean pasta is not available, you can try any of your favorite pasta with this recipe. And for a unique twist, the jumbo lump crab meat can be substituted for shrimp.

665. Spanish Style Salmon With Vegetables

Preparation Time: 10 minutes
Cooking Time: 20 minutes
Servings: 4

Ingredients:

2 small red onions, thinly sliced
1 cup shaved fennel bulbs
1 cup cherry tomatoes
15 green pimiento-stuffed olives
1 teaspoon cumin seeds
½ teaspoon smoked paprika

Salt and freshly ground black pepper, to taste
4 (8-ounce / 227-g) salmon fillets
½ cup chicken broth, low-sodium
2 to 4 tablespoons olive oil
2 cups cooked couscous

Directions:

Preheat the oven to 375°F (190°C).
Arrange the red onions, fennel bulbs, cherry tomatoes, and olives on two baking sheets. Sprinkle with cumin seeds, paprika, salt, and pepper.
Place the salmon fillets on top of the vegetables and sprinkle with salt. Pour the chicken broth evenly over the two baking sheets and drizzle with olive oil.
Bake in the preheated oven for 18 to 20 minutes until the vegetables are tender and the fish is flaky, checking regularly to ensure they don't overcook.
Divide the cooked couscous among four serving plates and top with vegetables and fillets, then serve.
TIP: If you can't find the salmon fillets, you can use other fish of your choice, like swordfish. The leftovers can be stored for salmon patties.

666. Swordfish With Lemon And Tarragon

Preparation Time: 5 minutes
Cooking Time: 15 minutes
Servings: 4

Ingredients:

1-pound (454 g) swordfish steaks, cut into 2-inch pieces
1 teaspoon salt, or more to taste
¼ teaspoon freshly ground black pepper
¼ cup olive oil and plus 2 tablespoons, divided
2 tablespoons unsalted butter
2 tablespoons fresh tarragon, chopped
Zest and juice of 1 lemon
Zest and juice of 2 clementine's

Directions:

Season the swordfish steaks with salt and pepper in a bowl.
Heat ¼ cup olive oil in a large skillet over medium-high heat. Sear the swordfish steaks for 2 to 3 minutes per side until lightly browned.
With a slotted spoon, remove the swordfish steaks from the heat to a plate.
Add 2 tablespoons olive oil and butter to the skillet over medium-low heat.
When the butter melts, fold in the tarragon, lemon and clementine zests and juices. Season with salt and stir well.
Return the swordfish steaks to the skillet. Cook for about 2 minutes more and let the swordfish steaks coat in the sauce thoroughly.
Remove from the heat and serve on plates.
TIP: You can try fresh sea scallops with this recipe and it tastes great paired with riced cauliflower or sautéed greens.

667. Stuffed Squid With Spinach And Cheese

Preparation Time: 15 minutes
Cooking Time: 30 minutes
Servings: 4

Ingredients:

4 tablespoons olive oil, divided
FILLING:
¼ cup olive oil
8 ounces (227 g) frozen spinach, thawed and drained
¼ cup sun-dried tomatoes, chopped
½ cup chopped pitted olives
4 ounces (113 g) goat cheese, crumbled
2 garlic cloves, finely minced
¼ cup fresh flat-leaf Italian parsley, chopped
¼ teaspoon freshly ground black pepper
2 pounds (907 g) baby squid, cleaned and tentacles removed

Directions:

Preheat the oven to 350°F (180°C). Coat the bottom of a baking dish with 2 tablespoons olive oil and set aside.
Make the filling: Mix together ¼ cup olive oil, spinach, tomatoes, olives, goat cheese, garlic, parsley, and pepper in a bowl until well combined.
On a clean work surface, spoon 2 tablespoons of the filling onto each baby squid, then arrange them on the prepared baking dish. Evenly pour the remaining olive oil over the squid.
Bake in the preheated oven for 25 to 30 minutes until cooked through.
Remove from the oven and cool for 8 minutes before serving.
TIP: If you can't find the baby squid, you can replace it with calamari steaks, but don't remember to increase the cook time.

668. Mediterranean Sheet Pan Fish Fillets

Preparation Time: 10 minutes
Cooking Time: 10 minutes
Servings: 4

Ingredients:

4 (4-ounce/ 113-g) fish fillets, such as cod or tilapia (½ inch thick)
2 tablespoons olive oil
1 tablespoon balsamic vinegar
2½ cups (about 12 ounces) green beans
1 pint (about 2 cups) cherry or grape tomatoes
Nonstick cooking spray

Directions:

Preheat the oven to 400°F (205°C). Spray two large baking sheets with nonstick cooking spray.
Arrange two fish fillets on each baking sheet and set aside.
Stir together the olive oil and vinegar in a bowl.
In a separate bowl, mix the green beans and tomatoes. Pour the olive oil and vinegar mixture into the bowl of vegetables. Toss gently to coat the vegetables in the mixture.
Divide the coated vegetables among the fish fillets and pour over the mixture.
Bake in the preheated oven for 5 to 8 minutes, or until the flesh is opaque and it flakes apart easily.
Allow to cool for 5 minutes and serve hot.
TIP: For additional zest, you can add a sprinkle of lemon juice and chopped parsley. You also can serve it with sautéed zucchini.

669. Quick Mussels With White Wine Sauce

Preparation Time: 5 minutes
Cooking Time: 10 minutes
Servings: 4

Ingredients:

2 pounds (907 g) small mussels
1 tablespoon olive oil
3 garlic cloves, sliced
1 cup thinly sliced red onion (about ½ medium onion)
2 (¼-inch-thick) lemon slices
1 cup dry white wine
¼ teaspoon kosher or sea salt
¼ teaspoon freshly ground black pepper
Fresh lemon wedges, for garnish

Directions:

Put the small mussels in a colander in the sink and run them under cold water. Discard the open shells or damaged shells. Set the mussels aside in the colander.

In a large skillet, heat the olive oil over medium-high heat. Add the garlic and onion, cook for 3 to 4 minutes until tender, stirring occasionally.

Add the lemon slices, wine, salt, and pepper. Stir well and allow to simmer for 2 minutes.

Pour in the mussels and cook covered until the mussels open their shells, giving the pan a shake from time to time, about 3 minutes.

With a slotted spoon, transfer the mussels to a serving bowl. Be sure to discard any mussels that are still closed.

Pour the wine sauce over the mussels in the bowl and serve garnished with lemon wedges.

TIP: To make this a complete meal, you can serve it with garlic bread or lemony broth on the side.

670. Marinated Shrimp With Orange

Preparation Time: 10 minutes
Cooking Time: 10 minutes
Servings: 6

Ingredients:

1½ pounds (680 g) fresh raw shrimp, shells and tails removed
3 tablespoons olive oil, divided
1 large orange, zested and peeled
3 garlic cloves, minced
1 tablespoon chopped fresh thyme (about 6 sprigs)
1 tablespoon chopped fresh rosemary (about 3 sprigs)
¼ teaspoon kosher or sea salt
¼ teaspoon freshly ground black pepper

Directions:

Put the shrimp, 2 tablespoons olive oil, orange zest, garlic, thyme, rosemary, salt, and pepper in a zip-top plastic bag. Seal the bag and shake until the shrimp is coated thoroughly. Set aside to marinate for 5 minutes.

In a large skillet, heat 1 tablespoon olive oil over medium heat. Add the shrimp and cook for 2 to 3 minutes per side, or until the flesh is totally pink and opaque.

Meanwhile, slice the peeled orange into bite-sized wedges on your cutting board, then place in a serving bowl.

Remove the shrimp from the pan to the bowl. Toss well. Serve immediately, or refrigerate to chill until you want to serve.

TIP: The orange zest can be replaced with lemon zest. For a distinct combination, you can use ¼ cup freshly chopped mint substituted for the thyme and rosemary in this recipe.

671. Poached Salmon With Mustard Sauce

Preparation Time: 15 minutes
Cooking Time: 20 minutes
Servings: 2

Ingredients:

MUSTARD SAUCE:
¼ cup plain Greek yogurt
2 tablespoons Dijon mustard
1½ teaspoons dried tarragon
Pinch salt
Pinch freshly ground black pepper
SALMON:
10 ounces (284 g) salmon fillets
1 tablespoon olive oil
Salt and freshly ground black pepper, to taste
½ fresh lemon, sliced
¼ cup dry white wine
Juice of ½ lemon
¼ cup water

Directions:

Make the mustard sauce: In a bowl, mix together the yogurt, Dijon mustard, tarragon, salt, and pepper until well combined. Set aside.

In a separate bowl, brush the salmon fillets with olive oil, salt, and pepper. Place the lemon slices on top of the fillets.

Add the white wine, lemon juice, and water to a skillet over medium-high heat. Bring them to a boil, then put in the salmon fillets.

Reduce the heat to medium and allow to simmer covered for 15 minutes, or until the fish is flaky.

Divide the salmon fillets between two serving plates. Pour the mustard sauce over the fillets, then serve warm.

TIP: You can try other fresh herbs of your choice, such as thyme, oregano or rosemary.

672. Grilled Halibut With Romesco Sauce

Preparation Time: 20 minutes
Cooking Time: 10 minutes
Servings: 2

Ingredients:

ROMESCO SAUCE:
½ cup jarred roasted piquillo peppers
¼ cup raw and unsalted almonds
2 tablespoons sun-dried tomatoes in olive oil with herbs
¼ teaspoon smoked paprika , or more to taste
2 small garlic cloves
¼ cup olive oil
2 tablespoons red wine vinegar
Pinch salt
HALIBUT:
2 (5-ounce / 142-g) halibut steaks
1 tablespoon olive oil, for greasing the grill grates
Salt and freshly ground black pepper, to taste

Directions:

Make the romesco sauce: In a food processor, put the piquillo peppers, almonds, tomatoes, paprika, garlic cloves, olive oil, vinegar, and salt. Pulse until all ingredients are combined into a smooth mixture. Transfer to a bowl and set aside.

Preheat the grill to medium-high heat. Lightly grease the grill grates with olive oil and set aside.

In a separate bowl, rub the halibut steaks with olive oil, salt, and pepper.

Grill the halibut steaks on the preheated grill for about 10 minutes, flipping the steaks halfway through, or until the fish flakes easily with a fork and juices run clear.

Transfer the halibut steaks to two plates and pour over the romesco sauce. Serve hot.

TIP: You can store the remaining Romesco sauce in a sealed airtight container in the fridge for up to one week.

673. Mackerel Niçoise Salad

Preparation Time: 10 minutes
Cooking Time: 20 minutes
Servings: 2

Ingredients:

DRESSING:
4 tablespoons olive oil
3 tablespoons red wine vinegar
1 teaspoon Dijon mustard

¼ teaspoon salt
Pinch freshly ground black pepper
SALAD:
2 teaspoons salt
2 small red potatoes
1 cup green beans
2 cups baby greens
2 hard-boiled eggs, sliced
½ cup cherry tomatoes, halved
1/3 cup Niçoise olives
2 (4-ounce / 113-g) cooked mackerel fillets

Directions:

Make the dressing: In a bowl, combine the olive oil, vinegar, mustard, salt, and pepper. Stir with a fork until mixed completely and set aside.
Make the salad: Fill a large pot with 3 inches of cold water, and add the salt. Bring it to a boil, then add the red potatoes and cook until they can be pierced easily with the tip of a sharp knife but are still firm, about 12 minutes. Remove the red potatoes from the heat to a colander. Blanch the green beans in the boiling water for 5 minutes, or until they start to soften. Transfer the green beans to the colander of potatoes. Let them cool under running cold water. When cooked, drain and dry with paper towels, then slice the potatoes on a flat work surface.
Spread out the baby greens on two serving plates. Top each plate with the sliced potatoes, green beans, and hard-boiled eggs. Scatter the tomatoes and olives over them, then place the mackerel fillets on top of the salad.
To serve, pour the prepared dressing over the salad and toss well.
TIP: To save time, you can buy the canned mackerel fillets directly in the market. And you can try any of your favorite fish, like grilled salmon or canned tuna.
Nutrition PER SERVING

674. Browned Salmon Cakes

Preparation Time: 15 minutes
Cooking Time: 15 minutes
Servings: 4

Ingredients:

1-pound (454 g) salmon fillets, spine, bones and skin removed
½ cup red onion, minced
1 large egg, whisked
2 tablespoons mayonnaise
1 ripe avocado, pitted, peeled, and mashed
½ cup almond flour
1 teaspoon garlic powder
1 to 2 teaspoons dried dill
½ teaspoon paprika
1 teaspoon salt
½ teaspoon freshly ground black pepper
Zest and juice of 1 lemon
¼ cup olive oil

Directions:

On a clean work surface, cut the salmon fillets into small pieces and transfer to a large bowl.
Add the minced red onion to the bowl and mash the salmon with a fork to break up any lumps. Add the whisked egg, mayo, and mashed avocado. Stir to combine well and set aside.
In a separate bowl, mix together the almond flour, garlic powder, dill, paprika, salt, and pepper.
Pour the dry ingredients into the bowl of salmon mixture, along with the lemon zest and juice. Mix well.
Make the salmon cakes: Scoop out equal-sized portions of the salmon mixture and shape into patties with your palm, about 2 inches in diameter. Set aside on a plate for 15 minutes.
Heat the olive oil in a large skillet over medium heat. Add the salmon patties and fry for 2 to 3 minutes on each side until the edges are lightly browned. Reduce the heat to low and cook covered until the patties are cooked through, about 7 minutes.
Remove from the heat and serve on plates.
TIP: To add more flavors to this meal, serve it alongside the broccoli salad with toasted walnuts. It also tastes great paired with the garlic aioli.

675. Shrimp Mojo de Ajo

Preparation Time: 10 minutes
Cooking Time: 40 minutes
Servings: 4

Ingredients

1/4 cup extra-virgin olive oil
10 garlic cloves, minced
1/8 teaspoon cayenne pepper, plus more as needed
8 ounces mushrooms, quartered
1-pound medium shrimp, peeled, deveined, and tails removed
Juice of 1 lime
1/2 teaspoon sea salt
1/4 cup chopped fresh cilantro leaves
2 cups cooked brown rice

Directions

Preparing the Ingredients. In a small saucepan over the lowest heat setting, bring the olive oil, garlic, and cayenne to a low simmer so bubbles just barely break the surface of the oil. Simmer for 30 minutes, stirring occasionally. Strain the garlic from the oil and set it aside.
Cooking. Add the olive oil to a large skillet over medium-high heat and heat it until it shimmers. Add the mushrooms. Cook for about 5 minutes, stirring once or twice, until browned. Add the shrimp, lime juice, and sea salt. Cook for about 4 minutes, stirring occasionally, until the shrimp are pink. Remove from the heat and stir in the cilantro and reserved garlic. Serve over the hot brown rice.

676. Weeknight Sheet Pan Fish Dinner

Preparation Time: 10 minutes
Cooking Time: 10 minutes
Servings: 4

Ingredients

Nonstick cooking spray
2 tablespoons extra-virgin olive oil
1 tablespoon balsamic vinegar
4 (4-ounce) fish fillets, such as cod or tilapia (½ inch thick)
2½ cups green beans (about 12 ounces)
1-pint cherry or grape tomatoes (about 2 cups)

Directions

Preparing the Ingredients
Preheat the oven to 400°F. Coat two large, rimmed baking sheets with nonstick cooking spray. In a small bowl, whisk together the oil and vinegar. Set aside. Place two pieces of fish on each baking sheet.
In a large bowl, combine the beans and tomatoes. Pour in the oil and vinegar, and toss gently to coat. Pour half of the green bean mixture over the fish on one baking sheet, and the remaining half over the fish on the other. Turn the fish over, and rub it in the oil mixture to coat. Spread the vegetables evenly on the baking sheets so hot air can circulate around them.
Cooking. Bake for 5 to 8 minutes, until the fish is just opaque and not translucent. The fish is done and ready to serve when it just begins to separate into flakes (chunks) when pressed gently with a fork.

CHAPTER 10: VEGETARIAN RECIPES

677. Italian Style Genoese Zucchini

Preparation Time: 10 minutes
Cooking Time: 2 minutes
Servings: 4

Ingredients:

2 medium zucchinis, spiralized
2 cups basil leaves
Juice from 1 lemon, freshly squeezed
3 cloves of garlic, minced
½ cup cashew nuts, soaked in water overnight then drained
Salt to taste

Directions:

Place zucchini strips on a plate.
Place the rest of the ingredients in a food processor and pulse until smooth.
Pour sauce over the zucchini then serve.

678. Wedding of Broccoli and Tomatoes

Preparation Time: 7 minutes
Cooking Time: 2 minutes
Servings: 3

Ingredients:

1 head broccoli, cut into florets then blanched
¼ cup tomatoes, diced
Salt and pepper to taste
Chopped parsley for garnish

Directions:

Place all ingredients in a bowl.
Toss to coat all ingredients.
Serve.

679. Green Buddha Smile

Preparation Time: 10 minutes
Cooking Time: 10 minutes
Servings: 6

Ingredients:

2 pounds boneless and skinless chicken breast
2 tablespoons lemon juice, freshly squeezed
Salt and pepper to taste
1-pound Brussels sprouts, trimmed and halved
3 cloves of garlic, minced
3/4 cup plain Greek yogurt
1 teaspoon stone-ground mustard
¼ cup balsamic vinegar
2 cups cooked quinoa
1 cup chopped red apple, cored, and chopped
¼ cup pepitas
1 avocado, sliced
1 ½ cup arugula
1 tablespoon fresh basil

Directions:

Place chicken and lemon juice in a bowl. Season with salt and pepper to taste. Allow marinating in the fridge for at least 30 minutes.
Fire up the grill to 3750F and cook the chicken for 6 minutes on each side. Add in the Brussels sprouts and cook for 3 minutes on each side. Set the chicken and Brussels sprouts aside.
In a bowl, mix together the garlic, yogurt, mustard, and vinegar. Season with salt to taste. Set aside.
On a bowl, place the quinoa and top with apple, pepitas, avocado, and arugula. Top with grilled chicken and Brussels sprouts.
Drizzle with the sauce and garnish with basil.

680. Zucchini Fettuccine with Mexican Taco

Preparation Time: 9 minutes
Cooking Time: 20 minutes
Servings: 6

Ingredients:

1 tablespoon olive oil
1-pound lean ground turkey
1 clove garlic, minced
½ small onion, chopped
1 tablespoon chili powder
¼ teaspoon garlic powder
¼ teaspoon onion powder
¼ teaspoon dried oregano
1 ½ teaspoon ground cumin
¼ cup water
¼ cup diced tomatoes
2 large zucchinis, spiralized
½ cup shredded cheddar cheese

Directions:

Place oil in a pot and heat over medium flame.
Sauté the turkey for 2 minutes before adding the garlic and onions. Stir for another minute.
Season with chili powder, garlic powder, onion powder, oregano, and ground cumin. Sauté for another minute before adding the water and tomatoes.
Close the lid and allow to simmer for 7 minutes.
Add in the zucchini and cheese and allow to cook for 3 more minutes.

681. Onion Green Beans

Preparation Time: 9 minutes
Cooking Time: 12 minutes
Servings: 4

Ingredients:

11 oz. green beans
1 tablespoon of onion powder 1 tablespoon of olive oil
½ teaspoon of salt
¼ teaspoon of red pepper flakes

Directions:

Wash the green beans thoroughly and put them in the bowl.
Sprinkle the green beans with lion's powder, salt, chilis, and olive oil.
Shake the green bean carefully.
Preheat the 400F air refrigerator.
Place the green beans in the deep fryer and cook for 8 minutes.
Next, shake the green beans and cook them for 4 minutes or more at 400 F. 7. When time remains: shake the green beans.
Serve them with joy!

682. Cream of Mushrooms Satay

Preparation Time: 9 minutes
Cooking Time: 2 minutes
Servings: 6

Ingredients:

7 oz. cremini mushrooms
2 tablespoon coconut milk
1 tablespoon butter
1 teaspoon chili flakes
½ teaspoon balsamic vinegar
½ teaspoon curry powder
½ teaspoon white pepper

Directions:

Wash the mushrooms carefully.
Then sprinkle the mushrooms with chili flakes, curry powder, and white pepper.
Preheat the air fryer to 400 F.
Toss the butter in the air fryer basket and melt it.
Put the mushrooms in the air fryer and cook for 2 minutes.
Shake the mushrooms well and sprinkle with the coconut milk and balsamic vinegar.
Cook the mushrooms for 4 minutes more at 400 F.
Then skewer the mushrooms on the wooden sticks and serve.

683. Tortoreto Mushrooms with Cheddar

Preparation Time: 10 minutes
Cooking Time: 6 minutes
Servings: 2

Ingredients:

2 Portobello mushroom hats
2 slices Cheddar cheese
¼ cup panko breadcrumbs
½ teaspoon salt
½ teaspoon ground black pepper
1 egg
1 teaspoon oatmeal
2 oz. bacon, chopped cooked

Directions:

Crack the egg into the bowl and whisk it.
Combine the ground black pepper, oatmeal, salt, and breadcrumbs in a separate bowl.
Dip the mushroom hats in the whisked egg.
After this, coat the mushroom hats in the breadcrumb mixture.
Preheat the air fryer to 400 F.
Place the mushrooms in the air fryer basket tray and cook for 3 minutes.
After this, put the chopped bacon and sliced cheese over the mushroom hats and cook the meal for 3 minutes.
When the meal is cooked – let it chill gently.

684. Lentil Triumph Hamburger with Carrots

Preparation Time: 10 minutes
Cooking Time: 12 minutes
Servings: 4

Ingredients:

6 oz. lentils, cooked
1 egg
2 oz. carrot, grated
1 teaspoon semolina
½ teaspoon salt
1 teaspoon turmeric
1 tablespoon butter

Directions:

Crack the egg into the bowl and whisk it.
Add the cooked lentils and mash the mixture with the help of the fork.
Then sprinkle the mixture with the grated carrot, semolina, salt, and turmeric.
Mix it up and make the medium burgers.
Put the butter into the lentil burgers. It will make them juicy.
Preheat the air fryer to 360 F.
Put the lentil burgers in the air fryer and cook for 12 minutes.
Flip the burgers into another side after 6 minutes of cooking.
Then chill the cooked lentil burgers and serve them.

685. Stir-Fried Sweet Potatoes with Parmesan

Preparation Time: 10 minutes
Cooking Time: 35 minutes
Servings: 2

Ingredients:

2 sweet potatoes, peeled
½ yellow onion, sliced
½ cup cream
¼ cup spinach
2 oz. Parmesan cheese, shredded
½ teaspoon salt
1 tomato
1 teaspoon olive oil

Directions:

Chop the sweet potatoes.
Chop the tomato.
Chop the spinach.
Spray the air fryer tray with the olive oil.
Then place on the layer of the chopped sweet potato.
Add the layer of the sliced onion.
After this, sprinkle the sliced onion with the chopped spinach and tomatoes.
Sprinkle the casserole with salt and shredded cheese.
Pour cream.
Preheat the air fryer to 390 F.
Cover the air fryer tray with the foil.
Cook the casserole for 35 minutes.
When the casserole is cooked, serve it.

686. Cauliflower Sprinkled with Curry

Preparation Time: 10 minutes
Cooking Time: 5 hours
Servings: 4

Ingredients:

1 cauliflower head, florets separated
2 carrots, sliced
1 red onion, chopped
¾ cup coconut milk
2 garlic cloves, minced
2 tablespoons curry powder
A pinch of salt and black pepper
1 tablespoon red pepper flakes
1 teaspoon garam masala

Directions:

In your slow cooker, mix all the ingredients.
Cover, cook on high for 5 hours, divide into bowls and serve.

687. Rosemary Scent Cauliflower Bundles

Preparation Time: 10 minutes
Cooking Time: 30 minutes
Servings: 4

Ingredients:

1/3 cup of almond flour
4 cups of riced cauliflower
1/3 cup of reduced-fat, shredded mozzarella or cheddar cheese
2 eggs
2 tablespoons of fresh rosemary, finely chopped
½ teaspoon of salt

Directions:

Preheat your oven to 400°F
Combine all the listed ingredients in a medium-sized bowl
Scoop cauliflower mixture into 12 evenly-sized rolls/biscuits onto a lightly-greased and foil-lined baking sheet.
Bake until it turns golden brown, which should be achieved in about 30 minutes.

688. Avocado in Garlic and Paprika Breading

Preparation Time: 10 minutes
Cooking Time: 10 minutes
Servings: 2

Ingredients:

2 avocados cut into wedges 25 mm thick

50g Pan crumbs bread
2g garlic powder
2g onion powder
1g smoked paprika
1g cayenne pepper
Salt and pepper to taste
60g all-purpose flour
2 eggs, beaten
Nonstick Spray Oil
Tomato sauce or ranch sauce, to serve

Directions:

Cut the avocados into 25 mm thick pieces.
Combine the crumbs, garlic powder, onion powder, smoked paprika, cayenne pepper, and salt in a bowl.
Separate each wedge of avocado in the flour, then dip the beaten eggs and stir in the breadcrumb mixture.
Preheat the air fryer.
Place the avocados in the preheated air fryer baskets, spray with oil spray and cook at 205°C (400°F) for 10 minutes.
Turn the fried avocado halfway through cooking and sprinkle with cooking oil.
Serve with tomato sauce or ranch sauce.
Nutrition: 123 Calories 11g Fat 4g Protein

689. Tomatoes in the Mushrooms

Preparation Time: 10 minutes
Cooking Time: 50 minutes
Servings: 4

Ingredients:

8 large mushrooms
250g of minced meat
4 cloves of garlic
Extra virgin olive oil
Salt
Ground pepper
Flour, beaten egg, and breadcrumbs
Frying oil
Fried tomato sauce

Directions:

Remove the stem from the mushrooms and chop it. Peel the garlic and chop. Put some extra virgin olive oil in a pan and add the garlic and mushroom stems.
Sauté and add minced meat. Sauté well until the meat is well cooked and season.
Fill the mushrooms with the minced meat.
Press well and take the freezer for 30 minutes.
Pass the mushrooms with flour, beaten egg, and breadcrumbs.
Place the mushrooms in the basket of the air fryer.
Select 20 minutes, 180°C (350°F).
Distribute the mushrooms once cooked in the dishes.
Heat the tomato sauce and cover the stuffed mushrooms.

690. Brown Rice and Baby Spinach

Preparation Time: 10 minutes
Cooking Time: 15 minutes
Servings: 6

Ingredients:

2 tablespoons extra-virgin olive oil
1 onion, chopped
4 cups fresh baby spinach
1 garlic clove, minced
Zest of 1 orange
Juice of 1 orange
1 cup unsalted vegetable broth
½ teaspoon sea salt
2 cups cooked brown rice

Directions:

In a large skillet over medium-high heat, heat the olive oil until it shimmers.
Add the onion and cook for about 5 minutes, stirring occasionally, until soft.
Add the spinach and cook for about 2 minutes, stirring occasionally, until it wilts.
Add the garlic and cook for 30 seconds, stirring constantly.
Stir in the orange zest and juice, broth, sea salt, and pepper. Bring to a simmer.
Stir in the rice and cook for about 4 minutes, stirring, until the rice is heated through and the liquid is absorbed.

691. Delicious Feta with Fresh Spinach

Preparation Time: 10 minutes
Cooking Time: 0 minutes
Servings: 6

Ingredients:

6 cups fresh baby spinach, chopped
¼ cup scallions, white and green parts, chopped
1 (16-ounce) package orzo pasta, cooked according to package directions, rinsed, drained, and cooled
3/4 cup crumbled feta cheese
1/4 cup halved Kalamata olives
1/2 cup red wine vinegar
1/4 cup extra-virgin olive oil
1½ teaspoons freshly squeezed lemon juice
Sea salt
Freshly ground black pepper

Directions:

In a large bowl, combine the spinach, scallions, and cooled orzo.
Sprinkle with the feta and olives.
In a small bowl, whisk the vinegar, olive oil, and lemon juice. Season with sea salt and pepper.
Add the dressing to the salad and gently toss to combine. Refrigerate until serving.

692. Celeriac Mix with Cauliflower

Preparation Time: 10 minutes
Cooking Time: 12 minutes
Servings: 6

Ingredients:

1 head cauliflower
1 small celery root
¼ cup butter
1 tablespoon. chopped rosemary
1 tablespoon. chopped thyme
1 cup cream cheese

Directions:

Skin the celery root and cut it into small pieces.
Cut the cauliflower into similar sized pieces and combine.
Toast the herbs in the butter in a large pan, until they become fragrant.
Add the cauliflower and celery root and stir to combine.
Season and cook at medium-high until whatever moisture in the vegetables releases itself, then cover and cook on low for 10-12 minutes.
Once the vegetables are soft, remove them from the heat and place them in the blender.
Make it smooth, then put the cream cheese and puree again.
Season and serve.

693. Cheddar Fondue with Tomato Sauce

Preparation Time: 10 minutes
Cooking Time: 30 minutes
Servings: 4

Ingredients:

1 garlic clove, halved
6 medium tomatoes, seeded and diced
2/3 cup dry white wine
6 tablespoons. Butter, cubed
1-½ teaspoons. Dried basil

Dash cayenne pepper
2 cups shredded cheddar cheese
1 tablespoon. All-purpose flour
Cubed French bread and cooked shrimp

Directions:

Rub the bottom and sides of a fondue pot with a garlic clove.
Set aside and discard the garlic.
Combine wine, butter, basil, cayenne, and tomatoes in a large saucepan.
On a medium-low heat, bring the mixture to a simmer, then decrease the heat to low.
Mix cheese with flour.
Add to tomato mixture gradually while stirring after each addition until cheese is melted.
Pour into the preparation fondue pot and keep warm.
Enjoy with shrimp and bread cubes.

694. Quick Spinach Focaccia

Preparation Time: 10 minutes
Cooking Time: 25 minutes
Servings: 12

Ingredients:

10 eggs
2 cups spinach, chopped
¼ tsp garlic powder
¼ tsp onion powder
½ tsp dried basil
1 ½ cups parmesan cheese, grated
Salt

Directions:

Preheat the oven to 400 F. Grease muffin tin and set aside.
In a large bowl, whisk eggs with basil, garlic powder, onion powder, and salt.
Add cheese and spinach and stir well.
Pour egg mixture into the prepared muffin tin and bake 15 minutes.
Serve and enjoy.

695. Triumph of Cucumbers and Avocados

Preparation Time: 10 minutes
Cooking Time: 15 minutes
Servings: 4

Ingredients:

12 oz cherry tomatoes, cut in half
5 small cucumbers, chopped
3 small avocados, chopped
½ tsp ground black pepper
2 tbsp olive oil
2 tbsp fresh lemon juice
¼ cup fresh cilantro, chopped
1 tsp sea salt

Directions:

Add cherry tomatoes, cucumbers, avocados, and cilantro into the large mixing bowl and mix well.
Mix together olive oil, lemon juice, black pepper, and salt and pour over salad.
Toss well and serve immediately.

696. Delicious Tomato Broth

Preparation Time: 10 minutes
Cooking Time: 15 minutes
Servings: 2

Ingredients:

14 oz can fire-roasted tomatoes
½ tsp dried basil
½ cup heavy cream
½ cup parmesan cheese, grated
1 cup cheddar cheese, grated
1 ½ cups vegetable stock
¼ cup zucchini, grated
½ tsp dried oregano
Pepper
Salt

Directions:

Add tomatoes, stock, zucchini, oregano, basil, pepper, and salt into the instant pot and stir well.
Seal pot and cook on high pressure for 5 minutes.
Release pressure using quick release. Remove lid.
Set pot on sauté mode. Add heavy cream, parmesan cheese, and cheddar cheese and stir well and cook until cheese is melted.
Serve and enjoy.

697. Rustic Cauliflower and Carrot Hash

Preparation Time: 10 minutes
Cooking Time: 10 minutes
Servings: 4

Ingredients:

1 large onion, chopped
1 tablespoon garlic, minced
2 cups carrots, diced
4 cups cauliflower pieces, washed
½ teaspoon ground cumin

Direction

Using big skillet over medium heat, cook 3 tbsps. of olive oil, onion, garlic, and carrots for 3 minutes.
Cut the cauliflower into 1-inch or bite-size pieces. Add the cauliflower, salt, and cumin to the skillet and toss to combine with the carrots and onions.
Cover and cook for 3 minutes.
Throw the vegetables and continue to cook uncovered for an additional 3 to 4 minutes.
Serve warm.

698. Moussaka

Preparation Time: 55 minutes
Cooking Time: 40 minutes
Servings: 6

Ingredients:

2 large eggplants, onions
10 cloves garlic, sliced
2 (15-ounce) cans diced tomatoes
1 (16-ounce) can garbanzo beans
1 teaspoon dried oregano

Direction

Slice the eggplant horizontally into ¼-inch-thick round disks. Sprinkle the eggplant slices with 1 teaspoon of salt and place in a colander for 31minutes.
Preheat the oven to 450°F. Pat the slices of eggplant dry with a paper towel and spray each side with an olive oil spray or lightly brush each side with olive oil.
Spread eggplant in a layer on a baking sheet. Bake for 10 minutes.
With a spatula, turn it over and bake for 12 minutes.
Using big skillet add the olive oil, onions, garlic, and remaining 1 teaspoon of salt. Cook for 3 minutes. Add the tomatoes, garbanzo beans, oregano, and black pepper. Simmer for 11 minutes.
Using a deep casserole dish, begin to layer, starting with eggplant, then the sauce. Repeat until all ingredients have been used. Bake in the oven for 20 minutes.
Remove from the oven and serve warm.

699. Vegetable-Stuffed Grape Leaves

Preparation Time: 50 minutes
Cooking Time: 45 minutes
Servings: 7

Ingredients:

2 cups white rice, rinsed

2 large tomatoes, finely diced
1 (16-ounce) jar grape leaves
1 cup lemon juice
4 to 6 cups water

Direction

Incorporate rice, tomatoes, 1 onion, 1 green onion, 1 cup of parsley, 3 garlic cloves, salt, and black pepper.
Drain and rinse the grape leaves.
Prepare a large pot by placing a layer of grape leaves on the bottom. Lay each leaf flat and trim off any stems.
Place 2 tablespoons of the rice mixture at the base of each leaf. Fold over the sides, then roll as tight as possible. Situate the rolled grape leaves in the pot, lining up each rolled grape leaf. Continue to layer in the rolled grape leaves.
Gently pour the lemon juice and olive oil over the grape leaves, and add enough water to just cover the grape leaves by 1 inch.
Lay a heavy plate that is smaller than the opening of the pot upside down over the grape leaves. Cover the pot and cook the leaves over medium-low heat for 45 minutes. Let stand for 20 minutes before serving.
Serve warm or cold.

700. Grilled Eggplant Rolls

Preparation Time: 30 minutes
Cooking Time: 10 minutes
Servings: 5

Ingredients:

2 large eggplants
4 ounces goat cheese
1 cup ricotta
¼ cup fresh basil, finely chopped

Directions:

Slice the tops of the eggplants off and cut the eggplants lengthwise into ¼-inch-thick slices. Sprinkle the slices with the salt and place the eggplant in a colander for 15 to 20 minutes.
In a large bowl, combine the goat cheese, ricotta, basil, and pepper.
Preheat a grill, grill pan, or lightly oiled skillet on medium heat. Pat the eggplant slices dry using paper towel and lightly spray with olive oil spray. Place the eggplant on the grill, grill pan or skillet and cook for 3 minutes on each side.
Take out the eggplant from the heat and let cool for 5 minutes.
To roll, lay one eggplant slice flat, place a tablespoon of the cheese mixture at the base of the slice, and roll up. Serve immediately or chill until serving.

701. Crispy Zucchini Fritters

Preparation Time: 15 minutes
Cooking Time: 20 minutes
Servings: 6

Ingredients:

2 large green zucchinis
1 cup flour
1 large egg, beaten
½ cup water
1 teaspoon baking powder

Direction

Grate the zucchini into a large bowl.
Add the 2 tbsp. of parsley, 3 garlic cloves, salt, flour, egg, water, and baking powder to the bowl and stir to combine.
In a large pot or fryer over medium heat, heat oil to 365°F.
Drop the fritter batter into 3 cups of vegetable oil. Turn the fritters over using a slotted spoon and fry until they are golden brown, about 2 to 3 minutes.
Strain fritters from the oil and place on a plate lined with paper towels.
Serve warm with Creamy Tzatziki or Creamy Traditional Hummus as a dip.

702. Cheesy Spinach Pies

Preparation Time: 20 minutes
Cooking Time: 40 minutes
Servings: 5

Ingredients:

2 tablespoons extra-virgin olive oil
3 (1-pound) bags of baby spinach, washed
1 cup feta cheese
1 large egg, beaten
Puff pastry sheets

Direction

Preheat the oven to 375°F.
Using big skillet over medium heat, cook the olive oil, 1 onion, and 2 garlic cloves for 3 minutes.
Add the spinach to the skillet one bag at a time, letting it wilt in between each bag. Toss using tongs. Cook for 4 minutes. Once cooked, strain any extra liquid from the pan.
Mix feta cheese, egg, and cooked spinach.
Lay the puff pastry flat on a counter. Cut the pastry into 3-inch squares.
Place a tablespoon of the spinach mixture in the center of a puff-pastry square. Turn over one corner of the square to the diagonal corner, forming a triangle. Crimp the edges of the pie by pressing down with the tines of a fork to seal them together. Repeat until all squares are filled.
Situate the pies on a parchment-lined baking sheet and bake for 25 to 30 minutes or until golden brown. Serve warm or at room temperature.

703. Instant Pot Black Eyed Peas

Preparation Time: 6 minutes
Cooking Time: 25 minutes
Servings: 4

Ingredients

2 cups black-eyed peas (dried)
1 cup parsley, dill
2 slices oranges
2 tbsp. tomato paste
4 green onions
2 carrots, bay leaves

Direction

Clean the dill thoroughly with water removing stones.
Add all the ingredients in the instant pot and stir well to combine.
Lid the instant pot and set the vent to sealing.
Set time for twenty-five minutes. When the time has elapsed release pressure naturally.
Serve and enjoy the black-eyed peas.

704. Green Beans and Potatoes in Olive Oil

Preparation Time: 12 minutes
Cooking Time: 17 minutes
Servings: 4

Ingredients

15 oz. tomatoes (diced)
2 potatoes
1 lb. green beans (fresh)
1 bunch dill, parsley, zucchini
1 tbsp. dried oregano

Direction

Turn on the sauté function on your instant pot.

Pour tomatoes, a cup of water and olive oil. Stir in the rest of the ingredients and stir through.
Close the instant pot and click the valve to seal. Set time for fifteen minutes.
When the time has elapsed release pressure. Remove the Fasolakia from the instant pot. Serve and enjoy.

705. Nutritious Vegan Cabbage

Preparation Time: 35 minutes
Cooking Time: 15 minutes
Servings: 6

Ingredients

3 cups green cabbage
1 can tomatoes, onion
Cups vegetable broth
3 stalks celery, carrots
2 tbsp. vinegar, sage

Direction

Mix 1 tbsp. of lemon juice. 2 garlic cloves and the rest of ingredients in the instant pot and. Lid and set time for fifteen minutes on high pressure.
Release pressure naturally then remove the lid. Remove the soup from the instant pot.
Serve and enjoy.

706. Instant Pot Horta and Potatoes

Preparation Time: 12 minutes
Cooking Time: 17 minutes
Servings: 4

Ingredients

2 heads of washed and chopped greens (spinach, Dandelion, kale, mustard green, Swiss chard)
6 potatoes (washed and cut in pieces)
1 cup virgin olive oil
1 lemon juice (reserve slices for serving)
10 garlic cloves (chopped)

Direction

Position all the ingredients in the instant pot and lid setting the vent to sealing.
Set time for fifteen minutes. When time is done release pressure.
Let the potatoes rest for some time. Serve and enjoy with lemon slices.

707. Instant Pot Jackfruit Curry

Preparation Time: 1 hour
Cooking Time: 16 minutes
Servings: 2

Ingredients

1 tbsp. oil
Cumin seeds, Mustard seeds
2 tomatoes (purred)
20 oz. can green jackfruit (drained and rinsed)
1 tbsp. coriander powder, turmeric.

Direction

Turn the instant pot to sauté mode. Add cumin seeds, mustard, ten nigella seeds and allow them to sizzle.
Add 2 red chilies and 2 bay leaves and allow cooking for a few seconds.
Add chopped 1 onion, 5 garlic cloves, ginger and salt, and pepper to taste. Stir cook for five minutes.
Add other ingredients and a cup of water then lid the instant pot. Set time for seven minutes on high pressure.
When the time has elapsed release pressure naturally, shred the jackfruit and serve.

708. Butter Potatoes

Preparation Time: 10 minutes
Cooking Time: 30 minutes
Servings: 6

Ingredients:

1.5-pound finger potatoes
1 tablespoon dried rosemary
3 tablespoons butter, softened
1 teaspoon salt

Directions:

Wash the finger potatoes well.
With the help of the big knife crush every potato.
Place the crushed potatoes in the tray and sprinkle with salt and dried rosemary. Mix up well.
Bake the finger potatoes for 30 minutes at 375F. The cooked potatoes will be soft and have a light crust.

709. Easy And Healthy Baked Vegetables

Preparation Time: 5 minutes
Cooking Time: 1 Hour And 15 minutes
Servings: 6

Ingredients:

2 lbs. Brussels sprouts, trimmed
3 lbs. Butternut Squash, peeled, seeded and cut into same size as sprouts
1 lb Pork breakfast sausage
1 tbsp fat from fried sausage

Directions:

Grease a 9x13 inch baking pan and preheat oven to 350F.
On medium high fire, place a large nonstick saucepan and cook sausage. Break up sausages and cook until browned.
In a greased pan mix browned sausage, squash, sprouts, sea salt and fat. Toss to mix well. Pop into the oven and cook for an hour.
Remove from oven and serve warm.

710. Mozzarella Eggplants

Preparation Time: 20 minutes
Cooking Time: 40 minutes
Servings: 4

Ingredients:

2 large eggplants
3 tomatoes
4 Mozzarella balls
1 tablespoon olive oil
1 teaspoon salt

Directions:

Trim the eggplants and make the cross cuts to get the Hasselback eggplants.
Sprinkle the vegetables with salt.
After this, slice the tomatoes and Mozzarella balls.
Fill the eggplant cuts with Mozzarella and tomatoes and sprinkle with olive oil.
Then wrap every eggplant in foil.
Bake the vegetables for 40 minutes at 375F.
Discard the foil from the eggplants and cut them on 4 servings (1/2 part of eggplant = 1 serving).

711. Greek Style Beans

Preparation Time: 10 minutes
Cooking Time: 10 Hours And 40 minutes
Servings: 8

Ingredients:

3 cups white beans
1/4 cup olive oil
1 onion, diced
1 clove garlic, peeled
28 oz. canned crushed tomatoes

Directions:

Pour 8 cups of water into the Instant Pot.
Add the white beans.
Season with a pinch of salt.
Let the beans soak for up to 10 hours.
Seal the pot. Set it to manual. Choose bean/chili function.
Adjust time to 15 minutes at high pressure. Release the pressure naturally.
Transfer the white beans into a bowl and set aside.
Take 1 cup of the cooking liquid and set aside.
Drain the remaining liquid.
Press the sauté setting. Heat the olive oil.
Cook the onion, garlic and tomatoes for 5 minutes.
Add the reserved cooking liquid and the tomatoes.
Put the beans back. Stir well. Secure the pot.
Choose bean/chili function for 5 minutes at high pressure.
Release the pressure naturally.
Season with salt and pepper.

712. Simple Baked Okra

Preparation Time: 20 minutes
Cooking Time: 10 minutes
Servings: 2

Ingredients:

8 oz okra, chopped
½ teaspoon ground black pepper
½ teaspoon salt
1 tablespoon olive oil

Directions:

Line the baking tray with foil.
Place the okra in the tray in one layer.
Sprinkle the vegetables with ground black pepper and salt Mix up well.
Then drizzle the okra with olive oil.
Roast the vegetables in the preheated to the 375F oven for 10 minutes.
Stir the okra with the help of spatula every 3 minutes.

713. Instant Pot Stuffed Sweet Potatoes

Preparation Time: 10 minutes
Cooking Time: 22 minutes
Servings: 2

Ingredients:

2 sweet potatoes (washed thoroughly)
cup chickpeas, onions
2 spring onions
1 avocado
cooked couscous

Directions:

Pour a cup and half of water in your instant pot then place steam rack in place.
Place the sweet potatoes on the rack. Set the valve to sealing and time for seventeen minutes under high pressure.
Meanwhile, roast the chickpeas on your pan with olive oil.
Add salt and pepper to taste then paprika.
Stir until chickpeas are coated evenly.
Cook for a minute then put off the heat.
When the instant pot time elapses, release pressure naturally for five minutes. Let the sweet potatoes cool then remove them from the instant pot.
Cut the sweet potatoes lengthwise and use a fork to mash the inside creating a space for toppings.
Add the pre-prepared toppings then serve with feta cheese lemon wedges.

714. Instant Pot Millet Pilaf

Preparation Time: 20 minutes
Cooking Time: 11 minutes
Servings: 4-5

Ingredients:

1 cup millet
Cup apricot and shelled pistachios (roughly chopped)
1 lemon juice and zest
tbsp olive oil
Cup parsley (fresh)

Directions:

Pour one and three-quarter cup of water in your instant pot. Place the millet and lid the instant pot.
Adjust time for 10 minutes on high pressure. When the time has elapsed, release pressure naturally.
Remove the lid and add all other ingredients. Stir while adjusting the seasonings.
Serve and enjoy

715. Sweet Potato Puree

Preparation Time: 10 minutes
Cooking Time: 15 minutes
Servings: 6

Ingredients:

2 pounds sweet potatoes, peeled
1 ½ cups water
5 Medjool dates, pitted and chopped

Directions:

Place all ingredients in a pot.
Close the lid and allow to boil for 15 minutes until the potatoes are soft.
Drain the potatoes and place in a food processor together with the dates.
Pulse until smooth.
Place in individual containers.
Put a label and store in the fridge.
Allow to thaw at room temperature before heating in the microwave oven.

716. Chickpea & Lentil Salad

Preparation Time: 10 minutes
Cooking Time: 3 Hours And 50 minutes
Servings: 4

Ingredients:

1 1/2 cups dried chickpeas, rinsed and drained
1 cup green lentils
1 teaspoon herbs de Provence
2 cups vegetable broth
12 oz. cherry tomatoes, sliced in half

Directions:

Combine the chickpeas, 2 cups water and 1 tablespoon olive oil in the Instant Pot.
Mix well.
Choose manual mode.
Cook at high pressure for 38 minutes.
Drain the chickpeas and set aside.
Add the lentils, vegetable broth and seasoning.
Press slow cook.
Adjust time to 3 hours.
Toss the lentils, tomatoes and chickpeas in a salad bowl.

717. Leek and Garlic Cannellini Beans

Preparation Time: 15 minutes
Cooking Time: 22 minutes
Servings: 4

Ingredients

1-pound cannellini beans, soaked overnight
1 onion, peeled and chopped
2 large leeks, finely chopped
3 garlic cloves, whole
1 teaspoon pepper
1 teaspoon salt
4 tablespoons vegetables oil, for toppings
2 tablespoons flour, for toppings

1 tablespoon cayenne pepper, for toppings

Directions:

Add all ingredients except the toppings ingredients into your instant pot
Press Manual/Pressure Cook
Cook for 20 minutes on High
Take a skillet and heat 4 tablespoons oil
Then add cayenne pepper and flour
Stir-fry for 2 minutes and keep them aside
Once done, quick release the pressure
Pour in the cayenne mixture and give it a good stir
Let it sit for 15 minutes before you serve
Serve and enjoy!

718. Sweet Chickpea and Mushroom Stew

Preparation Time: 10 minutes
Cooking Time: 8 minutes
Servings: 4

Ingredients

½ tablespoon button mushrooms, chopped
1 cup chickpeas, cooked
2 carrots, chopped
2 garlic cloves, crushed
4 cherry tomatoes
1 onion, peeled and chopped
A handful of string beans, trimmed
1 apple, cut into 1-inch cubes
½ cup raisins
A handful of fresh mint
1 teaspoon ginger, grated
½ cup orange juice, squeezed
½ teaspoon salt

Directions:

Place all ingredients in your instant pot
Pour water to cover
Cook on High pressure for 8 minutes
Quick-release the pressure over 10 minutes
Serve and enjoy!

719. Vegetable Stew

Preparation Time: 10 minutes
Cooking Time: 45 minutes
Servings: 4

Ingredients:

1-pound potatoes, peeled and cut into bite-sized pieces
2 tablespoons coconut oil, unsalted
3 tablespoons olive oil
2 cups vegetable broth
2 carrots, peeled and chopped
3 celery stalks, chopped
2 onions, peeled and chopped
1 zucchini, cut into ½ inch thick slices
1 tablespoon paprika
1 tablespoon salt
1 teaspoon black pepper
A handful of fresh celery leaves

Directions:

Warm oil on Sauté mode
Stir-fry onions for 3-4 minutes
Add celery, zucchini, carrots, and ¼ cup broth
Cook for 10 minutes more and keep stirring continuously
Stir in potatoes, cayenne pepper, bay leaves, remaining broth, celery leaves, salt and pepper
Close the lid
Cook at Meat/Stew for 30 minutes on High
Quick-release the pressure
Serve and enjoy!

720. Colorful Vegetable Medley

Preparation Time: 10 minutes
Cooking Time: 3 minutes
Servings: 4

Ingredients

1 small head broccoli, broken into florets
16 asparagus, trimmed
1 small head cauliflower, broken into florets
5 ounces green beans
2 carrots, peeled and cut on the bias
1 cup of water
Salt to taste

Directions:

Add water and set trivet on top of the water
Place steamer basket on top
Spread green beans, cauliflower, asparagus, carrots, broccoli in a steamer basket
Close the lid
Steam for 3 minutes on High
Release the pressure quickly
Season with salt
Serve and enjoy!

721. Asparagus with Feta

Preparation Time: 10 minutes
Cooking Time: 5 minutes
Servings: 4

Ingredients

1 cup feta cheese, cubed
1-pound asparagus spears end trimmed
1 tablespoon olive oil
1 cup of water
1 lemon
Salt and freshly ground black pepper, to taste

Directions:

Add water into a pot and set trivet over the water
Place steamer basket on the trivet
Place the asparagus into the steamer basket
Close the lid
Cook for 1 minute on high pressure
Release the pressure quickly
Take a bowl and add olive oil into it
Toss in asparagus until well-coated
Season with pepper and salt
Serve with feta cheese and lemon
Enjoy!

722. Rosemary Sweet Potato Medallions

Preparation Time: 10 minutes
Cooking Time: 18 minutes
Servings: 4

Ingredients

4 sweet potatoes
2 tablespoons coconut oil
1 cup of water
1 tablespoon rosemary
1 teaspoon garlic powder
Salt, to taste

Directions:

Add water and place steamer rack over the water
Using a fork, prick sweet potatoes all over
Then set on a steamer rack
Close the lid and cook for 12 minutes on High pressure
Release the pressure quickly
Cut the sweet potatoes into ½ inch
Melt the coconut oil on Sauté mode
Add in the medallions
Cook each side for 2 to 3 minutes until browned
Season with salt and garlic powder
Add rosemary on top
Serve and enjoy!

723. Artichoke with Garlic Mayo

Prep Time: 10 minutes
Cook Time: 12 minutes
Servings: 4

Ingredients:

2 large artichokes
½ cup mayonnaise
2 cups of water
2 garlic cloves, smashed
1 lime juice
Salt and black pepper, to taste

Directions:

Using a serrated knife, trim about 1 inch from the artichoke's top
Take a top, add water and set trivet over
Place the artichoke on the trivet
Close the lid and cook for 12 minutes on High pressure
Release the pressure quickly
Mix the mayonnaise with garlic and lime juice
Season with salt and pepper
Serve with garlic mayo and enjoy!

724. Steamed Artichoke with Lemon Aioli

Prep Time: 10 minutes
Cook Time: 10 minutes
Servings: 4

Ingredients:

4 artichokes, trimmed
1 lemon, halved
1 teaspoon lemon zest
1 tablespoon lemon juice
3 cloves garlic, crushed
½ cup mayonnaise
1 cup of water
1 handful parsley, chopped
Salt, to taste

Directions:

Cut the artichoke's ends, rub with lemon
Add water into the pot
Set steamer basket on top
Add artichoke into your basket and point this upward
Then sprinkle with salt
Close the lid and cook for 10 minutes on High pressure
Release the pressure quickly
Take a mixing bowl and add lemon juice, garlic, mayonnaise, and lemon zest
Season with salt
Serve with parsley on top and enjoy!

725. Herby-Garlic Potatoes

Prep Time: 10 minutes
Cook Time: 15 minutes
Servings: 4

Ingredients:

1½ pounds of potatoes
3 tablespoons coconut oil
½ cup vegetable broth
2 tablespoons fresh rosemary, chopped
3 cloves garlic, thinly chopped
½ teaspoon fresh thyme, chopped
½ teaspoon fresh parsley, chopped
¼ teaspoon black pepper, ground

Directions:

Take a small knife and pierce each potato to ensure there are no blowouts
Then place under pressure
Melt coconut oil on Sauté mode
Add in potatoes, rosemary, thyme, garlic, parsley and pepper
Cook for 10 minutes
Take a bowl and mix miso paste and vegetable stock
Stir in the mixture in the instant pot
Then close the lid and cook for 5 minutes on High pressure
Release the pressure quickly
Serve with parsley on top and enjoy!

726. Mashed Potatoes with Spinach

Prep Time: 10 minutes
Cook Time: 10 minutes
Servings: 6

Ingredients

2 cups spinach, chopped
3 pounds potatoes, peeled and quartered
½ cup almond milk
1/3 cup coconut oil
2 tablespoons fresh chives, chopped
1½ cups of water
Salt and black pepper, to taste

Directions:

Add water, salt, and potatoes in your cooker
Close the lid
Cook for 8 minutes on High pressure
Release the pressure quickly
Take a bowl, drain the potatoes and reserve the liquid in the bowl
Take another bowl and mash the potatoes
Mix with coconut oil and almond milk
Season with salt and pepper
Then add the reserved cooking liquid and thin the potatoes to attain the desired consistency
Put the spinach in the remaining potato liquid and keep stirring
Season it
Drain and serve with potato mash
Garnish with chives and black pepper
Serve and enjoy!

727. Mediterranean Veggie Bowl

Preparation Time: 10 minutes
Cooking Time: 20 minutes
Servings: 4

Ingredients:

1 cup quinoa, rinsed
1½ teaspoons salt, divided
2 cups cherry tomatoes, cut in half
1 large bell pepper, cucumber
1 cup Kalamata olives

Direction

Using medium pot over medium heat, boil 2 cups of water. Add the bulgur (or quinoa) and 1 teaspoon of salt. Close and cook for 18 minutes.
To arrange the veggies in your 4 bowls, visually divide each bowl into 5 sections. Place the cooked bulgur in one section. Follow with the tomatoes, bell pepper, cucumbers, and olives.
Scourge ½ cup of lemon juice, olive oil, remaining ½ teaspoon salt, and black pepper.
Evenly spoon the dressing over the 4 bowls.
Serve.

728. Grilled Veggie and Hummus Wrap

Preparation Time: 15 minutes
Cooking Time: 10 minutes
Servings: 6

Ingredients:

1 large eggplant
1 large onion
1/2 cup extra-virgin olive oil
6 lavash wraps or large pita bread
1 cup Creamy Traditional Hummus

Directions:

Preheat a grill, large grill pan, or lightly oiled large skillet on medium heat.
Slice the eggplant and onion into circles.
Rub the vegetables with olive oil and sprinkle with salt.

Cook the vegetables on both sides, about 3 to 4 minutes each side.
To make the wrap, lay the lavash or pita flat. Scoop 3 tablespoons of hummus on the wrap.
Evenly divide the vegetables among the wraps, layering them along one side of the wrap. Gently fold over the side of the wrap with the vegetables, tucking them in and making a tight wrap.
Lay the wrap seam side-down and cut in half or thirds.
You can also wrap each sandwich with plastic wrap to help it hold its shape and eat it later.

729. Spanish Green Beans

Preparation Time: 10 minutes
Cooking Time: 20 minutes
Servings: 4

Ingredients:

1 large onion, chopped
4 cloves garlic, finely chopped
1-pound green beans, fresh or frozen, trimmed
1 (15-ounce) can diced tomatoes

Direction

In a huge pot over medium heat, cook olive oil, onion, and garlic; cook for 1 minute.
Cut the green beans into 2-inch pieces.
Add the green beans and 1 teaspoon of salt to the pot and toss everything together; cook for 3 minutes.
Add the diced tomatoes, remaining ½ teaspoon of salt, and black pepper to the pot; continue to cook for another 12 minutes, stirring occasionally.
Serve warm.

730. Roasted Cauliflower and Tomatoes

Preparation Time: 5 minutes
Cooking Time: 25 minutes
Servings: 4

Ingredients:

4 cups cauliflower, cut into 1-inch pieces
6 tablespoons extra-virgin olive oil, divided
4 cups cherry tomatoes
½ teaspoon freshly ground black pepper
½ cup grated Parmesan cheese

Direction

Preheat the oven to 425°F.
Add the cauliflower, 3 tablespoons of olive oil, and ½ teaspoon of salt to a large bowl and toss to evenly coat. Fill onto a baking sheet and arrange the cauliflower out in an even layer.
In another large bowl, add the tomatoes, remaining 3 tablespoons of olive oil, and ½ teaspoon of salt, and toss to coat evenly. Pour onto a different baking sheet.
Put the sheet of cauliflower and the sheet of tomatoes in the oven to roast for 17 to 20 minutes until the cauliflower is lightly browned and tomatoes are plump.

Using a spatula, spoon the cauliflower into a serving dish, and top with tomatoes, black pepper, and Parmesan cheese. Serve warm.

731. Roasted Acorn Squash

Preparation Time: 10 minutes
Cooking Time: 35 minutes
Servings: 6

Ingredients:

2 acorn squash, medium to large
2 tablespoons extra-virgin olive oil
5 tablespoons unsalted butter
¼ cup chopped sage leaves
2 tablespoons fresh thyme leaves

Direction

Preheat the oven to 400°F.
Cut the acorn squash in half lengthwise.
Scoop out the seeds and cut it horizontally into ¾-inch-thick slices.
In a large bowl, drizzle the squash with the olive oil, sprinkle with salt, and toss together to coat.
Lay the acorn squash flat on a baking sheet.
Situate the baking sheet in the oven and bake the squash for 20 minutes. Flip squash over with a spatula and bake for another 15 minutes.
Cook the butter in a medium saucepan over medium heat.
Sprinkle the sage and thyme to the melted butter and let them cook for 30 seconds.
Transfer the cooked squash slices to a plate. Spoon the butter/herb mixture over the squash. Season with salt and black pepper. Serve warm.

732. Sautéed Garlic Spinach

Preparation Time: 5 minutes
Cooking Time: 10 minutes
Servings: 4

Ingredients:

1/4 cup extra-virgin olive oil
1 large onion, thinly sliced
3 cloves garlic, minced
6 bags of baby spinach, washed
1 lemon, cut into wedges

Directions

Cook the olive oil, onion, and garlic in a large skillet for 2 minutes over medium heat.
Add one bag of spinach and ½ teaspoon of salt. Cover the skillet and let the spinach wilt for 30 seconds. Repeat (omitting the salt), adding 1 bag of spinach at a time.
When all is added, open and cook for 3 minutes, letting some of the moisture evaporate.
Serve warm with lemon juice over the top.

733. Garlicky Sautéed Zucchini with Mint

Preparation Time: 5 minutes
Cooking Time: 10 minutes
Servings: 4

Ingredients:

3 large green zucchinis
3 tablespoons extra-virgin olive oil
1 large onion, chopped
3 cloves garlic, minced
1 teaspoon dried mint

Direction

Cut the zucchini into ½-inch cubes.
Using huge skillet, place over medium heat, cook the olive oil, onions, and garlic for 3 minutes, stirring constantly.
Add the zucchini and salt to the skillet and toss to combine with the onions and garlic, cooking for 5 minutes.
Add the mint to the skillet, tossing to combine. Cook for another 2 minutes. Serve warm.

734. Stewed Okra

Preparation Time: 5 minutes
Cooking Time: 25 minutes
Servings: 4

Ingredients:

4 cloves garlic, finely chopped
1 pound fresh or frozen okra, cleaned
1 (15-ounce) can plain tomato sauce
2 cups water
½ cup fresh cilantro, finely chopped

Direction

In a big pot at medium heat, stir and

cook ¼ cup of olive oil, 1 onion, garlic, and salt for 1 minute.
Stir in the okra and cook for 3 minutes.
Add the tomato sauce, water, cilantro, and black pepper; stir, cover, and let cook for 15 minutes, stirring occasionally.
Serve warm.

735. Sweet Veggie-Stuffed Peppers

Preparation Time: 20 minutes
Cooking Time: 30 minutes
Servings: 6

Ingredients:

6 large bell peppers, different colors
3 cloves garlic, minced
1 carrot, chopped
1 (16-ounce) can garbanzo beans
3 cups cooked rice

Direction

Preheat the oven to 350°F.
Make sure to choose peppers that can stand upright. Cut off the pepper cap and remove the seeds, reserving the cap for later. Stand the peppers in a baking dish.
In a skillet over medium heat, cook up olive oil, 1 onion, garlic, and carrots for 3 minutes.
Stir in the garbanzo beans. Cook for another 3 minutes.
Take out the pan from the heat and spoon the cooked ingredients to a large bowl.
Add the rice, salt, and pepper; toss to combine.
Stuff each pepper to the top and then put the pepper caps back on.
Wrap the baking dish using aluminum foil and bake for 25 minutes.
Pull out the foil and bake for 6 minutes.
Serve warm.

736. Brussels Sprouts Chips

Preparation Time: 20 minutes
Cooking Time: 20 minutes
Servings: 3

Ingredients:

½ pounds Brussels sprouts, sliced thinly
4 tablespoons olive oil
2 tablespoons mozzarella cheese, grated
1 teaspoon garlic powder
Salt and pepper to taste

Directions:

Preheat the oven to 400F.
In a bowl, combine all ingredients.
Toss to coat the ingredients
Place in a baking sheet and bake for 20 minutes or until golden brown.
Place in individual containers.
Put a label and store in the fridge.
Allow to warm at room temperature before heating in the microwave oven.

CHAPTER 11: LEGUMES

737. White Bean Dip

Preparation Time: 5 minutes
Cooking Time: 2 minutes
Servings: 2 cups

Ingredients:

¼ cup extra-virgin olive oil, plus more for drizzling
2 garlic cloves, chopped
3 fresh sage leaves
½ teaspoon dried oregano
2 (19-ounce) cans cannellini beans, rinsed and drained
1 teaspoon salt
¼ teaspoon freshly ground black pepper
¼ teaspoon red pepper flakes (optional)
1 to 2 tablespoons water

Directions:

In a small saucepan, heat the olive oil over low heat. Add the garlic, sage, and oregano and cook for 1 minute, until fragrant.
Turn off the heat. Add the beans to the pan and toss to coat with the seasonings.
Transfer the mixture to a food processor. Add the salt, black pepper, and red pepper flakes (if using). Process until smooth, adding water as needed to get the consistency you want.
Transfer the dip to a serving bowl and drizzle with a little more olive oil.

738. Classic Hummus

Preparation Time: 10 minutes
Cooking Time: 0 minutes
Servings: 1 cup

Ingredients:

½ cup toasted sesame seeds
2 tablespoons extra-virgin olive oil
1 garlic clove, peeled
1 teaspoon freshly squeezed lemon juice
1 (19-ounce) can chickpeas, rinsed and drained
¼ cup extra-virgin olive oil
1 teaspoon salt
2 tablespoons water

Directions:

In a food processor, combine the sesame seeds, olive oil, garlic, and lemon juice and process until the mixture becomes a paste. If needed, scrape down the sides of the bowl and repeat a few times. Don't worry if the paste is not completely smooth yet.
Add the chickpeas, olive oil, and salt to the tahini sauce in the food processor and blend until smooth. Add the water and blend again until soft and fluffy.
VARIATION TIP: Hummus lends itself to a variety of added flavors, as shown in these variations:
FAVA BEAN HUMMUS: When you remove fava beans from their padded pods, they are still enclosed in a thick skin that should be peeled off. Put 12 unpeeled fava beans in a pot of boiling water and boil for 3 minutes. Drain and cool, then pop the beans out of their skins. In a food processor or blender, combine about ½ cup hummus and the fava beans and blend until smooth.
LEMON HUMMUS: Lay 4 lemon slices on a rimmed baking sheet lined with parchment paper. Remove and discard any seeds. Brush the lemons with olive oil on both sides and roast at 350°F for 20 minutes. In a food processor or blender, combine about ½ cup hummus and the roasted lemon slices and blend until smooth.
MAKE-AHEAD TIP: Store the hummus in an airtight container in the refrigerator for up to 5 days or in the freezer for up to 6 months.

739. Three-Bean Salad

Preparation Time: 15 minutes, plus 1 hour to chill
Cooking Time: 0 minutes
Servings: 6

Ingredients:

1 (19-ounce) can chickpeas, rinsed and drained
1 (19-ounce) can cannellini beans, rinsed and drained
1 (19-ounce) can red kidney beans, rinsed and drained
½ red onion, finely chopped
¼ cup extra-virgin olive oil
3 tablespoons red wine vinegar
½ teaspoon salt
½ teaspoon dried oregano
¼ teaspoon freshly ground black pepper

Directions:

In a large bowl, combine the chickpeas, cannellini beans, kidney beans, and red onion.
In a small bowl, whisk together the olive oil, vinegar, salt, oregano, and pepper. Pour the dressing over the bean mixture and toss to combine.
Cover and refrigerate for 1 hour before serving.
MAKE-AHEAD TIP: This salad is best when prepared in advance. It will keep in the refrigerator for up to 3 days.
VARIATION TIP: You can substitute black beans for the cannellini beans and swap out the oregano for cilantro for a slightly different flavor profile.

740. Gigantea Beans In Tomato Sauce

Preparation Time: 5 minutes
Cooking Time: 5 minutes
Servings: 2

Ingredients:

1 (12-ounce) jar gigante beans, undrained
1 (6-ounce) can tomato paste
¾ cup water
½ teaspoon dried oregano

Directions:

Pour the beans and their liquid into a small saucepan and bring to a boil over medium-high heat. Remove the pan from the heat and drain the liquid.
In another small saucepan, combine the tomato paste and water and bring to a simmer to heat through.
Arrange the beans on a serving dish. Spoon over the tomato sauce and sprinkle with the dried oregano.
INGREDIENT TIP: If you can't find gigante beans, good substitutes are corona beans or large butter beans.

741. Mashed Fava Beans

Preparation Time: 15 minutes
Cooking Time: 10 minutes
Servings: 4

Ingredients:

3 pounds fava beans, removed from the pods but unpeeled
¼ cup water
½ teaspoon salt
¼ cup extra-virgin olive oil

3 garlic cloves, chopped
1 tablespoon finely chopped fresh rosemary
¼ teaspoon freshly ground black pepper

Directions:

Bring a large pot of water to a boil over high heat and cook the beans for 3 minutes. Drain the beans and rinse under cold running water to cool.
Peel the outer skin off the beans. The inner bean should pop out easily. You are going to be mashing the beans, so you can be messy during this step.
Put the beans in a food processor, add the water and salt, and puree.
In a skillet, heat the olive oil over low heat. Add the fava bean puree, garlic, rosemary, and pepper. Stir to combine and cook for about 5 minutes, until most of the water evaporates.

742. Spicy Borlotti Beans

Preparation Time: 10 minutes, plus overnight to soak
Cooking Time: 1 hour 30 minutes
Servings: 8

Ingredients:

1-pound dried borlotti beans, soaked overnight, drained, and rinsed
1 teaspoon salt, divided
2 tablespoons extra-virgin olive oil
1 large onion, chopped
½ green bell pepper, seeded and chopped
1 (14.5-ounce) can diced tomatoes, undrained
3 garlic cloves, minced
1 (1-inch) piece fresh red chile, seeded and minced
¼ teaspoon freshly ground black pepper
¼ teaspoon red pepper flakes

Directions:

Put the beans in a large soup pot, cover with water, and add ½ teaspoon of salt. Bring to a boil over medium-high heat, then reduce the heat to low and simmer for 1 to 1½ hours, until the beans soften. Drain.
In a large skillet, heat the olive oil over medium heat. Cook the onion and bell pepper for about 10 minutes, until softened.
Add the beans, tomatoes and their juices, garlic, chile, remaining ½ teaspoon of salt, black pepper, and red pepper flakes. Bring to a boil, then reduce the heat and simmer for 10 minutes.

743. Black Beans With Cherry Tomatoes

Preparation Time: 5 minutes
Cooking Time: 15 minutes
Servings: 2

Ingredients:

1 (15-ounce) can black beans, undrained
1 cup halved cherry tomatoes
1 teaspoon salt
1 tablespoon dried oregano
1 teaspoon red pepper flakes

Directions:

Pour the black beans and their liquid into a large skillet and bring to a low boil over medium-high heat. Reduce the heat to low and simmer for 5 minutes.
Stir in the cherry tomatoes, salt, oregano, and red pepper flakes. Cook for 10 minutes.

744. Warm Lentil Salad

Preparation Time: 15 minutes
Cooking Time: 20 minutes
Servings: 4

Ingredients:

For the lentils
1 cup lentils
2½ cups water
1 bay leaf
2 tablespoons extra-virgin olive oil
1 cup chopped onion
1 cup chopped carrot
1 garlic clove, minced
For the dressing
¼ cup extra-virgin olive oil
2 tablespoons white wine vinegar
1 teaspoon Dijon mustard
1 teaspoon salt
¼ teaspoon freshly ground black pepper

Directions:

To make the lentils
In a large saucepan, combine the lentils, water, and bay leaf and bring to a boil over medium-high heat. Reduce the heat to low and simmer for 20 minutes, until tender.
Drain the lentils and discard the bay leaf.
Meanwhile, in a skillet, heat the olive oil over medium heat and add the onion and carrot. Sauté for about 5 minutes, until softened. Add the garlic and cook for 1 more minute.
To make the dressing
In a small bowl, whisk together the olive oil, vinegar, mustard, salt, and pepper.
In a bowl, combine the warm lentils with the onion-carrot-garlic mixture. Add the dressing and toss to combine.

745. Moroccan Lentil Soup

Preparation Time: 10 minutes
Cooking Time: 40 minutes
Servings: 4

Ingredients:

1 tablespoon extra-virgin olive oil
1 cup chopped onion
1 cup chopped celery
1/2 cup chopped carrot
2 garlic cloves, minced
2 teaspoons ground cumin
2 teaspoons smoked paprika
1 teaspoon salt
1 teaspoon freshly ground black pepper
1 teaspoon ground turmeric
1 teaspoon ground ginger
1/2 teaspoon ground cinnamon
4 cups chicken broth
2 cups water
2 tablespoons tomato paste
2 cups brown lentils
¼ cup nonfat plain Greek yogurt
Chopped fresh flat-leaf parsley, for garnish

Directions:

In a soup pot, heat the olive oil over medium heat. Add the onion, celery, and carrot and cook for 5 to 7 minutes, until they start to soften. Add the garlic and cook for 1 minute.
Stir in the cumin, paprika, salt, pepper, turmeric, ginger, and cinnamon. Cook for 2 minutes to wake up the spices.
Add the broth, water, and tomato paste and stir until the tomato paste incorporates into the liquid. Stir in the lentils.
Bring everything to a boil, then reduce the heat to low and simmer for about 30 minutes, until the lentils are tender.
Serve each bowl with a dollop of yogurt and a sprinkling of parsley.

746. Vegetarian Chili

Preparation Time: 15 minutes
Cooking Time: 1 hour 10 minutes
Servings: 8

Ingredients:

2 tablespoons extra-virgin olive oil
2 medium onions, finely chopped
1 medium leek, finely chopped
1 fresh red chile, seeded and minced
4 garlic cloves, minced

2 tablespoons ground cumin
2 tablespoons ground coriander
2 tablespoons smoked paprika
2 tablespoons dried oregano
1 teaspoon ground cinnamon
1/4 teaspoon ground nutmeg
2 tablespoons tomato paste
2 tablespoons water
6 cups vegetable broth
1 cup green lentils
1 cup red lentils
2 (15-ounce) cans red kidney beans, rinsed and drained
2 (15-ounce) cans black beans, rinsed and drained
2 (14.5-ounce) cans chopped tomatoes, undrained
1 teaspoon salt

Direction;

In a large soup pot, heat the olive oil over medium heat. Add the onions and cook for about 4 minutes, until they start to soften. Add the leek, chile, and garlic and cook for about 1 minute, until fragrant.
Add the cumin, coriander, paprika, oregano, cinnamon, and nutmeg and cook for another minute, stirring to wake up the spices.
Stir in the tomato paste and water. Cook for about 2 minutes, until warmed through.
Add the broth, lentils, kidney beans, black beans, tomatoes and their juices, and salt. Bring the pot to a boil, then reduce to a simmer and cook for 1 hour, stirring every 15 minutes or so.
INGREDIENT TIP: If you crave more heat in your chili, you can leave the seeds in the chile.

747. Black-Eyed Peas With Mint

Preparation Time: 10 minutes
Cooking Time: 10 minutes
Servings: 8

Ingredients:

4 (15-ounce) cans black-eyed peas, undrained
1 cup baby spinach
1 cup chopped fresh mint
1/2 red onion, finely chopped
1 carrot, grated
3 scallions, thinly sliced
1/2 cup extra-virgin olive oil
3 tablespoons white wine vinegar
1 teaspoon salt
1/2 teaspoon freshly ground black pepper

Directions:

In a large saucepan, bring the black-eyed peas and their liquid to a boil over medium heat. Cook for about 5 minutes, until heated through. Drain.
Return the beans to the saucepan and stir in the spinach, mint, red onion, carrot, and scallions. Heat until warmed through.
In a small bowl, whisk together the olive oil, vinegar, salt, and pepper. Pour the mixture over the beans and stir to combine.
MAKE-AHEAD TIP: This dish can also be eaten cold and will keep in an airtight container in the refrigerator for up to 3 days.

748. Chickpea And Avocado Salad

Preparation Time: 10 minutes
Cooking Time: 0 minutes
Servings: 4

Ingredients:

1 (15-ounce) can chickpeas, rinsed and drained
2 avocados, pitted, peeled, and chopped
¼ cup chopped fresh cilantro
1 scallion, thinly sliced
2 tablespoons extra-virgin olive oil
Juice of 1 lime
½ teaspoon salt
¼ teaspoon freshly ground black pepper
¼ teaspoon red pepper flakes
¼ cup crumbled feta cheese

Directions:

In a large bowl, combine the chickpeas, avocado, cilantro, and scallion.
In a small bowl, whisk together the olive oil, lime juice, salt, black pepper, and red pepper flakes.
Pour the dressing over the chickpea-avocado mixture and toss to combine.
Sprinkle the feta cheese over the top.
VARIATION TIP: You can use onion or shallot instead of the scallion if preferred.

749. Peas And Tubetti With Pancetta

Preparation Time: 5 minutes
Cooking Time: 10 minutes
Servings: 4

Ingredients:

Salt
1-pound tubetti
3 tablespoons extra-virgin olive oil
½ cup diced pancetta
2 scallions, thinly sliced
12 ounces frozen peas
¼ cup water
¼ cup finely grated Parmesan cheese

Directions:

Bring a large pot of water to a boil over high heat. Once boiling, salt the water to your liking, stir, and return to a boil. Add the tubetti and cook according to package directions until al dente. Drain, reserving about ¼ cup of the cooking water.
In a large skillet, heat the olive oil over medium heat. Cook the pancetta for 2 minutes, then add the scallions and cook for another 2 minutes, until the pancetta is completely cooked.
Add the peas and water. Cover and cook for 5 minutes, stirring occasionally.
Add the cooked pasta and toss to combine. Add the reserved pasta water a little at a time as needed.
Sprinkle with the Parmesan cheese.
INGREDIENT TIP: If you can't find tubetti, you can substitute ditalini, orzo, or any other tiny pasta shape.

750. Crispy Black-Eyed Peas

Preparation Time: 10 minutes
Cooking Time: 10 minutes
Servings: 6

Ingredients:

15-ounces black-eyed peas
1/8 teaspoon chipotle chili powder
¼ teaspoon salt
½ teaspoon chili powder
1/8 teaspoon black pepper

Directions:

Rinse the beans well with running water then set aside. In a large bowl, mix the spices until well combined. Add the peas to spices and mix.
Place the peas in the wire basket and cook for 10-minutes at 360°Fahrenheit. Serve and enjoy!

751. Spicy Nuts

Preparation Time: 10 minutes
Cooking Time: 4 minutes
Servings: 8

Ingredients:

2 cups mixed nuts

1 teaspoon chipotle chili powder
1 teaspoon salt
1 teaspoon pepper
1 tablespoon butter, melted
1 teaspoon ground cumin

Directions:

In a bowl, add all ingredients and toss to coat. Preheat your air fryer to 350°Fahrenheit for 5-minutes. Add mixed nuts into air fryer basket and roast for 4-minutes.

752. Lemony Green Beans

Preparation Time: 5 minutes
Cooking Time: 12 minutes
Servings: 4

Ingredients:

1 lb. green beans washed and destemmed
Sea salt and black pepper to taste
1 lemon
¼ teaspoon extra virgin olive oil

Directions:

Preheat your air fryer to 400°Fahrenheit.
Place the green beans in the air fryer basket. Squeeze lemon over beans and season with salt and pepper.
Cover ingredients with oil and toss well.
Cook green beans for 12-minutes and serve!

753. Chickpea & Zucchini Burgers

Preparation Time: 20 minutes
Cooking Time: 10 minutes
Servings: 4

Ingredients:

1 can of chickpeas, strained
1 red onion, diced
2 eggs, beaten
1-ounce almond flour
3 tablespoons coriander
1 teaspoon garlic puree
1-ounce cheddar cheese, shredded
1 Courgette, spiralized
1 teaspoon chili powder
Salt and pepper to taste
1 teaspoon mixed spice

Directions:

Add your ingredients to a bowl and mix well. Shape portions of the mixture into burgers. Place in the air fryer for 15-minutes until cooked.

754. French Beans With Walnuts & Almonds

Preparation Time: 15 minutes
Cooking Time: 27 minutes
Servings: 6

Ingredients:

1 ½ lbs. of French green beans (stems removed)
¼ cup slivered almonds (lightly toasted)
¼ cup walnuts, finely chopped
½ teaspoon ground white pepper
½ lb. shallots, peeled and quartered
1 teaspoon sea salt
2 tablespoons olive oil

Directions:

Boil some water in a pan, adding the green beans to it. Cook beans for 2-minutes with salt. Drain the beans.
Place the green beans into a bowl and toss with the rest of the ingredients except the walnuts and almonds.
Mix nuts together in small bowl and set aside.
Place into air fryer basket and cook for 25-minutes at 400°Fahrenheit. Toss twice during cook time. Serve garnished with mixed nuts.

755. Cheesy Chickpea & Courgette Burgers

Preparation Time: 45 minutes
Cooking Time: 10 minutes
Servings: 4

Ingredients:

1 can chickpeas (drained)
3 tablespoons coriander
1-ounce cheddar cheese, shredded
2 eggs, beaten
1 teaspoon garlic puree
1 zucchini (spiralized)
1 red onion, diced
1 teaspoon chili powder
1 teaspoon mixed spice
Salt and pepper to taste
1 teaspoon cumin

Directions:

Mix your ingredients in a mixing bowl. Shape portions of the mixture into burgers. Place in the air fryer at 300°Fahrenheit for 15-minutes.

756. Garlic & Ginger Snow Peas

Preparation Time: 20 minutes
Cooking Time: 8 minutes
Servings: 4

Ingredients:

2 cups snow peas, trimmed
1 teaspoon olive oil
1 teaspoon pepper
1 teaspoon sea salt
1 tablespoon rice vinegar
1 tablespoon tamari sauce
2 cloves garlic, minced
3-inches of ginger root, minced

Directions:

Wash the snow peas with cold running water, then trim. Clean ginger and garlic with water, then slice them into small pieces. Set them aside.
In a large bowl, add a tablespoon tamari sauce, a tablespoon rice vinegar, salt, pepper, and olive oil. Mix in the minced ginger and garlic.
Add trimmed snow peas and toss to combine. Soak the peas in the marinade for about an hour before air frying them.
Preheat your air fryer to 380°Fahrenheit for 2-minutes. Transfer the marinated peas in a pan into air fryer and cook for 4-minutes.
Toss snow peas and cook for an additional 4-minutes.

757. Bulgur with Chickpeas, Spinach, and Za'atar (Instant Pot)

Preparation Time: 22 minutes
Cooking Time: 1 Minute
Servings: 4 To 6

Ingredients

3 tablespoons extra-virgin olive oil, divided
1 onion, chopped fine
½ teaspoon table salt
3 garlic cloves, minced
2 tablespoons za'atar, divided
1 cup medium-grind bulgur, rinsed
1 (15-ounce) can chickpeas, rinsed
1½ cups water
5 ounces (5 cups) baby spinach, chopped
1 tablespoon lemon juice, plus lemon wedges for serving

Directions

Using highest sauté function, heat 2

tablespoons oil in Instant Pot until shimmering. Add onion and salt and cook until onion is softened, about 5 minutes. Stir in garlic and 1 tablespoon za'atar and cook until fragrant, about 30 seconds. Stir in bulgur, chickpeas, and water.
Lock lid in place and close pressure release valve. Select high pressure cook function and cook for 1 minute. Turn off Instant Pot and quick-release pressure. Carefully remove lid, allowing steam to escape away from you.
Gently fluff bulgur with fork. Lay clean dish towel over pot, replace lid, and let sit for 5 minutes. Add spinach, lemon juice, remaining 1 tablespoon za'atar, and remaining 1 tablespoon oil and gently toss to combine. Season with salt and pepper to taste. Serve with lemon wedges.

758. Mediterranean Lentils and Rice

Preparation Time: 10 minutes
Cooking Time: 20 minutes
Servings: 4

Ingredients

2¼ cups low-sodium or no-salt-added vegetable broth
½ cup uncooked brown or green lentils
½ cup uncooked instant brown rice
½ cup diced carrots (about 1 carrot)
½ cup diced celery (about 1 stalk)
1 (2.25-ounce) can sliced olives, drained (about ½ cup)
¼ cup diced red onion (about 1/8 onion)
¼ cup chopped fresh curly-leaf parsley
1½ tablespoons extra-virgin olive oil
1 tablespoon freshly squeezed lemon juice (from about ½ small lemon)
1 garlic clove, minced (about ½ teaspoon)
¼ teaspoon kosher or sea salt
¼ teaspoon freshly ground black pepper

Directions

Preparing the Ingredients
In a medium saucepan over high heat, bring the broth and lentils to a boil, cover, and lower the heat to medium-low. Cook for 8 minutes.
Raise the heat to medium, and stir in the rice. Cover the pot and cook the mixture for 15 minutes, or until the liquid is absorbed. Remove the pot from the heat and let it sit, covered, for 1 minute, then stir.
While the lentils and rice are cooking, mix together the carrots, celery, olives, onion, and parsley in a large serving bowl.
In a small bowl, whisk together the oil, lemon juice, garlic, salt, and pepper. Set aside.
When the lentils and rice are cooked, add them to the serving bowl. Pour the dressing on top, and mix everything together. Serve warm or cold, or store in a sealed container in the refrigerator for up to 7 days.

759. Brown Rice with Tomatoes and Chickpeas

Preparation Time: 5 minutes
Cooking Time: 35 minutes
Servings: 6

Ingredients

12 ounces grape tomatoes, quartered
5 scallions, sliced thin
¼ cup minced fresh cilantro
4 teaspoons extra-virgin olive oil
1 tablespoon lime juice
Salt and pepper
2 red bell peppers, stemmed, seeded, and chopped fine
1 onion, chopped fine
1 cup long-grain brown rice, rinsed
4 garlic cloves, minced
Pinch saffron threads, crumbled
Pinch cayenne pepper
3¼ cups chicken or vegetable broth
2 (15-ounce) cans chickpeas, rinsed

Directions

Preparing the Ingredients.
Combine tomatoes, scallions, cilantro, 2 teaspoons oil, and lime juice in bowl. Season with salt and pepper to taste; set aside for serving.
Cooking
Heat remaining 2 teaspoons oil in large saucepan over medium-high heat until shimmering. Add bell peppers and onion and cook until softened and lightly browned, 8 to 10 minutes. Stir in rice, garlic, saffron, and cayenne and cook until fragrant, about 30 seconds.
Stir in broth and bring to simmer. Reduce heat to medium-low, cover, and simmer, stirring occasionally, for 25 minutes.
Stir in chickpeas, cover, and simmer until rice is tender and broth is almost completely absorbed, 25 to 30 minutes. Season with salt and pepper to taste. Serve, topping individual portions with tomato mixture.

760. Cannellini Bean Salad (Instant Pot)

Preparation Time: 30 minutes
Cooking Time: 3 minutes, Plus Brining Time
Servings: 6 To 8

Ingredients

1½ tablespoons table salt, for brining
1 pound (2½ cups) dried cannellini beans, picked over and rinsed
¼ cup extra-virgin olive oil, divided
¾ teaspoon table salt, divided
¼ cup tahini
3 tablespoons lemon juice
1 tablespoon ground dried Aleppo pepper, plus extra for sprinkling
8 ounces cherry tomatoes, halved
¼ red onion, sliced thin
½ cup fresh parsley leaves
1 recipe hard-cooked eggs, quartered (optional)
1 tablespoon toasted sesame seeds

Directions

Preparing the Ingredients. Dissolve 1½ tablespoons salt in 2 quarts cold water in large container. Add beans and soak at room temperature for at least 8 hours or up to 24 hours. Drain and rinse well. Add beans, 8 cups water, 1 tablespoon oil, and ½ teaspoon salt to Instant Pot. Lock lid in place and close pressure release valve. Select low pressure cook function and cook for 3 minutes. Turn off Instant Pot and quick-release pressure. Carefully remove lid, allowing steam to escape away from you. Drain beans, rinse with cold water, and drain again. Meanwhile, whisk remaining 3 tablespoons oil, tahini, lemon juice, Aleppo pepper, 1 tablespoon water, and remaining ¼ teaspoon salt in large bowl until combined; let sit for 15 minutes. Add beans, tomatoes, onion, and parsley and gently toss to combine. Season with salt and pepper to taste. Transfer salad to serving dish and arrange eggs on top, if using. Sprinkle with sesame seeds and extra Aleppo pepper to taste.

761. French Lentils with Swiss Chard (Instant pot)

Preparation Time: 30 minutes
Cooking Time: 11 minutes
Servings: 6

Ingredients

2 tablespoons extra-virgin olive oil, plus

extra for drizzling
12 ounces Swiss chard, stems chopped fine, leaves sliced into ½-inch-wide strips
1 onion, chopped fine
½ teaspoon table salt
2 garlic cloves, minced
1 teaspoon minced fresh thyme or ¼ teaspoon dried
2½ cups water
1 cup French green lentils, picked over and rinsed
3 tablespoons whole-grain mustard
½ teaspoon grated lemon zest plus 1 teaspoon juice
3 tablespoons sliced almonds, toasted
2 tablespoons chopped fresh parsley

Directions

Using highest sauté function, heat oil in Instant Pot until shimmering. Add chard stems, onion, and salt and cook until vegetables are softened, about 5 minutes. Stir in garlic and thyme and cook until fragrant, about 30 seconds. Stir in water and lentils.
Lock lid in place and close pressure release valve. Select high pressure cook function and cook for 11 minutes. Turn off Instant Pot and let pressure release naturally for 15 minutes. Quick-release any remaining pressure, then carefully remove lid, allowing steam to escape away from you.
Stir chard leaves into lentils, 1 handful at a time, and let cook in residual heat until wilted, about 5 minutes. Stir in mustard and lemon zest and juice. Season with salt and pepper to taste. Transfer to serving dish, drizzle with extra oil, and sprinkle with almonds and parsley. Serve.

762. Greek Chickpeas with Coriander and Sage (Instant Pot)

Preparation Time: 30 minutes
Cooking Time: 10 minutes, Plus Brining Time
Servings: 6 To 8

Ingredients

1½ tablespoons table salt, for brining
1 pound (2½ cups) dried chickpeas, picked over and rinsed
2 tablespoons extra-virgin olive oil, plus extra for drizzling
2 onions, halved and sliced thin
¼ teaspoon table salt
1 tablespoon coriander seeds, cracked
¼–½ teaspoon red pepper flakes
2½ cups chicken broth
¼ cup fresh sage leaves
2 bay leaves
1½ teaspoons grated lemon zest plus 2 teaspoons juice
2 tablespoons minced fresh parsley

Directions

Dissolve 1½ tablespoons salt in 2 quarts cold water in large container. Add chickpeas and soak at room temperature for at least 8 hours or up to 24 hours. Drain and rinse well.
Using highest sauté function, heat oil in Instant Pot until shimmering. Add onions and ¼ teaspoon salt and cook until onions are softened and well browned, 10 to 12 minutes. Stir in coriander and pepper flakes and cook until fragrant, about 30 seconds. Stir in broth, scraping up any browned bits, then stir in chickpeas, sage, and bay leaves.
Lock lid in place and close pressure release valve. Select low pressure cook function and cook for 10 minutes. Turn off Instant Pot and let pressure release naturally for 15 minutes. Quick-release any remaining pressure, then carefully remove lid, allowing steam to escape away from you.
Discard bay leaves. Stir lemon zest and juice into chickpeas and season with salt and pepper to taste. Sprinkle with parsley. Serve, drizzling individual portions with extra oil.

763. Barley with Lentils, Mushrooms, and Tahini-Yogurt Sauce

Preparation Time: 5 minutes
Cooking Time: 45 minutes
Servings: 4

Ingredients

½ ounce dried porcini mushrooms, rinsed
1 cup pearl barley
½ cup black lentils, picked over and rinsed
2 tablespoons extra-virgin olive oil
1 onion, chopped fine
2 large portobello mushroom caps, cut into 1-inch pieces
3 (2-inch) strips lemon zest, sliced thin lengthwise
¾ teaspoon ground coriander
Salt and pepper
2 tablespoons chopped fresh dill
½ cup Tahini-Yogurt Sauce

Directions

Preparing the Ingredients
Microwave 1½ cups water and porcini mushrooms in covered bowl until steaming, about 1 minute. Let sit until softened, about 5 minutes. Drain mushrooms in fine-mesh strainer lined with coffee filter, reserving soaking liquid, and chop mushrooms.
Bring 4 quarts water to boil in Dutch oven. Add barley, lentils, and 1 tablespoon salt, return to boil, and cook until tender, 20 to 40 minutes. Drain barley and lentils, return to now-empty pot, and cover to keep warm.
Meanwhile, heat oil in 12-inch nonstick skillet over medium heat until shimmering. Add onion and cook until softened, about 5 minutes. Stir in portobello mushrooms, cover, and cook until portobellos have released their liquid and begin to brown, about 4 minutes.
Uncover, stir in lemon zest, coriander, ½ teaspoon salt, and ¼ teaspoon pepper, and cook until fragrant, about 30 seconds. Stir in porcini and porcini soaking liquid, bring to boil, and cook, stirring occasionally, until liquid is thickened slightly and reduced to ½ cup, about 5 minutes. Stir mushroom mixture and dill into barley-lentil mixture and season with salt and pepper to taste. Serve, drizzling individual portions with Tahini-Yogurt Sauce.

764. French Lentils with Carrots and Parsley

Preparation Time: 5 minutes
Cooking Time: 50 minutes
Servings: 4 To 6

Ingredients

2 carrots, peeled and chopped fine
1 onion, chopped fine
1 celery rib, chopped fine
2 tablespoons extra-virgin olive oil
Salt and pepper
2 garlic cloves, minced
1 teaspoon minced fresh thyme or ¼ teaspoon dried
2½ cups water
1 cup lentilles du Puy, picked over and rinsed
2 tablespoons minced fresh parsley
2 teaspoons lemon juice

Directions

Preparing the Ingredients
Combine carrots, onion, celery, 1 tablespoon oil, and ½ teaspoon salt in large saucepan. Cover and cook over medium-low heat, stirring occasionally,

until vegetables are softened, 8 to 10 minutes. Stir in garlic and thyme and cook until fragrant, about 30 seconds.
Stir in water and lentils and bring to simmer. Reduce heat to low, cover, and simmer gently, stirring occasionally, until lentils are mostly tender, 40 to 50 minutes.
Uncover and continue to cook, stirring occasionally, until lentils are completely tender, about 8 minutes. Stir in remaining 1 tablespoon oil, parsley, and lemon juice. Season with salt and pepper to taste and serve.

765. Lentils with Spinach and Garlic Chips

Preparation Time: 5 minutes
Cooking Time: 30 minutes
Servings: 6

Ingredients

2 tablespoons extra-virgin olive oil
4 garlic cloves, sliced thin
Salt and pepper
1 onion, chopped fine
1 teaspoon ground coriander
1 teaspoon ground cumin
2½ cups water
1 cup green or brown lentils, picked over and rinsed
8 ounces curly-leaf spinach, stemmed and chopped coarse
1 tablespoon red wine vinegar

Directions

Preparing the Ingredients
Cook oil and garlic in large saucepan over medium-low heat, stirring often, until garlic turns crisp and golden but not brown, about 5 minutes. Using slotted spoon, transfer garlic to paper towel–lined plate and season lightly with salt; set aside. Add onion and ½ teaspoon salt to oil left in saucepan and cook over medium heat until softened and lightly browned, 5 to 7 minutes. Stir in coriander and cumin and cook until fragrant, about 30 seconds. Stir in water and lentils and bring to simmer. Reduce heat to low, cover, and simmer gently, stirring occasionally, until lentils are mostly tender but still intact, 45 to 55 minutes. Stir in spinach, 1 handful at a time. Cook, uncovered, stirring occasionally, until spinach is wilted and lentils are completely tender, about 8 minutes. Stir in vinegar and season with salt and pepper to taste. 5. Transfer to serving dish, sprinkle with toasted garlic, and serve.

766. Spiced Lentil Salad with Winter Squash

Preparation Time: 5 minutes
Cooking Time: 60 minutes
Servings: 6

Ingredients

Salt and pepper
1 cup black lentils, picked over and rinsed
1-pound butternut squash, peeled, seeded, and cut into ½-inch pieces (3 cups)
5 tablespoons extra-virgin olive oil
2 tablespoons balsamic vinegar
1 garlic clove, minced
1/2 teaspoon ground coriander
1/4 teaspoon ground cumin
1/4 teaspoon ground ginger
1/8 teaspoon ground cinnamon
1 teaspoon Dijon mustard
1/2 cup fresh parsley leaves
1/4 cup finely chopped red onion
1 tablespoon raw pepitas, toasted

Directions

Preparing the Ingredients
Dissolve 1 teaspoon salt in 4 cups warm water (about 110 degrees) in bowl. Add lentils and soak at room temperature for 1 hour. Drain well. Meanwhile, adjust oven racks to middle and lowest positions and heat oven to 450 degrees. Toss squash with 1 tablespoon oil, 1½ teaspoons vinegar, ¼ teaspoon salt, and ¼ teaspoon pepper. Arrange squash in single layer in rimmed baking sheet and roast on lower rack until well browned and tender, 20 to 25 minutes, stirring halfway through roasting. Let cool slightly. Reduce oven temperature to 325 degrees. Cook 1 tablespoon oil, garlic, coriander, cumin, ginger, and cinnamon in medium oven safe saucepan over medium heat until fragrant, about 1 minute. Stir in 4 cups water and lentils. Cover, transfer saucepan to upper rack in oven, and cook until lentils are tender but remain intact, 40 to 60 minutes.
Drain lentils well. Whisk remaining 3 tablespoons oil, remaining 1½ tablespoons vinegar, and mustard together in large bowl. Add squash, lentils, parsley, and onion and toss to combine. Season with salt and pepper to taste. Transfer to serving platter and sprinkle with pepitas. Serve warm or at room temperature.

767. Lentil Salad with Olives, Mint, and Feta

Preparation Time: 5 minutes
Cooking Time: 60 minutes
Servings: 4 To 6

Ingredients

Salt and pepper
1 cup lentilles du Puy, picked over and rinsed
5 garlic cloves, lightly crushed and peeled
1 bay leaf
5 tablespoons extra-virgin olive oil
3 tablespoons white wine vinegar
½ cup pitted kalamata olives, chopped coarse
½ cup chopped fresh mint
1 large shallot, minced
1-ounce feta cheese, crumbled (¼ cup)

Directions

Preparing the Ingredients
Dissolve 1 teaspoon salt in 4 cups warm water (about 110 degrees) in bowl. Add lentils and soak at room temperature for 1 hour. Drain well. Adjust oven rack to middle position and heat oven to 325 degrees. Combine lentils, 4 cups water, garlic, bay leaf, and ½ teaspoon salt in medium oven safe saucepan.
Cover, transfer saucepan to oven, and cook until lentils are tender but remain intact, 40 to 60 minutes.
Drain lentils well, discarding garlic and bay leaf.
In large bowl, whisk oil and vinegar together. Add lentils, olives, mint, and shallot and toss to combine. Season with salt and pepper to taste. Transfer to serving dish and sprinkle with feta. Serve warm or at room temperature.

768. Chickpeas with Garlic and Parsley

Preparation Time: 5 minutes
Cooking Time: 10 minutes
Servings: 4 To 6

Ingredients

1/4 cup extra-virgin olive oil
4 garlic cloves, sliced thin
1/8 teaspoon red pepper flakes
1 onion, chopped fine
Salt and pepper
2 (15-ounce) cans chickpeas, rinsed
1 cup chicken or vegetable broth
2 tablespoons minced fresh parsley
2 teaspoons lemon juice

Directions

Preparing the Ingredients
Cook 3 tablespoons oil, garlic, and pepper flakes in 12-inch skillet over medium heat, stirring frequently, until garlic turns golden but not brown, about 3 minutes. Stir in onion and ¼ teaspoon salt and cook until softened and lightly browned, 5 to 7 minutes. Stir in chickpeas and broth and bring to simmer. Reduce heat to medium-low, cover, and cook until chickpeas are heated through and flavors meld, about 7 minutes.
Uncover, increase heat to high, and continue to cook until nearly all liquid has evaporated, about 3 minutes. Off heat, stir in parsley and lemon juice. Season with salt and pepper to taste and drizzle with remaining 1 tablespoon oil. Serve.

769. Stewed Chickpeas with Eggplant and Tomatoes

Preparation Time: 5 minutes
Cooking Time: 60 minutes
Servings: 6

Ingredients

1/4 cup extra-virgin olive oil
2 onions, chopped
1 green bell pepper, stemmed, seeded, and chopped fine
Salt and pepper
3 garlic cloves, minced
1 tablespoon minced fresh oregano or 1 teaspoon dried
2 bay leaves
1-pound eggplant, cut into 1-inch pieces
1 (28-ounce) can whole peeled tomatoes, drained with juice reserved, chopped coarse
2 (15-ounce) cans chickpeas, drained with 1 cup liquid reserved

Directions

Preparing the Ingredients
Adjust oven rack to lower-middle position and heat oven to 400 degrees. Heat oil in Dutch oven over medium heat until shimmering. Add onions, bell pepper, ½ teaspoon salt, and ¼ teaspoon pepper and cook until softened, about 5 minutes. Stir in garlic, 1 teaspoon oregano, and bay leaves and cook until fragrant, about 30 seconds.
Stir in eggplant, tomatoes and reserved juice, and chickpeas and reserved liquid and bring to boil. Transfer pot to oven and cook, uncovered, until eggplant is very tender, 45 to 60 minutes, stirring twice during cooking.
Discard bay leaves. Stir in remaining 2 teaspoons oregano and season with salt and pepper to taste.

770. Spicy Chickpeas with Turnips

Preparation Time: 5 minutes
Cooking Time: 35 minutes
Servings: 4 To 6

Ingredients

2 tablespoons extra-virgin olive oil
2 onions, chopped
2 red bell peppers, stemmed, seeded, and chopped
Salt and pepper
¼ cup tomato paste
1 jalapeño chile, stemmed, seeded, and minced
5 garlic cloves, minced
¾ teaspoon ground cumin
¼ teaspoon cayenne pepper
2 (15-ounce) cans chickpeas
12 ounces turnips, peeled and cut into ½-inch pieces
¾ cup water, plus extra as needed
¼ cup chopped fresh parsley
2 tablespoons lemon juice, plus extra for seasoning

Directions

Preparing the Ingredients
Heat oil in Dutch oven over medium heat until shimmering. Add onions, bell peppers, ½ teaspoon salt, and ¼ teaspoon pepper and cook until softened and lightly browned, 5 to 7 minutes. Stir in tomato paste, jalapeño, garlic, cumin, and cayenne and cook until fragrant, about 30 seconds.
Stir in chickpeas and their liquid, turnips, and water. Bring to simmer and cook until turnips are tender and sauce has thickened, 25 to 35 minutes.
Stir in parsley and lemon juice. Season with salt, pepper, and extra lemon juice to taste. Adjust consistency with extra hot water as needed.

771. Chickpea Salad with Carrots, Arugula, and Olives

Preparation Time: 5 minutes
Cooking Time: None
Serves 6

Ingredients

2 (15-ounce) cans chickpeas, rinsed
1/4 cup extra-virgin olive oil
2 tablespoons lemon juice
Salt and pepper
Pinch cayenne pepper
3 carrots, peeled and shredded
1 cup baby arugula, chopped coarse
1/2 cup pitted kalamata olives, chopped coarse

Directions

Preparing the Ingredients
Microwave chickpeas in medium bowl until hot, about 2 minutes. Stir in oil, lemon juice, ¾ teaspoon salt, ½ teaspoon pepper, and cayenne and let sit for 30 minutes.
Add carrots, arugula, and olives and toss to combine. Season with salt and pepper to taste. Serve.

772. Chickpea Cakes

Preparation Time: 5 minutes
Cooking Time: 10 minutes
Servings: 6

Ingredients

2 (15-ounce) cans chickpeas, rinsed
½ cup plain Greek yogurt
2 large eggs
6 tablespoons extra-virgin olive oil
1 teaspoon ground coriander
1/8 teaspoon cayenne pepper
1/8 teaspoon salt
1 cup panko bread crumbs
2 scallions, sliced thin
3 tablespoons minced fresh cilantro
1 shallot, minced
1 recipe Cucumber-Yogurt Sauce

Directions

Preparing the Ingredients
Pulse chickpeas in food processor until coarsely ground, about 8 pulses. Whisk yogurt, eggs, 2 tablespoons oil, coriander, cayenne, and salt together in medium bowl. Gently stir in chickpeas, panko, scallions, cilantro, and shallot until just combined. Divide mixture into 6 equal portions and gently pack into 1-inch-thick patties.
Heat 2 tablespoons oil in 12-inch nonstick skillet over medium heat until shimmering. Carefully lay 3 patties in skillet and cook until well browned and firm, 4 to 5 minutes per side.
Transfer cakes to paper towel–lined plate and tent loosely with aluminum foil. Repeat with remaining 2 tablespoons oil and remaining 3 patties. Serve with yogurt sauce.

773. Black-Eyed Peas with Walnuts and Pomegranate

Preparation Time: 5 minutes
Cooking Time: None
Servings: 4 To 6

Ingredients

3 tablespoons extra-virgin olive oil
3 tablespoons dukkah
2 tablespoons lemon juice
2 tablespoons pomegranate molasses
Salt and pepper
2 (15-ounce) cans black-eyed peas, rinsed
½ cup walnuts, toasted and chopped
½ cup pomegranate seeds
½ cup minced fresh parsley
4 scallions, sliced thin

Directions

Preparing the Ingredients
Whisk oil, 2 tablespoons dukkah, lemon juice, pomegranate molasses, ¼ teaspoon salt, and 1/8 teaspoon pepper together in large bowl until smooth. Add peas, walnuts, pomegranate seeds, parsley, and scallions and toss to combine. Season with salt and pepper to taste. Sprinkle with remaining 1 tablespoon dukkah and serve.

774. Cranberry Beans with Fennel, Grapes, and Pine Nuts

Preparation Time: 5 minutes
Cooking Time: 1 Hour 30 minutes
Servings: 6 To 8

Ingredients

Salt and pepper
1 pound (2½ cups) dried cranberry beans, picked over and rinsed
3 tablespoons extra-virgin olive oil
½ fennel bulb, 2 tablespoons fronds chopped, stalks discarded, bulb cored and chopped
1 cup plus 2 tablespoons red wine vinegar
½ cup sugar
1 teaspoon fennel seeds
6 ounces seedless red grapes, halved (1 cup)
½ cup pine nuts, toasted

Directions

Preparing the Ingredients
Dissolve 3 tablespoons salt in 4 quarts cold water in large container. Add beans and soak at room temperature for at least 8 hours or up to 24 hours. Drain and rinse well. Bring beans, 4 quarts water, and 1 teaspoon salt to boil in Dutch oven. Reduce to simmer and cook, stirring occasionally, until beans are tender, 1 to 1½ hours. Drain beans and set aside.
Wipe Dutch oven clean with paper towels. Heat oil in now-empty pot over medium heat until shimmering. Add fennel, ¼ teaspoon salt, and ¼ teaspoon pepper and cook until softened, about 5 minutes. Stir in 1 cup vinegar, sugar, and fennel seeds until sugar is dissolved. Bring to simmer and cook until liquid is thickened to syrupy glaze and edges of fennel are beginning to brown, about 10 minutes. Add beans to vinegar-fennel mixture and toss to coat. Transfer to large bowl and let cool to room temperature. Add grapes, pine nuts, fennel fronds, and remaining 2 tablespoons vinegar and toss to combine. Season with salt and pepper to taste and serve.

775. Mashed Fava Beans with Cumin and Garlic

Preparation Time: 5 minutes
Cooking Time: 10 minutes
Servings: 4 To 6

Ingredients

4 garlic cloves, minced
1 tablespoon extra-virgin olive oil, plus extra for serving
1 teaspoon ground cumin
2 (15-ounce) cans fava beans
3 tablespoons tahini
2 tablespoons lemon juice, plus lemon wedges for serving
Salt and pepper
1 tomato, cored and cut into ½-inch pieces
1 small onion, chopped fine
2 tablespoons minced fresh parsley
2 hard-cooked large eggs, chopped

Directions

Preparing the Ingredients Cook garlic, oil, and cumin in medium saucepan over medium heat until fragrant, about 2 minutes. Stir in beans and their liquid and tahini. Bring to simmer and cook until liquid thickens slightly, 8 to 10 minutes.
Off heat, mash beans to coarse consistency using potato masher. Stir in lemon juice and 1 teaspoon pepper. Season with salt and pepper to taste. Transfer to serving dish, top with tomato, onion, parsley, and eggs, if using, and drizzle with extra oil. Serve with lemon wedges.

776. Gigante Beans with Spinach and Feta

Preparation Time: 5 minutes
Cooking Time: 30 minutes
Servings: 6 To 8

Ingredients

Salt and pepper
8 ounces (1½ cups) dried gigante beans, picked over and rinsed
6 tablespoons extra-virgin olive oil
2 onions, chopped fine
3 garlic cloves, minced
20 ounces curly-leaf spinach, stemmed
2 (14.5-ounce) cans diced tomatoes, drained
¼ cup minced fresh dill
2 slices hearty white sandwich bread, torn into quarters
6 ounces feta cheese, crumbled (1½ cups)
Lemon wedges

Directions

Preparing the Ingredients
Dissolve 3 tablespoons salt in 4 quarts cold water in large container. Add beans and soak at room temperature for at least 8 hours or up to 24 hours. Drain and rinse well. Bring beans and 2 quarts water to boil in Dutch oven. Reduce to simmer and cook, stirring occasionally, until beans are tender, 1 to 1½ hours. Drain beans and set aside.
Wipe Dutch oven clean with paper towels. Heat 2 tablespoons oil in now-empty pot over medium heat until shimmering. Add onions and ½ teaspoon salt and cook until softened, about 5 minutes. Stir in garlic and cook until fragrant, about 30 seconds. Stir in half of spinach, cover, and cook until beginning to wilt, about 2 minutes. Stir in remaining spinach, cover, and cook until wilted, about 2 minutes. Off heat, gently stir in beans, tomatoes, dill, and 2 tablespoons oil. Season with salt and pepper to taste. Meanwhile, adjust oven rack to middle position and heat oven to 400 degrees. Pulse bread and remaining 2 tablespoons oil in food processor to coarse crumbs, about 5 pulses. Transfer bean mixture to 13 by 9-inch baking dish and sprinkle with feta, then bread crumbs. Bake until bread crumbs are golden brown and edges are bubbling, about 20 minutes. Serve with lemon wedges.

777. Minty Chickpea Salad

Preparation Time:5 minutes
Cooking Time:20 minutes
Serves: 6

Ingredients:

1 can chickpeas, drained
½ pound cherry tomatoes, halved
1 cucumber, diced
¼ cup green olives, sliced
¼ cup black olives, sliced
1 shallot, sliced
2 tablespoons chopped mint
½ cup chopped parsley
½ cup walnuts, chopped
4 oz. short pasta, cooked and drained
2 cups arugula
1 lemon, juiced
2 tablespoons extra virgin olive oil
Salt and pepper to taste

Directions:

Combine the chickpeas and the rest of the ingredients in a salad bowl.
Drizzle with lemon juice and oil then sprinkle with salt and pepper and mix well.
Serve the salad fresh or keep in the refrigerator in a sealed container for up to 2 days.

778. Chickpea Arugula Salad

Preparation Time:5 minutes
Cooking Time:15 minutes
Servings: 4

Ingredients:

1 can chickpeas, drained
1 cup cherry tomatoes, halved
1/2cup sun-dried tomatoes, chopped
2 cups arugula
1 pita bread, cubed
½ cup black olives, pitted
1 shallot, sliced
½ teaspoon cumin seeds
½ teaspoon coriander seeds
¼ teaspoon chili powder
1 teaspoon chopped mint
Salt and pepper to taste
4 oz. goat cheese, crumbled

Directions:

Combine the chickpeas, tomatoes, arugula, pita bread, olives, shallot, spices and mint in a salad bowl.
Add salt and pepper to taste and mix well then stir in the cheese.
Serve the salad fresh.

779. Mixed Cherry Chickpea Salad

Preparation Time:5 minutes
Cooking Time:15 minutes
Servings: 4

Ingredients:

1 can chickpeas, drained
2 cups mixed cherry tomatoes, halved
2 tablespoons chopped parsley
1 pinch chili flakes
1 teaspoon sumac spices
2 tablespoons extra virgin olive oil
1 teaspoon sherry vinegar
Salt and pepper to taste
4 oz. mozzarella cheese, crumbled

Directions:

Combine the chickpeas, tomatoes, parsley, chili, sumac, oil and vinegar in a salad bowl.
Add salt and pepper to taste and mix well.
Top with mozzarella cheese and serve the salad fresh.

780. Kale White Bean Soup

Preparation Time:5 minutes
Cooking Time:50 minutes
Serves: 10

Ingredients:

2 tablespoons olive oil
1 sweet onion, chopped
2 celery stalk, sliced
2 carrots, diced
1 fennel bulb, sliced
2 garlic cloves, chopped
2 cans cannellini beans, drained
1 thyme sprig
¼ teaspoon chili flakes
½ teaspoon dried marjoram
4 cups vegetable stock
4 cups water
8 kale leaves, shredded
Salt and pepper to taste

Directions:

Heat the oil in a soup pot and stir in the onion, celery, carrots, fennel and garlic.
Cook for 5 minutes then stir in the beans, chili flakes, marjoram, stock, water, salt and pepper.
Cook for 20 minutes then add the kale. Cook for another 5 minutes then serve the soup warm.

781. Grilled Turkey with White Bean Mash

Preparation Time:5 minutes
Cooking Time:45 minutes
Serves: 4

Ingredients:

4 turkey breast fillets
1 teaspoon chili powder
1 teaspoon dried parsley
Salt and pepper to taste
2 cans white beans, drained
4 garlic cloves, minced
2 tablespoons lemon juice
3 tablespoons olive oil
2 sweet onions, sliced
2 tablespoons tomato paste

Directions:

Season the turkey with salt, pepper and dried parsley.
Heat a grill pan over medium flame and place the turkey on the grill. Cook on each side for 7 minutes.
For the mash, combine the beans, garlic, lemon juice, salt and pepper in a blender and pulse until well mixed and smooth.
Heat the oil in a skillet and add the onions. Cook for 10 minutes until caramelized. Add the tomato paste and cook for 2 more minutes.
Serve the grilled turkey with bean mash and caramelized onions.

782. Chicken Chickpea Stew

Preparation Time:5 minutes
Cooking Time:1 ½hours
Servings: 8

Ingredients:

3 tablespoons olive oil
3 pounds chicken thighs
2 sweet onions, chopped
4 garlic cloves, chopped
½ teaspoon cumin powder
½ teaspoon chili powder
½ teaspoon ground coriander
1 red chili, chopped
1 bay leaf
1 cinnamon stick
2 cups vegetable stock
1 can diced tomatoes
1 can chickpeas, drained
Salt and pepper to taste

Directions:

Heat the oil in a heavy saucepan or skillet and add the chicken. Cook on all sides until golden.

Add the onions and garlic and cook for 5 minutes.
Stir in the remaining ingredients and season with salt and pepper.
Cook on low heat for 1 hour.
Serve the stew warm and fresh.

783. Parsnip Chickpea Veal Stew

Preparation Time:5 minutes
Cooking Time:2 hours
Servings: 10

Ingredients:

2 pounds veal meat, cubed
3 tablespoons olive oil
2 shallots, chopped
4 garlic cloves, chopped
2 red bell peppers, cored and sliced
2 yellow bell peppers, cored and sliced
4 parsnips, peeled and sliced
2 carrots, sliced
1 can diced tomatoes
1 ½ cups beef stock
1 bay leaf
1 rosemary sprig
1 oregano sprig
1 can chickpeas, drained
Salt and pepper to taste

Directions:

Heat the oil in a heavy saucepan and stir in the veal. Cook for 5 minutes until slightly browned.
Add the shallots, garlic, bell peppers, parsnips and carrots.
Cook for another 5 minutes then stir in the rest of the ingredients.
Season with salt and pepper and cook for 1 ½ hours on low heat.
Serve the stew warm and fresh.

784. Vegan Lentil Bolognese

Preparation Time: 15 minutes
Cooking Time: 50 minutes
Servings: 2

Ingredients:

1 medium celery stalk
1 large carrot
½ large onion
1 garlic clove
2 tablespoons olive oil
1 (28-ounce / 794-g) can crushed tomatoes
1 cup red wine
½ teaspoon salt, plus more as needed
½ teaspoon pure maple syrup
1 cup cooked lentils (prepared from ½ cup dry)

Directions:

Add the celery, carrot, onion, and garlic to a food processor and process until everything is finely chopped.
In a Dutch oven, heat the olive oil over medium-high heat. Add the chopped mixture and sauté for about 10 minutes, stirring occasionally, or until the vegetables are lightly browned.
Stir in the tomatoes, wine, salt, and maple syrup and bring to a boil.
Once the sauce starts to boil, cover, and reduce the heat to medium-low. Simmer for 30 minutes, stirring occasionally, or until the vegetables are softened.
Stir in the cooked lentils and cook for an additional 5 minutes until warmed through.
Taste and add additional salt, if needed.
Serve warm.
Tip: You can use 1 cup of cooked bulgur wheat or minced mushrooms to substitute for the lentils.

785. Lentil and Tomato Collard Wraps

Preparation Time: 15 minutes
Cooking Time: 0 minutes
Servings: 4

Ingredients:

2 cups cooked lentils
5 Roma tomatoes, diced
1/2 cup crumbled feta cheese
10 large fresh basil leaves, thinly sliced
1/4 cup extra-virgin olive oil
1 tablespoon balsamic vinegar
2 garlic cloves, minced
1/2 teaspoon raw honey
1/2 teaspoon salt
1/4 teaspoon freshly ground black pepper
4 large collard leaves, stems removed

Directions:

Combine the lentils, tomatoes, cheese, basil leaves, olive oil, vinegar, garlic, honey, salt, and black pepper in a large bowl and stir until well blended.
Lay the collard leaves on a flat work surface. Spoon the equal-sized amounts of the lentil mixture onto the edges of the leaves. Roll them up and slice in half to serve.
Tip: If you want to make the collard leaves easier to wrap, you can steam them for 1 to 2 minutes before wrapping.

786. Vegetable and Red Lentil Stew

Preparation Time: 10 minutes
Cooking Time: 35 minutes
Servings: 6

Ingredients:

1 tablespoon extra-virgin olive oil
2 onions, peeled and finely diced
6½ cups water
2 zucchinis, finely diced
4 celery stalks, finely diced
3 cups red lentils
1 teaspoon dried oregano
1 teaspoon salt, plus more as needed

Directions:

Heat the olive oil in a large pot over medium heat.
Add the onions and sauté for about 5 minutes, stirring constantly, or until the onions are softened.
Stir in the water, zucchini, celery, lentils, oregano, and salt and bring the mixture to a boil.
Reduce the heat to low and let simmer covered for 30 minutes, stirring occasionally, or until the lentils are tender.
Taste and adjust the seasoning as needed.
Tip: You can try this recipe with different lentils such as brown and green lentils, but they need additional cooking time, about 20 minutes.

787. Sautéed Green Beans with Tomatoes

Preparation Time: 10 minutes
Cooking Time: 20 minutes
Servings: 4

Ingredients:

1/4 cup extra-virgin olive oil
1 large onion, chopped
4 cloves garlic, finely chopped
1 pound (454 g) green beans, fresh or frozen, cut into 2-inch pieces
1½ teaspoons salt, divided
1 can diced tomatoes
1/2 teaspoon freshly ground black pepper

Directions:

Heat the olive oil in a large skillet over medium heat.
Add the onion and garlic and sauté for 1 minute until fragrant.

Stir in the green beans and sauté for 3 minutes. Sprinkle with ½ teaspoon of salt.
Add the tomatoes, remaining salt, and pepper and stir to mix well. Cook for an additional 12 minutes, stirring occasionally, or until the green beans are crisp and tender.
Remove from the heat and serve warm.
Tips: To add more flavors to this meal, top the green beans with a sprinkle of toasted pine nuts or almonds before serving. For a spicy kick, you can sprinkle with ½ teaspoon red pepper flakes.

788. Baked Tomatoes and chickpeas

Preparation Time: 15 minutes
Cooking Time: 40 to 45 minutes
Servings: 4

Ingredients:

1 tablespoon extra-virgin olive oil
½ medium onion, chopped
3 garlic cloves, chopped
¼ teaspoon ground cumin
2 teaspoons smoked paprika
2 (15-ounce / 425-g) cans chickpeas, drained and rinsed
4 cups halved cherry tomatoes
½ cup plain Greek yogurt, for serving
1 cup crumbled feta cheese, for serving

Directions:

Preheat the oven to 425ºF (220ºC).
Heat the olive oil in an ovenproof skillet over medium heat.
Add the onion and garlic and sauté for about 5 minutes, stirring occasionally, or until tender and fragrant.
Add the paprika and cumin and cook for 2 minutes. Stir in the chickpeas and tomatoes and allow to simmer for 5 to 10 minutes.
Transfer the skillet to the preheated oven and roast for 25 to 30 minutes, or until the mixture bubbles and thickens.
Remove from the oven and serve topped with yogurt and crumbled feta cheese.
Tips: If you want to make it a vegan dish, you can skip the plain Greek yogurt and feta cheese topping. To add more flavors to this dish, serve the chickpeas and tomatoes over the cauliflower rice or quinoa.

789. Garlic and Parsley Chickpeas

Preparation Time: 10 minutes
Cooking Time: 18 to 20 minutes
Servings: 4 to 6

Ingredients:

¼ cup extra-virgin olive oil, divided
4 garlic cloves, sliced thinly
1/8 teaspoon red pepper flakes
1 onion, chopped finely
¼ teaspoon salt, plus more to taste
Black pepper, to taste
2 (15-ounce / 425-g) cans chickpeas, rinsed
1 cup vegetable broth
2 tablespoons minced fresh parsley
2 teaspoons lemon juice

Directions:

Add 3 tablespoons of the olive oil, garlic, and pepper flakes to a skillet over medium heat. Cook for about 3 minutes, stirring constantly, or until the garlic turns golden but not brown.
Stir in the onion and ¼ teaspoon salt and cook for 5 to 7 minutes, or until softened and lightly browned.
Add the chickpeas and broth to the skillet and bring to a simmer. Reduce the heat to medium-low, cover, and cook for about 7 minutes, or until the chickpeas are cooked through and flavors meld.
Uncover, increase the heat to high and continue to cook for about 3 minutes more, or until nearly all liquid has evaporated.
Turn off the heat, stir in the parsley and lemon juice. Season to taste with salt and pepper and drizzle with remaining 1 tablespoon of the olive oil.
Serve warm.

790. Black-Eyed Peas Salad with Walnuts

Preparation: time: 10 minutes
Cooking Time: 0 minutes
Servings: 4 to 6

Ingredients:

3 tablespoons extra-virgin olive oil
3 tablespoons dukkah, divided
2 tablespoons lemon juice
2 tablespoons pomegranate molasses
¼ teaspoon salt, or more to taste
1/8 teaspoon pepper, or more to taste
2 (15-ounce / 425-g) cans black-eyed peas, rinsed
½ cup pomegranate seeds
½ cup minced fresh parsley
½ cup walnuts, toasted and chopped
4 scallions, sliced thinly

Directions:

In a large bowl, whisk together the olive oil, 2 tablespoons of the dukkah, lemon juice, pomegranate molasses, salt and pepper.
Stir in the remaining ingredients. Season with salt and pepper.
Sprinkle with the remaining 1 tablespoon of the dukkah before serving.

791. Mashed Beans with Cumin

Preparation Time: 10 minutes
Cooking Time: 10 to 12 minutes
Servings: 4 to 6

Ingredients:

1 tablespoon extra-virgin olive oil, plus extra for serving
4 garlic cloves, minced
1 teaspoon ground cumin
2 (15-ounce / 425-g) cans fava beans
3 tablespoons tahini
2 tablespoons lemon juice, plus lemon wedges for serving
Salt and pepper, to taste
1 tomato, cored and cut into ½-inch pieces
1 small onion, chopped finely
2 hard-cooked large eggs, chopped
2 tablespoons minced fresh parsley

Directions:

Add the olive oil, garlic and cumin to a medium saucepan over medium heat. Cook for about 2 minutes, or until fragrant.
Stir in the beans with their liquid and tahini. Bring to a simmer and cook for 8 to 10 minutes, or until the liquid thickens slightly.
Turn off the heat, mash the beans to a coarse consistency with a potato masher. Stir in the lemon juice and 1 teaspoon pepper. Season with salt and pepper.
Transfer the mashed beans to a serving dish. Top with the tomato, onion, eggs and parsley. Drizzle with the extra olive oil.
Serve with the lemon wedges.

792. Green Bean and Lentil Stew

Preparation Time: 10 minutes
Cooking Time: 25 minutes
Servings: 5

Ingredients:

2 tablespoons olive oil
1/2 cup celery stalks, chopped
1/2 cup parsnips, chopped
1 green bell pepper, seeds and chopped
1 red bell pepper, seeds and chopped
1 poblano pepper, seeds and finely chopped
1/2 cup leeks, chopped
1 teaspoon ginger-garlic paste
1/2 teaspoon dried basil
1/2 teaspoon dried oregano
1/2 teaspoon dried rosemary
1/2 teaspoon curry paste
2 cups brown lentils
3 cups vegetable broth
1/2 cup tomato paste
Sea salt and freshly cracked black pepper, to taste
2 cups green beans, trimmed and halved

Directions:

Press the "Sauté" button to preheat your Instant Pot. Heat the olive oil and sauté the celery, parsnip, peppers, and leeks until they are tender.
Stir in the aromatics, curry paste, lentils, broth, and tomato paste. Season with salt and pepper to taste.
Secure the lid. Choose the "Manual" mode and cook for 10 minutes at High pressure. Once cooking is complete, use a natural pressure release for 5 minutes; carefully remove the lid.
Add the green beans to the inner pot. Seal the lid, press the "Sauté" button, and adjust to "Less" temperature. Let it simmer until thoroughly heated. Bon appétit!

793. Traditional Greek Arakas Latheros

Preparation Time: 10 minutes
Cooking Time: 35 minutes
Servings: 4

Ingredients:

4 tablespoons Greek olive oil
1/2 cup shallots, chopped
1 red bell pepper, seeded and chopped
1/2 cup celery stalks and ribs, chopped
1 fennel, chopped
1 cup roasted vegetable broth, preferably homemade
2 tablespoons tomato paste
1 ½ cups overripe tomatoes, pureed
1 tablespoon Greek seasoning mix
1/4 teaspoon mustard seeds
1 bay laurel
1 ½ pounds sugar snap peas
4 thick slices bread, cubed
1/4 teaspoon coarse sea salt
2 tablespoons extra-virgin olive oil
1 teaspoon dried oregano

Directions:

Press the "Sauté" button to preheat your Instant Pot. Heat the olive oil and sweat the shallots for 3 to 4 minutes. Then, add the bell pepper, celery, and fennel to the inner pot; continue cooking until they have softened.
Next, stir in the roasted vegetable broth, tomato paste, pureed tomatoes, Greek seasoning mix, mustard seeds, bay laurel, and sugar snap peas.
Secure the lid. Choose the "Manual" mode and cook for 18 minutes at High pressure. Once cooking is complete, use a quick pressure release; carefully remove the lid.
Meanwhile, crisp the bread cubes in a pan over moderate heat; fry your croutons with sea salt, olive oil, and dried oregano, stirring periodically.
Serve the warm peas with homemade croutons on the side.

794. Old-Fashion Snow Pea Chowder

Preparation Time: 10 minutes
Cooking time 25 minutes
Servings: 4

Ingredients:

1 tablespoon olive oil
1 red bell pepper, chopped
1 green bell pepper, chopped
2 carrots, trimmed and chopped
1 celery rib, chopped
1 cup leeks, chopped
2 garlic cloves, minced
3/4-pound snow peas
1 teaspoon cayenne pepper
1/4 teaspoon ground bay leaf
1/4 teaspoon ground cumin
1/4 teaspoon dried rosemary, crushed
1/2 teaspoon dried mint, crushed
Sea salt and ground black pepper, to taste
1/2 cup plain Greek yogurt

Directions:

Press the "Sauté" button to preheat your Instant Pot. Heat the olive oil and cook the peppers, carrot, celery, and leeks until they are tender and fragrant.
Stir in the garlic and continue sautéing for a further 30 seconds. Add the snow peas, cayenne pepper, bay leaf, cumin, rosemary, mint, salt, and black pepper.
Secure the lid. Choose the "Manual" mode and cook for 18 minutes at High pressure. Once cooking is complete, use a natural pressure release for 5 minutes; carefully remove the lid. Serve with Greek yogurt on the side. Enjoy!

795. Sloppy Lentils in Pita

Preparation Time: 15 minutes
Cooking Time: 30 minutes
Servings: 4

Ingredients:

4 tablespoons marinara sauce
2 vegetable bouillon cubes
1/4 teaspoon cumin
1/2 teaspoon mustard seeds
1/2 teaspoon red pepper flakes
2 cups water
1 cup red lentil
4 whole-wheat pita bread (flatbread)
2 tomatoes, sliced
1 Lebanese cucumber, sliced
2 tablespoons fresh parsley
2 cups fresh lettuce leaves
1 tablespoon yellow mustard
4 tablespoons Greek yogurt
1 teaspoon honey
1 tablespoon olive oil
1 teaspoon fresh garlic, pressed

Directions:

Place the marinara sauce, bouillon cubes, cumin, mustard seeds, red pepper flakes, water and lentils in the inner pot of your Instant Pot.
Secure the lid. Choose the "Manual" mode and cook for 10 minutes at High pressure. Once cooking is complete, use a quick pressure release for 5 minutes; carefully remove the lid.
Divide the lentil mixture between pitas; top with the tomato, cucumber, parsley, and lettuce. In a small mixing bowl, whisk the yellow mustard, Greek yogurt, honey, olive oil, and fresh garlic.
Drizzle the sauce over the vegetables; wrap each pita in foil and serve immediately. Enjoy!

796. Barbunya Pilaki (Turkish Bean Stew)

Preparation Time: 25 minutes
Cooking time 40 minutes
Servings: 6

Ingredients:

2 tablespoons olive oil
1 bell pepper, sliced
1/2 cup leeks, chopped
1 parsnip, sliced
1 celery stalk, sliced
1 teaspoon fresh garlic, minced
1-pound white beans, soaked at least 6 hours
2 tablespoons red pepper paste
10 ounces canned tomatoes, crushed
Sea salt and freshly ground black pepper, to taste
1 cup vegetable broth
1 dry bay laurel leaf

Directions:

Press the "Sauté" button to preheat your Instant Pot. Heat the olive oil and sauté the pepper, leeks, parsnip, celery until they are tender and fragrant.

Stir in the minced garlic and continue sautéing for a further 30 seconds, stirring continuously.

Add in the beans, followed by the red pepper paste, tomatoes, salt, black pepper, vegetable broth, and bay laurel leaf.

Secure the lid. Choose the "Bean/Chili" mode and cook for 30 minutes at High pressure. Once cooking is complete, use a quick pressure release; carefully remove the lid. Serve over hot rice if desired. Enjoy!

CHAPTER 12: SOUPS

797. Seafood Corn Chowder

Preparation Time: 10 minutes
Cooking Time: 12 minutes
Servings: 4

Ingredients:

1 tablespoon butter
1 cup onion
1/3 cup celery
½ cup green bell pepper
½ cup red bell pepper
1 tablespoon white flour
14 ounces chicken broth
2 cups cream
6 ounces evaporated milk
10 ounces surimi imitation crab chunks
2 cups frozen corn kernels
½ teaspoon black pepper
½ teaspoon paprika

Directions:

Place a suitably-sized saucepan over medium heat and add butter to melt.
Toss in onion, green and red peppers, and celery, then sauté for 5 minutes.
Stir in flour and whisk well for 2 minutes.
Pour in chicken broth and stir until it boils.
Add evaporated milk, corn, surimi crab, paprika, black pepper, and creamer.
Cook for 5 minutes.
Serves warm.

798. Classic Minestrone

Preparation Time: 12 minutes
Cooking Time: 25 minutes
Servings: 6

Ingredients:

2 tablespoons olive oil
3 cloves garlic
1 onion, diced
2 carrots
2 stalks celery
1 1/2 teaspoons dried basil
1 teaspoon dried oregano
1/2 teaspoon fennel seed
6 cups low sodium chicken broth
1 (28-ounce) can tomatoes
1 (16-ounce) can kidney beans
1 zucchini
1 Parmesan rind
1 bay leaf
1 bunch kale leaves, chopped
2 teaspoons red wine vinegar
1/3 cup freshly grated Parmesan
2 tablespoons chopped fresh parsley leaves

Directions:

Preheat olive oil in the insert of the Instant Pot® on Sauté mode.
Add carrots, celery, and onion, sauté for 3 minutes.
Stir in fennel seeds, oregano, and basil. Stir cook for 1 minute.
Add stock, beans, tomatoes, parmesan, bay leaf, and zucchini.
Secure and seal the Instant Pot® lid then select Manual mode to cook for minutes at high pressure.
Once done, release the pressure completely then remove the lid.
Add kale and let it sit for 2 minutes in the hot soup.
Stir in red wine, vinegar, pepper, and salt.
Garnish with parsley and parmesan.
Serve.

799. Beetroot and Carrot Soup

Preparation Time: 12 minutes
Cooking Time: 32 minutes
Servings: 6

Ingredients:

4 beets
2 carrots
2 potatoes
1 medium onion
4 cups vegetable broth
2 cups water
2 tbsp yogurt
2 tbsp olive oil

Direction

Peel and chop the beets.
Heat olive oil in a saucepan over medium high heat and sauté the onion and carrot until onion is tender.
Add beets, potatoes, broth and water and bring to the boil.
Reduce heat to medium and simmer, partially covered, for 30-40 minutes, or until beets are tender. Cool slightly.
Blend the soup in batches until smooth.
Return it to pan over low heat and cook, stirring, for 4 to 5 minutes or until heated through.
Season with salt and pepper.
Serve soup topped with yogurt and sprinkled with spring onions.

800. Roasted Red Pepper Soup

Preparation Time: 16 minutes
Cooking Time: 23 minutes
Servings: 7

Ingredients:

5-6 red peppers
1 large brown onion
2 garlic cloves
4 medium tomatoes
3 cups chicken broth
3 tbsp olive oil
2 bay leaves

Directions:

Grill the peppers or roast them in the oven at 450 °F (230°C) until the skins are a little burnt.
Place the roasted peppers in a brown paper bag or a lidded container and leave covered for about 10 minutes. This makes it easier to peel them.
Peel the skins and remove the seeds.
Cut the peppers in small pieces.
Heat oil in a large saucepan over medium-high heat.
Add onion and garlic and sauté, stirring, for 3 minutes or until onion has softened.
Add the red peppers, bay leaves, tomato and simmer for 5 minutes.
Add in the broth and season with pepper.
Bring to the boil then reduce heat and simmer for 20 more minutes.
Set aside to cool slightly.
Blend, in batches, until smooth.
Serve.

801. Spinach and Feta Cheese Soup

Preparation Time: 8 minutes
Cooking Time: 24 minutes
Servings: 4

Ingredients:

14 oz frozen spinach

oz feta cheese
1 large onion or 4-5 scallions
2 -3 tbsp light cream
3-4 tbsp olive oil
1-2 cloves garlic
4 cups water

Directions:

Heat the oil in a cooking pot.
Add the onion and spinach and sauté together for a few minutes, until just softened.
Add garlic and stir for a minute. Remove from heat.
Add about 2 cups of hot water and season with salt and pepper.
Bring back to the boil, then reduce the heat and simmer for around 30 minutes.
Blend soup in a blender.
Crumble the cheese with a fork.
Stir in the crumbled feta cheese and the cream.
Serve hot.

802. Moroccan Pumpkin Soup

Preparation Time: 7 minutes
Cooking Time: 54 minutes
Servings: 6

Ingredients:

1 leek, white part only
3 cloves garlic
½ tsp ground ginger
½ tsp ground cinnamon
½ tsp ground cumin
2 carrots
2 lb. pumpkin
1/3 cup chickpeas
5 tbsp olive oil
juice of ½ lemon

Directions:

Heat oil in a large saucepan and sauté leek, garlic and 2 teaspoons of salt, stirring occasionally, until soft.
Add cinnamon, ginger and cumin and stir.
Add in carrots, pumpkin and chickpeas. Stir to combine.
Add 5 cups of water and bring the soup to the boil, then reduce heat and simmer for 50 minutes.
Pullout from heat, add lemon juice and blend the soup.
Heat again over low heat for 4-5 minutes.
Serve topped with parsley sprigs.

803. Roasted Root Vegetable Soup

Preparation Time: 10 minutes
Cooking Time: 35 minutes
Servings: 6

Ingredients:

2 parsnips, peeled and sliced
2 carrots, peeled and sliced
2 sweet potatoes, peeled and sliced
1 teaspoon chopped fresh rosemary
1 teaspoon chopped fresh thyme
1 teaspoon sea salt
½ teaspoon freshly ground black pepper
2 tablespoons extra-virgin olive oil
4 cups low-sodium vegetable soup
½ cup grated Parmesan cheese, for garnish (optional)

Directions:

Preheat the oven to 400ºF (205ºC). Line a baking sheet with aluminum foil.
Combine the parsnips, carrots, and sweet potatoes in a large bowl, then sprinkle with rosemary, thyme, salt, and pepper, and drizzle with olive oil. Toss to coat the vegetables well.
Arrange the vegetables on the baking sheet, then roast in the preheated oven for 30 minutes or until lightly browned and soft. Flip the vegetables halfway through the roasting.
Pour the roasted vegetables with vegetable broth in a food processor, then pulse until creamy and smooth.
Pour the puréed vegetables in a saucepan, then warm over low heat until heated through.
Spoon the soup in a large serving bowl, then scatter with Parmesan cheese. Serve immediately.
Tip: If you don't have vegetable soup, just use the same amount of water to replace it.

804. Super Mushroom and Red Wine Soup

Preparation Time: 40 minutes
Cooking Time: 35 minutes
Servings: 6

Ingredients:

2 ounces (57 g) dried morels
2 ounces (57 g) dried porcini
1 tablespoon extra-virgin olive oil
8 ounces (227 g) button mushrooms, chopped
8 ounces (227 g) portobello mushrooms, chopped
3 shallots, finely chopped
2 cloves garlic, minced
1 teaspoon finely chopped fresh thyme
Sea salt and freshly ground pepper, to taste
1/3 cup dry red wine
4 cups low-sodium chicken broth
1/2 cup heavy cream
1 small bunch flat-leaf parsley, chopped

Directions:

Put the dried mushrooms in a large bowl and pour in enough water to submerge the mushrooms. Soak for 30 minutes and drain.
Heat the olive oil in a stockpot over medium-high heat until shimmering.
Add the mushrooms and shallots to the pot and sauté for 10 minutes or until the mushrooms are tender.
Add the garlic and sauté for an additional 1 minute or until fragrant. Sprinkle with thyme, salt, and pepper.
Pour in the dry red wine and chicken broth. Bring to a boil over high heat.
Reduce the heat to low. Simmer for 20 minutes.
After simmering, pour half of the soup in a food processor, then pulse until creamy and smooth.
Pour the puréed soup back to the pot, then mix in the cream and heat over low heat until heated through.
Pour the soup in a large serving bowl and spread with chopped parsley before serving.
Tip: If you don't have dry red wine, you can use white wine to replace it, such as sherry.

805. Rich Chicken and Small Pasta Broth

Preparation Time: 10 minutes
Cooking Time: 4 hours
Servings: 6

Ingredients:

6 boneless, skinless chicken thighs
4 stalks celery, cut into ½-inch pieces
4 carrots, cut into 1-inch pieces
1 medium yellow onion, halved
2 garlic cloves, minced
2 bay leaves
Sea salt and freshly ground black pepper, to taste
6 cups low-sodium chicken stock
½ cup stelline pasta
¼ cup chopped fresh flat-leaf parsley

Directions:

Combine the chicken thighs, celery, carrots, onion, and garlic in the slow cooker. Spread with bay leaves and

sprinkle with salt and pepper. Toss to mix well.
Pour in the chicken stock. Put the lid on and cook on high for 4 hours or until the internal temperature of chicken reaches at least 165°F (74°C).
In the last 20 minutes of the cooking, remove the chicken from the slow cooker and transfer to a bowl to cool until ready to reserve.
Discard the bay leaves and add the pasta to the slow cooker. Put the lid on and cook for 15 minutes or until al dente.
Meanwhile, slice the chicken, then put the chicken and parsley in the slow cooker and cook for 5 minutes or until well combined.
Pour the soup in a large bowl and serve immediately.
Tip: If you don't have stelline pasta, you can use any other small pastas, such as alphabet pasta.

806. Pumpkin Soup with Crispy Sage Leaves

Preparation Time: 15 minutes
Cooking Time: 10 minutes
Servings: 4

Ingredients:

1 tablespoon olive oil
2 garlic cloves, cut into 1/8-inch-thick slices
1 onion, chopped
2 cups freshly puréed pumpkin
4 cups low-sodium vegetable soup
2 teaspoons chipotle powder
1 teaspoon sea salt
½ teaspoon freshly ground black pepper
½ cup vegetable oil
12 sage leaves, stemmed

Directions:

Heat the olive oil in a stockpot over high heat until shimmering.
Add the garlic and onion, then sauté for 5 minutes or until the onion is translucent.
Pour in the puréed pumpkin and vegetable soup in the pot, then sprinkle with chipotle powder, salt, and ground black pepper. Stir to mix well.
Bring to a boil. Reduce the heat to low and simmer for 5 minutes.
Meanwhile, heat the vegetable oil in a nonstick skillet over high heat.
Add the sage leaf to the skillet and sauté for a minute or until crispy. Transfer the sage on paper towels to soak the excess oil.
Gently pour the soup in three serving bowls, then divide the crispy sage leaves in bowls for garnish. Serve immediately.
Tip: You can make your own chipotle powder by combining freshly ground chipotle chiles with garlic powder and herbs you like.

807. Mushroom and Soba Noodle Soup

Preparation Time: 15 minutes
Cooking Time: 10 minutes
Servings: 4

Ingredients:

2 tablespoons coconut oil
8 ounces (227 g) shiitake mushrooms, stemmed and sliced thin
1 tablespoon minced fresh ginger
4 scallions, sliced thin
1 garlic clove, minced
1 teaspoon sea salt
4 cups low-sodium vegetable broth
3 cups water
4 ounces (113 g) soba noodles
1 bunch spinach, blanched, rinsed and cut into strips
1 tablespoon freshly squeezed lemon juice

Directions:

Heat the coconut oil in a stockpot over medium heat until melted.
Add the mushrooms, ginger, scallions, garlic, and salt. Sauté for 5 minutes or until fragrant and the mushrooms are tender.
Pour in the vegetable broth and water. Bring to a boil, then add the soba noodles and cook for 5 minutes or until al dente.
Turn off the heat and add the spinach and lemon juice. Stir to mix well.
Pour the soup in a large bowl and serve immediately.
Tip: If you can't find the soda noodles, just use common long pastas to replace it.

808. Creamy Corn Soup

Preparation Time: 60 minutes
Cooking Time: 20 minutes
Servings: 4,

Ingredients

4 slices crisp cooked bacon, crumbled
2 tbsp cornstarch
1/4 cup water
2 tsp soy sauce
4 cups chicken broth
1 (14.75 oz) can cream-style corn
2 egg whites
1/4 tsp salt
1 tbsp sherry
1/2 lb. skinless, boneless chicken breast meat, finely chopped

Directions

Combine chicken with the sherry, egg whites, salt in a bowl. Stir in the cream style corn. Mix well.
Boil the soy sauce and chicken broth in a wok. Then stir in the chicken mixture, while continue boiling. Then simmer for about 3 minutes, stir frequently to avoid burning.
Mix corn starch and water until well combined. Mix to the simmering broth, while constantly stirring until it slightly thickens. Cook for about 2 minutes more.
Serve topped with the crumbled bacon.

809. Roasted Mushroom Creamy Soup

Preparation Time: 20 minutes
Cooking Time: 55 minutes
Servings: 8

Ingredients:

3 tablespoons olive oil
4 garlic cloves, chopped
2 shallots, chopped
½ teaspoon chili powder
½ teaspoon cumin powder
1 ½ pounds mushrooms, halved
2 cups vegetable stock
½ cup heavy cream
Salt and pepper to taste

Directions:

Combine the oil, garlic, shallots, chili powder, cumin and mushrooms in a baking tray.
Cook in the preheated oven at 350F for 20 minutes.
Transfer the mushrooms in a soup pot and stir in the stock, as well as salt and pepper.
Cook for 10 more minutes then add the cream and puree the soup with an immersion blender.
Serve the soup warm.

810. White Bean Kale Soup

Preparation Time: 1hour
Cooking Time: 1 Hour
Servings: 8

Ingredients:

2 tablespoons olive oil

1 shallot, chopped
2 garlic cloves, chopped
1 red pepper, chopped
1 celery stalk, diced
2 carrots, diced
1 can white beans, drained
2 tablespoons lemon juice
1 can diced tomatoes
2 cups vegetable stock
6 cups water
Salt and pepper to taste
1 bunch kale, shredded

Directions:

Heat the oil in a soup pot and stir in the shallot, garlic, red pepper, celery and carrots. Cook for 2 minutes until softened.
Add the rest of the ingredients and season with salt and pepper.
Cook on low heat for 30 minutes.
Serve the soup warm or chilled.

811. White Wine Fish Soup

Preparation Time: 30 minutes
Cooking Time: 50 minutes
Servings: 8

Ingredients:

3 tablespoons olive oil
2 shallots, chopped
2 garlic cloves, chopped
1 celery stalk, sliced
2 red bell peppers, cored and sliced
2 carrots, sliced
2 tomatoes, sliced
1 cup diced tomatoes
½ cup tomato juice
2 cups chicken stock
2 cups water
1 cup dry white wine
2 cod fillets, cubed
2 flounder fillets, cubed
1-pound fresh mussels, cleaned and rinsed
1 bay leaf
1 thyme sprig
Salt and pepper to taste

Directions:

Heat the oil in a soup pot and stir in the shallots, garlic, celery, bell peppers and carrots.
Cook for 10 minutes then add the tomatoes and tomato juice, as well as stock, water and wine.
Cook for 15 minutes then add the cod, flounder and fresh mussels, as well as the bay leaf and thyme.
Adjust the taste with salt and pepper and cook for another 5 minutes.
Serve the soup warm and fresh.

812. Smoked Ham Split Pea Soup

Preparation Time: 10 minutes
Cooking Time: 1 Hour
Servings: 8

Ingredients:

2 tablespoons olive oil
4 oz. smoked ham, diced
1 sweet onion, chopped
1 jalapeno pepper, chopped
2 red bell peppers, cored and diced
2 garlic cloves, chopped
2 carrots, diced
1 parsnip, diced
2 tomatoes, peeled and diced
2 cups vegetable stock
6 cups water
½ cup split peas
Salt and pepper to taste
1 lemon, juiced
Crème fraiche for serving

Directions:

Heat the oil in a soup pot and stir in the ham. Cook for 5 minutes then add the rest of the ingredients.
Season with salt and pepper and cook on low heat for 30 minutes.
Serve the soup warm, topped with crème fraiche.

813. Mushroom Spinach Soup

Preparation Time: 25 mins
Cooking Time: 10 minutes
Servings: 4

Ingredients

1 cup spinach, cleaned and chopped
1 cup mushrooms, chopped
1onion
6 garlic cloves
½ teaspoon red chili powder
Salt and black pepper, to taste
3 tablespoons buttermilk
1 teaspoon almond flour
2 cups chicken broth
3 tablespoons butter
¼ cup fresh cream for garnish

Directions

Heat butter in a pan and add onions and garlic.
Sauté for about 3 minutes and add spinach, salt and red chili powder.
Sauté for about 4 minutes and add mushrooms.
Transfer into a blender and blend to make a puree.
Return to the pan and add buttermilk and almond flour for creamy texture.
Mix well and simmer for about 2 minutes.
Garnish with fresh cream and serve hot.

814. Delicata Squash Soup

Preparation Time: 45mins
Cooking Time: 20 minutes
Servings: 5

Ingredients

1½ cups beef bone broth
1small onion, peeled and grated.
½ teaspoon sea salt
¼ teaspoon poultry seasoning
2small Delicata Squash, chopped
2 garlic cloves, minced
2tablespoons olive oil
¼ teaspoon black pepper
1 small lemon, juiced
5 tablespoons sour cream

Directions

Put Delicata Squash and water in a medium pan and bring to a boil.
Reduce the heat and cook for about 20 minutes.
Drain and set aside.
Put olive oil, onions, garlic and poultry seasoning in a small sauce pan.
Cook for about 2 minutes and add broth.
Allow it to simmer for 5 minutes and remove from heat.
Whisk in the lemon juice and transfer the mixture in a blender.
Pulse until smooth and top with sour cream.

815. Cod Potato Soup

Preparation Time: 10 minutes
Cooking Time: 1 Hour
Servings: 8

Ingredients:

2 tablespoons olive oil
2 shallots, chopped
1 celery stalk, sliced
1 carrot, sliced
1 red bell pepper, cored and diced
2 garlic cloves, chopped
1 ½ pounds potatoes, peeled and cubed
1 cup diced tomatoes
1 bay leaf
1 thyme sprig
½ teaspoon dried marjoram
2 cups chicken stock
6 cups water

Salt and pepper to taste
4 cod fillets, cubed
2 tablespoons lemon juice

Directions:

Heat the oil in a soup pot and stir in the shallots, celery, carrot, bell pepper and garlic.
Cook for 5 minutes then stir in the potatoes, tomatoes, bay leaf, thyme, marjoram, stock and water.
Season with salt and pepper and cook on low heat for 20 minutes.
Add the cod fillets and lemon juice and continue cooking for 5 additional minutes.
Serve the soup warm and fresh.

816. Keto French Onion Soup

Preparation Time: 40 mins
Cooking Time: 35 minutes
Servings: 6

Ingredients

5 tablespoons butter
500 g brown onion medium
4 drops liquid stevia
4 tablespoons olive oil
3 cups beef stock

Directions

Put the butter and olive oil in a large pot over medium low heat and add onions and salt.
Cook for about 5 minutes and stir in stevia.
Cook for another 5 minutes and add beef stock.
Reduce the heat to low and simmer for about 25 minutes.
Dish out into soup bowls and serve hot.

817. Minestrone Soup

Preparation Time: 10 minutes
Cooking Time: 1 hour
Servings: 4

Ingredients:

1 small white onion
4 cloves garlic
1/2 cup carrots
1 medium zucchini
1 medium yellow squash
2 tablespoons minced fresh parsley
1/4 cup celery sliced
3 tablespoons olive oil
2 x 15 oz. cans cannellini beans
2 x 15 oz. can red kidney beans
1 x 14.5 oz. can fire-roasted diced tomatoes, drained
4 cups vegetable stock
2 cups of water
1 1/2 teaspoons oregano
1/2 teaspoon basil
1/4 teaspoon thyme
1 teaspoon salt
1/2 teaspoon pepper
3/4 cup small pasta shells
4 cups fresh baby spinach
1/4 cup Parmesan or Romano cheese

Directions:

Grab a stockpot and place over medium heat. Add the oil then the onions, garlic, carrots, zucchini, squash, parsley, and celery. Cook for five minutes until the veggies are getting soft.
Pour in the stock, water, beans, tomatoes, herbs, and salt and pepper. Stir well. Decrease heat, cover, and simmer for 30 minutes.
Add the pasta and spinach, stir well then cover and cook for a further 20 minutes until the pasta is cooked through. Stir through the cheese then serve and enjoy.

818. Chicken Wild Rice Soup

Preparation Time: 10 minutes
Cooking Time: 15 minutes
Servings: 6

Ingredients:

2/3 cup wild rice, uncooked
1 tablespoon onion, chopped finely
1 tablespoon fresh parsley, chopped
1 cup carrots, chopped
8-ounces chicken breast, cooked
2 tablespoon butter
1/4 cup all-purpose white flour
5 cups low-sodium chicken broth
1 tablespoon slivered almonds

Directions:

Start by adding rice and 2 cups broth along with ½ cup water to a cooking pot. Cook the chicken until the rice is al dente and set it aside. Add butter to a saucepan and melt it.
Stir in onion and sauté until soft then add the flour and the remaining broth.
Stir it and then cook for it 1 minute then add the chicken, cooked rice, and carrots. Cook for 5 minutes on simmer. Garnish with almonds. Serve fresh.

819. Classic Chicken Soup

Preparation Time: 10 minutes
Cooking Time: 25 minutes
Servings: 2

Ingredients:

1 1/2 cups low-sodium vegetable broth
1 cup of water
1/4 teaspoon poultry seasoning
1/4 teaspoon black pepper
1 cup chicken strips
1/4 cup carrot
2-ounces egg noodles, uncooked

Directions:

Gather all the ingredients into a slow cooker and toss it Cook soup on high heat for 25 minutes.
Serve warm.

820. Cucumber Soup

Preparation Time: 10 minutes
Cooking Time: 0 minute
Servings: 4

Ingredients:

2 medium cucumbers
1/3 cup sweet white onion
1 green onion
1/4 cup fresh mint
2 tablespoons fresh dill
2 tablespoons lemon juice
2/3 cup water
1/2 cup half and half cream
1/3 cup sour cream
1/2 teaspoon pepper
Fresh dill sprigs for garnish

Directions:

Situate all of the ingredients into a food processor and toss. Puree the mixture and refrigerate for 2 hours. Garnish with dill sprigs. Enjoy fresh.

821. Squash and Turmeric Soup

Preparation Time: 10 minutes
Cooking Time: 30 minutes
Servings: 4

Ingredients:

4 cups low-sodium vegetable broth
2 medium zucchini squash
2 medium yellow crookneck squash
1 small onion
1/2 cup frozen green peas
2 tablespoons olive oil

1/2 cup plain nonfat Greek yogurt
2 teaspoon turmeric

Directions:

Warm the broth in a saucepan on medium heat. Toss in onion, squash, and zucchini. Let it simmer for approximately 25 minutes then add oil and green peas.
Cook for another 5 minutes then allow it to cool. Puree the soup using a handheld blender then add Greek yogurt and turmeric. Refrigerate it overnight and serve fresh.

822. Leek, Potato, and Carrot Soup

Preparation Time: 15 minutes
Cooking Time: 25 minutes
Servings: 4

Ingredients:

1 - leek
¾ - cup diced and boiled potatoes
¾ - cup diced and boiled carrots
1 - garlic clove
1 - tablespoon oil
Crushed pepper to taste
3 - cups low sodium chicken stock
Chopped parsley for garnish
1 - bay leaf
¼ - teaspoon ground cumin

Directions:

Trim off and take away a portion of the coarse inexperienced portions of the leek, at that factor reduce daintily and flush altogether in virus water. Channel properly. Warmth the oil in an extensively based pot. Include the leek and garlic, and sear over low warmth for two-3 minutes, till sensitive.
Include the inventory, inlet leaf, cumin, and pepper. Heat the mixture, mix constantly. Include the bubbled potatoes and carrots and stew for 10-15minutes Modify the flavoring, eliminate the inlet leaf, and serve sprinkled generously with slashed parsley.
To make a pureed soup, manner the soup in a blender or nourishment processor till smooth Come again to the pan. Include ½ field milk. Bring to bubble and stew for 2-3minutes

823. Bell Pepper Soup

Preparation Time: 30 minutes
Cooking Time: 35 minutes
Servings: 4

Ingredients:

4 - cups low-sodium chicken broth
3 - red peppers
2 - medium onions
3 - tablespoon lemon juice
1 - tablespoon finely minced lemon zest
A pinch cayenne peppers
¼ - teaspoon cinnamon
½ - cup finely minced fresh cilantro

Directions:

In a medium stockpot, consolidate each one of the fixings except for the cilantro and warmth to the point of boiling over excessive warm temperature.
Diminish the warmth and stew, ordinarily secured, for around 30 minutes, till thickened. Cool marginally. Utilizing a hand blender or nourishment processor, puree the soup. Include the cilantro and tenderly heat.

824. Yucatan Soup

Preparation Time: 10 minutes
Cooking Time: 20 minutes
Servings: 4

Ingredients:

½ cup onion, chopped
8 cloves garlic, chopped
2 Serrano chili peppers, chopped
1 medium tomato, chopped
1 ½ cups chicken breast, cooked, shredded
2 six-inch corn tortillas, sliced
1 tablespoon olive oil
4 cups chicken broth
1 bay leaf
¼ cup lime juice
¼ cup cilantro, chopped
1 teaspoon black pepper

Directions:

Spread the corn tortillas in a baking sheet and bake them for 3 minutes at 400ºF. Place a suitably-sized saucepan over medium heat and add oil to heat.
Toss in chili peppers, garlic, and onion, then sauté until soft. Stir in broth, tomatoes, bay leaf, and chicken.
Let this chicken soup cook for 10 minutes on a simmer. Stir in cilantro, lime juice, and black pepper. Garnish with baked corn tortillas. Serve.

825. Zesty Taco Soup

Preparation Time: 10 minutes
Cooking Time: 7 hours
Servings: 2

Ingredients:

1 ½ pounds chicken breast
15 ½ ounces canned dark red kidney beans
15 ½ ounces canned white corn
1 cup canned tomatoes
½ cup onion
15 ½ ounces canned yellow hominy
½ cup green bell peppers
1 garlic clove
1 medium jalapeno
1 tablespoon package McCormick
2 cups chicken broth

Directions:

Add drained beans, hominy, corn, onion, garlic, jalapeno pepper, chicken, and green peppers to a Crockpot.
Cover the beans-corn mixture and cook for 1 hour on "high" temperature. Set heat to "low" and continue cooking for 6 hours. Shred the slow-cooked chicken and return to the taco soup. Serve warm.

826. Spring Vegetable Soup

Preparation Time: 10 minutes
Cooking Time: 45 minutes
Servings: 4

Ingredients:

1 cup fresh green beans
¾ cup celery
½ cup onion
½ cup carrots
1/2 cup mushrooms
1/2 cup of frozen corn
1 medium Roma tomato
2 tablespoons olive oil
1/2 cup of frozen corn
4 cups vegetable broth
1 teaspoon dried oregano leaves
1 teaspoon garlic powder

Directions:

Place a suitably-sized cooking pot over medium heat and add olive oil to heat. Toss in onion and celery, then sauté until soft. Stir in the corn and rest of the ingredients and cook the soup to boil.
Now reduce its heat to a simmer and cook for 45 minutes. Serve warm.

827. Beef Sage Soup

Preparation Time: 10 minutes
Cooking Time: 20 minutes
Servings: 4

Ingredients:

½ pound ground beef
½ teaspoon ground sage
½ teaspoon black pepper
½ teaspoon dried basil
½ teaspoon garlic powder
4 slices bread, cubed
2 tablespoons olive oil
1 tablespoon herb seasoning blend
2 garlic cloves, minced
3 cups chicken broth
1 ½ cups water
4 tablespoons fresh parsley
2 tablespoons parmesan cheese

Directions:

Preheat your oven to 375°F. Mix beef with sage, basil, black pepper, and garlic powder in a bowl, then set it aside. Throw in the bread cubes with olive oil in a baking sheet and bake them for 8 minutes.
Meanwhile, sauté the beef mixture in a greased cooking pot until it is browned. Stir in garlic and sauté for 2 minutes, then add parsley, water, and broth. Cover the beef soup and cook for 10 minutes on a simmer. Garnish the soup with parmesan cheese and baked bread. Serve warm.

828. Cabbage Borscht

Preparation Time: 10 minutes
Cooking Time: 90 minutes
Servings: 6

Ingredients:

2 pounds beef steaks
6 cups cold water
2 tablespoons olive oil
½ cup tomato sauce
1 medium cabbage, chopped
1 cup onion, diced
1 cup carrots, diced
1 cup turnips, peeled and diced
1 teaspoon pepper
6 tablespoons lemon juice
4 tablespoons sugar

Directions:

Start by placing steak in a large cooking pot and pour enough water to cover it. Cover the beef pot and cook it on a simmer until it is tender, then shred it using a fork. Add olive oil, onion, tomato sauce, carrots, turnips, and shredded steak to the cooking liquid in the pot.
Stir in black pepper, sugar, and lemon juice to season the soup. Cover the cabbage soup and cook on low heat for 1 ½ hour. Serve warm.

829. Ground Beef Soup

Preparation Time: 10 minutes
Cooking Time: 30 minutes
Servings: 4

Ingredients:

1-pound lean ground beef
½ cup onion, chopped
2 teaspoons lemon-pepper seasoning blend
1 cup beef broth
2 cups of water
1/3 cup white rice, uncooked
3 cups of frozen mixed vegetables
1 tablespoon sour cream

Directions:

Spray a saucepan with cooking oil and place it over medium heat. Toss in onion and ground beef, then sauté until brown. Stir in broth and rest of the ingredients, then boil it.
Reduce heat to a simmer, then cover the soup to cook for 30 minutes. Garnish with sour cream. Enjoy.

830. Mexican Tortilla Soup

Preparation Time: 7 minutes
Cooking Time: 40 minutes
Servings: 4

Ingredients:

1-pound chicken breasts
1 can (15 ounces) whole peeled tomatoes
1 can (10 ounces) red enchilada sauce
1 and 1/2 teaspoons minced garlic
1 yellow onion, diced
1 can (4 ounces) fire-roasted diced green chili
1 can (15 ounces) black beans
1 can (15 ounces) fire-roasted corn
1 container (32 ounces) chicken stock
1 teaspoon ground cumin
2 teaspoons chili powder
3/4 teaspoons paprika
1 bay leaf
1 tablespoon chopped cilantro

Directions:

Set your Instant Pot on Sauté mode.
Toss olive oil, onion and garlic into the insert of the Instant Pot.
Sauté for 4 minutes then add chicken and remaining ingredients.
Mix well gently then seal and lock the lid.
Select Manual mode for 7 minutes at high pressure.
Once done, release the pressure completely then remove the lid.
Adjust seasoning as needed.
Garnish with desired toppings.

831. Chicken Noodle Soup

Preparation Time: 9 minutes
Cooking Time: 35 minutes
Servings: 6

Ingredients:

1 tablespoon olive oil
1 1/2 cups carrots
1 1/2 cup diced celery
1 cup chopped yellow onion
3 tablespoons minced garlic
8 cups low-sodium chicken broth
2 teaspoons minced fresh thyme
2 teaspoons minced fresh rosemary
1 bay leaf
2 1/2 lbs. chicken thighs
3 cups wide egg noodles
1 tablespoon fresh lemon juice
1/4 cup chopped fresh parsley

Directions:

Preheat olive oil in the insert of the Instant Pot on Sauté mode.
Add onion, celery, and carrots and sauté them for minutes.
Stir in garlic and sauté for 1 minute.
Add bay leaf, thyme, broth, rosemary, salt, and pepper.
Seal and secure the Instant Pot lid and select Manual mode for 10 minutes at high pressure.
Once done, release the pressure completely then remove the lid.
Add noodles to the insert and switch the Instant Pot to sauté mode.
Cook the soup for 6 minutes until noodles are all done.
Pullout chicken and shred it using a fork.
Return the chicken to the soup then add lemon juice and parsley.

832. Cheesy Broccoli Soup

Preparation Time: 11 minutes
Cooking Time: 30 minutes
Servings: 4

Ingredients:

½ cup heavy whipping cream
1 cup broccoli
1 cup cheddar cheese
Salt, to taste
1½ cups chicken broth

Directions:

Cook chicken broth in a large pot and add broccoli.
Boil and stir in the rest of the ingredients.
Simmer on low heat for 21 minutes.
Ladle out into a bowl and serve hot.

833. Rich Potato Soup

Preparation Time: 6 minutes
Cooking Time: 30 minutes
Servings: 4

Ingredients:

1 tablespoon butter
1 medium onion, diced
3 cloves garlic, minced
3 cups chicken broth
1 can/box cream of chicken soup
7-8 medium-sized russet potatoes
1 1/2 teaspoons salt
1 cup milk
1 tablespoon flour
2 cups shredded cheddar cheese
Garnish:
5-6 slices bacon, chopped
Sliced green onions
Shredded cheddar cheese

Directions:

Heat butter in the insert of the Instant Pot on sauté mode.
Add onions and sauté for 4 minutes until soft.
Stir in garlic and sauté it for 1 minute.
Add potatoes, cream of chicken, broth, salt, and pepper to the insert.
Mix well then seal and lock the lid.
Cook this mixture for 10 minutes at Manual Mode with high pressure.
Meanwhile, mix flour with milk in a bowl and set it aside.
Once the instant pot beeps, release the pressure completely.
Remove the Instant Pot lid and switch the instant pot to Sauté mode.
Pour in flour slurry and stir cook the mixture for 5 minutes until it thickens.
Add 2 cups of cheddar cheese and let it melt.
Garnish it as desired.

834. Mediterranean Lentil Soup

Preparation Time: 9 minutes
Cooking Time: 20 minutes
Servings: 4

Ingredients:

1 tablespoon olive oil
1/2 cup red lentils
1 medium yellow or red onion
2 garlic cloves
1/2 teaspoon ground cumin
1/2 teaspoon ground coriander
1/2 teaspoon ground sumac
1/2 teaspoon red chili flakes
1/2 teaspoon dried parsley
3/4 teaspoons dried mint flakes
2.5 cups water
juice of 1/2 lime

Directions:

Preheat oil in the insert of your Instant Pot on Sauté mode.
Add onion and sauté until it turns golden brown.
Toss in the garlic, parsley sugar, mint flakes, red chili flakes, sumac, coriander, and cumin.
Stir cook this mixture for 2 minutes.
Add water, lentils, salt, and pepper. Stir gently.
Seal and lock the Instant Pot lid and select Manual mode for 8 minutes at high pressure.
Once done, release the pressure completely then remove the lid.
Stir well then add lime juice.

835. Sausage Kale Soup with Mushrooms

Preparation Time: 8 minutes
Cooking Time: 70 minutes
Servings: 6

Ingredients:

2 cups fresh kale
6.5 ounces mushrooms, sliced
6 cups chicken bone broth
1-pound sausage, cooked and sliced

Directions:

Heat chicken broth with two cans of water in a large pot and bring to a boil.
Stir in the remaining ingredients and allow the soup to simmer on low heat for about 1 hour.
Dish out and serve hot.

836. Turkey Meatball and Ditalini Soup

Preparation Time: 15 minutes
Cooking Time: 40 minutes
Servings: 4

Ingredients:

meatballs:
1 pound 93% lean ground turkey
1/3 cup seasoned breadcrumbs
3 tablespoons grated Pecorino Romano cheese
1 large egg, beaten
1 clove crushed garlic
1 tablespoon fresh minced parsley
1/2 teaspoon kosher salt
Soup:
1 teaspoon olive oil
1/2 cup onion
1/2 cup celery
1/2 cup carrot
3 cloves garlic
1 can San Marzano tomatoes
4 cups reduced sodium chicken broth
4 torn basil leaves
2 bay leaves
1 cup ditalini pasta
1 cup zucchini, diced small
Parmesan rind, optional
Grated parmesan cheese, optional for serving

Directions:

Thoroughly combine turkey with egg, garlic, parsley, salt, pecorino and breadcrumbs in a bowl.
Make 30 equal sized meatballs out of this mixture.
Preheat olive oil in the insert of the Instant Pot on Sauté mode.
Sear the meatballs in the heated oil in batches, until brown.
Set the meatballs aside in a plate.
Add more oil to the insert of the Instant Pot.
Stir in carrots, garlic, celery, and onion. Sauté for 4 minutes.
Add basil, bay leaves, tomatoes, and Parmesan rind.
Return the seared meatballs to the pot along with the broth.
Secure and sear the Instant Pot lid and select Manual mode for 15 minutes at high pressure.
Once done, release the pressure completely then remove the lid.
Add zucchini and pasta, cook it for 4 minutes on Sauté mode.
Garnish with cheese and basil.

837. Lentil and Spinach Soup

Preparation Time: 35 minutes
Cooking Time: 12 minutes
Servings: 4

Ingredients

6 cups baby spinach
1 cup onion, diced
4 teaspoons spice mixture
1 cup brown lentils
4 cups vegetable broth

Directions:

Press Sauté mode on your instant pot
Add 1 tablespoon olive oil
Cook onions for 2 minutes
Add the spice mixture and season with salt and pepper
Add lentils and broth
Close the lid
Select Manual mode
Cook for 12 minutes on High pressure
Release the pressure quickly
Serve and enjoy!

838. Carrot Soup

Preparation Time: 30 minutes
Cooking Time: 10 minutes
Servings: 3

Ingredients

1 onion, chopped
1-pound carrots, cubed
¼ teaspoon cumin powder
¼ teaspoon paprika, smoked
3 cups vegetable broth

Directions:

Press Sauté mode on your instant pot
Add 2 tablespoons olive oil
Cook onions for 2 minutes
Add remaining ingredients
Close the lid
Select Manual mode
Cook for 5 minutes on High pressure
Release the pressure quickly
Transfer into your blender and blend until smooth
Season with salt and pepper
Serve and enjoy!

839. Chickpea Soup

Preparation Time: 35 minutes
Cooking Time: 20 minutes
Servings: 6

Ingredients

2 cups chickpeas, dried, soak in water overnight
2 carrots
1 onion chopped
4 teaspoon herb mixture, dried
6 cups vegetable broth

Directions:

Drain your chickpeas and set them aside
Press Sauté mode on your instant pot
Add 2 tablespoons olive oil
Add carrots and onion
Cook for 5 minutes
Stir frequently
Add broth and chickpeas and close the lid
Cook for 15 minutes on High pressure
Release the pressure quickly
Serve and enjoy!

840. Chicken and Tomato Soup

Preparation Time: 30 minutes
Cooking Time: 15 minutes
Servings: 6

Ingredients

1-pound chicken breast, cubed
28 ounces crushed tomatoes, canned
3 cloves garlic, minced
6 cups chicken broth
1 teaspoon mixed onion and garlic powder

Directions:

Press Sauté mode on your instant pot
Add 1 tablespoon olive oil
Cook garlic for few minutes, then add chicken breast
Cook until it turns brown on each side
Pour in the remaining ingredients
Seal the pot
Press Manual
Cook for 10 minutes on High pressure
Release the pressure quickly
Serve and enjoy!

841. Chicken and Quinoa Stew

Preparation Time: 30 minutes
Cooking Time: 25 minutes
Servings: 6

Ingredients

1¼ pounds chicken thigh fillet, sliced into strips
4 cups coconut oil
Butternut squash, chopped
4 cups chicken stock
½ cup quinoa
1 cup onion, chopped

Directions:

Add chicken into your Instant pot
Add remaining ingredients except for the quinoa
Cover the pot
Press Manual
Cook for 8 minutes on High pressure
Release the pressure naturally
Stir the quinoa into the stew
Press Sauté mode on your instant pot
Cook for 15 minutes
Serve and enjoy!

842. Vegetable and Lentil Soup

Preparation Time: 30 minutes
Cooking Time: 20 minutes
Servings: 5

Ingredients

6 cups chicken stock
1¼ cup green lentils
6 cloves garlic, minced
4 cups mixed vegetables, chopped
5 tablespoons mixed spices

Directions:

Pour 2 tablespoons olive oil into the Instant pot
Cook the garlic for 2 minutes
Add the vegetables and spices
Season with salt
Cook for 5 minutes
Pour in the stock and add lentils
Seal the pot
Press Manual mode
Cook for 12 minutes on High pressure
Release the pressure naturally
Serve and enjoy!

843. Stewed Kidney Bean

Preparation Time: 10 minutes
Cooking Time: 13 minutes
Servings: 4

Ingredients:

6 ounces red beans, cooked
2 cups vegetable broth
1 onion, peeled and chopped
2 tablespoons tomato paste
1 bay leaf
3 tablespoons olive oil
2 carrots, chopped
2 celery stalks
1 teaspoon salt
Parsley, a handful

Directions:

Warm oil on Sauté mode

Stir-fry onions for 3 minutes
Add celery and carrots
Cook for 5 minutes more
Add 1 tablespoon broth, beans, bay leaf, tomato paste, parsley, salt
Stir in 1 tablespoon flour and add remaining broth
Close the lid
Cook on High pressure for 5 minutes
Quick-release the pressure over 10 minutes
Add fresh parsley on top
Serve and enjoy!

844. Lentil Soup

Preparation Time: 20 minutes
Cooking Time: 10 minutes
Servings: 2

Ingredients:

½ cup red lentil
3 cups vegetable broth
1 onion, chopped
2 cloves garlic, chopped
Dried herb mixture, ½ teaspoon of each (mint, parsley, sumac, cumin, coriander)

Directions:

Select the Sauté setting in the instant pot
Add 2 tablespoons olive oil
Add the onion and cook for 3 minutes
Then add garlic and herb mixture
Cook for 2 minutes
Stir frequently
Add lentils and broth
Season with salt and pepper
Close the lid
Press Manual mode
Cook for 8 minutes on High pressure
Release the pressure naturally
Serve and enjoy!

845. Simple Veggie Stew

Preparation Time: 40 minutes
Cooking Time: 16 minutes
Servings: 4

Ingredients:

1 package mixed vegetables, frozen
4 cups vegetable broth
1 onion, minced
20 ounces tomato sauce
2 teaspoons Italian seasoning

Directions:

Set the Instant pot to Sauté mode
Add 1 tablespoon olive oil
Cook onion for 1 minute
Add frozen vegetables and cook for 3 to 5 minutes
Then add remaining ingredients
Cover the pot and press Manual
Cook for 15 minutes on High pressure
Release the pressure naturally
Season with salt and pepper
Serve and enjoy!

846. Pumpkin Soup

Preparation Time: 30 minutes
Cooking Time: 8 minutes
Servings: 4

Ingredients

30 ounces pumpkin puree
1-quart chicken stock
1 onion, chopped
2 cups sweet potato, chopped
1 teaspoon garlic powder

Directions:

Add all ingredients into your instant pot
Close the pot and press Manual
Cook for 8 minutes on High pressure
Release the pressure naturally
Then transfer it to your blender and blend until smooth
Season with salt and pepper
Serve and enjoy!

847. White Bean and Kale Soup

Preparation Time: 30 minutes
Cooking Time: 15 minutes
Servings: 10

Ingredients:

4 cups kale
30 ounces white cannellini beans
1 white onion, chopped
4 cups vegetable stock
28 ounces tomatoes, canned and diced

Directions:

Pour 3 tablespoons olive oil into your instant pot
Sauté white onion for 3 minutes
Then add rest of the ingredients
Press the Manual setting and cover the pot
Cook for 10 minutes on High pressure
Release the pressure naturally
Stir in the kale, then cover to make kale wilt
Serve and enjoy!

848. Chickpea Instant Pot Soup

Preparation Time: 5 minutes
Cooking Time: 30 minutes
Servings: 6

Ingredients:

2 cups of dry chickpeas
2 tablespoons extra virgin olive oil
1 yellow onion, chopped
3 garlic cloves, minced
salt to taste
2 carrots, chopped
1 green bell pepper, cored and chopped
3-4 red chili peppers
1 teaspoon ground coriander
1 teaspoon ground cumin
a teaspoon of Aleppo pepper (A Middle Eastern spice)
½ teaspoon of ground turmeric
½ teaspoon of ground allspice
15 ounces of chopped tomatoes with the juice
6 cups of low-sodium vegetable broth
juice from 1 lemon
1-ounce fresh cilantro, chopped

Directions:

Place the dry chickpeas in a bowl and submerge them in water. Let them soak overnight and then drain well.
Preheat your instant pot using the sauté setting and adjust the heat to high. Add extra virgin olive oil and heat until simmering. Add the onions, garlic, and a pinch of salt. Cook for 3 minutes, while stirring regularly.
Add the carrots, bell peppers, and spices. Cook for another 4 minutes, while stirring until the vegetables have softened a bit.
Add the chickpeas, tomatoes, and the broth. Make sure to add the juice from the tomatoes too. Lock the instant pot lid, and put the pressure-cooking setting on high. Set a timer for 15 minutes.
After cooking, allow natural release of pressure. After 10 minutes, you can press the quick release to remove any extra pressure.
Carefully unlock and remove the lid. Stir in the lemon juice and fresh cilantro. Transfer the contents to serving bowls and drizzle a little extra olive oil.

849. Instant Pot Mediterranean Chicken And Quinoa Stew

Preparation Time: 22 minutes
Cooking Time: 8 minutes
Servings: 6

Ingredients:

1-¼ pounds of chicken thighs, boneless and skinless
4 cups of butternut squash, peeled and chopped
4 cups unsalted chicken stock
1 cup yellow onion, chopped
2 garlic cloves, chopped
1 bay leaf
1-¼ teaspoons of kosher salt
1 teaspoon of dried oregano
1 teaspoon of ground fennel seeds
½ cup of uncooked quinoa
1-ounce of olives, sliced and pitted

Directions:

Combine the chicken, squash, stock, onion, garlic, bay leaf, salt, ground fennel seeds, oregano, and pepper in your instant pot. Cover the lid, turn the valve to seal and cook on high pressure for 8 minutes.
Release the valve carefully, using mitts or tongs. Quick-release until the steam and pressure go down. Remove chicken, then add quinoa to the instant pot, turn to sauté and cook while occasionally stirring until the quinoa is tender.
Shred the chicken and stir into stew. Discard bay leaf.
Serve the soup up into separate bowls, and sprinkle sliced olives.

850. Greek Vegetable Soup

Total Time: 55 minutes
Servings: 4

Ingredients:

3 tablespoons of olive oil
1 onion, chopped
1 clove garlic, minced
3 cups of cabbage, shredded
2 medium carrots, chopped
2 celery stocks, chopped
2 cups of cooked chickpeas
4 cups of vegetable broth
15-ounce fire-roasted tomatoes, diced
salt and pepper to taste

Directions:

Add olive oil to the instant pot and set to medium heat sauté.
Add the onions and cook until soft. Add garlic and cabbage and cook for another 5 minutes. When the cabbage softens, add the carrots, celery, and chickpeas. Stir everything to combine and cook for 5 minutes longer
Add the broth and canned tomatoes, then season with salt and pepper.
Press cancel to end sauté mode and cover the pot with the lid set to sealing mode.
Set to soup mode and adjust the time to 10 minutes.
After completion, release the pressure manually and serve immediately.
You may garnish the soup with parsley, feta, or anything you like on soup.

851. Instant Pot Mediterranean Lentil And Collard Soup

Preparation Time: 20 minutes
Cooking Time: 20 minutes
Servings: 6

Ingredients:

2 tablespoons of extra virgin olive oil
1 medium yellow onion, chopped
2 medium celery stocks, diced
3 garlic cloves, minced
2 teaspoons of ground cumin
1 teaspoon of ground turmeric
4 cups of low-sodium vegetable broth
1 ¼ cup of water
1 1/2 cups dry brown lentils, rinsed in water
2 carrots, peeled and diced
1 bay leaf
1 teaspoon himalayan salt
½ teaspoon of ground black pepper
3 collard leaves, cut into strips
1 teaspoon of lemon juice

Directions:

Set instant pot to sauté, then add the olive oil, heat, and add onions and celery. Stir often for 5 minutes. Turn the instant pot off.
Stir in the garlic, cumin, and turmeric until combined.
Add broth, water, lentils, carrots, bay leaf, salt, and pepper. Lock the lid and close the valve. Set to manual and cook on high pressure for 13 minutes.
After completion, quick release the pressure, carefully remove the lid and stir in collards and lemon juice.
Close the lid and set to manual and cook for 2 more minutes on high. Quick-release the pressure, open the lid, and it's ready to serve.

852. Melon Gazpacho

Preparation Time: 10 minutes
Cooking Time: 0 minute
Servings: 5

Ingredients:

1-pound cantaloupe, peeled, chopped
1 tablespoon avocado oil
1 red onion, diced
¼ cup of water
1 teaspoon dried basil

Direction

Incorporate all ingredients in the blender until smooth.
Pour the cooked gazpacho in the serving bowls.

853. Chicken Soup

Preparation Time: 10 minutes
Cooking Time: 30 minutes
Servings: 6

Ingredients:

1-pound chicken breast, skinless, boneless, chopped
½ cup fresh parsley, chopped
½ teaspoon ground black pepper
1 onion, diced
6 cups of water

Direction

Melt the 1 tsp. olive oil in the pan and add the onion.
Cook it until light brown.
Add chicken breast, parsley, and ground black pepper.
Add water and simmer the soup for 25 minutes.

854. Spicy Tomato Soup

Preparation Time: 10 minutes
Cooking Time: 15 minutes
Servings: 4

Ingredients:

2 cups tomatoes, chopped
1 cup beef broth
1 teaspoon cayenne pepper, basil
1 teaspoon ground paprika
1 oz Parmesan, grated

Direction

Blend the tomatoes and pour the mixture in the saucepan.
Add all remaining ingredients except Parmesan and bring the soup to boil.

Then ladle the cooked soup in the bowls and top with Parmesan.

855. Chicken Strips Soup

Preparation Time: 5
Cooking Time: 30 minutes
Servings: 4

Ingredients:

8 oz. chicken fillet, cut into strips
2 tablespoons fresh cilantro, chopped
1 cup plain yogurt
2 cups of water
1 teaspoon chili flakes

Direction

Put all ingredients in the pan and simmer for 30 minutes on the low heat.

856. Tomato Bean Soup

Preparation Time: 10 minutes
Cooking Time: 40 minutes
Servings: 4

Ingredients:

5 oz. beef tenderloin, sliced
½ cup white beans, soaked
5 cups of water
½ teaspoon chili flakes
tablespoons tomato paste

Directions:

Put all ingredients in the saucepan and stir until tomato paste is dissolved
Close the lid and cook the soup for 40 minutes over the medium-low heat.

CHAPTER 13: SALADS

857. Olives and Lentils Salad

Preparation Time: 10 minutes
Cooking Time: 0 minutes
Servings: 2

Ingredients:

1/3 cup canned green lentils
1 tablespoon olive oil
2 cups baby spinach
1 cup black olives
2 tablespoons sunflower seeds
1 tablespoon Dijon mustard
2 tablespoons balsamic vinegar
2 tablespoons olive oil

Directions:

Mix the lentils with the spinach, olives, and the rest of the ingredients in a salad bowl, toss and serve cold.

858. Lime Spinach and Chickpeas Salad

Preparation Time: 10 minutes
Cooking Time: 0 minutes
Servings: 4

Ingredients:

16 ounces canned chickpeas
2 cups baby spinach leaves
½ tablespoon lime juice
2 tablespoons olive oil
1 teaspoon cumin, ground
½ teaspoon chili flakes

Directions:

Mix the chickpeas with the spinach and the rest of the ingredients in a large bowl, toss and serve cold.

859. Minty Olives and Tomatoes Salad

Preparation Time: 10 minutes
Cooking Time: 0 minutes
Servings: 4

Ingredients:

1 cup kalamata olives
1 cup black olives
1 cup cherry tomatoes
4 tomatoes
1 red onion, chopped
2 tablespoons oregano, chopped
1 tablespoon mint, chopped
2 tablespoons balsamic vinegar
¼ cup olive oil
2 teaspoons Italian herbs, dried

Directions:

In a salad bowl, mix the olives with the tomatoes and the rest of the ingredients, toss, and serve cold.

860. Beans and Cucumber Salad

Preparation Time: 10 minutes
Cooking Time: 0 minutes
Servings: 4

Ingredients:

15 oz canned great northern beans
2 tablespoons olive oil
½ cup baby arugula
1 cup cucumber
1 tablespoon parsley
2 tomatoes, cubed
2 tablespoon balsamic vinegar

Directions:

Mix the beans with the cucumber and the rest of the ingredients in a large bowl, toss and serve cold.

861. Tomato and Avocado Salad

Preparation Time: 10 minutes
Cooking Time: 0 minutes
Servings: 4

Ingredients:

1-pound cherry tomatoes
2 avocados
1 sweet onion, chopped
2 tablespoons lemon juice
1 and ½ tablespoons olive oil
Handful basil, chopped

Directions:

Mix the tomatoes with the avocados and the rest of the ingredients in a serving bowl, toss and serve right away.

862. Arugula Salad

Preparation Time: 5 minutes
Cooking Time: 0 minutes
Servings: 4

Ingredients:

Arugula leaves (4 cups)
Cherry tomatoes (1 cup)
Pine nuts (.25 cup)
Rice vinegar (1 tbsp.)
Olive/grapeseed oil (2 tbsp.)
Grated parmesan cheese (.25 cup)
Black pepper & salt (as desired)
Large sliced avocado (1)

Directions:

Peel and slice the avocado. Rinse and dry the arugula leaves, grate the cheese, and slice the cherry tomatoes into halves. Combine the arugula, pine nuts, tomatoes, oil, vinegar, salt, pepper, and cheese.
Toss the salad to mix and portion it onto plates with the avocado slices to serve.

863. Chickpea Salad

Preparation Time: 15 minutes
Cooking Time: 0 minutes
Servings: 4

Ingredients:

Cooked chickpeas (15 oz.)
Diced Roma tomato (1)
Diced green medium bell pepper (half of 1)
Fresh parsley (1 tbsp.)
Small white onion (1)
Minced garlic (.5 tsp.)
Lemon (1 juiced)

Directions:

Chop the tomato, green pepper, and onion. Mince the garlic. Combine each of the fixings into a salad bowl and toss well.
Cover the salad to chill for at least 15 minutes in the fridge. Serve when ready.

864. Chopped Israeli Mediterranean Pasta Salad

Preparation Time: 15 minutes
Cooking Time: 2 minutes
Servings: 8

Ingredients:

Small bow tie or other small pasta (.5 lb.)
1/3 cup Cucumber
1/3 cup Radish
1/3 cup Tomato
1/3 cup Yellow bell pepper
1/3 cup Orange bell pepper
1/3 cup Black olives
1/3 cup Green olives
1/3 cup Red onions
1/3 cup Pepperoncini
1/3 cup Feta cheese
1/3 cup Fresh thyme leaves
Dried oregano (1 tsp.)
Dressing:
0.25 cup + more, olive oil
juice of 1 lemon

Directions:

Slice the green olives into halves. Dice the feta and pepperoncini. Finely dice the remainder of the veggies.
Prepare a pot of water with the salt, and simmer the pasta until it's al dente (checking at two minutes under the listed time). Rinse and drain in cold water.
Combine a small amount of oil with the pasta. Add the salt, pepper, oregano, thyme, and veggies. Pour in the rest of the oil, lemon juice, mix and fold in the grated feta.
Pop it into the fridge within two hours, best if overnight. Taste test and adjust the seasonings to your liking; add fresh thyme.

865. Feta Tomato Salad

Preparation Time: 5 minutes
Cooking Time: 0 minutes
Servings: 4

Ingredients:

Balsamic vinegar (2 tbsp.)
Freshly minced basil (1.5 tsp.) or Dried (.5 tsp.)
Salt (.5 tsp.)
Coarsely chopped sweet onion (.5 cup)
Olive oil (2 tbsp.)
Cherry or grape tomatoes (1 lb.)
Crumbled feta cheese (.25 cup.)

Directions:

Whisk the salt, basil, and vinegar. Toss the onion into the vinegar mixture for 5 minutes
Slice the tomatoes into halves and stir in the tomatoes, feta cheese, and oil to serve.

866. Greek Pasta Salad

Preparation Time: 5 minutes
Cooking Time: 11 minutes
Servings: 4

Ingredients:

Penne pasta (1 cup)
Lemon juice (1.5 tsp.)
Red wine vinegar (2 tbsp.)
Garlic (1 clove)
Dried oregano (1 tsp.)
Black pepper and sea salt (as desired)
Olive oil (.33 cup)
Halved cherry tomatoes (5)
Red onion (half of 1 small)
Green & red bell pepper (half of 1 - each)
Cucumber (¼ of 1)
Black olives (.25 cup)
Crumbled feta cheese (.25 cup)

Directions:

Slice the cucumber and olives. Chop/dice the onion, peppers, and garlic. Slice the tomatoes into halves.
Arrange a large pot with water and salt using the high-temperature setting. Once it's boiling, add the pasta and cook for 11 minutes. Rinse it using cold water and drain in a colander.
Whisk the oil, juice, salt, pepper, vinegar, oregano, and garlic. Combine the cucumber, cheese, olives, peppers, pasta, onions, and tomatoes in a large salad dish.
Add the vinaigrette over the pasta and toss. Chill in the fridge (covered) for about three hours and serve as desired.

867. Pork and Greens Salad

Preparation Time: 10 minutes
Cooking Time: 15 minutes
Servings: 4

Ingredients:

1-pound pork chops
8 ounces white mushrooms, sliced
½ cup Italian dressing
6 cups mixed salad greens
6 ounces jarred artichoke hearts, drained
Salt and black pepper to the taste
½ cup basil, chopped
1 tablespoon olive oil

Directions:

Heat a pan with the oil over medium-high heat, add the pork, and brown for 5 minutes.
Add the mushrooms, stir, and sauté for 5 minutes more.
Add the dressing, artichokes, salad greens, salt, pepper, and basil, cook for 4-5 minutes, divide everything into bowls and serve.

868. Mediterranean Duck Breast Salad

Preparation Time: 10 minutes
Cooking Time: 20 minutes
Servings: 4

Ingredients:

3 tablespoons white wine vinegar
2 tablespoons sugar
2 oranges, peeled and cut into segments
1 teaspoon orange zest, grated
1 tablespoon lemon juice
1 teaspoon lemon zest, grated
3 tablespoons shallot, minced
2 duck breasts
1 head of frisée, torn
2 small lettuce heads
2 tablespoons chives

Directions:

Heat a small saucepan over medium-high heat, add vinegar and sugar, stir and boil for 5 minutes and take off the heat.
Add orange zest, lemon zest, and lemon juice, stir, and leave aside for a few minutes. Add shallot, salt, and pepper to taste and the oil, whisk well and leave aside for now.
Pat dry the duck pieces, score the skin, trim, and season with salt and pepper. Heat a pan over medium-high heat for 1 minute, arrange duck breast pieces skin side down, brown for 8 minutes, reduce heat to medium and cook for 4 more minutes.
Flip pieces, cook for 3 minutes, transfer to a cutting board, and cover them with foil. Put frisée and lettuce in a bowl, stir and divide between plates.
Slice duck, arrange on top, add orange segments, sprinkle chives, and drizzle the vinaigrette.

869. Creamy Chicken Salad

Preparation Time: 10 minutes
Cooking Time: 0 minute
Servings: 6

Ingredients:

20 ounces chicken meat
½ cup pecans, chopped
1 cup green grapes
½ cup celery, chopped
2 ounces canned mandarin oranges, drained
For the creamy cucumber salad dressing:
1 cup Greek yogurt cucumber, chopped garlic clove
1 teaspoon lemon juice

Directions:

In a bowl, mix cucumber with salt, pepper to taste, lemon juice, garlic, and yogurt, and stir very well.
In a salad bowl, mix chicken meat with grapes, pecans, oranges, and celery.
Add cucumber salad dressing, toss to coat, and keep in the fridge until you serve it.

870. Chicken and Cabbage Salad

Preparation Time: 10 minutes
Cooking Time: 6 minutes
Servings: 4

Ingredients:

3 medium chicken breasts
4 ounces green cabbage
5 tablespoon extra-virgin olive oil
Salt and black pepper to taste
2 tablespoons sherry vinegar tablespoon chives
¼ cup feta cheese, crumbled
¼ cup barbeque sauce
Bacon slices, cooked and crumbled

Directions:

In a bowl, mix 4 tablespoon oil with vinegar, salt and pepper to taste and stir well.
Add the shredded cabbage, toss to coat, and leave aside for now.
Season chicken with salt and pepper, heat a pan with remaining oil over medium-high heat, add chicken, cook for 6 minutes, take off heat, transfer to a bowl and mix well with barbeque sauce.
Arrange salad on serving plates, add chicken strips, sprinkle cheese, chives, and crumbled bacon, and serve right away.

871. Roasted Broccoli Salad

Preparation Time: 9 minutes
Cooking Time: 17 minutes
Servings: 4

Ingredients:

1 lb. broccoli
3 tablespoons olive oil, divided
1-pint cherry tomatoes
1 ½ teaspoons honey
3 cups cubed bread, whole grain
1 tablespoon balsamic vinegar
½ teaspoon black pepper
¼ teaspoon sea salt, fine
grated parmesan for serving

Directions:

Set the oven to 450, and then place a rimmed baking sheet.
Drizzle your broccoli with a tablespoon of oil, and toss to coat.
Take out from the oven, and spoon the broccoli. Leave oil at the bottom of the bowl and add in your tomatoes, toss to coat, then mix tomatoes with a tablespoon of honey. place on the same baking sheet.
Roast for fifteen minutes, and stir halfway through your cooking time.
Add in your bread, and then roast for three more minutes.
Whisk two tablespoons of oil, vinegar, and remaining honey. Season. Pour this over your broccoli mix to serve.

872. Tomato Salad

Preparation Time: 22 minutes
Cooking Time: 0 minute
Servings: 4

Ingredients:

1 cucumber, sliced
¼ cup sun-dried tomatoes, chopped
1 lb. tomatoes, cubed
½ cup black olives
1 red onion, sliced
1 tablespoon balsamic vinegar
¼ cup parsley, fresh & chopped
2 tablespoons olive oil

Directions:

Get out a bowl and combine all your vegetables. To make your dressing mix all your seasoning, olive oil, and vinegar. Toss with your salad and serve fresh.

873. Feta Beet Salad

Preparation Time: 16 minutes
Cooking Time: 0 minute
Servings: 4

Ingredients:

6 Red Beets, Cooked & Peeled
3 Ounces Feta Cheese, Cubed
2 Tablespoons Olive Oil
2 Tablespoons Balsamic Vinegar

Directions:

Combine everything, and then serve.

874. Chicken and Quinoa Salad

Preparation Time: 10 minutes
Cooking Time: 20 minutes
Servings: 2

Ingredients:

2 tablespoons olive oil
2 ounces quinoa
2 ounces cherry tomatoes, cut in quarters
3 ounces sweet corn
Lime juice from 1 lime
Lime zest from 1 lime, grated
2 spring onions, chopped
Small red chili pepper, chopped
Avocado
2 ounces chicken meat

Directions:

Fill water in a pan, bring to a boil over medium-high heat, add quinoa, stir, and cook for 12 minutes.
Meanwhile, put corn in a pan, heat over medium-high heat, cook for 5 minutes, and leave aside for now.
Drain quinoa, transfer to a bowl, add tomatoes, corn, coriander, onions, chili, lime zest, olive oil, and salt and black pepper to taste and toss.
In another bowl, mix avocado with lime juice and stir well.
Add this to quinoa salad, and chicken, toss to coat, and serve.

875. Melon Salad

Preparation Time: 20 minutes
Cooking Time: 0 minutes
Servings: 6

Ingredients:

¼ teaspoon sea salt
¼ teaspoon black pepper

1 tablespoon balsamic vinegar
1 cantaloupe
12 watermelons
2 cups mozzarella balls, fresh
1/3 cup basil, fresh & torn
2 tablespoons olive oil

Directions:

Spoon out balls of cantaloupe, then situate them in a colander over the bowl.
Using a melon baller to cut the watermelon as well
Drain fruits for ten minutes, then chill the juice.
Wipe the bowl dry, and then place your fruit in it.
Mix in basil, oil, vinegar, mozzarella, and tomatoes before seasoning.
Gently mix and serve.

876. Bean and Toasted Pita Salad

Preparation Time: 15 minutes
Cooking Time: 10 minutes
Servings: 4

Ingredients:

3 tbsp chopped fresh mint
3 tbsp chopped fresh parsley
1 cup crumbled feta cheese
1 cup sliced romaine lettuce
½ cucumber, peeled and sliced
1 cup diced plum tomatoes
2 cups cooked pinto beans, well-drained and slightly warmed
Pepper to taste
3 tbsp extra virgin olive oil
2 tbsp ground toasted cumin seeds
2 tbsp fresh lemon juice
1/8 tsp salt
2 cloves garlic, peeled
2 6-inch whole-wheat pita bread, cut or torn into bite-sized pieces

Directions:

In a large baking sheet, spread torn pita bread and bake in a preheated 400oF oven for 6 minutes.
With the back of a knife, mash garlic and salt until paste-like. Add into a medium bowl.
Whisk in ground cumin and lemon juice.
In a steady and slow stream, pour oil as you whisk continuously. Season with pepper.
In a large salad bowl, mix cucumber, tomatoes, and beans. Pour in dressing, toss to coat well.
Add mint, parsley, feta, lettuce, and toasted pita, toss to mix once again, and serve.

877. Salad With Pine Nuts And Mozzarella

Preparation Time: 20 minutes
Cooking Time: 0 minutes
Servings: 2

Ingredients:

300g mini mozzarella
100g cocktail tomatoes
40g pine nuts
80g rocket
150g mixed salad
2 teaspoons of olive oil
2 teaspoons of red wine vinegar
2 teaspoons of balsamic vinegar
4 tbsp olive oil
1 teaspoon mustard
1 tbsp yogurt
salt and pepper

Directions:

Drain the mozzarella. Thoroughly clean and spin lettuce and rocket. Quarter the cherry tomatoes and put everything in a salad bowl.
For the dressing: Mix the red wine vinegar, balsamic vinegar, olive oil, mustard and yogurt together. Season with salt and pepper and mix everything with the salad.
Then add the pine nuts. Finished! Serve and enjoy.

878. Mediterranean Salad With Feta

Preparation Time: 15 minutes
Cooking Time: 0 minutes
Servings: 2

Ingredients:

200g feta cheese
200g cocktail tomatoes
50g almond slivers
100g mixed salad
2 tbsp red wine vinegar
1 tbsp raspberry vinegar
1 tbsp green pesto
3 tbsp olive oil
1 teaspoon mustard
salt and pepper

Directions:

Drain and dice the feta. Clean the lettuce and spin dry. Quarter the cherry tomatoes and place everything in a salad bowl.
Mix red wine vinegar, raspberry vinegar, olive oil, mustard and pesto. Season with salt and pepper and pour over the salad.
Finally add the almond slivers. Finished! Serve and enjoy.

879. Tomato And Cucumber Salad With Feta

Preparation Time: 10 minutes
Cooking Time: 0 minutes
Servings: 4

Ingredients:

2 tomatoes
½ cucumber
½ bunch of spring onions
200g feta
6 tbsp olive oil
3 tbsp balsamic vinegar
salt and pepper

Directions:

Thoroughly clean the tomatoes and cucumber. Eight tomatoes. Cut the cucumber into thin slices. Cut the spring onion into thin rings. Chop the herbs. Dice the feta.
Put all ingredients in a salad bowl. Add oil and balsamic vinegar, season with salt and pepper and mix well. Done! Serve and enjoy.

880. Mediterranean Salad With Peppers And Tomatoes

Preparation Time: 35 minutes
Cooking Time: 30 minutes
Servings: 2

Ingredients:

1 eggplant
1 zucchini
1 bell pepper
4 tomatoes
1 onion
4 sprigs of rosemary
6 sprigs of thyme
4 stalks of sage
3 tbsp olive oil
3 tbsp balsamic vinegar
salt and pepper

Directions:

Quarter tomatoes. Cut the remaining vegetables into bite-sized pieces, halve the onion and chop it into small pieces. Line a baking sheet with parchment

paper, place the vegetables on top, drizzle with olive oil and mix well.
Season with salt and pepper. Scatter the herbs over the vegetables. Put the vegetables in the oven and bake at 200 degrees for about 30 minutes.
Remove and transfer to a large bowl and mix with olive oil with balsamic vinegar. Season with salt and pepper.
Let it draw covered. When the salad is still lukewarm, add the tomato quarters and mix well.
Serve the salad lukewarm.

881. Mediterranean Potato Salad With Beans

Preparation Time: 180 minutes
Cooking Time: 15 minutes
Servings: 4

Ingredients:

500g potatoes
300g green beans
1 tbsp rosemary
8 sun-dried tomatoes
40g bacon
3 tbsp red wine vinegar
200g olives
1 egg yolk
salt and pepper

Directions:

Wash green beans, break into short pieces and boil in salted water for about 10 minutes, then drain in a colander. Collect some boiled bean water.
Drain the tomatoes and cut into small pieces. Collect some tomato oil. Chop the rosemary and cut the bacon into thin strips. Fry bacon with chopped rosemary in olive oil and tomato oil in a pan. Pour in the vinegar and the bean water and add the tomato pieces. Heat the potatoes and beans, let them steep and wait until they have cooled down. Then pour off using a sieve and collect the vinaigrette. Mix the potato salad with the olives.
Whisk the vinaigrette with egg yolk and then heat gently, stirring constantly, until the sauce thickens. Season with salt and pepper and pour over the salad. Let it steep for an hour. Finished! Serve and enjoy.

882. Orzo Olive Salad

Preparation Time: 180 minutes
Cooking Time: 10 minutes
Servings: 4

Ingredients:

250g orzo
100g cocktail tomatoes
100g olives
onion
½ bunch of parsley
250g feta cheese
For the dressing
1 lemon, squeezed
salt and pepper
30ml olive oil
2 cloves of garlic

Directions:

Cook the pasta for about 10 minutes according to the instructions on the packet. Wash and halve cocktail tomatoes, core the olives, peel and chop the onion, crumble the feta.
For the dressing: lemon juice, olive oil, garlic, salt and pepper mixed together.
Mix the Orzo together with the dressing and finally add the remaining ingredients. Finished. Serve and enjoy.

883. Mediterranean Tortellini Salad

Preparation Time: 30 minutes
Cooking Time: 12 minutes
Servings: 6

Ingredients:

500g tortellini
300g dried tomatoes
2 onions
3 tbsp olive oil
3 tbsp white wine vinegar
1 teaspoon thyme
salt and pepper
200g rocket

Directions:

Cook the tortellini, drain and set aside.
Chop the onions and sauté them in olive oil with the thyme. Add the chopped sun-dried tomatoes and fry for about 2 minutes. Then add the tortellini and remove the pan from the heat.
Season to taste with salt, pepper and white wine vinegar. Finally add the tomatoes and rocket. Finished! Serve and enjoy.

884. Mediterranean Salad With Parsnips And Peppers

Preparation Time: 15 minutes
Cooking Time: 1 hour
Servings: 2

Ingredients:

2 parsnips
1 bell pepper
1 clove of garlic
50g dried tomatoes
1 tbsp balsamic vinegar
Basil and chili flakes
salt and pepper
olive oil

Directions:

Peel the parsnips and cut into thin slices and cook in a saucepan with a little water for about 5 minutes.
Clean, core and dice the peppers.
Heat olive oil in a pan and fry the chopped peppers and parsnip slices.
Peel and chop the garlic and add to the vegetables in the pan. Season to taste with chili flakes, basil, pepper and salt. As soon as the pepper cubes and the parsnip slices are golden brown, put all the ingredients in a bowl and mix the whole thing with the balsamic vinegar.
Finished! Serve and enjoy.

885. Fried Mushroom Salad

Preparation Time: 30 minutes
Cooking Time: 0 minutes
Servings: 4

Ingredients:

1 zucchini
125g mushrooms
1 bell pepper
2 tomatoes
200g feta cheese
1 small onion
Lemon juice and olive oil
Balsamic vinegar
salt and pepper

Directions:

Cut everything into small pieces. Fry the zucchini, bell pepper and mushrooms in a pan.
Put everything in a bowl and season with balsamic vinegar, olive oil, lemon juice, a pinch of sugar, as well as salt, pepper and garlic.

886. Mediterranean Chickpea Salad

Preparation Time: 15 minutes
Cooking Time:
Servings: 4

Ingredients:

265g chickpeas
200g feta cheese
1 onion

1 bell pepper
½ cucumber
2 tbsp olives
2 tbsp parsley
salt and pepper
For the dressing
100ml olive oil
50ml white wine vinegar
1 tbsp lime juice
1tsp chili flakes
salt and pepper

Directions:

Drain the chickpeas, wash them and place in a large bowl. Cut the cucumber into slices. Core and chop the olives. Dice the paprika and feta, chop the onion. Chop the parsley.
Combine all ingredients except for the dressing in a bowl.
For the dressing: mix olive oil, white wine vinegar, lime juice, chili flakes, salt and pepper well.
Add the dressing to the other ingredients and mix everything well. Finished! Serve and enjoy.

887. Mediterranean Tuna Salad

Preparation Time: 20 minutes
Cooking Time: 0 minutes
Servings: 4

Ingredients:

1 clove of garlic
4 tomatoes
2 onions
200g feta cheese
1 cucumber
3 tbsp olive oil
1 tin of tuna
1 teaspoon rosemary
2 tablespoons balsamic vinegar
salt and pepper

Directions:

Wash and dice tomatoes and cucumber. Peel and chop the garlic and onions. Crumble the feta. Drain the tuna.
Put the garlic, tomatoes, onions and cucumber in a bowl and season with rosemary and basil and add a little olive oil.
Add the tuna and feta cheese. Season to taste with salt, pepper and balsamic vinegar. Finished! Serve and enjoy.

888. Mediterranean Egg Broccoli Salad

Preparation Time: 40 minutes
Cooking Time:
Servings: 4

Ingredients:

5 eggs
800g broccoli
200g mushrooms
2 tbsp pine nuts
50g dried tomatoes
250g yogurt
2 tbsp olive oil
½ onion
10 basil leaves
salt and pepper

Direction

Hard boil eggs. Clean the broccoli and cut off the florets. Peel and cut the broccoli stalks. Cut the dried tomatoes into strips. Peel and chop the onion and garlic. Clean the mushrooms and cut them in slices.
Cook the broccoli in boiling salted water for about 12 minutes. Drain the water and let it cool down.
Roast pine nuts in a pan and then set aside.
For the dressing: mix yoghurt with olive oil, add onion and garlic, season everything with salt and pepper.
Mix the broccoli, mushrooms and tomato strips together. Fold in the dressing and let everything steep for about 15 minutes.
Peel the eggs, cut eighths and fold into the salad. Refine the salad with roasted pine nuts and fresh basil and serve. Good Appetite!

889. Mediterranean Salad With Baked Camembert

Preparation Time: 30 minutes
Cooking Time: 15 minutes
Servings: 4

Ingredients:

800g asparagus
200g rocket
200g cherry tomatoes
100g olives
3 tbsp balsamic vinegar
4 mini camembert
2 tablespoons cranberries
5 tbsp olive oil
1 teaspoon mustard
salt and pepper

Directions:

Clean and peel the asparagus and cut off the woody ends. Cook in boiling salted water for about 10 minutes. Then drain and drain.
Thoroughly clean the rocket and spin dry. Wash and quarter the tomatoes.
For the dressing: mix the balsamic vinegar, 3 tbsp olive oil, salt, mustard and pepper in a bowl.
Bake the Camembert in a preheated oven at 200 ° C. Then take it out, let it cool and cover with a few cranberries.
Arrange the rocket with asparagus, tomatoes and olives on a plate. Drizzle with the salad sauce and add the melted camembert with cranberries. Finished! Serve and enjoy.

890. Mushroom Arugula Salad

Preparation Time: 25 minutes
Cooking Time: 0 minutes
Servings: 4

Ingredients:

500g mushrooms
200g sheep cheese
75g rocket
60g pine nuts
3 tbsp olive oil
salt and pepper

Directions:

Wash the mushrooms and cut into thin slices. Clean the rocket and cut into small pieces. Dice the sheep's cheese.
Put everything in a salad bowl with olive oil and balsamic vinegar. Season to taste with salt and pepper.
Toast the pine nuts in a pan until they are golden brown.
Add the pine nuts to the salad. Finished! Serve and enjoy.

891. Italian Bread Salad

Preparation Time: 60 minutes
Cooking Time: 30 minutes
Servings: 4

Ingredients:

2 ciabatta
5 tomatoes
½ cucumber
1 bunch of parsley
2 tbsp olive oil
½ bunch of rosemary
2 cloves of garlic
salt and pepper

Directions:

Preheat oven to 220 degrees. Dice the ciabatta, spread on a baking sheet with baking paper and drizzle with olive oil. Toast the bread cubes in the oven, remove them and let them cool down.
Wash and dice tomatoes and cucumber.
For the dressing: finely chop the parsley and rosemary. Peel and squeeze the garlic and mix with salt, pepper, olive oil and herbs.
Add the dressing to the diced tomatoes and cucumber.
Let it steep in the refrigerator for about 30 minutes.
Fold the bread cubes into the salad.
Finished! Serve and enjoy.

892. Tomato And Bread Salad

Preparation Time: 20 minutes
Cooking Time: 0 minutes
Servings: 4

Ingredients:

750g tomatoes
1 bunch of spring onions
2 sprigs of basil
4 slices of ciabatta
3 tbsp olive oil
6 tbsp white wine vinegar
salt and pepper

Directions:

Cut tomatoes into thin slices. Also, cut the spring onions into thin rings.
Pluck the basil leaves and cut into strips.
Cut the ciabatta into small pieces.
For the dressing: press the garlic and mix with olive oil, white wine vinegar, salt and pepper.
Mix all ingredients with the dressing.
Finished! Serve and enjoy.

893. Rocket Avocado Salad

Preparation Time: 20 minutes
Cooking Time:
Servings: 4

Ingredients:

125g rocket
250g cocktail tomatoes
½ avocado
50g olives
1 onion
1 clove of garlic
4 tbsp balsamic vinegar
3 tbsp olive oil
salt and pepper
Some sugar

Directions:

Clean the rocket. Wash and halve cocktail tomatoes. Peel, core and dice the avocado.
Peel the garlic and onion and cut into small pieces.
Drain and add olives.
Mix with the other ingredients and then season with salt, pepper and sugar.

894. Mediterranean Sausage Salad

Preparation Time: 20 minutes
Cooking Time: 45 minutes
Servings: 6

Ingredients:

600g meat sausage
3 onions
1 bell pepper
2 tomatoes
250g feta cheese
½ cucumber
2 tbsp mixed herbs
1 pinch of vegetable stock powder
3 tbsp olive oil
4 tbsp raspberry vinegar
salt and pepper

Directions:

Dice the meat sausage. Peel and chop the onions. Wash and chop the bell pepper, cucumber and tomatoes. Crumble the feta cheese. Chop the herbs into small pieces. Put everything together in a salad bowl.
Mix with the raspberry vinegar, olive oil, vegetable stock powder, salt and pepper.
Finished! Serve and enjoy.

895. Mediterranean Orange Salad

Preparation Time: 20 minutes
Cooking Time:
Servings: 4

Ingredients:

2 oranges
2 bulbs of fennel
1 onion
20 black olives
2 tbsp balsamic vinegar
3 tablespoons of olive oil
1 teaspoon honey
½ lettuce
salt and pepper

Directions:

Peel oranges and cut into slices. Clean and finely slice the fennel bulbs. Peel the onion and cut into thin slices. Core the olives. Clean the lettuce and pluck it into bite-sized pieces. Mix everything in a bowl.
For the dressing: mix salt, pepper, honey, olive oil and balsamic vinegar in a bowl.
Add the dressing to the other ingredients in the bowl and mix everything well.
Finished! Serve and enjoy.

896. Fattoush Salad –middle East Bread Salad

Preparation Time: 15 minutes
Cooking Time: 15 minutes
Servings: 6

Ingredients:

2 loaves pita bread
1 tbsp Extra Virgin Olive Oil
1/2 tsp sumac, more for later
Salt and pepper
1 heart of Romaine lettuce, chopped
1 English cucumber, chopped
5 Roma tomatoes, chopped
5 green onions (both white and green parts), chopped
5 radishes, stems removed, thinly sliced
2 cups chopped fresh parsley leaves; stems removed
1 cup chopped fresh mint leaves
1 1/2 lime, juice of
1/3 cup Extra Virgin Olive Oil
Salt and pepper
1 tsp ground sumac
1/4 tsp ground cinnamon
scant 1/4 tsp ground allspice

Directions:

For 5 minutes toast the pita bread in the toaster oven. And then break the pita bread into pieces.
In a large pan on medium fire, heat 3 tbsp of olive oil in for 3 minutes. Add pita bread and fry until browned, around 4 minutes while tossing around.
Add salt, pepper and 1/2 tsp of sumac. Remove the pita chips from the heat and place on paper towels to drain.
Toss well the chopped lettuce, cucumber, tomatoes, green onions, sliced radish, mint leaves and parsley in a large salad bowl.
To make the lime vinaigrette, whisk together all ingredients in a small bowl.
Drizzle over salad and toss well to coat.
Mix in the pita bread.
Serve and enjoy.

897. Artichoke and Arugula Salad

Preparation Time: 10 minutes
Cooking Time: 0 minutes
Servings: 6

Ingredients:

Salad:
6 canned oil-packed artichoke hearts, sliced
6 cups baby arugula leaves
6 fresh olives, pitted and chopped
1 cup cherry tomatoes, sliced in half
Dressing:
1 teaspoon Dijon mustard
2 tablespoons balsamic vinegar
1 clove garlic, minced
2 tablespoons extra-virgin olive oil
For Garnish:
4 fresh basil leaves, thinly sliced

Directions:

Combine the ingredients for the salad in a large salad bowl, then toss to combine well.
Combine the ingredients for the dressing in a small bowl, then stir to mix well.
Dressing the salad, then serve with basil leaves on top.
Tip: If you don't like canned food, and good at dealing with or want to deal with the fresh artichokes, you can use the same amount of fresh artichoke to replace the canned artichoke hearts.

898. Baby Potato and Olive Salad

Preparation Time: 10 minutes
Cooking Time: 20 minutes
Servings: 6

Ingredients:

2 pounds (907 g) baby potatoes, cut into 1-inch cubes
1 tablespoon low-sodium olive brine
3 tablespoons freshly squeezed lemon juice (from about 1 medium lemon)
¼ teaspoon kosher salt
3 tablespoons extra-virgin olive oil
½ cup sliced olives
2 tablespoons torn fresh mint
1 cup sliced celery (about 2 stalks)
2 tablespoons chopped fresh oregano

Directions:

Put the tomatoes in a saucepan, then pour in enough water to submerge the tomatoes about 1 inch.
Bring to a boil over high heat, then reduce the heat to medium-low. Simmer for 14 minutes or until the potatoes are soft.
Meanwhile, combine the olive brine, lemon juice, salt, and olive oil in a small bow. Stir to mix well.
Transfer the cooked tomatoes in a colander, then rinse with running cold water. Pat dry with paper towels.
Transfer the tomatoes in a large salad bowl, then drizzle with olive brine mixture. Spread with remaining ingredients and toss to combine well.
Serve immediately.
Tip: You can toss the hot tomatoes with half of the olive brine mixture after patting dry and let it to infuse before combining with remaining ingredients.

899. Barley, Parsley, and Pea Salad

Preparation Time: 10 minutes
Cooking Time: 10 minutes
Servings: 4

Ingredients:

2 cups water
1 cup quick-cooking barley
1 small bunch flat-leaf parsley, chopped (about 1 to 1½ cups)
2 cups sugar snap pea pods
Juice of 1 lemon
½ small red onion, diced
2 tablespoons extra-virgin olive oil
Sea salt and freshly ground pepper, to taste

Directions:

Pour the water in a saucepan. Bring to a boil. Add the barley to the saucepan, then put the lid on.
Reduce the heat to low. Simmer the barley for 10 minutes or until the liquid is absorbed, then let sit for 5 minutes.
Open the lid, then transfer the barley in a colander and rinse under cold running water.
Pour the barley in a large salad bowl and add the remaining ingredients. Toss to combine well.
Serve immediately.
Tip: If you have enough time, you can use pearl barley to replace the quick-cooking barley, and it may cost 15 more minutes to simmer the barley.

900. Cheesy Peach and Walnut Salad

Preparation Time: 10 minutes
Cooking Time: 0 minutes
Servings: 1

Ingredients:

1 ripe peach, pitted and sliced
1/4 cup chopped walnuts, toasted
1/4 cup shredded Parmesan cheese
1 teaspoon raw honey
Zest of 1 lemon
1 tablespoon chopped fresh mint

Directions:

Combine the peach, walnut, and cheese in a medium bowl, then drizzle with honey. Spread the lemon zest and mint on top. Toss to combine everything well.
Serve immediately.
Tip: You can serve this salad as breakfast, and serve it with plain almond yogurt and toss with cubed whole wheat bread, if desired.

901. Greek Chicken, Tomato, and Olive Salad

Preparation Time: 10 minutes
Cooking Time: 0 minutes
Servings: 2

Ingredients:

Salad:
2 grilled boneless, skinless chicken breasts, sliced (about 1 cup)
10 cherry tomatoes, halved
8 pitted Kalamata olives, halved
½ cup thinly sliced red onion
Dressing:
¼ cup balsamic vinegar
1 teaspoon freshly squeezed lemon juice
¼ teaspoon sea salt
¼ teaspoon freshly ground black pepper
2 teaspoons extra-virgin olive oil
For Servings:
2 cups roughly chopped romaine lettuce
½ cup crumbled feta cheese

Directions:

Combine the ingredients for the salad in a large bowl. Toss to combine well.
Combine the ingredients for the dressing in a small bowl. Stir to mix well.
Pour the dressing the bowl of salad, then toss to coat well. Wrap the bowl in plastic and refrigerate for at least 2 hours.

Remove the bowl from the refrigerator. Spread the lettuce on a large plate, then top with marinated salad. Scatter the salad with feta cheese and serve immediately.
Tip: How to grill the chicken breast: Preheat the grill to medium high heat, then grease the grill grates with olive oil. Place the chicken breast on the grill grate and grill for 15 minutes or until the internal temperature of the chicken reaches at least 165ºF (74ºC). Flip the chicken breast halfway through. Allow to cool before using.

902. Ritzy Summer Fruit Salad

Preparation Time: 10 minutes
Cooking Time: 0 minutes
Servings: 8

Ingredients:

Salad:
1 cup fresh blueberries
2 cups cubed cantaloupe
2 cups red seedless grapes
1 cup sliced fresh strawberries
2 cups cubed honeydew melon
Zest of 1 large lime
1/2 cup unsweetened toasted coconut flakes
Dressing:
1/4 cup raw honey
Juice of 1 large lime
1/4 teaspoon sea salt
1/2 cup extra-virgin olive oil

Directions:

Combine the ingredients for the salad in a large salad bowl, then toss to combine well.
Combine the ingredients for the dressing in a small bowl, then stir to mix well.
Dressing the salad and serve immediately.
Tip: You can enjoy this fruit salad between breakfast and lunchtime. Because during this time, the nutritional value of the fruits is highest and they can also give you a bright day.

903. Roasted Broccoli and Tomato Panzanella

Preparation Time: 10 minutes
Cooking Time: 20 minutes
Servings: 4

Ingredients:

1-pound (454 g) broccoli (about 3 medium stalks), trimmed, cut into 1-inch florets and ½-inch stem slices
2 tablespoons extra-virgin olive oil, divided
1½ cups cherry tomatoes
1½ teaspoons honey, divided
3 cups cubed whole-grain crusty bread
1 tablespoon balsamic vinegar
¼ teaspoon kosher salt
½ teaspoon freshly ground black pepper
¼ cup grated Parmesan cheese, for serving (optional)
¼ cup chopped fresh oregano leaves, for serving (optional)

Directions:

Preheat the oven to 450ºF (235ºC).
Toss the broccoli with 1 tablespoon of olive oil in a large bowl to coat well.
Arrange the broccoli on a baking sheet, then add the tomatoes to the same bowl and toss with the remaining olive oil. Add 1 teaspoon of honey and toss again to coat well. Transfer the tomatoes on the baking sheet beside the broccoli.
Place the baking sheet in the preheated oven and roast for 15 minutes, then add the bread cubes and flip the vegetables. Roast for an additional 3 minutes or until the broccoli is lightly charred and the bread cubes are golden brown.
Meanwhile, combine the remaining ingredients, except for the Parmesan and oregano, in a small bowl. Stir to mix well.
Transfer the roasted vegetables and bread cubes to the large salad bowl, then dress them and spread with Parmesan and oregano leaves. Toss and serve immediately.
Tip: You can use sun-dried tomatoes, ripped yellow tomatoes, or just grape tomatoes to replace the cherry tomatoes. Remember to reserve the juice and drizzle the salad with the juice for more freshness.

904. Sumptuous Greek Vegetable Salad

Preparation Time: 20 minutes
Cooking Time: 0 minutes
Servings: 6

Ingredients:

Salad:
1 (15-ounce / 425-g) can chickpeas, drained and rinsed
1 (14-ounce / 397-g) can artichoke hearts, drained and halved
1 head Bibb lettuce, chopped (about 2½ cups)
1 cucumber, peeled deseeded, and chopped (about 1½ cups)
1½ cups grape tomatoes, halved
¼ cup chopped basil leaves
½ cup sliced black olives
½ cup cubed feta cheese
Dressing:
1 tablespoon freshly squeezed lemon juice (from about ½ small lemon)
¼ teaspoon freshly ground black pepper
1 tablespoon chopped fresh oregano
2 tablespoons extra-virgin olive oil
1 tablespoon red wine vinegar
1 teaspoon honey

Directions:

Combine the ingredients for the salad in a large salad bowl, then toss to combine well.
Combine the ingredients for the dressing in a small bowl, then stir to mix well.
Dressing the salad and serve immediately.
Tip: You can use ½ head romaine lettuce or other fresh leaves to replace the Bibb lettuce.

905. Brussels Sprout and Apple Slaw

Preparation Time: 15 minutes
Cooking Time: 0 minutes
Servings: 4

Ingredients:

Salad:
1-pound (454 g) Brussels sprouts, stem ends removed and sliced thinly
1 apple, cored and sliced thinly
½ red onion, sliced thinly
Dressing:
1 teaspoon Dijon mustard
2 teaspoons apple cider vinegar
1 tablespoon raw honey
1 cup plain coconut yogurt
1 teaspoon sea salt
For Garnish:
½ cup pomegranate seeds
½ cup chopped toasted hazelnuts

Directions:

Combine the ingredients for the salad in a large salad bowl, then toss to combine well.
Combine the ingredients for the dressing in a small bowl, then stir to mix well.
Dressing the salad. Let sit for 30 minutes, then serve with pomegranate seeds and toasted hazelnuts on top.
Tip: If you don't like pomegranate seeds, you can replace it with sunflower seeds, pumpkin seeds, or chia seeds.

906. Vitamin Chicken Salad

Preparation Time: 5 min
Cooking Time: 0 minutes
Servings: 4-5

Ingredients:

3 cooked chicken breasts, shredded
1 yellow bell pepper, thinly sliced
1 red bell pepper, thinly sliced
1/2 red onion, thinly sliced
1 small green apple, peeled and thinly sliced
1/2 cup toasted almonds, chopped
3 tbsp lemon juice
2 tbsp extra virgin olive oil
1 tbsp Dijon mustard
salt and pepper, to taste

Directions:

In a deep salad bowl, combine peppers, apple, chicken and almonds.
In a smaller bowl, whisk the mustard, olive oil, lemon juice, salt and pepper. Pour over the salad, toss to combine and serve.

907. Chicken, Lettuce and Avocado Salad

Preparation Time: 5 min
Cooking Time: 0 minutes
Servings: 4

Ingredients:

2 grilled chicken breasts, diced
1 avocado, peeled and diced
5-6 green lettuce leaves, cut in stripes
3-4 green onions, finely chopped
5-6 radishes, sliced
7-8 grape tomatoes, halved
3 tbsp lemon juice
3 tbsp extra virgin olive oil
1 tsp dried mint
salt and black pepper, to taste

Directions:

In a deep salad bowl, combine avocados, lettuce, chicken, onions, radishes and grape tomatoes.
Season with dried mint, salt and pepper to taste. Sprinkle with lemon juice and olive oil, toss lightly, and serve.

908. Mediterranean Beef Salad

Preparation Time: 5 min
Cooking Time: 15 minutes
Servings: 4-5

Ingredients:

8 oz quality roast beef, thinly sliced
1 avocado, peeled and diced
2 tomatoes, diced
1 cucumber, peeled and diced
1 yellow pepper, sliced
2 carrots, shredded
1 cup black olives, pitted and halved
2-3 fresh basil leaves, torn
2-3 fresh oregano leaves
1 tbsp balsamic vinegar
4 tbsp extra virgin olive oil
salt and black pepper, to taste

Directions:

Combine the avocado and all vegetables in a large salad bowl. Add in basil and oregano leaves.
Season with salt and pepper, drizzle with balsamic vinegar and olive oil, and toss to combine. Top with roast beef and serve.

909. Ground Beef Salad with Creamy Avocado Dressing

Preparation Time: 5 min
Cooking Time:
Servings: 4-5

Ingredients:

1 green lettuce, cut in stripes
2-3 green onions, finely cut
1 garlic clove, crushed
½ cup black olives, pitted and halved
4-5 radishes, sliced
8 oz ground beef
2 tbsp extra virgin olive oil
1/2 tsp ground cumin
1/2 tsp dried oregano
1 tsp paprika
salt and pepper, to taste
for the dressing:
1 avocado, peeled and cut
1 tbsp extra virgin olive oil
4 tbsp lemon juice
2 garlic cloves, cut
1 tbsp water
1/2 tsp salt

Directions:

Blend the dressing ingredients until smooth.
Heat olive oil in a medium saucepan and gently cook the ground beef and the seasonings, stirring, for 5-6 minutes, or until cooked through.
Place lettuce, cooked beef and all other salad ingredients in a bowl. Toss well to combine. Drizzle with dressing and serve.

910. Tuna Salad with Lettuce and Chickpeas

Preparation Time: 5 min
Cooking Time: 0 minutes
Servings: 4

Ingredients:

1 head green lettuce, washed cut in thin strips
1 cup chopped watercress
1 cucumber, peeled and chopped
1 tomato, diced
1 can tuna, drained and broken into small chunks
1/2 cup chickpeas, from a can
7-8 radishes, sliced
3-4 spring onions, chopped
juice of half lemon
3 tbsp extra virgin olive oil

Directions:

Mix all the vegetables in a large bowl. Add the tuna and the chickpeas and season with lemon juice, oil and salt to taste.

CHAPTER 14: SMOOTHIES

911. Sweet Kale Smoothie

Preparation Time: 10 minutes
Cooking Time: 15 minutes
Servings: 2

Ingredients:

1 cup low-fat plain Greek yogurt
½ cup apple juice
1 apple, cored and quartered
4 Medjool dates
3 cups packed coarsely chopped kale
Juice of ½ lemon
4 ice cubes

Directions:

In a blender, combine the yogurt, apple juice, apple, and dates and pulse until smooth.
Add the kale and lemon juice and pulse until blended. Add the ice cubes and blend until smooth and thick. Pour into glasses and serve.

912. Avocado-Blueberry Smoothie

Preparation Time: 5 minutes
Cooking Time: 0 minutes
Servings: 2

Ingredients:

½ cup unsweetened vanilla almond milk
½ cup low-fat plain Greek yogurt
1 ripe avocado, peeled, pitted, and coarsely chopped
1 cup blueberries
¼ cup gluten-free rolled oats
½ teaspoon vanilla extract
4 ice cubes

Directions:

In a blender, combine the almond milk, yogurt, avocado, blueberries, oats, and vanilla and pulse until well blended.
Add the ice cubes and blend until thick and smooth. Serve.

913. Cranberry-Pumpkin Smoothie

Preparation Time: 5 minutes
Cooking Time: 0 minutes
Servings: 2

Ingredients:

2 cups unsweetened almond milk
1 cup pure pumpkin purée
¼ cup gluten-free rolled oats
¼ cup pure cranberry juice (no sugar added)
1 tablespoon honey
¼ teaspoon ground cinnamon
Pinch ground nutmeg

Directions:

In a blender, combine the almond milk, pumpkin, oats, cranberry juice, honey, cinnamon, and nutmeg and blend until smooth.
Pour into glasses and serve immediately.

914. Sweet Cranberry Nectar

Preparation Time: 8 minutes
Cooking Time: 5 minutes
Servings: 4
Ingredients:

4 cups fresh cranberries

1 fresh lemon juice
½ cup agave nectar
1 piece of cinnamon stick
1-gallon water, filtered

Directions:

Add cranberries, ½ gallon water, and cinnamon into your pot
Close the lid
Cook on HIGH pressure for 8 minutes
Release the pressure naturally
Firstly, strain the liquid, then add remaining water
Cool, add agave nectar and lemon
Served chill and enjoy!

915. Hearty Pear and Mango Smoothie

Preparation Time: 10 minutes
Cooking Time: nil
Servings: 1

Ingredients:

1 ripe mango, cored and chopped
½ mango, peeled, pitted and chopped
1 cup kale, chopped
½ cup plain Greek yogurt
2 ice cubes

Directions:

Add pear, mango, yogurt, kale, and mango to a blender and puree.
Add ice and blend until you have a smooth texture.
Serve and enjoy!

916. Breakfast Almond Milk Shake

Preparation Time: 4 minutes
Servings: 2

Ingredients

3 cups almond milk
4 tbsp heavy cream
½ tsp vanilla extract
4 tbsp flax meal
2 tbsp protein powder
4 drops of liquid stevia Ice cubes to serve

Directions

In the bowl of your food processor, add almond milk, heavy cream, flax meal, vanilla extract, collagen peptides, and stevia.
Blitz until uniform and smooth, for about 30 seconds.
Add a bit more almond milk if it's very thick.
Pour in a smoothie glass, add the ice cubes and sprinkle with cinnamon.

917. Raspberry Vanilla Smoothie

Preparation Time: 5 minutes
Cooking Time: 5 minutes
Servings: over 2 cups

Ingredients:

1 cup frozen raspberries
6-ounce container of vanilla Greek yogurt
½ cup of unsweetened vanilla almond milk

Directions:

Take all of your ingredients and place them in an instant pot Ace blender.
Process until smooth and liquified.

918. Blueberry Banana Protein Smoothie

Preparation Time: 5 minutes
Cooking Time: 5 minutes
Servings: 1

Ingredients:

½ cup frozen and unsweetened blueberries
½ banana slices up
¾ cup plain nonfat Greek yogurt
¾ cup unsweetened vanilla almond milk
2 cups of ice cubes

Directions:

Add all of the ingredients into an instant pot ace blender.
Blend until smooth.

919. Chocolate Banana Smoothie

Preparation Time: 5 minutes
Cooking Time: 0 minutes
Servings: 2

Ingredients:

2 bananas, peeled
1 cup unsweetened almond milk, or skim milk
1 cup crushed ice
3 tablespoons unsweetened cocoa powder
3 tablespoons honey

Directions:

In a blender, combine the bananas, almond milk, ice, cocoa powder, and honey. Blend until smooth.

920. Fruit Smoothie

Preparation Time: 5 minutes
Cooking Time: 0 minutes
Servings: 2

Ingredients:

2 cups blueberries (or any fresh or frozen fruit, cut into pieces if the fruit is large)
2 cups unsweetened almond milk
1 cup crushed ice
½ teaspoon ground ginger (or other dried ground spice such as turmeric, cinnamon, or nutmeg)

Directions:

In a blender, combine the blueberries, almond milk, ice, and ginger. Blend until smooth.

921. Mango-Pear Smoothie

Preparation Time: 10 minutes
Cooking Time: 0 minutes
Servings: 1

Ingredients:

1 ripe pear, cored and chopped
½ mango, peeled, pitted, and chopped
1 cup chopped kale
½ cup plain Greek yogurt
2 ice cubes

Directions:

In a blender, purée the pear, mango, kale, and yogurt.
Add the ice and blend until thick and smooth. Pour the smoothie into a glass and serve cold.

922. Chia-Pomegranate Smoothie

Preparation Time: 5 minutes
Cooking Time: 0 minutes
Servings: 2

Ingredients:

1 cup pure pomegranate juice (no sugar added)
1 cup frozen berries
1 cup coarsely chopped kale
2 tablespoons chia seeds
3 Medjool dates, pitted and coarsely chopped
Pinch ground cinnamon

Directions:

In a blender, combine the pomegranate juice, berries, kale, chia seeds, dates, and cinnamon and pulse until smooth. Pour into glasses and serve.

923. Honey And Wild Blueberry Smoothie

Preparation Time: 5 minutes
Cooking Time: 10 minutes
Servings: 2

Ingredients:

1 whole banana
1 cup of mango chunks
½ cup wild blueberries
½ plain, nonfat Greek yogurt
½ cup milk (for blending)
1 tablespoon raw honey
½ cup of kale

Directions:

Add all of the above ingredients into an instant pot Ace blender. Add extra ice cubes if needed.
Process until smooth.

924. Oats Berry Smoothie

Preparation Time: 5 minutes
Cooking Time: 5 minutes
Servings: 2

Ingredients:

1 cup of frozen berries
1 cup Greek yogurt
¼ cup of milk
¼ cup of oats
2 teaspoon honey

Directions:

Place all ingredients in an instant pot Ace blender and blend until smooth.

925. Kale-Pineapple Smoothie

Preparation Time: 5 minutes
Cooking Time: 5 minutes
Servings: 2

Ingredients:

1 Persian cucumber
fresh mint
1 cup of coconut milk
1 tablespoon honey
1 ½ cups of pineapple pieces
¼ pound baby kale

Directions:

Cut the ends off of the cucumbers and then cut the whole cucumber into small

cubes. Strip the mint leaves from the stems.
Add all of the ingredients to your instant pot Ace blender and blend until smooth.

926. Moroccan Avocado Smoothie

Preparation Time: 5 minutes
Cooking Time: 0 minutes
Servings: 4

Ingredients:

1 ripe avocado, peeled and pitted
1 overripe banana
1 cup almond milk, unsweetened
1 cup of ice

Directions:

Place the avocado, banana, milk, and ice into your instant pot Ace blender.
Blend until smooth with no pieces of avocado remaining.

927. Mediterranean Smoothie

Preparation Time: 5 minutes
Cooking Time: 5 minutes
Servings: 2

Ingredients:

2 cups of baby spinach
1 teaspoon fresh ginger root
1 frozen banana, pre-sliced
1 small mango
½ cup beet juice
½ cup of skim milk
4-6 ice cubes

Directions:

Take all ingredients and place them in your instant pot Ace blender.

928. Anti-Inflammatory Blueberry Smoothie

Preparation Time: 5 minutes
Cooking Time: 5 minutes
Servings: 1

Ingredients:

1 cup of almond milk
1 frozen banana
1 cup frozen blueberries
2 handfuls of spinach
1 tablespoon almond butter
¼ teaspoon cinnamon
¼ teaspoon cayenne
1 teaspoon maca powder

Directions:

Combine all of these ingredients into your instant pot Ace blender and blend until smooth.

929. Pina Colada Smoothie

Preparation Time: 10 minutes
Cooking Time: 0 minutes
Servings: 4

Ingredients:

4 bananas
2 cups pineapple, peeled and sliced
2 cups mangoes, cored and diced
1 cup ice
4 tablespoons flaxseed
1¼ cups coconut milk

Directions:

Put all the ingredients in a blender and blend until smooth.
Pour into 4 glasses and immediately serve.

930. Kiwi Smoothie

Preparation Time: 10 minutes
Cooking Time: 0 minutes
Servings: 2

Ingredients:

1 cup basil leaves
2 bananas
1 cup fresh pineapple
10 kiwis

Directions:

Put all the ingredients in a blender and blend until smooth.
Pour into 2 glasses and immediately serve.

CHAPTER 15: DESSERTS

931. Apple Couscous Pudding

Preparation Time: 10 minutes
Cooking Time: 25 minutes
Servings: 4

Ingredients:

½ cup couscous
½ cups milk
¼ cup apple, cored and chopped
tbsps. stevia
½ tsp. rose water
1 tbsp. orange zest, grated

Directions:

Heat up a pan with the milk over medium heat, add the couscous and the rest of the ingredients, whisk, simmer for 25 minutes, divide into bowls and serve.

932. Ricotta Ramekins

Preparation Time: 10 minutes
Cooking Time: 1 hour
Servings: 4

Ingredients:

6 eggs, whisked
½ pounds ricotta cheese, soft
½ pound stevia
1 tsp. vanilla extract
½ tsp. baking powder
Cooking spray

Directions:

In a bowl, mix the eggs with the ricotta and the other ingredients except the cooking spray and whisk well.
Grease 4 ramekins with the cooking spray, pour the ricotta cream in each and bake at 360F for 1 hour.
Serve cold.

933. Papaya Cream

Preparation Time: 10 minutes
Cooking Time: 0 minutes
Servings: 2

Ingredients:

cup papaya, peeled and chopped
1 cup heavy cream
1 tbsp. stevia
½ tsp. vanilla extract

Directions:

In a blender, combine the cream with the papaya and the other ingredients, pulse well, divide into cups and serve cold.

934. Orange Cake

Preparation Time: 20 minutes
Cooking Time: 60 minutes
Servings: 8

Ingredients:

4 oranges
1/3 cup water
½ cup Erythritol
½ tsp. ground cinnamon
4 eggs, beaten
3 tbsps. stevia powder
10 oz. Phyllo pastry
½ tsp. baking powder
½ cup Plain yogurt
3 tbsps. olive oil

Directions:

Squeeze the juice from 1 orange and pour it in the saucepan.
Add water, squeezed oranges, water, ground cinnamon, and Erythritol. Bring the liquid to boil.
Simmer the liquid for 5 minutes over the medium heat. When the time is over, cool it.
Grease the baking mold with 1 tbsp. of olive oil. Chop the phyllo dough and place it in the baking mold.
Slice ½ of orange for decorating the cake. Slice it. Squeeze juice from remaining oranges.
Then mix up together, squeeze orange juice, Plain yogurt, baking powder, stevia powder, and eggs. Add remaining olive oil
Mix up the mixture with the help of the hand mixer.
Pour the liquid over the chopped Phyllo dough. Stir to distribute evenly.
Top the cake with sliced orange (that one which you leave for decorating).
Bake the dessert for 50 minutes at 370F.
Pour the baked cake with cooled orange juice syrup. Leave it for 10 minutes to let the cake soaks the syrup.
Cut it into servings.

935. Lemon Cream

Preparation Time: 1 hour
Cooking Time: 10 minutes
Servings: 6

Ingredients:

2 eggs, whisked
¼ cup stevia
10 tbsps. avocado oil
1 cup heavy cream
Juice of 2 lemons
Zest of 2 lemons, grated

Directions:

In a pan, combine the cream with the lemon juice and the other ingredients, whisk well, cook for 10 minutes, divide into cups, and keep in the fridge for 1 hour before Servings.

936. Blueberries Stew

Preparation Time: 10 minutes
Cooking Time: 10 minutes
Servings: 4

Ingredients:

2 cups blueberries
3 tbsps. stevia
½ cups pure apple juice
1 tsp. vanilla extract

Directions:

In a pan, combine the blueberries with stevia and the other ingredients, bring to a simmer and cook over medium-low heat for 10 minutes.
Divide into cups and serve cold.

937. Mandarin Cream

Preparation Time: 20 minutes
Cooking Time: 0 minutes
Servings: 8

Ingredients:

2 mandarins, peeled and cut into segments
Juice of 2 mandarins
2 tbsps. stevia
4 eggs, whisked
¾ cup stevia
¾ cup almonds, ground

Directions:

In a blender, combine the mandarins with the juice and the other ingredients, whisk well, divide into cups and keep in the fridge for 20 minutes before Servings.

938. Creamy Mint Strawberry Mix

Preparation Time: 10 minutes
Cooking Time: 30 minutes
Servings: 6

Ingredients:

Cooking spray
¼ cup stevia
½ cup almond flour
1 tsp. baking powder
1 cup almond milk
1 egg, whisked
cups strawberries, sliced
1 tbsp. mint, chopped
1 tsp. lime zest, grated
½ cup whipping cream

Directions:

In a bowl, combine the almond with the strawberries, mint and the other ingredients except the cooking spray and whisk well.
Grease 6 ramekins with the cooking spray, pour the strawberry mix inside, introduce in the oven and bake at 350F for 30 minutes.
Cool down and serve.

939. Vanilla Cake

Preparation Time: 10 minutes
Cooking Time: 25 minutes
Servings: 10

Ingredients:

3 cups almond flour
3 tsps. baking powder
cup olive oil
1 and ½ cup almond milk
1 and 2/3 cup stevia
cups water
1 tbsp. lime juice
Tsps. vanilla extract
Cooking spray

Directions:

In a bowl, mix the almond flour with the baking powder, the oil, and the rest of the ingredients except the cooking spray and whisk well.
Pour the mix into a cake pan greased with the cooking spray, introduce in the oven, and bake at 370F for 25 minutes.
Leave the cake to cool down, cut and serve!

940. Orange Butterscotch Pudding

Preparation Time: 10 minutes
Cooking Time: 15 minutes
Servings: 4

Ingredients:

4 caramels
2 eggs, well-beaten
1/4 cup freshly squeezed orange juice
1/3 cup sugar
1 cup cake flour
1/2 teaspoon baking powder
1/4 cup milk
1 stick butter, melted
1/2 teaspoon vanilla essence
Sauce:
1/2 cup golden syrup
2 teaspoons corn flour
1 cup boiling water

Directions:

Melt the butter and milk in the microwave. Whisk in the eggs, vanilla, and sugar. After that, stir in the flour, baking powder, and orange juice.
Lastly, add the caramels and stir until everything is well combined and melted.
Divide between the four jars. Add 1 ½ cups of water and a metal trivet to the bottom of the Instant Pot. Lower the jars onto the trivet.
To make the sauce, whisk the boiling water, corn flour, and golden syrup until everything is well combined. Pour the sauce into each jar.
Secure the lid. Choose the "Steam" mode and cook for 15 minutes under High pressure. Once cooking is complete, use a natural pressure release; carefully remove the lid. Enjoy!

941. Recipe for Ruby Pears Delight

Preparation Time: 10 minutes
Cooking Time: 10 minutes
Servings: 4

Ingredients:

4 Pears
Grape juice-26 oz.
Currant jelly-11 oz.
4 garlic cloves
Juice and zest of 1 lemon
4 peppercorns
2 rosemary springs
1/2 vanilla bean

Directions:

Pour the jelly and grape juice in your instant pot and mix with lemon zest and juice
In the mix, dip each pear and wrap them in a clean tin foil and place them orderly in the steamer basket of your instant pot
Combine peppercorns, rosemary, garlic cloves and vanilla bean to the juice mixture,
Seal the lid and cook at High for 10 minutes.
Release the pressure quickly, and carefully open the lid; bring out the pears, remove wrappers and arrange them on plates. Serve when cold with toppings of cooking juice.

942. Mixed Berry and Orange Compote

Preparation Time: 15 minutes
Cooking Time: 15 minutes
Servings: 4

Ingredients:

1/2-pound strawberries
1 tablespoon orange juice
1/4 teaspoon ground cloves
1/2 cup brown sugar
1 vanilla bean
1-pound blueberries
1/2-pound blackberries

Directions:

Place your berries in the inner pot. Add the sugar and let sit for 15 minutes. Add in the orange juice, ground cloves, and vanilla bean.
Secure the lid. Choose the "Manual" mode and cook for 2 minutes at High pressure. Once cooking is complete, use a natural pressure release for 10 minutes; carefully remove the lid.
As your compote cools, it will thicken. Bon appétit!

943. Streuselkuchen with Peaches

Preparation Time: 10 minutes
Cooking Time: 20 minutes
Servings: 6

Ingredients

1 cup rolled oats
1 teaspoon vanilla extract
1/3 cup orange juice

4 tablespoons raisins
2 tablespoons honey
4 tablespoons butter
4 tablespoons all-purpose flour
A pinch of grated nutmeg
1/2 teaspoon ground cardamom
A pinch of salt
1 teaspoon ground cinnamon
6 peaches, pitted and chopped
1/3 cup brown sugar

Directions:

Place the peaches on the bottom of the inner pot. Sprinkle with the cardamom, cinnamon and vanilla. Top with the orange juice, honey, and raisins.
In a mixing bowl, whisk together the butter, oats, flour, brown sugar, nutmeg, and salt. Drop by a spoonful on top of the peaches.
Secure the lid. Choose the "Manual" mode and cook for 8 minutes at High pressure. Once cooking is complete, use a natural pressure release for 10 minutes; carefully remove the lid. Bon appétit!

944. Fig and Homey Buckwheat Pudding

Preparation Time: 10 minutes
Cooking Time: 10 minutes
Servings: 4

Ingredients

1/2 teaspoon ground cinnamon
1/2 cup dried figs, chopped
1/3 cup honey
1 teaspoon pure vanilla extract
3 ½ cups milk
1/2 teaspoon pure almond extract
1 ½ cups buckwheat

Directions:

Add all of the above ingredients to your Instant Pot.
Secure the lid. Choose the "Multigrain" mode and cook for 10 minutes under High pressure. Once cooking is complete, use a natural pressure release; carefully remove the lid.
Serve topped with fresh fruits, nuts or whipped topping. Bon appétit!

945. Zingy Blueberry Sauce

Preparation Time: 5 minutes
Cooking Time: 20 minutes
Servings: 10

Ingredients

1/4 cup fresh lemon juice
1-pound granulated sugar
1 tablespoon freshly grated lemon zest
1/2 teaspoon vanilla extract
2 pounds fresh blueberries

Directions:

Place the blueberries, sugar, and vanilla in the inner pot of your Instant Pot.
Secure the lid. Choose the "Manual" mode and cook for 2 minutes at High pressure. Once cooking is complete, use a natural pressure release for 15 minutes; carefully remove the lid.
Stir in the lemon zest and juice. Puree in a food processor; then, strain and push the mixture through a sieve before storing. Enjoy!

946. Chocolate Almond Custard

Preparation Time: 10 minutes
Cooking Time: 15 minutes
Servings: 3

Ingredients

3 chocolate cookies, chunks
A pinch of salt
1/4 teaspoon ground cardamom
3 tablespoons honey
1/4 teaspoon freshly grated nutmeg
2 tablespoons butter
3 tablespoons whole milk
1 cup almond flour
3 eggs
1 teaspoon pure vanilla extract

Directions:

In a mixing bowl, beat the eggs with butter. Now, add the milk and continue mixing until well combined.
Add the remaining ingredients in the order listed above. Divide the batter among 3 ramekins.
Add 1 cup of water and a metal trivet to the Instant Pot. Cover ramekins with foil and lower them onto the trivet.
Secure the lid and select "Manual" mode. Cook at High pressure for 12 minutes. Once cooking is complete, use a quick release; carefully remove the lid.
Transfer the ramekins to a wire rack and allow them to cool slightly before serving. Enjoy!

947. Honey Stewed Apples

Preparation Time: 5 minutes
Cooking Time: 5 minutes
Servings: 4

Ingredients

2 tablespoons honey
1 teaspoon ground cinnamon
1/2 teaspoon ground cloves
4 apples

Directions

Add all ingredients to the inner pot. Now, pour in 1/3 cup of water.
Secure the lid. Choose the "Manual" mode and cook for 2 minutes at High pressure. Once cooking is complete, use a quick pressure release; carefully remove the lid.
Serve in individual bowls. Bon appétit!

948. Greek-Style Compote with Yogurt

Preparation Time: 5 minutes
Cooking Time: 15 minutes
Servings: 4

Ingredients:

1 cup Greek yoghurt
1 cup pears
4 tablespoons honey
1 cup apples
1 vanilla bean
1 cinnamon stick
1/2 cup caster sugar
1 cup rhubarb
1 teaspoon ground ginger
1 cup plums

Directions:

Place the fruits, ginger, vanilla, cinnamon, and caster sugar in the inner pot of your Instant Pot.
Secure the lid. Choose the "Manual" mode and cook for 2 minutes at High pressure. Once cooking is complete, use a natural pressure release for 10 minutes; carefully remove the lid.
Meanwhile, whisk the yogurt with the honey.
Serve your compote in individual bowls with a dollop of honeyed Greek yogurt. Enjoy!

949. Butterscotch Lava Cakes

Preparation Time: 5 minutes
Cooking Time: 15 minutes
Servings: 6

Ingredients

7 tablespoons all-purpose flour
A pinch of coarse salt
6 ounces butterscotch morsels
3/4 cup powdered sugar
1/2 teaspoon vanilla extract
3 eggs, whisked
1 stick butter

Directions

Add 1 ½ cups of water and a metal rack to the Instant Pot. Line a standard-size muffin tin with muffin papers.
In a microwave-safe bowl, microwave butter and butterscotch morsels for about 40 seconds. Stir in the powdered sugar.
Add the remaining ingredients Spoon the batter into the prepared muffin tin.
Secure the lid. Choose the "Manual" and cook at High pressure for 10 minutes. Once cooking is complete, use a quick release; carefully remove the lid.
To remove, let it cool for 5 to 6 minutes. Run a small knife around the sides of each cake and serve. Enjoy!

950. Vanilla Bread Pudding with Apricots

Preparation Time: 5 minutes
Cooking Time: 15 minutes
Servings: 6

Ingredients

2 tablespoons coconut oil
1 1/3 cups heavy cream
4 eggs, whisked
1/2 cup dried apricots, soaked and chopped
1 teaspoon cinnamon, ground
1/2 teaspoon star anise, ground
A pinch of grated nutmeg
A pinch of salt
1/2 cup granulated sugar
2 tablespoons molasses
2 cups milk
4 cups Italian bread, cubed
1 teaspoon vanilla paste

Directions

Add 1 ½ cups of water and a metal rack to the Instant Pot.
Grease a baking dish with a nonstick cooking spray. Throw the bread cubes into the prepared baking dish.
In a mixing bowl, thoroughly combine the remaining ingredients Pour the mixture over the bread cubes. Cover with a piece of foil, making a foil sling.
Secure the lid. Choose the "Porridge" mode and High pressure; cook for 15 minutes. Once cooking is complete, use a quick pressure release; carefully remove the lid. Enjoy!

951. Mediterranean-Style Carrot Pudding

Preparation Time: 15 minutes
Cooking Time: 15 minutes
Servings: 4

Ingredients

1/3 cup almonds, ground
1/4 cup dried figs, chopped
2 large-sized carrots, shredded
1/2 cup water
1 ½ cups milk
1/2 teaspoon ground star anise
1/3 teaspoon ground cardamom
1/4 teaspoon kosher salt
1/3 cup granulated sugar
2 eggs, beaten
1/2 teaspoon pure almond extract
1/2 teaspoon vanilla extract
1 ½ cups jasmine rice

Directions

Place the jasmine rice, milk, water, carrots, and salt in your Instant Pot.
Stir to combine and secure the lid. Choose "Manual" and cook at High pressure for 10 minutes. Once cooking is complete, use a natural release for 15 minutes; carefully remove the lid.
Now, press the "Sauté" button and add the sugar, eggs, and almonds; stir to combine well. Bring to a boil; press the "Keep Warm/Cancel" button.
Add the remaining ingredients and stir; the pudding will thicken as it sits. Bon appétit!

952. Phyllo Cups

Preparation Time: 25 minutes
Cooking Time: 8 minutes
Servings: 12

Ingredients:

8 sheets (14 x 9-inch) frozen phyllo dough, thawed
Nonstick cooking spray
4 tsps. sugar
For the lemon cheesecake filling:
package (8 ounce) cream cheese, softened
tbsps. lemon curd
1/3 cup sugar
For the berry-honey filling:
3 oz. cream cheese, softened
½ cup whipping cream
½ tsp. vanilla
2 tbsps. honey
Fresh strawberries, sliced (or other berries)
For thee macadamia espresso coconut filling:
package (8 ounce) cream cheese, softened
1/3 cup sugar
½ cup whipping cream
1 tsp. espresso powder, instant
½ cup toasted coconut
¼ cup macadamia nuts, finely chopped

Directions:

For the phyllo cups:
Preheat the oven to 350F.
Lightly grease 12 pieces of 2 ½-inch muffin cups with the cooking spray; set aside.
Lay out 1 phyllo sheet, lightly grease with the cooking spray, sprinkle with some sugar, and then top with another 1 phyllo sheet. Repeat the process until 4 phyllo sheets are stacked, lightly greasing with the cooking spray, sprinkling with the sugar in the process. Repeat the procedure to make 2 stacks of 4-pieces phyllo sheets. Cut each stack lengthwise into halves. Then cut crosswise into thirds, making 12 rectangles.
Press 1 rectangle into each greased muffin cup, pleating the phyllo to form a cup, as necessary. Put the muffin cups in the oven and bake for about 8 minutes or until the phyllo cups are golden. When baked, remove the muffin tins from the oven and let cool in the pan for about 5 minutes. Remove the phyllo cups from the muffin tins and let cool completely. Fill each cup with desire filling. They can be filled for up to 1 hour before Servings.
For the lemon cheesecake filling:
Put the cream cheese and the sugar into a bowl; beat until the mixture is smooth. Beat in the lemon curd until mixed. Spoon the mixture into phyllo cups. If desired, garnish with lemon peel twists.
For the berry-honey filling:
Put the cream cheese in a bowl; beat until smooth. Beat in the vanilla and the honey. Add in the whipping cream; beat until stiff peaks form. Spoon the mixture into phyllo cups. Top with sliced

strawberries or with preferred berry. Drizzle with more honey, if desired.
For thee macadamia espresso coconut filling:
Put the cream cheese, sugar, and the espresso powder in a bowl; beat. Add in the whipping cream until stiff peaks form Stir in the nuts and toasted coconut.
Spoon the mixture into phyllo cups. If desired, garnish with additional toasted coconut and nuts.

953. Greek Almond Rounds Shortbread

Preparation Time: 45 minutes, plus 1hr chilling
Cooking Time: 12 minutes
Servings: 84

Ingredients:

½ cups butter, softened
cup blanched almonds, lightly toasted and finely ground
cup powdered sugar
egg yolks
tbsps. brandy or orange juice
tbsps. rose flower water, (optional)
Tsps. vanilla
½ cups cake flour
Powdered sugar

Directions:

Using an electric mixer, beat the butter on MEDIUM or HIGH speed for about 30 seconds in a large sized bowl. Add the 1 cup powdered sugar; beat until the mixture is light in color and fluffy, occasionally scraping the bowl as needed.
Beat in the yolks, vanilla, and the brandy until combined.
With a wooden spoon, stir in the flour and almonds until well incorporated. Cover and refrigerate for about 1 hour or until chilled and the dough is easy to handle.
Preheat the oven to 325F.
Shape the dough into 1-inch balls. Place the balls 2 inches apart init an ungreased cookie sheet. Dip a glass in the additional powdered sugar and use it to flatten each ball into ¼ -inch thickness, dipping the bottom of the glass every time you flatten a ball into cookies.
Place the cookie sheet into the preheated oven; bake for about 12-14 minutes or until the cookies are set.
When the cookies are baked, transfer them on wire racks. While they are still warm, brush with the rose water, if desired. Sprinkle with more powdered sugar. Let cool completely on the wire racks.
Notes: If using rose water, make sure that you use the edible kind. To store, layer the cookies with waxed paper between each cookie and keep on airtight containers. Close the container tightly and store at room temperature for up to 3 days or freeze for up to 3 months.

954. Cocoa Sweet Cherry Cream

Preparation Time: 2 hours
Cooking Time: 0 minutes
Servings: 4

Ingredients:

½ cup cocoa powder
¾ cup red cherry jam
¼ cup stevia
2 cups water
lb. cherries, pitted and halved

Directions:

In a blender, mix the cherries with the water and the rest of the ingredients, pulse well, divide into cups and keep in the fridge for 2 hours before serving.

955. Oatmeal Cakes With Mango

Preparation Time: 5 minutes
Cooking Time: 17 minutes
Servings: 2

Ingredients:

Hot cakes:
2 cups of oatmeal
3 eggs
1 tablespoon baking powder
1¼ cups of natural yogurt
1 teaspoon vanilla extract
1 cup chopped apple in small cubes
Oil spray
Mango honey (syrup):
2 cups diced mango
Orange juice
1 tablespoon maple honey
1 tablespoon vanilla extract
1 cinnamon stick

Directions:

In the pot, place all the ingredients of mango honey. Cover with valve open and cook at medium-high temperature until it whistles (in about 5 minutes). Reduce the temperature to low, remove the lid and continue cooking for 4 more minutes. Let cool a little and blend for a few seconds until you get a homogeneous mixture.
Also, blend all the ingredients of the hotcakes (except apple and oil spray) at speed 6, for 1 minute (until you get a homogeneous consistency). Pour into the Mixing Bowl and stir with the apple pieces, using the Balloon Whisk.
Preheat at medium-high temperature for 2 minutes. Reduce the temperature to low and sprinkle some oil spray.
Cook 6 to 8 hotcakes, for 2 minutes per side. Repeat with the remaining mixture.

956. Pumpkin Cream

Preparation Time: 5 minutes
Cooking Time: 5 minutes
Servings: 2

Ingredients:

2 cups canned pumpkin flesh
2 tbsps. stevia
tsp. vanilla extract
tbsps. water
A pinch of pumpkin spice

Directions:

In a pan, combine the pumpkin flesh with the other ingredients, simmer for 5 minutes, divide into cups and serve cold.

957. Vanilla Apple Compote

Preparation Time: 10 minutes
Cooking Time: 15 minutes
Servings: 6

Ingredients

3 cups apples, cored and cubed
1 tsp vanilla
3/4 cup coconut sugar
1 cup of water
2 tbsp fresh lime juice

Directions

Add all ingredients into the inner pot of instant pot and stir well.
Seal pot with lid and cook on high for 15 minutes.
Once done, allow to release pressure naturally for 10 minutes then release remaining using quick release. Remove lid.
Stir and serve.

958. Chocolate Rice

Preparation Time: 10 minutes
Cooking Time: 20 minutes
Servings: 4

Ingredients

1 cup of rice
1 tbsp cocoa powder
2 tbsp maple syrup
2 cups almond milk

Directions

Add all ingredients into the inner pot of instant pot and stir well.
Seal pot with lid and cook on high for 20 minutes.
Once done, allow to release pressure naturally for 10 minutes then release remaining using quick release. Remove lid.
Stir and serve.

959. Raisins Cinnamon Peaches

Preparation Time: 10 minutes
Cooking Time: 15 minutes
Servings: 4

Ingredients

4 peaches, cored and cut into chunks
1 tsp vanilla
1 tsp cinnamon
1/2 cup raisins
1 cup of water

Directions

Add all ingredients into the inner pot of instant pot and stir well.
Seal pot with lid and cook on high for 15 minutes.
Once done, allow to release pressure naturally for 10 minutes then release remaining using quick release. Remove lid.
Stir and serve.

960. Lemon Pear Compote

Preparation Time: 10 minutes
Cooking Time: 15 minutes
Servings: 6

Ingredients

3 cups pears, cored and cut into chunks
1 tsp vanilla
1 tsp liquid stevia
1 tbsp lemon zest, grated
2 tbsp lemon juice

Directions

Add all ingredients into the inner pot of instant pot and stir well.
Seal pot with lid and cook on high for 15 minutes.
Once done, allow to release pressure naturally for 10 minutes then release remaining using quick release. Remove lid.
Stir and serve.

961. Cold Lemon Squares

Preparation Time: 30 minutes
Cooking Time: 0 minutes
Servings: 4

Ingredients:

1 cup avocado oil + a drizzle
2 bananas, peeled and chopped
1 tablespoon honey
¼ cup lemon juice
A pinch of lemon zest, grated

Directions:

In your food processor, mix the bananas with the rest of the ingredients, pulse well and spread on the bottom of a pan greased with a drizzle of oil.
Put in the fridge for 30 minutes, slice into squares and serve.

962. Blackberry and Apples Cobbler

Servings: 6
Preparation Time: 10 minutes
Cooking Time: 30 minutes

Ingredients:

¾ cup stevia
6 cups blackberries
¼ cup apples, cored and cubed
¼ teaspoon baking powder
1 tablespoon lime juice
½ cup almond flour
½ cup water
3 and ½ tablespoon avocado oil
Cooking spray

Directions:

In a bowl, mix the berries with half of the stevia and lemon juice, sprinkle some flour all over, whisk and pour into a baking dish greased with cooking spray.
In another bowl, mix flour with the rest of the sugar, baking powder, the water and the oil, and stir the whole thing with your hands.
Spread over the berries, introduce in the oven at 375° F and bake for 30 minutes.
Serve warm.

963. Black Tea Cake

Servings: 8
Preparation Time: 10 minutes
Cooking Time: 35 minutes

Ingredients:

6 tablespoons black tea powder
2 cups almond milk, warmed up
1 cup avocado oil
2 cups stevia
4 eggs
2 teaspoons vanilla extract
3 and ½ cups almond flour
1 teaspoon baking soda
3 teaspoons baking powder

Directions:

In a bowl, combine the almond milk with the oil, stevia and the rest of the ingredients and whisk well.
Pour this into a cake pan lined with parchment paper, introduce in the oven at 350° F and bake for 35 minutes.
Leave the cake to cool down, slice and serve.

964. Green Tea and Vanilla Cream

Servings: 4
Preparation Time: 2 hours
Cooking Time: 0 minutes

Ingredients:

14 ounces almond milk, hot
2 tablespoons green tea powder
14 ounces heavy cream
3 tablespoons stevia
1 teaspoon vanilla extract
1 teaspoon gelatin powder

Directions:

In a bowl, combine the almond milk with the green tea powder and the rest of the ingredients, whisk well, cool down, divide into cups and keep in the fridge for 2 hours before serving.

965. Figs Pie

Servings: 8
Preparation Time: 10 minutes
Cooking Time: 1 hour

Ingredients:

½ cup stevia

6 figs, cut into quarters
½ teaspoon vanilla extract
1 cup almond flour
4 eggs, whisked

Directions:

Spread the figs on the bottom of a spring form pan lined with parchment paper.
In a bowl, combine the other ingredients, whisk and pour over the figs,
Bake at 375° F for 1 hour, flip the pie upside down when it's done and serve.

966. Cherry Cream

Servings: 4
Preparation Time: 2 hours
Cooking Time: 0 minutes

Ingredients:

2 cups cherries, pitted and chopped
1 cup almond milk
½ cup whipping cream
3 eggs, whisked
1/3 cup stevia
1 teaspoon lemon juice
½ teaspoon vanilla extract

Directions:

In your food processor, combine the cherries with the milk and the rest of the ingredients, pulse well, divide into cups and keep in the fridge for 2 hours before serving.

967. Strawberries Cream

Servings: 4
Preparation Time: 10 minutes
Cooking Time: 20 minutes

Ingredients:

½ cup stevia
2 pounds strawberries, chopped
1 cup almond milk
Zest of 1 lemon, grated
½ cup heavy cream
3 egg yolks, whisked

Directions:

Heat up a pan with the milk over medium-high heat, add the stevia and the rest of the ingredients, whisk well, simmer for 20 minutes, divide into cups and serve cold.

968. Picositos Brownies

Preparation Time: 5 minutes
Cooking Time: 15 minutes;
Servings: 8

Ingredients:

3 cups brownies mix
2 eggs
1/3 cup of milk
½ teaspoon cayenne pepper
1 teaspoon cinnamon
1 teaspoon vanilla extract
¼ cup chocolate sprinkles
Liquid candy to taste (decoration)
Chocolate sauce to taste (decoration)
Oil spray

Directions:

In a bowl, stir the following ingredients until a homogeneous mixture is obtained. Be sure to add them little by little, in the same order: mix for brownies, eggs, milk, cayenne pepper, cinnamon, vanilla and chocolate sprinkles.
Preheat the skillet at medium-high temperature for 2 and a half minutes. Cover the pot with the spray oil and reduce the temperature to low. Make sure the oil does not start to burn.
Add the previous mixture immediately, cover with the valve closed and cook for 15 minutes. Turn off the pot, remove the pan from the burner and let it sit for 3 minutes. Carefully invert the brownies on the Bamboo Cutting Board, slice it and serve with caramel or chocolate sauce.

969. Fruit Crepes

Preparation Time: 5 minutes
Cooking Time: 15 minutes
Servings: 4

Ingredients:

Crepes:
1 cup wheat flour
2 eggs
1¼ cups of milk
1 teaspoon vanilla extract
2 tablespoons melted butter
a pinch of salt
Powdered sugar to taste (powdered sugar)
Olive oil spray
Filling
2 cups of strawberries, sliced
½ cup sour cream
¼ cup brown sugar
1 teaspoon vanilla extract

Directions:

In a bowl, combine the flour and eggs. Add the milk gradually. Then add the vanilla extract, butter, salt and icing sugar. Beat well until you get a homogeneous mixture.
In the other bowl, combine the filling ingredients well with the help of the Spatula.
Preheat the skillet at medium-high temperature for about 2 and a half minutes and immediately lower the temperature to low. Cover the pan with olive oil spray.
With the help of the ladle, add approximately 1/8 cup of the mixture in the pan. Tilt the pan slightly to allow the mixture to spread evenly across the surface.
Cook the crepes for 40 to 45 seconds per side, or until lightly browned. Use the Silicone Spatula to flip them.
Repeat steps 4 and 5 with the remaining mixture. Add more spray oil, if necessary.
Fill the crepes and serve with syrup.

970. Crème Caramel

Preparation Time: 1 hour
Cooking Time: 1 hour
Servings: 12

Ingredients:

5 cups of whole milk
2 tsp vanilla extract
8 large egg yolks
4 large-sized eggs
2 cups sugar, divided
¼ cup 0f water

Directions:

Preheat the oven to 350°F
Heat the milk on medium heat until it is scalded.
Mix 1 cup of sugar and eggs in a bowl and add it to the eggs.
With a nonstick pan on high heat, boil the water and remaining sugar. Do not stir, instead whirl the pan. When the sugar forms caramel, divide it into ramekins.
Divide the egg mixture into the ramekins and place in a baking pan. Add water to the pan until it is half full. Bake for 30 minutes.
Remove the ramekins from the baking pan, cool, then refrigerate for at least 8 hours.
Serve.

971. Galaktoboureko

Preparation Time: 30 minutes
Cooking Time: 90 minutes
Servings: 12

Ingredients:

4 cups sugar, divided
1 tbsp. fresh lemon juice
1 cup of water
1 Tbsp. plus 1 ½ tsp grated lemon zest, divided into 10 cups
Room temperature whole milk
1 cup plus 2 tbsps. unsalted butter, melted and divided into 2
Tbsps. vanilla extract
7 large-sized eggs
1 cup of fine semolina
1 package phyllo, thawed and at room temperature

Directions:

Preheat oven to 350°F
Mix 2 cups of sugar, lemon juice, 1 ½ tsp of lemon zest, and water. Boil over medium heat. Set aside.
Mix the milk, 2 Tbsps. of butter, and vanilla in a pot and put on medium heat. Remove from heat when milk is scalded
Mix the eggs and semolina in a bowl, then add the mixture to the scalded milk.
Put the egg-milk mixture on medium heat. Stir until it forms a custard-like material.
Brush butter on each sheet of phyllo and arrange all over the baking pan until everywhere is covered. Spread the custard on the bottom pile phyllo
Arrange the buttered phyllo all over the top of the custard until every inch is covered.
Bake for about 40 minutes. cover the top of the pie with all the prepared syrup.
Serve.

972. Kourabiedes Almond Cookies

Preparation Time: 20 minutes
Cooking Time: 50 minutes
Servings: 20

Ingredients:

1 ½ cups unsalted butter, clarified, at room temperature 2 cups
Confectioners' sugar, divided
1 large egg yolk
2 tbsps. brandy
1 1/2 tsp baking powder
1 tsp vanilla extract
5 ⁄ cups all-purpose flour, sifted
1 cup roasted almonds, chopped

Directions:

Preheat the oven to 350°F
Thoroughly mix butter and ½ cup of sugar in a bowl. Add in the egg after a while. Create a brandy mixture by mixing the brandy and baking powder. Add the mixture to the egg, add vanilla, then keep beating until the ingredients are properly blended
Add flour and almonds to make a dough. Roll the dough to form crescent shapes. You should be able to get about 40 pieces. Place the pieces on a baking sheet, then bake in the oven for 25 minutes.
Allow the cookies to cool, then coat them with the remaining confectioner's sugar.
Serve.

973. Ekmek Kataifi

Preparation Time: 30 minutes
Cooking Time: 45 minutes
Servings: 10

Ingredients:

1 cup of sugar
1 cup of water
2 (2-inch) strips lemon peel, pith removed
1 tbsp. fresh lemon juice
½ cup plus 1 tbsp. unsalted butter, melted
½lbs. frozen kataifi pastry, thawed, at room temperature
2 ½ cups whole milk
½ tsp. ground mastiha
2 large eggs
¼ cup fine semolina
1 tsp. of cornstarch
¼ cup of sugar
½ cup sweetened coconut flakes
1 cup whipping cream
1 tsp. vanilla extract
1 tsp. powdered milk
3 tbsps. of confectioners' sugar
½ cup chopped unsalted pistachios

Directions:

Set the oven to 350°F. Grease the baking pan with 1. Tbsp of butter.
Put a pot on medium heat, then add water, sugar, lemon juice, lemon peel. Leave to boil for about 10 minutes. Reserve.
Untangle the kataifi, coat with the leftover butter, then place in the baking pan.
Mix the milk and mastiha, then place it on medium heat. Remove from heat when the milk is scalded, then cool the mixture.
Mix the eggs, cornstarch, semolina, and sugar in a bowl, stir thoroughly, then whisk the cooled milk mixture into the bowl.
Transfer the egg and milk mixture to a pot and place on heat. Wait for it to thicken like custard, then add the coconut flakes and cover it with a plastic wrap. Cool.
Spread the cooled custard-like material over the kataifi. Place in the refrigerator for at least 8 hours.
Strategically remove the kataifi from the pan with a knife. Remove it in such a way that the mold faces up.
Whip a cup of cream, add 1 tsp. vanilla, 1tsp. powdered milk, and 3 tbsps. Of sugar. Spread the mixture all over the custard, wait for it to harden, then flip and add the leftover cream mixture to the kataifi side.

974. Revani Syrup Cake

Preparation Time: 30 minutes
Cooking Time: 3 hours
Servings: 24

Ingredients:

1 tbsp. unsalted butter
2 tbsps. all-purpose flour
1 cup ground rusk or bread crumbs
1 cup fine semolina flour
¾ cup ground toasted almonds
3 tsp baking powder
16 large eggs
2 tbsps. vanilla extract
3 cups of sugar, divided
3 cups of water
5 (2-inch) strips lemon peel, pith removed
3 tbsps. fresh lemon juice
1 oz of brandy

Directions:

Preheat the oven to 350°F. Grease the baking pan with 1 Tbsp. of butter and flour.
Mix the rusk, almonds, semolina, baking powder in a bowl.
In another bowl, mix the eggs, 1 cup of sugar, vanilla, and whisk with an electric mixer for about 5 minutes. Add the semolina mixture to the eggs and stir.
Pour the stirred batter into the greased baking pan and place in the preheated oven.
With the remaining sugar, lemon peels, and water make the syrup by boiling the mixture on medium heat. Add the lemon juice after 6 minutes, then cook for 3 minutes. Remove the lemon peels and set the syrup aside.

After the cake is done in the oven, spread the syrup over the cake.
Cut the cake as you please and serve.

975. Almonds and Oats Pudding

Preparation Time: 10 minutes
Cooking Time: 15 minutes
Servings: 4

Ingredients:

1 tablespoon lemon juice
Zest of 1 lime
1 and ½ cups almond milk
1 teaspoon almond extract
½ cup oats
2 tablespoons stevia
½ cup silver almonds, chopped

Directions:

In a pan, combine the almond milk with the lime zest and the other ingredients, whisk, bring to a simmer and cook over medium heat for 15 minutes.
Divide the mix into bowls and serve cold.

976. Chocolate Cups

Preparation Time: 2 hours
Cooking Time: 0 minutes
Servings: 6

Ingredients:

½ cup avocado oil
1 cup, chocolate, melted
1 teaspoon matcha powder
3 tablespoons stevia

Directions:

In a bowl, mix the chocolate with the oil and the rest of the ingredients, whisk really well, divide into cups and keep in the freezer for 2 hours before serving.

977. Mango Bowls

Preparation Time: 30 minutes
Cooking Time: 0 minutes
Servings: 4

Ingredients:

3 cups mango, cut into medium chunks
½ cup coconut water
¼ cup stevia
1 teaspoon vanilla extract

Directions:

In a blender, combine the mango with the rest of the ingredients, pulse well, divide into bowls and serve cold.

978. Apples and Plum Cake

Servings: 4
Preparation Time: 10 minutes
Cooking Time: 40 minutes

Ingredients:

7 ounces almond flour
1 egg, whisked
5 tablespoons stevia
3 ounces warm almond milk
2 pounds plums, pitted and cut into quarters
2 apples, cored and chopped
Zest of 1 lemon, grated
1 teaspoon baking powder

Directions:

In a bowl, mix the almond milk with the egg, stevia, and the rest of the ingredients except the cooking spray and whisk well.
Grease a cake pan with the oil, pour the cake mix inside, introduce in the oven and bake at 350° F for 40 minutes.
Cool down, slice and serve.

979. Cinnamon Chickpeas Cookies

Preparation Time: 10 minutes
Cooking Time: 20 minutes
Servings: 12

Ingredients:

1 cup canned chickpeas, drained, rinsed and mashed
2 cups almond flour
1 teaspoon cinnamon powder
1 teaspoon baking powder
1 cup avocado oil
½ cup stevia
1 egg, whisked
2 teaspoons almond extract
1 cup raisins
1 cup coconut, unsweetened and shredded

Directions:

In a bowl, combine the chickpeas with the flour, cinnamon and the other ingredients, and whisk well until you obtain a dough.
Scoop tablespoons of dough on a baking sheet lined with parchment paper, introduce them in the oven at 350° F and bake for 20 minutes.
Leave them to cool down for a few minutes and serve.

980. Cocoa Brownies

Preparation Time: 10 minutes
Cooking Time: 20 minutes
Servings: 8

Ingredients:

30 ounces canned lentils, rinsed and drained
1 tablespoon honey
1 banana, peeled and chopped
½ teaspoon baking soda
4 tablespoons almond butter
2 tablespoons cocoa powder
Cooking spray

Directions:

In a food processor, combine the lentils with the honey and the other ingredients except the cooking spray and pulse well.
Pour this into a pan greased with cooking spray, spread evenly, introduce in the oven at 375° F and bake for 20 minutes.
Cut the brownies and serve cold.

981. Cardamom Almond Cream

Preparation Time: 30 minutes
Cooking Time: 0 minutes
Servings: 4

Ingredients:

Juice of 1 lime
½ cup stevia
1 and ½ cups water
3 cups almond milk
½ cup honey
2 teaspoons cardamom, ground
1 teaspoon rose water
1 teaspoon vanilla extract

Directions:

In a blender, combine the almond milk with the cardamom and the rest of the ingredients, pulse well, divide into cups and keep in the fridge for 30 minutes before serving.

982. Banana Cinnamon Cupcakes

Preparation Time: 10 minutes
Cooking Time: 20 minutes
Servings: 4

Ingredients:

4 tablespoons avocado oil
4 eggs

½ cup orange juice
2 teaspoons cinnamon powder
1 teaspoon vanilla extract
2 bananas, peeled and chopped
¾ cup almond flour
½ teaspoon baking powder
Cooking spray

Directions:

In a bowl, combine the oil with the eggs, orange juice and the other ingredients except the cooking spray, whisk well, pour in a cupcake pan greased with the cooking spray, introduce in the oven at 350° F and bake for 20 minutes. Cool the cupcakes down and serve.

983. Rhubarb and Apples Cream

Preparation Time: 10 minutes
Cooking Time: 0 minutes
Servings: 6

Ingredients:

3 cups rhubarb, chopped
1 and ½ cups stevia
2 eggs, whisked
½ teaspoon nutmeg, ground
1 tablespoon avocado oil
1/3 cup almond milk

Directions:

In a blender, combine the rhubarb with the stevia and the rest of the ingredients, pulse well, divide into cups and serve cold.

984. Almond Rice Dessert

Preparation Time: 10 minute
Cooking Time: 20 minutes
Servings: 4

Ingredients:

1 cup white rice
2 cups almond milk
1 cup almonds, chopped
½ cup stevia
1 tablespoon cinnamon powder
½ cup pomegranate seeds

Directions:

In a pot, mix the rice with the milk and stevia, bring to a simmer and cook for 20 minutes, stirring often.
Add the rest of the ingredients, stir, divide into bowls and serve.

985. Peach Sorbet

Preparation Time: 2 hours
Cooking Time: 10 minutes
Servings: 4

Ingredients:

2 cups apple juice
1 cup stevia
2 tablespoons lemon zest, grated
2 pounds peaches, pitted and quartered

Directions:

Heat up a pan over medium heat, add the apple juice and the rest of the ingredients, simmer for 10 minutes, transfer to a blender, pulse, divide into cups and keep in the freezer for 2 hours before serving.

986. Cranberries and Pears Pie

Preparation Time: 10 minutes
Cooking Time: 40 minutes
Servings: 4

Ingredients:

2 cup cranberries
3 cups pears, cubed
A drizzle of olive oil
1 cup stevia
1/3 cup almond flour
1 cup rolled oats
¼ avocado oil

Directions:

In a bowl, mix the cranberries with the pears and the other ingredients except the olive oil and the oats, and stir well.
Grease a cake pan with a drizzle of olive oil, pour the pears mix inside, sprinkle the oats all over and bake at 350° F for 40 minutes.
Cool the mix down, and serve.

987. Chia and Berries Smoothie Bowl

Preparation Time: 5 minutes
Cooking Time: 0 minutes
Servings: 2

Ingredients:

1 and ½ cup almond milk
1 cup blackberries
¼ cup strawberries, chopped
1 and ½ tablespoons chia seeds
1 teaspoon cinnamon powder

Directions:

In a blender, combine the blackberries with the strawberries and the rest of the ingredients, pulse well, divide into small bowls and serve cold.

988. Minty Coconut Cream

Preparation Time: 4 minutes
Cooking Time: 0 minutes
Servings: 2

Ingredients:

1 banana, peeled
2 cups coconut flesh, shredded
3 tablespoons mint, chopped
1 and ½ cups coconut water
2 tablespoons stevia
½ avocado, pitted and peeled

Directions:

In a blender, combine the coconut with the banana and the rest of the ingredients, pulse well, divide into cups and serve cold.

989. Watermelon Cream

Preparation Time: 15 minutes
Cooking Time: 0 minutes
Servings: 2

Ingredients:

1-pound watermelon, peeled and chopped
1 teaspoon vanilla extract
1 cup heavy cream
1 teaspoon lime juice
2 tablespoons stevia

Directions:

In a blender, combine the watermelon with the cream and the rest of the ingredients, pulse well, divide into cups and keep in the fridge for 15 minutes before serving.

990. Pistachio Balls

Preparation Time: 10 minutes
Cooking Time: 5 minutes
Servings: 16

Ingredients:

½ cup pistachios, unsalted
1 cup dates, pitted
½ tsp ground fennel seeds
½ cup raisins
Pinch of pepper

Directions:

Add all ingredients into the food processor and process until well combined.
Make small balls and place onto the baking tray.
Serve and enjoy.

991. Roasted Almonds

Preparation Time: 10 minutes
Cooking Time: 20 minutes
Servings: 12

Ingredients:

2 ½ cups almonds
¼ tsp cayenne
¼ tsp ground coriander
¼ tsp cumin
¼ tsp chili powder
1 tbsp fresh rosemary, chopped
1 tbsp olive oil
2 ½ tbsp maple syrup
Pinch of salt

Directions:

Preheat the oven to 325 F.
Spray a baking tray with cooking spray and set aside.
In a mixing bowl, whisk together oil, cayenne, coriander, cumin, chili powder, rosemary, maple syrup, and salt.
Add almond and stir to coat.
Spread almonds onto the prepared baking tray.
Roast almonds in preheated oven for 20 minutes. Stir halfway through.
Serve and enjoy.

992. Chocolate Matcha Balls

Preparation Time: 10 minutes
Cooking Time: 5 minutes
Servings: 15

Ingredients:

2 tbsp unsweetened cocoa powder
3 tbsp oats, gluten-free
½ cup pine nuts
½ cup almonds
1 cup dates, pitted
2 tbsp matcha powder

Directions:

Add oats, pine nuts, almonds, and dates into a food processor and process until well combined.
Place matcha powder in a small dish.
Make small balls from mixture and coat with matcha powder.
Enjoy or store in refrigerator until ready to eat.

993. Healthy & Quick Energy Bites

Preparation Time: 10 minutes
Cooking Time: 0 minutes
Servings: 20

Ingredients:

2 cups cashew nuts
¼ tsp cinnamon
1 tsp lemon zest
4 tbsp dates, chopped
1/3 cup unsweetened shredded coconut
¾ cup dried apricots

Directions:

Line baking tray with parchment paper and set aside.
Add all ingredients in a food processor and process until the mixture is crumbly and well combined.
Make small balls from mixture and place on a prepared baking tray.
Serve and enjoy.

994. Creamy Yogurt Banana Bowls

Preparation Time: 10 minutes
Cooking Time: 0 minutes
Servings: 4

Ingredients:

2 bananas, sliced
½ tsp ground nutmeg
3 tbsp flaxseed meal
¼ cup creamy peanut butter
4 cups Greek yogurt

Directions:

Divide Greek yogurt between 4 serving bowls and top with sliced bananas.
Add peanut butter in microwave-safe bowl and microwave for 30 seconds.
Drizzle 1 tablespoon of melted peanut butter on each bowl on top of the sliced bananas.
Sprinkle cinnamon and flax meal on top and serve.

995. Chocolate Mousse

Preparation Time: 10 minutes
Cooking Time: 6 minutes
Servings: 5

Ingredients:

4 egg yolks
½ tsp vanilla
½ cup unsweetened almond milk
1 cup whipping cream
¼ cup cocoa powder
¼ cup water
½ cup Swerve
1/8 tsp salt

Directions:

Add egg yolks to a large bowl and whisk until well beaten.
In a saucepan, add swerve, cocoa powder, and water and whisk until well combined.
Add almond milk and cream to the saucepan and whisk until well mix.
Once saucepan mixtures are heated up then turn off the heat.
Add vanilla and salt and stir well.
Add a tablespoon of chocolate mixture into the eggs and whisk until well combined.
Slowly pour remaining chocolate to the eggs and whisk until well combined.
Pour batter into the ramekins.
Pour 1 ½ cups of water into the instant pot then place a trivet in the pot.
Place ramekins on a trivet.
Seal pot with lid and select manual and set timer for 6 minutes.
Release pressure using quick release method than open the lid.
Carefully remove ramekins from the instant pot and let them cool completely.
Serve and enjoy.

996. Carrot Spread

Preparation Time: 10 minutes
Cooking Time: 10 minutes
Servings: 4

Ingredients:

¼ cup veggie stock
A pinch of salt and black pepper
1 teaspoon onion powder
½ teaspoon garlic powder
½ teaspoon oregano, dried
1 pound carrots, sliced
½ cup coconut cream

Directions:

In your instant pot, combine all the ingredients except the cream, put the lid on and cook on High for 10 minutes. Release the pressure naturally for 10 minutes, transfer the carrots mix to food processor, add the cream, pulse well, divide into bowls and serve cold.

997. Decadent Croissant Bread Pudding

Preparation Time: 5 minutes
Cooking Time: 15 minutes
Servings: 6

Ingredients

1/2 cup double cream
6 tablespoons honey
1/4 cup rum, divided
2 eggs, whisked
1 teaspoon cinnamon
A pinch of salt
A pinch of grated nutmeg
1 teaspoon vanilla essence
8 croissants, torn into pieces
1 cup pistachios, toasted and chopped

Directions

Spritz a baking pan with cooking spray and set it aside.
In a mixing bowl, whisk the eggs, double cream, honey, rum, cinnamon, salt, nutmeg, and vanilla; whisk until everything is well incorporated.
Place the croissants in the prepared baking dish. Pour the custard over your croissants. Fold in the pistachios and press with a wide spatula.
Add 1 cup of water and metal rack to the inner pot of your Instant Pot. Lower the baking dish onto the rack.
Secure the lid. Choose the "Manual" mode and cook for 12 minutes at High pressure. Once cooking is complete, use a quick pressure release; carefully remove the lid.
Serve at room temperature or cold. Bon appétit!

998. Poached Apples with Greek Yogurt and Granola

Preparation Time: 5 minutes
Cooking Time: 15 minutes
Servings 4

Ingredients

4 medium-sized apples, peeled
1/2 cup brown sugar
1 vanilla bean
1 cinnamon stick
1/2 cup cranberry juice
1 cup water
1/2 cup 2% Greek yogurt
1/2 cup granola

Directions

Add the apples, brown sugar, water, cranberry juice, vanilla bean, and cinnamon stick to the inner pot of your Instant Pot.
Secure the lid. Choose the "Manual" mode and cook for 5 minutes at High pressure. Once cooking is complete, use a natural pressure release for 5 minutes; carefully remove the lid. Reserve poached apples.
Press the "Sauté" button and let the sauce simmer on "Less" mode until it has thickened.
Place the apples in serving bowls. Add the syrup and top each apple with granola and Greek yogurt. Enjoy!

999. Jasmine Rice Pudding with Cranberries

Preparation Time: 5 minutes
Cooking Time: 15 minutes
Servings 4

Ingredients

1 cup apple juice
1 heaping tablespoon honey
1/3 cup granulated sugar
1 ½ cups jasmine rice
1 cup water
1/4 teaspoon ground cinnamon
1/4 teaspoon ground cloves
1/3 teaspoon ground cardamom
1 teaspoon vanilla extract
3 eggs, well-beaten
1/2 cup cranberries

Directions

Thoroughly combine the apple juice, honey, sugar, jasmine rice, water, and spices in the inner pot of your Instant Pot.
Secure the lid. Choose the "Manual" mode and cook for 4 minutes at High pressure. Once cooking is complete, use a natural pressure release for 5 minutes; carefully remove the lid.
Press the "Sauté" button and fold in the eggs. Cook on "Less" mode until heated through.
Ladle into individual bowls and top with dried cranberries. Enjoy!

1000. Orange and Almond Cupcakes

Preparation Time: 5 minutes
Cooking Time: 20 minutes
Servings 9

Ingredients

Cupcakes:
1 orange extract
2 tablespoons olive oil
2 tablespoons ghee, at room temperature
3 eggs, beaten
2 ounces Greek yogurt
2 cups cake flour
A pinch of salt
1 tablespoon grated orange rind
1/2 cup brown sugar
1/2 cup almonds, chopped
Cream Cheese Frosting:
2 ounces cream cheese
1 tablespoon whipping cream
1/2 cup butter, at room temperature
1 ½ cups confectioners' sugar, sifted
1/3 teaspoon vanilla
A pinch of salt

Directions

Mix the orange extract, olive oil, ghee, eggs, and Greek yogurt until well combined.
Thoroughly combine the cake flour, salt, orange rind, and brown sugar in a separate mixing bowl. Add the egg/yogurt mixture to the flour mixture. Stir in the chopped almonds and mix again.
Place parchment baking liners on the bottom of a muffin tin. Pour the batter into the muffin tin.
Place 1 cup of water and metal trivet in the inner pot of your Instant Pot. Lower the prepared muffin tin onto the trivet.
Secure the lid. Choose the "Manual" mode and cook for 11 minutes at High pressure. Once cooking is complete, use a quick pressure release; carefully remove the lid. Transfer to wire racks.
Meanwhile, make the frosting by mixing all ingredients until creamy. Frost your cupcakes and enjoy!

1001. Bread Pudding

Preparation Time: 5 minutes
Cooking Time: 25 minutes
Servings: 4

Ingredients:

4 egg yolks
3 cups brioche, cubed
2 cups half and half

½ teaspoon vanilla extract
1 cup sugar
2 tablespoons butter, softened
1 cup cranberries
2 cups warm water
½ cup raisins
Zest from 1 lime

Directions:

Grease a baking dish with some butter and set the dish aside. In a bowl, mix the egg yolks with the half and half, cubed brioche, vanilla extract, sugar, cranberries, raisins, and lime zest and stir well. Pour this into greased dish, cover with some aluminum foil and set aside for 10 minutes. Put the dish in the steamer basket of the Instant Pot, add the warm water to the Instant Pot, cover, and cook on the Manual setting for 20 minutes. Release the pressure naturally, uncover the Instant Pot, take the bread pudding out, set it aside to cool down, slice, and serve it.

1002. Ruby Pears

Preparation Time: 10 minutes
Cooking Time: 10 minutes
Servings: 4

Ingredients:

4 pears
Juice and zest of 1 lemon
26 ounces grape juice
11 ounces currant jelly
4 garlic cloves, peeled
½ vanilla bean
4 peppercorns
2 rosemary sprigs

Directions:

Pour the jelly and grape juice into the Instant Pot and mix with lemon zest and lemon juice. Dip each pear in this mix, wrap them in aluminum foil and arrange them in the steamer basket of the Instant Pot. Add the garlic cloves, peppercorns, rosemary, and vanilla bean to the juice mixture, cover the Instant Pot and cook on the Manual setting for 10 minutes. Release the pressure, uncover the Instant Pot, take the pears out, unwrap them, arrange them on plates, and serve cold with cooking juice poured on top.

1003. Grapes Stew

Preparation Time: 10 minutes
Cooking Time: 10 minutes
Servings: 4

Ingredients:

2/3 cup stevia
1 tablespoon olive oil
1/3 cup coconut water
1 teaspoon vanilla extract
1 teaspoon lemon zest, grated
2 cup red grapes, halved

Directions:

Heat up a pan with the water over medium heat, add the oil, stevia and the rest of the ingredients, toss, simmer for 10 minutes, divide into cups and serve.

1004. Vegan Whipped Cream

Preparation Time: 10 minutes
Cooking Time: 0 minutes
Servings: 2

Ingredients:

1 (13- to 14-ounce) can unsweetened, full-fat coconut milk
3 teaspoons sugar or any vegan sweetener
1 teaspoon pure vanilla extract

Directions:

Put the can of full-fat coconut milk overnight in the refrigerator.
Place it in a large metal bowl and electric beaters from an electric hand mixer in the freezer for an hour, then prepare the whipped cream.
Open a cold can of coconut milk (make sure to not shake it). The coconut cream solids will have hardened on the top. Spoon just the solids into the cold mixing bowl, avoiding the liquid.
Use an electric mixer in mixing coconut cream until stiff peaks form.
Then add sugar and vanilla, then beat another minute. Taste and add more sweetener if needed.
Leftovers: This whipped cream will stay fresh for 3 to 5 days in a sealed container in the refrigerator.

1005. Patty's Three-Minute Fudge

Preparation Time: 10 minutes
Cooking Time: 0 minutes
Servings: 6

Ingredients:

Vegan butter
2 cups dark semisweet vegan chocolate chips
1 (14.5-ounce) can vegan sweetened condensed milk
1 teaspoon vanilla extract

Directions:

Grease an 8-inch square pan with vegan butter and line with parchment paper.
In a microwave-safe two-quart bowl, heat the chocolate chips and condensed milk on high for 1 minute. Let rest for a minute, then stir to combine. If needed, heat an additional 30 seconds. Stir until completely melted and the chocolate is smooth. Stir in the vanilla.
Pour the fudge into the prepared pan. Make it cool and set for about 1 hour. Then cut into squares.
The fudge will keep at room temperature, covered, for 1 to 2 days.

1006. Healthy Avocado Chocolate Pudding

Preparation Time: 5 minutes
Cooking Time: 0 minutes
Servings: 4

Ingredients:

6 avocados, peeled, pitted, and cut into chunks
½ cup pure maple syrup, or more to taste
¾ cup unsweetened cocoa powder
2 teaspoons vanilla extract
Fresh mint leaves, optional

Directions:

In a food processor, purée the avocados, maple syrup, cocoa powder, and vanilla until smooth.
Garnish with mint leaves, if desired.
Ingredient Tip: Avoid leftovers and eat it all! The avocado will oxidize and turn brown after just a few hours.

1007. Mexican Chocolate Mousse

Preparation Time: 15 minutes
Cooking Time: 0 minutes
Servings: 4

Ingredients:

8 ounces bittersweet or semisweet vegan chocolate
1¾ cups (about 1 pound) silken tofu
½ cup pure maple syrup
1 teaspoon vanilla
1½ teaspoons ground cinnamon

Directions:

Create a double boiler by bringing a

medium pot filled halfway with water to a low simmer. Place a heatproof bowl above and make sure it is not touching the water. Add the chocolate to the bowl. Keep the pot over low heat and stir the chocolate until it is melted and silky smooth.
In a food processor, add all the ingredients. Blend until smooth.
Refrigerate before serving.
Substitution Tip: Substitute 1 teaspoon of chili powder for the ground cinnamon or add both for an authentic Mexican chocolate experience.

1008. Chocolate Peanut Butter Cups

Preparation Time: 20 minutes
Cooking Time: 0 minutes
Servings: 8

Ingredients:

5 ounces vegan semisweet chocolate, divided
½ cup smooth peanut butter
½ teaspoon vanilla
¼ teaspoon salt

Directions:

Line a muffin tray with 9 mini or regular paper cupcake liners.
Place half the chocolate in a microwave-safe bowl and microwave on high for 25 seconds, then take it out and stir.
Place bowl back in the microwave and repeat the process of cooking for 25 seconds, stopping and stirring, until the chocolate has melted.
Spoon 1 to 1½ teaspoons of melted chocolate into each cup. Place in the refrigerator for 10 minutes until solid.
Stir the peanut butter, vanilla, and salt together in a bowl. Transfer the peanut butter mixture to a resealable plastic bag and seal it tightly. Cut one corner of the plastic bag, then squeeze the bag to pipe 2 to 3 teaspoons of peanut butter in the middle of each cup. Smooth with a small spoon.
Melt the remaining chocolate. Spoon 1 to 1½ teaspoons of chocolate into the top of each cup. Smooth with a small spoon.
Refrigerate until solid, 30 to 40 minutes. Peel off the liners and enjoy. Remove it from the refrigerator. Let it sit for 15 or a few minutes if you like a softer chocolate.
Leftovers: Store leftovers in the refrigerator for up to 2 weeks or in the freezer for up to 1 month.

1009. Banana Ice Cream with Chocolate Sauce

Preparation Time: 10 minutes
Cooking Time: 0 minutes
Servings: 4

Ingredients:

½ cup raw unsalted cashews
¼ cup pure maple syrup
1 tablespoon unsweetened cocoa powder
1 teaspoon vanilla extract
¼ teaspoon salt
¼ cup water
6 ripe bananas, peeled and frozen

Directions:

Place cashews in a bowl and put water. Soak cashews for two hours or overnight. Drain and rinse.
In a food processor or blender, place the cashews, maple syrup, cocoa powder, vanilla, and salt. Blend, adding the water a couple of tablespoons at a time until you get a smooth consistency.
Transfer to an airtight container, then refrigerate. Bring to room temperature before using.
Place frozen bananas in the food processor. Process until you have smooth banana ice cream. Serve topped with chocolate sauce.
Ingredient Tip: The best way to freeze a banana is to start with ripe peeled bananas. Slice them into 2-inch chunks and arrange them in a single layer on a parchment-lined baking sheet. Pop them in the freezer. Once frozen, transfer to freezer-safe bags. Frozen bananas are also a delicious, healthy addition to smoothies. Individually freeze chunks of one banana, and you'll always be ready to create an icy, rich, creamy smoothie.

1010. Raspberry Lime Sorbet

Preparation Time: 15 minutes, plus 5 hours or more to chill
Cooking Time: 0 minutes
Servings: 4

Ingredients:

3 pints fresh raspberries or 2 (10-ounce) bags frozen
½ cup fresh orange juice
4 tablespoons pure maple syrup
3 tablespoons fresh lime juice
Dark chocolate curls, optional

Directions:

In a glass dish, combine the raspberries, orange juice, maple syrup, and lime juice. Stir well to mix. Cover then put in the freezer until frozen solid, about 5 hours.
Get it from the freezer and let it sit for 10 minutes. Crush chunks with a knife or large spoon and transfer the mixture to a food processor. Process this until smooth and creamy for 5 minutes. Serve immediately. The sorbet will freeze solid again, but can be processed again until creamy just before serving.
To serve, place a scoop into an ice cream dish. Garnish with fresh raspberries and dark chocolate curls, if using.
Preparation Tip: To make chocolate curls, use a vegetable peeler, and scrape the blade lengthwise across a piece of solid chocolate to create pretty, delicate curls. Refrigerate the curls until ready to use.

1011. Baked Apples with Dried Fruit

Preparation Time: 10 minutes
Cooking Time: 1 hour
Servings: 4

Ingredients:

4 large apples, cored to make a cavity
4 teaspoons raisins or cranberries
4 teaspoons pure maple syrup
1/2 teaspoon ground cinnamon
1/2 cup unsweetened apple juice or water

Directions:

Preheat the oven to 350°F.
Place apples in a baking pan that will hold them upright. Put the dried fruit into the cavities and drizzle with maple syrup. Sprinkle with cinnamon. Pour apple juice or water on the apples.
Cover loosely with foil and bake for 50 minutes to 1 hour, or until the apples are tender when pierced with a fork.
Servings: Suggestion: Serve the apples topped with Vegan Whipped Cream.

1012. Hemp Seed Brittle

Preparation Time: 10 minutes
Cooking Time: 10 minutes
Servings: 6

Ingredients:

¼ cup hemp seeds
2½ tablespoons brown rice flour
3 tablespoons melted coconut oil
2½ tablespoons pure maple syrup
Pinch salt

Directions:

Preheat the oven to 350°F. Line a baking sheet with parchment paper.
In a bowl, combine all ingredients, then mix well. Spread into an even layer on the baking sheet. Try to quickly else edges will burn.
Bake for 10 minutes and make sure the brittle doesn't burn. Turn off the oven and leave it for 30 minutes to cool down.
When it's completely cooled, break it into bite-size pieces with a sharp knife or your fingers.
Leftovers: Store leftovers in a sealed container at room temperature for 5 days or freeze for up to 1 month.

1013. Cardamom Date Bites

Preparation Time: 15 minutes, plus time to soak
Cooking Time: 15 minutes
Servings: 8

Ingredients:

1 cup pitted dates
3 cups old-fashioned rolled oats
¼ cup ground flaxseed
1 teaspoon ground cardamom
3 ripe bananas, mashed (about 1½ cups)

Directions:

Preheat the oven to 350°F. Line a baking sheet with parchment paper.
In a small bowl, place the dates and cover with hot water. Let it sit until softened, 10 to 30 minutes, depending on the dates, and then drain. Purée in a food processor or blender. Set the date paste aside.
In the food processor, grind the oats and ground flaxseed until they resemble flour.
In a large bowl, mix together the cardamom and mashed bananas. Stir in the ground oat-flaxseed mixture.
Form into walnut-size balls and flatten a little. Place on the baking sheet and form an indentation in the middle using a ¼ teaspoon measuring spoon. Fill each indentation with about ½ teaspoon of date paste.
Bake 15 minutes or until the bites are golden.

1014. Blueberry Frozen Yogurt

Preparation Time: 10 minutes
Cooking Time: 30 minutes
Servings: 6

Ingredients:

1-pint blueberries, fresh
2/3 cup honey
1 small lemon, juiced and zested
2 cups yogurt, chilled

Directions:

In a saucepan, combine the blueberries, honey, lemon juice, and zest.
Heat over medium heat and allow to simmer for 15 minutes while stirring constantly.
Once the liquid has reduced, transfer the fruits in a bowl and allow to cool in the fridge for another 15 minutes.

1015. Delectable Strawberry Popsicle

Preparation Time: 5 minutes
Cooking Time: 10 minutes
Servings: 5

Ingredients:

2 ½ cups fresh strawberry
½ cup almond milk

Directions:

Blend all ingredients until smooth.
Pour into the popsicle molds with sticks and freeze for at least 4 hours.
3 Serve chilled.

1016. Deliciously Cold Lychee Sorbet

Preparation Time: 0 minutes
Cooking Time: 5 minutes
Servings: 4

Ingredients:

2 cups fresh lychees, pitted and sliced
2 tablespoons honey
Mint leaves for garnish

Directions:

Place the lychee slices and honey in a food processor.
Pulse until smooth.
Pour in a container and place inside the fridge for at least two hours.
Scoop the sorbet and serve with mint leaves.

1017. Easy Fruit Compote

Preparation Time: 5 minutes
Cooking Time: 15 minutes
Servings: 2

Ingredients:

1-pound fresh fruits of your choice
2 tablespoons maple syrup
A dash of salt

Directions:

Slice the fruits thinly and place them in a saucepan.
Add the honey and salt.
Heat the saucepan over medium low heat and allow the fruits to simmer for 15 minutes or until the liquid has reduced.
Make sure that you stir constantly to prevent the fruits from sticking at the bottom of your pan and eventually burning.
Transfer in a lidded jar.
Allow to cool.
Serve with slices of whole wheat bread or vegan ice cream.

1018. Five Berry Mint Orange Infusion

Preparation Time: 10 minutes
Cooking Time: 10 minutes
Servings: 12

Ingredients:

½ cup water
3 orange pekoe tea bags
3 sprigs of mint
1 cup fresh strawberries
1 cup fresh golden raspberries
1 cup fresh raspberries
1 cup blackberries
1 cup fresh blueberries
1 cup pitted fresh cherries
1 bottle Sauvignon Blanc
½ cup pomegranate juice, natural
1 teaspoon vanilla

Directions:

In a saucepan, bring water to a boil over medium heat. Add the tea bags, mint and stir. Let it stand for 10 minutes.
In a large bowl, combine the rest of the ingredients.
Put in the fridge to chill for at least 3 hours.

CHAPTER 16: KETOGENIC MEDITERRANEAN RECIPES

1019. Beef and Cabbage Roast

Preparation Time: 10 minutes.
Cooking Time: 7 hours on low + 1 hour on low.
Servings: 10

Ingredients:

1 red onion, quartered
2 garlic cloves, minced
2-3 stocks celery, diced (approximately 1 cup)
4-6 dry pimento berries
2 bay leaves
5.5 pounds beef brisket (two pieces)
1 teaspoon chili powder
1 teaspoon ground cumin
2 cups broth, beef + 2 cups hot water
Salt and pepper to taste
1 medium cabbage (approximately 2.2 pounds), cut in half, then quartered

Directions:

Add all ingredients, except cabbage, to crock-pot in order of list.
Cover, cook on low for 7 hours.
Uncover, add the cabbage on top of the stew.
Re-cover, cook for 1 additional hour.

1020. Simple Chicken Chilli

Preparation Time: 10 minutes.
Cooking Time: 6 hours on low.
Servings: 8

Ingredients:

1 Tablespoon butter
1 red onion, sliced
1 bell pepper, sliced
2 garlic cloves, minced
3 pounds boneless chicken thighs
8 slices bacon, chopped
1 teaspoon chili powder
Salt and pepper to taste
1 cup chicken broth
¼ cup coconut milk
3 Tablespoons tomato paste

Directions:

Add all ingredients to the crock-pot, starting with the butter.
Cover, cook on low for 6 hours.
Shred the chicken with a fork in the crock-pot. Serve.

1021. Swordfish in Tarragon-Citrus Butter

Preparation Time: 5 minutes
Cooking Time: 20 minutes
Servings: 4

Ingredients:

1-pound swordfish steaks, cut into 2-inch pieces
1 teaspoon salt
¼ teaspoon freshly ground black pepper
¼ cup extra-virgin olive oil, plus 2 tablespoons, divided
2 tablespoons unsalted butter
Zest and juice of 2 clementine's
Zest and juice of 1 lemon
2 tablespoons chopped fresh tarragon
Sautéed greens, Riced Cauliflower, or Zucchini Noodles, for serving

Directions:

In a bowl, toss the swordfish with salt and pepper.
In a large skillet, heat ¼ cup olive oil over medium-high heat. Add the swordfish chunks to the hot oil and sear on all sides, 2 to 3 minutes per side, until they are lightly golden brown. Using a slotted spoon, remove the fish from the pan and keep warm.
Add the remaining 2 tablespoons olive oil and butter to the oil already in the pan and return the heat to medium-low. Once the butter has melted, whisk in the clementine and lemon zests and juices, along with the tarragon. Season with salt. Return the fish pieces to the pan and toss to coat in the butter sauce. Serve the fish drizzled with sauce over sautéed greens, Riced Cauliflower, or Zucchini Noodles.

1022. Escabeche

Preparation Time: 10 minutes
Cooking Time: 20 minutes, plus 15 minutes to rest
Servings: 4

Ingredients:

1 pound wild-caught Spanish mackerel fillets, cut into four pieces
1 teaspoon salt
½ teaspoon freshly ground black pepper
8 tablespoons extra-virgin olive oil, divided
1 bunch asparagus, trimmed and cut into 2-inch pieces
1 (13.75-ounce) can artichoke hearts, drained and quartered
4 large garlic cloves, peeled and crushed
2 bay leaves
¼ cup red wine vinegar
½ teaspoon smoked paprika

Directions:

Sprinkle the fillets with salt and pepper and let sit at room temperature for 5 minutes.
In a large skillet, heat 2 tablespoons olive oil over medium-high heat. Add the fish, skin-side up, and cook 5 minutes. Flip and cook 5 minutes on the other side, until browned and cooked through. Transfer to a serving dish, pour the cooking oil over the fish, and cover to keep warm.
Heat the remaining 6 tablespoons olive oil in the same skillet over medium heat. Add the asparagus, artichokes, garlic, and bay leaves and sauté until the vegetables are tender, 6 to 8 minutes.
Using a slotted spoon, top the fish with the cooked vegetables, reserving the oil in the skillet. Add the vinegar and paprika to the oil and whisk to combine well. Pour the vinaigrette over the fish and vegetables and let sit at room temperature for at least 15 minutes, or marinate in the refrigerator up to 24 hours for a deeper flavor. Remove the bay leaf before serving.
Substitution Tip: You can use mackerel fillets canned in oil and skip the cooking step for convenience, or substitute cod or halibut and follow the recipe as-is.

1023. Tuna Slow-Cooked in Olive Oil

Preparation Time: 5 minutes
Cooking Time: 45 minutes
Servings: 4

Ingredients:

1 cup extra-virgin olive oil, plus more if needed
4 (3- to 4-inch) sprigs fresh rosemary
8 (3- to 4-inch) sprigs fresh thyme
2 large garlic cloves, thinly sliced
2 (2-inch) strips lemon zest
1 teaspoon salt
½ teaspoon freshly ground black pepper

1-pound fresh tuna steaks (about 1 inch thick)

Directions:

Select a thick pot just large enough to fit the tuna in a single layer on the bottom. The larger the pot, the more olive oil you will need to use. Combine the olive oil, rosemary, thyme, garlic, lemon zest, salt, and pepper over medium-low heat and cook until warm and fragrant, 20 to 25 minutes, lowering the heat if it begins to smoke.

Remove from the heat and allow to cool for 25 to 30 minutes, until warm but not hot.

Add the tuna to the bottom of the pan, adding additional oil if needed so that tuna is fully submerged, and return to medium-low heat. Cook for 5 to 10 minutes, or until the oil heats back up and is warm and fragrant but not smoking. Lower the heat if it gets too hot.

Remove the pot from the heat and let the tuna cook in warm oil 4 to 5 minutes, to your desired level of doneness. For a tuna that is rare in the center, cook for 2 to 3 minutes.

Remove from the oil and serve warm, drizzling 2 to 3 tablespoons seasoned oil over the tuna.

To store for later use, remove the tuna from the oil and place in a container with a lid. Allow tuna and oil to cool separately. When both have cooled, remove the herb stems with a slotted spoon and pour the cooking oil over the tuna. Cover and store in the refrigerator for up to 1 week. Bring to room temperature to allow the oil to liquify before serving.

1024. Shrimp Ceviche Salad

Preparation Time: 15 minutes, plus 2 hours to marinate
Cooking Time: 30 minutes
Servings: 4

Ingredients:

1-pound fresh shrimp, peeled and deveined
1 small red or yellow bell pepper, cut into ½-inch chunks
½ English cucumber, peeled and cut into ½-inch chunks
½ small red onion, cut into thin slivers
¼ cup chopped fresh cilantro or flat-leaf Italian parsley
1/3 cup freshly squeezed lime juice
2 tablespoons freshly squeezed lemon juice
2 tablespoons freshly squeezed clementine juice or orange juice
½ cup extra-virgin olive oil
1 teaspoon salt
½ teaspoon freshly ground black pepper
2 ripe avocados, peeled, pitted, and cut into ½-inch chunks

Directions:

Cut the shrimp in half lengthwise. In a large glass bowl, combine the shrimp, bell pepper, cucumber, onion, and cilantro.

In a small bowl, whisk together the lime, lemon, and clementine juices, olive oil, salt, and pepper. Pour the mixture over the shrimp and veggies and toss to coat.

Cover and refrigerate for at least 2 hours, or up to 8 hours. Give the mixture a toss every 30 minutes for the first 2 hours to make sure all the shrimp "cook" in the juices.

Add the cut avocado just before serving and toss to combine.

1025. Greek Stuffed Squid

Preparation Time: 15 minutes
Cooking Time: 30 minutes
Servings: 4

Ingredients:

8 ounces frozen spinach, thawed and drained (about 1½ cup)
4 ounces crumbled goat cheese
½ cup chopped pitted olives (I like Kalamata in this recipe)
½ cup extra-virgin olive oil, divided
¼ cup chopped sun-dried tomatoes
¼ cup chopped fresh flat-leaf Italian parsley
2 garlic cloves, finely minced
¼ teaspoon freshly ground black pepper
2 pounds baby squid, cleaned and tentacles removed

Directions:

Preheat the oven to 350°F.

In a medium bowl, combine the spinach, goat cheese, olives, ¼ cup olive oil, sun-dried tomatoes, parsley, garlic, and pepper.

Pour 2 tablespoons olive oil in the bottom of an 8-inch square baking dish and spread to coat the bottom.

Stuff each cleaned squid with 2 to 3 tablespoons of the cheese mixture, depending on the size of squid, and place in the prepared baking dish.

Drizzle the tops with the remaining 2 tablespoons olive oil and bake until the squid are cooked through, 25 to 30 minutes. Remove from the oven and allow to cool 5 to 10 minutes before serving.

Substitution Tip: This recipe calls for baby squid, which are cylindrical in shape and easy to stuff, much like a large pasta shell, but I have also made this using calamari steaks, placing filling in the center and rolling like an enchilada before placing in the baking dish. Since the steaks are thicker, you will need to increase the cooking time by 10 to 15 minutes.

1026. Beef Shoulder in BBQ Sauce

Preparation Time: 5 minutes
Cooking Time: 10 hours on low
Servings: 12

Ingredients:

8 pounds beef shoulder, whole
1 Tablespoon butter
1 yellow onion, diced
1 garlic bulb, peeled and minced
4 Tablespoons red wine vinegar
2 Tablespoons Worcestershire sauce
4 Tablespoons Swerve (or suitable substitute)
1 Tablespoon mustard
1 teaspoon salt
1 teaspoon fresh ground black pepper

Directions:

In a bowl, mix seasoning together. Set aside.

In a pan, melt the butter, add the meat. Brown on all sides. Transfer to crock-pot.

In the same pan, fry the onion for 2-3 minutes, pour over the meat.

Pour in the seasoning.

Cover, cook on low for 10 hours.

Remove from crock-pot, place on a platter, cover with foil, let it rest for 1 hour.

Turn the crock pot on high, reduce the remaining liquid by half and serve with the shredded beef.

1027. Dressed Pork Leg Roast

Preparation Time: 5 minutes.
Cooking Time: 8 hours on high.
Servings: 14

Ingredients:

8 pounds pork leg
1 Tablespoon butter
1 yellow onion, sliced

6 garlic cloves, peeled and minced
2 Tablespoons ground cumin
2 Tablespoons ground thyme
2 Tablespoons ground chili
1 teaspoon salt
1 teaspoon fresh ground black pepper
1 cup hot water

Directions:

Butter the crock-pot. Slice criss-crosses along top of pork leg.
Arrange onion slices and minced garlic along the bottom of the crock-pot.
Place meat on top of vegetables.
In a small bowl, mix the herbs. Rub it all over the pork leg.
Add the water. Cover, cook on high for 8 hours.
Remove from crock pot, place on a platter, cover with foil. Let it rest for 1 hour.
Shred the meat and serve.

1028. Rabbit & Mushroom Stew

Preparation Time: 10 minutes.
Cooking Time: 6 hours on high.

Servings: 6
Ingredients:

1 rabbit, in portion size pieces
2 cups spicy Spanish sausage, cut in chunks
2 Tablespoons butter, divided
1 red onion, sliced
1 cup button mushrooms, washed and dried
1 teaspoon cayenne pepper
1 teaspoon sweet paprika
1 teaspoon salt
1 teaspoon fresh ground black pepper
1 cup chicken broth+1 cup hot water

Directions:

Butter the crock-pot.
In a large pan, melt the butter, add the pieces of rabbit, brown on all sides. Transfer to crock-pot.
In the same pan, sauté the onions, sausage chunks, and spices for 2-3 minutes. Pour in chicken broth to deglaze the pan, heat on high for 1 minute then pour the mixture over the rabbit.
Add the mushrooms. Adjust the seasoning, if needed.
Add the water. Cover, cook on high for 6 hours. Serve.

1029. Italian Spicy Sausage & Bell Peppers

Preparation Time: 10 minutes.
Cooking Time: 6 hours on low.
Servings: 5

Ingredients:

2 Tablespoons butter
2 red onions, sliced
4 bell peppers, sliced
2 regular cans Italian tomatoes, diced
2.2 pounds spicy Italian sausage
1 teaspoon dry oregano
1 teaspoon dry thyme
1 teaspoon dry basil
1 teaspoon sweet paprika
1 teaspoon salt
1 teaspoon fresh ground black pepper

Directions:

Butter the crock-pot.
Add the sliced onions and peppers. Salt.
Pour the tomatoes over them. Toss well.
Add seasoning. Mix it in.
Arrange sausages in middle of the pepper and onion mixture.
Add ¼ cup hot water.
Cover, cook on low for 6 hours. Serve.

1030. Chicken in Salsa Verde

Preparation Time: 10 minutes.
Cooking Time: 6 hours on low.
Servings: 4

Ingredients:

2.2 pounds chicken breasts
3 bunches parsley, chopped
¾ cup olive oil
¼ cup capers, drained and chopped
3 anchovy fillets
1 lemon, juice and zest
2 garlic cloves, minced
1 teaspoon salt
1 teaspoon fresh ground black pepper

Directions:

Place the chicken breasts in the crock-pot.
In a blender, combine rest of ingredients, pour over the chicken.
Cover, cook on low for 6 hours. Shred with a fork and serve.

1031. Salmon Poached in White Wine and Lemon

Preparation Time: 5 minutes.
Cooking Time: 1 hour on low + 1 hour on low.
Servings: 4

Ingredients:

2 cups water
1 cup cooking wine, white
1 lemon, sliced thin
1 small mild onion, sliced thin
1 bay leaf
1 mixed bunch fresh tarragon, dill, and parsley
2.2 pounds salmon fillet, skin on
1 teaspoon salt
1 teaspoon fresh ground black pepper

Directions:

Add all ingredients, except salmon and seasoning, to the crock-pot. Cover, cook on low for 1 hour.
Season the salmon, place in the crock-pot skin-side down.
Cover, cook on low for another hour. Serve.

1032. Butcher Style Cabbage Rolls – Pork & Beef Version

Preparation Time: 20 minutes.
Cooking Time: 8.5 hours on low.
Servings: 6

Ingredients:

1 large head of white cabbage – 3 pounds
1 ¾ cups beef, chopped in small pieces
1 ¾ cups pork, chopped in small pieces
1 sweet onion, cut into small pieces
1 red bell pepper, cut into small cubes
1 cup mushrooms, chopped small
2 Tablespoons olive oil
1 cup beef broth
½ cup cooking cream
Salt and pepper to taste
1 heaping teaspoon ground cumin

Directions:

Cut out the stalk of the cabbage head like a cone shape, place the cabbage in a pot with the hole up, boil some water and pour it over the cabbage. Let it soak in the hot water for 10 minutes. This will soften it considerably and the leaves will separate easily.

Chop the meats into small pieces; place them in a mixing bowl.
In a pan, heat the olive oil. Sauté the onion, the bell pepper, and the mushrooms for 5 minutes, cool them in the pan and add to the meats.
Add the seasoning, mix well with your hands.
Separate 8-10 leaves of cabbage, lay each one flat, cut the thick part of the stalk and stuff the leaf with about 2 tablespoons of meat mixture. Roll and put aside until meat mixture used up.
Finely cut the remaining cabbage and place in the crock-pot. Place the prepared cabbage rolls seam-side down, pour the broth and the cream evenly over the cabbage rolls. Cover, cook on low for 8.5 hours.

1033. One-pot Oriental Lamb

Preparation Time: 10 minutes.
Cooking Time: 4 hours on high.
Servings: 4

Ingredients:

3 cups lamb, de-boned and diced
2 Tablespoons almond flower
2 cups fresh spinach
4 small red onions, halved
2 garlic cloves, minced
¼ cup yellow turnip, diced
2 Tablespoons dry sherry
2-3 bay leaves
1 teaspoon hot mustard
¼ teaspoon ground nutmeg
1 teaspoon chopped fresh thyme
1 teaspoon chopped fresh rosemary
5-6 whole pimento berries
1 1/3 cups broth of your choice – beef, chicken, or lamb
Salt and pepper to taste
8 baby zucchini, halved
2 Tablespoons olive oil

Directions:

Preheat the crock-pot on high.
Place the lamb in the crock-pot, cover with almond flour. Add the remaining ingredients to crock-pot.
Cover, cook on high for 4 hours.

1034. Zucchini Lasagne with Minced Pork

Preparation Time: 20 minutes.
Cooking Time: 8 hours on low.
Servings: 6

Ingredients:

4 medium-sized zucchini
1 small onion, diced
1 garlic clove, minced
2 cups lean ground pork, minced
2 regular cans diced Italian tomatoes
2 Tablespoons olive oil
2 cups grated Mozzarella cheese
1 egg
Small bunch of fresh basil or 1 Tablespoon dry basil
Salt and pepper to taste
2 Tablespoons butter to grease crock-pot

Directions:

Cut the zucchini lengthwise making 6 slices from each vegetable. Salt and let drain. Discard the liquid.
In a pan, heat the olive oil. Sauté the onion and garlic for 5 minutes.
Add minced meat and cook for another 5 minutes. Add tomatoes and simmer for another 5 minutes.
Add seasoning and mix well. Add basil leaves. Cool slightly.
Beat the egg, mix in 1 cup of cheese.
Grease the crock-pot with butter and start layering the lasagna. First, the zucchini slices, then a layer of meat mixture, top it with cheese, and repeat. Finish with zucchini and the second cup of cheese.
Cover, cook on low for 8 hours.

1035. Mediterranean Meatloaf

Preparation Time: 10 minutes.
Cooking Time: 6 hours on low + 3 hours on high.
Servings: 6-8

Ingredients:

3 cups lean ground pork
2 large eggs
2 small zucchini, shredded and drained
1 red onion, cut small
1 red bell pepper, cut in small cubes
1 cup hard cheese of your preference – Parmesan or Cheddar, shredded
2 Tablespoons olive oil
1 Tablespoon dry oregano
Salt and pepper to taste
Topping:
¼ cup of ketchup
2 Tablespoons shredded cheese

Directions:

Place all ingredients, except topping, in a mixing bowl and combine well by hand.
Make 4 folded strips of aluminum foil and lay across bottom of crock-pot in a crisscross pattern.
Sprinkle olive oil across the foil, bottom of the crock-pot and sides.
Form one meat loaf from meat mixture, place on top of foil grid.
Cover, cook on low for 6 hours or on high for 3 hours.
Remove the lid, spread the ketchup on top of meatloaf. Sprinkle with cheese, cook for an additional 5 minutes to melt the cheese.

1036. Stuffed Bell Peppers Dolma Style

Preparation Time: 10 minutes.
Cooking Time: 6 hours on low.
Servings: 6

Ingredients:

1 cup lean ground beef
1 ¾ cup lean ground pork
1 small white onion, diced
6 bell peppers in various colors
1 small head cauliflower
1 small can tomato paste – 28 fl ounces
4 garlic cloves, crushed
2 Tablespoons olive oil
Salt and pepper to taste
1 Tablespoon dried thyme

Directions:

Cut off tops of the bell peppers, set aside. Clean inside the peppers.
Chop the cauliflower in very small pieces resembling rice grains, place in a mixing bowl.
Add the onion, crushed garlic, dried herbs. Combine thoroughly.
Add the meats, tomato paste, and seasoning. Mix well with your hands.
Sprinkle olive oil along the bottom and sides of the crock-pot.
Stuff the bell peppers with the mixture and set them in the crock-pot. Carefully place the top back on each pepper. If you have any meat and cauliflower mixture left, spoon it between the peppers in the crock-pot.
Cover, cook on low for 6 hours.

1037. Tuna Salad

Preparation Time: 20 minutes
Cooking Time: 5 minutes
Servings: 5

Ingredients:

1-pound green beans, trimmed and halved
1/3 cup water
Salt, as required

1 (12-ounce) can water packed solid white tuna, drained
1 (6-ounce) can sliced black olives, drained
¼ medium onion, sliced thinly
6 tablespoons olive oil
3 tablespoons fresh lemon juice
½ teaspoon lemon zest, grated finely
1 teaspoon dried oregano
Ground black pepper, as required
4 large organic hard-boiled eggs, peeled and quartered

Directions:

In a pan, add the green beans, water and a large pinch of salt over high heat and bring to a boil.
Cook for about 5 minutes.
Remove from the heat and drain the green beans completely.
Immediately, place the green beans onto a paper towels-lined baking sheet to cool.
In a bowl, add the tuna, olives and onion and mix.
In another bowl, add the oil, lemon juice, lemon zest, oregano, salt and black pepper and beat until well combined.
Place the dressing over the salad and gently stir to combine.
Divide the tuna salad, green beans and eggs onto serving plates and serve.
Nutrition: Per Servings: Net Carbs: 5.4g; Calories: 400; Total Fat: 30.1g; Saturated Fat: 5.3g

1038. Tuna Stuffed Avocado

Preparation Time: 15 minutes
Cooking Time: 0 minutes
Servings: 4

Ingredients:

1 (12-ounce) can solid white tuna packed in water, drained
1 tablespoon mayonnaise
3 scallions, sliced
½ red bell pepper, seeded and chopped
Dash of balsamic vinegar
Ground black pepper, as required
Pinch of garlic salt
2 ripe avocados, halved and pitted

Directions:

In a bowl, add all the ingredients except the avocado and mix well.
Stuff each avocado half with the tuna mixture and serve.

1039. Salmon Salad

Preparation Time: 15 minutes
Cooking Time: 9 minutes
Serves: 4

Ingredients:

4 tablespoons olive oil, divided
1 (8-ounce) salmon fillet
10 ounces cherry tomatoes, halved
1 large cucumber, chopped
8 ounces mozzarella balls
½ cup fresh basil leaves, chopped
Salt and ground black pepper, as required
1 tablespoon balsamic vinegar
1-2 tablespoons pesto

Directions:

In a skillet, heat 1 tablespoon of the oil over medium-high heat.
Place the salmon fillet, skin side down and cook for about 5 minutes.
Flip and cook for about 3-4 minutes.
Remove from the skillet and transfer the salmon fillet onto a plate.
Carefully, remove the skin salmon fillet and chop into bite sized pieces.
Set aside to cool.
In a large bowl, add the remaining oil and all ingredients and toss to coat well.
Add the salmon pieces and gently toss to coat well.
Serve immediately.

1040. Pesto Salmon

Preparation Time: 15 minutes
Cooking Time: 15 minutes
Servings: 2

Ingredients:

2 (6-ounce) salmon fillets
½ teaspoon fish rub
1 teaspoon butter, melted
4 teaspoons basil pesto
1 large tomato, cut into ¼-inch thick slices

Directions:

Preheat oven to 450 F. Place a baking sheet in the oven to heat.
Arrange 1 large piece onto a smooth surface.
Now, place another large greased piece of foil on top of first one.
Season the salmon fillets with fish rub evenly and drizzle with butter.
Place pesto over each salmon fillet evenly.
Arrange tomato slices over pesto evenly.
Wrap the foil pieces around salmon fillets to secure.
Arrange the salmon parcel onto the heated baking sheet.
Bake for about 15 minutes.
Remove from the oven and set aside for about 2-3 minutes.
Carefully, open the parcel and serve immediately.

1041. Salmon with Yogurt Sauce

Preparation Time: 15 minutes
Cooking Time: 12 minutes
Servings: 4

Ingredients:

½ cup plain Greek yogurt
3 garlic cloves, minced
2 tablespoons fresh dill, minced
2 tablespoons fresh lemon juice
1 tablespoon olive oil
1½ teaspoons ground coriander
1½ teaspoons ground cumin
Salt and ground black pepper, as required
4 (6-ounce) skinless salmon fillets
2 tablespoons fresh basil leaves

Directions:

In a large bowl, add all the ingredients except the salmon and basil and mix until well combined.
Transfer half of the yogurt mixture into another bowl and reserve in refrigerator for serving.
In the large bowl of the remaining yogurt mixture, add the salmon fillets and coat with the mixture well.
Refrigerate for about 25-30 minutes, flipping once halfway through.
Preheat the grill to medium-high heat. Lightly, grease the grill grate.
Remove the salmon fillets from the bowl and with the paper towels, discard the excess yogurt mixture.
Place the salmon fillets onto the grill and cook for about 4-6 minutes per side.
Remove from the grill and transfer the salmon fillets onto the serving plates.
Garnish with the basil and serve with the topping of the reserved yogurt mixture.

1042. Salmon with Dill

Preparation Time: 15 minutes
Cooking Time: 25 minutes
Servings: 2

Ingredients:

¼ cup fresh dill, chopped and divided
1 teaspoon fresh lemon zest
½ teaspoon smoked paprika
½ teaspoon fennel seeds, crushed lightly
Salt and ground black pepper, as required

2 (6-ounce) skin on salmon fillets
1 tablespoon fresh lemon juice
3 tablespoons olive oil

Directions:

In a bowl, 2 tablespoons of dill, lemon zest, paprika, fennel seeds, salt and black pepper and mix well.
Season the salmon fillet with dill mixture evenly and then drizzle with lemon juice.
Squeeze a lemon half over each fillet.
In a large skillet, heat the oil over medium heat and place the salmon fillets in a single layer.
Reduce the heat to the low and cook for about 20 minutes.
Flip and cook for about 5 minutes more.
With a slotted spoon, transfer the salmon fillets onto a paper towel-lined plate to drain.
Serve immediately with the topping of remaining dill.

1043. Moist and Spicy Pulled Chicken Breast

Preparation Time: 5 minutes
Cooking Time: 6 hours on low
Servings: 8

Ingredients:

1 teaspoon dry oregano
1 teaspoon dry thyme
1 teaspoon dried rosemary
1 teaspoon garlic powder
1 teaspoon sweet paprika
½ teaspoon chili powder
Salt and pepper to taste
4 tablespoons butter
5.5 pounds chicken breasts
1 ½ cups ready-made tomato salsa
2 Tablespoons of olive oil

Directions:

Mix dry seasoning, sprinkle half on the bottom of crock-pot.
Place the chicken breasts over it, sprinkle rest of spices.
Pour the salsa over the chicken.
Cover, cook on low for 6 hours.

1044. Whole Roasted Chicken

Preparation Time: 10 minutes
Cooking Time: 8 hours on low
Servings: 6

Ingredients:

1 whole chicken (approximately 5.5 pounds)
4 garlic cloves
6 small onions
1 Tablespoon olive oil, for rubbing
2 teaspoons salt
2 teaspoons sweet paprika
1 teaspoon Cayenne pepper
1 teaspoon onion powder
1 teaspoon ground thyme
2 teaspoons fresh ground black pepper
4 Tablespoons butter, cut into cubes

Directions:

Mix all dry ingredients well.
Stuff the chicken belly with garlic and onions.
On the bottom of the crock-pot, place four balls of aluminum foil.
Set the chicken on top of the balls. Rub it well with olive oil.
Cover the chicken with seasoning, drop in butter pieces.
Cover, cook on low for 8 hours.

1045. Pot Roast Beef Brisket

Preparation Time: 5 minutes
Cooking Time: 12 hours on low
Servings: 10

Ingredients:

6.6 pounds beef brisket, whole
2 Tablespoons olive oil
2 Tablespoons apple cider vinegar
1 teaspoon dry oregano
1 teaspoon dry thyme
1 teaspoon dried rosemary
2 Tablespoons paprika
1 teaspoon Cayenne pepper
1 tablespoon salt
1 teaspoon fresh ground black pepper

Directions:

In a bowl, mix dry seasoning, add olive oil, apple cider vinegar.
Place the meat in the crock-pot, generously coat with seasoning mix.
Cover, cook on low for 12 hours.
Remove the brisket from the liquid, place on a pan. Sear it under the broiler for 2-4 minutes, watch it carefully so the meat doesn't burn.
Cover the meat with foil, let it rest for 1 hour. Slice and serve.

1046. Seriously Delicious Lamb Roast

Preparation Time: 5 minutes
Cooking Time: 8 hours on low
Servings: 8

Ingredients:

12 medium radishes, scrubbed, washed and cut in half
Salt and pepper to taste
1 red onion, diced
2 garlic cloves, minced
1 lamb joint (approximately 4.5 pounds) at room temperature
2 Tablespoons olive oil
1 teaspoon dry oregano
1 teaspoon dry thyme
1 sprig fresh rosemary
4 cups heated broth, your choice

Directions:

Place cut radishes along bottom of crock-pot. Season. Add onion and garlic.
In a small bowl, combine the herbs and olive oil. Mix until a paste develops.
Place the meat on top of radishes. Rub the paste over the surface of the meat.
Heat the stock, pour it around the meat.
Cover, cook on low for 8 hours. Let it rest for 20 minutes. Slice and serve.

1047. Lamb Provençal

Preparation Time: 5 minutes.
Cooking Time: 8 hours on low
Servings: 4

Ingredients:

2 racks lamb, approximately 2 pounds
1 Tablespoon olive oil
2 Tablespoons fresh rosemary, chopped
1 Tablespoon fresh thyme, chopped
4 garlic cloves, minced
1 teaspoon dry oregano
1 lemon, the zest
1 teaspoon minced fresh ginger
1 cup (Good) red wine
Salt and pepper to taste

Directions:

Preheat the crock-pot on low.
In a pan, heat 1 tablespoon olive oil. Brown the meat for 2 minutes per side.
Mix remaining ingredients in a bowl.
Place the lamb in the crock-pot, pour remaining seasoning over meat.
Cover, cook on low for 8 hours.

1048. Greek Style Lamb Shanks

Preparation Time: 10 minutes.
Cooking Time: 6 hours on medium high.
Servings: 8

Ingredients:

3 Tablespoons butter
4 lamb shanks, approximately 1 pound each

2 Tablespoons olive oil
8-10 pearl onions
5 garlic cloves, minced
2 beef tomatoes, cubed
¼ cup green olives
4 bay leaves
1 sprig fresh rosemary
1 teaspoon dry thyme
1 teaspoon ground cumin
1 cup fresh spinach
¾ cup hot water
½ cup red wine, Merlot or Cabernet
Salt and pepper to taste

Directions:

In a pan, melt the butter, brown the shanks on each side.
Remove from pan, add oil, onions, garlic. Cook for 3-4 minutes. Add tomatoes, olives, spices. Stir well. Add liquids and return the meat. Bring to boil for 1 minute.
Transfer everything to the crock-pot.
Cover, cook on medium-high for 6 hours.

1049. Homemade Meatballs and Spaghetti Squash

Preparation Time: 15 minutes
Cooking Time: 8 hours on low
Servings: 8

Ingredients:

1 medium-sized spaghetti squash, washed
1 Tablespoon butter, to grease crock-pot
2.2 pounds lean ground beef
2 garlic cloves
1 red onion, chopped
½ cup almond flour
2 Tablespoons of dry Parmesan cheese
1 egg, beaten
1 teaspoon ground cumin
Salt and pepper to taste
4 cans diced Italian tomatoes
1 small can tomato paste, 28 fl ounces
1 cup hot water
1 red onion, chopped
¼ cup chopped parsley
½ teaspoon each, salt and sugar (optional)
1 bay leaf

Directions:

Cut the spaghetti squash in half, scoop out seeds with a spoon.
Grease the crock-pot, place both halves open side down in crock-pot.
Mix meatball ingredients in a bowl. Form approximately 20 small meatballs.
In a pan, heat the olive oil. Brown the meatballs for 2-3 minutes on each side. Transfer to the crock-pot.
In the small bowl, add the tomatoes, tomato paste, oil, water, onion and parsley, add ½ teaspoon each of salt and sugar. Mix well.
Pour the marinara sauce in the crock-pot around the squash halves.
Cover, cook on low for 8 hours.

1050. Salmon with Avocado Cream

Preparation Time: 15 minutes
Cooking Time: 8 minutes
Servings: 4

Ingredients:

For Avocado Cream
2 medium ripe avocados, peeled, pitted and chopped
1 cup plain Greek yogurt
2 garlic cloves, chopped
3-4 tablespoons fresh lime juice
Salt and ground black pepper, as required
For Salmon
2 teaspoons ground cumin
1 teaspoon red chili powder
1 teaspoon paprika
1 teaspoon garlic powder
Salt and ground black pepper, as required
4 (6-ounce) skinless salmon fillets
2 tablespoons unsalted butter

Directions:

For avocado cream: in a food processor, add all the ingredients and pulse until smooth.
For salmon: in a small bowl, add the spices, salt and black pepper and mix well.
Coat the salmon fillets with the spice mixture evenly.
In a nonstick skillet, melt the butter over medium-high heat and cook the salmon fillets for about 3 minutes.
Flip and cook for about 4-5 minutes or until the desired doneness of the salmon.
Transfer the salmon fillets onto the serving plates.
Top with avocado cream and serve.

1051. Salmon with Veggies

Preparation Time: 15 minutes
Cooking Time: 22 minutes
Servings: 4

Ingredients:

4 (6-ounce) (1-inch thick) skinless salmon fillets
Salt and ground black pepper, as required
1 (2¼-ounce) can sliced black olives, drained
½ cup zucchini, chopped finely
2 cups cherry tomatoes, halved
2 tablespoons canned capers with liquid
1 tablespoon olive oil

Directions:

Preheat the oven to 425 degrees F.
Grease an 11x7-inch baking dish
Season the salmon fillets with salt and black pepper generously.
In a bowl, add the remaining ingredients and toss to coat well.
Place the salmon fillets into the prepared baking dish in a single layer and top with the veggie mixture evenly.
Bake for about 22 minutes.
Serve hot.

1052. Almond Crusted Tilapia

Preparation Time: 15 minutes
Cooking Time: 10 minutes
Servings: 4

Ingredients:

1 cup almonds, chopped finely and divided
¼ cup ground flax seeds
4 (6-ounce) tilapia fillets
Salt and ground black pepper, as required
2 tablespoons olive oil

Directions:

In a shallow bowl, add ½ cup of the almonds and ground flax seeds and mix well.
Season the tilapia fillets with the salt and black pepper evenly.
Now, coat the tilapia fillets with the almond mixture evenly.
In a large heavy skillet, heat the oil over medium heat and cook the tilapia fillets for about 4 minutes per side.
Transfer the tilapia fillets onto a serving plate.
In the same skillet, add the remaining almonds and cook for about 1 minute, stirring frequently.
Remove the almonds from the heat and sprinkle over fish.
Serve warm.

1053. Parmesan Tilapia

Preparation Time: 15 minutes
Cooking Time: 11 minutes
Servings: 4

Ingredients:

4 (6-ounce) tilapia filets
Salt and ground black pepper, as required
½ cup Parmesan cheese, grated
¼ cup basil pesto
1 cup fresh tomatoes, chopped
2 tablespoons butter, melted

Directions:

Preheat the broiler of oven. Line a baking sheet with a greased piece of foil
Season the tilapia fillets with the salt and black pepper lightly.
Arrange the tilapia fillets onto the prepared baking sheet line in a single layer and top each with Parmesan cheese evenly.
Broil for about 10-11 minutes.
Remove from the oven and transfer the tilapia fillets onto the serving plates.
Top each fillet with the pesto and tomatoes evenly.
Drizzle with the melted butter and serve.

1054. Tilapia with Artichokes

Preparation Time: 15 minutes
Cooking Time: 14 minutes
Servings: 4

Ingredients:

1 tablespoon butter
4 (4-ounce) frozen tilapia fillets, thawed and pat dried
12 ounces jarred artichokes, drained and chopped
1 cup fresh baby spinach, chopped
1/3 cup sun-dried tomatoes, chopped
2 tablespoons capers
1 teaspoon garlic, crushed

Directions:

In a skillet, melt the butter over medium-high heat and cook the tilapia fillets for 2 minutes per side.
Add the remaining ingredients and gently, stir to combine.
Reduce the heat to medium and cook for about 5-10 minutes or until desired doneness of fish.

1055. Tilapia Casserole

Preparation Time: 15 minutes
Cooking Time: 14 minutes
Servings: 4

Ingredients:

2 (14-ounce) cans sugar-free diced tomatoes with basil and garlic with juice
1/3 cup fresh parsley, chopped and divided
¼ teaspoon dried oregano
½ teaspoon red pepper flakes, crushed
4 (6-ounce) tilapia fillets
2 tablespoons fresh lemon juice
2/3 cup feta cheese, crumbled

Directions:

Preheat the oven to 400 degrees F.
In a shallow baking dish, add the tomatoes, ¼ cup of the parsley, oregano and red pepper flakes and mix until well combined.
Arrange the tilapia fillets over the tomato mixture in a single layer and drizzle with the lemon juice.
Place some tomato mixture over the tilapia fillets and sprinkle with the feta cheese evenly.
Bake for about 12-14 minutes.
Serve hot with the garnishing of remaining parsley.

1056. Cod & Capers Bake

Preparation Time: 10 minutes
Cooking Time: 15 minutes
Servings: 4

Ingredients:

1½ teaspoons paprika
1½ teaspoons ground cumin
Salt and ground black pepper, as required
2 shallots, chopped finely
3 garlic cloves, minced
2 tablespoons fresh lemon juice
1½ tablespoons unsalted butter, melted
1-pound tilapia, cut into 8 pieces
¼ cup capers

Directions:

Preheat the oven to 375 degrees F. Line a rimmed baking sheet with a greased parchment paper.
In a small bowl, add the paprika, cumin, salt and black pepper and mix well.
In another small bowl, add the butter, shallots, garlic, lemon juice and butter and mix until well combined.
Season the tilapia fillets with the spice mixture evenly and coat with the butter mixture generously.
Arrange the tilapia fillets onto the prepared baking sheet in a single layer and top each with the capers.
Bake for about 10-15 minutes or until the desired doneness of fish.
Remove from the oven and serve hot.

1057. Spicy Cod

Preparation Time: 15 minutes
Cooking Time: 35 minutes
Servings: 5

Ingredients:

1 teaspoon dried dill weed
2 teaspoons sumac
2 teaspoons ground coriander
1½ teaspoons ground cumin
1 teaspoon ground turmeric
2 tablespoons olive oil
1 yellow onion, chopped
8 garlic cloves, chopped
2 jalapeño peppers, chopped
4 large tomatoes, chopped
2 tablespoons fresh lime juice
½ cup water
Salt and ground black pepper, as required
5 (6-ounce) boneless cod fillets

Directions:

For spice mixture: in a small bowl, add the dill weed and spices and mix well.
In a large, deep skillet, heat the oil over medium-high heat and sauté the onion for about 2 minutes.
Add the garlic and jalapeno and sauté for about 2 minutes.
Stir in the tomatoes, lime juice, water, half of the spice mixture, salt and black pepper and bring to a boil.
Reduce the heat to medium-low and cook, covered for about 10 minutes, stirring occasionally.
Meanwhile, season the cod fillets with the remaining spice mixture, salt and pepper evenly.
Place the fish fillets into the skillet and gently, press into the tomato mixture.
Increase the heat to medium-high and cook for about 2 minutes.
Reduce the heat to medium and cook, covered for about 10-15 minutes or until the desired doneness of the fish.
Remove from the heat and serve hot.

1058. Mahi-Mahi with Mayonnaise & Parmesan

Preparation Time: 15 minutes
Cooking Time: 16 minutes
Servings: 4

Ingredients:

4 (6-ounce) (½-inch thick) frozen Mahi-Mahi fillets, thawed and pat dried
1 teaspoon fish rub
½ cup mayonnaise
4 tablespoons Parmesan cheese, grated
½ teaspoon garlic powder
Ground black pepper, as required

Directions:

Preheat the oven to 400 degrees F. Arrange a rack in the upper half of the oven. Lightly, grease a baking dish.
Season the fish fillets with the fish rub evenly.
In a bowl, add the mayonnaise, Parmesan, garlic powder and black pepper and mix well.
Arrange the fish fillets into the prepared baking dish in a single layer.
Top each fillet with Parmesan mixture evenly.
Bake for about 12 minutes.
Now, set the oven to broiler.
Broil for about 3-4 minutes.
Serve hot.

1059. Halibut with Capers

Preparation Time: 15 minutes
Cooking Time: 15 minutes
Servings: 4

Ingredients:

1 tablespoon olive oil
2 (8 ounce) halibut fillets
¼ cup homemade chicken broth
¼ cup butter, chopped
3 tablespoons capers, with liquid
1 teaspoon garlic, minced
Salt and ground black pepper, as required

Directions:

In a large skillet, heat the oil over medium-high heat and cook the halibut steaks for about 2-3 minutes per side or until browned.
With a slotted spoon, transfer the halibut steaks onto a plate.
In the same skillet, add the broth and cook for about 2-3 minutes, scraping the browned bits from the bottom.
Stir in the butter, capers, salt and black pepper and cook for about 1-2 minutes.
Stir in the halibut steaks and cook for about 3-4 minutes or until desired doneness of fish.
Serve immediately.

1060. Parmesan Halibut

Preparation Time: 10 minutes
Cooking Time: 24 minutes
Servings: 2

Ingredients:

2 (6-ounce) halibut fillets
Salt and ground black pepper, as required
3 tablespoons sour cream
2 tablespoons Parmesan cheese, grated
3 tablespoons scallion, sliced and divided
¼ teaspoon dried dill weed
¼ teaspoon garlic powder

Directions:

Preheat the oven to 375 degrees F. Lightly, grease a baking sheet.
Season each halibut fillet with salt and black pepper lightly.
In a bowl, add the sour cream, Parmesan cheese, 2 tablespoons of scallion, dill weed and garlic powder and mix well.
Coat each halibut fillet with Parmesan mixture evenly.
Arrange the halibut fillets onto the prepared baking sheet.
Bake for about 24 minutes.
Serve hot with the garnishing of remaining scallion.

1061. Halibut, Capers & Olives Bake

Preparation Time: 15 minutes
Cooking Time: 40 minutes
Servings: 4

Ingredients:

1 yellow onion, chopped
1 large tomato, chopped
1 (5-ounce) jar pitted Kalamata olives
¼ cup capers
¼ cup olive oil
1 tablespoon fresh lemon juice
Salt and ground black pepper, as required
4 (6-ounce) halibut fillets
1 tablespoon Greek seasoning

Directions:

Preheat the oven to 350 degrees F.
In a bowl, add the onion, tomato, onion, olives, capers, oil, lemon juice, salt and black pepper and mix well.
Season the halibut fillets with the Greek seasoning evenly.
Arrange the halibut fillets onto a large piece of foil.
Top the fillets with the tomato mixture.
Carefully, fold all the edges of to create a large packet.
Arrange the foil packet onto a baking sheet.
Bake for about 30-40 minutes or until desired doneness of the fish.
Remove from the oven and serve hot.

1062. Sea Bass with Olives & Tomatoes

Preparation Time: 15 minutes
Cooking Time: 10 minutes
Servings: 4

Ingredients:

3 medium heirloom tomatoes diced
1/3 cup mixed pitted olives, chopped
1 tablespoon capers
1 garlic clove, minced
2 tablespoons olive oil
1 tablespoon balsamic vinegar
Salt, as required
4 (6-ounce) skin on sea bass fillets
1 teaspoon Herbs de Provence
1 tablespoon Dijon mustard
¼ cup feta cheese, crumbled

Directions:

Preheat the broiler of oven.
In a bowl, add the tomatoes, olives, capers, garlic, olive oil, vinegar, and a little and mix well.
Season the fish fillets with the herbs de Provence and salt evenly and then, coat with the Dijon mustard.
Arrange the fish fillets onto a baking sheet in a single layer and top with the olives mixture.
Broil for about 10 minutes, rotating the baking sheet once halfway through.
Remove from the oven and immediately, sprinkle with the cheese.
Serve immediately.

1063. Stuffed Swordfish

Preparation Time: 15 minutes
Cooking Time: 20 minutes
Servings: 2

Ingredients:

1 (8-ounce) (2-inch thick) swordfish steak

1½ tablespoons olive oil, divided
1 tablespoon fresh lemon juice
2 cups fresh spinach, torn
1 garlic clove, minced
¼ cup feta cheese, crumbled

Directions:

Preheat the outdoor grill to high heat. Lightly, grease the grill grate.
Carefully, cut a slit on one side of fish steak to create a pocket.
In a bowl, add 1 tablespoon of the oil and lemon juice and mix.
Coat both sides of fish with oil mixture evenly.
In a small skillet, add the remaining oil and garlic over medium heat and cook until heated.
Add the spinach and cook for about 2-3 minutes or until wilted.
Remove from the heat and set aside to cool slightly.
Stuff the fish pocket with spinach, followed by the feta cheese.
Grill the fish pocket for about 8 minutes.
Flip and cook for about 5-6 minutes or until desired doneness of fish.
Cut the fish pocket into 2 equal sized pieces and serve.

1064. Super Simple Vegetables Salad

Preparation Time: 4 minutes
Cooking Time: 7 minutes
Servings: 4

Ingredients:

¾ cup chopped red tomatoes
1 cucumber
½ cup chopped green bell pepper
½ cup chopped onion
¼ cup pitted Kalamata olives
¼ cup extra virgin olive oil
2 tablespoons red vinegar
¼ cup mayonnaise
½ teaspoon oregano

Directions:

Cut the cucumber into thin slices then place in a salad bowl.
Next, add chopped red tomatoes, chopped green bell pepper, chopped onion, and kalamata olives to the salad bowl then drizzle extra virgin olive oil and red vinegar over the vegetables. Toss to combine.
Once it is done, transfer the salad to a serving dish then drizzle mayonnaise and sprinkle oregano on top.
Serve and enjoy!

1065. Mushroom Black Pepper in Cabbage Blanket

Preparation Time: 11 minutes
Cooking Time: 22 minutes
Servings: 4

Ingredients:

2 cups mushroom
3 tablespoons extra virgin olive oil
1 teaspoon minced garlic
½ cup sliced onion
3 tablespoons coconut aminos
2 teaspoons cayenne pepper
¾ cup coconut milk
¼ teaspoon black pepper
¼ lb. cabbage

Directions:

Cut the mushroom s into small pieces then set aside.
Preheat a skillet over medium heat then pour extra virgin olive oil into it.
Once the olive oil is hot, stir in minced garlic and sliced onion to the skillet then sauté until aromatic and lightly golden brown.
Next, add mushrooms to the skillet then season with black pepper.
Pour coconut milk over the mushrooms then cook until the coconut milk is completely absorbed into the mushrooms.
In the meantime, place the cabbage in the steamer then steam until wilted.
Remove the steamed cabbage from the steamer and let it cool.
Next, return back to the mushroom.
Once the coconut milk is completely absorbed into the mushroom, season with cayenne pepper and coconut aminos then stir well. Remove from heat and let it cool.
Place a sheet of steamed cabbage on a flat surface then put the cooked mushroom on it.
Wrap the mushrooms with steamed cabbage and roll it tightly. Repeat with the remaining steamed cabbage and mushrooms.
Serve and enjoy.

1066. Tasty Vegetables Soup in Coconut Gravy

Preparation Time: 4 minutes
Cooking Time: 11 minutes
Servings: 4

Ingredients:

2 cups chopped spinach
1 cup chopped cabbage
1 medium carrot
1/4 cup cooked kidney beans
2 tablespoons chopped celeries
1 teaspoon minced garlic
1-teaspoon cayenne pepper
1/2 teaspoon red chili flakes
3/4 cup coconut milk
1-cup water

Directions:

Peel the carrot then cut into slices. Set aside.
Pour water into a pot then season with minced garlic, cayenne pepper, and red chili flakes then bring to boil.
Once it is boiled, add kidney beans, chopped cabbage, and carrot to the soup.
Pour coconut milk into the soup then bring to a simmer.
Next, stir in chopped spinach to the soup and cook until the spinach is just wilted.
Transfer the soup to a serving bowl then serve warm.
Enjoy immediately.

1067. Avocado Cream Soup with Chipotle

Preparation Time: 4 minutes
Cooking Time: 12 minutes
Servings: 4

Ingredients:

4 ripe avocados
2 cups water
2 cups Greek yogurt
1-teaspoon chipotle

Directions:

Cut the avocados into halves then remove the seeds.
Scoop out the avocado flesh then place in a blender.
Pour Greek yogurt to the blender then blend until smooth. Set aside.
Next, pour water into a saucepan then season with chipotle. Bring to boil.
Once it is boiled, stir in avocado mixture then stir well.
Transfer the avocado cream soup to a serving bowl then serve immediately.
Enjoy warm.

1068. 5 minutes Crispy Spinach

Preparation Time: 4 minutes
Cooking Time: 2 minutes
Servings: 4

Ingredients:

2 bunches spinach

½ cup almond flour
¼ teaspoon pepper
1-cup water
½ cup extra virgin olive oil, to fry

Directions:

Season the almond flour with pepper then stir well. Set aside.
Cut the spinach leaves and remove the stem.
Coat the spinach leaves with almond flour mixture then dip into the water.
Take the spinach out of the water then coat again with almond flour. Repeat with the remaining spinach and almond flour.
Preheat a frying pan over medium heat then pour olive oil into it.
Once the oil is hot, put the coated spinach in the hot oil and fry for approximately 2 minutes each side.
Remove the fried spinach from the frying pan and strain the oil.
Serve and enjoy.

1069. Sautéed Broccoli with Onion and Mushroom

Preparation Time: 8 minutes
Cooking Time: 6 minutes
Servings: 4

Ingredients:

3 cups broccoli florets
1 cup chopped mushroom
2 tablespoons extra virgin olive oil
½ cup chopped onion
¼ teaspoon pepper
½ teaspoon sesame seeds

Directions:

Preheat a skillet over medium heat then pour extra virgin olive oil into it.
Once the oil is hot, stir in chopped onion and sauté until aromatic and lightly golden brown.
Next, stir in chopped mushroom and broccoli florets then cook until wilted.
Season the mushroom and broccoli with pepper then stir well. Cook until the broccoli is done but not too soft.
Remove the sautéed broccoli and mushroom from heat and transfer to a serving dish.
Sprinkle sesame seeds on top and serve immediately.
Enjoy warm.

1070. Almond Pecan Porridge with Cinnamon

Preparation Time: 4 minutes
Cooking Time: 16 minutes
Servings: 4

Ingredients:

2 cups unsweetened almond milk
½ cup almond butter
2 tablespoons extra virgin olive oil
2 tablespoons hemp seeds
½ cup chopped pecans
1-teaspoon cinnamon

Directions:

Preheat an oven to 250°F (121°C)) and line a baking tray with parchment paper.
Toss the pecans with extra virgin olive then spread over the prepared baking tray.
Bake the pecans until tender then remove from the oven. Let it cool.
Once the toasted pecans are cool, transfer to a food processor then process until becoming crumbles. Set aside.
Preheat almond milk over medium heat then add almond butter to it.
Wait until the butter is melted then transfer the mixture to a serving bowl.
Add pecans crumbles to the bowl then sprinkle hemp seeds and cinnamon on top.
Serve and enjoy immediately.

1071. Green Veggie Salad with Brown Cashew Sauce

Preparation Time: 5 minutes
Cooking Time: 7 minutes
Servings: 4

Ingredients:

2 cups chopped spinach
½ cup chopped long beans
1 cup chopped cabbage
½ cup beans sprouts
¼ cup shredded carrots
2 tablespoons extra virgin olive oil
1-teaspoon minced garlic
¼ cup roasted cashews
½ cup coconut milk
2 teaspoons red chili flakes
2 tablespoons coconut aminos

Directions:

Preheat a steamer over medium heat then alternately steam the vegetables.
Remove the steamed vegetables then arrange on a serving dish. Set aside.
Place the roasted cashews in a blender then pour coconut milk into the blender. Blend until smooth then set aside.
Preheat a skillet over medium heat then pour olive oil into it.
Stir in minced garlic then sauté until lightly golden brown and aromatic.
Pour cashews and coconut milk mixture into the skillet then season with red chili flakes. Bring to a simmer.
Once it is done, pour the cashews sauce over the steamed vegetables then drizzle coconut aminos on top.
Serve and enjoy immediately.

1072. Carrot Omelet with Avocado Topping

Preparation Time: 6 minutes
Cooking Time: 8 minutes
Servings: 4

Ingredients:

½ cup grated carrots
½ cup chopped spinach
3 tablespoons coconut flour
½ cup coconut milk
3 tablespoons extra virgin olive oil
2 ripe avocados
½ teaspoon cinnamon

Directions:

Cut the avocados into halves then remove the seeds.
After that, scoop out the avocado flesh then mash until smooth. Set aside.
Combine coconut flour with coconut milk then stir until incorporated and smooth.
Add grated carrot and chopped spinach to the mixture then stir until combined.
Next, preheat a pan over medium heat then pour extra virgin olive oil into the pan.
Once the oil is hot, pour coconut mixture to the pan then fry until both sides are lightly golden and the omelets cooked through.
Place the carrots omelets on a serving dish then top with the avocado topping.
Sprinkle cinnamon over the avocado then serve.
Enjoy!

1073. Light Sour Soup with Kabocha

Preparation Time: 8 minutes
Cooking Time: 6 minutes
Servings: 4

Ingredients:

1 cup chopped Kabocha
½ cup chopped long beans
¼ cup chopped carrots
¾ cup chopped cabbage
½ cup pecans
1-tablespoon extra-virgin olive oil
½ teaspoon minced garlic
1-teaspoon sliced shallot
1-teaspoon red chili flakes
¼ cup chopped green tomatoes
3 cups water

Directions:

Pour water into a pot then bring to boil.
Once it is boiled, add pecans to the pot then cook the pecans until tender.
Remove the pecans from the pot and strain the water. Set aside.
Next, preheat a pot over medium heat then pour olive oil into the pot.
Once the oil is hot, stir in minced garlic and sliced shallots then sauté until aromatic and lightly golden.
Pour water into the pot then season with red chili flakes. Bring to boil.
Once it is boiled, reduce the heat and add kabocha, long beans, carrots, cabbages, pecans, and chopped green tomatoes to the pot. Cook for approximately 3 minutes or until the vegetables are tender.
Transfer the soup to a serving bowl then serve immediately.
Enjoy warm.

1074. Spiced Coconut Carrot Fritter

Preparation Time: 4 minutes
Cooking Time: 12 minutes
Servings: 4

Ingredients:

½ cup coconut flour
2 tablespoons coconut milk
2 tablespoons water
2 tablespoons grated coconut
2 tablespoons shredded carrots
¼ teaspoon coriander
¼ cup olive oil, to fry

Directions:

Place coconut flour in a bowl then pour water and coconut milk over the flour.
Season the flour with coriander then mix until incorporated.
Add grated coconut and shredded carrots to the mixture then stir until just combined.
Next, preheat a frying pan over medium heat then pour olive oil into it.
Once the oil is hot, drop about 2 tablespoons of mixture and fry for approximately 2 minutes.
Flip the fritter and fry until both sides of the fritter are lightly golden brown.
Remove the fritter and strain the excessive oil. Repeat with the remaining mixture.
Once it is done, arrange the fritters on a serving dish and serve.
Enjoy warm.

1075. Savory Kale Garlic with Crispy Coconut Cubes

Preparation Time: 6 minutes
Cooking Time: 22 minutes
Servings: 4

Ingredients:

1-cup coconut flour
½ cup water
5 tablespoons minced garlic
1-teaspoon pepper
¼ cup extra virgin olive oil, to sauté and fry
3 cups chopped kale
2 tablespoons coconut aminos
1 teaspoon red chili flakes

Directions:

Preheat a steamer over medium heat and wait until it is ready.
In the meantime, combine coconut flour with water, 2 tablespoons of minced garlic, and ½ teaspoon pepper. Mix well until becoming a soft dough.
Wrap the dough with aluminum foil then place in the steamer. Steam for about 10 minutes or until set.
Remove the cooked dough from the steamer and let it cool.
Once the cooked coconut dough is cool, unwrap it and cut into cubes. Set aside.
Preheat a frying pan over medium heat then pour olive oil into it.
Once the oil is hot, put the coconut cubes in the frying pan and fry until lightly golden brown and crispy.
Remove the crispy coconut cubes from the frying pan then strain the excessive oil. Set aside.
Next, take 2 tablespoons of olive oil and pour into a skillet.
Preheat the skillet to medium heat then stir in the remaining minced garlic into it. Sauté until aromatic and lightly golden brown.
Add chopped kale to the skillet then season with pepper, red chili flakes, and coconut aminos. Stir well and cook until the kale is wilted.
Once it is done, remove the sautéed kale from the skillet and transfer to a serving dish.
Serve and enjoy.

1076. Scrumptious Zucchini Noodles with Avocado Pecans Sauce

Preparation Time: 4 minutes
Cooking Time: 14 minutes
Servings: 4

Ingredients:

4 medium zucchinis
2 tablespoons extra virgin olive oil
1 fresh avocado
1-cup fresh basil leaves
½ cup roasted pecans
2 teaspoons minced garlic
2 tablespoons lemon juice
¼ cup water

Directions:

Cut the avocado into halves then remove the seed.
Scoop out the avocado flesh then place in a blender.
Add fresh basil leaves and roasted pecans to the blender then season with minced garlic and lemon juice.
Pour water into the blender then blend until smooth. Set aside.
Peel the zucchinis then cut into halves lengthwise.
Using a julienne peeler cut the zucchini into noodles form then set aside.
Next, preheat a skillet over medium heat then pour olive oil into it.
Once the oil is hot, stir in the zucchini noodles and mix well.
Sauté the zucchini until wilted then remove from heat. Transfer to a salad bowl.
Drizzle avocado pecans sauce over the zucchini noodles then toss to combine.
Serve and enjoy.

1077. Healthy Veggie Rolls with Dill Sauce

Preparation Time: 4 minutes
Cooking Time: 12 minutes
Servings: 4

Ingredients:

4 fresh collard green leaves
1 cucumber
½ red bell pepper
¼ cup diced onion
1 tablespoon sliced olives
¼ cup cherry tomatoes
½ cup almond yogurt
¾ teaspoon garlic powder
½ teaspoon vinegar
2 tablespoons extra virgin olive oil
5 sprigs fresh dill
¼ teaspoon pepper

Directions:

Combine almond yogurt with garlic powder, vinegar, olive oil, fresh dill, and pepper in a blender then blend until smooth. Set aside.
Peel the cucumber and remove the seeds.
Using a julienne peeler cut the cucumber into noodle forms then set aside. Do the same thing with the bell pepper.
Arrange collard green leaves on a flat surface then spread the almond yogurt mixture over the leaves.
After that, arrange cucumber noodles and bell pepper noodles on the leaves then sprinkle diced onion, sliced olives, and cherry tomatoes on top.
Carefully roll the leaves then cut into halves.
Arrange the rolls on a serving dish then serve. Enjoy!

1078. Baked Spaghetti Squash with Spicy Almond Sauce

Preparation Time: 6 minutes
Cooking Time: 24 minutes
Servings: 4

Ingredients:

½ spaghetti squash
2 tablespoons sesame oil
¼ cup almond butter
2 tablespoons coconut aminos
1 ½ tablespoons extra virgin olive oil
¼ teaspoon garlic powder
1 teaspoon red chili flakes
2 tablespoons chopped roasted almonds

Directions:

Preheat an oven to 250°F (121°C) and cover a baking tray with aluminum foil.
Brush the spaghetti squash with sesame oil then place on the prepared baking tray.
Bake the spaghetti squash for approximately 15 minutes or until tender then remove from the oven and let it cool.
Using a julienne peeler cut the spaghetti squash into noodle forms then place in a salad bowl. Set aside.
Next, combine almond butter with coconut aminos, extra virgin olive oil, garlic powder, and red chili flakes then stir until incorporated.
Drizzle the sauce over the baked spaghetti squash then sprinkle chopped roasted almonds on top.
Serve and enjoy!

1079. Savory and Nutritious Fried Cauliflower Rice

Preparation Time: 6 minutes
Cooking Time: 23 minutes
Servings: 4

Ingredients:

3 cups cauliflower florets
2 tablespoons extra virgin olive oil
½ teaspoon minced garlic
½ teaspoon pepper
2 tablespoons coconut aminos
1 lemon grass
1 cup chopped mushroom
½ cup sliced cabbage
¼ cup shredded carrots

Directions:

Place the cauliflower florets in a steamer then steam until soft.
Remove the steamed cauliflower florets from the steamer and transfer to a food processor. Process until smooth.
Next, preheat a skillet over medium heat then pour extra virgin olive oil into the skillet.
Once the oil is hot, stir in minced garlic and sauté until wilted and aromatic.
Add chopped mushrooms, sliced cabbage, and shredded carrots to the skillet then sauté until wilted.
After that, stir in cauliflower rice to the skillet then season with pepper, coconut aminos, and lemon grass. Cook until combined.
Once it is done, transfer the fried cauliflower rice to a serving dish then serve warm.
Enjoy immediately.

1080. Fresh Green in Red Curry Gravy

Preparation Time: 4 minutes
Cooking Time: 16 minutes
Servings: 4

Ingredients:

2 cups broccoli florets
1 cup chopped spinach
1 cup chopped kale
2 tablespoons chopped celeries
2 tablespoons extra virgin olive oil
¼ cup chopped onion
2 teaspoons minced garlic
1-teaspoon ginger
1-teaspoon red curry paste
¾ cup coconut milk
½ cup water

Directions:

Preheat a skillet over medium heat then pour extra virgin olive oil into it.
Once the oil is hot, stir in chopped onion and minced garlic then sauté until lightly golden brown and aromatic.
Next, pour water into the skillet then season with ginger and red curry paste. Bring to boil.
Once it is boiled, stir in broccoli florets, chopped spinach, and chopped kale to the skillet then pour coconut milk over the vegetables. Bring to a simmer.
Once it is done, remove the vegetable curry from heat and transfer to a serving bowl.
Serve and enjoy warm.

1081. Coconut Creamy Pumpkin Porridge

Preparation Time: 6 minutes
Cooking Time: 14 minutes
Servings: 4

Ingredients:

3 cups chopped pumpkin
2 cups water
½ cup coconut milk
¼ cup extra virgin olive oil
¼ teaspoon pepper
½ teaspoon garlic
½ teaspoon thyme
2 tablespoons chopped parsley
2 tablespoons coconut flakes
¼ cup chopped roasted almonds

Directions:

Preheat an oven to 250°F (121°C) and line a baking tray with aluminum foil.

Toss the pumpkin cubes with extra virgin olive oil then spread on the prepared baking tray.
Bake the pumpkin until tender then remove from the oven. Set aside.
Pour water into a pot then season with pepper, garlic, and thyme. Bring to boil.
Once it is boiled, add baked pumpkin to the pot and pour coconut milk over the pumpkin. Bring to a simmer.
Once it is done, remove the cooked pumpkin and the gravy from heat then transfer to a blender. Blend until smooth and becoming porridge.
Pour the creamy pumpkin to a serving bowl then sprinkle coconut flakes and roasted almonds on top.
Garnish with fresh parsley then serve immediately.
Enjoy warm.

1082. Spicy Eggplant in Coconut Gravy

Preparation Time: 4 minutes
Cooking Time: 14 minutes
Servings: 4

Ingredients:

2 cups chopped eggplants
2 tablespoons extra virgin olive oil
2 cloves garlic
2 shallots
¼ cup red chili flakes
1-inch galangal
2 lemon grasses
2 bay leaves
1 kaffir lime leaf
1-cup coconut milk

Directions:

Place garlic, shallots, and red chili flakes in a food processor then process until smooth.
Next, preheat a skillet over medium heat then pour olive oil into it.
Once the oil is hot, stir in the spice mixture then sauté until aromatic.
Add chopped eggplants to the skillet then season with galangal, lemon grasses, bay leaves, and kaffir lime leaves.
Pour coconut milk over the eggplants then bring to a simmer.
Once it is done, transfer the cooked eggplants together with the gravy to a serving dish.
Serve and enjoy!

1083. Zucchini Beef Casserole

Preparation Time: 14 minutes
Cooking Time: 38 minutes
Servings: 4

Ingredients:

½ cup goat cheese
2 tablespoons coconut yogurt
2 eggs
1-cup ground beef
2 tablespoons extra virgin olive oil
¼ cup chopped onion
1-cup water
½ teaspoon pepper
¼ teaspoon ginger
¼ teaspoon turmeric
¾ cup coconut flour
4 tablespoons coconut oil
½ cup sliced zucchini

Directions:

Preheat a skillet over medium heat then pour extra virgin olive oil into the skillet.
Once the oil is hot, stir in chopped onion and sauté until lightly golden brown and aromatic.
Add ground beef to the skillet then season with pepper, ginger, and turmeric. Stir until the beef is no longer pink.
Pour water over the beef then bring to boil.
Once it is boiled, reduce the heat and cook until the water is completely absorbed into the beef.
Once it is done, remove the beef from heat and let it cool.
Preheat an oven to 400°F (204°C) and coat a casserole dish with cooking spray. Set aside.
Transfer the cooked beef to the prepared casserole dish then spread evenly.
Combine goat cheese with eggs and coconut yogurt then stir until incorporated.
Pour the cheese mixture over the beef and arrange sliced zucchini on it.
Pour coconut oil over the coconut flour then mix until becoming crumbles.
Sprinkle the crumbles on top then bake the casserole for approximately 35 minutes or until set.
Once it is done, remove the casserole from the oven and let it cool.
Serve and enjoy.

1084. Mediterranean Cauliflower Tabbouleh

Preparation Time: 15 minutes, plus 30 minutes to chill
Cooking Time: 5 minutes
Servings: 6

Ingredients:

6 tablespoons extra-virgin olive oil, divided
4 cups Riced Cauliflower
3 garlic cloves, finely minced
1½ teaspoons salt
½ teaspoon freshly ground black pepper
½ large cucumber, peeled, seeded, and chopped
½ cup chopped mint leaves
½ cup chopped Italian parsley
½ cup chopped pitted Kalamata olives
2 tablespoons minced red onion
Juice of 1 lemon (about 2 tablespoons)
2 cups baby arugula or spinach leaves
2 medium avocados, peeled, pitted, and diced
1 cup quartered cherry tomatoes

Directions:

In a large skillet, heat 2 tablespoons of olive oil over medium-high heat. Add the rice cauliflower, garlic, salt, and pepper and sauté until just tender but not mushy, 3 to 4 minutes. Remove from the heat and place in a large bowl.
Add the cucumber, mint, parsley, olives, red onion, lemon juice, and remaining 4 tablespoons olive oil and toss well. Place in the refrigerator, uncovered, and refrigerate for at least 30 minutes, or up to 2 hours.
Before serving, add the arugula, avocado, and tomatoes and toss to combine well. Season to taste with salt and pepper and serve cold or at room temperature.

1085. Garlicky Broccoli Rabe with Artichokes

Preparation Time: 5 minutes
Cooking Time: 10 minutes
Servings: 4

Ingredients:

2 pounds fresh broccoli rabe
1/2 cup extra-virgin olive oil, divided
3 garlic cloves, finely minced
1 teaspoon salt
1 teaspoon red pepper flakes
1 can artichoke hearts, drained and quartered
1 tablespoon water

2 tablespoons red wine vinegar
Freshly ground black pepper

Directions:

Trim away any thick lower stems and yellow leaves from the broccoli rabe and discard. Cut into individual florets with a couple inches of thin stem attached.
In a large skillet, heat ¼ cup olive oil over medium-high heat. Add the trimmed broccoli, garlic, salt, and red pepper flakes and sauté for 5 minutes, until the broccoli begins to soften. Add the artichoke hearts and sauté for another 2 minutes.
Add the water and reduce the heat to low. Cover and simmer until the broccoli stems are tender, 3 to 5 minutes.
In a small bowl, whisk together remaining ¼ cup olive oil and the vinegar. Drizzle over the broccoli and artichokes. Season with ground black pepper, if desired.

1086. Roasted Eggplant with Mint and Harissa

Preparation Time: 10 minutes
Cooking Time: 35 minutes
Servings: 4

Ingredients:

2 medium eggplants, cut into ½-inch cubes
4 tablespoons extra-virgin olive oil
1 teaspoon salt
¼ teaspoon freshly ground black pepper
1 cup chopped fresh mint
¼ cup Harissa Oil or store-bought harissa
¼ cup chopped scallions, green part only

Directions:

Preheat the oven to 425°F. Line a baking sheet with parchment paper.
In a large bowl, place the eggplant, olive oil, salt, and pepper and toss to coat well.
Place the eggplant on the prepared baking sheet, reserving the bowl, and roast for 15 minutes. Remove from the oven and toss the eggplant pieces to flip.
Return to the oven and roast until golden and cooked through, another 15 to 20 minutes.
When the eggplant is cooked, remove from the oven and return to the large bowl. Add the mint, harissa, and scallions and toss to combine. Serve warm or cover and refrigerate for up to 2 days.

1087. Shakshuka

Preparation Time: 10 minutes
Cooking Time: 30 minutes
Servings: 4

Ingredients:

½ cup plus 2 tablespoons extra-virgin olive oil, divided
½ small yellow onion, finely diced
1 red bell pepper, finely diced
1 (14-ounce) can crushed tomatoes, with juices
6 ounces frozen spinach, thawed and drained of excess liquid (about 1½ cups)
2 garlic cloves, finely minced
1 teaspoon smoked paprika
1 to 2 teaspoons red pepper flakes (optional)
1 tablespoon roughly chopped capers
6 large eggs
¼ teaspoon freshly ground black pepper
¾ cup crumbled feta or goat cheese
¼ cup chopped fresh flat-leaf parsley or cilantro

Directions:

Heat broiler on low setting.
In a medium, deep oven-safe skillet, heat 2 tablespoons olive oil over medium-high heat. Add the onion and bell pepper and sauté until softened, 5 to 8 minutes.
Add the crushed tomatoes and their juices, ½ cup olive oil, spinach, garlic, paprika, red pepper flakes (if using), and capers, stirring to combine. Bring to a boil, then reduce the heat to low, cover, and simmer for 5 minutes.
Uncover the pan and gently crack each egg into the simmering sauce, allowing the egg to create a crater in the sauce and being careful to not let eggs touch. Add the pepper, then cover and cook, poaching the eggs until the yolks are just set, eight to 10 minutes. Eight minutes will yield softer yolks, while a longer cooking time will yield firmer yolks.
Uncover the pan and spread the crumbled cheese over top of the eggs and sauce. Transfer to the oven and broil under low heat until the cheese is just slightly browned and bubbly, 3 to 5 minutes. Drizzle with the remaining 2 tablespoons olive oil, top with chopped parsley, and serve warm.
Prep Tip: For an even quicker preparation, substitute 1 jar low-sugar marinara sauce (less than 6 grams) for the onion, bell pepper, crushed tomatoes, and garlic. Skip steps 2 and 3, season the marinara sauce with paprika and red pepper flakes, and bring to a simmer before cracking in the eggs.

1088. Crustless Spanakopita

Preparation Time: 15 minutes
Cooking Time: 45 minutes
Servings: 6

Ingredients:

12 tablespoons extra-virgin olive oil, divided
1 small yellow onion, diced
1 (32-ounce) bag frozen chopped spinach, thawed, fully drained, and patted dry (about 4 cups)
4 garlic cloves, minced
½ teaspoon salt
½ teaspoon freshly ground black pepper
1 cup whole-milk ricotta cheese
4 large eggs
¾ cup crumbled traditional feta cheese
¼ cup pine nuts

Directions:

Preheat the oven to 375°F.
In a large skillet, heat 4 tablespoons olive oil over medium-high heat. Add the onion and sauté until softened, 6 to 8 minutes.
Add the spinach, garlic, salt, and pepper and sauté another 5 minutes. Remove from the heat and allow to cool slightly.
In a medium bowl, whisk together the ricotta and eggs. Add to the cooled spinach and stir to combine.
Pour 4 tablespoons olive oil in the bottom of a 9-by-13-inch glass baking dish and swirl to coat the bottom and sides. Add the spinach-ricotta mixture and spread into an even layer.
Bake for 20 minutes or until the mixture begins to set. Remove from the oven and crumble the feta evenly across the top of the spinach. Add the pine nuts and drizzle with the remaining 4 tablespoons olive oil. Return to the oven and bake for an additional 15 to 20 minutes, or until the spinach is fully set and the top is starting to turn golden brown. Allow to cool slightly before cutting to serve.
Leftovers Tip: Pine nuts can be expensive, but I like to buy them in bulk and store them in my freezer for use in various dishes. Sprinkle them on salads for extra crunch or use them to make homemade pesto. The Israeli Salad with Nuts and Seeds uses a variety of seeds and nuts, including pine nuts, to create a satisfying crunch and a satiating main course salad.

1089. Zucchini Lasagna

Preparation Time: 15 minutes
Cooking Time: 1 hour
Servings: 8

Ingredients:

½ cup extra-virgin olive oil, divided
4 to 5 medium zucchini squash
1 teaspoon salt
8 ounces frozen spinach, thawed and well drained (about 1 cup)
2 cups whole-milk ricotta cheese
¼ cup chopped fresh basil or 2 teaspoons dried basil
1 teaspoon garlic powder
½ teaspoon freshly ground black pepper
2 cups shredded fresh whole-milk mozzarella cheese
1¾ cups shredded Parmesan cheese
½ (24-ounce) jar low-sugar marinara sauce (less than 5 grams sugar)

Directions:

Preheat the oven to 425°F.
Line two baking sheets with parchment paper or aluminum foil and drizzle each with 2 tablespoons olive oil, spreading evenly.
Slice the zucchini lengthwise into ¼-inch-thick long slices and place on the prepared baking sheet in a single layer. Sprinkle with ½ teaspoon salt per sheet. Bake until softened, but not mushy, 15 to 18 minutes. Remove from the oven and allow to cool slightly before assembling the lasagna.
Reduce the oven temperature to 375°F.
While the zucchini cooks, prep the filling. In a large bowl, combine the spinach, ricotta, basil, garlic powder, and pepper. In a small bowl, mix together the mozzarella and Parmesan cheeses. In a medium bowl, combine the marinara sauce and remaining ¼ cup olive oil and stir to fully incorporate the oil into sauce.
To assemble the lasagna, spoon a third of the marinara sauce mixture into the bottom of a 9-by-13-inch glass baking dish and spread evenly. Place 1 layer of softened zucchini slices to fully cover the sauce, then add a third of the ricotta-spinach mixture and spread evenly on top of the zucchini. Sprinkle a third of the mozzarella-Parmesan mixture on top of the ricotta. Repeat with 2 more cycles of these layers: marinara, zucchini, ricotta-spinach, then cheese blend.
Bake until the cheese is bubbly and melted, 30 to 35 minutes. Turn the broiler to low and broil until the top is golden brown, about 5 minutes. Remove from the oven and allow to cool slightly before slicing.
Substitution Tip: You can use eggplant in place of the zucchini, using the same method of cooking ahead before layering in the dish. You could even use a combination of the two for extra variety!

1090. Moroccan Vegetable Tagine

Preparation Time: 20 minutes
Cooking Time: 1 hour
Servings: 6

Ingredients:

½ cup extra-virgin olive oil
2 medium yellow onions, sliced
6 celery stalks, sliced into ¼-inch crescents
6 garlic cloves, minced
1 teaspoon ground cumin
1 teaspoon ginger powder
1 teaspoon salt
1/2 teaspoon paprika
1/2 teaspoon ground cinnamon
1/4 teaspoon freshly ground black pepper
2 cups vegetable stock
1 medium eggplant, cut into 1-inch cubes
2 medium zucchini, cut into ½-inch-thick semicircles
2 cups cauliflower florets
1 (13.75-ounce) can artichoke hearts, drained and quartered
1 cup halved and pitted green olives
1/2 cup chopped fresh flat-leaf parsley, for garnish
1/2 cup chopped fresh cilantro leaves, for garnish
Greek yogurt, for garnish (optional)

Directions:

In a large, thick soup pot or Dutch oven, heat the olive oil over medium-high heat. Add the onion and celery and sauté until softened, 6 to 8 minutes. Add the garlic, cumin, ginger, salt, paprika, cinnamon, and pepper and sauté for another 2 minutes.
Add the stock and bring to a boil. Reduce the heat to low and add the eggplant, zucchini, and cauliflower. Simmer on low heat, covered, until the vegetables are tender, 30 to 35 minutes. Add the artichoke hearts and olives, cover, and simmer for another 15 minutes.
Serve garnished with parsley, cilantro, and Greek yogurt (if using).
Substitution Tip: You can replace the spice combination used in this recipe with garam masala, an Indian spice blend found in many grocery stores.

1091. Citrus Asparagus with Pistachios

Preparation Time: 10 minutes
Cooking Time: 15 minutes
Servings: 4

Ingredients:

5 tablespoons extra-virgin olive oil, divided
Zest and juice of 2 clementine's or 1 orange (about ¼ cup juice and 1 tablespoon zest)
Zest and juice of 1 lemon
1 tablespoon red wine vinegar
1 teaspoon salt, divided
¼ teaspoon freshly ground black pepper
½ cup shelled pistachios
1-pound fresh asparagus
1 tablespoon water

Directions:

In a small bowl, whisk together 4 tablespoons olive oil, the clementine and lemon juices and zests, vinegar, ½ teaspoon salt, and pepper. Set aside.
In a medium dry skillet, toast the pistachios over medium-high heat until lightly browned, 2 to 3 minutes, being careful not to let them burn. Transfer to a cutting board and coarsely chop. Set aside.
Trim the rough ends off the asparagus, usually the last 1 to 2 inches of each spear. In a skillet, heat the remaining 1 tablespoon olive oil over medium-high heat. Add the asparagus and sauté for 2 to 3 minutes. Sprinkle with the remaining ½ teaspoon salt and add the water. Reduce the heat to medium-low, cover, and cook until tender, another 2 to 4 minutes, depending on the thickness of the spears.
Transfer the cooked asparagus to a serving dish. Add the pistachios to the dressing and whisk to combine. Pour the dressing over the warm asparagus and toss to coat.

1092. Herbed Ricotta–Stuffed Mushrooms

Preparation Time: 10 minutes
Cooking Time: 30 minutes
Servings: 4

Ingredients:

6 tablespoons extra-virgin olive oil, divided

4 portobello mushroom caps, cleaned and gills removed
1 cup whole-milk ricotta cheese
1/3 cup chopped fresh herbs (such as basil, parsley, rosemary, oregano, or thyme)
2 garlic cloves, finely minced
½ teaspoon salt
¼ teaspoon freshly ground black pepper

Directions:

Preheat the oven to 400°F.
Line a baking sheet with parchment or foil and drizzle with 2 tablespoons olive oil, spreading evenly. Place the mushroom caps on the baking sheet, gill-side up.
In a medium bowl, mix together the ricotta, herbs, 2 tablespoons olive oil, garlic, salt, and pepper. Stuff each mushroom cap with one-quarter of the cheese mixture, pressing down if needed. Drizzle with remaining 2 tablespoons olive oil and bake until golden brown and the mushrooms are soft, 30 to 35 minutes, depending on the size of the mushrooms.
Prep Tip: To make this a super-quick meal, replace the herbs and 2 tablespoons olive oil with 4 ounces jarred pesto.

1093. Braised Greens with Olives and Walnuts

Preparation Time: 5 minutes
Cooking Time: 20 minutes
Servings: 4

Ingredients:

8 cups fresh greens (such as kale, mustard greens, spinach, or chard)
2 to 4 garlic cloves, finely minced
½ cup roughly chopped pitted green or black olives
½ cup roughly chopped shelled walnuts
¼ cup extra-virgin olive oil
2 tablespoons red wine vinegar
1 to 2 teaspoons freshly chopped herbs such as oregano, basil, rosemary, or thyme

Directions:

Remove the tough stems from the greens and chop into bite-size pieces. Place in a large rimmed skillet or pot.
Turn the heat to high and add the minced garlic and enough water to just cover the greens. Bring to a boil, reduce the heat to low, and simmer until the greens are wilted and tender and most of the liquid has evaporated, adding more if the greens start to burn. For more tender greens such as spinach, this may only take 5 minutes, while tougher greens such as chard may need up to 20 minutes. Once cooked, remove from the heat and add the chopped olives and walnuts.
In a small bowl, whisk together olive oil, vinegar, and herbs. Drizzle over the cooked greens and toss to coat. Serve warm.

1094. Pesto Cauliflower Sheet-Pan "Pizza"

Preparation Time: 10 minutes
Cooking Time: 35 minutes
Servings: 4

Ingredients:

1 head cauliflower, trimmed
¼ cup extra-virgin olive oil
1 teaspoon salt
½ teaspoon freshly ground black pepper
1 teaspoon garlic powder
4 tablespoons Arugula and Walnut Pesto or store-bought pesto
1 cup shredded whole-milk mozzarella or Italian cheese blend
½ cup crumbled feta cheese

Directions:

Preheat the oven to 425°F.
Remove the stem and bottom leaves from a head of cauliflower and carefully break into large florets—the larger, the better. Thinly slice each floret from top to stem to about ¼-inch thickness.
Line a large rimmed baking sheet with aluminum foil and drizzle with the olive oil, spreading the oil around with your fingers to coat the foil. Lay the cauliflower out in a single layer on the oiled sheet. Sprinkle with salt, pepper, and garlic powder.
Place in the oven and roast until softened, 15 to 20 minutes. Remove from the oven and spread the pesto evenly over top of the cauliflower. Sprinkle with the shredded cheese and feta, return to the oven, and roast for 10 more minutes, or until the cheese is melted and the cauliflower is soft.
Turn the broiler to low and broil until browned and bubbly on top, 3 to 5 minutes. Remove from the oven, allow to cool slightly, and cut into large squares to serve.

1095. Greek Stewed Zucchini

Preparation Time: 5 minutes
Cooking Time: 40 minutes
Servings: 4 to 6

Ingredients:

¼ cup extra-virgin olive oil
1 small yellow onion, peeled and slivered
4 medium zucchini squash, cut into ½-inch-thick rounds
4 small garlic cloves, minced
1 to 2 teaspoons dried oregano
2 cups chopped tomatoes
½ cup halved and pitted Kalamata olives
¾ cup crumbled feta cheese
1/4 cup chopped fresh flat-leaf Italian parsley, for garnish (optional)

Directions:

In a large skillet, heat the oil over medium-high heat. Add the slivered onion and sauté until just tender, 6 to 8 minutes. Add the zucchini, garlic, and oregano and sauté another 6 to 8 minutes, or until zucchini is just tender.
Add the tomatoes and bring to a boil. Reduce the heat to low and add the olives. Cover and simmer on low heat for 20 minutes, or until the flavors have developed and the zucchini is very tender.
Serve warm topped with feta and parsley (if using).

1096. Roasted Brussels Sprouts with Tahini-Yogurt Sauce

Preparation Time: 10 minutes
Cooking Time: 35 minutes
Servings: 4

Ingredients:

1-pound Brussels sprouts, trimmed and halved lengthwise
6 tablespoons extra-virgin olive oil, divided
1 teaspoon salt, divided
½ teaspoon garlic powder
¼ teaspoon freshly ground black pepper
¼ cup plain whole-milk Greek yogurt
¼ cup tahini
Zest and juice of 1 lemon

Directions:

Preheat the oven to 425°F. Line a baking sheet with aluminum foil or parchment paper and set aside.

Place the Brussels sprouts in a large bowl. Drizzle with 4 tablespoons olive oil, ½ teaspoon salt, the garlic powder, and pepper and toss well to coat.
Place the Brussels sprouts in a single layer on the baking sheet, reserving the bowl, and roast for 20 minutes. Remove from the oven and give the sprouts a toss to flip. Return to the oven and continue to roast until browned and crispy, another 10 to 15 minutes. Remove from the oven and return to the reserved bowl.
In a small bowl, whisk together the yogurt, tahini, lemon zest and juice, remaining 2 tablespoons olive oil, and remaining ½ teaspoon salt. Drizzle over the roasted sprouts and toss to coat. Serve warm.

1097. Asparagus Frittata

Preparation Time: 10 minutes
Cooking Time: 20 minutes
Servings: 4

Ingredients:

8 tablespoons extra-virgin olive oil, divided
¼ cup finely chopped white onion (about ½ small onion)
1-pound medium-thin asparagus, rough stalks trimmed, cut into 1-inch pieces
2 medium garlic cloves, minced
6 large eggs
2 tablespoons vegetable broth
1 teaspoon salt
½ teaspoon freshly ground black pepper
4 tablespoons Zesty Orange or Roasted Garlic Aioli, for serving
½ cup chopped herbs (basil, parsley, or mint), for garnish (optional)

Directions:

In an 8- to 10-inch skillet, heat 4 tablespoons olive oil over medium heat. Add the onion and sauté for 3 to 4 minutes, until the onion begins to soften. Add the asparagus and garlic and cook until asparagus is tender, 5 to 6 minutes. Transfer the cooked vegetables to a bowl and let cool. Wipe any cooked food from the skillet, but do not wash.
In a medium bowl, whisk together the eggs, vegetable broth, salt, and pepper. Add the cooled asparagus and mix until well combined.
In the same skillet, heat 2 tablespoons of olive oil over medium-high heat. Pour the egg mixture into the skillet and reduce the heat to medium-low. Let the eggs cook undisturbed for 2 to 3 minutes, or until the bottom begins to set.
Run a thin spatula around the edge to allow the uncooked eggs to move towards the bottom of the pan. Cook, continuously moving the uncooked egg mixture until the top is a little wet but not liquid, 3 to 5 minutes.
Run the thin spatula under the cooking tortilla to make sure that no part of the bottom is stuck to the skillet. Place a large flat plate or cutting board on top of the skillet and quickly invert the tortilla to the flat surface.
Add the remaining 2 tablespoons olive oil to the skillet and carefully slide the tortilla back into the pan, uncooked-side down. Cook over low heat until cooked through, another 2 to 3 minutes.
Transfer back to the plate or cutting board. Allow to rest for 5 minutes before slicing.
Serve warm or at room temperature with aioli and chopped fresh herbs (if using).

1098. Garlicky Shrimp with Mushrooms

Preparation Time: 10 minutes
Cooking Time: 15 minutes
Servings: 4

Ingredients:

1 pound peeled and deveined fresh shrimp
1 teaspoon salt
1 cup extra-virgin olive oil
8 large garlic cloves, thinly sliced
4 ounces sliced mushrooms (shiitake, baby bella, or button)
½ teaspoon red pepper flakes
¼ cup chopped fresh flat-leaf Italian parsley
Zucchini Noodles or Riced Cauliflower, for serving

Directions:

Rinse the shrimp and pat dry. Place in a small bowl and sprinkle with the salt.
In a large rimmed, thick skillet, heat the olive oil over medium-low heat. Add the garlic and heat until very fragrant, 3 to 4 minutes, reducing the heat if the garlic starts to burn.
Add the mushrooms and sauté for 5 minutes, until softened. Add the shrimp and red pepper flakes and sauté until the shrimp begins to turn pink, another 3 to 4 minutes.
Remove from the heat and stir in the parsley. Serve over Zucchini Noodles or Riced Cauliflower.
Leftovers Tip: Serve the shrimp chilled over mixed greens for an easy lunch. Whisk 1 to 2 tablespoons red wine vinegar or lemon juice into the garlic oil for an easy vinaigrette.

1099. Crème Anglaise

Preparation Time: 5 minutes;
Cooking Time: 10 minutes
Servings: 2

Ingredients:

6 tablespoons Erythritol
1 teaspoon vanilla extract, unsweetened
5 egg yolks, pasture-raised
2 cups coconut milk, unsweetened and full-fat

Directions:

Place a medium saucepan over medium heat, add vanilla and coconut milk and whisk until combined and bring to simmer.
In the meantime, whisk together egg yolks and Erythritol until blended.
Slowly whisk in milk mixture, then return this mixture to pan over medium heat and cook for 3 to 5 minutes or until thickened to the desired level.
When done, let the custard cool slightly and then serve with sliced fruits.

1100. Keto Chocolate Mousse

Preparation Time: 2 hours and 5 minutes
Cooking Time: 5 minutes
Servings: 4

Ingredients:

3.5-ounce dark chocolate, chopped
1 tablespoon Erythritol
1/2 teaspoon vanilla extract, unsweetened
2 cups Greek yogurt
3/4 cup almond milk, unsweetened and full-fat

Directions:

Place a medium saucepan over medium heat, add chocolate and simmer for 3 to 5 minutes or until chocolate melts completely, whisking frequently.
Then whisk in vanilla and sweetener until dissolved and then remove the pan from heat.
Place yogurt in a large bowl, pour in chocolate mixture and mix until well combined.
Divide this mixture evenly between 4 serving bowls and let chill in the refrigerator for 2 hours.
When done, top with raspberries and serve.

1101. Mint Chocolate Chip Ice Cream

Preparation Time: 3 hours;
Cooking Time: 0 minutes
Servings: 1

Ingredients:

2 tablespoons chocolate chips, unsweetened
1 teaspoon cocoa powder, unsweetened
1/16 teaspoon salt
1/16 teaspoon Erythritol
1/4 teaspoon vanilla extract, unsweetened
6 drops peppermint extract, unsweetened
1 cup coconut milk, unsweetened and full-fat

Directions:

Place all the ingredients in a large bowl and whisk using a stand mixer until well combined.
Pour this mixture in a freezer proof container, seal the container and place in freezer for 2 to 3 hours until frozen.
Then remove bowl from the freezer, let rest at room temperature for 15 minutes or until slightly softened and then blend again with a stand mixer.
Serve straightaway.

1102. Chocolate Avocado Pudding

Preparation Time: 5 minutes;
Cooking Time: 20 minutes
Servings: 2

Ingredients:

1 medium avocado, pitted
1/4 cup cocoa powder, unsweetened
1 teaspoon sea salt
1/2 teaspoon vanilla extract, unsweetened
10 drops liquid stevia

Directions:

Remove it from avocado, then scoop out its flesh and place in a bowl.
Add remaining ingredients and blend using a stick blender until well combined.
Serve immediately.

1103. Vanilla Frozen Yogurt

Preparation Time: 35 minutes
Cooking Time: 0 minute
Servings: 8

Ingredients:

4 tablespoons monk fruit sweetener, grounded
2 teaspoons vanilla extract, unsweetened
1 tablespoon lemon juice
1 tablespoon olive oil
3 cups chilled plain yogurt, full fat

Directions:

Place all the ingredients in a blender and pulse for 1 to 2 minutes or until blended and creamy.
Spoon this mixture into a freezer safe container, cover with its lid and chill for 30 minutes or until soft but firm ice cream comes together.
Serve straightaway.

1104. Chia Berry Yogurt Parfaits

Preparation Time: 10 minutes;
Cooking Time: 0 minutes;
Servings: 4

Ingredients:

1 cup mixed berries, frozen
1/3 cup flaked coconut, toasted
1/3 cup chia seeds
2 tablespoons sunflower seeds
2 tablespoons pumpkin seeds
1 tablespoon Erythritol
1/4 teaspoon ground cinnamon
1/2 teaspoon vanilla extract, unsweetened
1/2 cup coconut cream, full-fat
1 cup Greek yogurt
2/3 cup water

Directions:

Stir together chia seeds, Erythritol, cinnamon, vanilla, coconut cream, and water until well combined and then spoon in a bottom of a serving bowl.
Mix berries and yogurt with a fork until crushed and smooth paste form and then spoon this mixture in an even layer on top of the chia seed layer.
Stir together sunflower seeds, pumpkin seeds and coconut flakes and top this mixture on the berries-yogurt layer.
Serve straightaway.

1105. Lemon Meringue Cookies

Preparation Time: 2 hours and 10 minutes;
Cooking Time: 1 hour
Servings: 15

Ingredients:

1/4 cup Erythritol
1/2 tablespoon lemon zest
1/2 teaspoon lemon juice
2 egg whites, pasture-raised

Directions:

Set oven to 200 degrees F and let preheat.
In the meantime, place egg whites in a large bowl and blend using a stick blender until stiff peaks forms.
Then beat in lemon juice until hard peaks forms and then beat in sweetener, 1 tablespoon at a time, until well mixed and slowly beat in lemon zest.
Spoon this mixture into a piping bag and form cookies on a baking sheet, lined with a parchment sheet.
Place the baking sheet into the heated oven and bake for 1 hour, then switch off the oven and let cookies rest in oven for 1 to 2 hours until cool completely.
Serve straightaway.

1106. Strawberry Cheesecake Jars

Preparation Time: 1 hour and 10 minutes;
Cooking Time: 0 minutes;
Servings: 4

Ingredients:

1 cup and 1 tablespoon strawberry and basil chia jam
1/4 cup powdered Erythritol
1 teaspoon lemon zest
1/2 teaspoon vanilla extract, unsweetened
1 tablespoon lemon juice
1 cup coconut cream, full-fat
1 cup cream cheese, full-fat
1/2 cup sour cream, full-fat

Directions:

Beat together lemon zest, vanilla, coconut cream, and cream cheese with a stick blender until smooth.
Divide this mixture evenly into 6 jars, each about 4-ounce, then top with 2 tablespoons of strawberry and basil chia jam.

Place these jars in the refrigerator for 1 hour or until chilled and then serve.

1107. Chocolate Truffles

Preparation Time: 10 minutes
Cooking Time: 6 minutes
Servings: 22

Ingredients

1 cup sugar free- chocolate chips
2 tablespoons butter
2/3 cup heavy cream
2 teaspoons brandy
2 tablespoons swerve
¼ teaspoon vanilla extract
Cocoa powder

Directions

Put heavy cream in a heat proof bowl, add swerve, butter and chocolate chips, stir, introduce in your microwave and heat up for 1 minute.
Leave aside for 5 minutes, stir well and mix with brandy and vanilla.
Stir again, leave aside in the fridge for a couple of hours.
Use a melon baller to shape your truffles, roll them in cocoa powder and serve them.
Enjoy!

1108. Keto Doughnuts.

Preparation Time: 10 minutes
Cooking Time: 15 minutes
Servings: 24

Ingredients

¼ cup erythritol
¼ cup flaxseed meal
¾ cup almond flour
1 teaspoon baking powder
1 teaspoon vanilla extract
2 eggs
3 tablespoons coconut oil
¼ cup coconut milk
20 drops red food coloring
A pinch of salt
1 tablespoon cocoa powder

Directions

In a bowl, mix flaxseed meal with almond flour, cocoa powder, baking powder, erythritol and salt and stir.
In another bowl, mix coconut oil with coconut milk, vanilla, food coloring and eggs and stir.
Combine the 2 mixtures, stir using a hand mixer, transfer to a bag, make a hole in the bag and shape 12 doughnuts on a baking sheet.
Introduce in the oven at 350 degrees F and bake for 15 minutes.
Arrange them on a platter and serve them.
Enjoy!

1109. Chocolate Bombs

Preparation Time: 10 minutes
Cooking Time: 10 minutes
Servings: 12

Ingredients

10 tablespoons coconut oil
3 tablespoons macadamia nuts, chopped
2 packets stevia
5 tablespoons unsweetened coconut powder
A pinch of salt

Directions

Put coconut oil in a pot and melt over medium heat.
Add stevia, salt and cocoa powder, stir well and take off heat.
Spoon this into a candy tray and keep in the fridge for a while.
Sprinkle macadamia nuts on top and keep in the fridge until you serve them.
Enjoy!

1110. Amazing Jello Dessert

Preparation Time: 2 hours 10 minutes
Cooking Time: 5 minutes
Servings: 12

Ingredients

2 ounces packets sugar free jello
1 cup cold water
1 cup hot water
3 tablespoons erythritol
2 tablespoons gelatin powder
1 teaspoon vanilla extract
1 cup heavy cream
1 cup boiling water

Directions

Put jello packets in a bowl, add 1 cup hot water, stir until it dissolves and then mix with 1 cup cold water.
Pour this into a lined square dish and keep in the fridge for 1 hour.
Cut into cubes and leave aside for now.
Meanwhile, in a bowl, mix erythritol with vanilla extract, 1 cup boiling water, gelatin and heavy cream and stir very well.
Pour half of this mix into a silicon round mold, spread jello cubes, then top with the rest of the gelatin.
Keep in the fridge for 1 more hour and then serve.
Enjoy!

1111. Strawberry Pie

Preparation Time: 2 hours and 10 minutes
Cooking Time: 5 minutes
Servings: 12

Ingredients

For the crust:
1 cup coconut, shredded
1 cup sunflower seeds
¼ cup butter
A pinch of salt
For the filling:
1 teaspoon gelatin
8 ounces cream cheese
4 ounces strawberries
2 tablespoons water
½ tablespoon lemon juice
¼ teaspoon stevia
½ cup heavy cream
8 ounces strawberries, chopped for serving
16 ounces heavy cream for serving

Directions

In your food processor, mix sunflower seeds with coconut, a pinch of salt and butter and stir well.
Put this into a greased spring form pan and press well on the bottom.
Heat up a pan with the water over medium heat, add gelatin, stir until it dissolves, take off heat and leave aside to cool down.
Add this to your food processor, mix with 4 ounces strawberries, cream cheese, lemon juice and stevia and blend well.
Add ½ cup heavy cream, stir well and spread this over crust.
Top with 8 ounces strawberries and 16 ounces heavy cream and keep in the fridge for 2 hours before slicing and serving.
Enjoy!

1112. Delicious Chocolate Pie

Preparation Time: 3 hours 10 minutes
Cooking Time: 20 minutes
Servings: 10

Ingredients

For the crust:

½ teaspoon baking powder
1 and ½ cup almond crust
A pinch of salt
1/3 cup stevia
1 egg
1 and ½ teaspoons vanilla extract
3 tablespoons butter
1 teaspoon butter for the pan
For the filling:
1 tablespoon vanilla extract
4 tablespoons butter
4 tablespoons sour cream
16 ounces cream cheese
½ cup cut stevia
½ cup cocoa powder
2 teaspoons granulated stevia
1 cup whipping cream
1 teaspoon vanilla extract

Directions

Grease a spring form pan with 1 teaspoon butter and leave aside for now.
In a bowl, mix baking powder with 1/3 cup stevia, a pinch of salt and almond flour and stir.
Add 3 tablespoons butter, egg and 1 and ½ teaspoon vanilla extract, stir until you obtain a dough.
Press this well into spring form pan, introduce in the oven at 375 degrees F and bake for 11 minutes.
Take pie crust out of the oven, cover with tin foil and bake for 8 minutes more.
Take it again out of the oven and leave it aside to cool down.
Meanwhile, in a bowl, mix cream cheese with 4 tablespoons butter, sour cream, 1 tablespoon vanilla extract, cocoa powder and ½ cup stevia and stir well.
In another bowl, mix whipping cream with 2 teaspoons stevia and 1 teaspoon vanilla extract and stir using your mixer.
Combine the 2 mixtures, pour into pie crust, spread well, introduce in the fridge for 3 hours and then serve.

1113. Tasty Cheesecakes

Preparation Time: 10 minutes
Cooking Time: 15 minutes
Servings: 9

Ingredients

For the cheesecakes:
2 tablespoons butter
8 ounces cream cheese
3 tablespoons coffee
3 eggs
1/3 cup swerve
1 tablespoon caramel syrup, sugar free
For the frosting:
3 tablespoons caramel syrup, sugar free
3 tablespoons butter
8 ounces mascarpone cheese, soft
2 tablespoons swerve

Directions

In your blender, mix cream cheese with eggs, 2 tablespoons butter, coffee, 1 tablespoon caramel syrup and 1/3 cup swerve and pulse very well.
Spoon this into a cupcakes pan, introduce in the oven at 350 degrees F and bake for 15 minutes.
Leave aside to cool down and then keep in the freezer for 3 hours.
Meanwhile, in a bowl, mix 3 tablespoons butter with 3 tablespoons caramel syrup, 2 tablespoons swerve and mascarpone cheese and blend well.
Spoon this over cheesecakes and serve them.
Enjoy!

1114. Raspberry and Coconut Dessert.

Preparation Time: 10 minutes
Cooking Time: 5 minutes
Servings: 12

Ingredients

½ cup coconut butter
½ cup coconut oil
½ cup raspberries, dried
¼ cup swerve
½ cup coconut, shredded

Directions

In your food processor, blend dried berries very well.
Heat up a pan with the butter over medium heat.
Add oil, coconut and swerve, stir and cook for 5 minutes.
Pour half of this into a lined baking pan and spread well.
Add raspberry powder and also spread.
Top with the rest of the butter mix, spread and keep in the fridge for a while.
Cut into pieces and serve.
Enjoy!

1115. Tasty Chocolate Cups

Preparation Time: 30 minutes
Cooking Time: 5 minutes
Servings: 20

Ingredients

½ cup coconut butter
½ cup coconut oil
3 tablespoons swerve
½ cup coconut, shredded
1.5-ounce cocoa butter
1 ounces chocolate, unsweetened
¼ cup cocoa powder
¼ teaspoon vanilla extract
¼ cup swerve

Directions

In a pan, mix coconut butter with coconut oil, stir and heat up over medium heat.
Add coconut and 3 tablespoons swerve, stir well, take off heat, scoop into a lined muffins pan and keep in the fridge for 30 minutes.
Meanwhile, in a bowl, mix cocoa butter with chocolate, vanilla extract and ¼ cup swerve and stir well.
Place this over a bowl filled with boiling water and stir until everything is smooth.
Spoon this over coconut cupcakes, keep in the fridge for 15 minutes more and then serve.
Enjoy!

1116. Simple and Delicious Mousse.

Preparation Time: 10 minutes
Cooking Time: 0 minutes
Servings: 12

Ingredients

8 ounces mascarpone cheese
¾ teaspoon vanilla stevia
1 cup whipping cream
½ pint blueberries
½ pint strawberries

Directions

In a bowl, mix whipping cream with stevia and mascarpone and blend well using your mixer.
Arrange a layer of blueberries and strawberries in 12 glasses, then a layer of cream and so on.
Serve this mousse cold!
Enjoy!

1117. Simple Peanut Butter Fudge

Preparation Time: 2 hours and 10 minutes
Cooking Time: 2 minutes
Servings: 12

Ingredients

1 cup peanut butter, unsweetened
¼ cup almond milk

2 teaspoons vanilla stevia
1 cup coconut oil
A pinch of salt
For the topping:
2 tablespoons swerve
2 tablespoons melted coconut oil
¼ cup cocoa powder

Directions

In a heat proof bowl, mix peanut butter with 1 cup coconut oil, stir and heat up in your microwave until it melts.
Add a pinch of salt, almond milk and stevia, stir well everything and pour into a lined loaf pan.
Keep in the fridge for 2 hours and then slice it.
In a bowl, mix 2 tablespoons melted coconut with cocoa powder and swerve and stir very well.
Drizzle the sauce over your peanut butter fudge and serve.
Enjoy!

1118. Lemon Mousse.

Preparation Time: 10 minutes
Cooking Time: 0 minutes
Servings: 5

Ingredients

1 cup heavy cream
A pinch of salt
1 teaspoon lemon stevia
¼ cup lemon juice
8 ounces mascarpone cheese

Directions

In a bowl, mix heavy cream with mascarpone and lemon juice and stir using your mixer.
Add a pinch of salt and stevia and blend everything.
Divide into dessert glasses and keep in the fridge until you serve.
Enjoy!

1119. Keto Broccoli Soup

Preparation Time: 10 minutes
Cooking Time: 30 minutes
Servings: 4

Ingredients

olive oil
1 cup chicken broth
1 cup heavy whipping cream
6 oz. shredded cheddar cheese
salt
5-ounces broccoli
1 celery stalk
1 small carrot
½ onion

Directions

In a pot add olive oil over medium heat
Add onion, carrot, celery and cook for 2-3 minutes
Add chicken broth and simmer for 4-5 minutes
Stir in broccoli and cream
Sprinkle in cheese and season with salt

1120. Keto Taco Soup

Preparation Time: 10 minutes
Cooking Time: 10 minutes
Servings: 8

Ingredients

2 lbs. ground beef
1 onion
1 cup heavy whipping cream
1 tsp chili powder
14 oz. cream cheese
1 tsp garlic
1 tsp cumin
2 10 oz. cans tomatoes
16 oz. beef broth

Directions

Cook for a couple of minutes, onion, garlic and beef
Add cream cheese and stir until fully melted
Add tomatoes, whipping cream, beef broth, stir and bring to boil

1121. Keto Chicken Soup

Preparation Time: 10 minutes
Cooking Time: 30 minutes
Servings: 4

Ingredients

2 boneless chicken breast
20-ounces diced tomatoes
½ tsp salt
1 cup salsa
6-ounces cream cheese
Avocado
2 tablespoons taco seasoning
1 cup chicken broth

Directions

In a slow cooker place all ingredients and cook for 5-6 hours or until chicken is tender
Whisk cream cheese into the broth
When ready, remove and serve

1122. Keto Spinach Soup

Preparation Time: 5 minutes
Cooking Time: 15 minutes
Servings: 2

Ingredients

¼ lbs. spinach
2 oz. onion
¼ lbs. heavy cream
½ oz. garlic
1 chicken stock cube
1,5 cup water
1 tablespoons butter

Directions

In a saucepan melt the butter and sauté the onion
Add garlic, spinach and stock cube and half the water
Cook until spinach wilts
Pour everything in a blender and blend, add water
Serve with pepper and toasted nuts

1123. Keto Toscana Soup

Preparation Time: 10 minutes
Cooking Time: 30 minutes
Servings: 4

Ingredients

1 lb. Italian sausage
½ cup whipping cream
1 tsp garlic
2 cup kale leaves
1 bag radishes 16-ounces
1 onion
30-ounces vegetable broth

Directions

Cut radishes into small chunks and blend until smooth
In a pot add onion and sausage, cook until brown, add radishes, broth
Cook on medium heat, add heavy whipping cream, kale leaves
Cook for a couple minutes
Remove and serve

1124. Keto Parmesan Soup

Preparation Time: 10 minutes
Cooking Time: 30 minutes
Servings: 4

Ingredients

1 broccoli
1 tsp pepper
1 tablespoon butter
1 tablespoon cheese

1 onion
½ cup warm
1 tsp salt
½ cup heavy cream

Directions

In a saucepan add onion and cook
Stir in broccoli and cook until soft
Combine with heavy cream and place in a blender, blend until smooth
Return the soup to the saucepan, season with salt
Serve and sprinkle with parmesan

1125. Keto Cauliflower Soup

Preparation Time: 10 minutes
Cooking Time: 30 minutes
Servings: 4

Ingredients

½ head of cauliflower
½ cup heavy cream
½ red bell pepper
1 tsp salt
1 tsp pepper
1 tablespoon butter
1 tablespoons parmesan cheese
1 tsp herbs

Directions

In a saucepan melt butter, add cauliflower and cook until soft
Remove from saucepan and set aside
Melt butter and sauté and bell pepper
In a food processor add cauliflower mixture, pepper and cook for 4-5 minutes
Season with salt and pepper
Garnish with parmesan and serve

1126. Keto Broccoli Cheese Soup

Preparation Time: 10 minutes
Cooking Time: 20 minutes
Servings: 2

Ingredients

2 cups broccoli
3 cups chicken broth
1 onion
1 cup heavy cream
6 oz. cream cheese
1 tablespoon hot sauce
3 tablespoons butter
1 clove garlic
6 oz. cheddar cheese

Directions

In a saucepan melt butter, add onion, garlic and sauté until soft
Pour in heavy cream, chicken broth, stir in broccoli
Cover and continue cooking for 12-15 minutes
Add cheese and cook until melted
Stir in hot sauce and enjoy

1127. Keto Queso Soup

Preparation Time: 10 minutes
Cooking Time: 30 minutes
Servings: 4

Ingredients

1 lb. chicken breast
1 tablespoon taco seasoning
1 tablespoon avocado oil
1 can diced green chilies
6-ounces cream cheese
½ cup heavy cream
salt
2 cups chicken broth

Directions

In an iron Dutch oven heat oil over medium heat stir in taco seasoning and cook for 1-2 minutes
Add broth, chicken and simmer for 20 minutes, remove chicken and shred
Stir in cream cheese and heavy cream into the soup, once the cheese has melted, add the chicken back to the soup, season with salt and serve

Made in the USA
Columbia, SC
30 November 2021